MORE PRAISE FOR

Legends of the American Desert

"A fascinating and sometimes bewildering profusion of themes that appear, join, separate and disappear like the braided channels of a Southwestern river. It is also an impressive exercise in graceful journalism."

—*Time*

"An entertainingly synoptic cultural portrait of the Southwest."
—*Outside*

"Part journalism and part history, part memoir and part travel writing, part John McPhee and part William Least Heat-Moon. . . . Shoumatoff's energetic storytelling and taste for piquant detail keep one bouncing along cheerfully. . . ."
—*Boston Globe*

"Alex Shoumatoff delivers an elegant, fact-happy bag of travelogue, memoir, history and did-you-knowness, while capturing all the grit and grandeur of the Southwest."
—*New York Post*

"An enchanting melange of portraits of the extraordinary region and people of the Southwest."
—*Publishers Weekly*

"Shoumatoff has accrued a considerable reputation for varied and perceptive travel writing, and his latest book will not disappoint his avid fans."
—*Booklist*

"Alex Shoumatoff has given those of us who love high, dry empty country a valuable addition to our libraries."

—TONY HILLERMAN

"*Legends of the American Desert* is the big enchilada of a book-that the American Southwest has always needed. It is stuffed with sharp-eyed social commentary, memorable characters, and Shoumatoff's legendary curiosity and good humor. No one else could have rolled together Santa Fe trustafarians, Clayton Lonetree, Yale-educated cowboys, Jesuit missionaries, and Zuni witchcraft into such an entertaining and illuminating read."

—THURSTON CLARKE, author of *California Fault*

"Alex Shoumatoff is a great historian, a travel writer without peer, a scholarly naturalist, a keen and perceptive and quirky observer—a brazen original. In this rich and wonderful book, past and present merge in a sweeping, often frightening, always intriguing, very savvy (and savory!), insightful, and swiftly paced narrative. A major-league history lesson. *Legends of the American Desert* is also outright fun."

—JOHN NICHOLS, author of *The Milagro Beanfield War*

"*Legends of the American Desert* is Shoumatoff at his best—eclectic, canny, witty, urbane without pretense, folksy without corn, and a splendid read. He manages, as only a few writers can, to embrace whole worlds while keeping a cool weather eye on the hard cogent facts."

—TIMOTHY FERRIS, author of *The Whole Shebang*

Legends *of the* American Desert

Legends
of the American
Desert

SOJOURNS IN THE GREATER SOUTHWEST

ALEX SHOUMATOFF

 HarperPerennial
A Division of HarperCollinsPublishers

Legends of the *American Desert*

SOJOURNS IN THE GREATER SOUTHWEST

ALEX SHOUMATOFF

HarperPerennial

A hardcover edition of this book was published in 1997 by Alfred A. Knopf, Inc. It is reprinted here by arrangement with Alfred A. Knopf, Inc.

First HarperPerennial Edition, 1999

Library of Congress Cataloging-in-Publication Data

ISBN 0-06-097769-8

00 01 02 03 ❖/RRD 10 9 8 7 6 5 4 3

For the two new children born to our family since this work was undertaken: Oliver Shema and Zachary Shyaka— may the Southwest still be there for you to delight in and ponder when you grow up and hit the road in search of your place in the world

Contents

Part One

The Absence of Water

A few days before the Fourth of July 1980, forty-three Salvadorans fleeing the crossfire of their country's civil war toward a vague, mouthwatering picture of America received from television, glossy magazines, and their Mexican arranger arrived at a funky little outpost on the Arizona border called San Luis Río Colorado. There they were informed of a "last-minute change." Instead of being flown to Los Angeles, which had been part of the twelve-hundred-dollar package each of them had already paid for up front, they were going to have to walk in. But only nineteen miles, their arranger assured them—a piece of cake. All they had to do was walk to Ajo, a dying copper town in the desert hills west of Tucson, where a truck would be waiting to take them the rest of the way.

Fifteen of the Salvadorans decided to stay in San Luis. The other twenty-eight, accompanied by four Mexican coyotes, as alien smugglers are called in border slang, were taken by truck to an even smaller outpost called El Papalote (the Kite), and from there, at about ten o'clock on the night of Thursday, the third, they struck out for Ajo. Several of the men had gotten tanked up at a local bar—not a smart thing to do on the eve of a desert trek, as alcohol accelerates dehydration. One of the women was seriously overweight. She would be the first to die. Another had high heels on. Several others wore sneakers with the toes cut out for ventilation. Only a few of the Salvadorans had thought to bring water.

July in southern Arizona, as any local will tell you, is "blowtorch city," "hellacious," "hotter than a jalapeño." Ground temperatures at midday can hit 145 degrees Fahrenheit. That weekend they hovered at 115. By nine o'clock the next morning, the Salvadorans were weaving and staggering. By eleven the expedition had ground to a halt. Two of the men and one of the coyotes took most of the remaining water and kept going, promising to return with help. The others sat and waited. As the day wore on, the strands of the social contract, of basic human decency, began to unravel. Two of the women threatened to kill a third if she didn't produce urine for them to drink. Three other women were raped by one of the coyotes as they lay prostrate in the heat. The coyote died from the exertion not long afterward.

That night, the beginning of the holiday weekend, the three men who had gone on were apprehended by La Migra, the border patrol, in an abandoned house in a little place called Why, ten miles south of Ajo (which is at a Y whose right-hand fork leads to Tucson). After lengthy grilling, they broke down and told about the others. The next morning one of La Migra's planes flew low over the vast creosote-bush flats south of Ajo. From the passenger seat, Agent Gerry Scott spotted a trail of discarded clothes—an ominous sign, because in the latter stages of dehydration the contact of cloth on the skin becomes unbearable. Farther south lay the suitcases several of the Salvadorans had packed with heavy winter clothes and books, in anticipation of their new life in El Norte, "the North." These were the first things to have been abandoned.

Other agents, who had set out on horses, found the bodies. Three dead men were propped against a telephone pole. Ten others were scattered on the desert floor. It wasn't a pretty sight. Some had eaten toothpaste. Some had drunk cologne or aftershave lotion. Dirt, cactus, paloverde twigs, were stuffed in the mouths of others. Their skin was gray and completely inelastic. If you had pinched it, it would have stayed pinched, Agent Scott told me. Four of the women and eight of the men were still barely alive. The other four have never been accounted for.

Just before midnight, in the same eyeball-drying, nostril-searing desert on the Arizona-Mexico border that did in the Salvadorans, a sidewinder has crossed a sandy wash (or empty streambed, also known as an arroyo or a draw) in the peculiar manner these highly specialized rattlesnakes have perfected for moving over loose, shifting surfaces: planting the front of its body in the sand, flipping the rear forward and to the side, then planting the rear and flipping the front—and now, having left in its wake an angled trail of parallel J's, it lies coiled and motionless under a creosote bush.

Along comes a kangaroo rat, hopping back to its burrow, its cheeks bulging with seeds, stopping often to listen for danger with its ultra-sensitive hearing, ready to avoid fangs or talons by leaping vertically into the air, or to flick sand into the eyes of an attacker with its long, tufted tail. But the pinkish-mauve sidewinder is perfectly camouflaged on the pinkish-mauve sand. It looks like an inanimate, innocuous bump—like an anthill, maybe—and the rat's attempt to dodge its sudden lunge is a split second late. As the sun rises, the snake has already swallowed the rat and is absorbing water from its tissue.

One of the easiest ways for a desert animal to obtain water is to eat a plant or another animal (the high water content of all living things being a legacy of their marine origins). Kangaroo rats not only drink surface water—licking beads of dew from stones or leaves, for instance—they manufacture "metabolic water" from seeds and other dry plant material, painstakingly extracting hydrogen and oxygen from their carbohydrates and recombining them into H_2O. And this isn't the only refinement of these remarkable desert specialists: their nostrils have ridges that trap the moisture they exhale; their kidneys secrete a concentrated paste instead of liquid urine. They even go so far as to eat their own fecal pellets to recapture whatever moisture they contain.

Two days later the sluggish sidewinder, still bulging with the partially digested rat, is no match for another southwestern desert specialist—a roadrunner, which circles like a mongoose and suddenly, seeing its moment, darts in and grabs the snake behind the head in its beak. Then shaking the snake violently and flinging it around a few times to break its back, it gulps it down. For the next few days the roadrunner strides around jauntily with several inches of snake tail protruding from its mouth, while its gastric juices work at dissolving the other end and absorbing the sidewinder's (and the kangaroo rat's) water.

For the last thousand years or so, the Hopi Indians have lived on four spectacular mesas in northeastern Arizona. Two of their thirteen villages are thought to be the oldest continuously inhabited communities in the Americas. Except for a few springs, seeps, and intermittent washes, there is no surface water in Hopi country. No one in his right mind would want to live in such a dry land unless, like the Hopi, he had special reasons. The Hopi believe that they are living in the Fourth World, three previous ones having been destroyed because of the wickedness of their ancestors, and that the scant rainfall on which their survival depends will only come through prayer, through everybody's heart being right. They have chosen to live in such a punishing environment because they don't want the evil traits that brought their ancestors down to surface again. They don't want to fail in this world, too.

For the Hopi growing corn is an act of faith. Some of their cornfields, down on the desert floor, are miles from the villages. Well into this century, the women would walk to them with jugs of water balanced on their heads and lovingly, making each drop count, water each plant with gourd ladles fastened to poles (now they take plastic water cans out to the cornfields in pickups). Before planting, the Hopi study the sky carefully, and just before it looks as if it is going to rain, they bury the kernels deep in the sandy soil. If it doesn't rain, the corn doesn't come up.

The Hopi believe as well that when they die they become benevolent beings known as kachinas and eventually take the form of clouds, becoming Cloud People, whose substance, or *navala,* is liquid and is manifested as rain. As Cloud People who send down their life-giving fluid to their kin, the dead continue to play a vital role in the order of things. Their kin must perform certain ceremonies and smoke pipes known as cloud-blowers before they plant their corn. They must summon the Cloud People and beseech them to release their *navala.*

Or this is what I had learned from Frank Waters's *Book of the Hopi* and *The Handbook of North American Indians.* Whenever I found myself among actual Hopi, I tried to discover if they still held these beliefs. Late one afternoon in the spring of 1992, for instance, I was sitting in my pickup on Second Mesa, waiting for some people, and I got into a discussion with two young Hopi men and a girl who were sitting in a car next to me, passing a joint. I asked if "you guys" were still into reggae. (In the mideighties a reggae craze swept the Hopi and Havasupai Reservations, transforming their youth cultures). One of them said they were, but live concerts were no longer allowed on the reservation; now they had to drive down to Tempe (near Phoenix). "And the clouds," I asked. "Do you still believe they're the ancestors?" Yes, the young man said in a tone of great reverence.

A few months later, I drove out to the Hopi mesas for a meeting with a religious leader from the village of Shongopovi, but he didn't show up at our rendezvous. I drove around with his sister, looking for him, but he wasn't at any of his usual haunts. I decided to wait in front of his house in case he turned up there.

The woman next door was beating a rug in front of her house. I explained that I was waiting for her neighbor, and idly looked up at the sky. Dozens of small fleecy clouds were hovering over the mesa. It was almost as if they were keeping an eye on things. Suddenly the belief made sense. It seemed perfectly reasonable that when you died and were buried, your corpse would soon dry up, and your fluids would rise into the sky and become one of these little cloud puffs. The ancestors are out in force today, I thought, but none of them is big enough to let down a shower. I could understand the frustration of having these little clouds hanging around day after day and it never raining.

You don't pray to them as much as you harangue them, a Navajo man later explained to me (the Navajo came down from the Pacific Northwest roughly five hundred years ago and subsequently adopted many Hopi beliefs, including the one about the ancestors being clouds). You tell them, I am alive, I have a right to be here, so give me your rain.

The woman next door clearly wanted me to move along. "I don't know when he's coming back," she told me. "He may have gone very far away."

I looked up at the clouds and said to her, "Those are the ancestors, aren't they?" and she said, nervously, as if she weren't sure she should be revealing this to a *bahana,* a white man, "Yes."

By the turn of this century the advent of modern techniques for damming and diverting rivers had opened up vast areas of the desert to ranching and farming, and there was a rush on the Southwest's very limited surface water. An era of water hustling and rustling began. All kinds of treachery was committed on behalf of cities that did not even exist yet. Los Angeles was already off and running, however, spreading into its arid basin so rapidly that the immediate water sources were unable to keep up with it. The Los Angeles River—not a big one to begin with (it only accounts for .005 percent of California's surface water)—was reduced to half its flow in the 1880s by artesian pumping of the aquifer beneath it. In 1904 William Mulholland, the superintendent of the City of Los Angeles Water Company, declared, "The time has come when we shall have to supplement the supply from some other source."

Mulholland and his colleague Joseph Lippincott, the regional engineer for the Reclamation Service, cast their eyes up to the Sierra Nevada. Two hundred and fifty miles northeast, at four thousand feet above sea level, there was a big lake, Owens Lake, fed by the Owens River. Thanks to irrigation water from the river, the Owens Valley was verdant with citrus groves planted by homesteaders, who had defrauded and massacred the local Paiute Indians. Mulholland and Lippincott conceived the idea of siphoning off the Owens River into an aqueduct and running it down to Los Angeles and the adjacent San Fernando Valley—it was downhill most of the way—and they invited a select group of Los Angeles businessmen to go in with them. Quietly the syndicate bought up the worthless desert real estate in the San Fernando Valley and persuaded the farmers in the Owens Valley to part with their water rights, dynamiting the private reservoirs of reluctant ones until they agreed to sell at condemnation prices.

The Los Angeles Aqueduct was laid across "some of the most scissile, fractionated, fault-splintered topography in North America," Marc Reisner writes in his history of water usage in the West, *Cadillac Desert*. Fifty-three miles of it ran through tunnels. It went on-line in 1913, even before the city had acquired legal control of the Owens River's flow, with armed guards patroling it day and night. Soon the irrigated land in the San Fernando Valley increased by more than a factor of ten, the real estate shot up to as much as a thousand dollars for a lot in one of the elegant new subdivisions that Mulholland and Lippincott's buddies in the construction business were putting in, and everyone in the syndicate became a millionaire. By 1918 there were palms along Santa Monica Boulevard. Bungalow courts with lush lawns and tropical landscaping sprouted in the desert, pink haciendas that supposedly replicated the sumptuous homes of the dons in Spanish Colonial California, the fledgling motion picture industry, barrios, ghettos, cafeterias, pet cemeteries, hamburger joints, neon-lit strips, shopping centers, golf courses, winding streets lined with single-story, single-family "ranch" houses, coalesced into a sprawling megalopolis of intimate pseudovillages inhabited by strangers and linked by freeways. By 1930 the aqueduct was providing 1.3 million Angeleños with 50 gallons a day, and the San Fernando Valley, with 88,000 acre-feet for irrigated agriculture (an acre-foot of water covers an acre to a depth of one foot, with approximately 326,000 gallons of water).

There was plenty of water for everybody until the twenties, when droughts left the Owens Valley farmers high and dry three times. Apologists of the aqueduct argued that it provided "the greatest good for the greatest number," but the farmers were unpersuaded, and in 1924 they armed themselves and drove in a caravan to the aqueduct's gatehouse. Inside, they spun five huge wheels and returned the Owens River to its valley. But the river was rediverted, so in 1927 they dynamited a section of the aqueduct called No Name Siphon. The following year the San Francisquito Dam, part of the aqueduct's diversion system, burst, and an avalanche of water swept through the Santa Clara Valley, taking with it trees, houses, bridges, railroad tracks, telephone poles, towns, bodies, mud. The disaster claimed 385 lives, and Mulholland's career was ruined. But the aqueduct was repaired, and the growth it made possible continued. Today the Owens Valley is desert, as the San Fernando Valley used to be; Owens Lake is a saline pond; and clouds of alkali dust sweep through the abandoned citrus groves.

Later in the century, when new technology for pumping water in pipes over mountains was perfected, Los Angeles received an additional 5.6 million acre-feet from the Colorado River, hundreds of miles to the east. The Colorado is the lifeblood of the modern Southwest. The most utilized and litigated band of moving fresh water on the planet, it is diverted at dozens of points—to Las Vegas and San Diego, to Phoenix and Tucson, to Tijuana and the vast truck farms in the Imperial and Coachella Valleys. Half of it is whisked away before it even leaves Colorado. A century ago paddle wheelers ascending the Colorado to provision mining camps, wagon trains, and army outposts had to plow through the turbulent tidal bore at its mouth, created by the collision of its mighty discharge with the surf of the Gulf of California. Today the Colorado Delta is, most of the time, as dry as a sandbox. Except in years of heavy spring runoff, not a drop of the Colorado reaches the gulf anymore. The river (like the Yellow River in China) is completely used.

The absence of water has largely determined the behavior and morphology of not only individual species in the Southwest, but entire cultures. Everything comes down to the dryness. I should probably clarify before proceeding just what I mean by "the Southwest," because dozens of animals answer to that name. I am talking about a region centered on Arizona and New Mexico, whose heart is perhaps the Navajo Reservation, but also embracing southern California, southern Nevada, southern Utah, and southern Colorado and much of Texas and extending east to mid-Missouri and south over the border to include Chihuahua and Sonora—the part of the ethnographic continuum known as the Greater Southwest that is in northern Mexico, in other words, and is sometimes referred to as "the Other Southwest."

By this definition, the fifty thousand, or maybe twice that many, Tarahumara Indians, who live up in the craggy, canyon-riddled Sierra Madre Occidental, for instance, are a southwestern tribe. The Tarahumara have had much less contact with the modern world than their cousins in the States. "The Tarahumara have a traditional society in which nature is paramount," a half-Tarahumara man recently explained. "Even rocks can be alive. It is a different concept of everything." According to Tarahumara belief, heterosexual men have three souls, heterosexual women have four, and homosexuals have seven and are therefore even more powerful than peyote. Death was introduced at the request of a potbellied, slow-moving man who became worried that with humanity multiplying unchecked he was going to be squashed, so he asked God to start taking lives. (This man later became the horned toad.) After he dies, every Tarahumara must make a journey to every place he ever lived and gather his footprints so that he can present them, along with his hair, to God.

I am reminded of this belief now as I try to retrieve my own twenty-seven-year-old footprints—who I was in November 1970, when I drove across New Mexico and Arizona in a battered station wagon with my dog Willie. But that young man is mostly a blur. This was my first encounter with the Southwest. I had no interest in it yet per se. I had just turned twenty-four, and had just split up with a woman I'd been living with in New Hampshire and was on my way to California. I knew I wanted to be a writer of some kind and had tried my hand at poetry. Now I was writing songs reminiscent of the young Bob Dylan's at the rate of three or four a day. Nature had hit me, and as Willie and I made our way through the rural South, I would often stop to identify birds with my binoculars and field guide. Somewhere in south Texas, I made a watercolor of a scissor-tailed flycatcher sitting on a power line. Looking back, I realize I was exactly the sort of person who is drawn to the Southwest. My choice of that particular cross-country route seems now not so much accidental as in character and providential.

This was my first desert, and I didn't quite know what to make of it. As I cruised around northeastern Arizona, I repeatedly had the sensation that I was traveling along an old seafloor. The landscape would seem to be thirsting for the water that had once been everywhere; the canyons would seem to plunge to murky depths; the mesas and monuments to be remnant shallows. Even the vegetation contributed to the illusion: sinuous wands of ocotillo wavered like seaweed, cacti bristled like sea urchins encrusted on the rock. Ship rocks—the ancient volcanic necks eroded in Gibraltar-like slants that crop up here and there on the Colorado Plateau—seemed to belong to a fleet sailing a ghost sea.

I was hardly the first to have this intuition, as I would discover in time. Here is the young Georgia O'Keeffe, for instance, writing to a friend in New York in 1916, having just arrived in the Southwest to teach art at West Texas Normal College, in the Texas Panhandle:

> Tonight I walked into the sunset—to mail some letters—and the whole sky—and there is so much of it out here—was just blazing—and grey blue clouds were rioting all through the hotness of it. . . . I walked out past the last house—past the last locust tree—and sat on the fence for a long time—looking—just looking at—the lightning—you see there was nothing but sky and flat prairie land—land that seems more like the ocean than anything else I know.

The Navajo, Hualapai, and Havasupai all sensed this marine past and have myths about a great flood long ago. The Hualapai's flood ended when the culture hero Packithaawi split the ground open with his club, creating the Grand Canyon, which drained it off deep into the earth. The Colorado, the Big Water meandering on the canyon floor a mile below, is its final runoff, being sucked down into the underworld.

In fact, during the last 150 million years or so, the Southwest has been repeatedly invaded by the sea and is littered with evidence of these submerged periods: sharks' teeth and imprints of giant seaweed are embedded in an Arizona mountaintop; an arroyo outside Galisteo, New Mexico, is lined with fossil shells of snail-like ammonites, thirty-six inches across. Much of the more recent bedrock is ancient coral reef, made up of the shells and secretions of marine animals subsequently compressed into limestone. These porous formations often hold reservoirs of water, oil, or natural gas.

My first clear recollection of being in the Southwest is the night I cruised into Arizona on Route 66, the two-lane motor route from Chicago to Los Angeles that would be displaced by a series of interstates fifteen years later. The moon was full and so bright that I turned off the headlights and drove across the desert floor in its ghostly light. East of Holbrook, I found myself in a lurid badlands littered with the trunks of thousands of enormous, petrified trees—the Painted Desert—and after we pulled off the highway, Willie and I crashed behind a russet-and-gray-banded mound. In the morning I took a monumental crap and photographed the huge brown bomber as it lay gleaming on the pock-marked sand, with a snowcapped peak in the background, like a Dali composition. Willie and I walked among the trees—two-hundred-foot-long conifers of the long-extinct genus *Aucarioxylon,* part of a logjam in the floodplain of a broad, shallow river that had flowed here some 200 million years ago and had subsequently been buried under many feet of sand and mud, where they were slowly shot with silica and turned into stone, and only now were they coming to the surface, exposed by millennia of slashing summer-monsoon rain. In those days the continents had not yet separated, and the "Southwest" was seventeen hundred miles closer to the equator. Most of it was a teeming swamp. Dinosaurs had browsed and mated and tangled in mortal combat under these towering evergreens.

The next morning I walked out to the edge of the Grand Canyon and was so dumbfounded that I sat there for several hours trying to process the stupendous abyss, and when I finally stood to my feet, my sense of time and of the visually possible and of my importance in the scheme of things had been permanently altered. I took a snapshot of myself, holding out the camera as I stood at the South Rim—bearded, squinting under a woolen hat, and jauntily clenching a pipe full of homegrown marijuana. Far below, gleaming segments of the Colorado snaked around buttes and multicolored spurs.

A few days later I took a dirt road that went for fifty miles or so through the desert. On the map it had looked like a shortcut, but the road became rough, and after an hour there was nothing human in sight. Traversing an alluvial fan that sloped down to the desert floor, I came upon a young Indian man with long black hair, sitting on a boulder, facing away from me, looking out over the vastness. I have no idea what tribe he was—maybe Navajo, maybe Pima, O'odham, or Chemehuevi. He was about my age. I stopped and asked if he wanted a lift, but he didn't answer the question or acknowledge my presence in any way. Maybe he was waiting for a vision. I stayed there for an awkward moment, then drove on. This was my first encounter with a Native American.

A Gallery of Fugitives

The Southwest is the least American part of the United States; as the WPA guide to New Mexico observed in 1940, "The veneer of Americanization in places runs thin indeed." So it attracts people from modern Anglo-America or Europe who are looking for what anthropologists call the Other. The Southwest offers two basic categories of Other for such people to embrace—the Indians and the Hispanics—without their even having to leave the country, so it is a logical starting point. In 1970 I didn't know it yet, but I was one of these fugitives myself. My disaffection with the dominant culture had only evolved to the point where I didn't want to live in its cities; I was "not a pavement person," as Georgia O'Keeffe—another member of the breed—put it. But over the next twenty-five years my fascination with the Other, my quest to find and reinvent myself in an alternative culture, would take me all over the world. There are four classic meccas for people on such quests—the American Southwest, the Amazon, Africa, and Tibet—and I would touch base with them all, returning to the Southwest more than a dozen times. The Southwest would serve as a way of reviewing my progress, and there I would meet, or learn about, Anglos much like myself, kindred souls, fellow fugitives, who had been drawn to this mystical, sunny part of the world, vast sections of which are not on the American wavelength. And it was in the Southwest that I would ultimately decide that my quest was misframed, because there is no independent Other apart from one's own projections, and would abandon it. By then I had traveled so extensively that nothing was exotic anymore. No society, I had realized, is without its venal side. I had met the Other, you could say, and he was me.

Everett Ruess, a young artist from southern California who began to take solo trips into the desert Southwest in 1929, was a prototypical Other Questor. Ruess roamed and painted in the Canyonlands of southern Utah, a fantastic rock desert of nubs and spires, mesas and monuments, and gaping canyons whose scalloped beige walls are streaked with lucent blue-black streamers of long-solidified iron- and magnesium-rich drip known as desert varnish, where at every turn there's a balanced rock, a natural bridge, or a desert window eaten clean through a flying buttress of red sandstone, or some other spectacular erosional artifact. Edward Abbey, a later fugitive—from Hoboken, New Jersey, no less—who reinvented himself in the Canyonlands as a desert dissident in the fifties and sixties, describes them as "the least inhabited, least inhibited, least governed, least priest-ridden, most arid, hostile, most lonesome, most grim bleak desolate and savage quarter of the state." Mormon boys gone bad—cattle rustlers and stagecoach holdup artists like Butch Cassidy—laid low in back branch canyons. The Mormon farmers who founded communities with names like Orderville and began to irrigate and grow crops on the larger canyon floors in the 1870s found the landscape diabolical, judging from the place-names they bestowed on it—Devil's Rock Garden, Death Hollow, Carcass Wash. But Everett Ruess found it hauntingly beautiful.

On November 11, 1934, Ruess rode out of the little Mormon town of Escalante on the back of a burro. A lanky, blond twenty-year-old, with his cowboy boots grazing the ground from the back of his mount and his boyish face shaded by a gigantic black ten-gallon hat, he looked quite the dude. This time, he was planning an indefinite stay in the desert. He had loaded his pack burro with ample grub and had written his parents that day, "I may not have a post office for a couple of months," and his brother Waldo, "As to when I shall visit civilization, it will not be soon, I think."

Eight days later Ruess turned up at Clayton Porter and Addlin Lay's sheep camp, in Soda Gulch, a branch of Escalante Canyons about fifty miles to the southeast. He spent two nights with the sheepherders, asking a million questions—about the scenery and the Indian ruins and the distances between water—and the next morning he headed south, toward Hole-in-the-Wall, where the Escalante River runs into the Colorado. He told Porter and Lay that he was going to do some sketching. That was the last anyone saw of him.

Ruess's parents, especially his mother, were supportive of their son's desert forays, and they didn't become worried about his failure to check in until February of the following year. On March 1 a search party was sent out, and it found Ruess's burros in Davis Gulch, another branch of the Escalante Canyons, below Soda Gulch. The burros were fat and healthy. Davis Gulch is a lush oasis blessed with a cottonwood-lined stream, brilliant wildflowers—columbine, sego lily—and plenty of pasture. Two sandstone arches buttress its north wall, and there are several small cliff dwellings that were built by the Anasazi people and abandoned in the thirteenth century. Near one of the dwellings the searchers found candy wrappers, empty condensed-milk cans, and a jumble of size-nine boot prints—evidently Ruess's campsite. The words NEMO NOV, 1934, scratched over a doorway, were probably his work and may have referred to the name ("Nobody" in Latin) Ulysses used to deceive the Cyclops; Ruess had been reading *The Odyssey* in T. E. Lawrence's translation. Or they could have referred to Captain Nemo, the Jules Verne hero who checks out of Western civilization and creates his own submarine Other. Ruess was continuously trying out new names on himself and his burros.

There was no sign of Ruess, however. Some evidence (a confusion of moccasin and size-nine boot prints on a nearby ledge; a boast reportedly made years later in the Phoenix penitentiary) suggests that he was murdered by a Navajo named Jack Crank, who hated whites and needed the scalp of a "blood enemy" for a ceremony. Or he may have been done in by rustlers known to be working the Escalante drainage and to be on the lookout for an undercover agent who they had heard was going to try to infiltrate their operation. Some think Ruess was flash flooded—swept away by the torrential runoff of a distant rainstorm that had come racing down an arroyo from out of the blue. Or maybe he fell into one of the slits—just too wide to jump over and too deep to climb out of, cut by the abrasive action of swirling, gritty water—that riddle the Canyonlands. In 1985, after spending the night at the Fly Canyon Motel in Utah, just over the Arizona border, I followed one of these baby canyons as it veered all over the place, across miles of gray slickrock. After several hours I was dehydrated, and having lost all sense of direction, I began to panic. But suddenly everything began to look familiar. There was the motel. I realized that I was just a dozen yards from where I had started.

Ruess could also have fallen off a precipice. A daredevil, he loved to shock people by dashing up cliffs and dangling over drops. The previous May he had written a friend, "Yesterday I did some miraculous climbing on a near-vertical rock wall, and escaped from that, too. One way or other, I have been flirting pretty heavily with death, the old clown."

Or it could be that Ruess faked his disappearance, crossed the Colorado into Navajo country, and, one theory goes, settled down with a Navajo woman on a remote part of the reservation. Another woman swore she met Ruess and talked with him near Monterrey, Mexico, in

1937. Periodic sightings of a wild old man up in the rocks still come out of the Canyonlands, fueling rumors that Ruess is alive.

A final possibility is that Ruess climbed way up some cliff, settled into an alcove or down on some ledge out of sight from below, and, having no further interest in living, simply checked out, and his remains haven't been found yet. His letters that fall suggest that this may have been what happened. Ruess writes that he has gone "too far alone" to connect with Frances (a girl he had fallen in love with that summer from across a room in San Francisco), college, an art career, or anything, and he resolves to follow "the lone trail" wherever it leads, to "the end of the horizon."

People who met him had the impression that he wasn't all there—"a strange kid," one man recalled, who "loved the Navajos and everybody, loved animals, burros, dogs, kids, and everything." Ruess himself at one point couldn't remember where he had been for the last couple of days. The colors in his strongest descriptions—vermilion cliffs, claret shadows—seem almost too intense, like verbal Van Goghs. In one letter he expresses a wish to dissolve into landscape and become the beauty around him.

Taos is a magnet for modern fugitives. The Athens of the Southwest, it was where the cultures of the Plains Indians and the Pueblos, and later Eastern and Amerindian mysticism, met and cross-fertilized. Early in the century the young Swiss psychoanalyst C. G. Jung, seeking perspectives on the European psyche, visited Taos, the northernmost of the pueblos. Jung was deeply impressed by the serenity and the dignity of "the Indians who stood wrapped in blankets on the highest roofs of the pueblo, mute and absorbed in the sight of the sun." A chief named Ochwiay Biano explained to him that "we are a people who live on the roof of the world; we are the sons of Father sun, and with our religion we daily help our father to go across the sky. We do this not only for ourselves, but for the whole world. If we were to cease practising our religion, in ten years the sun would no longer rise. Then it would be night forever."

Jung concluded that the serenity of Taoseños was derived from the belief that their lives were "cosmologically meaningful," that their prayers really mattered, that they had a central place in an orderly scheme of transformations and correspondences, of propitiations and reciprocations. The chief also told Jung what he thought of white people: how sharp and cruel their features were, how uneasy and restless they seemed, how they thought with their heads instead of with their hearts.

In 1921, the British novelist D. H. Lawrence came to Taos at the invitation of the Bohemian heiress Mabel Dodge Sterne (later Luhan). A bearded, sunken-eyed, thirty-six-year-old wraith, stricken with "t.b. in the third degree," as a Mexican doctor would describe it, Lawrence brought his free-thinking German wife, Frieda, a cousin of Baron von Richthofen, the flying ace. Lawrence had been longing to leave Europe—particularly the dank, grimy ugliness of industrialized England and his "cultured ego," his "finished self"—behind, and to awaken his "vital, innermost being" through mystic communion with the Indians in America. But the First World War had delayed his plans. Stuck in England, he had consoled himself with the novels of James Fenimore Cooper.

Mabel packed the Lawrences into a big open Cadillac touring car, and they set off "across desert and mesa, down cañons and up divides and along arroyos and so forth." After two days they reached some Apache, who put on a dance for them. Lawrence found the show more "primordial" than anything Cooper had prepared him for. "Listening [to the *pat-pat* of the drums and the *hie-hie-hie-away* of the singers], an acute sadness, and a nostalgia, unbearably yearning for something, and a sickness of the soul came over me," he wrote. "The gobble-gobble chuckle in the whoop surprised me in my very tissues. Then I got used to it, and could hear in it the humanness, the playfulness, and then, beyond that, the mockery and the diabolical, pre-human, pine-tree fun of cutting dusky throats and letting the blood spurt out unconfined."

Mabel was involved with an Indian from Taos Pueblo, Tony Luhan, who would become her fourth husband. She was a little too pushy and spoiled for Lawrence, too conscious of the power her inheritance of a Buffalo banking fortune gave her. He wrote his mother-in-law in Berlin after a few months:

> Mabel . . . is . . . another "culture-carrier," likes to play the patroness, hates the white world and loves the Indian out of hate . . . these people have only money, nothing else but money, and because all the world wants money, all the money, America has become strong, proud and over-powerful.
>
> If one would only say: "America, your money is shit, go and shit more"—then America would be a nothing.

Nevertheless, Lawrence accepted Mabel's invitation to return to Taos in the spring of 1924. His insights into the local ethnic tensions deepened:

> The Indian is not in line with us. . . . And the minute you set eyes on him you know it. . . . The Indian way of consciousness is different from and fatal to our way of consciousness. Our way of consciousness is different from and fatal to the Indian. The two ways . . . are never . . . to be reconciled. . . . [And there are two reactions a white man can have.] You can detest the insidious devil for having an utterly different way from our own great way. Or you can perform the mental trick, and fool yourself and others into believing that the befeathered and bedaubed darling is nearer to the true ideal gods than we are.

And yet it was the Indians of New Mexico, more than anyone else in his travels, who finally connected Lawrence with the basic race experience:

> New Mexico, the picturesque reservation and playground of the eastern states, very romantic, old Spanish, Red Indian, desert mesas, pueblos, cowboys, penitentes, all that film-stuff. Very nice, the great South-West, put on a sombrero and knot a red kerchief round your neck, to go out in the great free spaces!
>
> That is New Mexico wrapped in the absolutely hygienic and shiny mucous-paper of our trite civilization. That is the New Mexico known to most of the Americans who know it at all. But break through the shiny sterilized wrapping, and actually *touch* the country, and you will never be the same again.
>
> I think New Mexico was the greatest experience from the outside world that I have ever had. It certainly changed me for ever. Curious as it may sound, it was New Mexico that liberated me from the present era of civilization, the great era of material and mechanical development. Months spent in holy Kandy, in Ceylon, the holy of holies of southern Buddhism, had not touched the great psyche of materialism and idealism which dominated me. And years, even in the exquisite beauty of Sicily, right among the old Greek paganism that still lives there, had not shattered the essential Christianity on which my character was established.

What Lawrence admired about the Indians was that they had the "oldest religion," which he defined as "the whole life-effort . . . to . . . come into sheer naked contact, *without a mediator or an intermediary* . . . with the elemental life of the cosmos, mountain-life, cloud-life, thunder-life, air-life, earth-life, sun-life." But apart from Tony Luhan and apart from watching the Indians' dances and races from the sidelines, he seems to have had little contact with them. "The point is, what is the feeling that passes from an Indian to me, when we meet?" he asked. In fact, Lawrence's own reaction, "the feeling of most ordinary farmers and ranchers . . . it is only honesty to admit it," was "instinctive but tolerant repulsion." The earthiness of the Indian in the end offended Lawrence's squeamish sensibilities, and he didn't succeed in liberating himself from the kind of racist interjections that were almost expected of an Englishman abroad, about "the silly dark people" of "nauseous" Ceylon, or the Apache, who "have a cult of water-hatred, they never wash flesh or rag. So never in my life have I smelt such an unbearable sulphur-human smell as comes from them when they cluster: a smell that takes the breath from the nostrils."

And yet he clearly appreciated what the Indians represented. After a visit to Taos Pueblo, he declared, "In the dust where we have buried the silent races and their abominations, we have buried so much of the delicate magic of life." The negative feelings about European civilization he had brought to New Mexico were reinforced:

> But here it is: the newest democracy ousting the oldest religion! And once the oldest religion is ousted, one feels the democracy and all its paraphernalia will collapse, and the oldest religion, which comes down to us from man's pre-war days, will start again. The sky-scraper will scatter on the winds like thistledown, and the genuine America, the America of New Mexico, will start on its course again. This is an interregnum.

One evening in the spring of 1992, my wife and I had dinner at a restaurant in Taos. As my wife ordered, our waitress, a handsome woman of about sixty with an English accent, asked her if her accent isn't Ugandan. It is: my wife is Rwandan, but she grew up in a refugee village in Uganda. Our waitress, whose name was Marceline, told us that she had once been the mistress of the brother of King Freddy, Uganda's last monarch. Marceline invited us back to her house, and we stayed up late listening to the incredible story of her life. She had first been married to a chieftain in northern Pakistan, from whom when the marriage deteriorated she had to flee for her life, leaving their little daughter (who, Muslim Pakistan's being a patrilineal society, belonged to the father; she would not see her daughter for thirty years, when by a complete fluke they ran into each other in a hotel in Chicago). Then she had toured Africa as a stripper for the Folies Bergères ("I had no talent as a singer or dancer, so all I could do was take off my clothes," she explained sheepishly), where she attracted the notice of King Freddy's brother. Later on, she had married an Italian, then a Sioux chief, who brought her to Taos, and they were no longer together. "I love everything that isn't me," Marceline told us, adding that the best way to understand a culture is to marry into it.

It isn't surprising that this woman has ended up in Taos. Taos is still the raw frontier, where few questions are asked, and it attracts all kinds of fugitives. Like sixty-nine-year-old Lawrence "Howie" Krantz, who was arrested in Taos for having stolen $270,000 from a church treasury in Suffern, New York, ten years earlier, back when he was Clyde Womer. Or charming, handsome Judd Adam Platt, who turned up in Taos in 1986. Before long he moved in with the ex-wife of the manager of the ski area, and they converted her home into an upscale bed-and-breakfast. But by the end of 1991 the relationship was over, and while getting a court order to restrain Platt from conducting further business on behalf of the inn, the woman mentioned to the judge that he seemed to be concealing his true identity. This led to the discovery that Platt was really Mark Allen Sampson, a Minnesota lawyer wanted for mail fraud and stealing around $400,000 from twenty clients' trust accounts.

Santa Fe is also a big reinvention center, where people come to start over and be themselves. The trail from the East is well worn. It has long been a haven for gays. "During the 1920s and 1930s," writes Jeffrey Hogrefe in his biography of Georgia O'Keeffe,

> Santa Fe and Taos were to American lesbians what Capri was to British homosexuals at the same time—a place away from the constraints of organized society, which discouraged homosexual unions. For many years on Canyon Road, a bar for women operated with the unlikely name of Claude's. Claude was a woman, rumored to be a scion of an old New York family, sent west to pursue her style of life away from the disapproving glare of her family's social circle. Men were allowed in Claude's only by a special arrangement when a white flag was raised outside the adobe house. In Broadway crowds at this time a woman who had switched her sexual preference was said to have "gone Santa Fe."

Another category of people came to the Southwest because of the brightness and clarity of the light. This would include the Navajo (according to one of their origin myths), the motion picture industry, Frank Lloyd Wright, Georgia O'Keeffe, and the eccentric astronomer Percival Lowell. The brother of the president of Harvard and of the imagist poet Amy, Lowell retired in 1894 to Flagstaff, Arizona, where he set up an eighteen-inch telescope on a hill outside of town and focused it on Mars. Over the next twenty years, he developed the theory that the elaborate tracery of canals he thought he saw etching the red planet could only be the work of a high civilization; their purpose, he conjectured, was to pump water from the poles to the equator. The planet was dying because it was drying up; the only water was at the poles, and the Martians, he further conjectured, must have put aside their fratricidal nationalism to have developed this global network of irrigation ditches. Lowell's theory had a moral, and his mission became spreading the word about it: the earth could dry up too someday, and we should take heed and learn from the Martian experience to live in peace and harmony. The canals proved to be optical illusions, however. About a third of the observers of Mars report seeing them. One wonders to what degree his theory was subliminally influenced by his living in the high desert of northern Arizona.

Another group of fugitives was persecuted for their religion, the Sephardic Jews who fled the Inquisition in Mexico City and came with the first Hispanic settlers of New Mexico in 1590. The descendants of these *conversos,* so named because they converted to Catholicism but secretly kept their faith alive, are only now beginning to discover (finally understanding the strange vestigial rituals they were brought up with) who they are and are reembracing their hidden Judaic roots. Or the Latter-Day Saints—the Mormons—whose founder and prophet, Joseph Smith, was mob-lynched in Carthage, Illinois, in 1844 for practicing and advocating "plural marriage," and who were then led by the Moses-like Brigham Young on an epic trek into the western desert in search of their promised land, which they found three years later in the valley of the Great Salt Lake, Utah, and called the Kingdom of Deseret.

Then there were those who came to take the desert cure—victims of tuberculosis and other respiratory ailments, who were fleeing the sooty cities and the miasmal climates of the East and Europe; dry air was the only therapy until the discovery of penicillin. Many of these "lungers" took the train to Las Vegas, New Mexico, and checked into sumptuous sanitoriums like the 270-room, Queen Anne–style Montezuma Hotel (now the Armand Hammer United World College), where because nothing could really be done for them, they generally died. But the desert cure worked for John C. Van Dyke, who arrived in Los Angeles in 1897, forty-two years old and suffering from an unspecified respiratory disease, as he later recalled, "just ill enough not to care about perils and morbid enough to prefer dying alone in the sand, to passing out in a hotel with a room-maid weeping on the foot of the bed." Early that summer Van Dyke set out alone, undaunted by warnings of heat and dehydration, with a fox terrier and an Indian desert-bred pony, over the San Gorgonio Pass into the Mojave Desert. "I went into the desert to get well," he wrote. "Many of my days in there were ill days. But I kept busy making notes and studying vegetation and animals. Why did I go alone? Because I could find no one to go with me. They were all afraid of—nothing."

Van Dyke had no set itinerary or timetable, and because he only took out his notebook "at odd intervals, when I lay with my back against a rock or propped up in the sand . . . I cannot well remember the exact route of my odyssey, for . . . I was not traveling by map." Of course the location of water was a major determinant of his route. Van Dyke dug for it in empty washes, he followed the flight of doves to *tinajas,* natural catchments of rainwater (also known as tanks) lingering in shadowy rock crevices. Reaching the Colorado River, he made a raft of reeds and poled across it.

For one sixty-day stretch, he didn't meet a soul. "At first it was a relief to be alone, to be out of sight and sound of civilization, to be able to stop and think and examine values and try to find out the real worth of things human. But there came a time when the instinct to get back into the herd asserted itself. I never tired of the beauty of the desert," Van Dyke confessed. "Its fiery dawns and orange sunsets and opalescent air with the grim grandeur of its tall mountains never paled. But I began to long for the sight of familiar faces, and the sound of friendly voices."

Still, Van Dyke continued his "strange wanderings" for several more seasons, until he realized that he had regained his health (much as the naturalist John Muir cured himself of his pulmonary problems with arduous climbs in the Sierra Nevada). In 1901, Scribners published *The Desert: Further Studies in Natural Appearance,* his account of four years of "wandering for health and desert information"; it was the eleventh of his thirty-five now all-but-forgotten books. Some of the purpler passages are typical of the Victorian prose of the day:

> What tongue shall tell the majesty of it, the poetry of its widespread chaos, the sublimity of its lonely desolation! And who shall paint the splendor of its lights; and from the rising sun to the going down of the moon on the iron mountains the glory of its wondrous colorings! It is a gaunt land of splintered peaks, torn valleys, and hot skies. And at every step there is the suggestion of the fierce, the defiant, the defensive . . .

At times Van Dyke, endorsing the prevalent view of "nature red in tooth and claw," sounds like Henry Morton Stanley slashing his way through "darkest Africa":

The life . . . on the desert is peculiarly savage. It is a show of
teeth in bush and beast and reptile. At every turn one feels the
presence of the barb and thorn, and jaw and paw, the beak
and talon, and sting and poison thereof. There is no living in
concord or brotherhood here. Everything is at war with its
neighbor, and the conflict is unceasing. . . . Everything pur-
sues or is pursued. Every muscle is strung to the highest tension. The bounding deer must get away; the swift-following
wolf must not let him. The grey lizard dashes for a ledge of
rock like a flash of light; but the bayonet bill of the roadrunner must catch him before he gets there.

At other times Van Dyke affects a sharp-eyed indolence, like Thoreau:
"I may confess . . . to having stretched myself for hours upon granite
bowlders [sic] while following the play of indigo lizards in the sand."

In one of his finest passages, he describes the desert's cruelest ruse,
the rain that never lands:

After many nights of heat, long skeins of white stratus will
gather along the horizons, and out of them will slowly be
woven forms of the cumulus and the nimbus. And it will rain
in short squalls of great violence in the lomas, mesas, and bordering mountains. But usually the cloud that drenches a
mountain top eight thousand feet up will pass over an intervening valley, pouring down the same flood of rain, and yet
not a drop reaching the ground. The air is always dry and the
raindrop that has to fall through eight thousand feet of it
before reaching the earth, never arrives. It is evaporated and
carried up to its parent cloud again. During the so-called
"rainy season" you may frequently see clouds all about the
horizon and overhead that are "raining"—letting down long
tails and sheets of rain that are plainly visible; but they never
touch the earth. The sheet lightens, breaks, and dissipates two
thousand feet up. It rains, true enough, but there is no water,
just as there are desert rivers, but they have no visible stream.

Thus, he concludes, the desert is not only terrestrial, but aerial. Van
Dyke perceived the fusion of the land and the sky—a fundamental
characteristic of the southwestern landscape that the Indians had long
been aware of. The Jicarilla Apache, for instance, speak of the earth as
a woman and the sky as a man lying on top of her.

At the other end of the literary spectrum, perhaps, but in his own way
also a fugitive, was Ernie Pyle, a nationally syndicated columnist who
settled in Albuquerque during the Depression and became one of its

important culture heroes—the only middle school in Albuquerque not named for a U.S. president is named for him. Pyle had the perfect voice for this unpretentious working town. In *Ernie Pyle's Southwest,* which introductory "trail notes" by Ed Ainsworth describe as a collection of "some of Ernie's timeless word pictures describing his wandering trips through the desert corner of the Southwest he loved so much," Pyle writes about his First Contact, in 1926, during a "crazy kid tour of America" in a Model-T Ford roadster. The following decade he became a roving reporter, and with his wife, who had a drinking problem, he made sure to swing through the Southwest at least once a year. The Pyles made some friends in Albuquerque, and "there grew in us an overwhelming warmth of feeling for the uncanny sweeps of empty space in this part of the world," Pyle explains. "Out here you actually see the clouds and the stars and the storms, instead of just reading about them in the newspapers. They become a genuine part of your daily life, and half the entire horizon is yours in one glance just for the looking, and the distance sort of gets into your soul and makes you feel that you too are big inside."

Pyle's "expeditions into the realm of solitude," as Ainsworth calls them, took place between 1935 and 1939. Saddened by the suffering of the Depression, he saw himself, according to Ainsworth, as "a vicarious emissary of the destitute," and he himself wrote in straight-shooting prose, "There has been building within me an obsession that the only way to peace of mind is to go somewhere in the desert, far away from things, and just sit down."

In 1943 the Pyles built a modest three-room bungalow out in the high desert east of town. Nothing was out there but "rabbits and sagebrush." The main motive for remoteness was the missus's alcoholism. It was a long walk to the liquor store, and the town was small enough that, once people understood the problem, nobody would serve her. America had entered the war, and Ernie was frequently gone on long, dangerous assignments, reporting on the Pacific theater from the beachheads and the trenches. His dispatches from the American fighting man were syndicated by Scripps Howard in two hundred papers and won him a Pulitzer Prize. On April 8, 1945, Pyle himself was cut down by a Japanese sniper bullet on the tiny South Pacific island of Ie-Shima. His wife attempted suicide by repeatedly stabbing herself with scissors and died of pneumonia six months after him. The house is now a library on Santa Cruz, a crowded street of bungalows, ranches, and adobes, in Ridgecrest, one of Albuquerque's swanker neighborhoods.

Pyle doesn't seem to have established much rapport with the Indians. "The way the Indians stare at you," he wrote after one of his desert forays. "It isn't a stare of curiosity. They see plenty of white peo-ple. It's an unearthly steady stare, like somebody in a trance. They just stare you to death." D. H. Lawrence had been the recipient of similar looks. "And one of these *braves* shoved his glittering eyes close to mine," Lawrence wrote. "He'd have killed me then and there, had he dared. He didn't dare; and I knew it and he knew it."

If Pyle had any mystical experiences at the Anasazi's abandoned sites, he didn't compromise his hard-nosed journalistic image by admitting to them. After a visit to Chaco Canyon, the Anasazi's elabo-rate ritual center, Pyle remarked, "I think I shan't go see any more Indian ruins. For they are exasperating. They raise a question, and leave it unanswered.

"Here at Chaco Canyon, the two great questions are, 'Where did they come from? Where did they go?' You ask with tiredness and res-ignation, for there is no answer. Nobody knows."

Then there was my generation. Many of my peers dropped out of the dominant culture in the sixties and created their own countercultural Other. The movement, which sent the largest wave of Anglo questers to the Southwest to date, had in fact begun in the late forties, with the beatniks. Not long before his death I spoke with the poet Allen Gins-berg, one of its catalysts, about the movement's origins, and he recalled how he and Jack Kerouac and William Burroughs had been deeply impressed by Oswald Spengler's *Decline of the West*. "We read how at the end of the Roman empire the young aristocrats were no longer interested in what was happening in Rome and started exploring the empire's far reaches, to make contact with people like the Visigoths, and we could see the parallel. The energy was going out of American civilization and the young people were repelled by its hyperscientific rationality into a second religiousness and were turning to substrates of what Kerouac called Fellahin humanity, like the blacks and the Mexicans and the Indians."

Ginsberg referred me to a passage near the end of Kerouac's *On the Road*. The narrator, Sal, and two friends have driven over the Mexican border and are nearing the city of "Gregoria," where they will score some marijuana and girls and have an epic debauch. Sal is at the wheel, and while the others are asleep, he thinks how this is

not like driving across Carolina, or Texas, or Arizona, or Illi-nois; but like driving across the world and into the places where we would finally learn ourselves among the Fellahin

Indians of the world, the essential strain of the basic primitive, wailing humanity that stretches in a belt around the equatorial belly of the world from Malaya (the long fingernail of China) to India the great subcontinent to Arabia to Morocco to the selfsame deserts and jungles of Mexico and over the waves to Polynesia to mystic Siam of the Yellow Robe and on around, on around, so that you hear the same mournful wail by the rotted walls of Cádiz, Spain, that you hear 12,000 miles around in the depths of Benares the Capital of the World.

The awe in which Kerouac held these Fellahin Indians is revealed in the next sentences:

These people were unmistakably Indians and were not at all like the Pedros and Panchos of silly civilized American lore— they had high cheekbones, and slanted eyes, and soft ways; they were not fools, they were not clowns; they were great, grave Indians and they were the source of mankind and the fathers of it. The waves are Chinese, but the earth is an Indian thing. As essential as rocks in the desert are they in the desert of "history."

Ruins

My old college buddy Don married the sister of a California classmate right after we graduated in 1968, and after spending the rest of the sixties on the Coast, he and Katie decided to homestead deep in the Hispanic recesses of northern New Mexico. "We went around with topo maps, looking for *ranchos* that weren't being worked," Don recalled. In Coyote (pronounced Ki-yo-TAY), a mountain village of sixty families, whose senior members didn't speak English, "we hit it off with one family, the Martinezes, and they sort of adopted us." The Martinezes sold Don and Katie, for twenty-eight dollars an acre, some land on a spectacular mesa high above Coyote, and they built themselves an adobe house. When I dropped in on them in the spring of 1971, they were planting peas. I remember Don and me riding horses to the edge of a deep canyon and tethering them to an ancient, gnarled piñon tree, and Don prying a chunk of hardened waxy yellow sap from one of its cracks with his folding knife and giving it to me to chew, which he said the Indians did. We jigged down to the canyon floor and sat beside a clear stream tumbling in a series of pools and watched a stubby-tailed bird known as a dipper or water ouzel, bobbing on a boulder, doing about one deep knee bend per second; then it flew downstream for twenty feet, dove into a pool, and walked along the bottom snapping up aquatic insects, possibly caddis flies. That evening the three of us sat on a limestone ledge and watched the sun go down. Don put a match to a stack of dead, gray piñon branches, and it exploded into fragrant, popping, purple flames. Within minutes the branches had crumpled up like burnt scraps of paper, and by the time the sun disappeared, all that was left of them was a smudge on the ledge. Across the arroyo a coyote walked out on a shelf, and closing its eyes, flattening its ears behind its head, and raising its muzzle to the sky, it cut loose with a long, dolorous aria, punctuated with frenzied barks and yips, and exultantly informed the world that it was alive, that it "has a right to be here," as a Navajo friend I made years later would have put it. But then it caught sight of us and immediately clammed up and, with exaggerated insouciance, eyeballing us insolently, melted back into the mesquite.

I admired Don and Katie. They had found their Other years before I would take up my quest. We lost touch with each other. Fifteen years passed. I didn't have the opportunity to return to the Rio Arriba—the Upper Rio Grande Valley—until the summer of 1986. Driving through Coyote in a rented car, I wondered if Don and Katie were still there. The chances of their even being together still, let alone still living on the mesa, I knew were statistically very slim. I stopped at Coyote's little grocery store. A woman named Cecilia Salazar was sitting at a loom, weaving a heavy, striped Rio Grande–style rug. "I weave in the way our Spanish ancestors did," she told me proudly. "This is my great-grandmother's loom. I card and spin the wool myself. It comes out thicker that way, and I dye it with local herbs." I asked if she knew Don and Katie, and she asked back, "Who wants to know? I won't tell, because the last people who were looking for Katie were FBI." (Katie had been active in the Students for a Democratic Society at Berkeley.) I assured her I was just an old friend, and Cecilia said she didn't think they were living on the mesa anymore.

On the way up, I stopped to ask directions of a toothless silver-haired woman dressed in black who spoke only Spanish—the rural Castilian of three centuries ago, mixed with some Basque expressions and occasional borrow words from Nahuatl and Rio Grande Pueblo. She was standing outside a Penitente *morada,* or church. The Penitente Brothers of the Third Order of Saint Francis arose in Spain in the fourteenth century during the Black Death. During Holy Week, its members, known as Penitentes or Hermanos, flagellate themselves to atone for their sins and those of the community. The practice may have come, like many aspects of Old New Mexican culture, from the Moors. Shirtless Shiite Muslims still parade through the streets of Peshawar, Pakistan, during Ramadan, flogging themselves to a crimson pulp. The vows of the Penitentes are known as *alavados,* an Arabic word, and are intoned by a mullahlike cantor. By 1833, when the Franciscans left New Mexico, most of the mountain villagers in the Rio Arriba had joined the order. Through the 1950s, the Penitentes would put themselves through excruciating ordeals during Holy Week, flailing themselves with whips, or *disciplinas,* made of cholla, yucca, leather, or wire, some studded with glass or metal tines, carrying huge crosses to hilltops and hanging from them for days. The order's Holy Week observances became, along with the snake dance of the Hopi, one of the Southwest's early tourist attractions. Many *moradas* phased out flagellation in 1959, but the Penitentes are still very active, helping out the needy, praying for the sick, holding seventy-two-hour wakes, meting out punishment for crimes like stealing.

Farther on, I met a family crammed into an old beat-up Chevy. One of the children in the backseat looked retarded; congenital abnormalities crop up with some frequency in the isolated *poblaciónes*, or settlements, of the Rio Arriba, where cousin marriage is common, and everyone is related to one another in several ways. How you doin'? I asked the man at the wheel, and he said, Doin' without. I asked the way to Don and Katie's, and he said, "When you get up on the *flatecito*, it's the first road after the acequia."

The acequia—another Arabic word—was a stone-lined irrigation ditch that ran for miles down to the valley below. A thousand of the old Spanish and Mexican acequia districts are still apportioning water in the Rio Arriba. They make up the oldest irrigation system in the country. The turnoff ended in a blazing-yellow meadow of three-foot-tall sweet clover. I waded out to the wreck of an old Saab. There was a book on the front seat—Katie's copy of *The Joyous Cosmology,* one of the major countercultural texts. The house looked on the meadow. It was padlocked, and its adobe walls were melting. Obviously, this scene had not been happening for some time. It was a ruin in progress—one of New Mexico's many. The archaeologist David Stuart estimates there are eighty-two thousand prehistoric ruins in the state. There are also numerous derelict windmills, main frames of abandoned uranium mines, and defunct vehicles. Once the roof of an adobe caves in, its walls melt quickly. A lot of mud structures of varied vintage are deliquescing out in the desert. Each ruin represents a defeat, a promise that did not hold. That is the history of the Southwest: a continuous series of boom-and-bust cycles, one group of people coming in and bravely making a go of it for a while, but ultimately being forced to bail out for one reason or other—a prolonged drought, a meteor strike, or, in the most recent case, the end of the Cold War (which has been extinguishing missile ranges and military labs in New Mexico).

I wrote Don a note and stuck it in the door, and a few months later my phone back east rang; it was Don. He told me that he and Katie had split up and had both remarried and divorced, and now they were living in different parts of Santa Fe. They had a boy in college and a girl in high school. After I left in 1971, he told me, Katie got pregnant, but the baby, delivered by Rafaelita Martinez, a *partera,* or midwife, who lived down the road, had been stillborn. The women of Coyote, dressed in black and ululating in the Moorish fashion, had held a seventy-two-hour wake.

"Things started getting rough," Don went on. "The younger generation had stopped growing pumpkins and was living off food stamps. But then they started talking about La Raza [the Race, the People, in the sense of 'we Chicanos'], and there was this back-to-the-land resurgence. 'Hey man this is beautiful, my granddaddy lived in this shack. This is our country.' Other Anglos were burned out or robbed repeatedly, their fences were cut, and their gardens were overrun. One guy's Carminghia was torched, but that was because he was stupid and left it on the road. We never had any trouble; I guess because we were accepted. I'm building another house on the land and I keep tight with Daniel Lujan, who became the *compadre* [godfather] of our son José. I just bought two horses from him."

There was a lot of indigenous violence in Coyote, Don told me. "Almost every family has lost someone in a blood feud. After Daniel's brother was murdered in 1974, Daniel gunned down two of the Ortegas, and that particular cycle ended with a shoot-out at a distance of fifty yards between the Archuletas and the Garcias, with one man killed in each family. The dying words of Claudio Velarde, who was stabbed in the Rancho Allegre Bar, were '*Deme venganza,*' 'Give me vengeance.' Coyote was founded by renegades, and it's still seriously Wild West. There are tons of Salazars and Martinezes. They have an expression that means 'We're all cousins.' My theory is because many of them still don't have television, they have to create drama among themselves for entertainment." The last time I visited Don, in August of 1995, there was a big funeral for Nestor Martinez, the gentle sixty-three-year-old village half-wit, who was shot point-blank in the forehead by one of the young Salazars over a bottle of wine. Nestor used to stand for hours on a ridge with his three dogs looking at the sky, and there was talk he fucked goats. It seemed almost an obligatory rite of passage in Coyote to kill someone in the kindred your people were feuding with. On the side of an old barn someone had sprayed

VIVA LA CAUSA
LA RAZA
LOS MOCHOS

Los Mochos were a branch of the Martinezes whose common ancestor, El Mocho, had lost one of his hands.

. . .

During the 1991–92 academic year I lived in Albuquerque, and Don and I saw quite a bit of each other. Don had explored most of the prehistoric sites around Coyote and had become very knowledgeable about the Anasazi by then, and he was making paintings of their ancient towns as he imagined them to have been in their heyday—powerful paintings, with swirling purple skies. One morning he took me up to a ruined citadel called Tsipin, which sits on a mesa behind Cañones, the *población* between Coyote and Abiquiu. "Tsipin" means "Chipping Place" in Tewa, the language of five present-day Pueblo groups in the Rio Grande Valley who are vaguely descended from the Proto-Puebloan-Anasazi subculture, known as the Pajarito (Little Bird), that built this three-hundred-room complex out on a remnant rib of the plateau overlooking the Chama Valley. Tree rings on pine poles incorporated in the construction date the period of occupation at A.D. 1200 to 1325 or 1350. These Pajarito were master knappers of chert and flint. Perhaps the town specialized in manufacturing projectiles and tools—spearheads, ax heads, arrowheads. The site was superficially excavated in 1905 by the archaeologist Edgar Lee Hewitt and has since been picked over many times by pothunters, but even so, sifting through rubble beneath the city walls, Don found a small, exquisitely faceted, clear quartz-crystal arrowhead.

Of the 82,000 prehistoric ruins in New Mexico, only 300 have been systematically excavated, and there are reliable dates on just 120 to 150. (The term "prehistoric," of course, is completely Eurocentric. On one of my visits to Acoma, a pueblo which was thriving at the same time as Tsipin and is still going—along with several of the Hopi villages, it has the most direct connection to the Anasazi—I stopped to admire an intricately painted bowl that an old man had set out on a table in a narrow winding alley of the adobe complex. I asked the man if the design was prehistoric, and he just look pained and refused to dignify the question with an answer.)

The mesa Tsipin sits on is called Polvadera Mesa (Powdered Mesa), because it is made of porous, aerated, light volcanic tuff. The top is about five hundred feet above the arroyo from which Don and I scrambled up forty-five minutes of steep scree, rising one step for every two. Halfway up, the elements had eaten a perfectly proportioned alcove out of a pocked white-cinder wall. From the top there was a sweeping view of the Chama Valley—Georgia O'Keeffe country. Her Ghost Ranch was down there in Abiquiu. The main entrance to Tsipin came up the other side and rose to the top in a flight of wide stone steps that, Don pointed out, lined up beautifully with the Pedernal, a flat-topped mountain that was one of O'Keeffe's favorite subjects. "God told me if I painted that mountain enough, I could have it," she declared. Like Acoma, the site was both militarily and religiously strategic; it had "the same eccentric shopping list of requirements," David Stuart told me later. The thirteenth century was a time of stress for the Anasazi. By the end of it the entire San Juan Valley, where the culture had evolved (the San Juan drains the Four Corners area, where New Mexico, Arizona, Utah, and Colorado meet), was in the throes of a terrible drought; Chaco Canyon, the great ceremonial center to the southeast, would be abandoned in 1300. That the Pajarito people were suffering from the progressive desiccation of their plateau, too, is reflected in their pottery, whose prevailing motif is the great prayer plume of the mythic guardian of springs and streams, the preserver of water and of life, Awanyu. As the century progresses and the water fails and life becomes more precarious for the Pajarito, the plumes painted in bands on their ollas, or earthen water jars, become more numerous and elaborate. Modern Tewans believe the Pajarito disappeared because they fell out of favor with Awanyu (who subsequently threw himself across the sky, becoming the Milky Way). But why had the Pajarito needed such an impregnable fortress? The Navajo, who would make hit-and-run raids on the Anasazi as they worked in their cornfields and wreak havoc on their already stressed towns, had not yet swept down from the north. Were they competing with other Anasazi for dwindling resources? Down in the Chama Valley, a contemporaneous, probably closely related population had recently been discovered to have practiced an ingenious dry-farming technique called cobble farming, which extends the growing season in agriculturally marginal areas. In the spring these people paved their fields with cobblestones and sowed their crops among them. The stones absorbed the sun's heat and accelerated germination, giving the shoots a boost. But as summer came on, the leaves of the growing plants shaded and cooled the stones, and they took on a new function as condensation plates, providing a moist microclimate. These cobble farmers were such "masters of dryness," as Don put it, they grew even thirsty crops like cotton in their cobble fields.

Don and I joined a deeply grooved track worn smooth by tens of thousands of yucca-fiber sandals that wound through a section of pockmarked pumice that had been cut into cavate chambers, a twenty-room, one-story hotel that Don suggested was maybe for visiting traders. Caravans of *pochtecas,* Aztec merchants who traveled all over Anasazi land and even to the Mound Builders on the Mississippi, probably stayed here. The *pochtecas* were especially interested in turquoise—the prize *chalchihuitl*—and in the sacred peyote, which the Aztec priesthood used to contact the gods and to obtain the revelations and prophesies that enabled it to keep the rest of the population in fear and obedience. They brought military macaws (the green-and-blue species, *Ara militaris,* which ranges as far north as the Sierra Madre) and copper bells, which Anasazi dancers strapped to their ankles or upper calves.

This compound was outside the citadel walls, which we came to farther out on the mesa spur. "A formidable concept," pronounced Don, admiring the 360-degree view. We looked into some rubble-filled pits; Tsipin had had sixteen to eighteen kivas, subterranean ceremonial chambers. Most of the ceremonies probably had to do with keeping on good terms with the clouds and with monitoring the progress of the corn. Eventually, the Pajarito might well have become persuaded, like the Hopi and the Taoseños, that their ceremonies played a central role in the order of things, that the sun wouldn't come up unless they prayed it up.

While men performed increasingly esoteric ceremonies in the smoky darkness of their kivas, the women had an unusual degree of power and recognition in the post-Anasazi, Pueblo society of "historical" times. They were in charge of caring for the enemy scalps, which involved feeding them cornmeal and baring their buttocks at them and touching them to their nipples and vaginas. Ritual intercourse robbed the scalps of their power and converted them into beneficent fetishes, useful for bringing rain. Earth being Mother, and the pueblo being of the earth, it belonged to the women. If a woman wanted to throw out her no-good man, she just placed his blanket and his sandals outside the door.

"Anasazi" is a Navajo word meaning "Enemy Ancestors," which has two possible interpretations. The Enemy Ancestors could either be the forebears of the Navajo's current enemies, especially the Hopi (who are directly descended from the Anasazi and who bear long-standing animosity toward the Navajo; the Navajo word for the Hopi means "Enemy," and the Hopi's own name for the Anasazi is the less charged Histasimon, which simply means "the Ancestors"), or they are the Navajo's own inimical forebears. One afternoon, two Navajo men, Tom and John, and I hiked up to a ridge overlooking Dinnebito Wash, in northeastern Arizona. At the end of the ridge, a small Anasazi ruin surveyed the drainage. "They sure knew how to site 'em," I said to my companions and suggested we go over and check it out. But Tom said no way, the ruin was an "omen," and it was "just a good idea" to steer clear of it. "The Anasazi are people from the past whose time was up, and the Creator took them back," he explained. Something had caused them to be wiped off the face of the earth, and it was best to have no contact with them in case it was transmissible.

John said it wasn't drought—the usual explanation—but "death by fire." In fact, a volcanic spattercone had exploded violently in 1066 (the year William the Conqueror took England), leaving a big hole known as Sunset Crater, north of present-day Flagstaff and about eighty miles southwest of where we were sitting. The cinders that spewed from its cone settled in a fine black mat over hundreds of square miles, hastily driving Anasazi from their pueblos. "Some of the people who lived in Betatakin [a 115-room cliff dwelling thirty miles north] hiked down here. The Red House clan, which is part of the Towering House clan, is their descendants."

In 1851 some Mojave Indians told two young sisters, Olive and Mary Oatman, whom they had abducted from a wagon train, about a now-extinct family from which they and all the races except whites originated. They steered clear of one of this family's ruins on a nearby mountain, which they called "the abode of the spirits," who were, Olive wrote after she had been ransomed and returned to the white world, "perfectly acquainted with all the doings, and even the secret motives and character, of each individual of the tribe." If anyone went there without authorization, "a fire would burst forth from the mountain and instantly consume them."

The view of the Anasazi as somewhat sinister carries over to some Anglo writers. In *Enchanted Mesa,* the last novel of the prolific writer of westerns Louis L'Amour and a departure from his other work, the Anasazi are still alive. They live in a subterranean world that is entered through a hole at the back of a certain remote canyon. Their race is dying, however, and so they are coming out into this world, taking the form of seductive (but cold and heartless) women who kidnap humans so they can interbreed with them and keep themselves going until they reach the Fifth World.

Tree-ring and pollen tests have established that between 1256 and 1279 the Colorado Plateau was gripped by severe drought. Three or four years of drought in a row would have been enough to drive most people away, as when Oklahoma became a dust bowl in the 1930s. By 1300 Chaco Canyon had been abandoned. The cliff towns at Mesa Verde held on a little longer. By 1350, as a result of social turmoil, another volcanic eruption, and a meteor strike, Casas Grandes, the commercial hub of the Greater Southwest, down in what is now Chihuahua, Mexico, had bottomed out.

But the drought may have dealt only the coup de grâce to already debilitated cultures. Corn is an incomplete protein, and overdependence on it produces iron-deficiency anemia, arthritis, shortened life span, and high infant mortality, all of which the Anasazi were suffering from, as well as tooth and gum infections that spread into their jawbones from masticating the hard kernels. The Anasazi didn't know they had to eat beans, too, to get a healthy lysine quota, and they went on eating and worshiping corn and not knowing what to attribute their failing health to. They had come to the end of a long evolutionary trail that had begun five thousand years earlier with the domestication of maize, a wild grass with cobs the size of your forefinger, in the Tehuacán Valley of central Mexico. The stabilization of a plentiful food supply had fueled a population boom—the greatest conurbation on the planet at that point, with pyramids, built by slaves from vassal states, staggered along a mile-and-a-quarter-long Avenue of the Dead. Kernels of the revolutionary plant made their way slowly to the rude, barbarian tribes in the north—the *chichimecos,* the sons-of-dog lineage, as the Aztecs haughtily called them. By 3600 they reached some of the Desert Culture people in the high, rugged pine forest of southeastern New Mexico. But these people were making out fine as hunter-gatherers. They were spreading large nets and catching dozens of erratically bolting jackrabbits, driving deer with moving walls of flame, harvesting some three hundred species of wild edible plants, digging wells, which enabled them to spend more time in waterless areas. They were in the process of switching from spears and atlatls, thong spear-throwers, to the bow and arrow, which were lighter, smaller tipped, and more portable and could be fired from a crouch in the underbrush. So it took three thousand years before maize began to make a dent on the Desert Culture.

At first its members treated maize as another wild grain on their collecting round. In the spring they would bury a few kernels beside a riverbank, and that fall they would come back to see how they had done. But gradually some of the women began to stay around during the summer months and keep the deer, birds, and rodents away from the growing plants. New, improved strains kept coming up from Mexico, and gradually the agricultural revolution took hold. As the Desert Culture people settled into farming, their dwellings became more permanent. They gave up sleeping in caves, windbreaks, crudely lashed stacks of brush, or wherever night found them and began to build a more substantial shelter, the pit house—a dome of slathered mud and brush on a pole frame over a recessed floor—which kept them cool in summer and snug in winter. In the last centuries before Christ, clusters of pit houses—the first farming villages in the Southwest—were built by three different peoples—the Anasazi, the Hohokam, and the Mogollon, on the Colorado Plateau, the Sonoran Desert, and the pine-forested Mogollon Highlands along the New Mexico–Arizona border. In the next thousand years, pottery styles, irrigation techniques, the many-chambered, tiered masonry complex that the Spaniards would call pueblo, pyrite-encrusted mirrors used by shamans for self-hypnosis, and many other elements and artifacts would arrive from the agricultural states to the south.

"Hohokam" means "Not There Anymore," "All Used Up"—as when you've shaken the last drop out of your canteen—in the language of the Pima Indians, who moved into much of the Hohokam area or, some think, may be the Hohokam themselves, who had undergone cultural devolution and reverted to being desert foragers by the time Jesuit missionaries encountered them in the seventeenth century. At their height, during their classic period, around 1450, the Hohokam had hundreds of thousands of acres of the Sonoran Desert under cultivation, and they were tending hundreds of miles of canals. Their life centered on the ditches—mending breaks, desilting, remodeling. The later, more refined ditches were deeper and narrower, which reduced seepage and water loss from evaporation, and they were raised up on levees, so laterals could be run off on both sides. Their settlements tended to be sited at weak points in the system, where a break could create a sudden need for manpower. One canal took off from the Gila River and delivered water to several towns. There must have been an understanding among these communities, some simple agreement on water rights, perhaps even an allotment system.

The Hohokam played, in oblong pits two hundred feet long, pelota, the Mesoamerican ball game that reenacts the defeat of the lords of death. The ball was the size of a cantaloupe and was made of the latex of the guayule bush and could not be kicked or thrown but had to be butted with the hips, knees, or elbows through one of several stone rings set in the pit's walls. Around 1000, they hit on the technique for acid etching, some three hundred years before it was discovered by European armor engravers. The technique involved daubing pitch, usually in the shape of an animal, on the back of a cockle (to get the cockle the Hohokam trekked regularly to the Gulf of California); dunking the cockle into the fermented juice of saguaro-cactus fruit, whose acid ate around the pitch; then prying off the pitch to reveal an intaglio horned toad, frog, snake, or bird.

Even more artistic was a group of Mogollon known as the Mimbres people, who, at the turn of this millennium, began to turn out exquisite pottery: pitchers, jars, crocks, ladles, effigy vessels painted with black-on-white birds, insects, fish, turkeys, mountain lions, water bugs, composite creatures (a toad that is also a rattlesnake, a bat with beaks for ears and human feet), fleurs-de-lis, rotating patterns of detached wings, narratives, scenes from daily life. Around the rim of one bowl, some people are making arrows. On others, a child is being born, a man is being beheaded, birds are being snared in a thicket. A good Mimbres pot these days can fetch twenty-five thousand dollars. By 1200 the Mimbres had spread as far east as Albuquerque and El Paso. Then they lost definition and were apparently absorbed by the Anasazi.

At the same time, the Anasazi were having a golden age. They built Cliff Palace, a fantastic complex with two hundred rooms, twenty-three kivas, and several turrets, on Mesa Verde, in the corner of southwestern Colorado. Mushrooming, budding off daughter communities, at their height three hundred thousand or so Anasazi were scattered over hundreds of thousands of square miles in hundreds of pueblos.

In the tenth century the Anasazi built twelve Great Pueblos and a number of smaller ones in Chaco Canyon and came close to high civilization. The largest, Pueblo Bonito, was on the scale of the Coliseum. Chaco Canyon was the center of an economic, ritual, and social system spread out over an estimated hundred thousand square miles. Communications were maintained by smoke signals sent from mesa to mesa. Recently, infrared scanners on balloons floating above the site remote-sensed five hundred miles of dead-straight, perfectly level, thirty-foot-wide roads leading from the pueblos. Two spiral petroglyphs scored on top of Fajada Butte, at the canyon's southern entrance, were bisected by shafts of sunlight at midday on the solstices and equinoxes, so the Chachoans were closely monitoring celestial events. Don, naturally, has made many pilgrimages to Chaco Canyon. He calls it a "brainful." The historic Pueblos call it Itiwanna, the "Center Place," where Grandmother, Spider Woman, set down her heart and spread her legs out to the four directions.

But by 1300 the time of the Anasazi and the Hohokam was up. The drought may have been only one of the factors in their disappearance. The corn diet, deforestation, internal discord, and the depredations of Ute, Paiute, Navajo, and Apache might have also contributed. Some of the Hohokam canals by then were already fifteen hundred years old. Two things happen to old irrigation systems, especially ones like the Hohokam's, which had no outlet and didn't feed back into the river: waterlogging (after a while, the water that is let out into the fields stops draining into the ground) and salinization (eventually, salts left behind by evaporation ruin the soil). Such problems could well have beset the Hohokam. Erosion, the nemesis of many an agricultural society, was also a problem. The natural process of river-channel deepening, known as arroyo cutting in the Southwest, is accelerated by both irrigation and drought. Some of the rivers could have sunk so low in their beds that water could no longer have been easily brought up from them without techniques the Hohokam didn't have.

Finally, there is evidence of a second dry spell, in the fifteenth century. From the absence of waterbird bones in the fifteenth-century geologic strata along the Gila River, it looks as if the river dried up completely. For the Hohokam, this would have spelled disaster. Their culture by then was overspecialized. After centuries of irrigation farming, drought resistance (a quality of other breeds of corn, like the ones now used by the Hopi) had been bred out of their seeds. Everything about the state of the abandoned Hohokam settlements along the Gila suggests a gradual departure consistent with drought. No unburied skeletons were lying around; few jars were left full of grain.

At the end of the seventeenth century, Jesuit missionaries came up into the Sonoran Desert and found, camped among the ruined pueblos and sand-smothered canals of what had obviously been a sophisticated culture, some poor nomadic Indians who called themselves, like the Navajo, like most tribal peoples the world over, the People. The men were naked; the women wore rabbit skins. The People lived in flimsy brush huts and ate wild sweet potatoes, roots, insects, honey, and mesquite beans. Their way of life was not unlike that of the Desert Culture people, before the arrival of corn. In Spanish, one of the missionaries asked one of the People what tribe he belonged to, and the Indian, who of course had never heard Spanish, said, "*Pimach,*" which in his tongue meant "I don't know," that is, "I don't understand what this man is saying." As a result of this all-too-common failure of communication (which has only been compounded with the arrival of a second European culture), the People became known as the Pima.

For many years, it was thought that the Pima were the descendants of the Hohokam, who had regressed to nomadic foraging. But cultural regression is usually associated with migration. The Amazon Indians, for instance, who at the time of European contact in 1541 were living in densely packed agricultural and fishing chiefdoms that went on for as many as sixty leagues along the main Amazon, retreated (or those who survived) to the headwaters of tributaries, where, protected from slavery, epidemics, and missionaries by daunting rapids, they regressed to hunter-gatherers. Regression rarely happens in place, an anthropologist told me. Evidence has been mounting that the Pima were a Mexican tribe that came up into Arizona and filled the void after the collapse of Hohokam culture. Indeed, why would the Pima have called the Hohokam the Not There Anymore people if they were them?

Maybe some of the Hohokam went up to the Hopi mesas and joined them. The Hopi have a story about how one of their clans—the Cloud or Water clan, nicknamed the Flood clan (the version that follows was collected in the thirties by a Hopi named Edmund Nequatewa)—lived many years ago at a place to the south called Palotquopi, which is thought to have been one of the Hohokam's towns in the Gila or Salt Valley. The people of Palotquopi were very prosperous. They diverted water from the river that ran through their country into canals they had dug, and everybody worked on the canals together. The eventual collapse of Palotquopi, however, wasn't due to drought or failure of the irrigation system. One time the people down at Palotquopi put on a butterfly dance. The Hopi butterfly dance is performed by unmarried girls as a demonstration that they are ready for husbands. This dance was so successful that it went on several days. Some of the young married women began to take part in it. Gradually the festivities moved from the dance plaza into the cozy darkness of the kivas. Nobody cared who was whose wife or husband anymore. Finally several of the men got it on with the chief's wife. Respect for the chief was what kept the community—any community—together, and when this happened, Palotquopi promptly fell apart.

As for what became of the Mogollon, most of them were probably absorbed by the Anasazi, but some of them may have headed south in the Sierra Madre and morphed into the Tarahumara.

The Anasazi are still in the Southwest. They became the Pueblos. Some of the prehistoric pueblos—Acoma, Zuñi, and several of the Hopi villages—were never abandoned. Dental and genetic comparisons of the Anasazi and the Hopi show no important differences. There is a straight transition from Chaco Canyon to the Zuñi in the redware pottery of both as well. The Pajarito came down into the Rio Grande Valley and became the Tewans. The governor of San Felípe Pueblo told me his ancestors took the "middle road" from Mesa Verde, and the Navajo claim that their Red House clan is Anasazi from Betatakin (and thus Enemy Ancestors?). "Are you going to let the Hopi tell you they're the only ones descended from the Anasazi?" my Navajo friend Tom asked.

It isn't so hard to imagine moving to the river when the countryside is drying up. The Anasazi-Pueblo connection seems more of a problem for the archaeologist, who requires harder evidence than does oral history. "What happened to the Anasazi is no mystery to us," a Pueblo told me. "We are the Anasazi." The Anasazi are not only genetically but culturally alive. The essential ethos, the ancient common world-view, is still operative. As Edward P. Dozier, an anthropologist of the Pueblos, remarks, "The Pueblos would appear to mirror the past rather well." But the culture has become of necessity more secretive and inaccessible, more fossorial and hermetic, since the arrival of Europeans four centuries ago.

The thousand-year record of what could be cannibalism on the Colorado Plateau may be related to the deficiency of the corn diet. Ten mass-burial sites with from five to eighty-nine violently dismembered skeletons have been discovered in the last few years. The most recent, near one of the Hopi's village, carbon-dates to A.D. 1700. While cannibalism can't be proven from bones, the only scenario that satisfactorily explains the state of the skeletons is that the bones were taken apart and eaten. "The long bones were broken open and appear to have been scraped for their marrow content," the archaeologist Christy Turner told me. "Crania were split. Teeth were blown out. There is near-total destruction of the face and heads; one skull received nine high-velocity blows from a club or boulder. Parts of the skeletons are missing. Half a body at one site was stuffed up a fireplace ventilator. The bones are charred, yet there is no evidence of general conflagration at the sites, which suggests that they were roasted, and their excellent state of preservation indicates that the soft tissue was not left to disintegrate around them. Some have been gnawed by what may have been human teeth. All the skeletons are those of plateau people, Anasazi."

The Hopi themselves do not accept Turner's conclusions and deeply resent archaeologists digging their ancestors' graves, which they have since successfully put a stop to. "This is just Anglo disinformation to make us look like savages," a Hopi told me. During the Pueblo Revolt of 1680, when the Spaniards were driven out of New Mexico, the Hopi razed one of their villages, Amatovi, for wholeheartedly collaborating with the Franciscan missionaries. The corpses were mutilated but not cannibalized.

It is unclear why Anasazi would have eaten each other, if indeed they did (which I don't have any problem believing). Maybe they were given to ritual or revenge cannibalism—the sort of torture and mutilation practiced by many of the historic southwestern tribes, who danced around scalp poles, wore long bones as trophies, and shot arrows into the eyes, ears, tongues, and genitals of strung-up captives. Cannibalism is the most terrible humiliation that can be inflicted on a hated enemy, and it generally intensifies at the chiefdom stage, when communities subjugate and exact tribute from one another, and a paramount chief arises who controls several communities—the stage the Anasazi had reached when they disappeared.

. . .

The most powerful Anasazi ruins, for me, are down in the converging canyons of de Chelly and del Muerto, in northeastern Arizona. The canyons are also a gallery. For two thousand years the inhabitants of these canyons—the Anasazi; their ancestors, who are known as the Basket Makers; and the Navajo, who came later and still live there— let their imaginations run wild on their walls, pecking or painting hundreds of images. Some of the petroglyphs and pictographs are so high up you wonder how the artists reached them.

Late one afternoon a few Julys back, my wife and I and Don and his friend Abby and her two daughters went to see the canyons. On the way down Route 64 to their junction at Chinle, our two-car caravan pulled over to check out the Antelope House Overlook. Walking south a few hundred yards on the rocky piñon-and-juniper-studded plateau, we suddenly found ourselves at the edge of the stupendous Canyon del Muerto. Six hundred feet below, a cottonwood-lined river curved among tan cliffs and buttresses streaked with desert varnish, only now, it being the height of summer, the river had been reduced to a few interbraided streamlets meandering on its sandy bed (in spring the whole canyon floor becomes a torrent). We could hear a dove cooing and a dog barking on the wind and women's laughter coming up from a pickup full of Navajo—an erosion-control crew that had knocked off for the day—careening merrily on the canyon floor. A fine rain was sifting down through the sunlight. Through this gleaming curtain we could see, nestled under a gargantuan streaked wall at a bend of the river, a cluster of small, round or square, roofless adobe structures, the same khaki color as the cliff and completely dwarfed by it. These were the ruins of Antelope House, once the home of forty or so Anasazi. It was one of the most astonishing and resonant frames I had laid eyes on. If I had to choose a single image to represent the passage of the human species on this earth, this would be it. My wife said it was like a dream, and that night she dreamed that some very holy people, dressed in white, told her she could live in the canyon for the rest of her life.

In the morning we rode on horses down into the canyon with a Navajo named Dennis and spent the day looking at the rock art. There are all kinds of amazing images: headless birds; wingless birds whose angled bodies and dangling legs make them seem as if they were in flight; turkeys; ducks; cranes; fret designs; maps of the night sky; birdheaded men; men with birds on their heads; polychrome men; looparmed men; women with pincerlike labia between their legs; the humpbacked flute player Kokopeli—a Mesoamerican figure who crops up on walls all over the Southwest—here with a huge erection; positive and negative handprints (dark on light background and vice versa); men; dogs; bighorn sheep stuck with arrows. One of the most recent panels, a masterpiece historic mural by an unknown Navajo, portrays a cavalcade of Spanish soldiers in cloaks and flat-brimmed hats with muskets held aloft—the Narbona expedition of 1805, sent out to take care of the "Navajo problem." Ninety Navajo men and twenty-five women huddled in a cave were gunned down by these caballeros on the rim of what came to be called as a result the Canyon del Muerto. The terrible new menace that was in store for the native southwesterners, just as they were coming out of the devastating decades of drought, seemed embodied in this sinister column of horsemen. It clarified why the Navajo call Spaniards *nakai,* travelers, those who move around in groups.

After galloping us up a sandbar of the Canyon de Chelly, Dennis reigned up before another rendering of Kokopeli, here lying on his back, tickling his tube, while a squatting woman to his right was giving birth, the baby emerging from between pincer labia.

My wife told us about some prehistoric people who lived along the Kagera River in Rwanda and were called the Chwezi, and about how her people, the Tutsi, feared them because they were reputed to steal children. Navajo believe the same thing about the Anasazi, but Dennis didn't seem to be afraid of them. He called them the Ancient Ones. Who were they? I asked.

"I've heard that they may have been aliens whose ship crashed," he said. "They made do with what was around until another ship came and picked them up, somewhere around 1200."

The twin canyons are among the Navajo's most sacred places, and they became the focus of resistance in 1863 when General James H. Carleton launched a campaign to round up the Navajo and their equally troublesome cousins, the Mescalero Apache. "All Indian men . . . are to be killed," Carleton ordered, and the women and children were to be marched three hundred miles down to an internment camp at Bosque Redondo, in the parched desert of southeastern New Mexico. The idea behind what the Navajo call the Long Walk was that if you took the Navajo "away from their haunts and hills and hiding places of their country" to a reorientation center and "there be kind to them; there teach their children how to read and write; teach them the arts of peace; teach them the truths of Christianity"—they would in time become model citizens. "Fair Carletonia," however, as the camp was called, fell tragically short of its utopian mandate, and in fact became a model for the Third Reich's concentration camps.

The leader of the Navajo campaign was fifty-three-year-old Kit Carson, the old Indian fighter; this was his last hurrah. The Navajo called him Rope Thrower, because he lassoed them. Detachments of bluecoats, augmented by Ute and *nakai* irregulars, fanned out over Dinetah, the sacred Navajo homeland, torching hogans and crops and running off stock. By winter Carson's scorched-earth policy had left the People facing starvation. Finally Carson and his men entered the Canyon de Chelly, where they met with fierce resistance from a new cult founded by a thirty-five-year-old man known as Hashkenneniinii, the Angry One, who thought he would be able to enlist the supernatural being Monster Slayer as an ally. As search-and-destroy missions of bluecoats rode up and down the twin canyons, Navajo threw rocks down on them and whooped and taunted them from above. Occasionally there would be skirmishes, and the attackers would disappear up the canyon walls, using secret handholds. Peach orchards were destroyed; a grandmother was shot in the head as she chanted one of her witchcraft songs, and her bundle of poison was burned. Piles of bodies accumulated on the canyon floor. At last the People realized that their only alternative to extermination was to submit to removal, and they began to come out in groups of three to ten and surrender to the *bilagaana* (as *americanos* had come out sounding in their language).

"When I'm in this canyon, I feel like I'm with my grandmother, my *nali*," said Dennis a few bends on. His maternal grandmother had summered and grown corn up the canyon at Spider Rock, the abode of the Navajo culture hero Spider Woman (as opposed to the Pueblo Spider Woman, who set down her heart at Chaco Canyon), who taught the women how to weave. His grandmother had told him that long ago the canyons were made by huge, hippopotamus-like creatures wallowing in the mud of what was then a vast quagmire. After they had gouged out the canyons, they sent the epic-sized Hummingbird to check if the walls were dry, which explains why some of them are scored with stuttering parenthetical gashes that look like the imprint of huge wings.

Enter Man

opi traditionally believe (as do Havasupai) that they issued from the Place of Emergence in the Grandmother Canyon—the Grand Canyon. Navajo believe they emerged from Navajo Lake, the navel of the universe. The prevailing Anglo theory during most of the nineteenth century about the origin of the Indians was that they were one of the Lost Tribes of Israel. The Mormons considered them to be the Lamanites, a Lost Tribe that had been blighted with dark skin for turning away from the Lord and for routing the Nephites, whose history, the Book of Mormon, engraved on two golden tablets in "reformed Egyptian" hieroglyphs, was given by the angel Moroni to twenty-two-year-old Joseph Smith to translate.

By the end of the century evidence had accumulated that at least half a dozen times during the ice ages, from a million and a half to perhaps eleven thousand years ago, the Bering Strait had frozen solid, creating a corridor between Alaska and Asia that enabled many forms of life to cross continents. During early congelations of the strait, camels and three-toed horses traveled from the Americas to Asia, and ancestral coyotes trotted over, giving rise to African jackals and all the fetching breeds of the domestic dog, while herds of woolly mammoths, musk oxen, primitive bison, caribou, moose, deer, elk, and antelope fanned down into the Americas, and various reptiles—frogs, snakes, including the pit viper—hopped or slithered over the bridge. The grizzly bear was one of the most recent arrivals from the Old World—within the last twenty thousand years—as were the ancestors of bighorn sheep and man.

The date of humans' arrival in the New World is still hotly debated. Conservative paleoanthropologists say there was no one until twelve thousand years ago, but a growing number of their colleagues believe it could be much earlier—possibly as long as seventy thousand years ago.

Strong dental evidence—thirty characters shared by ancient jaw-bones in Siberia and North America—suggests that the initial groups (the first group may not have contained more than a hundred people) were nomadic mammoth hunters from the Lena Basin of northeastern Siberia. These nomads, who probably followed the game across the strait, would multiply into almost all the fourteen million or so native peoples living in the Americas by the time of Columbus's "discovery." The Eskimo and the Apacheans were of different Siberian stock and came in separate waves. The first wave was the ancestral Paleo-Indians. Most Native Americans are of Paleo-Indian, that is, Lena Basin, stock.

What else is known about these people? The men averaged five feet, four inches. They had the epicanthic fold—eyelids whose drooping inner corners possibly evolved as protection from snow glare. They wore hides stitched with bird-bone needles and sinew threads. Dogs pulled their sleds and travois, guarded their camps, and brought their game to bay. They had fire, but it is unclear whether they knew how to make fire from scratch or just took along smoldering sticks from their last camp, whether the genealogy of their nightly fires was ultimately traceable to a lightning strike or a volcanic eruption in Siberia years before. Around the fires they told stories. They seem to have been fully capable of articulate speech, to have had more or less the same emotional and intellectual range as modern humans. The care with which they buried their dead children, for instance, suggests that they felt love and grief. Their culture was that of the Upper Paleolithic. Among the ideas and technics they brought with them to the New World were the pit house, the spear-thrower, the bull-roarer, the cult of the bear, the "X-ray" style of depicting animals, the frog as a water symbol. There was probably in each of their bands someone who played a specialized spiritual role, a shaman who, by establishing a relationship with the animal powers, with the world of hidden causes, attempted to foretell the future, including the outcome of hunts and raids; to influence weather patterns and the movement of game; to diagnose and treat the sick; and to cause injury to enemies by sorcery and magic.

As these nomadic hunters fanned down into North America, they found a hunter's paradise. There were no other humans to compete with, only vast herds of large, shaggy, dull-witted beasts that had never seen man before and had no reason to fear him. "I can almost imagine a party of Paleo-Indians walking up to a mammoth and lighting a fire under it," a paleoanthropologist told me.

In such abundance their numbers grew quickly. Some left the parent band and formed a new band, and when that band got too large, a third band formed, and the scattered bands made their way south, remaining in friendly running contact, their collective population growing at an explosive rate, maybe even by 4 percent a year. Moving slowly, in no great hurry, skirting ice barriers, feeling their way into new life zones, discovering the properties of new plants (and sometimes, undoubtedly, paying for the price of this knowledge with their lives), their senses fully engaged, their minds and bodies constantly challenged, stopping to establish a temporary base for a season or two, then picking up and moving on, proceeding an average of perhaps no more than five or six miles a year, they began to show up in the Southwest no later than eleven thousand years ago and maybe a lot earlier.

Some of the bands came down the Great Basin into the Basin Ranges country. A greater number stayed east of the Rockies, in what are now the Great Plains. Some of these rounded the southern tip of the Rockies, New Mexico's Sangre de Cristo Mountains, and entered the Southwest that way. By 10,500 years ago some of them were already in sight of Tierra del Fuego, at the tip of South America, and there may have been as many as six thousand Paleo-Indians scattered over the New World, with a density of one per square mile—the maximum density for a viable hunter-gatherer population—at the front of the line.

The Southwest at that time was maybe ten degrees cooler. What is now desert was steppe. The piñon-juniper woodland and some of the pine forests were more extensive. Dryness did not define the country and its possibilities as it does now. More rivers and streams flowed year-round. A strong, wide river could present a serious barrier, and it was at the places where the animals crossed the rivers, and at the water holes where they came to drink, that they were most vulnerable. Most of the Paleo-Indian archaeological sites are kill sites near water. One of the earliest, in eastern New Mexico, is a little spring-fed pond that overflowed into Blackwater Draw, a tributary of the Brazos, about 10,000 years ago, but has since dried up and been covered with sand. Here, about 11,500 years ago, a number of mammoths and bison were slaughtered. First the hunters hamstrung the beasts, then they went for their throats with spears. The animals were butchered on the spot. In the centuries that followed, their missile-riddled carcasses were covered with a mat of black silt, and much later they were exposed again by erosion. Five leaf-shaped spear points, made of percussion-flaked chert, several of them five inches long, were found embedded in a pachyderm's rib cage. The site was dug in the thirties, and the people who had made the points were called Clovis, after a nearby stop on the Atchison, Topeka, and Santa Fe Railroad that had been known until

1907 as Riley's Switch and was renamed by the daughter of a railroad official who had been studying about the fifth-century king of the Franks. (It was in Clovis in the fifties, in the recording studio of a local rock-and-roll aficionado named Norman Penny, that Buddy Holly recorded "That'll Be the Day" and other classics, his four previous singles having bombed in Nashville.)

There are earlier dates for the arrival of man. Some want to knock Clovis man from his pedestal, and others want him there forever. The first attempt to dislodge Clovis, an archaeological coup because you would then be the man with the oldest man, was made in the late thirties by the archaeologist Frank C. Hibben, who claimed to have found twenty-five-thousand-year-old artifacts in a cave in the Sandia Mountains, overlooking Albuquerque. The artifacts did not hold up to subsequent radiocarbon dating, which was developed after the war. Nor could Hibben's conclusions be verified. A responsible archaeologist is supposed to leave part of the site intact so it can be sifted through by a "replication team," and Hibben dug the cave clean. "Hibben was charismatic and he had the reputation of being a heavy hitter," one of his colleagues told me, "but he had a peculiar radiocarbon date that couldn't be replicated."

"An archaeologist is like a gold prospector," the first colleague explained. "All he's doing is making a claim, and he has to submit the claim to the community of investigators so it can be verified."

Equally controversial is the 1990 discovery by the archaeologist Richard MacNeish, in a cave in southern New Mexico, of what he claims are signs of human occupation going back at least forty thousand years. One afternoon in February 1992, I drove down to the site where MacNeish had just arrived to supervise the third and final digging season. The site is on the McGregor missile-testing range, 125 miles south of the Trinity Site at White Sands, where "the Gadget," the first atomic bomb, was detonated on July 16, 1945. Here the bugs were taken out of Nike Atlas and Zeus missiles; the Falcons, Matadors, Rascals, and Aerobee Hi's, Honest Johns, Little Johns, Sergeants, Lacrosses, Hawks, Darts, and the Patriots that had proven so effective in the recent showdown with Saddam Hussein were tested; and research on laser-beam death rays, part of the Star Wars program, was conducted until 1989. The death ray was "a failed effort," Bill Broad, who had written a book on the program, told me, but Star Wars, "like Frankenstein, has taken on a life of its own." The most money yet—$4.15 billion—had just been budgeted

for it. The new concept was an interceptor rocket called the Brilliant
Pearl, which was probably going to be tested here.

I drove over the Organ Mountains, a tiara of jagged brown spires
east of Las Cruces, and down into the next intermontane basin, which
is known as the Tularosa (from the Spanish *tule,* for cattail). But no
wet spots with cattails were visible from here, only vast creosote flats
receding to the distant, hazy silhouette of the Jarilla Mountains to the
east. "In all the sun-scorched and sand-blasted reaches of the Southwest there is no grimmer region . . . ," writes the historian C. L. Sonnichsen. "The Tularosa country is a parched desert where everything,
from cactus to cowman, carries a weapon of some sort, and the only
creatures who sleep with both eyes closed are dead." This is Billy the
Kid country, one of the last pockets of the wild frontier, which persisted even after Hollywood began to immortalize it in celluloid shoot-
'em-ups. Here Pat Garrett, who gunned down Billy the Kid in his long
johns in 1881 as he was heading to Pete Maxwell's meat room in Fort
Sumner to cook himself a steak, met his own violent end twenty-seven
years later during an altercation with a neighbor on the other side of a
countywide feud. There was a series of other murders that so destabi-
lized the political scene that they delayed New Mexico's statehood.
Now most of the Tularosa, along with about a third of the state,
belongs to the federal government—the Department of Defense or the
Bureau of Land Management.

A soldier guarding the entrance to the missile range waved me
through without even asking for an ID. It's over, I realized. The Cold
War is over. The whole operation seemed to have pretty much wound
down. I turned left at a white stand of the various models of missiles
that had been put out over the years and headed down a road that
ran straight through creosote bushes for the next twenty miles.
Every so often a patch of creosote would be singed (Zapped by a death
ray? I wondered), or a road would shoot off to the right or left, with
a sign identifying it as the way to the Launching Command Center or
the Armaments, Munitions, and Chemical Command, to Missile
Assembly, Telemetry, or the Nuclear Effects Directorate, or there
would be a yellow diamond-shaped road sign that announced an
upcoming TANK CROSSING. The flats were littered with shrapnel—
twisted shiny metal fragments of what I supposed were capsules, can-
isters, and casings of sophisticated experimental weapons or their
targets, slow-flying unpiloted craft known as drones. Thirty thousand
years from now the archaeologists are going to have a field day here,
I reflected.

What a weird overlap, a wild time line, what an escalation—from the spear-thrower to the six-gun to the death ray—there was in this parched, empty basin. How much nastier the world had become. But maybe the whole modern scene, here so precariously dependent on water and war contracts, really is an "interregnum," as Lawrence called it. I wondered what it would have been like to have been Mac-Neish's discovery—or creation—Pendejo man.

MacNeish and his team of four were quartered in a cinder-block barracks outside Orogrande (Big Gold), population sixty-three. The name refers to a nugget reportedly the size of a finger that was found there in 1905 and sparked a brief gold rush that ended a year later when the ore-bearing veins gave out. The place today consists of a bar, a café, a post office, a gas station, a convenience store, and about fifteen families. MacNeish, "up in his seventies and running around like an antelope," in an admiring colleague's description, was in traditional archaeologist garb—khakis and a wide-brimmed straw hat. His bushy mustache and bully dynamism reminded me of Teddy Roosevelt (Mac-Neish had even boxed in his youth, like Roosevelt; he had been a Golden Gloves champion in Binghamton, New York, in 1938). He clearly enjoyed being the maverick, the heretic, reveled in the outrage and the attention. A classic southwestern mental outlaw, if ever there was one. He knew exactly what he had here, and fuck the archconservatives in Tucson, fuck the fuddy-duddy Clovis-firsters. His use of the F word became more frequent as we sat up late into the night with a bottle of Jack Daniel's.

"So you want to know about the origin of man in the New World?" Scotty, as he insisted I call him, asked. "You're embarking on a stormy sea I've been a sailor on for many years, since Tamaulipas, Mexico, 1949. At that time I was looking for the origin of corn. We knew that the valley with the first domesticated cobs was somewhere between Chile and the St. Lawrence River, so we just kept bracketing, until on a high terrace in Tamaulipas we found some little ones that carbon-dated from four thousand to four thousand five hundred years ago. The technology had just been developed, and this was one of the first hundred carbon dates. We continued to dig, and under the layer with the corn we found pre-Clovis material, evidence of a pre-projectile-point man more than twelve thousand years old—in fact, considerably more than twenty thousand. Later, in 1968, we found a cave in Peru where a ground sloth had been killed twenty-five thousand years ago. Other early dates began to come in from colleagues: Chile, thirty-three thousand years ago; Pennsylvania, twenty-five thousand years ago;

Brazil, twenty-five to thirty thousand years ago, with one date estimated at forty-two thousand—which may not be any earlier than what we've got here. The lowest of our four levels is at the end of the scale of what carbon-fourteen dating can accurately deal with. Over thirty-two to thirty-three thousand years ago the dates are meaningless.

"But in the fifties Clovis began to crystallize in some people's minds as the earliest big-game hunter, and as evidence accumulated to the contrary, these people began to dig in. And forty years later they still won't admit they're wrong. They've got whole theories based on nobody being around before twelve thousand years ago, and they don't know what to do with these data, which say they're wrong. It's very hard for these people to say, 'Mea culpa, my career for the last forty years has been on the wrong track.'

"You have to understand that the same thing happened when Clovis was discovered in 1931. At that time the dictators of archaeology were two men named Holmes and Hrdlička. They had risen to prominence in the 1890s and had decided, on the basis of American Indians' skulls, on the lack of Neanderthal remains, that there were no Ice Age men in the New World, that man could not have been contemporaneous with the extinct Ice Age animals, and every time somebody came up with a mammoth or an extinct horse or bison with a projectile point in it, Holmes and Hrdlička shot him down. They went to their graves refusing to admit that man arrived earlier than six thousand years ago. Of course up to 1860, when Darwin and Spenser applied evolutionary theory to the origin of man, and a half-million-year-old ape-man was found in Java, the entire world was only five thousand years old when God created Adam and Eve and the Garden of Eden, and the Indians were thought to be one of the lost ten tribes. The Bering Strait theory had been proposed earlier in that century by Jefferson, Franklin, and other luminaries of the American Philosophical Society. It was important that the Indians not be very old in the New World, that before they arrived there had been civilized Mound Builders, whom the barbarian Indians had done in, and there was Church dogma to back this up, because this justified shooting every Indian on sight."

In the morning we drove out to the site. The McGregor range had been off-limits to humans without clearance from 1974 to 1989 while the Patriot and the death ray were being tested, and MacNeish, who was looking for some undisturbed caves that "the looters from Texas" hadn't had the opportunity to visit, where there might still be some early plant remains, thought there might be some on this 600,000-plus-acre tract. In 1990 he found one in a dolomite limestone cliff above the desert floor and named it Pendejo Cave. *Pendejo* is Mexican-Spanish slang for pubic hair and, by some metaphoric leap that no one has been able to explain to me, idiot or fuckup; addressed to the wrong person, without checking how much he has had to drink, it can get you into trouble. It is one of the choice *nuevomejicano* swears.

One of MacNeish's scoffers told me that he named his discovery Pendejo Cave because "anybody who believes him is a fool," but MacNeish explained that the arroyo below the cave was called Pendejo Wash on his map.

Clearing the owl and bat droppings and pack-rat middens from the floor of the cave, the team soon found a layer of yucca-fiber sandals, corncobs, acorns, beans, piñon nuts, projectile points, and potsherds dating as far back as 1000 B.C. Then one day one of the diggers came running with a large bone that MacNeish recognized as belonging to a horse that had been extinct for eleven thousand years. In the weeks that followed, bones of all kinds of extinct animals—tapir, llamas, skunks, weasels, magpies, giant turtles, a new kind of horse, "big, fat, and ploddy like a western range horse"—forty species in all, amid what appeared to be ancient fireplaces and lithics, were unearthed.

"Oh hell," MacNeish told me he had said, as we climbed up to the cave. "The shit's hit the fan again. Early man is a hornet's nest. Let's do it right this time so all these niggling objections can be resolved. Bring in the objectioners to tell us why they don't like it and bring in experts to test their hypotheses against mine."

So MacNeish invited the big guns to come and look at his site, and as they had with every other one claimed to be more than twelve thousand years old, they didn't buy it. "They didn't think the artifacts were artifacts. They said they were slivers of rock that had fallen from the roof of the cave and had been stomped and chipped by animals. We tried stomping on some rocks ourselves, but we couldn't get them to look anything like the lithics we'd been finding. We just had a mineralogist here who said some of the rocks in the cave came from thirty miles away; forty-four percent of the lithics are foreign.

"They said the bones must have been dragged in by a saber-toothed tiger or a dire wolf. 'And what about this piece of whittled bone sticking in the heel bone of this horse, which we did a CAT scan on and is thirty-two thousand five hundred years old?' I asked. They said they didn't think the date was very good, or that the point had been put there by somebody, but it had been sunk a inch and a half into the horse, really smacked with at least forty pounds of pressure.

" 'And what about all these fireplaces?' I asked. 'Did the tiger roast the animals, too?' 'They aren't fireplaces,' the objectioners said, 'they're

the remains of forest fires or lightning strikes.' Imagine, twenty-four
lightning strikes that landed right in the middle of twenty-four rings of
stone, laid out just like hearths. I've excavated eight hundred fireplaces,
goddammit, don't you think I know a fireplace when I see one? But just
to make them happy, we're having thermoluminescence tests performed
on the stones. Thermoluminescence dates are good back to forty thousand years. They can tell you how hot the fire was and the direction of
the burn. If the sides of the stones facing inside the rings were hotter
than the outsides, then we've got 'em."

We passed the wreck of a drone and a flag marking something that
had not exploded. MacNeish showed me an agave called lechuguilla,
quids of whose stiff, pointed basal leaves, dating fifteen to eighteen
thousand years ago had turned up in the cave. He indicated three
species of milletlike *Setaria* grass, which he said was as nutritious as
wheat. He pointed down to the edge of the wash. "That's an abnormal
amount of *Opuntia* [prickly pear] down there. It's probably due
to human disturbance. In Mexico they let a big fire go down to ash,
then they put their food on *Opuntia* paddles and the paddles right on
the cinders. The paddles are called *nopales*. They're pretty high in
protein."

He explained how from twenty-nine thousand to fifty or sixty thousand years ago there had been a grassland desert in the Tularosa, something like the one presently around Abilene, Texas, but with camels,
little horses, midget goats, great big long-extinct Aztlan jackrabbits;
then from twenty-nine thousand to eighteen thousand years ago there
had been a wet period, and the basin had turned into a woodland with
oak trees and a series of lakes, with mammoths mucking around them.
Then around nineteen thousand years ago, as the huge sheet of the
Wisconsin glacier far to the north had begun to recede, the lakes had
become smaller and smaller, and the desert had returned, but a different kind of desert, with giant tortoises, buffalo, agave, and cactus.
Then between twelve and ten thousand years ago, as the last glacier
advanced, there had been a juniper woodland.

Each of these periods was reflected in the layered contents of the
cave floor. Although MacNeish's critics accuse him of being cavalier
with his carbon dating and sloppy with his science, the interior of the
cave was impressively sectioned off with strings, plumb lines, and let-
tered series in accordance with the La Perra technique, and two members of the team were carefully brushing off a shelf. The precise
location was noted and a drawing was made of any artifact before it
was removed, and if it was a really good one, it was photographed.
MacNeish pointed out in Zone C—around the time of Christ—a bed

of leaves, a pallet that some Archaic Indian had slept in. He showed me the twelve-thousand-year-old stratum. "This is where some of my colleagues begin to get nervous. We found a palm and a fingerprint in clay fired into brick in Zone I, twenty-eight thousand nine hundred years ago. The objectioners suggested they were ours, so we had ourselves fingerprinted. Zone N had a nice orangy fireplace outlined by river pebbles that I'd guesstimate is forty-two thousand to forty-five thousand years old. You get humans—or their pebble choppers—to the top of O, which is beyond the range of most of the machines." He showed me part of the cave that had not been excavated and was going to be boarded up so a replication team could have at it.

"How far back will we go in the end?" he asked. "In this cave, at least fifty thousand years. But I'm convinced that the arrival of man in the New World will turn out to have been much earlier: more like seventy thousand." Then he attacked the theories that were making some of his colleagues hold at twelve thousand years ago. One of the theories has the Paleo-Indians moving from the Bering Strait to Tierra del Fuego in just a thousand years. "I lived with Eskimo for ten years, and I saw how slow their migrations are. It's a population-pressure process. By the third generation, when your family has grown from four members to twenty-four, one of the sons has to move twenty miles away. When you reach a new ecological zone, when you have to leave the tundra and live in the boreal forest or the plains, you're reluctant to leave what you're adapted to. We're talking five to six thousand years to Patagonia at a minimum. And look at the diversity of the descendants of the Paleo-Indians—their many blood types and differences in DNA. There are twelve separate races—six-foot, two-inch Algonquins, Mayans, Aztecs, five-foot, two-inch, squat fatty ones in Brazil. They're more diverse than even the Caucasians. They've got a hundred and fifty languages. They had to be sitting around a lot longer than twelve thousand years for that to happen."

I polled some of MacNeish's colleagues on his dates. They fell into three groups: those who didn't seem to be interested in being objective; those who had no theoretical problems with an earlier time arrival, but wanted to see hard data; and those who thought MacNeish was definitely on the right track. The thing that impressed me more than the cave itself, a triangular niche maybe fifteen feet on a side and maybe forty deep, was its site. The cave was above what was now a waterless arroyo, but was probably during much of the period when it was occupied a full-time stream, in a branch of a narrow defile known as Rough Canyon. MacNeish's theory was that it was only used in the fall, when the game came down from the highlands through the canyon to winter on the basin floor (which explained why there were no human bones, only "debatable tools"—another of the objections). We hiked over to a promontory that MacNeish figured was a lookout on the other side of the draw. "Something comes down the canyon, two or three guys take off at a run and dispatch it with their atlatls, then they bring it up to the cave and butcher it," he conjectured. We sat there taking in the view of the basin spreading out for a hundred miles beyond the canyon walls. Far to the north, we could make out the dunes of White Sands, the world's largest gypsum dune field, rank after rank of clean white gypsum crystal spread over thousands of acres of the Tularosa Valley floor. As gypsum-laden streams from the surrounding mountains empty into nearby Lake Lucero and the lake evaporates, gypsum is swept up by the wind and is continually being added to the dunes, which are migrating northeast at the rate of twenty feet a year. There are four types of dune: dome-shaped; ripplelike transverse; crescent-shaped barchan; and hairpin-shaped parabolic.

Maybe twenty miles out there we spotted a slowly moving horizontal line, like a line being dragged across a computer screen by a mouse: an interminable freight train on the South Pacific line creeping across the desert floor, which snapped us out of our Pendejo reveries.

Several months later, MacNeish left the dig with seven hazy fingerprints that he claims are about twenty-eight thousand years old—new ammunition. The following year, 1993, the skeletal remains of a robust man about five feet, four inches tall, possibly an ancestor of the southern Ute, was found in a cave in southern Colorado. Hailing the find as "among the oldest human remains in North America," John Noble Wilford wrote in *The New York Times,* "From the evidence of spear points and other artifacts, people arrived in North America twelve thousand years ago and probably much earlier." In 1994 the seven-and-a-half-foot tusk of a butchered mastodon was found buried in sediments in the Aucilla River near Tallahassee, Florida. Radiocarbon testing of gourd seeds found near the tusk put the age at 12,200 years, making it "the earliest known butchering site in North America," according to Wilford. But two replication teams were unable to confirm the fifty-thousand-year-old dates for stone tools, hearths, and wall paintings at the Pedra Furada in northeastern Brazil. In February 1997, however, Wilford reported two new finds: a 12,500-year-old child's footprint in Chile, and 300,000-year-old stone tools in northern Siberia, blowing away the previous oldest-known date for humans in Siberia of thirty to forty thousand years ago. The battle rages, but slowly, it seems, the dam is cracking on the Clovis-firsters.

Adaptations

O ver in Arizona, the Sonoran Desert was enjoying the most spectacular spring in years. As I drove west of Tucson that March in 1992, the winter rains had brought out blazing slopes of wildflowers—Mexican golden poppy, aster, lupine, fairy duster, bloodweed, peppergrass, clamoring weed, silver puffs, owl clover, desert dandelion—in the forests of columnar cacti, among the plumes and rosettes of yucca and agave, in the thickets of mesquite, ironwood, catclaw acacia, paloverde, and *palo blanco*. Acres and acres of globe mallow, yellow bladderpod, desert marigold, Parry's penstemon, were accented with purple-padded Santa Rita prickly pear. Waxy yellow or carmine flowers, devoured by ants, fringed the paddles of other prickly-pear species. The slender arms of teddy-bear cholla cacti had a luminous stubble of platinum-blond needles. The Ajo lilies were in bloom and under them microspecies only an inch or two high, like woolly daisies and Mojave desert stars. Each species flowers in sequence, awakened by rain. Rarely is there enough rain continuously, from October on, for all of them to flower in a given year. Out of a ten, this was a seven, one botanist had told me; a colleague of his said such springs come on average only every seventeen years.

There are twenty-five hundred species of higher plants in the Sonoran Desert. So much of the vegetation rises over your head that it is known as an arboreal desert. The Navajo, who live on the sagebrush steppe to the north of the Sonoran, have a word for it that means "Summer All the Time." The O'odham Indians, who live in it, used to eat 450 species of its flora, until they switched to store food. They attribute the dryness of their world to the anger of Cloud Man. According to one of their legends, one day their ancestors went to I'toi, the coyote-like being who had brought them into the world, and asked him to move back the mountains and widen the valley where they lived so they could have more land to farm. I'toi granted their request. But this meant that Cloud Man, who had been delivering water to the valley from the mountains, would have a longer trip and more water to haul, and he decided he wasn't going to do it anymore. Without water from him, the valley soon became a desert.

The Sonoran Desert is the hottest and driest of the Southwest's four deserts. The other three—the Great Basin, the Mojave, and the Chihuahuan—are classic rain-shadow deserts. Between eight and five million years ago, the coastal ranges of California, which had been heaved up by the collision of North America with tectonic plates in the Pacific, had risen high enough to interrupt the eastward flow of clouds off the ocean and to keep moisture from reaching their lee sides. The Great Basin developed in the rain shadow of the Sierra Nevada, the Mojave Desert emerged in the rain shadow of the San Gabriel Mountains, and farther south and inland the Chihuahuan Desert, a tongue of which protrudes into southern New Mexico, formed in the arid gap between the eastern and western chains of the Sierra Madre. The Sonoran Desert, which spreads up from the Gulf of California into southwestern Arizona, is influenced more by a subtropical high-pressure system known as the Hadley cell than by the orographic effect that created the other deserts. The main rain it gets is during the brief summer monsoon, when big gyres loop across Panama and track storms up from the Gulf of Mexico, and, in the northern part, around Tucson, when winter winds raft clouds in from the Pacific over the coastal mountains. It has several patches of 100 percent Sahara-type desert: the Algodones (Cotton) Dunes, a five-by-fifty-mile strip of whipped reddish-brown sand east of Yuma, Arizona, and El Gran Desierto, east of the upper Gulf of California, the largest sea of sand in North America, with windswept "star" dunes—pronged, with peaked centers—up to several hundred feet high.

Just below the Arizona border, there's a lunar, crater-pocked collection of mountains known as the Sierra de Piñacate, which get practically no rain at all. Yuma got only .28 inches one year, but the record for consecutive days without rain—767—goes to Baghdad, California, a little oasis in the Mojave Desert. (According to historian Richard E. Lingenfelter, Death Valley, California, "is in fact the driest spot in the country. The average rainfall since 1912, when the first records were kept, is only 1.66 inches per year—the lowest recorded anywhere in the Western Hemisphere. There have been years, such as 1929 and 1953, when not a drop of rain was seen in the valley.") But it is the Sonoran Desert south and east of Yuma and on down to the Gulf of

California that is generally regarded as the hot center, the torrid heart, of the Southwest.

So how does all this vegetation manage to survive? What a collective testament to the tenacity of life all these plants represent, I thought, marveling at the desert's counterintuitive lushness as I drove out to Ajo (the destination of the doomed Salvadorans twelve years earlier). The basic strategy is to conform to Liebig's law of the minimum, which simply states that the growth of a plant varies with the nutrients (including water) it is provided, and when the plant is deprived of nutrients, it cuts back. One of the most successful examples of this is the creosote bush, also known as greasewood. It can go for a year without water, dying back to half its size, its resin-coated leaves brown and shriveled yet still alive. When rain finally comes, shoots and yellow flowers burst forth from dead-seeming buds, and the desert smells of the waxy, soapy, emulsified pungence given off by its leaves. To the O'odham, it is a welcome smell. They know that rain may be on the way when this scent from a nearby cloudburst is borne on the wind. Which was the case now: vast creosote flats, looking like nurseries devoted to this drab, low-key, supremely drought-resistant shrub, were in yellow flower. The Mexicans call it *el gobernador* because it dominates their landscape. One-fourth of Mexico, seventy-four million acres, is covered with it, and another forty-four million in the United States.

Creosote bushes do not grow on top of each other; they give each other space, so each bush can suck up the moisture around it with its elaborate tracery of shallow roots. They often grow in rings that can be seventy-five feet in circumference and are all the same genetic individual, clones of a parent plant that died out in the center years ago. Some clonal rings in the Mojave Desert are estimated to be eleven or twelve thousand years old, which makes them the oldest living organisms on earth.

With the myopic arrogance typical of frontier *meligan* (as *americanos* came out in language of the O'odham), an 1882 dictionary dismissed the creosote bush as "foul-smelling and worthless except to hold loose sand in place." In fact, it has served as a desert pharmacy for generations of indigenous desert peoples. From the ethnobotanist Gary Nabhan's books, *The Desert Smells Like Rain* and *Gathering the Desert*, and other sources, one learns that during a summer storm a creosote bush releases fifty-some volatile oils, including vinyl and methyl ketones, camphor, and limonene, into the ozone-charged air. Its resin, an "amber, tacky syrup exuded as droplets on its stems," is a complex mix not only of these oils, but of flavonoids, lignins, saponins, and waxes. In addition, the bush attracts a certain scale insect that produces a viscous substance known as lac, which was traditionally used to mend ollas. Since the arrival of the internal-combustion engine, the crusty lac has even been used to seal cracked engine casings. According to O'odham legend, Earth Maker took soil from his breast and flattened the soil into tortillas, from which the creosote bush sprang; then he took the lac of the scale insect and formed the mountains in his fingers. The plant has antimicrobial, analgesic, and vasodepressant properties and has been used by Indians as a contraceptive and to treat at least fourteen ailments, including menstrual cramps, cancer, and, after its introduction by the Spaniards, syphilis.

The resin of the creosote bush and the waxy coating of its leaves also serve to keep the plant from dehydrating. It is one of many plants that migrated from South America, already adapted to dryness, like the grasses, sunflowers, peas, buckthorns, and nightshades that had evolved low water budgets in savannas, thorn forests, and other tropical biomes where there was a pronounced dry season. Other southwestern desert plants are local species that developed new structures and responses as the aridity became more severe. The cacti are thought to have evolved from an air plant in the South American rain forest that grew in the crotches of trees and, in this surprisingly moisture-deficient environment, developed internal organs for storing water—succulence. Once they reached the Southwest, they radiated on and on. Arizona alone has sixty-eight species. The hillsides that I was passing through were choked with them—tall columnar saguaros and organ-pipe cacti, teddy-bear and jumping and pencil and chain-fruit chollas, prickly pears, barrel cacti, hedgehog cacti, galloping cacti.

Most cacti have no leaves—leaves transpire and are a major source of water loss—or their leaves have evolved into needles, which fend off thirsty animals and function as "dripsticks," collecting rainwater and directing it to their roots. Many have a columnar form, which has the lowest ratio of surface area to mass and thus further reduces water loss through transpiration. Most columnar cacti are pleated, like accordion bellows, so they can expand as they fill with water. They have shallow, wide-spreading root systems that suck up percolating downpours, and they are designed to die back without dying completely, growing in segments that wither and drop off in times of serious drought without harm to the rest of the plant.

The tallest cactus in the Southwest—and in the world—is the saguaro; some saguaros reach for the Arizona sky with fifty-foot, bristly green candelabra and live for two hundred years. Their root systems can spread over an area of a hundred feet, and they can double their size, becoming bloated, baobablike blimps, until they weigh up to two tons, 75 percent of which is water. After a single summer downpour, a saguaro can go for a year without further intake of water due to a special refinement: it transpires at night. During the day, when most plants lose copious amounts of water through their stomates (the plant equivalent of pores), the saguaro's stomates remain closed.

Each saguaro is a miniature ecosystem, a five-story hotel, for a host of creatures. Elf owls nest in holes that Gila woodpeckers, going after insects, bore into the columns. Coyotes, white-winged doves, and ground squirrels love the saguaro's sweet red fruit so much that of the four million seeds a saguaro can produce, only three or four may make it to maturity. So do the O'odham, who classify as human these colossal cacti that dominate their landscape. With long poles they knock off the ripe fruit that blossoms on the tips of the saguaros in June and July and make a wine from it, which they drink in their annual rainmaking ceremony. The drinking of saguaro wine is an act of purging. The O'odham keep drinking until they vomit and "throw up the clouds," as one member of the tribe put it; they make themselves like saturated thunderheads that finally burst with the summer rains they need to grow their crops. The Spanish missionaries who came into the Sonoran Desert and set out trying to convert the O'odham saw the saguaro as an omen that their work would go well. Its occasionally cruciform branching pattern reminded them of their god. To my youngest son, however, the plants seem to be giving you the finger.

Saguaros spend their lives under siege, until finally their hole-riddled columns, full of healed-over black nicks, knotted burls where an arm fell off (unless it was replaced by the twisted spokes of several new arms), keel over and lie on the ground in a heap of expiring, deliquescing geometry as their green sheaths weather to diamond-latticed gray strings that look like the frame of a dirigible or a stomach wall. The ribs are used in traditional Sonoran Ranch–style houses as *latillas,* or ceiling lattices. The northern limit of the saguaro's range is around Bumblebee, Arizona. Down by Phoenix they come into play on many of the Valley of the Sun's hundred-and-counting golf courses. Dozens of the plants have suffered the indignity of being plugged by Titleists, Maxflis, Pinnacles, Ultras, and so on. The squamous *thok* of a golf ball smacking a saguaro is as distinctive as—let me think—the gobble of a *chachalaca* (an arboreal cousin of the turkey that inhabits thickets in northern Mexico).

Some cacti have no need of soil and fasten themselves to gray rock, from which they are nearly indistinguishable. The small, spineless, gray-green, napiform peyote cactus, which grows in the Chihuahuan Desert, possesses a number of psychotropic alkaloids, the most important of which is mescaline. When several peyote "buttons" are eaten, after an initial phase of nausea often accompanied by violent retching, a feeling of creamy well-being ensues. Spectacular visions, ecstatic rushes, kaleidoscopic plays of scintillating color, mandalas, paisleys, whorls, and other vague forms—some sexually arousing, some grotesque, some utterly terrifying—begin to pulse before the eye, often accompanied by hallucinations of sound, taste, smell, and touch.

The Indians discovered the properties of peyote early on—peyote bags recently dug up in southern Texas and northern Mexico carbondate to eight thousand years ago—and they came to believe that God spoke to them through it. The Aztecs had been longtime users of peyote when the Spaniards burst upon them, and it is still taken ritually by a number of tribes in the Sierra Madre and by members of the Native American Church, which has a strong following in the Southwest, particularly among Navajo.

The adaptations of the Southwest's desert animals are equally ingenious. Each came to terms with the dryness in its own way. The Gila monster developed the ability to store water in its fatty tail, as camels (which actually evolved in the Southwest, but died out on this continent around ten thousand years ago) do in their humps, and the desert tortoise evolved two sacs under its carapace for the same purpose; a pint of water will last a desert tortoise the whole summer. The reptiles—lizards, tortoises, and snakes—have the art of thermoregulation and water retention down best. They pass semisolid wastes and are sheathed in scaly, plated skin, so their water loss is minimal. They don't perspire, and they don't overheat, because they can vary their body temperature. Slipping into a torpid state, they go for long periods without food or water. Each reptile is a beautiful, nearly self-contained system, insulated from dryness and heat. But no creature has a more elegantly simple survival strategy than the Piñacate beetle: it collects the water it needs by merely tilting its oval, hard-shell body into the air and holding it there for several hours before dawn, until dew condenses on it and gradually trickles down its back and legs into its waiting mouth (which is just what the convergent Namibian beetle of North Africa does).

Another denizen of the Sierra de Piñacate—one of the few that can survive in such a water-deprived habitat—is the desert bighorn sheep. Radiating from the Caucasus of Asia Minor, its ancestors spread into the high plateau of Tibet and the deserts of Mongolia, then, within the last twenty thousand years, crossed over into Alaska via the Bering ice bridge. Eventually a magnificent new species, *Ovis canadensis,* arose, whose rams bear massive horns that curl back in spirals. The bighorn came as far down as the Sonoran and Chihuahuan Deserts and Baja California, settling in the high mountains and the low desert ranges, where steep, rugged terrain provides the grasses, browse, and forbs that they require and freedom from the competition of other grazers. Four desert subspecies—*Ovis canadensis nelsoni, mexicana, cremnobates,* and *weemsi*—developed remarkable abilities to cope with discontinuous water intake. Coming upon one of the rare tanks (natural cisterns) in a shady rock cavity early in the morning, a small herd of *mexicana* in the Sierra de Piñacate can drink up to 20 percent of their body weight in three minutes, and this, supplemented by the metabolic water they manufacture from their plant food (as do kangaroo rats) and by the preformed water on dew-drenched vegetation, will hold them for several weeks or even months.

But most of the warm-blooded animals had to modify their behavior, mainly by lying low during the day. At night the desert is alive with bats, rats, owls, raccoon, skunks, badgers (which aren't even desert species, strictly speaking), and seldom-seen creatures like the ringtail or coatimundi, the ocelot, and the kit fox. The kit fox is small (reduced size, in accordance with Bergman's rule, decreases the body surface from which water can be lost) and white (increasing its albedo, or reflectivity), with big ears, like the kangaroo rat's (the better to pass off body heat and pick up faint audio frequencies).

The jackrabbit has incredibly long, black-tipped, paper-thin, veinmeshed ears through which, lacking sweat glands, it dissipates body heat. There was a population of black-tailed jackrabbits at the University of New Mexico's South Golf Course that I saw a good deal of during our stay in Albuquerque. They were habituated to the golfers, so you could walk right up to them as they sat in the tumbleweed-infested natural-desert rough, or "gunge," as my golfing buddy Patrick Markwith calls it, or stood in groups of three or four, frozen on the fairway, with their ears erect, radiating the noonday heat through dilated blood vessels, the sun-shot membranes lit a translucent watermelon pink. The jackrabbit has special muscles that expose the underfur on its flanks, enabling it to flash from tan to white, and with its ears folded back and the eye on the side of its head wide with fright, it zigzags in dizzying bursts up to thirty miles an hour and hops up to twenty feet (an adaptation that has been called directive camouflage). I've watched jackrabbits run joggers' dogs in circles. Also, like kangaroo rats, they are autocaprophagous—that is, they eat their own feces.

Sometimes there are astonishing numbers of antelope jackrabbits (which, like the black-tailed species, are actually hares) in the creosote flats. You wonder how the desert is able to support so much life. The Mimbres people of southwestern New Mexico, the most artistic of the vanished cultures, made bowls depicting the hare in the moon. If you look closely at the full moon, it seems to be impressed with the silhouette of a jackrabbit.

The rodents, especially, have become fossorial, burrowing into the ground and creating cooler, moister secondary environments for themselves. There are even burrowing owls, burrowing tree frogs, and a huge wasp, the tarantula hawk (*Hemipepsis* sp.), which attacks and paralyzes tarantulas and drags them into its burrow, where its larvae feed on their vital fluids. The holes that the burrowers make are havens for all sorts of other animals, especially reptiles. The animals that don't retire to holes during the heat of the day generally take to the shade of a bush and wriggle and shuffle to make contact with cooler, moister soil. Many animals, especially the predators, with their keen sense of smell, have a preternatural ability to locate groundwater. They start digging—in the depression between two dunes, for instance. After a few feet, they hit a layer of moist sand, and the hole fills with water.

Another important strategy is dormancy. Just as many desert plants weather the driest months as seeds, waiting to be germinated by rain, the desert spadefoot toad digs itself a hole four to six feet deep and stays there, estivating, without food or water, for all but two weeks of the year. (In their viscous amphibian skin, they would shrivel up if they remained active aboveground.) During the brief monsoon season, in August, the rains seep down and revive the dormant toads, and they surface by the thousands. The males gather in the evanescent pools of rainwater and begin to call to the females, sounding something like frantically bleating sheep. The females arrive and, because there is little time, forgo the rituals of courtship common in the animal world and allow the males to mount them immediately. Soon the females, with the bleating males still clinging to them, begin spewing out the fertilized egg masses, until the pools are a foaming broth. After two days the stench at the pools, which is something like burnt peanut butter, is overpowering, and the thousands of eggs hatch into tadpoles.

These tadpoles have an extraordinary refinement. They all start out as vegetarians, feeding on the algae that have quickly bloomed in the water. But if the tiny eggs of fairy shrimp, blowing in the desert dust sometimes from hundreds of miles away (another amazing example of dormancy), happen to land and hatch in their pool, the mouths of some of the tadpoles enlarge so that they can eat the shrimp, and they turn into carnivores. If the rains continue, the algae thickens until the carnivorous tadpoles can no longer see their prey, and the vegetarian ones outcompete them. But if the rains stop, all the tadpoles struggle for a place in the center of the drying pool. Some are stranded on the edges and bake to death, and the carnivorous tadpoles become cannibalistic, turning on their own kind. Few of the original teeming broods, in any case, survive to the third stage of their life cycle and become toads (in a matter of eleven days, as opposed to the months or years other species require), and most of those that do are snapped up by birds or snakes before they can dig down into the safety of the earth with their specialized spadelike feet, not to be seen until the next monsoon.

From toads to humans, predation is probably the most common strategy for cornering the limited supply of nutrients or resources. Georgia O'Keeffe wrote to a friend in 1939:

> I brought home the bleached bones as my symbols of the desert. To me they are as beautiful as anything I know. To me they are strangely more living than the animals walking around—hair, eyes, all with their tails switching. The bones seem to cut sharply to the center of something that is keenly alive on the desert even tho' it is vast and empty and untouchable—and knows no kindness with all its beauty.

The frequency and the naturalness of predatory violence, in turn, seems to have colored the attitudes of the desert people. "Evil isn't down in the underworld for us," a Navajo friend told me. "It's part of everyday life and is all around you. There has to be the positive and the negative in any land-based religion."

And so there is a more accepting attitude when bad things happen, when situations take a violent turn, as they often do among people whose circumstances are precarious and marginal. Even the ultimate and most horrible consequence of violence—death—somehow doesn't seem like such a big deal in the Southwest. Not only Navajo, but Chicanos and Anglos seem to recognize that this is a hermetic desert world in which surreptitious acts of violence sporadically occur. Perhaps this attitude in itself is an adaptation, as if the dryness were the organizing principle of violence and death, too.

The most intelligent and adaptable, the most seemingly human, of the Southwest's animals is the coyote. Slinking around in its salt-and-pepper-gray fur, almost invisible in the barren landscape, it moves easily from life zone to life zone, eating just about anything, dead or alive: mice; rats; gophers; jackrabbits; rodents of all kinds; snakes, including rattlesnakes; horned toads; skunks; armadillos; bumblebees; crayfish;

turtles; birds and bird eggs; ground squirrels; antelope squirrels; juniper berries; pods of honey mesquite and screwbean mesquite; the sweet, juicy tunas, or red fruit of the prickly pear. This "scrawny, coarse-haired, living, breathing allegory of Want," as Mark Twain characterized the "varmint," loves sheep—newborn lambs especially—which doesn't make it popular with animal husbanders in any of the three cultures—Native American, Hispano, or Anglo. The ranchers around Farmington, New Mexico, for instance, sponsor an annual nineteen-day coyote hunt in the Four Corners area. The 1991 purse was ten thousand dollars, 50 percent of which went to the person who brought in the most carcasses. The excuse for the event, which has come under fire from environmentalists and animal protectionists, is that the coyotes are supposedly responsible for the dearth of deer, which the New Mexico Game and Fish Department says is not true; the decline in deer is due to loss of habitat—or maybe, the seasoned coyote trapper Walt Sinclair had the temerity to suggest, to an overabundance of deer hunters.

The writer Frank Waters has compared the coyote's cadenzas to "a wolf's howl bitten into pieces." Few mammalian self-expressions conjure more effectively, to the modern ear at least, the ecstasy of wildness (which the yipping and whooping of Indians is perhaps an attempt to enter). The Paleo and Apachean hunters watched Coyote play dead and suddenly spring to life and pounce on a mouse that had ventured too near his scrawny, mangy, motionless carcass. They saw how he could go for days and great distances without food or water, and they described a good sense of direction as "Coyote sense." Coyote became a central character in their myths, a protohuman who ushered them into the world, a god, a savior, an evil trickster, a bungling prankster whose ruses always backfired. (Hanna-Barbera's coyote-and-roadrunner cartoons are the latest telling of the ancestral myth.) He became the totem of their clans, their model, their divine hunter tutelary, their alter ego. They made up and recited epic poems, trickster cycles, about the adventures of Coyote that went on for days. The Greek, Chinese, Japanese, and Hebrew storytellers had a similar character, who was, as Paul Rodin describes in his book *The Trickster,*

> at one time creator and destroyer, giver and negator, he who dupes and is always duped himself. He wills nothing. At all times he is constrained from impulses over which he has no control. He knows neither good nor evil yet he is responsible for nothing. He possesses no values, moral or social, is at the mercy of his passions and appetites, yet through his actions all values come into being.

The O'odham have a story about a flood caused by the tears of an abandoned child that rose to the level of the woodpecker's tail (which explains why the woodpecker's tail is so conspicuously banded). After the flood subsided, Coyote and Elder Brother made new people of clay like those who had been washed away. To a number of California tribes, the Milky Way is dust kicked up by a race between Coyote and Wildcat. The Navajo have a story about how the Canyon de Chelly was made—by Coyote, not the wallowing hippolike creatures Dennis told us about. One day Coyote went to the People and begged them to show him how to use fire. The People gave him their flint stones. Coyote tried and tried to make a fire with them, but with no luck. In anger he flung the stones to the ground, which started a fire so big and hot that the earth split. Then Water Pourer poured water into the crack, and the washing action of the water gradually enlarged it. In another Navajo myth, Coyote is sent to find the source of dawn.

Coyote is two-faced, and as such he embodies the balance of opposites, the basic duality of all existence, the way all elements are paired: male-female, night-day, life-death, earth-sky, good-evil. He created the earth—which was good—but either as a blunder or a joke he also gave us death. According to one Navajo story, Coyote tossed a stone into a lake. If it came back up, people could stay in this world forever.

"We Navajo understand Coyote is always waiting out there, just out of sight. And Coyote is always hungry," explains Alex Etcitty of the Water Not Far clan. "Coyote lives off somewhere," another Navajo says. "He just wanders around because he is everybody's uncle."

In *Going Back to Bisbee,* Richard Shelton describes a race between several coyotes, a Doberman, and a Great Dane: "The coyotes would let the dogs gain on them a little, and then put on a burst of speed and leave the dogs behind. Once, when they had a considerable lead on the dogs, they stopped for a few seconds and one of them actually sat down, waiting for the dogs to catch up." Then they took off like "the sudden splitting of a long crack through the atmosphere."

Whether a coyote is prowling, loping, or racing full throttle, its bushy tail is always down between its legs.

Humans are among the most poorly equipped animals for dealing with desiccating heat. We overheat quickly, not only from the ambient heat, but from the metabolic heat we generate in the effort to stay cool. The only way we can dissipate the heat is by evaporative cooling—sweating. In the desert we sweat prodigiously, at up to fifty times our normal rate, although, with the beads evaporating from our skin almost as soon as they form, we may hardly be aware of doing it. On a really hot day, we can lose more than three gallons. All this water must be made up—and soon—or we will begin to experience the agony of what the ethnologist William McGee called, in the classic monograph on the effects of dehydration on the human system, "desert thirst."

McGee developed cancer, and he made periodic treks into the Sonoran Desert, hoping that the strong sunlight would cure it. On the morning of August 23, 1905, he was camped seventy-five miles south of Yuma, along El Camiño del Diablo, the Devil's Highway, as the Spaniards called this particularly torrid and waterless section of the route to their missions in California. Fifty-seven years earlier, during the California gold rush, hundreds of Mexican "argonauts," or prospectors, had underestimated their water needs and died along the Camiño and had either been buried in shallow graves or picked apart by vultures.

As he lay by his burnt-out campfire, McGee was awakened by, as he later wrote, a "deep guttural moaning or roaring," magnified in the desert stillness, from behind some boulders a quarter mile off. Rushing to the spot, he found a withered Mexican campesino barely clinging to life. The campesino's name was Pablo Valencia. Valencia was stark naked, and his ashen-purple skin was covered with "great livid blotches," as McGee would report in the monograph. His ribs, femurs, tendons, and joints were outlined in detail. His lips had shriveled to thin lines of black tissue, exposing his gums, which were the same color, as were his conjunctivas, from which the skin around his eyes had contracted. No longer able to blink, his eyes were set in a fixed stare, and he was blind except for being dimly aware that it was daylight. He was also nearly deaf and could only hear loud noises.

McGee sloshed water over Valencia's face, head, chest, and abdomen and poured dilute whiskey into his mouth. After an hour, Valencia began to make feeble swallowing motions, and McGee gave him some digitalis-nitroglycerin-belladonna tablets to stimulate his heart. After two hours, Valencia had recovered the ability to speak and was begging pathetically, "*Agua, agua.*"

As he gained strength in the days that followed, he told McGee the story of his ordeal. He had been out in the desert for eight days, the last seven without water. After his water was gone, he hallucinated that he met Jesus, and Jesus showed him where to find water, but when he got there, there wasn't any water, and he became obsessed with finding and killing Jesus for deceiving him. The strength of Valencia's desire for revenge, McGee speculates, probably helped keep him alive. The only source of water he found was a scorpion, which he killed and greedily devoured. At last, when he was too weak to get up, he crossed himself and, with a pang of regret that there was no holy water to bless his departing soul, waited for the end. As the dawn of the eighth day came, he had what would be known today as an out-of-body experience: he had the sensation that his body was lying there lifeless, while his consciousness hovered over it, reluctant to leave it to the buzzards that had begun to gather. It was at that point that McGee found him.

McGee's monograph was called "Desert Thirst As Disease," and it broke the process of dehydration into five stages: clamorous, cotton-mouth (a prospectors' expression), swollen-tongue, shriveled-tongue, and blood-sweat. The modern approach is to track body-weight loss. At 2 percent loss, thirst may be violent. At 4 percent, your throat and mouth are parched. You become groggy and sluggish, and as the electrolyte balance that governs the transmission of impulses along nerves goes out of whack, concerted effort like walking purposefully in one direction or following a train of thought becomes more and more difficult. You begin to lag and weave. Your mind plays tricks on you. Perhaps, like Valencia, you begin to soliloquize in whispered curses. At 8 percent you reach the cottonmouth stage: your salivary glands seize, your tongue swells, and you can barely talk. You start to hallucinate, "especially the delectable pictures engendered by the desert mirage," writes McGee. And then, passing from "functional derangement" to the final phase, "structural degeneration," at last you become a victim of "death in its cruellest form—from the torture of thirst."

There is precious little a human can do physically to make it easier for himself in the desert. Dark skin, which all desert people (and all tropical people, for that matter) have, offers some protection against ultraviolet rays. In the mideighties, there was a theory that the O'odham seem to have evolved, during centuries in the Sonoran Desert, an extra roll or packet of fat around their gut that has a water-storage function like the camel's hump, the Gila monster's tail, and the bulbous, steatopygic buttocks of Pygmies and Bushmen. It was invaluable, the theory went, when they covered great distances on foot and burned tremendous amounts of energy running down game, but now that they were bombing around in pickups and not getting enough exercise and eating lots of junk food, it was killing them. Obesity and diabetes (the O'odham have one of the worst rates in the world, and "taking a ton of insulin doesn't seem to solve the problem," their longtime ethnologist Bernard Fontana told me) are terrible problems in the tribe.

This theory was really a variant of the "thrifty gene" hypothesis, originally applied to the Bushmen of the Kalahari Desert. In a 1986 article reporting that, according to the Indian Health Service, members of some western tribes were seven to ten times as likely to get diabetes as non–Native Americans, *The New York Times* explained that "over centuries of hunting and marginal farming . . . [the Indians'] bodies evolved so that they could store fat efficiently, enabling them to survive long periods of famine between harvests or successful hunts." But in 1986 fully half of the O'odham and their cousins the Pima over the age of twenty-five had diabetes, as did one-fourth of the Zuñi, while the incidence in non-Indians was only 4 percent. The article also suggested that the diabetes was "a life style disease," brought on by sitting for hours at television sets and eating junk food loaded with sugar and fat. Cultural barriers to dieting and the attitude that being fat was a sign of health and prosperity (also prevalent in Africa) were proposed as contributing factors. The Zuñi started a program to revive long-distance running. Participants got T-shirts that said I OUTRAN SUGAR SICKNESS.

I had seen a lot of obesity among the Havasupai, down in their Eden-like branch of the Grand Canyon, and a White Mountain (formerly Coyotero) Apache had shown me the meat section of the tribe's supermarket in Whiteriver, Arizona. There was almost no red meat; it was practically total lard. "This is what's killing us," he had told me. It wasn't just that the cheap cuts were being unloaded on his people, he explained; they loved fat, perhaps as a throwback to when it was a treat. But I have also seen the same sort of fatty cuts in the supermarkets of Harlem. Minorities in general have a greater propensity for obesity and diabetes—and alcoholism. So maybe there are psychological factors as well. A doctor with the Indian Health Service had told me that the homicide, alcohol-related-accident, and suicide rates among Native American males between the ages of fifteen and thirty are almost double the national average. Out on the Navajo Reservation, someone who is drunk gets hit by a car or freezes to death in an arroyo on average once a day. There is also a theory that Indians, like other Mongoloids (including Japanese and Tibetans) have a hereditary low tolerance for alcohol, but the evidence is inconclusive. Indians do "flush" (their skin becomes uncomfortably red) under the effects of alcohol, and heavy drinking is certainly widespread in the Indian community, but it's also widespread in the Southwest's Hispanic community, and there are other factors: Indians often drink to get drunk, like Russians; they are traditionally interested in altered states; and some of them explain that they drink as a form of social protest, because the white man destroyed their culture, and because the early traders deliberately addicted them to firewater, the way the British East India Company addicted the Chinese to opium in the nineteenth century.

I was on my way to see the ethnobotanist Gary Nabhan, who lived out in Ajo and had done a lot of work with the O'odham and had developed a new, nongenetic theory about their diabetes. The road to Ajo is single lane, and cars come at each other at great speed. Most of the traffic is O'odham, and alcohol-related collisions are frequent. The most famous O'odham is Ira Hayes, the Congressional Medal of Honor winner who was one of the GIs in the famous photograph of the American flag being raised on Iwo Jima. Hayes ended up drinking himself to death.

I picked up an old O'odham man thumbing a ride. He was blind drunk, and he, too, it turned out, was a World War II veteran. "I fought for you," he kept telling me. We drove past Quijotoa (which means "Mountain Shaped Like a Carrying Basket" in O'odham), where there was a fabulous gold and silver strike in 1883. Boomtowns called Logan City, Allen City, New Virginia, and Brooklyn had sprung up overnight and had lasted a few years; now they were smothered by sand. The old vet was in no condition to talk about his culture, or what was left of it. I wanted to ask him about the annual salt pilgrimage the O'odham used to make to the Gulf of California until the twenties, when commercial salt became available to the tribe. Half a dozen young men would go down with an older man who had made the trip before, like "a quail with her young," one of them recalled years later. The pilgrims wore nothing and took nothing with them except for little pottery canteens, some of which they cached along the way so they would have water on the way back. They weren't just after the crusts of salt in evaporated tide pools and along the high-tide line, but were hoping for a vision that would bring them luck or power. Their guide instructed them to put all thoughts of home from their minds and warned against stepping on animal tracks lest the animal become angry and make them sick. When they reached the gulf, the young men, who had never seen such a vast body of water before, couldn't believe their eyes. The ultimate test of the pilgrimage was for them to go into the water. Quaking with fear, they waded in up to their armpits.

The O'odham had also been masters of dryness. They had practiced *ak chin* farming, planting their crops at the mouths of arroyos, and sheet-flood farming, where a sudden heavy rain spread out over the desert floor. They had directed runoff into catchment basins and waffle gardens, grids of little squares with raised edges, in which they buried their seeds. In 1913 they had ten thousand acres of the Sonoran Desert devoted to floodwater farming. Now there were fewer than a hundred. I knew that while the O'odham had a sixty-day corn with small ears and low water needs, what they were famous for was grow-ing beans. They grew all kinds—lima, scarlet runner, the common tepary, pinto, great northern, black, Jaco's cattle, and string beans, all of which were natives, and later, Old World species like favas and chickpeas, or garbanzos, which they got from Jesuit missionaries. Plus they ate hundreds of wild desert plants, like the pods of three species of mesquite, one of which, velvet mesquite, has pods that taste like carob; there are two flushes of them, summer and late summer, and when they come out you can grab them by the handful.

I wanted to ask the old vet whether it was true, as the linguist William Pilcher has proposed, that the sparsity and unpredictability of rain colors the O'odham's entire outlook, making them reluctant to give black-and-white statements; not saying, "It is going to rain on us," for instance, until the downpour is just about to cut loose, but speaking in hedgy, hesitant terms, such as "It looks like it may be going to rain on us." I wanted to ask him if he believed that it was the spi-ders who bring down the rain, by spinning webs from the ocean to the sky, then chewing holes in the clouds. But he just wanted me to take him to Tucson. After we passed Why, he changed his mind and asked me to drop him off at a *rancheria* a couple of miles off the road, so I drove him there and continued to Ajo, which consisted of little more than the big open pit and white slag heap of an old copper mine, a trailer park for overwintering midwestern retirees, and a Mexican food stand called El Torro, shaped like a big bull whose flank opened and that was where you went up and placed your order.

It was O'odham Day at the Organ Pipe Cactus National Monu-ment, south of Ajo, and I found Nabhan and his friend Caroline Wil-son, a naturalist for the park service, busy with the displays. While waiting for a chance to talk with him, I sat beside an old man named Albert Gomez who told me he was a Hiaced O'odham, a Gila River Papago, as opposed to a Tohono O'odham, a Sand Papago. There are about twelve hundred Hiaced O'odham and another thousand or so Mexican O'odham just over the border. A high percentage of the ones in Mexico farm, but the Hiaced were traditionally hunter-gatherers whose main source of food was the fish in the Gila River and the Gulf of California, and they farmed only supplementarily. Because they were often on the move, the Bureau of Indian Affairs (BIA) hadn't rec-ognized them as a separate group with their own ancestral home range and hadn't given them a reservation. Gomez was waging what was probably by now a losing battle to rectify the situation. He gave me a brochure that explained the injustice.

We went to Nabhan's house, and he explained how he had started looking into the O'odham's diabetes problem and had discovered that desert peoples around the world are particularly prone to the disease. The Australian Aborigines have even higher rates. But it also plagues the desert-dwelling tribes of Ethiopia and Yemen, and the Yuma and the Cocopa of Arizona, and he wondered why.

"The answer is simple," he told me, "but it took three or four years to figure out. The O'odham traditionally ate an abnormal amount of slow-release carbohydrates that protected them from radical rises of blood sugar. The same gummy mucilage that slows down water loss in desert plants like the prickly pear, that water gloms on to, causing succulence, slows down sugar release in people who eat it. So the O'odham never had to develop genetic resistance to diabetes, because the plants they ate protected them from it. Their diet included members of forty families of mucilaginous plants that have five to ten times more soluble fiber than there is in oat bran and that stretch the digestion of sugar over six to nine hours instead of the half-hour pancreas-stressing peaks you get from modern processed food."

So the solution was to persuade the O'odham to return to their traditional diet. But the chance of this happening at this late date was probably no better than that of Congress's deciding to give the Hiaced O'odham their own reservation. My impression of the O'odham, a superficial one but supplemented by people who knew them well, was that there was not much left of their culture. Their traditional subsistence pattern, dependent on rain falling in the hottest and driest of the Southwest deserts, had always been iffy and had probably been one of the first to go when an alternative, however unhealthy in the long run, had presented itself. After years of working with them, Nabhan was only beginning to realize the extraordinary breadth and sophistication of their botanical knowledge, sadly just as it was dying out. For instance, of the millions of individual plants belonging to several thousand species that are scattered over the Organ Pipe Cactus National Monument, there are 25 exceedingly rare species with only 150 or so individuals, and Nabhan had found several elderly informants who could identify 17 of them and "who know things about their distribution that have been completely glossed over by Western science. There are two kinds of science," he said, "and they're completely complementary."

Hooked on Chile

One of the most important wild edible plants of the Sonoran Desert is the *chiltepin*—the tiny, ardent chile pepper that grows on bushes. Mexicans pickle it in vinegar with diced onions and carrots and sell the mixture in old tequila bottles. It is a variety, and perhaps the wild ancestor, of a single Mesoamerican species, *Capsicum annuum,* which has produced "almost any pepper you can think of—bell, jalapeño, pimiento, New Mexico Anaheim type, yellow wax, six-four, ancho, poblano, *pasilla,*" Paul Bosland, a chile researcher at New Mexico State University in Las Cruces, tells me over the phone. *Chiltepins* are very hot (but not as hot as *Capsicum chinensis,* the excoriating *habanero* of the Amazon). They are the ones bandidos flip into their mouths like peanuts and pretend to be unaffected, but their flushed faces give them away; the ones macho Texans carry in little pillboxes and pop periodically. "We're suspicious of strangers' affectations about chile," an Amarillo man told me. "We think they're trying to make fun of us." This variety is also called *chile piquín, piquín,* and *tepin. Tepin* is round, like a pea; *piquín* is more bullet shaped. One of the *piquíns* from north of Tampico, Mexico, dropped into a two- or three-gallon pot of beans, is guaranteed to bring tears to your eyes.

The mestizos of Oaxaca, Mexico, grow dozens of varieties of chile (which can also be spelled "chili" and is a colloquial collective noun embracing several species of hot pepper with a multitude of varieties and preparations) in their gardens, but the plant doesn't seem to have been so important in the native Southwest. The Tarahumara Indians, Gary Nabhan reports, use chile to ward off witchcraft, the way garlic was used in Old New Mexico; a man who won't eat a chile is suspected of being a sorcerer. Sonoran campesinos treat earaches with it, and women apply it to their nipples to wean their babies. The Cora Indians of the Pacific Coast have a legend that the testes of the first man,

Narama, turned into chile pods. The Pima Indians of the Sonoran Desert make a pancake known as *pasadol* from the pulp of whole green chiles, but it's unclear whether the Indians of New Mexico had the long green chile now associated with the state or whether the Spaniards brought it with them when they came up from Mexico. At any rate, the *nuevomejicanos* began to grow it in the Hatch Valley, a branch of the Rio Grande Valley above Las Cruces, a century or two ago. The green chile is the immature fruit, like a green tomato, picked before it is ripe. The New Mexicans began to use it more as a vegetable, as the main ingredient in many of their dishes, perhaps because they had fewer crops and other food choices, such as seafood, than the Mexicans, who treat it more as a spice. They made a green chile stew with pork or other meat, potatoes, tomatoes, onions, and garlic, seasoned perhaps with oregano, cumin, and cilantro. They mixed a little diced green chile sauce in the filling of their enchiladas (omelettes seasoned with chiles) and poured a bunch more over them. They served chiles with corn, zucchini, and onions. They made *chile pasado,* roasting the pods until they blistered, then peeling and drying them so they could later be reconstituted as a vegetable. In the north, they developed thin-walled varieties—Chimayo, Dixon, Velarde—whose pods weren't harvested until they turned red and were hung to dry in strings known as *ristras.* Today the *ristra* is an essential part of the southwestern look and performs a decorative as well as a culinary function. No adobe home in Santa Fe is authentic without a *ristra* or two hanging on the porch. The pods are ground into powder and used in dishes like *carne adovado,* strips of pork marinated overnight in chile-powdered water and roasted in a slow oven, and *posole,* a Christmas dish resembling black-eyed peas, with lime-dried corn and chile-cured meat. To most Americans, "chile" is a bowl of ground beef and/or beans seasoned with red powder. This is Texas chili, a very different kettle of fish from New Mexico chile.

Red chile is rich in vitamin A (from its carotene), and fresh green chile has more vitamin C ounce for ounce than an orange. Both have a number of amino acids and minerals that round out the "big three"— corn, squash, and beans, the aboriginal staples of Mesoamerica—and both contain seven related compounds known as capsaicinoids, which give them their bite, pungency, and *potencia*. The principal compound, capsaicin, triggers the release in your body of something called Substance P, which causes pain, then, by a negative feedback process, activates opioids that turn the Substance P off, and endorphins that produce a state akin to runner's high, a rush similar to jumping into an icy pool after taking a sauna. The second process becomes stronger with each dose of capsaicin, so chiles are mildly addictive: you can become dependent on them for the secondary effect. A Santo Domingo Pueblo Indian who goes to Washington, D.C., a couple of times a year told me that he always takes his chile with him. "After two or three days without chile, I start wanting it real bad. The food just don't taste." Paul Bosland says "addiction" is a loaded word; chile withdrawal is no more acute than an unsatisfied craving for chocolate doughnuts. "It's not like you have to check yourself into the Betty Ford Clinic."

But I found myself rather seriously hooked on chile after a few months in Albuquerque. I got my daily fix at places like El Patio, Barelos, Los Cuates, and the Frontier restaurant, or if I was dining at home, I slathered frozen green Bueno brand on whatever I was eating, the way Brazilians sprinkle manioc farinha on everything. My wife learned to make burritos with chicken, fajitas, and half a dozen other New Mexican dishes; a friend taught her the secret of tortillas: they should be rolled from dough the size of a golf ball and the texture of an earlobe. All these were enhanced with green chile. Even Albuquerque's McDonald's, recognizing the importance of chile in the New Mexican diet, offer green chile stew and chile burgers, a rare regional variant in their also subtly addictive fast-food formulas. People who come to New Mexico for a visit and end up staying—of which I met many examples—speak of being "enchanted." Chile is part of the enchantment process. As a New Mexican told me, "It keeps you coming back."

Chile raises the threshold of pain and stimulates the appetite. It spices a dull meal. Its antioxidants keep meat from spoiling and disguise the smell and taste of meat that's going bad. *Capsicum frutescens,* a closely related Brazilian species that's the source of Tabasco and malageta peppers) was taken by the Portuguese to Africa, where *pilip-ili,* as it is known, is the main meat preservative in the refrigeratorless bush, and from there to India, where it was such a hit that a misconception arose that it is a native species, and to the rest of Asia, where it helped give rise to the hot cuisine of Szechwan, for instance. Now there's a chile belt around the world, which corresponds roughly to Kerouac's equatorial underbelly, and New Mexican restaurants with a heavy accent on chile are packing 'em in in Los Angeles, New York, Dallas, and Miami. The country Chile, by the way, was named for a local chief and has nothing to do with *Capsicum.* In Central American slang, a *chile* is a lie.

The FRIENDLY CHILE CAPITOL [*sic*] OF THE WORLD, as a billboard on the interstate proclaims, and the center of New Mexico's $250-million-a-year chile industry is Hatch. When I blew into Hatch, in early February, the growers were getting their beds ready for planting. More than a dozen varieties are grown in the Hatch Valley: sweet ones (bell peppers), mild ones (New Mexico six-four, R-Naki, Tam jalapeños), medium-hot ones (Big Jim, Mexi-Bell), hot ones (Sandia), very hot and spicy ones (serranos, *piquíns*), and extra-hot ones (Barker, Santa Fe Grande, Española Improved, jalapeños, yellow hots). I stopped at a diner, and while chowing down on bean burritos smothered in green chile sauce, read the local paper, *The Courier,* which covers Doña Ana and Sierra Counties. Most of the articles were about the chile crop, how the wettest winter in memory was going to add to the already skyrocketing cost of getting it in, how the agronomists at the state university were still trying to come up with new hybrids that would be resistant to chile wilt, a fungus that attacks the plants' roots and did in a quarter of last year's crop. Jimmy Lytle, whose wife, Jo, is president of the Hatch Chile Growers' Association, told me that "the demand for chile is a lot more than what we can grow, so stopping the wilt is our top priority." When I passed through Hatch a few weeks later, Mexican braceros (men who come up from south of the border and do the work nobody else wants to do) were hoeing the rows.

Gary Nabhan tells me a recent study finds that women on a high chile diet have difficulty reaching orgasm by vaginal self-stimulation because the capsaicin blocks endorphin release. He writes that Sonorans pop *chiltepins* to keep cool, as a method of "internal air-conditioning," but we found that a bowl of green chile stew was also a great way to warm up after a morning of skiing on Sandia Peak (which looms over Albuquerque), and we therefore endorse the message of a billboard on the way to Santa Fe: CHILLY? CHILE. One of my golf partners in Albuquerque had a great game except for a tendency to "chile-dip" his chips, to hit too far behind the ball, to "hit the big ball first," as he put it, so his shot landed way short of the pin. I'm still trying to trace the genesis of chile-dip. I have a hunch it originated in Texas. (I have this image of a cocktail party at a country club in Austin. The waiter comes up with a chile dip, which I dig deep into with a stalk of celery.) In any case, it has transcended the Southwest and is used by golfers all over the land.

Getting to Know Some Navajo

In 1519, when a handful of indifferently armed and equipped Spanish adventurers led by Hernán Cortés conquered Mexico, there were about thirty million people in that part of the world. Most of them were unhappy subjects of the Aztec emperor, Moctezuma II, a delicate man who was himself a deity and lived, secluded from public view, with an inner circle of high priests and relatives in a fabulous metropolis in the middle of a huge lake, with canals insteads of streets, floating gardens, and aviaries of astonishing birds. From there he presided over a bureaucracy of byzantine complexity. Thousands of his agents roamed the countryside collecting taxes and rounding up people to sacrifice to the sun, who required a regular tribute of still-beating human hearts.

On the northern fringes of the empire were the barbarian *chichimecos,* the sons-of-dog lineage. The region had been in a dark age since the collapse of the Hohokam and the Anasazi. The Spaniards would find some forty-five tribal groups there, speaking about twenty mutually unintelligible languages, and yet with enough in common that they would be considered to belong to a single culture area—the Greater Southwest, spreading from Pueblo, New Mexico, to the southern Sierra Madre, almost as far down as Guadalajara.

In his seminal book *Cycles of Conquest,* Edward H. Spicer divides the people of the northern fringes into four basic types. Three-quarters of them, maybe 150,000 souls—were Rancheria People. They lived in loose farming communities, or *rancherias,* as the Spaniards would call them, each family compound within shouting distance of the next. The Pimans, the Yumans, the Yaqui, the Opata—just about everyone in northern Mexico—were Rancheria People.

Then there were probably forty or fifty thousand (although some estimates run as high as two hundred thousand) Village People, who lived in the multistoried cellular adobe complexes that the Spaniards would call pueblos. Most of them lived in the Rio Grande Valley, and six or seven thousand—the Hopi—were on West Mesa, in the barren rock desert of northeastern Arizona.

Third were the completely different Band People, the Apacheans, who roamed in small groups on the fringes of Pueblo country and maintained a volatile relationship with the Village People, trading or raiding, depending on their circumstances. They had split into seven tribes, each of which was divided into subgroups, in turn composed of bands that were clusters of families related through their women. Each family lived in a hide tepee or a cone of stacked brush known as a wickiup. The bands were highly independent and mobile, coming together only in emergencies, when they were hurting for food and a raid had to be made or a death avenged.

Finally, there were the preagricultural bands who were still way back in the Paleolithic (the Apacheans did some farming, particularly the Navajo), the roving collectors of wild food, like the Toboso, the Guasave, and the Seri. The Seri lived along the Gulf of California and on desert islands in the gulf, and until a few decades ago, when con-dominium developers moved in on the pristine beaches of Tiburón Island, their ancient way of life was virtually undisturbed. They ate deer, rabbit, fish, giant sea turtles, seaweed seeds, and cactus fruit. It was not a lack of protein that kept them at their rudimentary stage—the swarming marine life in the gulf was there for the taking—but the extreme scarcity of fresh water. When the first Spaniards found them, they were wearing lip disks, and they believed they were descended from giants who were compulsive gamblers and had finally died out because they kept betting their lives and losing.

Most of these peoples, like tribal peoples the world over, called themselves the People. The Seri called themselves Comaac, the Navajo were Diné, the Pima and the Papago were O'odham. Seri, Navajo, Pima, and Papago were the names the Spaniards gave them.

Scientists maintain that the Apacheans are descended from a later wave of Siberians, ethnically different than the Paleo-Indians—the Na-dene migration—which crossed the Bering Strait maybe ten or eleven thousand years ago (Richard MacNeish says sixteen thousand). Their dental characters and blood groups trace to the forested region between the Amur and Lena Basins. The Apacheans are a late, flat-faced, slant-eyed group of specialized Mongoloids. Unlike the Paleo-Indians, they have heavy shovel-shaped incisors that look like coal scuttles, they aren't 100 percent type O, and they lack the diego factor, a blood char-acter that influences the genetics of skin color and resistance to disease.

The Na-dene, or Athabascans, as they are also called, settled in the Mackenzie Valley of the Pacific Northwest, where they fished for salmon and sorted themselves into castes and hewed long oceangoing canoes and monumental totem poles from the towering coastal cedars. Within the last thousand years, some of them—the Apacheans—broke away and began to drift south in loose, highly mobile bands. Whether they were driven out or defected, there was, evidently, no love lost. The Apacheans separated from the Sarsees of northern Alberta very recently. So close are their languages—about as different as French and Italian—that Richard MacNeish in the forties was able to communicate pretty well in Navajo with the slave group of Sarsees. "We're supposed to be rainbow people," Edgar Perry, a White Mountain (formerly Coyotero) Apache told me. "But I think we're Athabascans. One time I was up in Fairbanks, Alaska, and I got talking with some Indians, and I couldn't believe how many of the words were the same. 'How come you speak our language?' they kept asking me." In the twenties the anthropologist Edward Sapir also found a linguistic kinship between Navajo and Tibetan. Both have subtle tonal differences the Anglo-Saxon ear can't hear. The same Sarsee word rising means "wood," and falling means "vagina."

In the early centuries of the millennium, when the Anasazi were already suffering hit-and-run raids from the Shoshonean ancestors of the Ute and the Paiute, nomadic foragers who had never converted to farming, and had withdrawn to defensive positions, a fierce new group of marauders—the Apacheans—swept down from the north. There's a lot of disagreement about when they arrived in the Southwest. Estimates range from 900 to 1525, with most recent estimates putting entry by 1400. By the mid–fourteenth century, when the Pajarito people bailed out of Tsipin, their fortress above Cañones that Don had taken me to, most of the Apacheans were probably still in the Plains. They had abandoned the coastal culture and were doing the Plains trip—hunting buffalo and antelope with sinew-backed bows, schlepping their possessions on dog-drawn travois, slipping their dwelling hides over a conical forked-pole frame, decorating their deer- and antelope-skin clothes and moccasins with porcupine quills, focusing their religion on a shaman who cured with visions and counteracted pathogenic spells of lightning, bears, and other natural forces and animals. Gradually, they developed a subsistence pattern based on raiding. Glottochronological studies suggest that in 1300 the Apacheans were still a single or several closely related groups. Eventually they would break up into the Navajo, the Chiricahua, the Jicarilla, the Kiowa Apache, the Lipan, the Mescalero, and the Western Apache, of which there were eventually five subtribal groups. "Apache" is the Zuñi word for "Enemy." In the coming centuries the Zuñi would become one of the Apacheans' favorite targets, and through the late nineteenth century a Zuñi had to take a Navajo scalp to be admitted to manhood. The Hopi called the Navajo Tusa-hutva, the "Head Pounders," because Navajo raiding parties would periodically descend on the mesas and club them to death. Relations between the Hopi and the Navajo are still strained because both claim the same area as their homeland. The Navajo have their own names for the Hopi: the House People, Cliff Shitters (a reference to the outhouses that hang over the edges of the mesas). One Navajo punster I met calls them Hopeless.

The earliest tree-ring date for a hogan, the characteristic Navajo dwelling, in the Southwest is 1485, plus or minus fifty years. The earliest archaeological evidence for direct contact between the Anasazi and the Apacheans is 1525. By then the Apacheans had begun to attack the eastern pueblos, in eastern New Mexico, on the edge of the Plains. The Apacheans would make hit-and-run raids on the Anasazi in their fields, and the existence of the Anasazi became more circumscribed, more dependent on corn, as it became increasingly dangerous to hunt game. Sometimes a band of Apacheans would suddenly appear with meat to trade for produce, and the Anasazi would host a wary feast for them. The Navajo saw the advantages of having a stable food supply and started to grow corn themselves. "Navaju," in fact, is a Tewa Pueblo word meaning "Great Planted Fields." The first reference to the *apaches de navaju* is in a 1626 report on Franciscan missionary activities in California and New Mexico.

The Navajo were also intrigued by the Village People's horticultural mysticism and adopted the Pueblo belief in three previous worlds and four cardinal points and much of their ceremonialism, while the Pueblos incorporated the vision quest and other aspects of Navajo shamanism. The next centuries would be a period of extraordinary religious cross-fertilization and syncretic ferment. This was the Navajo's outstanding trait—a remarkable cultural fluidity: if they saw something another culture had or was doing that looked good, they adopted it. "The Navajo are beggarly nomads, the sponges in American Indian culture," an anthropologist explained. "They stole sheep from the Spaniards and became the greatest sheepherders in the world. They stole horses and became the preeminent cowboys of the Southwest. They learned sandpainting from the Pueblos and silversmithing from the Spaniards and brought both to new artistic levels. They took the

rifle and the pickup and the television and the junk food of the modern
Anglo culture. Progress is their most important product."

It was no accident that the omnivorous, ubiquitous predator-
scavenger Coyote was one of their main culture heroes. Their resilience
enabled the Navajo to rebound spectacularly from near extinction in
the 1860s, after the Long Walk to Fort Sumner at Bosque Redondo (or,
as they call it, Hweeldi, the place of confinement). Today they are the
largest traditional nation in the United States. According to the last
census, 155,276 were enrolled. To belong officially to the tribe, you
have to have at least one-quarter blood. But there are undoubtedly
many more Navajo out there.

Horses are thought to have been introduced to the Southwest by
colonists who came up into New Mexico with Juan de Oñate in 1598.
It didn't take long for the Apacheans—the Kiowa and the Lipan on the
Plains, the ever-adapting Navajo—to pick up on the possibilities of the
steeds. The earliest record of an apparently Navajo raid on Spanish livestock was in 1609, when the herds of the colonist Juan Martínez de
Montoya were carried off. Montoya had been granted some of the
Jemez Pueblos in *encomienda* and was working them hard. (The
encomienda was a land grant by the Spanish crown that included whatever Indians happened to be living there.) Runaway Jemez—*renegados*
(renegades)—were probably in on the raid as well. The colonists' virtual enslavement of their charges and the missionaries' practice of
whipping members of their new flocks for skipping mass and other
infractions encouraged some Pueblos to flee into the mountains and
join their enemies, the Navajo, and often the *renegados* took the mission's or the colonist's horses and cattle with them. And the Spaniards
themselves deliberately and foolishly contributed to the Apacheans'
growing herds. By 1650 they were trading horses and tobacco regularly
to the Lipan and Kiowa for buffalo robes and meat. By 1680 Apache
were coming to Pecos Pueblo and buying horses with women they had
abducted from other Plains tribes. It took only a few decades for the
Apache to become what General George Crook would call admiringly
"the finest light cavalry in the world."

Extending their range and striking power tremendously, the horse
confirmed their choice of raiding as the most rewarding and stimulating
way to make a living. For the next two centuries, mounted Apacheans
would prey on Village People, Rancheria People, other Band People like
the Ute and Paiute, Spaniards, Mormons, wagon trains—they weren't
particular. They became an ever-present danger, a major thorn in the

side of progress, as important a retardant of civilization and progress on the southwestern frontier as the absence of water, making any large-scale farming or ranching impossible throughout much of the region right up to the 1880s. The Apacheans' turf, their roaming and raiding area, included most of Mexico and Arizona, west Texas, and northern New Mexico. It was roughly equivalent to the modern Southwest, in other words. The Spaniards, huddled in their fortified enclaves, called it Apacheria.

A Western Apache raiding party usually consisted of five to fifteen men. The preparations for the raid were elaborate, according to interviews with old-timers conducted by Grenville Goodwin, a brilliant, largely self-taught ethnologist who died in 1940 of a brain tumor at the age of thirty-three: the raiders mended the soles of their moccasins and took along a couple of extra pairs in case they wore out and painted "wind tracks" along their outside to make them light and swift. They skinned the necks of deer and cut the skins up in thin spirals to get single long strips of rawhide, which they later used to make rope. They prepared food: mescal, dry seeds, dry cakes of prickly-pear tunas, and painted white, black, or red stripes across their faces, over their noses, and under their eyes. Certain taboos were observed: the husband of a pregnant woman couldn't go, for instance, and you couldn't scratch yourself with your fingers on the warpath; you had to use a stick. Special warpath language had to be used, with different words for "woman," "horse," "Mexican," "white man," and "water" (the latter, *nahina*, "it keeps moving"). The shaman was consulted as to the outcome of the raid, and depending on his auguries, it might be postponed, or you wouldn't go at all. You got the shaman to give you "bat power," which made you elusive, and to infuse your gun or bow and arrow with "star power." You purified yourself with sweat baths and went off by yourself to talk to your power. "Enemies–against power" supposedly made a knife equal to a gun.

Just before daybreak several of the raiders, on foot, would gently open the corrals of the settlement they had decided to hit and quickly move the herd out. The others, on horseback, would then surround the herd and drive it off, and everybody would hightail it, sometimes spending four or five days without stopping to sleep, until they got back to camp. If they had taken scalps, they danced with them on poles, which generated enemies–against power. Once home, there was a wild victory party. Widows and divorcées danced naked. One of these women-without-husbands might cut a piece of stomach from a horse and dance with it between her legs. The men would butcher a horse and smear themselves with its blood and guts. The loot was distributed matrilineally. Adults who were taken captive (if the foray was not a raid, but a war party to avenge the death of a slain kinsman) were turned over to the women for slow torture. The kinsman's sister or female relatives had the satisfaction of delivering the coup de grâce. One of the old-timers recalled how two Mexican soldiers, one of them a captain, who had been taken captive were forced to dance with two women. As they danced the chief came up and asked them, "Do you know that these two women you are dancing with will be the ones to kill you in a little while?" The captain said, "No woman is going to kill me." Soon afterward, the captives were tied up, and the women dismembered and then shot them, then the women came back with their arms and legs to where everyone was dancing and danced with them.

The Navajo established themselves in a roughly rectangular homeland they called Dinetah, the land of the People, bounded by four sacred mountains (North Mountain, or Debe'nitsaa, the La Plata Mountains of Colorado; South Mountain, or Tso Dzil, Mount Taylor, near Grants, New Mexico; East Mountain, or Sis Naajin'i, Sierra Blanca, Colorado; and West Mountain, Dook Oslid, the San Francisco Peaks, near Flagstaff, Arizona) and four sacred rivers (the Colorado, the Little Colorado, the San Juan, and the Rio Grande). After they were released from Bosque Redondo, in 1868, a reservation much smaller than the original Dinetah, but still larger than West Virginia, was created for the Navajo. On their sagebrush steppe, scored with awesome canyons, occasionally uplifted into a craggy, pine-clad range, and spectacularly open to the sky, they evolved a distinctive culture— myths full of wisdom and humor, fifty-eight elaborate ceremonials, each of which is chanted by a *hataali,* or specialized singer. One of these "sings," Night Way, for instance, takes nine days and consists of 576 songs that must be intoned perfectly, word for word, in order to accomplish its purpose, which is to initiate boys and girls between the ages of seven and thirteen into the ceremonial life of adults. It must be performed between first frost and first thunderstorm, while the snakes are hibernating, and the slightest mistake can result in self-hexing: crippling, paralysis, loss of sight or hearing.

The central idea of the Navajo belief system is *hozho* (which to the European ear sounds something like the French *haut jean*), which is often rendered as "walking in beauty." One woman described it to me as "being in harmony with everything—yourself, mainly, all the living things, the air, Father Sky, moon, and on and on." The writer Tony Hillerman, whose mysteries are set on the Navajo Reservation and are full of ethnographic detail, explains *hozho* as "a sort of blend of being in harmony with one's environment, at peace with one's circumstances, content with the day, devoid of anger, and free from anxieties." At this point it would be a mistake to talk about "the Navajo" as if all 155,000 of them belong to a single, uniform culture and are frozen in some kind of fixed, idealized "ethnographic present." In fact, there is tremendous diversity within the Navajo nation, and the culture is changing all the time. One meets all kinds of Navajo: born-again ones, peyote "roadmen," old dope-smoking hippies, gung ho World War II vets, heavy-metal freaks. There are important cultural and dialect differences depending on what part of the vast "rez," which of the 109 chapters, or local jurisdictions, you are in. But whatever their persuasion, it is my impression that most Navajo, even progressives who live in the cities of the Southwest, still live by the Navajo Way and are "tight in their practice," as a Tibetan Buddhist lama I met in Santa Fe put it. The differences among Navajo seem more to do with strategies for relating to the dominant culture, for dealing with "the almighty dollar, the ownership thing," as my friend Tom put it, "this is my property and I got the papers to prove it." *Hozho* is still the goal, but the reality, for many of the Navajo I came into contact with, was that besides the usual problems—marital, family, money, and so on—they were also saddled with the peculiar ones that went with belonging to a defeated culture; they were, in one anthropologist's description of the modern Native American dilemma, "stumbling between cosmologies." But I found them the most approachable of the native southwestern peoples, and the most helpful in my quest for the Other.

By 1985, when I spent a month traveling around Arizona and met my first Navajo, they were wary and weary of Anglo wanna-bes prying into their ceremonial life. I heard stories of Navajo who had their kinship charts already printed up and ready to sell to anthropologists, of the following exchange between a tourist who walks into a trading post on the rez where a woman is feeding her red-haired baby: "Was the father red-haired?" the tourist asks in a crude attempt to start a conversation, and the woman retorts, "I wouldn't know. He never took his hat off."

By this time I was thirty-eight—in a different stage of life from the rudderless young songwriter who had drifted up to the edge of the Grand Canyon almost fifteen years earlier. If adulthood can be divided, after Erich Fromm, into three stages—becoming, getting, and being— I was now in getting mode. I had two sons and seven books to my credit, and I had come to Arizona to report book eight—a "sweeping hydrohistory" of the American Southwest, as I described this early conception of the present work.

With my wife and boys I had several brief encounters with Navajo that summer. The first was with a lovely woman named Lavina Ohls, who lived on a quiet street in Scottsdale, Arizona. While thoroughly modernized, Lavina told us that she still lived according to the old Navajo Way, which "emphasizes the purity of your walk from sunrise to sundown, and being thankful that the day is here again. The door of the hogan always faces east, toward the rising sun. It gives you a twinge in your heart to say, 'I'm alive again.' You take a walk and see a bird; excitement surges from your own thoughts. There are no swear words in Navajo. The worst is 'You go to the devil.' You don't cuss nature, 'cause the only thing you do is destroy yourself." She explained how "if something is wrong with your body, or people can't get together, you call in a medicine man," to make the appropriate sand-paintings, which takes six to nine days. The patient sits on the painting, and the medicine man rubs sand on the afflicted portion of his body. But "when a person is sick and there is no wound, he treats himself by resting and being calm and zeroing in on what is hurting him."

A few days later we were driving through the desert above Flagstaff and stopped to look at the weavings that several Navajo men had strung out under a juniper-bough ramada. Navajo "rugs," which are in fact blankets or wall hangings, are woven almost exclusively by the women, who according to legend learned the craft from Spider Woman, the primordial being who lived in the Canyon de Chelly. According to ethnohistorians, however, they may have picked it up from Pueblo women, who wove blankets from wild cotton on crude upright looms; these mantas, as the Spaniards called them, were important trade and tribute items. The weavings were colored with vegetal dyes—alder bark, piñon gum, dock weed—and later with indigo and cochineal brought up by the Spaniards from Mexico. After the introduction of the *churro* sheep in the sixteenth century, they were made of wool. They are not only works of art, but visual records of the People's history, encoded in horizontal bands of zigzags, diamonds, and stripes.

While I was talking with a man about the rugs—his prices, which he quoted with the deadpan of a toll collector, translated to something like a thousand dollars a square foot—suddenly there was an explosion of laughter behind the ramada. My two boys, five and six, had gathered the other men around them and were putting on a little show with their Gobots, must-have toys for white suburban kids in the mideighties. André, the oldest, had just, with a few twists, magically transformed his Gobot from a truck into a robot.

That evening I stopped at a fork in a frost-heaved highway that led like a roller coaster across a golden plain. Is this the turnoff to the

Painted Desert? I wondered. I was looking forward to a reunion with that extraordinary landscape I had passed through fifteen years earlier. Behind a hillock I noticed a Navajo compound, or outfit, as it is called, consisting of several hogans and a brush ramada, and drove up to ask directions. These were "male" hogans, typical of the western reservation, with six sides of adobe-chinked logs and dome-shaped roofs of cribbed, mud-smothered logs, with a hole in the center for smoke to exit. An ancient little woman—a *shimishani,* or grandmother, with silver hair and a wrinkled, leathery face and dressed in the traditional pleated skirt, velveteen blouse, and turquoise-and-silver jewelry—was tending a pot of mutton stew over a fragrant, crackling fire. The whole scene had a high-altitude austerity to it that reminded me of the Quechua of the Peruvian Andes.

Out of one of the hogans came a tall man, radiant, welcoming, and blind. "It's been a while since we had visitors," he said, and he invited us to stay for supper. But I was on this tight touristic schedule. We had to make Sanders, Arizona, by nightfall, I figured, so I declined, and we drove back to the fork and took the turnoff, which turned out to be the way to the Painted Desert. A few miles farther we passed a young man standing against a store with his arms folded across his chest and time on his hands—a different sense of time, undoubtedly, than my fast eastern mind-set, and I realized that we should have stayed and had supper with the blind man and his mother. What was I expecting to learn by this rushing around?

Early the next morning, leaving my wife asleep, the boys and I went for a walk behind the motel, which was about all there was to Sanders. It had rained hard in the night, and the sky was gray and overcast. Crossing some tracks, we reached the bank of the Rio Puerco, a long, intermittent river that rises in the pine-clad uplands of northwestern New Mexico, hundreds of miles to the east, and eventually contributes (when it has anything to contribute) to the Colorado. The riverbed was maybe a hundred feet across and was completely empty except for a few interbraided trickles on the near side, ten feet below us. And this was the major drainer of the region—"a miserable dirty & little stream of brackish water," in the description of the artist Richard H. Kern, who was attached to an expedition of United States Army Corps of Topographical Engineers exploring a wagon route in 1849 and was killed by Pahvant Indians in Utah four years later, at the age of thirty-two. (Which is what *puerco* in fact means: filthy.)

Sliding down the bank, we walked across the riverbed. By the time we reached the other side, several inches of sticky beige mud—good adobe mud—were caked on the soles of our sneakers. We climbed a bluff whose beige shale was so brittle that it crumbled in my hands. A family of Gambel's quail, beautifully camouflaged against the shale in their earth grays and browns, scuttled into the nearby underbrush. I was thinking how things come around, how mud hardens into shale and then thousands of years later the shale dissolves back into mud, when suddenly I began to hear a grinding, sloshing roar, which was soon followed by the appearance, from around a bend maybe a hundred yards upstream, of a six-foot-high wall of foamy chocolate water, with all kinds of debris tossing in it—bottles, boards, tires, boulders, branches, a large, barkless tree trunk.

The wall was advancing very slowly—it seemed almost in slow motion—spreading into the gap between the banks. I realized that if we didn't get back across the riverbed, we would be stranded on this side—there was no bridge in sight—and my wife would have no idea what had happened to us. So I sized up our chances, and we made a run for it. We beat the wall by twenty feet.

The memory of that near escape always makes me shudder. If we were Navajo, we would have believed that we had somehow gotten out of sync with the water spirits and would have had to hire a *hataali* to sing a Tohee, or Water Way, ceremony for us. There are few left who know it. This sing is for people who survive drowning or flash flooding, for sickness from rain or thunder, for injury from eating corn struck by lightning, from inhaling flag (iris) pollen and losing your voice, from cooking with wood shattered by lightning, from eating the meat of lightning-struck sheep or horses, or for dreaming of drowning. The cutting of prayer sticks for Water Horse and Rain Boy is all that is left of a once much more elaborate ceremony.

"Water is the blood vein of Mother Earth. It's one of the four elements and is in a lot of prayers," my Navajo friend Tom would tell me six years later. "Clouds, lightning, and rainbows have their earth counterparts—springs, serpents, and natural bridges. When they dammed the Colorado River at Glen Canyon Dam and other Anglo dams, the Water People bored their way to freedom as many small droplets. My brother fell into a mountain torrent one time," Tom went on, "and was tumbled around and nearly drowned. He needed to make peace with the Water People." And his cousin Sally, John's sister, told me that in 1982 her brother Roy drowned when his canoe capsized in a lake because "he did something to anger the Water People."

That fall—1991—I came to Albuquerque to do further research on the book. A lot had happened in those six years. My marriage with the

Brazilian woman, the mother of our boys, had ended, and I was now married to a Tutsi refugee from Uganda. At the time it happened, I had sensed the flash flood was a message of some kind; many people live their whole lives in the Southwest without seeing a wall of water like the one we outran in the Rio Puerco. Having taken on this ambitious hydrohistory, I wondered if it was a show of force by the Water People, either to give me a taste of what I had gotten into or to warn me off the project. But now I wonder if it wasn't perhaps an omen of turbulence to come. Forty-five now, I had progressed from the "getting" to the "being" stage, in Fromm's typology; or as my Navajo friend Sally would have put it, I had "become real." Having your family blow up in your face will do that to you.

There had been changes in the scholarly approaches to the Southwest and in its very climate as well. Thanks to the explosion of Mount Pinatubo in the Philippines and the cyclic return of El Niño, the warm current in the Pacific, the drought years of the eighties had ended, and there was less talk about water problems and global warming and new interest in the Southwest as a multicultural model. Up to now, the frontier had always been portrayed from the Anglo point of view. Now the focus was on collecting the conquered peoples'—the Indians' and the Mexicans'—versions. Anthropology itself had become less dyadic, less the dispassionate, paternalistic scientist come to study the primitive Other, and more self-analytical and participatory. Reflexive anthropology—deconstructing the anthropologist, looking at who was asking the questions—was in vogue, and the anthropologists were becoming more involved in the political and environmental struggles of the peoples they were studying. My trips through the Southwest and northern Mexico seemed inadequate; the region was much too sophisticated for a traveler's once-over-lightly treatment. I had been distracted from the book during the late eighties by the demands of deadline journalism. I needed to get back out there and to immerse myself in the Southwest, so with credentials as a visiting scholar at the University of New Mexico in Albuquerque, I packed my wife and my two boys, now eleven and twelve—our reconstituted Luso-Slavic-Watusi-American family of four, as I described us, into our Chevy pickup and our Ford Explorer and we headed West.

Soon after our arrival, I came into contact with some Navajo through a visit to the site of the worst radioactive spill in history, sixty miles up the Rio Puerco from where the boys and I had barely escaped being flash flooded. The Churchrock Incident, as it is known, happened on July 19, 1979, when a dam burst, releasing a hundred million gallons of water and eleven hundred tons of tailings from a uranium mine into the Rio Puerco and contaminating it for ninety miles downstream.

This was one of the many tragedies in what Lori Goodman, a Navajo environmental activist, has called the Indian Resource War. A 1975 inventory of the 25,000-square-mile Navajo Reservation estimated that it had 100 billion barrels of oil, 232 billion cubic feet of natural gas, 5 billion tons of coal, and 80 million pounds of uranium. The war over these riches began in the twenties with the tapping of oil and natural gas, which led to the creation of the Navajo tribal council in 1934, because there had to be an entity that would sign the leases. Then there was the uranium boom, which began with the mining of more than 11,000 tons of uranium-bearing ore in Monument Valley. The ore was trucked to the Smelter Mountain Mill in Durango, Colorado, to be processed into uranium oxide, or "yellowcake," then trucked down to Los Alamos, to produce, among other things, the first three atomic bombs. From 1946 to 1968, more than thirteen million tons of uranium ore were mined on the rez to make nuclear warheads. Over ninety thousand acres of tribal land were leased for uranium exploration and development. Today, windblown thorium 230 and radon 226, not to mention nonradioactive arsenic, barium, vanadium, and so on, spread from more than a thousand abandoned mines on the reservation. Dozens of Navajo miners who handled and processed yellowcake have died of leukemia and lung cancer, and birth defects plague their children. Twenty communities, and some six hundred scattered dwellings, are radiologically contaminated.

In the sixties new sources of energy were needed to fuel the growth of the Southwest, and the tribal council was persuaded to sign away its coal for a royalty of fifteen cents a ton, a tenth of what the federal government gets for the coal on its land. Today, the Navajo Reservation boasts five of the largest open-pit coal mines in the world. Since 1971, three million gallons of water have been pumped daily from the Navajo aquifer (which underlies the central Navajo Reservation and the Hopi Reservation in the middle of it) to flush crushed coal from one of them—the Black Mesa Mine—down a 273-mile slurry line to the Mojave power plant in Laughlin, Nevada, which provides juice for southern California, Arizona, and Nevada. As a result, sacred springs and washes whose water the Hopi and Navajo depend on to grow their crops have dried up. ("Moenkopi Wash," for instance, along whose banks the Hopi grow most of their corn, means "Full-Time River"; now it has become intermittent.)

One morning that fall, I drove to Thoreau, New Mexico (named after the author of *Walden Pond,* but pronounced "ther-oo"), to see a

Navajo activist named Ray Morgan, who was doing follow-up on the Churchrock Incident. Heading west from Albuquerque on Interstate 40, I passed 11,301-foot Mount Taylor, the southeast corner of Dinetah and sacred to the Acoma as well the Navajo and the most prominent feature of the Grants Mineral Belt, which contains half the nation's uranium; then the malpais, the badlands of ancient black lava that extend down to Quemado; then Grants, whose streetlights, at the height of the uranium boom in the fifties, were decorated with effigies of Santa Claus with a bag of uranium slung over his shoulder. By 1957, Grants Belt uranium was already fueling the first of an eventual total of 110 nuclear reactors. By 1979, the year of the spill, thirty-eight mines and five mills were operating on the reservation in what is known as the "checkerboard" area to the east, where Navajo land intercalates with other properties, and on the Laguna Reservation, which boasted the largest open-pit uranium mine on earth. In 1986 a Hispano man from Grants whose well had been contaminated perched on a cross for two months until the situation was investigated and he was compensated.

The boom was over by 1990, when the price for yellowcake dropped from forty to ten cents a pound, but the subsequent signing of NAFTA, the free-trade agreement with America's neighbors, opened a new market for yellowcake—Mexican reactors—so the mining may be starting up again soon.

The uranium is down in the water-bearing Gallup sandstone, and the mines had to be dewatered, Ray explained as we passed the mounds of old ammunition at Fort Wingate. The fort was originally a cavalry post whose purpose was to keep an eye on the Navajo after they came back from Bosque Redondo. During World War II it was converted to an ordnance depot, due to the proximity of the railroad. Some of the ammo there, buried in rows of gumdrop mounds in the desert and still live, goes back to the First World War. Leaving the interstate at Churchrock, we ascended through spectacular red-rock formations covered with snow into the high steppe, where the Perky, as local Navajo call the Rio Puerco, rises. In its natural state, the Perky, which meanders down from Hosta Butte, on the Continental Divide, was an ephemeral stream. Fed by snowmelt and summer rains, it only ran two months of the year. But between 1969 and 1986, it flowed year-round, thanks to millions of gallons of contaminant-laden water pumped into its north fork from three mines above Churchrock. The local people came to depend on this water for their sheep, goats, and cattle. Some used it to irrigate their crops. Children played in it and drank it. No one told them it was contaminated, and they would have had trouble believing it if someone had, Ray said, because according to the traditional Navajo concept of water pollution, "it has to be related to something physical. It has to be something that can be tasted or smelled or that changes the water's color." How could water—something a Navajo woman had described to me not as fluid, but a prayer, a blessing—be poisoned?

The mining distressed the elders, Ray went on, "but they didn't say anything because their sons were making eight or nine dollars an hour. Agents from the United Nuclear Corporation went around to the families living in the North Fork drainage and paid them a thousand dollars and promised to build them a house and a road, but nothing was on paper; it was a verbal type of promise, and the majority of the People didn't speak English and were misled by interpreters and moved off the only homes they knew of." As we drove along the tranquil, but now toxic, wash, it was difficult to sense the horror of what had happened here. The horror was all the more insidious because it was invisible. Ray pointed out the abandoned head frame where United Nuclear had run a thousand-foot shaft down to the Gallup sandstone. The contaminants moved through such shafts from one water table to another. Water contaminated by contact with ore, wasterock overburden (the rock or soil dug through or removed to get to the higher-grade ore; usually there is three to ten times as much wasterock as there is ore), and dust from mining operations leached or seeped or was pumped into other water-bearing layers. At their peak the dewatering pumps were sucking up a hundred thousand acre-feet a day. They drained one zone that happened to be the best water supply between Laguna and Gallup. The Ojo de Gallo Wash at the village of San Rafael, just south of Grants, where Francisco Vásquez de Coronado, the leader of the first Spanish expedition into the Southwest, had stopped in 1541, became dry (it has started flowing again since the mining stopped).

The spill made the already poisoned arroyo even more lethal. Ninety miles downstream, across the Arizona border, the Puerco's radioactive levels still exceed the state's acceptable standards of thirty picocuries per liter. Ray showed me where it happened. It is now an Environmental Protection Agency superfund site. The polluted water is sprayed into the air to evaporate. Twenty-one million dollars have been spent to prevent further damage, but less than 1 percent of the volume of the spill has been cleaned up, and a subterranean plume of contamination has been spreading throughout the drainage. Its rate of spread depends on the weather. The drier it is, the higher the plume rises.

The immediate effects of the spill on the people in the drainage were devastating. They were told to stop using their shallow, hand-dug wells, to stop grazing their stock or letting them drink from the river, and to stop their children from playing in it. A ban was imposed on selling Rio Puerco stock. The local Navajo lost a big part of their income and had to buy their meat and haul water from great distances or pipe it over the divide. A small out-of-court settlement was reached with United Nuclear, but there has been no follow-up on the long-term health effects of the spill. Uranium poisoning is slow acting. Some effects can take twenty years to show up. They include, Ray said, pattern baldness, nausea, cancer, weakening of the stomach lining, and increased vulnerability to ulcers. Many of the victims are long gone, and so is United Nuclear, and to prove that a certain condition had been caused by the spill would be difficult.

A few old-timers were still around. We passed the hogan of Tom Lewis, a *hataali*. His windmill wasn't yet contaminated. Mrs. Arviso, who was eighty-four or -five, had running water piped from Smith Lake, twenty miles away. The niece of the old Parker lady, who died five years ago, still felt complications from having walked in the river the day after the spill; she still had burning itches between her toes. When I asked if it would be possible to talk to her, Ray said she didn't live here anymore. As for the others, he said he didn't want to just barge in on them, and besides, the weather was kind of nice, and they were probably all in Gallup, shopping before the storm that was coming in from California. He seemed very protective of his people. I asked whether Tohee, Water Way, had been performed to heal the people who had become ill from being exposed to the contaminated water, but this was something he clearly didn't want to talk about with a *bilagaana*.

We agreed to meet again to talk to the elders, particularly the *hataali* and a man named Arsenio Smiley, who was one of the famous Navajo code talkers on the Pacific theater; the Japanese could never break the code they were using over the radio because it wasn't a code: they were just talking Navajo. I called the day before to confirm the appointment, but Ray said there was too much snow, so we made another date. That day came, and I drove the two hours to Thoreau, and he wasn't there. I tracked down Ray's wife, who worked in the kitchen of the Indian boarding school. Are any of you Mrs. Morgan? I asked a group of women eating lunch. Silence. At last she giggled. She said Ray was probably at the Aztec Laundromat. We phoned there, and he was. "I tried to call you yesterday," he told me. "Arsenio's sisters told me he's been under the weather for the last couple of weeks, so we can't see him." Well, we could go see Tom Lewis, I suggested. Ray wasn't enthusiastic, but he agreed to meet me at a turnoff in Churchrock. I drove there and waited, but he never showed.

Ray didn't come out and say it (this isn't etiquette in many tradi-tional societies), but the message was clear: our business with each other was over; the next level of interaction, of penetration into the Navajo world, wasn't going to happen. Ray had sensed that I was after more than just the story of the spill, which was true: I wanted to get to know some Navajo, to learn about their belief system and to what extent the People still live by it. I decided, having come all the way out here, to track down Arsenio Smiley myself. Ray had said he spoke English and could tell me some good stories, and I had been looking forward to meeting him. The Upper Puerco is in Pinedale Chapter; each of the 109 chapters has a thousand or more residents and elects a delegate to the tribal council in Window Rock. I asked a man on a tractor turning over a field how to get to the Pinedale chapter house, and he said he didn't know, which was undoubtedly a lie. After some driving around, I found the chapter house. A woman there told me the last she heard Arsenio was living at Mariano Lake, but I drove up there, and nobody had heard of him, so I went to the Crownpoint police, who sent me back to the chapter house, and this time another woman gave me a map to Arsenio's trailer, which was past the Happy Valley Church. I pulled up to the trailer and gave my horn a few blasts, which is Navajo etiquette. Two little girls, Adaline and Alva, came out. I asked if they knew Arsenio Smiley. Alva said, "He's our father." (In Anglo kinship terminology, he was their paternal grandfather. Many traditional people use "father" in this way.) She said he lived down in the old Churchrock barracks, and I asked the two of them if they would take me there.

The barracks had been built in 1940 for the workers at the Fort Wingate ordnance depot. They were in a sorry state, but people still lived in them. Arsenio, a sixty-six-year-old with a mischievous gleam in his eyes, was sitting beside a little woodstove. As I had suspected, Ray had slung me the bit about his being under the weather to protect his privacy.

I said, "I hear you are one of the famous code talkers," and Arsenio said, "It's kind of a long story, so you may as well stay a few days." He was hoping his granddaughters would stay around and listen, but they weren't interested, and they went outside to play. "When I was a boy, we learned how to outwit animals, how to put yourself inside an animal's skull," Arsenio told me. "We were taught patience and endurance. Nowadays our kids are more on quick electronic Western-civilization type of stuff. They throw their food into a microwave and eat on the run, and you can't get them to sit still for five minutes." He put on my felt hat and said, "Hey I've got an idea. Let's trade hats. Maybe that way we can get into each other's heads."

Arsenio related how he was drafted into the Marines in 1943 at the age of eighteen. "I didn't want to go. Our feeling was that's not our war, but a whole bunch of us went." He spent most of his tour handling supplies and only sent one radio message, on Saipan. After the war Arsenio went to work for the tribe's environmental health department. He collected water from washes and wells and sent it to the tribal lab in Fort Defiance for bacterial analysis. After the mining started, he would hold a Geiger counter to plants and to the dust on the trucks that had been hauling uranium ore, and "it showed there was content." Sometime in the early seventies, some Anglo men from New York offered his parents, who were living on the Upper Puerco, two hundred dollars if they moved, and they agreed, affixing their thumbprints to a piece of paper that the men provided but not understanding that they were being paid to move so United Nuclear could put in a uranium mill on the site. One day a front loader came and toppled their corral and hogan, and they moved with their belongings to Ram Mesa, two miles away. Some days, Arsenio claimed, a fog of tailings would envelope the mesa. "The waste sand emits alpha particles that won't penetrate a piece of paper," he explained, "but when inhaled will deliver large amounts of radiation to lung tissue."

One day about ten years ago Billy Yazee, who lived on the other side of the barracks, and a friend were taking a shortcut across a tailings pile, and they sank to the waist in soggy sand. When they got out, their legs were covered with a red rash and were stinging badly. Billy had been having his legs treated ever since, and the rash still hadn't gone away. Billy was a *hataali*, and he knew Water Way, but Arsenio wasn't sure if he did the male or the female ceremony. "Male rain makes thunder," he explained, "but female rain don't make any sound. It just rains quietly." There were several different water clans—Big Water, Bitter Water, Sweet Water, Salt Water, Waters Flow Together. "Water is sacred. We believe that we originate from Mother Earth and were consolidated with rain from our Heavenly Father. We are the children of water."

Arsenio was completely open about the traditional beliefs. When he went off to war, he told me, his parents had a Protection Way ceremony performed for him. "During training we did ceremonies, and when we were released from the war, other prayers were said so that whatever was done during that war would not be with our memories." Some of the men had needed to take a scalp to be initiated into their warrior society, and they had returned to Dinetah with Japanese scalps. I wondered how Native Americans felt about fighting "for your country," joining the army that had defeated them. But it was the only way for many to get off the rez and learn a trade, to break out of "internal exile," as Murray Kempton described the situation of American Communists, and the only way, these days, to get an enemy scalp. I knew that Cayapo Indian adolescents in the Amazon were in a similar bind because they needed to kill somebody to become a man, and this was frowned on by the dominant Brazilian society, and that the Zuñi's warrior priesthood was dying out for the same reason. Other sources confirmed that not only did code talkers take scalps in Okinawa, but Navajo sneaked into the Japanese-American internment camp in Leupp, Arizona, and scalped some of the prisoners there, and during the Korean War the warrior societies kept going by taking Korean scalps; I don't know about Vietnam or Desert Storm.

Big Mountain

One day, at the offices of Tonantzin, a traditional peoples' advocacy group in Albuquerque, I met two Navajo, Tom and John, who lived way out in the Arizona desert, off the modern grid, at a place called Big Mountain. Tom and John were cousins and my age—in their late forties. They wore their hair long and, having gone through the sixties, were practiced at jiving wanna-bes and talking about Mother Earth and Indian spirituality. "I can't tell you my Indian name or my ears would dry up," Tom kidded me. Tom could have passed for a Buryat Mongol, which belied his insistence that the People had emerged locally, from Navajo Lake. "Don't tell me you're falling for that Bering Strait stuff," he chided me. He had a memorable way of putting things. "For us every day is a thanksgiving day, a prayer in the cycle of life," he remarked as we were driving around Albuquerque a few days later. "But in the white world, every day is a slogan. 'Give me liberty or give me death.' 'I've just begun to fight.' 'The Uncola.' "

Albuquerque was certainly bristling with slogans. Billboards along its freeways hawked the services and wares of chiropractors (AMOR CHIROPRACTIC: SERVING YOU FROM THE HEART), car dealers (BOB TURNER'S FORD COUNTRY), and lawyers competing for the drunk-driver and drunk-driver-victim market. (Ron Bell's said INJURED? I SUE DRUNK DRIVERS and had a picture of a DWI handcuffed behind his back, the cuffs several feet in diameter and protruding from the billboard in 3-D. W. J. Cooney's simply said INJURED? and had the mangled butt end of an actual compact car smashed through it, while Bruce Barnett's relatively subdued billboard was spanned by an American eagle.) All kinds of businesses clamored for attention as we cruised the arteries of the oasis: RECOGNITION PLUS, where my sons and their teammates got trophies at the end of the soccer season; evangelical operations with signs like JESUS CHRIST TOUGHER THAN NAILS or MY BOSS IS A JEWISH CARPENTER. "Sloganworld," as I began to call it, was the perfect name for this hokey, chimeric outpost of the modern world that consists basically of cars, furniture, appliances, building materials, and produce trucked in on Interstate 40 from Chicago, Los Angeles, and other distant cities; of video and audio barrages from faraway media stations.

Tom had precisely the perspective on the Southwest's most recent overlay that I was looking for, and he tacitly took on me and my quest and let me hang out with him. He became my teacher, and I kept bombarding him with questions, which was not the Indian approach.

Finally one morning, Tom got impatient with me and my constant questions and snapped, "If you quit acting like the late Harry Reasoner, maybe you'd learn something."

Over the Thanksgiving break, Tom and John and my wife and the boys and I all drove out to Big Mountain together. It was a four-hour trip, and by the time we got there, we were fast friends; as Tom observed, "We've been having a small talking circle, and are feeling a lot better about each other." Tom's sense of where we came from— New York (at first he thought we lived in the city, not in the forested mountains upstate)—was "I know it's tough there. At every intersection someone has a bucket, a rag, and a squeegee, and the asphalts are like the roads on the rez."

Tom and John's people had lived on Big Mountain forever. There are about sixty Navajo clans, with many subclans; each Navajo belongs to his mother's clan and is "born for" his father's. Tom was Waters Flow Together born for Many Goats, and he was John's "father," or paternal uncle. They also shared a mutual great-grandfather, Old Gold Tooth, through their mothers, so they were double cousins. Old Gold Tooth's father had been rounded up by Kit "Rope Thrower" Carson and had marched on the Long Walk to Bosque Redondo and had been released when he was twelve.

The Bureau of Indian Affairs policy in the fifties had been to get the children off the reservation and integrate them into the mainstream, and from the ages of six to fourteen Tom had been sent to an Indian boarding school, where, he told us, "they made you eat a can of Skol chewing tobacco or a bar of gray laundry soap if they caught you talking your own language." After high school in Gallup, the notorious wide-open border town on the eastern edge of the rez, he went to computer college in Albuquerque, and there he got into the Red Power scene that was burgeoning in the early seventies. One of his close friends, with whom he would go up to the Sandia Mountains that loom over the city from the east to drum and dance and do ceremonies and get away from Sloganworld, was a fellow Navajo named Larry Casuse, "who wanted to do away with the booze and the whole exploitation scene, 'See the Indian do this, see the Indian do that,' " in Gallup, so on March 1, 1973, he took the mayor hostage and held him in Stearn's sporting-goods store, and there the state police blew his head off.

We stopped at a wholesale warehouse in Gallup where John, who was a silversmith, picked up some stones and silver for an order. Half the town was stores where "Genuine Reservation Pawn" and other jewelry were sold—"A-rabs" (Lebanese, actually) controlled the business, John told me, setting the prices every Thursday. The other half was a skid row with flophouses and bars where liquor, drugs, Navajo girls, pretty much anything you were looking for, could be scored. "Gallup is the major shopping area for the People," Tom explained. "It lives off the People." One grocer in town was rumored to have been selling rattlesnake meat, which was taboo for Navajo to eat; the Snake People are very feared. We passed the rambling Hotel El Rancho, where "Old Ronnie Reagan and lots of other movie stars stayed" while they were on location during the heyday of the Hollywood western in the forties and fifties. The Rio Puerco, coming down from Churchrock, ran right through town, between the interstate and the railroad tracks.

The first of every month there is an invasion of muddy pickups—people coming in for their social security, pension, or welfare checks. As we got back on the interstate, two falling-down drunks were thumbing at the entrance ramp. Something like five hundred intoxicated Indians freeze to death or are hit by cars in New Mexico every year. That winter a thirteen-year-old girl would be found frozen to death in a ditch behind a Gallup grocery store. In February ten-month-old Winona Kee would freeze after being carried out of the house by her four-year-old sister because drunk relatives were fighting inside. Some thought the solution for cleaning up Gallup was to legalize alcohol on the rez, where it is currently banned, but others feared this would lead to increased teenage drinking, fetal alcohol syndrome, domestic violence, and child abuse. As it was, on reservations nationwide, alcohol-related deaths were 5.6 percent higher than they were in the general population; the unemployment rate was 49 percent; the tuberculosis rate was eight times higher; the teen-suicide and infant-mortality rates were dramatically elevated. One study found that one in six Indian teenagers across the land attempted suicide, one in four had become a problem drinker by the end of high school, 18 percent reported being constantly sad, 11 percent confessed to extreme hope-lessness. Larry Casuse's martyrdom accomplished nothing.

On May 1, 1974, the federal government attempted to resolve a dispute that dated to the creation of the rez in 1868 and of the Hopi Reservation in 1882 by awarding a coal-rich, 1.8-million-acre tract that included Big Mountain to the Hopi, even though the area was inhabited almost entirely by Navajo. Commercial interests influenced the decision: the Navajo would have to leave, and with the area vacated, there would be few obstacles to mining companies getting at the coal on Black Mesa, a part of Big Mountain where the coal-bearing shale lies right on the surface. Twenty-three hundred Navajo families agreed to be relocated, but another 253 families, including Tom and John's, refused to leave. They decided that they would rather die making a last stand at Big Mountain than be forced to take a second Long Walk, as John put it.

"I was still in Albuquerque when Public Law 93531 [which gave Big Mountain to the Hopi] was passed," Tom recalled. "I knew my people were suffering because of relocation, and I was tired of the rat race anyway, of living from paycheck to paycheck, of living for the utility company and having to go up in the hills at night if I wanted to be alone, so I went back to my clan at Big Mountain, and we banded together to resist relocation. We resisted by being there."

The Bureau of Indian Affairs had been trying to smoke them out ever since, by fencing them out of their grazing land, by reducing the livestock quotas on their grazing permits by 90 percent, by forbidding them to make repairs or improvements on their homes. But they were still there, ready to fight to the death if necessary. From 1974 on, Big Mountain became a focus of Native American resistance and spiritual renewal. At one point early on, AIM, the militant American Indian Movement, anticipating a showdown like the one at Wounded Knee, South Dakota, in 1973, supplied them with arms from the Sandinistas. Every summer, in July, the people of Big Mountain put on a Sun Dance, and traditional peoples came from all over the Americas to express their solidarity.

In Window Rock Tom picked up a box of bullets for his ancient, long-barreled, single-shot .22-caliber "varmint gun" (the one he had been carrying for the last eighteen years whenever he went on Big Mountain in case the government came to throw him and his people off) and some provisions—mutton, cranberry juice, cilantro. In darkness we continued to Ganado, then up to Pinon and Forest Lake, where we hit a rutted dirt road that ran along Dinnebito Wash. Across the wash, and on the other side of a storm fence, were the lights of the houses of the Diné, or Navajo, who had agreed to be located. "We lost a lot of people through psychological warfare," John told me. On this side Tom and John's families and the other holdouts were living in some of the most primitive conditions in America. In summer they had to throw fifty-five-gallon oil drums into the back of their pickups and drive twenty miles for water; in winter they melted snow. "But we like it that way," John went on. "When water comes through pipes, people take it for granted. They don't respect it or appreciate it anymore. When you've got electric, you're a slave of the utility. If the electric goes off, there goes your refrigerator, your computer, your bank account."

We were pretty wiped out by the time we reached Tom's outfit. Tom and John wanted to watch the Hopi night dancers who they heard were dancing at Hotevilla, forty minutes away. My wife said there were night dancers in the village she grew up in in Uganda—people who, when their child was sick, would get a strand of hair or a finger-nail clipping of their child and would dance naked behind their hut in the darkness to pass the sickness over. A long, fascinating comparison of Navajo and Tutsi beliefs and customs ensued. It was amazing how many parallels there were—the taboo on speaking the name of the dead, the owl as a harbinger of death, and so on—considering that the cultures had evolved on separate continents, without being able to compare notes. It was clear that the Navajo's reputation for being obsessed with witchcraft was largely a product of their proximity to uncomprehending Anglos, like the stereotypes that have been attached to the Mexicans. We ended up talking till three in the morning and crashing in a spare hogan, made of piñon faggots plastered with mud, around a fire whose smoke exited through a hole in the roof.

A few weeks later I drove back out to Big Mountain to spend a few days with Tom and John. This time I could see how beautiful it was, the blinding glory of Glitter World, as Navajo call it. (They adopted the Pueblo belief that this is the Fourth World humans have lived in, the three previous ones being Black, Blue, and Yellow Worlds.) The piñon-spattered steppe was blanketed in snow. Two mustangs were frolicking below a tiara of tan, stress-cracked sandstone. The sunlight gave their choidal fractures a lucent, casein sheen. Magenta mesas dusted with snow rimmed the horizon. To the west, San Francisco Peaks, one of the four sacred mountains, the western corner of Dine-tah, rose as awesomely as one of the Himalayas from the Tibetan Plateau. Rush Limbaugh, who has a big following among the gung ho

Navajo World War II vets, was delivering a caustic right-wing rap on the radio.

This time Tom and I stayed at John's place, which wasn't a traditional hogan, but a free-form hippie-commune shack surrounded by automotive detritus and earthy in the extreme, almost like a nest. "For us the earth is not dirty," John explained. For two days we just kind of hunkered down there, drumming and chanting, feeding the woodstove, smoking white sage tobacco, picking various medical herbs and brewing tea from them, talking about the People and their way of looking at things and all the times they have been had by the white man. "The earth is Changing Woman," Tom explained. "By the end of winter, she is an old withered hag. In spring she becomes young again, dancing here, dancing there. The land is the Bible from which the stories of the origin can be read.

"We native people try to keep in harmony with all creation," he went on. "If you violate the natural laws of wind, rain, lightning, reptiles, it has to have a negative effect on you. If someone gets hit by a thunderbeam, their face gets twisted. You're not supposed to laugh at them—they're special people. If you brush a rattler with your boot or your stirrup and he reacts, you have to do a water ceremony. You have to tell the Water People, 'Hey cool it. I am here, I have a right to live. Don't make me one of those who belongs to you.' Like my son [John's brother] Roy, who drowned—he's with the Water People." In certain springs, Tom said, there were long water serpents that I should not let herpetologists know about.

It was lambing time, and we helped John's mother, Alice, an inscrutably wrinkled old *shimishani,* get the lambs to their mothers, who were waiting on one side of a round corral of interlocking, twisted piñon boughs that was a work of art, like a giant crown of thorns. Tom deftly lassoed (he was left-handed) a mother who was reluctant to give her milk and placed her lamb next to her. John skinned and cut up a lamb that hadn't survived—its eyes had already been pecked out by crows—and hung the strips of purple meat in a juniper tree, while a black dog lay panting gently beneath it; he planned to use the skin for a pouch. Down below, five cop cars suddenly pulled up to Alice's hogan. It was give-out day. The Navajo tribal police were bringing canned goods loaded with sugar and fat, contributed by various humanitarian agencies, for the people of Big Mountain. After they left, the three of us sat on a ledge and watched the sheep come home. "God this is beautiful," I said, and Tom rejoined, "I wouldn't know. I've lived here all my life."

One day in 1989, John told me, a German girl had appeared, and she ended up staying two years, helping his mother with the sheep. The Navajo name for "German" is "Steel Helmet"; it dates to World War I. Hitler is "He Smells His Mustache." Every so often, another German wanna-be would appear. "Why do the Germans keep coming here?" he mused. "'Cause over there there's nothing interesting anymore."

One of the outstanding Navajo traits is an irrepressible, buoyant sense of fun. Many Navajo love practical jokes, particularly those at the expense of *bilagaana,* and are masters of puns, achieving double or triple entendres with subtle shifts of pitch or the addition of prefixes. The language is so rich (and almost impossible for an Anglo to learn) that it has very few borrow words. Among them are *gohweĬ* (coffee, from Spanish *café*), *aloos* (rice, from Spanish *arroz*), and *nóomba* (number, from English). The first treaty negotiations and ethnological sessions with Anglos were conducted in Spanish, the lingua franca of the frontier through the turn of the century.

The next afternoon Tom, John, John's older brother Kee, and I had a sweat. We heated up some lava stones and put them in the sweat lodge, a dome of lashed sticks covered with rugs and blankets, and got in. As we stared down at the red-hot rocks, sweat pouring out of us, Tom and John and Kee started chanting in Navajo. In the middle of one of John's incantations, I heard the words "federal prison." We crawled out and rolled in the snow, which sent a shock to the system like biting into a *chiltepin,* one of the excoriating wild chile peppers of the Sonoran Desert. "My ears got really hot in there," I said to Tom. "That's 'cause you talk too much," he said. I asked John what the "federal prison" part of his prayer was all about, and he said, "My nephew, Clayton Lonetree. He's doing twenty-five years in Fort Leavenworth for espionage."

"Clayton Lonetree. . . . Wasn't he the Marine guard at the Moscow embassy who was seduced by a beautiful KGB Russian girl a couple of years ago and busted for passing secrets to the Commies?" I asked. That's him, John said. The story (alleged wild orgies in the embassy's secret code room and so on; a black Marine guard had also been recruited as a spy) had broken in 1987 and had been all over the papers. I recalled having the feeling at the time that Lonetree was being hung out to dry, sensing that the real story was probably quite different. Clayton was the son of John's older sister Sally, who lived in Tuba City, an hour from the family's outfit on Big Mountain.

The Captivity of Clayton Lonetree

Tom and John and I became like brothers. I would go out to see them whenever I had the chance, and the house my family and I had rented on La Hacienda Drive became the Waters Flow Together clan's Albuquerque pied-à-terre. Tom would come "for only a week" to "get laid," as he put it. I got involved in the whole extended family and its cosmological stumbling. One of John's young nephews came in from Tsaile, a community on the rez, to study carpentry at the Technical and Vocational Institute and rented an apartment not far from us. His wife got a job as a waitress at Wendy's. Their first foray into Sloganworld seemed to be going well, but then one of the nephew's brothers came for a visit and got drunk and rowdy, and they were thrown out of their apartment, and the nephew dropped out in midterm, and they all went back to Tsaile.

Tom nicknamed me "Mutton Man" because I'd always bring a leg of lamb whenever I came to Big Mountain. "Mutton Man" was the name of a Superman-like cartoon character in the *Navajo Times*. On my way out to Big Mountain, wending through Dinetah, I would often pick up hitchhikers. One time I gave a lift to a teenage couple that was going to Shiprock. They were heavy-metal freaks. "Heavy metal is the best thing that ever happened on the rez," the boy told me. I could see how the nihilism of heavy metal might appeal to existentially stymied young Navajo kids, the way it did to the post-Communist but still-mired youth of Eastern Europe. The girl said that some of the heavy-metal freaks in their high school were into Satanism and cut up drunks for ceremonies. Three years ago a dismembered corpse was found hanging from one of the soccer posts.

This was reminiscent of the Farmington incident. In Farmington, New Mexico, on the eastern edge of the rez, there was a local redneck rite of passage that consisted of rolling drunk Navajo. In April 1974 three tanked-up Navajo men were abducted from the streets of Farmington. Their mutilated bodies were found in Chokecherry Canyon, outside of town. Firecrackers had been set off in their nostrils, plastic had been melted on their naked buttocks, their groins had been gigged by a sharp instrument, and the uncircumcised penis of one had been charred like a candlewick. Rumors of an Indian finger being passed around at the high school led to the arrest and confessions of three Anglo boys, two of them fifteen and the third sixteen. They weren't tried as adults. All they got was light sentences to reform school, which precipitated a riot of Navajo and Navajo sympathizers in Farmington. They were all released in less than two years, but soon afterward each of them met with strange accidents. There was talk that they had been "witched" by Navajo shamans versed in the black arts.

I asked the boy if the redneck kids in Farmington had been killed by witchcraft, and he said, "That's what I heard." (He would have been a toddler in 1974.) Then I ran by him something I'd heard from a forensic pathologist who worked at the medical examiner's office in Albuquerque, that sometimes the Navajo tribal police would bring in the pulverized bodies of suspected skinwalkers. Skinwalkers are witches—*chindi*—who can take the form of animals, particularly wolves or coyotes, and can cause illness or death to those they dislike. They are believed to be people who want to become rich and have gone through an elaborate ceremony that includes the sacrifice, by untraceable magic means, of a relative, usually a brother or a sister.

"This happens," the boy said. "The skinwalkers get beaten beyond recognition so they won't come back." (I also ran this past Tom, and he said, "Witchcraft looks bad, but it's just the negative side of spirituality, combined with jealousy. A piece of hair has all your energy, contains a complete blueprint of you, like DNA. Navajo have a different relationship with evil. It's present all the time. You got to have the negative with the positive, the male and the female, day and night, earth and sky. There are male and female trees. Corn plants are male and female. Christians tell us, 'You worship ghosts,' but so do they. What about the Holy Ghost? Jesus Christ is not walking around here. My [great-great] grandfather knew a sing that would lock your trigger if you were trying to shoot him." One of John's sisters, who lived in Tsaile, told me that the real reason the Navajo were incarcerated at Bosque Redondo was to harass them into revealing the secret formula of an arrow poison that was so strong the arrow didn't even have to hit, and it killed you; but they never did.)

One morning I was sitting in front of a hogan with a Big Mountain traditionalist, and we noticed a skinny black dog with a white beard slinking behind a rise, two hundred yards off. "It's been here a couple of days," the traditionalist told me. "It's not a stray; it's a skinwalker," he said matter-of-factly, but asked not to be named, because the evil could be deflected back to him.

Late in February 1992, I drove out to Tuba City to see Sally and find out if anything could be done to help her son Clayton. Heading up to the Hopi mesas from Ganado, I passed a narrow butte on the valley floor called Steamboat and the turn off to Jeddito, which means "Antelope Spring." Having driven this way several times now, I was beginning to internalize the scenery. I had heard several versions of the meaning of "Huiye Toye," the name of the last spring before you enter the Hopi Reservation: an Anglo doctor who is married to a Navajo woman and lives in Ganado told me "Huiye Toye" means "Scary Place" or "Dreadful Place," either because of the eerie sound the spring makes in the canyon or because the spring is a Hopi shrine and Navajo who drank from it were sometimes ambushed by Hopi. Tom said it meant "Risky Place," or, literally, "Take a Risk to Get Water," because Ute bounty hunters would hide in the bushes, waiting to scalp Navajo. There was no love lost between the Navajo and the Ute, the Navajo word for whom means "They're Coming at You." In the 1830s, as the Navajo historian Raymond Friday Locke writes, the Mexican government, desperate to subdue the Navajo and to stop their depredations, "encouraged private citizens to become scalp hunters, paying a high bounty on Navajo scalps. But the government officials in Sante Fe couldn't tell one swatch of black hair from another and ended up paying silver for the scalps of their allies as well as quite a few that had been lifted by their own [i.e. Mexican] countrymen."

By the end of the eighteenth century, the Spanish policy toward the Navajo, who remained more or less persistently hostile, was one of outright extermination. In 1821, a year after Mexico gained independence, the tribe made overtures of peace. A delegation of sixteen chiefs came to the presidio at Jemez Pueblo. An American trader who was there, General Thomas James, recorded that the chiefs "requested the commander of the fort to allow them to pass on to the governor at Santa Fe, saying that they had come to make peace. The commander invited them into the fort." Peace pipes went around, then at a signal each chief was seized by two Spaniards, and a third stabbed him in the heart. "A Spaniard who figured in this butchery showed me his knife, which he said had killed eight of them," James continued.

Their bodies were thrown over the wall of the fort and covered with a little earth in a gully.

A few days afterwards five more of the same nation appeared on the bank of the river opposite the town, and inquired for their countrymen. The Spaniards told them they had gone to Santa Fe, invited them to come over the river, and said they would be well treated. They crossed, and were murdered in the same manner as the others. There again appeared three Indians on the opposite bank, inquiring for their chiefs. They were decoyed across, taken into the town under the mask of friendship, and also murdered in cold blood. In a few days two more appeared, but could not be induced to cross, when some Spanish horsemen went down the river to intercept them. Perceiving this movement, they fled, and no more embassies came.

After this treachery, for the two and half decades that New Mexico remained part of Mexico, the Navajo killed every white man, woman, and child they had the chance to.

A few miles farther, on my way to Tuba City, a young Navajo couple flagged me down. The woman's name was Darlene. She had just gone into labor, and they needed a lift up to the hospital at Keams Canyon. The man's name was Gary. "I was born on the Apache Rez," he told me with some irritation, "and now my kid is going to be born on the Hopi Rez." A quarter of a mile on we picked up Darlene's uncle George. Darlene was calm, centered. She was eighteen. This was her first child, but she obviously had the situation under control. There was no question she was going to have a bouncing baby. George asked, "Where you going?" "To see a woman in Tuba City," I said. When I let them out at the hospital, he gave my hand a big squeeze.

Tuba City, on the other side of the Hopi mesas, is the funky commercial hub of the western rez, a smaller, dry version of Gallup. Sally lived on the edge of town with her husband, Kee Richard, who drove a propane truck. I picked up an escort of stray dogs as I pulled up to their trailer. Sally, a handsome, down-to-earth woman of forty-seven, came out and yelled at them. "They bite. It's hard to walk around here."

Sally worked for the tribe as a nutrition educator, warning about the evils of junk food and polyunsaturated fat, and she was also on the board of a group that called itself, with the typical Navajo love of word play, the Handicapables. She had had Clayton when she was sixteen and living in Chicago, she told me. His father, Spencer Lonetree, was a Winnebago. They had two (he claims only one) more children. They never married, and she returned to Arizona with her children, where in the early seventies she met Kee Richard. Sally and Kee Richard married and had two boys and a girl. In 1974 Spencer came and took Clayton and his brother back to live with him in St. Paul, Minnesota. Clayton joined the marines six years later, right out of high school. "He always wanted to be in the service," Sally told me. "He used to play with toy soldiers."

On January 9, 1987, Clayton's kid brother called and said he was in trouble. "They were keeping him in a place called Quantico," Sally continued. "I flew to Washington and took the train to Quantico. 'It's my son they're picking on,' I told the conductor. 'They've got him up for espionage.'

"I hadn't seen Clayton in three years, and we spent two hours getting reacquainted. The next morning at dawn I did a Corn-Pollen ceremony. It was overcast. There was a little snow on the ground and a lot of tall trees, but I looked at a map and figured out where East was, and I faced that way and said a prayer. I said 'I have a reason to be here' and offered the pollen four times, to the earth, the sky, the water, and the air."

Sally sat through the whole trial, which lasted from July 21 to August 20. Sam Lonetree, Clayton's grandfather, a venerable old Winnebago chief, was also there, in his headdress, beating his drum outside the courtroom. One time in the middle of the trial he went up to Clayton and without a word slowly brushed him with an eagle feather.

The defense team included the legendary late champion of radicals and underdogs William Kunstler, who had defended Russell Means and Harold Banks and Leonard Peltier in the Wounded Knee affair. But the military court's mind appeared to be made up. Caspar Weinberger, the secretary of defense, was calling for the death penalty, and several gung ho marines had even volunteered for the firing squad. None of the defense's motions except those for recesses were granted, and none of its important witnesses were allowed to testify. Clayton was convicted and sentenced to thirty years, which were subsequently reduced to twenty-five.

After the verdict Spencer fired the entire defense team, and a lawyer named Lee Calligaro, who had helped prosecute Lieutenant Calley for the Mylai massacre, took over the appeal. But it had been five years. Nothing had happened, and Sally was starting to lose hope. "The feeling I get about Clayton and his predicament is that nobody cares," she told me. "Everybody's got their own lives and their own problems. I haven't gotten much support from Navajo. The World War Two vets think Clayton tarnished their image. One of them asked me, 'How could he be a disgrace to our people?' I said, 'Oh pooey.' " Even Sally's family had distanced itself from the tragedy. In traditional Navajo belief, if something happens, there's a reason for it.

"There's some screwed-up, weird people in the Pentagon," she went on. "I know what David felt going against Goliath. I know what the Crucifixion was like." And then she burst into tears. "I miss my boy."

It had been two years since Sally had seen Clayton, because of the distance and expense of getting to Kansas and because she had to take care of her husband, who had gotten cancer. She had become active in a support group called MOMS—Mothers of Mistreated Servicemembers. I filled Robert Redford, who had bought the movie rights to my last book and was interested in things Indian, in on Clayton's predicament, and he put up the money for me to drive Sally out to Fort Leavenworth, Kansas, and if it seemed appropriate, I could sound Clayton out about whether he was interested in having his life made into a movie.

On December 14, 1992 (by now we had left Albuquerque and were back home in upstate New York), I flew to Phoenix and picked up Sally at Tuba City in a rented Sunbird. We swung through Big Mountain to see if Tom or John was there. Clayton's umbilical was buried under a piñon up on the mountain, Sally told me. Big Mountain was really more like a big hill, a low bump on the horizon, whose top could be reached from Sally's mother's hogan in four hours if you didn't get lost in the canyons on the way up. It was named by a Navajo who had been wounded by a Ute and had to crawl its length, "inch by inch, so it seemed like a mountain to him," Sally explained.

Each outcrop and land feature had a story, and Sally seemed to know all of them. Even though she had left Big Mountain at an early age and had been out in Sloganworld most of her life, she was still Diné through and through.

"This place is called Hopi Fall because a Hopi fell off his donkey and died here," she told me as we drove along. "That box canyon is called John Horson's Corral. That's They Kill a Lot of Watermelon Wash because years ago some Indian farmers got upset and started kicking their watermelons. That rock is called Sam Wilson's Statue because it looks like this elder called Sam Wilson, who's still alive." We stopped to look at a pictograph made in the thirties of a man, a horse, and a police badge, depicting a police raid on a gambler.

Sally was more of a progressive than the rest of her family. She had spent years living outside Dinetah, but she was still traditional in many ways, and she knew her clan genealogies back four generations, to all sixteen of her great-great-grandparents. She held the traditional view that when something bad happens, it's no accident. Either you brought it on yourself—you transgressed the "way" of some animal or natural force, or you were delinquent in a ceremony, say, or you forgot to give thanks, or your wants got the better of you—or someone did it to you: black magic.

"You don't get real until something happens. You go too far, and then you know," she explained. In the case of her husband, Kee Richard, "When he got the tumor in his nose the doctor in Flagstaff said he's got cancer, and the doctor's cure was to zap him with radiation. But my aunt, who is a medicine woman, took one look at him and asked, 'Did you ever kill a porcupine?' and Kee Richard said, 'Well, yes—when I was ten. I clubbed a porcupine with a stick from the fire. It went off to die with blood pouring out of its nose.' The first sign something was wrong with Kee Richard was his nose started bleeding. My aunt told him he had to offer turquoise and abalone to the porcupine and make a confession and ask forgiveness.

"You can be in harmony and sailing along just fine when suddenly you run into something disharmonious, and there's always a reason for it. Like my brother Roy, who drowned. He got on bad terms with the Water People. Or my sister Lavine, who got bitten by a rattler on Big Mountain when she was little. Her arm got big and bloated, but she recovered, and after that every time I saw a snake, I would kill it. Snakes see everything purple, and one day at noon when I was out with the sheep, everything suddenly turned purple. A snake slithered up and asked, 'Why are you killing all of us brothers?' I explained because my sister got bitten. So the snake said, 'Let's make a deal. Don't kill us, and we won't bother you.' "

"What about Clayton?" I asked. "How do you see what happened to him?"

"As soon as I heard about Clayton's problem, I hired a relative to do a ceremony at Big Mountain. He used a dog as a medium. The dog went from hogan to hogan howling. He went all over the world. We looked up in the sky and saw seven stars streaking across it. And after the trial I looked into the fire in the woodstove in our trailer, and I saw seven soldiers. I feel those are the ones who said, 'Hey let's get that man in trouble. He's alone, and he's an Indian.' So they went after him."

What actually happened, I learned, was that Clayton's Russian girl-friend, Violetta, persuaded him to give floor plans and identities of the CIA agents at the embassy to her "uncle Sasha"—nothing they didn't already have. Months later, in Vienna, tormented by guilt, he turned himself in. The Naval Investigative Service (NIS) never would have found out what he did otherwise. In the end, as William Kunstler told me, Clayton lived up to the code of honor and was a "better marine than any of them."

But a scapegoat was needed for the incredible lapses in security at the Moscow station, especially for letting the new $186-million American embassy be so riddled with bugs by the KGB during its construction that it couldn't be occupied. Not until 1994 would the reason for the recent exposure and execution of dozens of CIA operatives in the Soviet imperium become clear: they were betrayed by one of their own, Aldrich Ames, in return for payments of more than a million dollars. But Clayton didn't do it for money. As the commandant of the Marine Corps put it in his recommendation for leniency, Clayton was just a lonely, confused, lovesick kid far from home. But the NIS needed someone to hang, a big score to cover up its own ineptness, and coerced from Clayton, by depriving him of sleep and interrogating him in teams, a confession to much more than he ever did, which he retracted the next day. But by then the NIS had announced to the media that it had made "the bust of the century," and it was too late.

Sally wasn't all that close to her family on Big Mountain. Her kid sister Louise resented her for not being more active in the struggle, even though Sally had done her bit, even going to prison for it. According to Louise, Sally, being the first child, "caught all the dysfunctional family feedback." Sally reflected as we drove along, "We Navajo are not together. The World War Two vets are over here; the Vietnam vets are over there. The Vietnam vets suffer silently. They drink to get drunk. My brother Ed was on the front line. I know there's something wrong, but he never talks about it. A friend of [her brother] John's was in Desert Storm. He wiped out some little kids over there because he was ordered to, and it changed him. He's really suffering. No job; he's been repo'd. 'To this day I still hear those kids crying,' he told me. He needs to do Enemy Way. He needs to forgive himself. Other Navajo are not behind the land dispute."

Sally told me that her mother had been an orphan and as a child had been passed from family to family of the Waters Flow Together clan. We reached Alice's hogan. Tom and John were not around. We "bounced," to use the Ugandan term for the common experience in pretelephone societies of going to see someone who isn't there. Inside, Sally's niece Lucinda was feeding her six-month-old baby, who was strapped to a cradle board, and looked as much like the archetypal mother goddess as Laura Gilpin's famous photograph of the Navajo Madonna in the thirties. When I last saw her, she had been waitressing at Wendy's on Central Avenue in Albuquerque. Now she and her child were staying with their grandmother on Big Mountain, contemplating their next move, as Sally had done a generation earlier with her two boys when her life with Spencer Lonetree in St. Paul exploded.

I greeted Alice, the sturdy, inscrutably wrinkled *shimishani* who spoke no English but, I suspected, understood a lot more than she let on, and she gave me, for the first time, knowing I'd been trying to help Clayton, a flicker of recognition, too fast to be considered a smile, but more than I'd ever gotten out of her before. She was dressed traditionally, belonging to the last generation to do so. Her daughters all wore jeans and other western duds.

Sally explained how the woman is the keeper of the hogan. "She keeps the fire burning for her family. She has her babies sitting a little way to the west, behind the fireplace, and buries the umbilical in some sacred place. The women make decisions in a lot of things, like where to move for better grazing. They can stand a lot of pressure. They are the ones that are talking, cooking, getting water in, supporting each other so these things can be carried out. I know my place as far as a woman is concerned. I put my two daughters through the puberty ceremony. My mother showed me so many nitty-gritty things. When we were doing the ceremony, we parched white corn and ground it, and ground it again into powder. The girls had to get up in the morning and run to keep in shape."

In 1979 Sally and her mother and some other women in the Waters Flow Together clan were arrested for harassing a Bureau of Indian Affairs crew stringing a fence that would cut them off from their traditional grazing land and give it to the Hopi. Alice fired a shotgun over their heads. As soon as the crew put in a post, the women would pull it out. They beat one man with a post and, screaming, "Rape, you are raping our mother," tried to tear off his clothes. "This land is all the old ones know," Sally told me. "Big Mountain is their life. Take them away from it, and they die."

Alice had eleven children. Roy drowned in the canoeing accident in 1982. Before that, in 1975, another son, Paul, was hit by a train in Wyoming. A third boy, Kenneth, died in a car accident in Louisiana. "I used to have a lot of brothers," Sally told me. And now Clayton. Alice was convinced that someone had put a curse on her family. "It's because of witchcraft that we suffer," she had explained through a translator in 1988 to an Anglo woman named Anita Parlow, who was writing a book on the land dispute for the Christic Institute. "The witches are skinwalkers. They change shape, especially they turn into coyotes. The people on the other side, the Hopi, they know how to do these things. One was caught not long ago in his skin by the coyote trapper. The power is being used against us. My brother was punished to death and then my sons. It's not just the skinwalkers. Relocation has caused destabilization in our power. We are preoccupied with relocation, and that interrupts the proper conduct of our ceremonies."

Since the Long Walk, Coyote's image with the Navajo has been falling into disrepute. As they gave up raiding and settled down and became sheepherders, Coyote stopped being a role model and became a varmint, and eventually a witch, the favorite form for skinwalkers to take. He became increasingly evil, as the Navajo became increasingly paranoid in their quest to find an explanation for their defeat. It is not a good idea at all, if you are a traditional Navajo, to step on a Coyote Person's tracks, and even more dangerous to come upon its carcass or putrid remains. This is how you get coyote illness. Even the sight of a coyote is a bad omen.

Another way to get coyote illness is to let a Coyote Person look you in the eye when you shoot it or to leave it writhing and twitching to death. The twitches will jump over into you, or one side of your mouth will drop permanently, or you'll go crazy and become unable to remember anything, or you'll take to the bottle and, if you're a woman (here the coyote is much like the Afro-Brazilian macumba spirit Mae Pombajeira), drop your panties for anybody in sight.

There was an outbreak of coyote illness (or perhaps rabies) in the conservative Big Mountain area of Dinetah after 1948, when the government started paying a bounty for coyote skins. This preserved the now-practically-extinct ceremony for curing victims of coyote illness, in time for the anthropologist Karl W. Luckert to learn it from an old singer named Man with Palomino Horse. (It is from Luckert's book, *Coyoteway,* that most of the above material is taken.)

Dead coyotes can transmit actual disease. On February 8, 1975, eleven-year-old Danny Gallant was exploring the foothills of Sandia Peak, overlooking Albuquerque, after school with a friend, found a dead coyote, skinned it with a hunting knife, and took the skin home. A few days later an excruciatingly painful bubo swelled under his right armpit. He had contracted bubonic plague, a rare but endemic scourge of New Mexico.

Sally's fear of coyotes is not as great as some Navajo's. "Coyote says, 'If I'm going south, you have my blessing,' but if you see a coyote going north, it means wherever you are going is a problem. If you see a dead coyote, that's nothing. You just think, Poor coyote. But if I see a coyote going north, I make my own prayer.

"Coyote always wants to be first in everything," she explained, "but a lot of times it doesn't go the way he wants. Gambling, racing, politics, he always wants to win. He was there in the beginning, throwing up the planets, distributing everything, telling everybody, 'This is all you have to do; there's no need to discuss it.'

"I do a lot of medicine so Clayton can hold up," she told me. "I have some of his clothes and ceremonial objects. I do traditional and peyote ceremonies, and new ones that are coming out. I spent about three thousand dollars to fly this man out to Fort Leavenworth to sing some very long and ancient prayers.

"I try to imagine how it is for him in there. It's not just counting the days when you'll be coming back among the People. He is asking the spirit with calm, 'What are you trying to tell me? There's some people that did worse, and they didn't come here. Why did this really happen?' I guess he's looking for a vision."

As we drove east through Dinetah, Sally told me about the four worlds, how back in Black World "every organism spoke for itself and said, 'This is how I'm going to contribute.' There was no death, and nobody had feelings; nobody knew what we know today. Humans weren't fully formed, they didn't have fingers yet or feelings but could communicate with the other animals, and as they tried out various feelings ('Shall we have happiness? Shall we know sorrow and shed tears?') they separated from the animals and could no longer talk with them."

The present world, Glitter World, she went on, "has sunshine, different colors, snow, hail, rainbows. You can see each thing and know what it is. We have many flavors of everything. Only buzzards and crows overslept while other birds were decorating themselves down in creation, Black World. They were lazy and got up late, and there was hardly anything left except charcoal and white clay, which became the color of their droppings."

We drove past Gallup, then Mount Taylor, and left Dinetah. Sally noted a red haze of "polluzion" on the horizon, which had never been there when she was a child. We passed Laguna Pueblo, stopped for lunch in Albuquerque with some of my buddies, and made Amarillo by nightfall. Sally had never been to Amarillo, but she had just been reading about a gambler called Amarillo Slim in the *Navajo Times*. This was an adventure for her, driving across the country with a strange man, but for a semitraditional person she was unusually open to new experiences, and she welcomed the opportunity to talk to a sympathetic stranger. There was a lot she needed to get out.

"Mom married Twin Boy's son, of the Edgewater clan," she told me. "I was born sometime in the early forties; they don't know when.

I asked Mom, and she said the year that there was a lot of piñon harvested, five years later. I don't know how old I am, but I feel old.

"My original name was Shtady," she went on. "I rode a horse every
day to the Evangelical Navajo Mission Academy at Heartrock, where
my teacher, Miss Seacrest, gave me the name Sally. Then I was sent up
to the Intermountain School in Brigham, Utah." At that time, the
fifties, the Bureau of Indian Affairs was trying to get the young generation of Indians off the reservations, provide them with job training,
and integrate them into the mainstream. By 1980 there would be
827,000 Native Americans in the skid rows of a dozen cities. The program, recognized as a flop, has since been abandoned.

"The BIA wanted to modernize us," Sally went on. "So they sent me
to Chicago, a big city where I was an alien. It was culture shock. The
people looked mean. They ran fast to meet their C-train, to meet their
deadline. The first thing I noticed about Chicago, it was dirty. You
could taste the soot. And lonely." She went to dances at the dilapidated
Indian culture center, and there she met victims of relocation from all
over the country. It was out of networking sessions at this center and
those in Minneapolis and St. Paul that AIM arose. Spencer Lonetree
was the center's activities director, and before long he and Sally had
become involved.

After they split, they got into a typical modern American custody
struggle, but with a tribal twist: the Winnebago are patrilineal, and the
Navajo matrilineal, so each parent felt the kids were culturally his or
hers. Torn between warring parents as he was growing up, Clayton did
some serious cosmological stumbling. He tried to be a Navajo and a
Winnebago, then he became an "apple" (red on the outside, white on
the inside) after two years in an evangelical Baptist mission in Farmington, where he had the Indian whipped out of him. At high school in
St. Paul, he fell in with some skinheads and became a neo-Nazi; then
he became a marine and was such a good marine that he was chosen
for the elite Embassy Guard and was sent to Moscow. There he found
a harsh, oppressive grain of life that he could relate to. The U.S.S.R. was
more Asiatic, more communitarian, seemingly more morally focused
than Anglo-America. There was a lot of heavy drinking, just like on
the reservation. The ideology of communism—power to the people,
down with the imperialist oppressors—was attractive. Meanwhile,
Clayton's redneck staff sergeant kept picking on him for his heritage.
"At a certain point," I would ask him, "did you begin to wonder who
was the real enemy?" and Clayton said, "That's about it."

Sally and I crossed the Texas Panhandle, whose oceanic short-grass
was broken only by the occasional grain elevator or twirling Aermotor

windmill, and cruised up into Oklahoma. The rivers became wider and more frequent, the trees taller and their stands denser, and finally the Plains gave way to forest. At one point we got out to stretch, and beads of sweat broke out on my forearms. We were no longer in the Southwest, I realized. On the evening of the third day—the eighteenth of December 1992—Sally and I pulled into Fort Leavenworth, a sleepy antebellum installation on the banks of the Missouri, which had been at one time the extreme outpost on the western frontier, in the heart of Indian country. George Catlin, who painted the vanishing tribespeople in full feather, described it in 1832 as a "delightful cantonment," where the officers' wives and daughters could ride horses over beautiful green fields and pick strawberries, and flocks of prairie fowl extended "from the horizon, seeming almost to fill the air." From here Stephen Watts Kearny's Army of the West set out to conquer New Mexico and California in 1848, and many of the campaigns against the hostile tribes were launched. Leonard Peltier was serving consecutive life sentences in the federal pen a mile down the road from Fort Leavenworth, having been convicted of (and some said framed for) the shooting deaths of two FBI agents at Ogallala in 1975. It seemed ironic that Clayton, whose great-grandfather had been imprisoned at Bosque Redondo, should have ended up here, as if he had somehow come full circle.

Catlin described the prairie on fire at night at Fort Leavenworth: acres upon acres of "sparkling and brilliant chains of liquid fire . . . hanging suspended in graceful festoons from the skies." Now, a week before Christmas, thousands of little yellow bulbs, strung by the prisoners, were glittering in the trees and outlining the houses of Fort Leavenworth—an incredible display. We had been unable to get word to Clayton that we were coming. At first the commandant of the disciplinary barracks said it would not be possible to see him, but I told him that I had been a marine myself and was a friend of the family and how Clayton's mom hadn't seen him in two years and the opportunity had arisen to give her a lift here. Finally, the commandant relented, and we were buzzed through a series of grates into the visitors' room.

The inmates entered in brown uniforms and spit-shined shoes. Each was carrying a deck of cards or a checkerboard in case he and his visitors ran out of conversation. An Anglo hoisted his three children into the air at once. A muscular black man and his wife sat in a corner, devouring each other with their eyes.

At last Clayton came—a slight, sensitive, almost frail-looking man, he was thirty-one now, five-seven, 135 pounds. His black hair had turned salt-and-pepper since the court-martial. His glasses were fogged up from his walk across the chilly courtyard. Nobody had been to see him in two years, and the sight of children, women, bright clothes, and his mother was too much for him. His mouth trembled involuntarily, and it took him a while to think of the word for what he had been doing—"printmaking."

Talk of a movie was obviously premature. I didn't even bring it up. The fact that there was no resolution, no denouement, I knew, would be a problem for Hollywood. So was Clayton's brief adolescent infatuation with Hitler. That would not do at all. It flew in the face of the current stereotype of the Indian as spiritual ecologist. Indians these days are supposed to be too centered to take such a wrong turn. Hollywood was mainly preoccupied with atoning for its previous stereotypes, and for "what we did to them," and wasn't yet prepared to dignify the Indian with complexity.

A few months later I got *Esquire* magazine to send me for an article to Russia, where I tracked down Violetta in the hopes that she would say something that would help Clayton get released. They hadn't communicated since he had turned himself in at the Vienna embassy. Violetta was too scared to go into details, but she gave me a letter for him that said she loved him and was waiting for him and had been forced to do what she did. My article came out in November 1993. That same month the Military Court of Appeals ruled that Clayton's sentence was excessive and that he was eligible for immediate parole. But two years went by, and nothing happened; he was still in prison. He was just an Indian, with no friends in important places, and there didn't seem to be much sympathy for him. Leniency for someone who betrayed the Corps and the country apparently wasn't a priority. Sally went back to Fort Leavenworth for another hearing in March 1995, but there was still no word on when he would be released.

Part Two

Land Ho

What can we gain by sailing to the moon if we are not able to cross the abyss that separates us from ourselves? This is the most important of all voyages of discovery, and without it all the rest are not only useless but disastrous. Proof: the great travelers and colonizers of the Renaissance were, for the most part, men who perhaps were capable of things they did precisely because they were alienated from themselves. In subjugating primitive worlds they only imposed on them, with the force of cannons, their own confusion and alienation.

Thomas Merton, *Wisdom of the Desert*

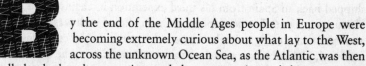y the end of the Middle Ages people in Europe were becoming extremely curious about what lay to the West, across the unknown Ocean Sea, as the Atlantic was then called: whether the water just ended at some point and ships venturing to its edge would fall off into nothingness, which the flat-earthers, who dominated the scientific establishment of the time, were convinced was the case, or whether the earth was, in fact, a sphere, for which there was growing evidence. If this was true, it was logical that if you kept sailing west you would eventually come to the Far East, from the other direction. And maybe this would prove a quicker route to the precious spices of Cathay than the long, arduous trek across Asia, forged by the Polos in the thirteenth century, that traders from Europe now had to make.

What no one suspected was that a whole other supercontinental landmass, stretching almost from pole to pole, blocked the way. The science and technology of measuring longitude were still in a primitive state, and the estimates of the earth's circumference by the few bold enough to accept the globe's roundness were thousands of miles short.

It was natural that the greatest curiosity about what lay to the west should have come from the westernmost point of Europe, the Iberian Peninsula. By 1440 the Portuguese had developed a new type of ship— the caravel—that could tack against the wind. No longer at the mercy of currents and prevailing winds, caravels struck out in every direction. They found islands hundreds of leagues from shore, explored the West African coast, and were well on the way to forging an eastern sea route to the Indies around Cape Horn, when, in the early months of 1492, the Moors were finally driven out of their last Spanish stronghold, Granada. After eight centuries under the Moorish yoke, Spain was free to devote herself to the race to the East, and since Portugal had the lead on the eastern route, Ferdinand and Isabella decided to give the Italian navigator Christoforo Colombo (Columbus) a shot at proving the wild theory he had been taking from one European court to another for the past twelve years, that the East could be reached more quickly by sailing west.

Columbus sailed to the Canaries, and from there the northeastern trades took him west, to the edge of the world. His three caravels continued into totally unknown waters. As the provisions gave out, the crew became increasingly mutinous. Columbus was on the verge of being beheaded when land was sighted. A small island off the Indies (as Asia was then called) mainland, Columbus thought. It was actually one of the Bahamas.

By 1500 the Admiral of the Ocean Sea was out of favor, and he was shipped back to Spain from his third expedition in chains. He died in obscurity in 1506. The hemisphere he had collided with was named for another Italian navigator who came in his wake. In the centuries that followed, Columbus's reputation was resuscitated, until he became an icon of European resourcefulness and daring.

The Duke Comes to Duke City

But by 1992, the quincentenary of the "discovery," the Great Navigator, as *The New York Times* reported on Columbus Day, was "under revisionist siege." Who the historical Columbus had been was probably irretrievable. What he had even looked like was anybody's guess. There were dozens of wildly differing artistic renditions. That he had been a brilliant sailor, with an uncanny ability to navigate uncharted waters by dead reckoning, there was no doubt. But once he hit land, he had been over his head. His administrative and political skills weren't up to the task of implanting a colony. He was probably more opportunistic than principled. He worked for Spain because he hadn't gotten any offers from Italy or Portugal.

In any case, who Columbus really was didn't matter so much at this point as what he had come to represent—the emblematic Columbus, who was nothing less than Europe and everything European, ideological, material, even viral (for many years Columbus had taken the rap for introducing syphilis, although new evidence points to Basques, making their way down the North American coast much earlier, as the probable culprits).

Politically and economically, the Spanish empire had been on the wane for three centuries, but culturally and demographically, in the Americas it was thriving. Florida and the Southwest were undergoing a sort of peaceful, uncombatable migratory *reconquista*. In Miami, which had become the new capital of Latin America, it was becoming hard to hear English. For a certain type of Spaniard and Latino, the blue-blooded antiquarian who gloried in the past and considered himself a criollo, an *español,* a *peninsular* of pure Iberian stock, unsullied by intermarriage with the natives, the quincentenary was a very big deal. It was becoming almost a sort of revitalization movement, like the Ghost Dance of the Paiute. Plans for massive celebration had been set rolling years ahead by gung ho Columbistas in each Latin American country and had been greeted for the most part by complete indifference on the part of the general population.

The Native Americans were even less excited about the quincentenary. As one Navajo put it, "For us to honor Columbus would be like the Jews rendering homage to Hitler, or the Japanese thanking Truman for dropping the atom bomb on them." What had Columbus brought but five hundred years of genocide and ethnocide, evangelization, colonization, bloodshed, massacre, enslavement, rape of Mother Earth, epidemic diseases to which Native Americans had no resistance, 378 broken treaties in the United States alone, a long list of extinct tribes, an estimated forty million dead from Alaska to Tierra del Fuego? The very term "discovery" was offensively Eurocentric. It was more like Columbus murdered the continent. As John from Big Mountain put it, "Some folks aren't too happy that Columbus discovered what we today call America."

At a meeting in Santa Fe the previous October, a Jemez Pueblo woman named Laura Fragua shed tears and said, "Forgive me for my anger. I cry for the lives that were lost—the children killed, the mothers killed, the grandmothers killed. But we are still here, Creator, and we thank you." A Navajo named Willy Baldwin performed a ceremony for dealing with feelings for the lost millions of brothers and sisters. Baldwin ignited a bundle of tobacco and wafted the smoke toward everybody's face with an eagle feather. Then he and five others sat around a large drum he had brought, pounding. "The long, strong drumbeats reverberated in the amphitheater, drowning out the sound of Santa Fe traffic," the Albuquerque *Journal* reported.

The Indigenous Peoples Alliance, made up of tribal peoples from both continents, was formed out of concern for the need for a response to the quincentenary, and all over the continent plans to disrupt the festivities with massive demonstrations were secretly laid. The alliance's North American coordinator was the small, interesting advocacy group in Albuquerque called Tonantzin, which operated out of an unobtrusive two-room office behind drawn blinds off Central Avenue, networking with the other allies on the bulletin board of an Apple computer. It was through Tonantzin that I hooked up with the people on Big Mountain.

One morning in February 1992, I read in the Albuquerque *Journal* that Christobal Colón de Carvajal, the young Spanish duke of Veraguas, twenty-second in direct line from Christopher (though a couple of times through females)—Christopher Columbus XXII, in other words—was coming to Duke City (Albuquerque having been named for the Spanish duke of Albuquerque) to try to smooth things over with the governors of the nineteen surviving Pueblo nations. The Pueblos had suffered terribly at the hands of the Spaniards, and the governors had rebuffed an earlier approach from Colón. This time he had come with nineteen gold-tipped canes personally inscribed to each of them. "My idea about the Indians is to offer a message of friendship and understanding for all the history and for the future," he declared in broken English.

Being the scion of such a symbol wasn't easy. Colón's father, who was apolitical but an admiral, had been killed by Basque separatists in 1986 because of his emblematic descent. Colón was in the navy himself and had agreed to go around the Americas on a sort of damage-control mission as 1992 turned from the quincentenary into the Year of the Native American.

David Lujan, the director of Tonantzin, was adamantly opposed to détente. "Colón is willing to let bygones be bygones, but we're not," he explained. "Nineteen ninety-two is the year to bring everybody together, to protect the sovereignty of our way of life, to heal, to seek spiritual unity and declare to the world that we continue to live and plan for our future, to call upon churches and government to cease further aggressions, upon historians to tell the truth, upon the entertainment and news industries and all those with influence in shaping popular culture to forgo the use of dehumanizing, stereotyping, cartooning images and information regarding our people, and to recognize their responsibility for the emotional violence their fields have perpetuated against our children, and to end all cultural and economic discrimination against native peoples." Lujan told me about encounters that were being organized in Ecuador, Guatemala, and Panama (hosted by Kuna Indians); about the peace and dignity walk (which Buddhists were joining) from the Shoshone Reservation to Fort Leavenworth, Kansas; about the "dual-star" relay race: one team was setting out from Argentina, another from Alaska, and they would meet in Mexico on October 12, the day Columbus made land.

I got hold of Andrés Romero, the chairman of the New Mexico Quincentenary Committee, who, with his long, Gothic face and flowing silver hair, looked like an El Greco. "There's some Columbus bashing going on," he complained, "and these things happened five hundred years ago." Not all Indians were anti-Columbus, he pointed out. Some had danced for Colón at the reception in the Governor's Palace in Santa Fe. Romero's take was that midwestern Indians, who had a more recent negative experience with whites, were stirring everybody up. "The Southwest Indians had a negative experience initially, but that was three hundred years ago. Since then there has been coexistence even to the point of intermarriage. I think we all should bury the hatchet, look to the future, and not repeat the mistakes of the past."

The duke and his petite blond wife, a *duquesa* and *marquesa* in her own right, were being squired around by state senator Tom Benavides, a *nuevomejicano* of the blue-blooded *español* type, who wore an eye patch and was descended from Alonso de Benavides, the *custodio*, or chief administrator, of New Mexico's Franciscan missions, who ran the Inquisition in the seventeenth century ("Our grandfathers were brothers," the senator told me), and from practically everybody else of importance in colonial New Spain. "I would have been related to Alvarez [the first European to sail the coast of the Gulf of Mexico], but his daughter died before she could bear one of my ancestor's children. I want the monarchy here. I am descended from King Alonso the Seventh." Benavides had introduced a bill to the legislature proposing that the southern half of Bernalillo County, which includes Albuquerque, be made a county of its own, named for him, and he was trying to get El Paso returned to New Mexico. Apparently a drunken surveyor named Clark back in the nineteenth century shot the New Mexico–Texas line seventy miles farther west than it should have been. A Texan told me the Benavides bill had a "fat chance. Texas without El Paso is like a chile relleno without the chile."

Benavides invited me to breakfast at the Holiday Inn with His Grace, as he referred to Colón, who was wearing a bola tie and was sweet, warm, impeccably mannered, and utterly charming, a central-casting young aristocrat who walked with his hands clasped behind his back and listened with his head cocked attentively—a perfect emissary to pay the guilt debt and accomplish this delicate diplomatic fence-mending mission. The duchess, however, was in a snit and had receded into her mink coat, speaking to no one. Apparently they'd been having a fight, which I gathered had to do with her feeling neglected. She and I and Benavides drove in one limousine to the All-Indian Pueblo Cultural Center, where the governors had finally agreed to meet with Colón, who followed in another limousine half an hour later. The delay, he explained apologetically, was that he had been waiting for the English translation of his speech to be faxed from Santa Fe. It still hadn't come, so he was going to ad-lib in halting *inglés*. His wife, livid at being kept waiting, lit into him in staccato Castilian in front of everybody. He calmed her down, and we all went in.

The duke explained to the governors that he himself had Aztec blood, through no less than Moctezuma II. "The fact that I have

Indian blood makes me proud," he said. "This makes me closer to you in my feeling, and I consider myself part of you. My idea is to help Indians, to work for the future. I'm a positive man. The most important thing isn't history, but the future." He hinted at the possibility of endowing an annual Christopher Columbus college scholarship for a deserving Pueblo high-school graduate.

One by one, the governors came up and were presented with their cane. They were the elders of their people, and they projected dignity, soft-spoken wisdom, and a sense of tragic loss. Canes had traditionally been given to the caciques of New Spain by the king in symbolic recognition of their authority and in the spirit of peace. The United States had kept up the tradition, periodically distributing presidential canes.

The governor of San Felípe, standing at the mike, welcomed the duke and wished "continued peace between our countries. I think all of us being mortals, we need the guidance of the person upstairs." Then he said a prayer in his pueblo's Eastern Keresan language. He was followed by the governor of San Juan. Acoma's governor invited the duke to come and see the two bells transported from Spain to the pueblo's mission of St. Stephen in the seventeenth century. Tesuque was next. Isleta's governor said, "It's a great honor to receive this cane from Spain." Cochiti's said, "Don't feel bad you can't speak English. I'm an Indian and in the same shoes." Laguna, Nambe, Picuris, Pojoaque, Santa Clara, Santo Domingo, San Ildefonso, Sandia, Santa Ana, Zia, followed. The governor of Taos said he'd add the duke's cane to the pueblo's collection. Its last cane was from Nixon. Only Jemez refused to accept the cane. Two young Jemez men sat snickering in the audience and walked out when the pueblo's name was called.

James Hena, the chairman of the All-Indian Pueblo Council, told the duke that the council had been going since 1598, a lot longer than the U.S. government, and he invited all the governors to "come up and pose with the duke and the other folks so they can have it for the papers. The events of the last five hundred years have variously been described as good or bad," he continued conciliatingly. "We governors agree that it's no special year for us. There's no reason to celebrate, and there's no reason to demonstrate. History is history. Let's make the next five hundred years for all the people of the world, reduce poverty and deprivation, promote justice and compassion and respect for native people." The son of the governor of Pojoaque asked the duke to autograph a *National Geographic* article on Columbus that asked, "Just who was this stubborn, single-minded enigma of a man?"

Then we drove up to Santo Domingo, forty-five miles north of Albuquerque, to watch one of the colorful dances on the pueblo's ritual

calendar. On the way Andrés Romero explained how the Spanish culture of New Mexico, due to centuries of isolation, was purer than any
other in Latin America, and by "establishing commonality and strength-
ening historical ties," New Mexico could become "the port of the Americas." Senator Benavides, as I later discovered, was deeply involved in
the business aspects of this vision. The negativism about Columbus,
Romero maintained, was really "a perpetuation of the Black Legend,
spread by England to discredit the Spanish empire, to make it look like
a genocide, using the [sixteenth-century] report of Bartolomé de Las
Casas on the atrocities to the Indians. I'll tell you how entrenched the
Black Legend is. If Columbus's sponsor had been English, the American
quincentenary would have come up with a lot more than seven million.
It would have been more like the Statue of Liberty."

The pueblo was only five minutes off the Albuquerque–Santa Fe freeway, but it was on a very different wavelength from Sloganworld—as
inspired by my Navajo friend Tom I had begun to call it—the modern
Anglo-American overlay and its high-speed autobahns. The pueblo's traditional communal architecture had been replaced by detached single-
family adobe homes, but the feeling of something very ancient, a Third
World fellah earthiness, was still there. Snow squalls whipped through
the plaza, which was lined with hundreds of people waiting for the winter dances to begin. Young people sat on the edges of the roofs; old
women wrapped in striped Pendleton blankets sat in rows of folding
chairs. They were all Indians—not a single tourist or even a single Anglo
in the entire crowd, perhaps because it was bitter cold.

The duke and his entourage entered the plaza and were shown to
their seats. No one paid them any attention. Two thuggish, dark-suited
nuevomejicano state troopers, who reminded me of the bodyguards for
the politicos of PRI, Mexico's ruling party, stayed with the limousine.

"How long's this going to take?" one asked.

"I don't know," said the other. "We better get out of here before
they scalp us."

The duchess had no interest in watching the dances and stood by
herself on a porch. Pacing distractedly in her furs and high heels, she
stepped in some dog shit, and that was the last straw. She became semi-
hysterical, and the troopers led her into one of the limousines.

I stood against an adobe wall beside a young man from the pueblo
who said his name was Dusty Rodez (pronounced "Roads"). He
opened a medicine pouch around his neck and put a pinch of corn
pollen in my palm and told me to blow and scatter it, which two people meeting for the first time do "for good health," he explained. Then
he showed me his fetishes. If I wanted to know about Indian spiritual-

ity, he was my man, he assured me. He asked for my telephone number in Albuquerque so he could come and see me. He reminded me of the local Rastafarians in Negril, Jamaica, circa 1971, sidling up and testing the waters with the new honky on the scene. Then he said, "Say, I'm kind of broke right now. You wouldn't happen to have a couple of dollars to spare?"

There was a commotion behind us. A man had fallen off a ladder and was lying in the fetal position with a crowd around him. Dusty explained, "He consumed too much." To the beat of drums and the ONE-two-three of gourd rattles, two soundless files of Matachines dancers came up the plaza, kicking to the right and then to the left in beaded moccasins. The costumes were Spanish. The men wore sombreros. A young bride had money pinned to her dress—*milagros*, offerings in the hope of a blessing, gifts of love and piety. But the miters some of the dancers wore, with black fringes over their eyes, were Moorish. A man was playing an accordion "to bring up the spirits of the Spanish," Dusty told me. I asked a woman what the Matachines dance represented. She said, politely, "I really can't tell you."

Later I learned that the dance reenacts the overthrow of the Moors, the stunning victory for Christianity. The *reconquista* of Spain was projected to the conquest of Mexico and from there used to acculturate the peaceful, welcoming Pueblos along the Rio Grande. Making the Indians themselves perform the pageant and play the Moors was one of the more fun ways of teaching them their place. The king figure was both the Moorish king Selin and the Aztec Moctezuma. But the clown dancers (introduced by the Pueblos from their own traditions) subtly mocked the Spaniards. One was dressed as Santa Claus, another as Zorro, in a flat black hat and mask. I wondered if any fun was being poked at the duke, who was watching appreciatively. Months later I asked the governor of the pueblo about this, and he said, mischievously, "That's classified."

The governor invited us into his house, where a huge feast was laid out. He took us to an alcove behind a wall where there was a shrine, with canes, old prayer sticks, plastic toy horses and cows used in prayers for the health of the herd. "You're the first white men in this century who have been allowed to see these things," he told us. He showed us the canes of the original Spanish and Mexican governors, and the one Lincoln had given, and told us, "They're alive for our people."

The Conquest

The realization that they were dealing with an entirely new hemisphere was slow to come to Columbus and the explorers who followed. As late as 1524 Giovanni da Verrazano would mistake Chesapeake Bay for the Pacific. The explorers kept looking for signs that they had arrived at the islands of the Amazons that Marco Polo had reported lay "on the right hand of the Indies."

Ignorance of what had landed in her lap, however, did not prevent Spain from winning a larger empire in the next fifty years than Rome did in five centuries, from achieving no less than the greatest territorial annexation in world history. Caravels sailed into the Caribbean and took one island after another—Hispaniola, Cuba, Jamaica. By 1518 Columbus had skirted the Caribbean rim three times, Balboa had sited the Pacific from the Isthmus of Panama, Ponce de León had gone to look for the Fountain of Youth and met death in Florida, and the eastern coast of South America had been descended as far as the mouth of the Río de la Plata. There were indications that something big lay west of Cuba. That year Juan de Grijalva traded with natives on the Mexican coast for some very sophisticated gold ornaments, and they told him that they came from a rich civilization in the interior. A few months later Hernán Cortés was dispatched by the viceroy of Cuba to see what was there.

How Cortés, accompanied by only a handful of indifferently armed and equipped adventurers, could have brought down an entire empire, with millions of subjects, was, as William H. Prescott reflects toward the end of his masterful narrative, *History of the Conquest of Mexico*, "a fact little short of the miraculous." Many things seemed to have contributed to the Aztecs' downfall. Having never seen a horse, they thought the Spaniards' mounts were gods in their own right, while the

Spaniards, with their gleaming armor and fire-breathing harquebuses, could only be the children of the Sun himself.

Moctezuma was especially terrified because he had been expecting strange, powerful beings from the east. A series of recent inexplicable occurrences had signaled unmistakably that the end of the Fourth Age was at hand: the lake on which the floating capital had been constructed had suddenly, without explanation, become violently agitated; a turret of the great temple had caught fire and kept burning despite all attempts to extinguish it; there had been three comets; and soon before the coming of the Spaniards, a strange light had appeared in the east. It was obvious who those men with their white skin and beards were: the relatives of Quetzalcoatl. They fit all the descriptions in the oracles. They had come to bring on the Fifth Age, and it was useless to resist them, Moctezuma reasoned. And so he did almost nothing to prevent Cortés and his men from entering the city, then his palace, and taking him prisoner.

Several other unfortunate coincidences facilitated the conquest and subsequent conversion of the Aztecs. They had a virgin-birth myth of their own; they already baptized in water and revered the cross, which was the emblem of their rain god. Their priests, like the Franciscans, practiced flagellation and self-mortification, whipping themselves with cactus thorns.

The Spaniards possessed superior weapons and martial skills, and having just overthrown the Moors, they were on a roll. The conquest of Mexico and, later on, of New Mexico became a holy cause, an extension of the Spanish *reconquista*. The conquistadores were convinced of their spiritual and racial superiority, and this gave them a psychological edge, like the Anglo-Americans who believed that it was their "manifest destiny" to acquire northern Mexico and subdue the savage tribes of the West. They also brought a plague with them: smallpox. The plague not only prevented the Aztecs from mopping up the Spaniards after a victorious battle that became known as the Noche Triste, the "Night of Sadness," it demonstrated the powerlessness of their gods.

An Incredible Odyssey

I t was every conquistador's dream to find and conquer "another Mexico." Perhaps there was one to the north. All kinds of things (some from European fable, some from the natives' equally imaginative geography) were rumored to be up there: a sea passage called the Strait of Anian, which allegedly led directly to the Indies; the Island of Pearls; another island, where gold was the only metal; a race of people who basked in the shade of their huge ears; another race that didn't have to eat, but fed on smells. Perhaps the Seven Cities of Antilla lay to the north. According to a medieval legend, centuries earlier seven Portuguese bishops had sailed west into the Ocean Sea and had each founded a city. This legend was one of the few things the Spaniards had to go on when they arrived in the New World. They named the West Indies the Antilles after the cities, although no trace of them was ever found.

The north's being terra incognita, its geography was completely vague. Not until 1535 would Fortún Jimenez sail up the Pacific coast in search of Indians with gold and discover the peninsula of Baja California, which he thought was an island—Polo's Island of the Female, no less. Jimenez's commander in chief, Cortés, named the "island" California, after Caliphia, the queen of the Amazons. It was assumed that Mesoamerica and La Florida, the "Land of Flowers," were separate landmasses, and in 1527 Pánfilo de Narváez set forth from Cuba with six hundred men to colonize the flat, humid peninsula that jutted down from the north. The expedition soon met with disaster. Having thoroughly alienated the locals and found no gold, or even enough food, Narváez finally gave the order for the remaining horses to be killed and eaten and for five boats to be stitched together from their hides, in which they all set sail for Cuba. But off what is now Galveston, Texas, the flotilla was caught in a hurricane. There were only four survivors. One was the expedition's treasurer, Alvar Núñez Cabeza de Vaca. Captured and enslaved by coastal Indians, Cabeza de Vaca escaped and fled inland. For five years he wandered from tribe to tribe, healing the sick with prayers and the sign of the cross, sometimes being taken captive, sometimes being taken for a god. One day he was thrown into a pen with three other survivors of the shipwreck he hadn't known about—Alonso del Castillo, Andrés Dorantes, and Dorantes's blackamoor slave, Estéban. The four of them decided to escape together and head west, in the direction of Mexico. But a year passed before they were able to make their break.

Traveling from village to village, trekking around with nomads and living off the bounty of the land, they were the first Europeans to see and eat buffalo. It was a wonderfully free life, and they found the Indians to be generous and fun loving and very good at what they did. Gradually they became like an itinerant medicine show. Estéban had a flair for languages and was a master of jive. He did the talking, shaking a magic rattle he had picked up from one of the Plains tribes. The others maintained a regal silence. As their act became tighter, they began to find crowds waiting for them with their sick or just for the chance to touch them, and they acquired an entourage.

One day, however, eight of the Indians with them suddenly died. A ninth, who seemed to be dead, recovered miraculously after Vaca whispered some magic words over him. The rest of the entourage concluded that the Spaniards had the power of life or death over them and fled in terror.

Proceeding to one of the villages of the Cow People—nomadic Indians who lived by following the buffalo—they found its residents "in an attitude of extreme dread and supplication sitting in their houses facing the wall with bowed heads, their hair pulled down over their eyes, and all their possessions piled in the middle of the floor," as Vaca would write in his memoir. Instead of waiting for them in throngs, the Indians now fled at the sight of them.

Wading through the Rio Grande, they made their way across the Chihuahuan Desert, over the craggy, canyon-riddled Sierra Madre Occidental, and down to the Pacific Coast. While waiting for the rain-swollen Yaquí River to become crossable, they met an Indian with a buckle around his neck, which Vaca realized could only have come from a Spanish sword belt. Trying to contain his excitement, he asked the Indian where he had gotten the buckle, and the Indian said, "From heaven." Two men from heaven, he explained, with beards and white skin and horses and lances, had recently passed through and killed several of his relatives.

The four of them had reached the northern frontier of the province of Nueva Galicia, in the viceroyalty of New Spain, as Mexico was now called. It had been eight years since they left Cuba.

Hallucinations of the North

n many ways the Southwest is a tongue, the northernmost projection, of Latin America. In remote mountain villages of northern New Mexico, the Spanish of Cervantes is still the lingua franca, and Tucson, despite a spreading rash of Florida-style and California Mission golf retirement communities, is still basically Mexican. For most of its recorded history, the Southwest has in fact been El Norte, so in the summer of 1986 I decided to start in Mexico City, the radiation center of the Southwest's second, Hispanic overlay, and to follow the northward expansion of the frontier of New Spain all the way up into southern Colorado. I planned to spend several weeks exploring the Other Southwest, as the Mexican part of the Greater Southwest culture area has been called, which retains more of the original continuum. The modern world has made fewer inroads, and frontier conditions still prevail in isolated pockets. One gets a better sense of what the area was like during the Spanish period, of course, and indeed during most of its history.

Traveling alone this time, I reached Mexico City on July 6. The city was recovering from a massive earthquake of a few months earlier. Much of the city was rubble. The colonial architecture, tilted and slumped by previous quakes, seemed on the whole to have held up a lot better than the modern stuff. After several days of consulting with viceregal, Franciscan, and Jesuit scholars, poring over documents, and inspecting sites and simply wandering the streets of the most surreal and anachronic conurbation on the planet—you never know what decade, what century, is around the corner—I headed west, in a series of buses, to Guadalajara, Tepic, and, finally, Compostela, the old capital of Nueva Galicia, where Cabeza de Vaca and his bedraggled companions' odyssey had ended in 1535.

The governor of Nueva Galicia was the sadistic Nuño de Guzmán, whose atrocities to the natives were unparalleled in the annals of the conquest. Guzmán had once nailed one of his men to a tree by his tongue for talking back to him. He was fond of siccing his mastiff, Amigo, on the local Tepehuano Indians and watching him tear them apart. Guzmán promptly arrested the six hundred Tepehuano who had insisted on escorting Cabeza de Vaca and his companions even though it was planting time, and had them marched off into slavery. He was intrigued by the guarded quality of Cabeza de Vaca's account of what he and the others had seen in their wandering in La Florida. Cabeza de Vaca characterized the region as "remote, malign, and devoid of resources." Guzmán suspected he was playing down what was really up there because he wanted to return for the gold and the turquoise himself. In fact, Cabeza de Vaca was just trying not to exaggerate. Having walked the land for eight years, he was under no illusions about it.

What most intrigued Guzmán and the viceroy in Mexico City, Antonio de Mendoza, in whose palace Cabeza de Vaca was soon to be a guest, was the part about six "emerald" arrowheads, which Cabeza de Vaca said he had regrettably left behind on the Sinaloa River, and the reports he had heard about seven fabulously rich pueblos with turquoise-studded doors not far to the north of where they had passed. These reports confirmed what Guzmán had heard from an Indian named Tejo, who claimed to have visited these very pueblos on a trading trip. It was the number "seven" that made the reports so convincing. Obviously these were the Seven Cities of Antilla.

Vaca rushed to Spain to secure the commission to conquer and settle La Florida, but he was too late. The plum had just been awarded to Hernando de Soto, who would pay for it with his life, expiring in 1542 on the west bank of the Mississippi, his health and spirit broken after three years of hunting vainly for the Seven Cities and the equally elusive Fountain of Youth. In consolation, the king, Carlos I, appointed Cabeza de Vaca *adelantado,* or governor-general, of the province of the Río de la Plata, in South America, where he embarked on a second, equally remarkable career in exploration, discovering the astonishing falls of Iguaçú and trying to stop his countrymen who were enslaving the local Guarani Indians. His years among the Indians had deepened his love and compassion for them. If Guzmán (who would have loved to mount his own expedition to the cities, but was arrested by Mendoza in 1537 on charges of barbarity and shipped back to Spain in chains) embodied the Black Legend stereotype, Cabeza de Vaca was the antithesis.

So was Mendoza himself, a man of high principle, versed in Thomas More and Italian humanism, who saw the New World as an opportunity to create an ideal society, far from the corruption of Europe, and believed that the Indians were as much God's children as were his countrymen. Exploration was not a priority for him, but if another Mexico lay to the north, Mendoza had no intention of letting others get there first. Cautious by nature, and recognizing that the Seven Cities could prove to be ignes fatui, he decided to send, rather than a full-scale expedition, a discreet reconnoitering party that would report to him, and him alone, on what it found.

Foreseeing how useful the blackamoor Estéban could be, Mendoza had already taken the precaution of buying him. Estéban was definitely up for a return trip, not that he had any say in the matter. But obviously a slave couldn't lead the *entrada,* so Mendoza turned to the Church. Men of the cloth had been in on the conquest from almost the beginning, accompanying, sometimes even preceding, the soldiers. The first had arrived in 1524—twelve Franciscan monks who became known as the Apostles. The missionary responsibilities in New Spain were soon divided among four orders. The Brown Robes, as the Franciscans were called, worked in the north, the Dominicans and Mercadorians in the south, and the Augustinians in the center.

One Brown Robe, Fray Marcos de Niza, came highly recommended to Mendoza as possessing the requisite fortitude, integrity, and frontier experience to lead the search for the cities. "Barefoot and indefatigable" were the words the bishop of Mexico had used about de Niza. He had served with Alvarado in Ecuador and with Pizarro in Peru. His report on the atrocities he had seen his countrymen commit against the Incas had been incorporated in the Dominican priest Bartolomé de Las Casas's *Destruction of the Indies,* an exposé that had tremendous impact on Mendoza and his king. On top of this, de Niza was skilled in celestial navigation, cosmography, and astronomy. Mendoza signed him up along with another Brown Robe, Fray Onorato, to keep him company. His instructions were to take possession of all significant landforms, bodies of water, and communities in the name of the viceroy, to inform the natives that they were now subjects of God and the king of Spain, and to keep Mendoza closely informed of his progress by foot messengers.

Setting out from Mexico City without fanfare, the de Niza party reached Compostela in December 1538, where they were welcomed by the new governor of Nueva Galicia, Guzmán's replacement, Francisco Vásquez de Coronado, a young hidalgo, or member of the lower nobility, from Salamanca who had come to New Spain in Mendoza's entourage. The buses I rode through Mexico followed more or less their route, zipping through country that must have taken them weeks to ride through, crossing bridges over deep gorges that had held them up for days, passing through fields bristling with orderly rows of blue-green-spiked maguey cactus, from which tequila is made, around bends of hairy mountain roads, where crates of tomatoes and bell peppers had fallen off trucks, shattered, and spilled their rotting contents. Rusty carcasses of smashed cars littered the curb, and ornate white crosses, some with offerings of plastic flowers, marked the sites of fatal accidents (a custom that spreads into northern New Mexico and is one of the more visible signs of the Latino continuum). Around one bend, a shirtless man was standing with an automatic pistol in his hand, perhaps an agent of the Federales, looking for a *narcotraficante* in the woods below. Every so often a spectacular vista of parched red land would open. *Una vasta tierra colorada,* a young man seated beside me said of a panorama that the rounding of a bend had just presented. He was a Combonian priest, training for missionary work in Uganda.

The first permanent European settlement on the Pacific Coast, Compostela is twenty miles inland, nestled in cool foothills that stay green year-round. The lava soils from the nearby dormant Volcán de Ceboruco are rich, and there is gold and silver in the vicinity. The future of Compostela was promising, but history would pass it by. In 1560 the provincial government, the *audiencia,* was moved, and Guadalajara became the capital of everything in the north. As the years passed, Compostela became just another small, sleepy Mexican town, *muy pacifico,* as one of its citizens described it. Its plan conformed to the 1537 Royal Ordinances Concerning the Laying Out of Towns on the frontier. Typically, four square leagues were allotted per settlement. First the missionaries came in and built the church, which became the centerpiece of the plaza and was, ideally, four hundred feet by six hundred, and around the plaza columned arcades went up, in which the women could sell goods and wares, hides and produce. Behind the arcades were public and private *palacios* with gracious inner courtyards, and shooting off at each of the plaza's corners, as extensions of its sides, were two streets. More streets and plazas were added as needed.

I blew into town just as the Sunday-evening *paseo* was materializing in Compostela's central plaza, with shy, lush teenage girls—beautiful, ripe, cinnamon *chicas,* some of them in white high heels—circumambulating, arm in arm, in one direction, and the boys taking a turn or two in the other, or whistling softly from benches, while on other benches parents and grandparents looked on approvingly, remembering the days of their youth and remarking how beautiful so-and-so's daughter had become. Most of the young men of Compostela had been to the States. Many were there now, doing jobs no one else wanted in New York, Washington, Trenton, Wisconsin, Pasadena, for ten times what they could make here. El Norte still beckoned.

I asked two old men in the main plaza if there was a local *historiador* who could fill me in on the town's history, and they sent me up a cobbled street to the house of the pharmacist, Salvador Gutiérrez Contreras. Doña Gutiérrez was tending the pharmacy, in a front room of the house. Within, behind an iron-grille gate, was a patio with a beautiful garden, roses and heliconia in bloom, colorful little finches in a bamboo cage. Señor Gutiérrez was sitting on the patio, reading. It was not every day that a *norteamericano* interested in the history of Nueva Galicia came to town, and he treated the occasion with solemnity. Presenting me with his history of the state of Nayarit, as this part of the long-extinct jurisdiction of Nueva Galicia is now called, he took me down to the little regional museum in the plaza, of which he was the curator, and thrust a huge key into the ancient padlock of its massive wooden door. Inside was a collection of Oltec-Aztec effigy statues, found locally; a 1919 photograph of nine original Zapatistas (from whom the Mayan guerrillas who burst onto the Mexican political stage out of the jungle of Chiapas on New Year's Day 1994 took their name) hanging by their necks from several limbs of the same tree; and tinted photos of Compostela's benefactors in this century. We proceeded to the church, where a dozen kneeling worshipers, most of them old women in black veils, were contemplating the miracle-working Señor de la Misericordia, a very important sixteenth-century Christ, Señor Gutiérrez told me, that had been brought from Seville by none other than the barbaric Nuño de Guzmán. At the front of the church a young girl in a radiant white gown was taking her First Communion. The church, like thousands of others in Mexico, offered a refuge from the squalid present in the splendor of the past, which was in turn a radiant, opulent vision of the future that the worshipers hoped would be their reward.

We continued past the cinema, which Señor Gutiérrez explained had been the house of the Conde de Miraballes, the biggest *haciendero* around before the revolution. He walked me to the only hotel in town, and politely took his leave.

The hotel was BGT—"below the grimness threshold," in my personal rating system of developing-world hostelries. My room was as barren as a jail cell. I went outside, but it did little good. The whole town was claustrophobic, what an anthropologist might have described as a "life-term social arena." Chasing tequila with tamarind juice in a restaurant up the street, I read Herbert Bolton's biography of Coronado. A huge man, with a fleshy, distinguished-looking, almost-patrician face, reminiscent of Charles Laughton's or Winston Churchill's, approached my table. His pants were held up with braces, the buttons of his fly were missing, and he kept scratching his back with a stick. No one paid him any mind. The village half-wit, presumably. Saying, *Mille perdones,* he asked to see my book. Outside a young couple clung to each other under a tall, swaying coco palm; hundreds of mayflies dive-bombed a street lamp and expired twitching on the pavement. A statue of a man holding forth in a frock coat surveyed the scene.

The next day I rode out of Compostela in a '64 Chevy *colectiva,* or makeshift bus, squashed beside a very large woman who had spent ten years as a floor supervisor in a Los Angeles dress factory and was taking her daughter up to Tepic to be treated for nerves (*nervosismo*). The road weaved through the *monte*—a low, thorny vine-smothered forest of hardwoods, palms, and palmettos, little changed from four centuries ago. It must have been tough going for the de Niza party. Coronado escorted them as far north as Culiacán, the northernmost outpost of Nueva Galicia—now a seething city of a million souls and the distribution center of the marijuana and opium poppy grown inland—in the foothills of the Sierra Madre Occidental. An Indian uprising was in progress. Coronado had the leader, Ayapin, captured and quartered, and peace was restored to the land.

From Compostela I continued up the coast to San Blas, a rustic fishing village with little memory that it had been the first Spanish port on the Pacific. The closest to a *historiador* I could find was a grizzled old cuss who lived in a shack below a ruined fort. For five hundred pesos up front he let me take a look at a paperback he kept wrapped in a plastic bag that he swore would deliver the historical goods on San Blas, and I sat on a stump in his yard among mountains of hubcaps, empty bottles, and all kinds of other *junque,* slapping at fierce little mosquitoes known as *sancudos,* dripping in the clammy heat, and gradually ascertaining the book was worthless. It wasn't till midnight, wandering down a dark street, that I finally gleaned some lowdown from a mural on the wall of what appeared to be a failed nightclub—in English, no less. From here ships had shot across the Gulf of California, rounded the tip of Baja California, and sailed up the California coast, provisioning missions as far north as Monterey; and the Philippine trade, which introduced all kinds of things from Asia, such as silk,

Chinese art motifs, and possibly marijuana, and had tremendous influence on the coalescing culture of New Spain (as important as the underappreciated legacy of the Moors), had begun. Pirate ships had lain in wait off San Blas for the Manila galleon to put in. Epic voyages by contemporaries of Captain Cook and Vitus Bering had set out from here. Juan Perez had discovered Nootka, Alaska, and called it San Lorenzo de Nootka; De la Bodega y Cuadra had met with the British navigator George Vancouver to establish what is now the U.S.–Canada border.

Following ancient, well-worn trading trails, the de Niza party passed through the land of the Tepehuano and the Opata. Estéban, done out in ankle bells, feathers, and body paint, with his magic rattle and a greyhound at either hand, wowed the natives. At the Sinaloa River, Fray Onorato fell sick and had to be carried back to Culiacán in a litter. The others proceeded, fording the Fuerte River.

More buses and *colectivas,* the last of them a pickup for five hours in the full moon, brought me to El Fuerte, "the Fort," on the banks of the River Fuerte—another once-important, forgotten installation on the northern frontier. El Fuerte had been important for only four years, beginning in 1820, right after the Revolution of Independence, when it became the capital of something called the Free State of the West. In 1824 El Estado Libre del Oriente was broken up into the present states of Sinaloa and Sonora. Since then, El Fuerte had been steadily mellowing into the sleepy backwater that it was today, like Compostela, like San Blas, and thousands of other towns in Latin America, only a particularly nice one. The following evening, cinnamon Sinaloan beauties in *paseo,* fourteen, fifteen years old, circumambulated the vintage colonial plaza, lined with columned arcades and with a wrought-iron bandstand in the middle, then repaired with their boyfriends to the disco in the tastefully restored hacienda where I was staying.

I called on Tito Gomez Torres, public defender, poet, and *historiador* of El Fuerte, at his office in the Municipal Building. A laid-back, silver-haired man in his sixties, he was known in town as Tito Tranquilino. It was late Sunday afternoon, and as we sat talking, every so often a languid, flatulent blat from a tuba would waft over from a nearby street through the large open window, as if the musician had nodded off with his lips on the mouthpiece and had just been nudged awake. The news had gone around that a gringo was in town, and a teenage boy came up to the window with a flyer in English that he wanted me to translate about how to avoid getting syphilis. Tito proposed we repair to an outdoor restaurant to eat the giant freshwater prawns, known as *cauques,* that swim in the River Fuerte. The prawns are native to the Philippines (Did they, too, arrive on the Manila galleon? I wondered) and get to be a foot long and, washed down with Dos Equis beer, are scrumptious. This was the kind of place you file away. I pictured myself white-haired and rocking in a hammock, like John Huston's father in *The Treasure of the Sierra Madre,* while a buxom beauty bent over and popped grapes into my mouth. This town is really mellow, I said to Tito.

"The people are of good character, but it's changed around here," he told me sadly. "The marijuana and poppy growers in the hills are coming into town and causing problems. The possibility of making quick money has eroded the value system. Now there are *gente floja,* people who don't work, and this has given rise to *deliquencia.* On the edge of town, four or five people are being rolled a week, mostly for their cars."

Ten miles inland, Tito told me, in the foothills of the sierra, there is a village of albinos descended from French soldiers who had been "invited by Mexican traitors" to install Maximilian, an Austrian Hapsburg, as emperor. In 1867 the soldiers landed on the Sinaloan coast, but they were soon driven back to their ships. Most of them sailed away, but thirty or forty of them had been stranded and had fled into the *monte.* They were from Alsace and "very blond," Tito Tranquilino went on. "For a while they lived on roots and wild animals, but the local people were *muy pacíficos* and took them in. They married the daughters of the campesinos and produced a new race, *una concreta población de albinos.*" My eyes widened. The women, he assured me, were knockouts, *muy guapas.* This was definitely worth a side trip, I decided.

The next morning I walked down to the market, picking up an entourage of shoe-shine boys, and negotiated with a taxi driver sitting on the hood of his old beat-up Chevy for a round-trip to Tetaroba. Not many gringos come to El Fuerte, and those who do are bass fishermen or dove hunters from Texas, or they want to buy the goatskin helmet masks that the outlying Mayo Indians make for their Lenten pageants. None had ever expressed an interest in seeing the albinos.

But *No problema, señor:* he holds open the passenger door, and soon we are kicking up dust in the desert thorn scrub, which is loaded with iguanas and curiously reptilian roadrunners motoring around on their powerful legs among mesquite, *guacaporo,* and *quinoto* trees and cardon, *hecho,* and *isnala* cacti and taking off on short bursts of flight over gullies. After half a dozen miles we begin to see, squatting in the doorways of mud-and-wattle huts, not dusky fellahin diluted and undiluted Indians, but fair-skinned Europeans.

We stop at the house of a man in his late fifties named Abelardo Blanchette. He isn't a full-blown albino, but he's definitely albinoid, with blue-gray eyes and blistered, beet-red skin, *Muy molestado por el sol,* my driver remarks. Blanchette's three daughters have not inherited the affliction. They are, as Tito Tranquilino promised, very handsome, and they look completely French, although culturally the family is pure campesino, can't speak a word of French, and knows nothing about its Alsatian ancestry except that Abelardo tells me he is a great-grandson of one of the soldiers. The real albinos, he says, live on a rancho called Yecorato, twenty miles farther on. I ask the taximan if we can go there, and he says the road is too bad for his car. That's how it always is. The real ones are always over the next rise.

So we drive on a mile to another place called El Reparito and visit with one of Abelardo's cousins, Segundino Blanchette, who is descended from the same soldier and has similar hypopigmented skin and eyes. The two most common forms of oculo-cutaneous albinism are recessive, so you need two copies of the gene, one from either parent, to get them. About one in forty thousand white Europeans is an albino. I don't know what the ratio is in Zaire, but I've seen a few of them there, and they are striking. On my list of projects is to travel across equatorial Africa collecting beliefs about albinos. In an isolated village where the population is inbred, the chances of the same gene meeting up with itself through a consanguineous union are much better, and albinism is more usual. The Swedish ethnographer Carl Lumholtz, who spent five years between 1890 and 1899 in the Sierra Madre looking for the descendants of the Anasazi, found a family of ten Tarahumara albinos living on a remote rancho. The woman's hair was yellowish white, her eyelids and lashes were snow white, and her skin was white and "disfigured with large red spots and small freckles." She was very shy and "kept her eyes more than half shut," so "it was not possible to ascertain the color of the iris."

Back in the States, I described the Blanchettes to three geneticists, and two of them thought they sounded like "manifesting heterozygotes." Abelardo and Segundino's fathers had probably inherited a double dose of the same gene from their common Blanchette grandfathers and had been full-blown albinos, and they themselves had probably received only one copy and were expressing only vestigial albinism. The third geneticist, however, told me that some genes for albinism, like the one that produces a white forelock, are dominant, and there are other, poorly described dominants for oculo-cutaneous hypopigmentation, which they could have inherited. The possibility of their being "a new type of mutant," he said, couldn't be ruled out either. "Sounds like interesting country back in there," he added.

Fray Marcos was beginning to run out of steam, and at the Mayo, the next big river north of the Fuerte that rushes down from the Sierra Madre into the Gulf of California, he decided to let Estéban go on ahead. He instructed the blackamoor to send back a messenger with a palm-high cross if he ran into anything important; a two-palm-high cross if it was something a bit more important; and if it was something of tremendous importance—"greater and better than New Spain"—he should send back a large cross. Four days after they separated, a large cross arrived. Estéban was on his way to "the greatest country in the world," the messenger told Fray Marcos. It was called Cíbola (a word of unclear origin, perhaps an approximation of the Zuñi name Shi-wona; *cíbolo* would eventually enter Spanish with the meaning buffalo). The first of the Seven Cities of Cíbola was only thirty days off. Estéban's informants confirmed that its doors were indeed studded with turquoise.

But it was Holy Week, and Fray Marcos refused to cross the Mayo until he had celebrated Easter. By now a second large cross, with a message to come quick, had arrived. A third cross, with the message that Estéban would be waiting at the end of the *despoblado,* the stretch of uninhabited desert that was coming up soon, met Fray Marcos on the way. The desert took four days to cross. At the other side there was a Tepehuano village that Cabeza de Vaca's companion Dorantes, on the way down, had called the Town of Hearts because its residents had given him six hundred deer hearts. But no sign of Estéban.

Free for the first time since his capture in North Africa, Estéban, in cabalistic drag, was becoming more and more outrageous. In each new village he demanded, and was given, the Indians' most valued possessions—their turquoise and their women—and as his harem grew, his entrées became grander and more flamboyant, and his loyalties to God and Spain became increasingly tenuous. North of the Town of Hearts, he traveled for two weeks through the uninhabited sagebrush and cactus country of southern Arizona, passing near the future sites of Fort Huachuca and Tombstone. At last he saw in the distance what his guides told him was the first of the Seven Cities—actually a Zuñi pueblo called Hawikuh. He sent messengers ahead with his rattle to proclaim that a great medicine man was on the way.

This was a big mistake. The Zuñi were fairly obsessed with witchcraft and were particularly wary of strangers with magic powers. The cacique of Hawikuh recognized the rattle as the work of a Plains tribe to the east that was the Zuñi's mortal enemy. He smashed it to the ground and sent back word for Estéban to come no closer if he valued his life. Estéban decided to ignore the warning and proceeded. The Zuñi seized him, stripped him of his possessions, and held him in a large house outside the city walls while they debated what to do. In the morning, as Estéban stepped out of the house, the Zuñi shot him full of arrows. Pieces of his body were sent to each of the seven pueblos as proof that the giant black kachina, who had told them that other, white kachinas, the Children of the Sun, were on the way, was mortal. The dismemberment was also a way of dispersing his magic powers.

Four and a half centuries later, Hawikuh is a pile of rubble, and the Zuñi, who are still going strong as a culture, live fourteen miles down the road, in a pueblo called Halona I'itiwana, or "Middle Ant Hill." The Zuñi are a unique community among the Pueblos. Their language is of a different stock, perhaps distantly related to California Penutian. They can be traced directly through their redware ceramics and their DNA to the people of Chaco Canyon. Their original territory was much larger than their present reservation. Zuñi petroglyphs turn up as far away as the South Valley of Albuquerque; the Zuñi apparently had close trading relations with extinct Pueblos there. They have the longest and one of the bloodiest histories of interaction with the Spaniards, and there is such lingering resentment that Mexicans and *nuevomejicanos,* whom they call *mehekuka,* are not welcome at their ceremonies. They still have a legend about a "black Mexican with chile lips" who came from "the land of everlasting summer" and was killed by their ancestors.

Christianity, which was introduced in the seventeenth century, left them cold. They killed two of their missionaries, and the Franciscans finally gave up on them in 1821. As Frank Hamilton Cushing, a brilliant young ethnologist who lived with them for four years, starting in 1879, wrote, "The Zuñi faith . . . is as a drop of oil in water, surrounded and touched at every point, yet in no place penetrated or changed inwardly by the flood of alien belief that descended upon it."

Cushing was a prototype of the modern fugitive, indeed one of the first Other questers to be drawn to the Southwest. A sickly child, he grew up in central New York. He spent much of his time alone in the woods, communing with the animals and birds in a special language he made up for the purpose. He had a sixth sense for finding Indian relics and sites. One of his colleagues would describe him as "intensive, intuitional, mystic, neurotic and in chronic ill health, with a streak of exhibitionism." By the age of nine he had become an expert on arrowheads.

Cushing arrived among the Zuñi at age twenty-two, having signed on as the ethnologist on a collecting expedition for the newly formed Bureau of American Ethnology. To everyone's consternation, instead of staying in the tent camp his colleagues had pitched on the edge of the village, he moved, uninvited, into the governor of the pueblo's house. So appalled were his colleagues that they left him there, without supplies, and without even saying goodbye. Cushing was supposed to spend around three months with the Zuñi, but he ended up staying until 1883. It took him two years to learn the language. By the end he was attending sacred ceremonies no *melika,* or Anglo (another corruption of *americano*), had ever seen. He dressed like a Zuñi, led an attack against Mexican-American horse thieves, collected his own enemy scalp (of an Apache; a special ceremony had to be performed to purge the scalp because it had been cut with a steel knife instead of a flint one), was inducted into the secret fraternity of war magicians—the Bow Priesthood—and offered a wife, whom he refused. He was the first "participant observer," the first anthropologist to live for an extended period with his subjects, to "get down with them," which is now standard practice. "The day is fast approaching," Cushing predicted, "when it will be demonstrated that the personal equation is the supremely essential thing in such researches as this." Jesse Green, who edited his writings on the Zuñi, credits Cushing with avoiding the projection that modern anthropologists, "so enamored of their neat formulas that they mistake them for facts," are sometimes guilty of, and the critic Edmund Wilson, who visited the pueblo in 1947, observed that "a good deal of Cushing's work has an autobiographical element, and his account of his queer dual life is a unique literary document on the struggle between white man and red man, not in the forest or on the plains, but in one dislocated human spirit."

Cushing butted heads with Senator John Logan of Illinois, whose son-in-law and some other army officers were trying to gain title to the tribe's land, and Logan threatened to bring down the whole Bureau of American Ethnology unless Cushing was recalled. He died at the age of forty-two, destroying his notes on the secrets he'd been privy to as a Bow Priest, which he felt ought not to be revealed.

Cushing's detailed depiction of the Zuñi's rich and complex social and ceremonial structures, of their "systems within systems," had tremendous influence on Claude Lévi-Strauss's structuralism. The pueblo is best known for its ten-foot-high, masked, beaked, horned, feather-tiaraed Shalako dancers, who perform at the midwinter festival. This is the most spectacular dance in the Southwest. The dancers carry their extra height with frames on their shoulders.

The Zuñi also have a strong berdache tradition. A berdache is a biological male with reduced genitals who dresses like a woman, acts like a woman, does work and hangs out with the women, and is sexually available to unmarried young men, is a sex teacher and a condoned extra outlet for married men. The Spaniards called the berdaches *putos,* male whores, or *sodomitas,* not understanding their spiritual importance. The Zuñi berdaches are revered as both male and female. Some have fathered children. They elect the role after having a sacred vision on the threshold of adulthood or are appointed by the community. The beloved berdache, Wéwha, who died in 1956, was taken to Washington, where he was received by Grover Cleveland and became a good friend of the Speaker of the House and his wife.

The Zuñi today have fourteen clans, six kiva groups, twelve curing societies, including eight societies of the Completed Path, and sixteen Rain Priesthoods. The Bow Priesthood is vestigial because the requirement that you have to have taken an enemy scalp to belong is still in effect, and scalping just isn't done anymore. In 1978 there were only two very old Bow Priests. There is an order of clowns, actually a medical fraternity, called the Néwekwe. Their principal business is to deal with digestive disorders. As Wilson wrote in 1947:

> They are supposed to possess the secret of an extremely potent medicine, and—apparently to demonstrate its efficacy—it is their custom to give public exhibition at which they drink urine and eat excrement, chew up pieces of cloth and wood, swallow pebbles and handfuls of ashes, bite the heads off live mice and devour the entrails of dogs, which they have just torn to pieces alive.

The fear of witchcraft is still strong. The witches are believed to have once had a secret society of their own, but now they operate as individuals, causing drought, floods, sickness, epidemics, and death, working magic with the hair, nails, excrement, or clothing of their victims, shooting foreign objects into their bodies. Until the federal government put a stop to the practice in 1925, people accused of being a witch by the Bow Priesthood were hung by their thumbs or elbows from a rafter in the abandoned Franciscan chapel until they confessed or died. Now the punishment is settled privately, between the witch and the accuser. The fate of an exposed witch is often unknown. He or she just disappears. Witches are considered to be "raw people" as opposed to humans, who are "cooked people" (a distinction in many tribal societies, which Lévi-Strauss has examined in great detail). Human form is only one of many they can take. Like the Navajo skinwalkers, witches can also turn into coyotes, crows, hawks, dogs, or cats. They can fly into a dust devil and commandeer it to go places. Wilson mentions an anthropologist who pried into the Zuñi's spiritual secrets and was expelled as a witch, his notes destroyed.

Like all tribal peoples, the Zuñi are observant naturalists. Their ethnoentomology is particularly interesting. Wilson writes of "sacred black butterflies which one of the orders of priests is supposed to put into their drums and which are said to drive the hearers to frenzy." Butterflies are the symbolic animal of summer warmth. Ants and water striders are also important beings. The writer Tony Hillerman retells a Zuñi parable about how those who were living in Hawikuh had a feast whose wastefulness offended the plants and the rain and the earth that had provided the food. Plus, the Corn Maidens who had shown up at the feast, disguised as old hags, weren't fed. So they sent a drought. Cloud Swallower drank up the clouds. The rain ceremonies were performed to no avail, and Hawikuh was abandoned by all but a young boy and his sister and an old woman, who had shared what little food they had with the Corn Maidens. The boy tried to make a butterfly to bring the warmth of summer, but ended up making a being-which-flies-on-double wings—a dragonfly, or *tsi-ni-thla,* which was in fact Cornstalk Being, and the Grandfather, as the children called the dragonfly, traveled over many mountains and across many plains to the Land of Everlasting Summer, where the Corn Maidens lived, and the dragonfly persuaded them to send rains that brought the crops back into fruition.

So calm, gentle, open, friendly, and accessible do the Zuñi appear on the surface that the anthropologist Ruth Benedict, who spent time with them in the thirties, described them (using Spengler's distinction) as Apollonian as opposed to Dionysian. The traditional Zuñi greeting is to breathe on one another's hand, to give each other a little blast of warm air from the spirit within. But I was told if a Zuñi senses you're after something, he will clam up. Wilson was told to hide the anthropological studies he'd brought with him and felt like someone who had come to a totalitarian dictatorship with contraband political tracts. The atmosphere of the pueblo as it was flooded with whites who had come for the Shalako dances reminded him of "Moscow on the eve of the purges." According to an anthropologist fluent in Zuñi, a violent dispute broke out in a clan kiva before a recent Shalako dance about how certain paraphernalia was traditionally used, and one of the disputants whipped out Ruth L. Bunzel's exhaustive *Introduction to Zuñi Ceremonialism* in the forty-seventh annual report of the Bureau of

American Ethnology, 1929–30, and found the page where the paraphernalia was discussed, which settled the matter.

As at Santo Domingo, the traditional Pueblo cellular adobe apartment complex has given way to detached single-family residences with
beige walls and sheet-metal roofs. The traditional pueblo was a communal fortress for protection mainly against the Navajo, an anthropologist told me, and it was given up by all but Acoma and Taos
Pueblos after the Navajo were neutralized in the 1860s. The houses
have running water, electricity, and telephones and are masted with
television aerials. Pickups are parked out front. The Zuñi are hooked
up to the modern Southwest; they draw off the grid, but they aren't
really part of it. In recent years, I was told, they have achieved one of
the big Indian education success stories, halting what had been one of
the leading teenage suicide rates. Now their basketball team, the Roadrunners, makes up in spunk and speed what it lacks in height.

I arrived at Zuñi a few weeks after my side trip to the albinos and was
taken to see the ruins of Hawikuh by José Sheyka, a jewelry maker
from the pueblo. We drove through cedar-studded grassland, a low
mesa country of bunchgrass and sage. Wild spinach, which the Zuñi
eat, was all over the place. Passing a marshy pond, the sort of wet
meadow known in the Southwest by its Spanish name, *ciénega,* we
turned right, onto a road whose red clay was too slick for the car, so
we parked and set out on foot.

The road led to a summer sheep camp. After maybe three-quarters
of a mile, we left the road and walked out on a spur, a high spot in the
middle of the prairie, smothered with rock and rubble, with a few
ancient, small, warped cedar trees sticking up here and there. The
rubble was full of sherds that had been painted in different colors
and styles. On a beige boulder an inscription—JOHN TSETHLICKI US
NAVY 1952–7—had been pecked. Gusts of wind sent wavy shudders
through acres of tall golden grass below, and a few buzzards teetered
overhead. José told me that when he was a young man his father and
his clan brothers would come out here for a couple of days without
food or water and run down wild horses to toughen themselves up, to
"try their strength." Interclan cross-country relay races are still held,
with the participants kicking three-inch sticks called *tikwa,* planting
prayer sticks, and leaving shell, tobacco, and cornmeal offerings at
shrines like Owl Spring. The spring got its name, the ethnographer
Peter Nabokov writes in his book *Indian Running,* after one racer

asked an owl grandmother to help him win, and the owl said, "Take one of the feathers from my left wing. My sleep will overcome the other runners."

"There isn't much to see here," José said. "All the winds covered it up." The pueblo was excavated in the twenties. No trace of any turquoise-studded door was found. The date of occupation was estimated at from 1300 to 1680. "All our ceremonies were probably started by these people," José went on. He invited me to watch a rain dance that afternoon, for which his nephews were already suiting up in his living room when we got back.

Only three of Estéban's three-hundred-person entourage escaped slaughter or captivity by the Zuñi, and they fled to Fray Marcos with the terrible news of what had happened. What Fray Marcos then did is unclear. Some think he turned tail and fled and never came within two hundred miles of Zuñi country. But that's not what he said he did when he got back to Mexico. His story was:

> In the end, seeing that I was determined, two chiefs said that they would go with me [on to Hawikuh]. With these and my own Indian interpreters, I pursued my journey until I came within sight of Cíbola, which is situated in a plain at the base of a round hill. It has the appearance of a very beautiful city, the best I have seen in these parts. The houses are of the style the Indians have described to me, all made of stone, with their stories and terraces, as it appeared to me from a hill where I was able to view it. The city is larger than the city of Mexico. At times I was tempted to go to it, because I knew that I risked only my life, which I had offered to God on the day I began this journey. But finally I realized, considering my danger, that if I died, I wouldn't be able to make my report of this country, which to me appears the greatest and best of the discoveries. I commented to the chiefs who had accompanied me; and they told me it was the poorest of the seven cities, and the Totonteac [thought to be one of the Hopi villages] is much larger and better than all the seven, and that it has so many houses and citizens it has no end. Under the circumstances, it seemed appropriate to me to call that country the new kingdom of Saint Francis; and there with the aid of the Indians, I made a great heap of stones, and on top of it I placed a cross, small and light only because I had not the means of making it larger, and I declared that I erected that cross and monument in the name of Don António de Mendoza, viceroy of New Spain, for the emperor, our Lord, as a

sign of possession, conforming to my instruction, and by which possession I proclaimed that I took all of the seven cities and the kingdoms of Totonteac and of Acus and of Marata, and that the reason I did not go to these latter places was in order to give an account of all I did and saw.

The more charitable historians argue that Fray Marcos may have received his exaggerated impression of the pueblo's size from the reflected brilliance of a dawn or a sunset. But maybe he couldn't face the idea of returning empty-handed to the viceroy. Or maybe he wasn't even aware of the distortion. The conquest was full of confirmed sightings, by more than one observer, of mermaids on beaches, monsters in the sea, and angels in the sky. Wishful thinking was exacerbated by cross-cultural misunderstanding, of seeing what one wanted to see and hearing what one wanted to hear from natives only too willing, for a variety of reasons beginning with politeness, to answer in the affirmative. The Spaniards' rocks fit in the Indians' holes. The convergence of the spiritually charged number 7—of central importance not only in the Zuñi's cosmic and community architecture, but in Western myth, going back to ancient Greece (seven legendary islands of the Hebrides, seven strings to the lyre, seven gates to Thebes, and so on)—was particularly supportive of projection. In a world so strange and marvelous, the distinction between what was real and what was not wasn't always clear. The desert was full of mirages. As Bernal Diaz, one of Cortés's companions, wrote at the end of his life in his memoir of the conquest, "If I had not lived through these events myself, I would have thought they were a dream."

The Cíbola Expedition

hen Fray Marcos got back to Compostela and told how Estéban and half his *compañeros* had been killed at the walls of a city bigger than Mexico, and that this was just the smallest of the Seven Cities, Coronado could scarcely contain his excitement. Swearing the friar to secrecy, Coronado rushed with him to Mexico City to tell Mendoza.

But no news so big could be kept under wraps. It leaked through such sources as Fray Marcos's barber, and soon all Mexico City was abuzz with it. To keep it from the ears of rival conquistadores in Cuba and Spain, the viceroy banned everyone from leaving the colony without his permission while he considered what to do. Clearly a full-scale military campaign was indicated this time.

Mexico City was full of idle young hidalgos, literally "sons of somebody," petty nobles like Coronado but without his connections, casualties of the Spanish law of primogeniture who stood to inherit neither land nor title from their parents and after a small settlement were packed off to the Indies, like the younger sons of the British aristocracy who were packed off to colonial Kenya or the trust-fund hippies of Santa Fe in this century. The hidalgos in Mexico City were "corks floating on the water," in the historian Matias Angel de la Mota Padilla's description. The citizens grew sick of having to feed them. Most were in their twenties. Coronado himself was only twenty-six. They were steeped in chivalric romances and dreamed of emulating the quixotic adventures of the first-wave conquistadores and of literary heroes like Amadis de Gaula. Most of them hailed from Estremadura, a province as dusty and rock strewn as the country they would be wandering in for the next two years, or from Don Quixote's equally bleak homeland, La Mancha (from the Moorish al-Manshash, the Parched

Land). They were, in a sense, preadapted to the Chihuahuan Desert's dryness.

Mendoza offered each man who signed on thirty pesos and a *repartimiento,* an estate on the land they would conquer. Rumors of a mountain of silver were already circulating around Mexico City. He had no trouble finding takers.

The expedition mustered at Compostela on February 22, 1540, and set out on schedule. Of the 336 Spaniards, 225 were mounted and 62 were on foot, a few took along wives and children, and they were accompanied by hundreds of Indian allies, 559 extra horses, thousands of pack mules, sheep, and dogs. Two ships under the command of Hernando de Alarcón were to sail up along the Gulf of California with extra supplies and provisions and to rendezvous with them in a couple of months. The *entrada* cost roughly the equivalent of a million dollars today and was the most ambitious treasure hunt ever launched from the capital of New Spain. Its captain general was Coronado, whose personal equipage alone included twenty-three horses and three or four suits of armor. "Such a noble body was never assembled in the Indies, nor so many men of quality in so small a body," its chronicler, Pedro de Castañeda, wrote. The indomitable Fray Marcos spearheaded the religious contingent.

Five months later the expedition crossed the great *despoblado*—not a desert, but the uninhabited White Mountains wilderness of eastern Arizona—thirty leagues of jagged peaks, twisting barrancas (large deep canyons), and icy torrents. The provisions gave out. Many of the horses dropped from exhaustion. Morale sank. Spinosa and two African slaves died after eating some tasty-looking herbs—probably the lethal water hemlock—at what afterward was named the Camp of Death. At this point the scouts were approached by four Indians who communicated in sign language that they were from Cíbola and that there was plenty of food a day ahead. Coronado gave crosses to two of the Indians and sent them back with the message that they were coming in the name of the emperor across the water to place the people of Cíbola under his dominion and to afford them a knowledge of God, and if the Cíbolans were agreeable to this, there would be no trouble. The other two he kept as hostages.

Warily, sensing that they were being watched, the expedition proceeded into Zuñi country. Coronado was impressed by how the smoke signals that were rising on mesas here and there "both give warning of our approach and identify us." He pronounced them "as good a method of communication as we could have devised ourselves." At midnight a large band of Cíbolans ambushed a party sent out to guard what is now known as Bad Pass, scattering many of the horses and rattling several tenderfoot caballeros so much that they put their saddles on backward.

At last they saw Cíbola—Hawikuh, probably. But instead of a great gleaming city, it was just an unimpressive little mud town, "all crumpled together" at the end of a spur. There were no roofs of gold, no turquoise-studded doors, no doors at all, in fact. Access seemed to be by the ladders leaning on the walls, which were terraced back to a height of six stories. Choice Castilian curses filled the air, and several of the men had to be restrained from strangling Fray Marcos.

The Cíbolans had hidden their women and jewelry, and two or three hundred warriors with leather shields were standing in formation before the pueblo, brandishing spears and aiming arrows from bent bows. They drew a line on the ground in front of them with sprinkled cornmeal and made it clear that the Spaniards were not to cross it.

In some senses this line is still drawn.

The Spaniards were exhausted and weak with hunger and were in no shape for a fight. They held out gifts and made conciliatory gestures, which the Cíbolans interpreted as a sign of fear, so they attacked, coming "almost to the heels of our horses to fire their arrows." At last Coronado sounded the traditional battle cry, *Santiago y a ellos* (Saint James and at them),* and the men returned the fire with their crossbows and harquebuses.

The Cíbolans, driven back to their pueblo, pulled up the ladders and pelted the Spaniards with rocks from the roofs. One of the rocks knocked Coronado, a conspicuous target in his plumed helmet and splendid armor, off his horse, and he was carried unconscious to a tent. When he came to, the battle was over. The Zuñi had taken to the hills, leaving "something we prized more than gold or silver; namely plentiful maize and beans, turkeys larger than those in New Spain, and salt better and whiter than any I have seen in my whole life." The turkeys

---

* James the Elder, possibly Christ's brother or cousin, was beheaded by Herod and became the first apostle to die for the Gospel. (This is explained in a collection of essays by Marc Simmons, Donna Pierce, and Joan Myers called *Santiago, Saint of Two Worlds*.) His relics ended up in Galicia, at a shrine called Santiago de Compostela, which is why the capital of Nueva Galicia was called Compostela, the "Field of the Star." At crucial engagements during the *reconquista* of Spain, there would sometimes be a break in the clouds, and Santiago ("Saint James" in Castilian)—radiant, haloed in golden light, mounted on a white horse, and suited in armor— would appear in the heavens and urge on the flagging troops. There were dozens of confirmed apparitions. And during the conquest of New Spain, time and again Santiago appeared to recharge the troops. He was big juju. In the centuries that followed, Santiago was gradually absorbed into the Indian pantheon along with the Virgin of Guadalupe. The Indians revered his gentler attributes, as a protector of flocks and a restorer of stray animals.

weren't raised for food, but for the magnificent robes that were made from their feathers. Coronado christened the place Granada, after Mendoza's birthplace.

After several days the Cíbolans were persuaded to come down from their impregnable sacred mesa, Corn Mountain, and their elders submitted to the Spanish God and king and explained that they had killed Estéban because he had molested their women. It turned out that the Cíbolans had been expecting light-skinned people to come from the south and conquer them for fifty years. Either they were waiting for the return of Quetzalcoatl, or word had reached them of the conquest of Mexico.

"Everything is the reverse of what Fray Marcos said," an extremely distressed Coronado reported to Mendoza. "He has not told the truth in a single thing." According to the friar's celestial calculations, the expedition's route would parallel the Gulf of California, never more than twenty miles inland. It was with this understanding that the two supply ships under Hernando de Alarcón had set sail from Acapulco on May 6, picking up a third vessel at Culiacán. But the coast kept veering northwest, and the land route kept heading northeast, and by the time Coronado reached Cíbola, he and Alarcón were hundreds of miles apart; but so primitive and unreliable was the technology of measuring longitude that neither was aware of the divergence. So both were on their own, although some supplies later did reach Coronado by land. Alarcón's voyage became one of pure exploration, and he made several important discoveries. He established that Baja California was a peninsula and not an island—a discovery that would not register with the mapmakers back in Spain for a century and a half.

At the neck of the gulf, Alarcón and his men found "a mighty river with a current so furious that we could scarcely sail against it." They called it the Buena Guia, or Unfailing Guide, but the name didn't take. It would become the Colorado (the Red) because of the redness of its water. Fighting its tidal bore, the clash of its discharge with the incoming tide, they entered the river. Tall Indians with magnificent physiques, with beads and shells dangling from their pierced nostrils, aiming drawn bows, brandishing maces and daggers, lined both banks. Alarcón put ashore in a dinghy. One of the Indians dashed into the water and embraced him.

These were the Yumans, whose descendants still live along the lower Colorado. They grew corn and lived in semisubterranean longhouses, roofed with straw, that could hold a hundred people. Alarcón estimated the population of one of their towns to be five or six thousand.

The Yumans took scalps and were continuously at war among themselves. They fasted for visions and put great stock in their dreams. When one of them died, his corpse and all his possessions were heaped on a huge pyre and incinerated. All memory of him was erased, and his name could never be mentioned again.

The Yumans were fascinated by Alarcón's magnificent beard. Perceiving, in spite of the language barrier, that they were sun worshipers, Alarcón cleverly identified himself as the Son of the Sun (an imposture for which he would later be censured by the Council of the Indies in Seville), and the Yumans' hospitality turned into reverence.

Coronado sent out reconnaissance parties in every direction, hoping they would find something to reverse the disgrace and justify the outing. One cavalcade set out for the Tusayans, who lived in seven (again the magic number) pueblos on four mesas. These people would later be called the Moquis by the Spaniards. Today they're known as the Hopi. They possessed no transportable physical wealth, only an exceptionally rich ceremonial life.

It turned out that the Tusayans, too, were waiting for a long-lost white brother. His name was Pahána, and he was twenty years overdue. At first they took the cavalcade's commander, Pedro de Tovar, to be Pahána. The contact went as it had at Cíbola: a line of sacred cornmeal was drawn, then there was a brief skirmish. The Spaniards prevailed with the help of Santiago, and peace was made. But it soon became clear to the Tusayans that Pahána didn't know the ceremonial shake with the Bear clan leader, or how to form *nakwach,* the ancient symbol of brotherhood, and he seemed to have totally forgotten the agreement he made with their grandfathers. The inevitable conclusion, that this was not Pahána, was not long coming. The Tusayans called them *castilas,* Castilians, and later *kachada,* white man, and *dodagee,* dictator, according to Frank Waters, whose 1963 *Book of the Hopi* revealed much of their complex mystical belief system, angering the traditionalists and becoming one of the major sixties New Age wanna-be texts. According to Edmund Nequatewa, who collected some of his people's legends in the thirties, the *castila* priests who came to the village of Shongopovi and forced the villagers to build a mission, burned their kachinas, and molested their wives, were called *tota-achi,* which means a grouchy person who won't do anything for himself, like a child. The current Hopi word for white man is *bahana.*

The Tusayans told the *castilas* about a great river to the west, and the *castilas* became excited. Maybe it would lead to the South Sea, the Strait of Anian, or some other passage to Cathay. They rode on until suddenly they found themselves at the rim of a stupendous barranca—the Grand Canyon. They were in desperate need of water and tried to get down to the river, which they could see a mile below, meandering among banded tiers of rock, but they succeeded in descending only part of the way, far enough to see that some spires that had looked from the rim to be the height of a man were in fact "higher than the great tower in Seville." They didn't get to meet the "tall people" the Tusayans had told them about, who lived down in the canyon—probably the Havasupai, who are still there. The Havasupai wouldn't be contacted until 1776.

Another column rose east until they reached the kingdom of Aku, now called Acoma, often translated as Sky City, although its real meaning is more like Place of Preparedness. Perched on a craggy, four-hundred-foot butte in the center of a cliff-lined bowl, the pueblo boasts one of the most spectacular and militarily and spiritually strategic sites on the planet. One of the Spaniards pronounced it "the greatest stronghold ever seen in the world." Seeing the advancing cavalcade, a swarm of warriors descended from the citadel and sprinkled the customary cornmeal line, but then one of them signed peace in the lingua franca known to the native peoples over much of the continent, crossing his second fingers (meaning "our meeting"), then placing one hand over the other (we are friends and will not harm each other). According to the anthropologist Wilhelm Wundt, complicated messages could be transmitted in North American "gesture speech," like "white soldiers, led by an officer of high rank but low intelligence, have taken the Mescalero Indians prisoner."

The Spaniards were led up three hundred stone steps to a series of hand- and footholds bored in the rock face and, passing through a crack, emerged on top of the mesa. There they found an elaborate pueblo complex with three or four stories of terraced cubes, ladders leaning on them like stairways to the sky, ample stashes of corn, cisterns full of rainwater and snowmelt (at the end of winter the Acoma would stuff them with huge snowballs). But Acoma possessed no precious metals or stones, or anything else of material value to the Spaniards, and they continued east, scouting locations where they all could spend the winter, until they came to a large (for this part of the world, anyway) brown river gliding serenely between cottonwood bosquets. They called it Nuestra Señora, the first of seventeen names it would have in its recorded history. Today Americans call this river, which describes their southern border from El Paso to the Gulf of Mexico, the Rio Grande, Mexicans the Río Bravo.

The Spaniards' Indian guides took them to a group of twelve pueblos called Tiguex—the largest and most prosperous settlement they had yet seen, with "maize, beans, melons, and turkeys in abundance." One of the pueblos, they sent word to Coronado, was seven stories high and had thirty-five thousand residents—almost certainly an overestimate. A later Spanish visitor to Tiguex, Gaspar Perez de Villagra, would describe its inhabitants as "quiet, peaceful people of good appearance and excellent physique, alert and intelligent. . . . The men dress in garments of cotton cloth, and the women wear beautiful shawls of many colors. . . . We saw no maimed or deformed people among them. The men and women alike are excellent swimmers. They live in complete equality, neither exercising authority nor demanding obedience." In fact, according to the ethnohistorian Ramón Gutiérrez, Pueblo women were free to sleep with whomever they wanted. Their husbands didn't seem to mind, which was very different from the extremely possessive, violently jealous Latin concept of love. The women's availability also had a Samson-and-Delilah element. They slept with the Spaniards to neutralize their power, and there was also a tacit understanding on the part of the Pueblos that in giving their women they would get something in return, but the Spaniards just took and took; there was no reciprocity. It was what Gutiérrez calls a "dyadic" relationship, which is unhealthy and unstable because it is unbalanced, and the flow of what anthropologists like to call "goodies" is one way, from the client to the patron, the servant to the master. Even though the dominant culture has changed, relations between it and the Southwest's native cultures are still basically dyadic. A useful bit of jargon for understanding this part of the world.

This was the place, Coronado decided, to hunker down for the winter. The main force moved in—twelve thousand mouths to feed, including Mexican Indian allies. The expeditionaries ate all the food and maltreated the women, taking those who didn't offer themselves; by now the respect for the natives, tightly enforced at the outset, had eroded. On top of this, it was an unusually cold winter. The Rio Grande froze "so thick loaded animals could cross it," and the Spaniards commandeered all the available buffalo robes and *mantas* (blankets) so they could keep warm.

At last the people of Tiguex could stand no more. They started by killing the Spaniards' horses outside one of the pueblos. The Spaniards retaliated by smoking out and massacring everyone who was barricaded in the pueblo. Two hundred men were tied to stakes and burned alive. The man who ordered the massacre, Garcia Lopez de Cardenas, would spend seven years in a Spanish prison for this appalling violation of the Law of the Indies, which expressly forbade such things. But the damage was done: Spanish-Pueblo relations were poisoned. One wonders how Coronado could have let it happen.

Of the twelve pueblos of Tiguex, only two remain, Sandia and Isleta. The others were displaced by the Spanish settlement of Bernalillo, founded in 1698. Bernalillo would have become a big city instead of Albuquerque, a dozen miles down the valley, but in 1878 the town fathers of Bernalillo tried to hold up the Atchison, Topeka, and Santa Fe Railroad for $425 an acre for a right-of-way (the going price for land in those parts in those days was $2 or $3 an acre), and the AT and SF men decided to bring the track down over the Sandia Mountains to Los Lunas instead. Albuquerque, which would have been a whistle stop, became the chief division point on the continental line, and Bernalillo was bypassed. The WPA guide to New Mexico reported in 1940 that the town "retains some of the atmosphere of the old Spanish days." Today it's a funky town of trailers and old adobes, with a few big farmhouses on its main drag. The local power structure is completely *nuevomejicano*. There are a few non-Hispanic hippies. Placitas, a bedroom community of Bernalillo, has become yuppified. It used to be a groovy scene. The poets Robert Creely and Gregory Corso lived there. There was a hippie bar called the Thunderbird Bar, but it burned down, which seems to be the fate of all hippie bars in New Mexico.

The *nuevomejicanos* were isolated from Mexico even when both were part of New Spain, and after their annexation by the United States, they were even more so. But now a new wave of Mexicans was moving north, refertilizing the Hispanic culture. The *nuevomejicanos* and the *mexicanos* had the same religion, basically the same language, the same mestizo mix. There was some friction between the *manitos* and *juareños,* as the two groups called each other (*manito* is short for *hermanito,* little brother of the Penitente sect, that is, hick; a *juareño* is someone who has crossed the Rio Grande at Ciudad Juárez, that is, wetback), mainly because of competition for jobs, but for the most part the Mexicans were taken in by the better-off *nuevos,* who felt compassion for their brothers and their dangerous odyssey to El Norte. When we were living in Albuquerque, exactly 450 years after the winter at Tiguex, the Albuquerque *Journal* had a story about a fourteen-year-old Mexican girl who had been found standing in a daze on one of the freeway ramps. She had crossed the border with her aunt, who had abandoned her, and the police were having no luck tracking down her grandmother in Guadalajara. Apparently she had no one in the world. Soon she was taken in by a *nuevomejicano* family.

Yolanda Medina of Bernalillo tried to help a *juareña* and ended up being murdered. This was a big story in the papers for a couple of days. It touched a lot of nerves: the immigrants-flooding-in nerve, the what-vile-human-beings-could-murder-a-Good-Samaritan nerve. Yolanda's nude body was found on October 20, 1991, by a bicyclist on the bank of an irrigation ditch outside of Bernalillo. She had been raped and asphyxiated and had been missing for five days, having disappeared a day short of her twenty-first birthday. Her murder was all the more horrible because she was such a pretty girl, with her hair fluffed up and sprayed in the luxuriant skyscraper hairdo favored by *cholas* of her age. Yolanda had last been seen leaving the Atlas travel agency in Albuquerque in the company of a woman. The police worked up a composite sketch of the woman and set up a hotline that received numerous calls, but they didn't recognize her from the composite when they arrested her two days after the murder for shoplifting a pair of boots worth $24.95. She was released after a bond company posted a hundred dollars. The APD blotter noted that she failed to provide credible documents for identification and that she was not sure of her local address. Which, it turned out a few days later, was the Nativity of the Blessed Virgin Mary Church.

The woman's name was Catalina Tarin. She was nineteen and a Mexican illegal, like her boyfriend, who gave his name as José de Jesus Dionicio Nuñez Hernandez, which may have been an alias. The couple said they were students from Veracruz, below Ciudad Juárez. Apparently they had been staying in a succession of churches supportive of aliens, taking advantage of religious agencies and of the good hearts of people like Yolanda. In the church the police found phony IDs, the radio from Yolanda's pickup, Yolanda's ID bracelet, her gold Del Norte High School ring, and a pair of fur-lined handcuffs. But "physical evidence" suggested she was killed in the basement of another church—the Apostolic Church in the Faith of Jesus Christ. Yolanda and Catalina had struck up a conversation in front of the travel agency, where Catalina was trying to cash a check. Yolanda explained it was closed because it was Columbus Day. The next day they met back at the agency, which refused to cash the check, and they drove off in Yolanda's pickup, even though Yolanda had told her dad she was scared because Catalina kept asking questions about the truck. The police speculated that either Yolanda may have been a witness to a crime, or Catalina wanted her ID. "These people, they wanted the American dream and they wanted it very quickly," said a member of the Bernalillo PD. "That's probably their motive. They were taking shortcuts to that dream and didn't want to work for it."

On May 6 of the following year, both Catalina and José downed poison in jail and killed themselves in a suspected suicide pact. José left a seven-page letter with a map to the bodies of other women he had killed down in Mexico. He seems to have been a serial killer; it turned out he had lured another woman into a church, but she escaped. "There are a whole lot of things I'm not feeling at ease about that make it seem cult-related," said Captain Greg Marcantel, who was running the investigation. Besides the fur-lined handcuffs, "there's it occurring in a church and some of the details from the autopsy." Bloodstain and pubic-hair analyses suggested that Yolanda Gody had been dragged and probably kept several days in the church before being dumped on the ditch bank in Bernalillo.

The next day the *Journal* revealed the translated contents of the suicide notes. José and Catalina said they were innocent and were killing themselves because they were unable to endure "the humiliation and bad treatment of the jailers," including being kept in solitary twenty-four hours a day, so they "decided to put an end to these intolerable sufferings which we are living, so far away from our Mexican land." They claimed they were framed by police, who, once they learned they were aliens, put Yolanda's clothes in the church. What the police's motive might have been they did not say, unless it was pressure to come up with a conviction. "We did not kill this woman and we did not know her," wrote José. "I am sure this is a punishment of God for my past sins." His map showed the woods outside Acatlán, a town southeast of Mexico City, where the previous July he hid the naked bodies of two women: one was a shoe salesgirl he had been having an affair with, the other a *campesina* who happened to be passing by and witnessed the crime.

I had lunch one day with Father Bill Sanchez, who attends to the earthly and spiritual needs of Pueblos, *juareños,* and Chicanos out of the Christian Motivation Center in Bernalillo.

"This was Tiguex, the place where it all started," he told me. "There were two kivas on our church grounds. Whenever it rains, pottery sherds are exposed. This was the plaza. The pueblo was destroyed twice in the 1600s because we couldn't stop the Indians' practices. The Inquisition was run out of here.

"It's strange that all the energy, all the wealth, was poured into buildings," Father Bill reflected. "Think of what it could have done to improve the lot of the poor. The more devoutly Christian Pueblos say we should celebrate the last five hundred years because they brought us Christ, but others say we already had Christ—we believed in a supreme God and that the essence of the person is the soul. We already had the Parousia, the doctrine of a Second Coming. But it wasn't until 1580 that there was a papal bull acknowledging that Indians had souls. To the Spaniards they didn't have souls until then."

In the spring of 1541 Coronado and his men set out after a final mirage, a last chance for glory—the kingdom of Quivira, where they had been told by a handsome Indian—whose head was swathed in a colorful turban, so they called him the Turk—there was a huge river with fish as big as horses and "a great number of very large canoes with twenty oarsmen on each side and bearing sails. The nobility traveled in the stern beneath canopies, and on the bow was a great eagle of gold . . . the lord of that land took his siestas under a large tree from which were hung numerous little bells of gold that played for him by themselves in the breeze. The common table service of everyone was wrought with silver, and the pitchers, plates, and bowls were of gold."

The Turk led them across the Texas and Oklahoma Panhandles, their curved, casque helmets glinting in the sun. They passed oceanic herds of buffalo, an uncountable number of pronghorn antelope and the gray wolves that preyed on them. The prairie was so flat you could see the sky between the buffalo's legs, Castañeda wrote, and if you lay down on your back you "lost sight of the ground." Somewhere in the vicinity of Lindsborg, Kansas—by now they were four thousand miles from Compostela and, unbeknownst to either of them, within only three hundred miles of de Soto's even more ill-fated expedition—the Turk admitted that he had been making the whole thing up, leading them on a wild-goose chase until they ran out of food and their horses died, and it would be easy for the people of Tiguex to kill them for what they had done to them. The Turk was like a mother killdeer leading a predator from the nest, sacrificing himself to save his people. One of the soldiers sneaked up behind him, slipped a rope around his neck, and garroted him.

And that was what the Coronado expedition came up with—zip. Back at Tiguex, Coronado was racing a friend on a horse when his saddle girth broke; he fell and was kicked in the head by his friend's steed. He never fully recovered from the concussion. Morose and convinced that a plot was afoot to remove him from command, all he wanted now was to return to his wife, Beatrice, in Compostela. In January 1542, he gave the order to clear out. Sixty of the men wanted to stay and try to make a go of it in this beautiful, desolate land. Some had fallen in love with Pueblo women. Others still hoped to find the gold over the next ridge. But Coronado denied their petitions, and they all left Tiguex together, except for three of the Franciscans, who stayed behind to begin missionary work. One of them went out on the Plains to bring the Gospel to the Wichitas and within the year was shot full of arrows by unknown Indians as he prayed on his knees for the Lord to receive his soul. The other two remained among the Pueblos. What became of them is not known.

Some months later, with Coronado confined to a litter and in deep depression, the expedition reached Compostela. As the leader of a costly two-year venture with nothing to show for it, Coronado fell quickly from favor. He was brought to trial for mismanagement and cruelty to the natives, and though acquitted of both charges, he died in obscurity twelve years later.

The Spiritual Conquista

With Coronado's failure to turn up any precious metals or stones or flourishing civilizations in the far north, interest in that part of the world dwindled. Exciting things were happening closer to home. Silver—rich veins of it—was struck in Zacatecas, north of Guadalajara, the very year Coronado returned, and the colony was transformed. Mexico City became the metropolis of the New World, rivaling in splendor the great European capitals.

Most of the loot from the mines was surrendered to God. It went into soaring spires and sixty-foot gilded altars, into flamboyant baroque visions of the glory to come that would serve for millions of poor devout mestizos, if nothing else, as refuges from the misery and squalor of the present. This magnificent flowering of ecclesiastical art could never have been achieved, of course, without native sweat and blood. The Church would proudly boast that in the first eighty years of Spanish rule the Indians built more than they had in the previous two thousand. Much of the loot was shipped back to the motherland and sunk into even more grandiose homages, like the Gothic cathedral of Seville. A deep otherworldliness was at the heart of the conquest.

Some of the loot was retained for worldly purposes, however. Not a few citizens of the viceroyalty became extremely rich, and those who did flaunted their wealth recklessly. By the early seventeenth century, two thousand or more coaches would circle the Alameda, one of the capital's great plazas, of an afternoon, the women done out in Chinese silks that had come on the Manila galleon, the men in rakish hats with pearl-and-diamond-embroidered bands.

Influenced by Bartolomé de Las Casas's exposé of the atrocities of the conquests of Peru, Mexico, and the Caribbean, the Council of the Indies in Seville outlawed the enslavement of cooperative Indians. The restriction did not apply to Africans and warlike Indians, however, and bodies were needed to extract the silver. The mine owners either ignored the law or got around it by taking advantage of several legal institutions. One was the *encomienda,* in which land was granted to a worthy individual by the crown and with the land came whatever Indians happened to be on it. The Indians were legally minors, and the *encomiendero* was theoretically their guardian: he was responsible for clothing and feeding them, educating them, and providing health care and religious instruction. In return for assuring their salvation in the world to come, they belonged to him in the here and now.

Eventually the *encomienda* was abolished, but there still remained the *repartimientos,* the estates granted to loyal subjects of the crown that became in effect feudal fiefdoms where the local Indians were treated as serfs, and the huge ranches, the haciendas and the latifundia, whose injustices would survive into this century and provoke the Mexican Revolution.

Some of the Indians resisted. Local tribes in central Mexico, north of the capital, held off the miners and colonists in the bloody but futile *chichimecos* wars until 1590. Others fled into mountains, deserts, and jungles. But most withdrew into themselves and submitted to physical subjugation, and most of them soon died. By 1568, less than fifty years after the arrival of the first Europeans, the native population of central Mexico had shrunk from an estimated 30 million to 3 million. By 1620 all but 1.6 million were dead from overwork, starvation, disease, and cultural demoralization—lack of will to live. Smallpox was the big killer. The Mayans called the plague *nohkakil,* the great fire. The only thing that kept the Indians of New Spain from being completely wiped out, like the Arawak and the Caribs in the Caribbean, were the efforts of the missionaries to keep the conquest "Christian and apostolic and not a butchery," and the fact that there was an awful lot of them scattered over a huge area. As my Navajo friend John put it, "Their immune system was zero for these types of diseases." Plague itself, introduced by ship rats, was also a sporadic problem.

The missionaries wanted the Indians' souls as badly as the miners and the colonists wanted their bodies, and in some places they were able to get to the Indians first and to offer them some protection against their more ruthless countrymen. It was these "barefoot men of god," as Herbert Bolton calls them, who became the pioneers of far northern New Spain. Barefoot like the meek and the poor, as a form of humbling themselves and mortifying the flesh. But did these padres actually walk barefoot hundreds of miles on searing desert sands? Meredith Dodge, a viceregal scholar at the University of New Mexico, familiar with the inventory lists of the wagon trains that came up to New Mexico from Chihuahua, told me that the Franciscans were issued one good pair of boots a year, and after these wore out, they wore sandals. The Jesuits, according to University of Arizona historian Bernard Fontana, weren't barefoot, either: they wore sandals.

Many of these priests were very dedicated, ready to give their lives to save the natives' heathen souls. As William Prescott wrote, the "reverend fathers" who came to New Spain to proselytize the Indians tended to be "godly persons," not "bishops and pampered prelates, who too often squandered the substance of the Church in riotous living," but "men of unblemished purity of life, nourished with the learning of the cloister," who "counted all personal sacrifices as little in the sacred cause to which they were devoted." In two hundred years of evangelizing in the north, 132 men of the cloth would be martyred. Yet it was they, of all the Spaniards, who had the most in common with their killers. Like the Indians, they had their own traditions of desert mysticism and self-denial, and they looked beyond the outer, material world for the meaning of life. When Fray Pedro de Ortega came to Taos Pueblo to offer his faith to them, he was refused a place to sleep and given ground-up field mice mixed with urine to eat. "For a good appetite there is no bad bread," he told his inhospitable hosts, cheerily downing the revolting fare. The Indians were impressed.

I spent a morning with the chronicler of the Jesuits in Mexico City, Padre Ignacio Peres Alonso, discussing the order's activities in New Spain. On a shelf in his book-lined study was a gilt-edged glass case containing the skull of the first Jesuit martyr, Padre Gonzalo de Tapia. He was decapitated in 1594 at the mission of San Félipe on the Sinaloa River, which was then the last outpost of civilization on the northern frontier, by a native shaman named Nacabeba who saw him as a threat to his power. The padre's preaching against polygamy had not gone over well at all. Also in the case were the femurs of two other Jesuits killed by Tepehuano Indians in the Sierra Madre in 1621. All three were canonized.

The Jesuits, who were known as Black Robes, came into the field in 1591, and they took on the evangelization of northwest Mexico (New Spain), Pimeria Alta, where the Pima lived, while the Brown Robes worked in the northeast, in New Mexico, in Pueblo country. The Jesuits were highly organized. Each man had seventeen years of training before he went into the field, Padre Ignacio told me. Starting at the age of seventeen, a Black Robe did three years of novitiate, then he studied the classics for the three years of his juniorate, maybe at the

College of Tepotzotlan, outside Mexico City. This college, which I visited a few days later, boasts one of the most beautiful churches in Mexico, with panels of gold-encrusted icons the height of five men and the
dress of the Virgin of Loreto on display in a downscaled replica of the
house where she appeared. From there the aspiring missionary went to
Mexico City or to nearby Puebla for three years of philosophy, then
four years of theology, capped by a year-long tertianship, in which he
mastered the complexities of canon law. Then after boning up on
Indian languages, missionary techniques, and arts and crafts that
would be useful on the frontier, at last he was ready for the field.

The Franciscan approach was different. The Franciscan evangelists'
training was mainly in self-denial. On my way to Compostela, I visited
one of the Franciscan training colleges that had been important for the
north in New Spain—the Apostolic College for the Propagation of the
Faith of the Most Holy Santa Cruz of the Miracles, a walled compound on the highest hill of Querétaro, a colonial city 140 miles northwest of Mexico City. One of the brothers interrupted a chess game to
show me around. He took me to a tree that, according to legend, had
miraculously sprouted from a cane one of his predecessors had thrust
in the ground centuries earlier, and then to one of the austere cells
where a trainee preparing for the field slept on a crude pallet and con-
templated a human skull placed on his bed table to remind him of
death, after which "the true life begins," the priest explained.

The first phase of fieldwork, the initial contact, was called, like the
conquistadores' forays, the *entrada*. Here is how the Jesuit father Eusebio Francisco Kino, who would spend two and a half decades spreading the faith in Sonora and southern Arizona, described his dicey
contact with the Guaicuros on the tip of Baja California in 1683. Kino
was fresh from Europe, and these were the first wild Indians he had
ever seen:

> On Tuesday morning . . . [we] heard some whoops of Indians
> who were coming toward this harbor . . . the Indians arrived
> shouting loudly, armed with bows and arrows, painted as a
> sign of war . . . and making signs that we should leave their
> lands. . . . We tried to make them understand that we came in
> peace and begged them to lay their weapons down on the
> ground, promising that we would do likewise, but they
> refused. Father Gony and I then went up to them, gave them
> maize, biscuits, and glass beads, which they refused to take
> from our hands, asking us to lay them down on the ground;
> but afterward they began to take them directly from our
> hands.

We now began to be very friendly and familiar and they gave us roasted mescal heads, which were very good,* little nets very well made, and feathers of birds which they wore on their heads, etc. We showed them a crucifix, and next day a statue of Our Lady of Guadalupe, but they gave no sign of being familiar with either of these things or anything else relating to the Catholic Faith. In the afternoon they went away very well content, although some of our men suspected that they could not be trusted.

Soon Father Kino had the Indians pronouncing "Jesus" and other Castilian words with s and f, even though their own language lacked these consonants. The work seemed to be progressing well. But then the missionaries' mulatto drummer boy disappeared. In fact he had found a fine pearl in one of the local oysters (the inner eastern shore of Baja abounds with pearls of fairly good quality and is therefore known as the Pearl Coast; see John Steinbeck's *The Sea of Cortez*), traded it to the Guaicuros for a canoe, and paddled across the gulf to freedom. The padres, however, suspected foul play on the part of the Guaicuros.

A few mornings later a hundred naked warriors showed up at the padres' camp. Thinking there was going to be trouble, the Spaniards dished out some *pozole,* or cornmeal mush, which the Guaicuros had shown a fondness for, and as they sat eating it, one of the soldiers who had come along to protect the padres gave the order for the small cannons to be fired into the unsuspecting group. Three Guaicuros were killed, the rest fled for their lives, and the mission was aborted.

The Jesuits specialized in dangerous contacts. In Paraguay they went alone into the jungle and lured the Guarani Indians from behind the trees with flutes and clarinets. In the hostile Apache country of Arizona, they carried a huge bell to a mountaintop and rang it. Smoke signals soon began to rise in the distance, and the next day hundreds of Apache came to see how the amazing sounds had been made.

The next phase of the missionaries' work was known as reducing. The Indians had to be persuaded to live together in one place, if they were not already doing so. It was explained to them through an interpreter that they would be fed and clothed and taught the true religion and would be better off medically, which wasn't true; in fact, living all

---

* "Mescal" is the Spanish generic word for maguey, century plant, or agave, of which there are dozens of species. It also refers to the tequila fermented from it. The hearts are densely fibrous, with a pulp that becomes deliciously sweet, like butterscotch or thickened custard, after being roasted for several days, and this is a popular dish in its range, northern Mexico, to this day.

together, with contagious Spaniards among them, they were sitting ducks for smallpox, measles, flu, and other European microbes to which they had no resistance. Those who were amenable were herded into large compounds known as *reducciones* and subjected to a spartan routine of fieldwork and worship. Disobedient Indians were to receive no more than sixteen lashes unless they were very disobedient; then they got twenty-five. Still, the native people were a lot better off with the padres than they would have been on the secular setups, the *repartimientos* and the *encomiendas*, or working in the mines.

The Christian message went over with varying success from tribe to tribe. The Spaniards taught the women of each tribe to weave and wear a *rebozo*, or shawl, in a special sequence of stripes, sort of like a regimental tie. These distinctive tribal *rebozos* are still worn by Indian women through Mexico. The *rebozo* of the Purepecha, a large tribe in the state of Michoacán, for instance, has purple and white stripes on a black background.

The missionaries were instructed to build the church near, or if possible right on top of, the Indians' traditional religious center. It was no accident that the dark-skinned Virgin of Guadalupe first appeared—on December 12, 1531, to an Aztec peon named Juan Diego—on the Hill of Tepeyac outside Mexico City, right near the sanctuary of the Aztec goddess Tonantzin. This sort of syncretic superimposition had been going on for centuries. The Church of the Virgin Sopra Minerva had been built over the Temple of Minerva in Rome, and the Copacaba Virgin just happened to appear on the island in Lake Titicaca where the Incas, who had to be dissuaded from their sun worship if the missionaries were going to get anywhere with them, believed the sun was born.

The traditional peoples' advocacy group in Albuquerque that put me in touch with the Navajo resisters on Big Mountain called itself Tonantzin, after the Aztec goddess catholicized into the Virgin of Guadalupe. Its symbol was a cross on the apex of a pyramid, a merging of spiritual traditions, Indians and Chicanos common-causing against the Anglo invader. One day I had lunch with the soft-spoken but intense director of Tonantzin, David Lujan, whose is of old *nuevomejicano* stock, and a young Navajo colleague named Lori, at Baca's on Central Avenue. Sitting with them, I could feel their deep sadness for their lost sovereignty, for their violated homelands, Aztlan (as Chicanos call the northern two-thirds of Mexico that was annexed by the United States) and Dinetah. I had the sensation that this restaurant and the traffic moving through the window down Central Avenue and the entire modern envelope we were in—Sloganworld—was an illusion, that underneath this thin, toxic layer of vinyl and tarmac, and the strident, tacky commercial assault, was something much older and deeper. I asked David if the merging of Christianity and traditional religion was good or bad, and he said, "Neither. That's just the way it is. At this point we can't do anything about it."

The appearance of a dark-skinned Aztec virgin was an important step in putting the Word over. Now the Indians had their own Virgin; the message was proprietary. If their heathen beliefs couldn't be completely abolished, they could at least be incorporated *poco a poco*. Get them singing the hymns, wearing the clothes. Often the best that could be done was a sort of compromise. The Indians came only partway. They believed, say, that if you were good, you went to heaven, but if you were bad, you went back into the desert as an animal. The Zuñi continued to worship their old idols for centuries, which, unknown to the Franciscans, were hidden behind the altar of the church.

Lapses into "paganism" were dealt with in the early years by the Holy Office of the Inquisition in Mexico. In 1539 the powerful Texcoco cacique, Don Carlos Chichimecatecuhtli, who had been inhibiting the work of the missionaries, was burned at the stake. In 1544 reports reached the ears of the Inquisitors that the nobles of Yanhuitalan were offering sacrifices with their own blood and hair, birds, and slaves, who were first cruelly tortured, in caves of the Suchitepéquez region. This was brutally stopped. Don Juan, the head cacique of the Mixtec, was caught performing and later eating human sacrifices to the rain god. His excuse was that he was only trying to alleviate the drought and famine that were ravaging his people. He, too, was put to death. That year, down in Oaxaca, a priest visited the shrine where the caciques of Coatlan were wont to offer sacrifices, and he found a large stone idol with a human heart, freshly torn from a child, in its mouth and sixteen human heads lying about. All these abominable infractions were summarily dealt with.

Most receptive to the Word were the Rancheria People, like the Opata, on the Pacific Coast. Already living in villages, these *indios de pueblo* were more readily reduced than the *indios barbaros,* the roving collectors of wild food like the Toboso, the Guasave, and the Seri, who bolted at the slightest interference with their freedom of movement. Certain tribes were hopeless. The Yaqui would resist all approaches from the *yori,* or white man, until early in this century.

The New Treasure of the Sierra Madre

o tribe in New Spain gave the missionaries a harder time than the Tarahumara. To this day most of the members of this tribe have little or nothing to do with Mexican society. Officially, there are some fifty thousand Tarahumara, but there may be twice as many, scattered along drainages in loose clusters of interrelated families known as *ranchos,* their flimsy, slapdash dwellings within shouting distance of one another. The most traditional people in the Greater Southwest continuum, and the largest indigenous group in North America after the Navajo, they are, in terms of their relationship with the modern world, where the Hopi were a hundred years ago.

The Tarahumara live in the rugged southwestern corner of the state of Chihuahua, in the heart of the Sierra Madre Occidental, in a rectangle roughly 375 miles by 150, which bears their name and remains one of the largest "unreduced" pockets, and one of the largest, least disturbed wildernesses, in North America. This is the jagged range immortalized by Bogart and Huston in the unforgettable movie of B. Traven's *The Treasure of the Sierra Madre* and celebrated among wilderness lovers for Copper Canyon, a system of tangled, immense chasms, four of which are deeper than the Grand. But in recent years drug growers have been taking over the back canyons and enslaving the local Tarahumara and Tepehuano, forcing them to grow marijuana and poppy and killing those who refuse. In 1994 an average of four Indians per week were reported murdered in the sierra.

I've gone up into this magical, canyon-riddled wilderness three times. The first was in 1986, after my visit to El Fuerte and the albinos. The following morning I joined a group of campesinos waiting for the train from Los Mochis, which goes up over the sierra to Chihuahua City and is one of the world's most scenic train rides. The campesinos were sitting on cardboard boxes tied with string and were keeping to their own thoughts under straw cowboy hats. In English this activity would be described as "hanging out," "hanging," or "chilling." In the Greater Southwest Hispanic continuum, there is a gradient of expressions, conforming to what might be described as zones of vernacular latitude. In central Mexico the expression is *tragando caña*—literally, sucking sugarcane; in Chihuahua it is *comiendo moscas,* eating flies; in the rural Rio Arriba of northern New Mexico, a Chicano would be more apt to say *chingando la borega,* fucking the sheep. *Ola Hieronimo.* Whazzappenin' *vato?* Whadyou binupto bro? Oh I jus' bin on the ranch *chingando la borega.*

I kept asking the stationmaster when the train was coming, and he kept holding up a small space between his thumb and forefinger and assuring me it would be here in *un ratito.* The morning passed. Unpacking my small portable library, I boned up on the native people I was about to meet. The word "Tarahumara" is a Spanish distortion of the people's word for themselves, Rarámuri, meaning "Footrunners." The men of the tribe play a game that consists of kicking a hard wooden ball the size of a croquet ball and chasing it in relays, sometimes for two days, until one team beats the other to a finish line often a hundred miles away. According to the anthropologist John G. Kennedy, "The ball . . . is not actually kicked, but is lifted into the air in a motion so rapid that it looks like kicking." The women, who also run, keep a hoop rolling for as many as forty miles, like the Acoma and Zuñi kick-stick racers. In his book *Indian Running,* Peter Nabokov writes that a crowd cheers the runners to the finish line, but there is no recognition of the winner. "Once the finish line is crossed it often seems as if the event had never happened. Observors are surprised when the Tarahumara who wins a two-day race for his team walks away virtually ignored. There is a sense of anticlimax as the victor assumes normal stature and life goes on."

The Tarahumara keep running well into their sixties. Carl Lumholtz in 1894 encountered Tarahumara running "easily 170 miles without stopping." The naturalist Ernest Thompson Seton reported a postman "who routinely covered 70 miles a day, seven days a week, bearing a heavy mailbag," and delivered letters and parcels "at an easy run." Several Tarahumara were recruited to run the marathon for Mexico in the 1928 summer Olympics, at Amsterdam, but they were a disappointment. Pacing themselves, they crossed the line minutes behind the front runners, and kept running. No one had explained that the race was only 26 miles, 385 yards long. "Too short," they complained. "It seemed the Tarahumaras, as with other Indians, found it difficult to extract their running prowess from its cultural context and reshape it to fit the white man's criteria for competitive sports," writes Nabokov. Moreover, "running in endless circles bored them" and gave them bad dreams. Their idea of running is to splash through streams and vault boulders.

Tall, lean, long legged, with high cheekbones and beaklike noses, the men wear white shirts untucked, wide woolen belts with geometric designs woven on them by their women, headbands, loincloths that resemble diapers, and the standard Latin American tire-tread sandals or huaraches. The women wear layers of colorful skirts. Of the 36,145 members of the tribe counted in 1980, 10,605 didn't speak Spanish. The preponderance of these were women. The most traditional Tarahumara, who have rejected Christianity or were never brought into the fold, live in the remote and inaccessible back canyons and are known as *gentiles*. Unfortunately, these practically unpoliceable canyons, where you can harvest two crops of *mota* and *chutama*, marijuana and opium poppy, a year, are the most desirable sites for illicit plantations, and it is the *gentiles* who are being done the most violence by the *narcotraficantes*. The modern world they are trying to check out of is pursuing them with a vengeance.

The Tarahumara are thought to be the descendants of the Mogollon, contemporaries of the Anasazi whose pit houses straggled the ridges of the Mogollon Highlands, along the New Mexico–Arizona border, and who fade out of the archaeological record around 1200. Their inner life, based on an ancient, rich animistic belief system, is as intricate as their outer existence, their material culture, is austere and rudimentary. Christianity, to the extent that it has penetrated the Tarahumara worldview at all, has become something quite different. Many of the baptized *(bautizados)* are only nominal Christians and still hold to the old beliefs. They follow the basic Tarahumara code: to walk in silence and not to steal or do bad things (that is, magic) that will make people sick.

The Tarahumara traditionally venerate the sun, the moon, lightning, wind, shooting stars, the spirits of certain trees, rocks, caves, and streams more than the Holy Trinity. They sacrifice roosters, lambs, goats, and cows to Father Sun so that he will not fall on them or bring drought or early snow. Solar eclipses make them uneasy because they believe the sun is sick, and if the sun dies, they will, too. An owl hooting in the night is a death omen, and a coyote crying at you is a warning sign, calling for family protection ceremonies. Rainbows are feared because they sneak up on men while they are tending sheep and make them faint, then grab their children. Each of the rainbow's bands is a stolen child. Women are kidnapped by little elves known as *rurubi*, by snakes that take the form of old boyfriends, and in the old days by bears, who used to wall them up in caves, until the Tarahumara chased all the bears away with rocks and slings.

The men drive deer over cliffs and run them down, yet they tell a story about a deer that was being chased by their dogs who turned into a beautiful woman and stopped the dogs in their tracks. Animals used to talk because they were in fact transformed humans, but one day humans suddenly lost the power to change into animals, and those who were at that moment in animal form were stuck that way forever. People still become animals when they die. You can tell which animal the deceased has become because its tracks will show up in the ashes sprinkled around his corpse, which is wrapped in a blanket with the eyes closed and the arms folded and is provided with *piñole* (cracked corn), corn beer, and tortillas—with plenty of food for your long journey, the mourners gathered round the body keep telling it, so there is no reason for you to come back and plague our sleep or bring us illness. Dreaming about the dead can cause miscarriage.

Central to the Tarahumara inner cosmos is the belief in multiple souls: heterosexual males have three; females four; and homosexuals, embodying both sexes, thus have seven. "Each of these souls enjoys some autonomy," writes ethnologist William L. Merrill in his fascinating study, *Rarámuri Souls*. "Different souls can be in different places at the same time and can experience different fates after they leave the body at death. In this view, the souls within a single body are of two kinds, large souls and small souls. The many small souls reside principally in the joints but can also be in other parts of the body." Some Tarahumara shamans specialize in peyote, which plays a key role in the tribe's spiritual life; others in medicinal plants, of which there are hundreds; and others in dream interpretation and tracking down errant souls.

Tarahumara have a long-standing, understandable distrust of *chabochi*, variously translated as spider faces or whiskered ones, their main term for white Europeans, either Hispanic or Anglo; another term means hairy asses. Gringos are *bringos*. The souls of *chabochi* go automatically to the underworld because they are the sons of the devil. They have no hope for redemption. But the soul of a *chabochi* who has slept with a Tarahumara goes to heaven, while the soul of a Tarahumara who has slept with a *chabochi* goes to live with the dead.

· · ·

At last the train pulled in, the *primero especial,* the showcase of the line, with a vista dome, dining car, plush air-conditioned cars with romantic music gushing from overhead speakers, and liveried porters who spoke English. But it was full. Another train was just behind, the conductor told me, apologetically, blocking the door. After another hour this train pulled in—the *pollero,* the chicken train, steerage class. It was even fuller, but there was always room for a few more. The campesinos and I got on. I found a spot in a packed aisle where I could sit on my duffel bag. The train lurched forward, and after several hours the monotonous thorn scrub began to acquire some relief as we rose into the *bajada,* the piedmont—prime marijuana-growing country.

Back to the books.

The history of Tarahumara-Spanish relations has been characterized by *mucho sangre e fuego,* a lot of blood and fire, in the words of one history of the evangelization of New Spain. Some of the bloodiest revolts and reprisals on the colonial frontier took place in the Tarahumara. The basic problem was that the Tarahumara lived, and still live, in scattered nuclear families with maybe twenty families per *rancho* and weren't amenable to being "reduced." The only time they see people from other *ranchos* is once every month or two when they get together for a corn beer party, an institutionalized blowout known as a *tesguinada,* where corn beer, or *tesguina,* is brewed in huge vats. These affairs enable the men from one *rancho* to meet the women from another and thus introduce new blood to communities, helping reduce inbreeding, and they make it possible for the Tarahumara to get out of themselves. The Tarahumara are very modest and inhibited and naturally shy, and there is a lot of sleeping around at these gatherings, everybody getting bombed and pairing off and sneaking into the bushes. Lumholtz remarks that if it wasn't for the *tesguinadas,* the race would have died out long ago. Sexual activity is said to be infrequent except on these occasions.

The problems with evangelizing such people were immense. The only part of the Christian message they could readily relate to was the concept of Satan; to this day, they have a healthy dread of the devil and his allies, the Water People, who kidnap the souls of the unwary along streams. Father Jacob Neumann wrote in 1682, a year after he had arrived in the Tarahumara:

> Our labors consist in converting and baptizing the natives, founding settlements, persuading the Indians to leave their caves and scattered hovels, and to adopt a civilized life, thus forming them, so to speak, into a corporate body. We compel them to live in villages near the church, which we build in

convenient locations where the country is more open. This is a very difficult task. For—to explain their character a little—while these people were still heathen ... they were accustomed to live, not in groups, but separately, far from one another. With their wives and children they dwelt in mountain caves or in huts built of straw, which seemed more suitable for catching birds than for human habitation.

Neumann would spend fifty years among the Tarahumara without, apparently, coming close to understanding them. Years later, he wrote:

These Indians are by nature and disposition a sly and crafty folk, from whom sincerity is not to be expected. They are accomplished hypocrites, and as a rule, the ones who seem most virtuous should be considered the most wicked of all. . . . In fact, I cannot deny that with these stoney-hearted people the result does not repay the hard labor of the valuable seed. . . . They show no aversion to sin, no anxiety about their eternal happiness, no eagerness to be persuaded by their relatives to be baptized. They show rather a lazy indifference to everything good, unlimited sensual desire [in fact the opposite seems to be the case], an irresistible habit of getting drunk, and stubborn silence in regard to hidden pagans [the *gentiles*], and so we cannot find them and bring them into the fold of Christ.

The initial contact was made by Father Juan Fonte, who wrote, optimistically, in 1607: "I am in a happy and enthusiastic state of mind, seeing the door now opened to us for numerous conversions, especially since these developments can go forward without the aid of captains and soldiers."

Fonte persuaded some of the Tarahumara to move into the San Pablo Valley with their old enemies, the Tepehuano. He and his successors gave them steel axes and plows, taught them how to make better use of their farmland, introduced the Spanish form of local government, and gave them sheep, which they hoped would make the Indians settle together in larger groups but had the opposite effect of dispersing them ever more widely; now that they had a portable source of protein, they weren't so completely dependent on corn.

After he had been there ten years, Father Fonte was killed in a rebellion led by a charismatic Tepehuano named Quantles, to whom God spoke through a small stone idol he carried with him, promising resurrection to all who died fighting the Spaniards.

Then silver was struck at Parral, in the southeastern Tarahumara, and many of the tribe were forced to work in the mines. By the middle of the seventeenth century the majority of the Tarahumara were disillusioned with the reduction program, and they realized that they would always be dependent on subsidies from the outside world if they lived as the missionaries wanted them to and that the only way to survive as Tarahumara was to live as they had always lived—scattered.

Revolts of apostates, bitterly opposed to everything Spanish, erupted in 1646, 1650, and 1652. A Neapolitan father was strung up on a cross and decapitated. Measles and smallpox epidemics in 1666 and 1668 deepened the disaffection, and more Jesuits were killed in 1690. More smallpox epidemics broke out in that decade. The rumor among the Tarahumara was that smallpox was spread by church bells; very possibly the actual vector was baptismal water. The 1695 epidemic, the worst of all, precipitated a revolt that took two years to quell. It ended with the severed heads of thirty of its leaders being posted on the road to the village of Comcomorach. This was the Tarahumara's last attempt at active resistance. From then on, they practiced avoidance and withdrawal, the mask that Octavio Paz describes in *The Labyrinth of Solitude* as a Mexican national trait, but that many marginalized and exploited Native Americans in Latin America, such as the Quechua of the Peruvian Andes, wear.

In 1767 the Jesuits were expelled from the New World, and the twenty-nine missions and at least fifty-five *visitas* (outposts that a padre would visit every month or so to minister to his flock) that they had established in the Tarahumara were left in the hands of the Indians. The tribe became progressively isolated until the beginning of this century, when missionaries returned and futile efforts to bring the Tarahumara into the fold began anew.

By midafternoon we were climbing up the magnificent gorge of the Septentrion River in a series of death-defying switchbacks, working our way up through a zone of small, warped oaks and cascades tumbling into limpid pools, until at last we reached the upper plateau, a realm of pines and pasture and pure mountain air, of log cabins and *ciénagas,* wet meadows ablaze with buttercups and irises. It seemed like Colorado, except the Indians still predominated, and there was a virtual absence of modern infrastructure.

The Sierra Madre, or Mother Range, is part of the cordillera running from Alaska to Patagonia that was heaved up a hundred million years ago as the Americas separated from the Pangaea supercontinent and slammed into submerged tectonic plates out in the Pacific. The Rockies disappear in the desert around Albuquerque, and after a hiatus of several hundred miles, the cordillera crops up again as the Sierra

Madre Occidental. The highest point of the range is 3,992-meter Mount Mohinora.

In the millennia that followed, west-flowing arteries of the Fuerte River ate through multicolored, cave-riddled bands of gray volcanic tuff, pink rhyolite, and laramide limestone, carving stupendous barrancas. According to the Tarahumara version, the barrancas were made by the feet of Crow as he walked across the land. The snow that blankets the sierra in winter melts in the air before it reaches the canyon floors more than a mile below, whose life-forms include figs and citrus trees, vampire bats and the malaria plasmodium. But on the upper plateau, whose average elevation is 7,500 feet, there is ponderosa parkland, as in Colorado, but with Mexican touches—hummingbirds zipping around wispy stalks of sotol. The Sierra Madre Occidental has twenty-three of Mexico's fifty-eight pine species—more than anywhere else in the world. Under the pines are two hundred–some kinds of oak and a host of jays and woodpeckers. The temperate zone and the tropics interdigitate here, producing weird juxtapositions: parrots screaming among maples, orchids and bromeliads sprouting in the crotches of walnuts. The sierra is a neglected megacenter of biodiversity, but rapacious lumber companies, drug growers, and the drug-eradication effort are causing a lot of damage. Species of birds, butterflies, and reptiles are going extinct, some of them before they have even been identified.

The Tarahumara call five kinds of small, spiny, gray, pincushion-like cacti that cling to rock peyote, but none of them are *Lophophora williamsii,* the one with psychotropic alkaloids. It grows down in the Chihuahuan Desert, east of the Sierra Madre Occidental. The Tarahumara used to make a two-week trek to get it. Now they go in trucks.

It was their peyote cult that attracted Antonin Artaud, the tormented French writer and founder of the Theater of Cruelty, into the Sierra Madre in 1936, or so he claimed. Disillusioned with Europe, where the Fascist curtain was falling, longing to meet people not yet "perverted by civilization," himself malnourished and suffering the torture of opium withdrawal, Artaud made his way on horseback up into the sierra, communicating with his Indian guide mainly through gesticulation. There, as he reported in a strange little book called *Les Tarahumaras,* he submitted to "the peyote cure" and spent three days that were "the happiest of my existence"—unless, as some scholars believe, he made the whole thing up, as Carlos Castañeda did his experiences with peyote under the direction of a fictitious Yaqui Indian whom he called Don Juan.*

The train stopped at a point on the Continental Divide called El Divisadero. Everyone got out and walked to the edge of the stupendous Copper Canyon, plunging six thousand feet in cave-riddled tiers. Tarahumara women in kerchiefs and voluminous skirts sat along the path to the overlook before displays of baskets, dolls, and sashes they had made—early tourist stuff, with no cultural meaning, like the dolls the Hopi started to make in the fifties for the tourists who came to their snake dance. The women wore the same blank expression as the Otomis and Mixtec women I had seen sitting on the sidewalks of Mexico City, waiting for passersby to flip them a coin. I aligned a topographical map I had picked up in the capital with the view. Two barrancas over, there was an old silver-mining town called Batopilas, where I hoped to hire a guide and some burros and poke around in the back barrancas for a few days.

I got back on the train, and after dark, it pulled into Creel, the main town in the high sierra, founded by the wealthy turn-of-the-century banker, miner, landowner, and governor of Chihuahua, Enrique C. Creel. The serflike conditions in which the *peónes* lived on his 1.7-million-acre hacienda helped spark the Mexican Revolution. The Creels were the inspiration of the Mirandas in Carlos Fuentes's novel *The Old Gringo*. But Enrique's motive for founding Creel was allegedly humanitarian. In 1906 the Tarahumara were being encroached on by miners for the umpteenth time. "Scarcely a month, week, or day passes but that there comes to this government a deputation of Indians complaining of dispossession of their small and deteriorating land," he wrote, and he decided to start a colony to "congregate and educate" the Tarahumara and "economically better their lives."

But none of this happened. Creel became a mestizo center, not a Tarahumara center, assuming a role comparable to the one Gallup,

---

* The Yaqui, who live in the foothills of the Sierra Madre to the north of the Tarahumara, do not traditionally take peyote. Not to diminish his achievement, but Castañeda, according to his debunkers, apparently never left the UCLA library and subsequently dodged attempts to locate or produce his guru. The southwestern "hooey" tradition, as a friend in Sedona, Arizona, calls it, is a rich one and spreads into many domains—literature, real estate, mining, mysticism. The psychologist and writer Richard de Mille exposed Don Juan as a hoax in two books, *Castañeda's Journey* and *The Don Juan Papers*. But in a later essay, collected in *The Invented Indian*, edited by James A. Clifton, which distinguishes between two components of truth—validity and authenticity—de Mille concedes that Don Juan's teachings are valid because they ring true, even though the ethnology is spurious and they are inauthentic because their source is not the fictitious Don Juan.

New Mexico, has for the Navajo except that Creel is smaller, less rowdy, and dry (the sale of liquor to the Tarahumara is forbidden, although there's a tradition of bootlegging going back at least to the time of Lumholtz).

I got off the train. It was raining hard. A boy came up to me and asked me if I was looking for a place to stay. I said I was, and shouldering my duffel bag, he led me through muddy streets redolent of wood smoke, past poncho-wrapped forms huddling under dripping eaves, to a tin-roofed log cabin—his mother's house. She took in guests. I ended up bunking in an outbuilding with a young mestizo from an outlying town who had just come down from Salt Lake City, returning triumphantly with booty from *el otro lado*—flashy cowboy boots, a big ghetto blaster, and a suitcase of presents for his brothers and sisters, which he had bought with wages for illegal work on an assembly line.

The next morning I caught a succession of rides to a *rancho* about thirty miles away, where a Tarahumara woman, whose name I had been given by an anthropologist, lived. She had lived in Denver and was used to dealing with *bringos*. We talked for a couple of hours, after which she arranged for me to walk back to Creel with her cousin, who had not been to Creel in several years, but he wanted to buy an ax head he had been saving up for. The man and I spent that afternoon and the following morning in each other's company and spent the night on the kitchen floor of some mestizos, and during this whole time we must not have exchanged more than a dozen words. We parted company in Creel. A few hours later, I saw him sitting on a curb in the plaza, staring off into space and fingering his ax head. Eventually, having had the Creel experience, he got up and headed back home.

The following morning I set off on foot for Batopilas. After several hours a mestizo family in a pickup stopped for me, and I got in back with a little old leather-faced Tarahumara man. I extended my hand, and he grazed my palm timidly with his fingers.

The old man had with him a gnarled walking stick, a long bamboo pole for knocking off pitahaya cactus fruit, which were ripening, and, in a small plastic shopping bag, a snail, a string of large orange mushrooms (*Amanita caesarea,* one of the few edible members of an otherwise lethal genus), and a hard wooden ball the size of a croquet ball, which I gathered from his pidgin Spanish he had carved from the burl of an oak tree. I asked what the ball was for, and he said for *rajalipame,* the kick-ball relay race. The balls are also made of madrona. The old man's face was as wrinkled as a prune, and his glittering eyes were full of mischief.

The driver stopped and tried to hit a rock squirrel—a delicacy for both Tarahumara and mestizos—with stones, but it dived into some boulders, and we drove on. Soon afterward, in the middle of nowhere, the old man tapped the roof of the cab, the driver stopped, and he got out. I asked where he was going. He pointed east, at miles of pine-fringed crags, and set out walking in the Tarahumara way—ramrod straight, even leaning slightly backward, and picking his feet up high, almost goose-stepping, so as not (if my theory is correct) to trip in his huaraches and stub his bare toes.

Late in the afternoon, we reached the rim of Batopilas Canyon, a wild, awesome gorge, though a little smaller than Copper Canyon. Thousands of feet below, a twisted segment of the Batopilas River slithered in a scrub-slathered crevice, appearing, by an optical illusion having to do with the diminishing height of the receding canyon walls, to be flowing toward us, into the depths of the canyon; in fact, it was going the other way, toward El Fuerte, which was maybe a week downstream, if you made it past the rapids and the *traficantes*.

The road into the canyon zigzagged vertiginously down the sequence of life zones, back into desert scrub, with roadrunners scuttling under thirty-foot *mescales,* or century plants, and it descended the mile-thick sequence of volcanic strata to the limestone, sandstone, quartzite, and granitoid basement rock on the canyon floor. These heavily fractured lower units of the Sierra Madre Occidental were intruded some forty-five million years ago by slanted fissure veins of dacite and porphyry, and in these veins there occur, in podlike concentrations, coils, balls, ferns, and herringbone spikes of crystalline silver. The Sierra Madre is the world's richest epithermal silver province, and Batopilas has been one of its most productive districts, yielding, over three and a half centuries, an estimated three hundred million ounces of silver from more than three hundred mines, many of whose locations are lost, as the town's records burned twice in the eighteenth century. You can still supposedly wash a third of an ounce of tracings from your hair after bathing in the river.

In 1632 a small party of Spanish fortune seekers spotted polished nuggets of snow-white silver glittering in the river. A century later Don Rafael Alonso de Pastrana made such a fortune from an outcropping vein he was working that he laid a sidewalk of solid ingots in the village. In 1861 an American company hit an even-richer blind vein. This Veta Grande, or Great Vein, as it was called, was held at one point for two months by bandits, who extracted an estimated hundred thousand dollars' worth of the metal before "tiring of the mining life," as

Wendell E. Wilson and Chris E. Panczner relate in an article on Batopilas for the *Mineralogical Record.*

In 1880 an American, Alex R. Shepherd, bought up twelve square miles of the canyon, dug the Porfirio Díaz tunnel, which was the longest mine shaft on earth, and built the Hacienda San Miguel, at the time one of the most imposing structures in the North American west. The ore was sent for smelting to Aurora, Illinois, in wetted leather bags known as *zurrónes,* and Shepherd had an upright piano carried in by twenty-five Tarahumara who, spelling each other every thirty minutes, took several weeks to make the 185-mile delivery. After the revolution, the market for Mexican silver bottomed out, sending Batopilas into, Wilson and Panczner continue, "a more or less permanent decline." Today it is yet another town living in the shadow of its former greatness, like Compostela, San Blas, El Fuerte, like many a Mexican place, like Mexico in general. Its eight hundred souls tend goats and grow corn, beans, and squash and probably other things on the canyon's upper slopes. A few lone panners still sift sludge along the river, making just enough to get by. The new treasure of the Sierra Madre is vegetable, and as in El Fuerte, the local economy and moral fabric, such as they are, have been subverted by the *traficantes,* who are becoming increasingly brutal and brazen. In 1992 a group of naturalists from Tucson botanizing in the canyon strayed too close to some poppy fields. Two of the men were pistol-whipped, and one of the women was raped. The following year Alan Weisman, who was doing a piece for the *Los Angeles Times Magazine,* walked into a dead-silent restaurant in Batopilas where four gold-festooned *traficantes* in lizard-skin cowboy boots were eating. They had stacked their semiautomatics on the cook's lap. Five Tarahumara had just been massacred, and another two were hiding in the ruins of the Jesuit mission. "Beautiful place, bad people" was one Sierra Madre native's verdict on Batopilas.

The floor of Batopilas Canyon was tropical, with citrus and bamboo crowding the riverbank, roots of tescalama figs dripping down road cuts and boulders like wax from melted candles. After several hours of driving along the river, we spotted an elaborate stone aqueduct—one of Shepherd's improvements—running along the opposite bank, and several miles later we crossed a bridge and pulled into Batopilas, a long, straggling line of whitewashed, tile-roofed colonial buildings, with bougainvillea offsetting their decay, the single narrow street full of burros and piglets, a young Tarahumara in a white blouse and loincloth bent under a dresser several times his weight that he was carrying with a tumpline, an albino in a doorway, two men looking up from a pool table and taking in the new gringo who just blew into town.

I hung out for two days in Batopilas, followed the Porfirio Díaz tunnel for half a mile until I shined up a snake with my flashlight, tubed the warm, shallow, riffled river with some kids, went to the weekly movie, an old black-and-white Mexican western projected on a sheet, which most of the town turned out for, and made discreet inquiries about the drug trade, which had evidently arrived in the midseventies, although the citizens of Batopilas had grown poppies on their windows long before that, because the flower was pretty. At last I found a man who owned a mule and two pack burros and was up for taking me to the town of Urique, in the next canyon—a day or two's trip. His name was Chalo Diaz, and he was hard-bitten and around fifty. The closest thing to a smile, the only rise I ever managed to get out of him, was a slight curl of the upper lip. He took along his son Martín to help drive the burros. Martín was a sullen twelve-year-old who beat the life out of toads and harmless snakes in the path with his stick. He was not a child in the pampered, bracketed First World sense.

We passed a cactus wren burbling from the tip of a pitahaya cactus, its head thrown back, and at dusk reached the homestead of a gold prospector who Chalo knew had gone to Chihuahua City to sell his monthly pouch of dust and wouldn't mind if we crashed on his porch. The man's wife had died a few years back, Chalo told me, and he lived here alone. It was a beautiful spot, with fireflies flickering in the boulder-strewn riverbed below. In the morning Martín rounded up the animals. Packing each burro was a three-man job, with Chalo and Martín on either side, tying down the load, while I held the animal's ears. I pointed out to Chalo a bleeding puncture wound on one of the burro's necks. *Vampiro,* he explained. We finished our coffee and beans and started up the narrow canyon—Chalo, agile as a goat, scrambling up the steep, rocky trail and driving the burros with mournful yips and curses, prodding and whacking them with a branch, Martín behind him, hurrying to keep up, and me on the mule.

At ten we reached the dozen huts of Cerro Colorado. Only women and children, mestizos shyly crowding doorways, were in the village. A child ran to its mother in tears as we approached. I asked Chalo where the men were. *Quien sabe?* he said. "Is this one of the areas where they grow marijuana and poppy?" I asked innocently.

"No. Not here," he said quickly. The trail, in places barely a foot wide, now led up to a series of treacherous talus slopes. It may have been the same path that Lumholtz took when he came over into the Batopilas Canyon and two of his burros lost their footing and careened over precipices. Lumholtz didn't have much luck with his animals. On another occasion, one of the mules slipped and got wedged in a tree several hundred feet below the trail. The crate containing Lumholtz's library burst open, "scattering the wisdom of the ages to the winds."

We rose out of the tropics into the temperate zone, through dense acacia thickets into a stunted forest of gray oak, emory oak, Mexican live oak, manzanita, and two kinds of red-limbed madrone. Chalo unpacked the burros and let them graze in a patch of ragweed. I watched two iridescent beetles at my feet roll a ball of goat dung many times their size. Looking back across the canyon, Chalo pointed out the shacks of some *gentiles* on an alplike grassy slope just below the opposite rim, at roughly eye level, several miles away as the crow flies. Wondering how people could live in such isolation, I asked how often they came down to the little village, hours below, and he said hardly ever. The trail continued along a ridge above a branch canyon, the Barranca de Plantana, which plunged thousands of feet off to the right and was so deep and narrow we couldn't see its bottom, then led under the soaring cliffs of the Cerro El Manzano, which were encrusted with shocks of wild pineapple and tangled whorls of maguey, until, at last, we came up on the plateau. The rest of the day passed through an open, level parkland, an unearthly bower of ponderosa pines and gamma grass, with hummingbirds zipping around among wispy stalks of sotol (the preferred fiber for baskets and sombreros), raucous flocks of Mexican jays, streams tumbling in deep, greenish pools just the right temperature for skinny-dipping, which I did while Chalo and his son, too inhibited to strip in front of a gringo, waited uncomfortably.

Toward evening we reached the summer farm of some people from Batopilas whom I shall call the Muñozes, a warm, tight, wholesome family who welcomed us with hot chocolate and seemed right out of *Little House on the Prairie*. A handsome young man had just hiked up from the bottom of the Barranca de Urique to pitch woo to their pretty auburn-haired eighteen-year-old daughter. He seemed like a serious young man who planned to make something of himself; the family clearly approved of the courtship. The kitchen was earthy and soot-blackened but immaculately neat and organized, like those of wood-burning fellahin, tribal and posttribal, the world over.

Here I was definitely separated from my Black Stallion folding knife, a beautiful razor-sharp blade that had already been stolen from my side bag once before, while I was dancing in a village deep in the Ituri forest of Zaire. But my guides, sterling young men of the Walese tribe, were furious and had refused to leave the village without it. Finally, one of them found it stuffed in the thatch of the *barazza* (the African equivalent of a ramada). The Muñozes were mortified, and everyone started looking for it, but this time it was gone.

One suspect was the Tarahumara man who lived with his family over a small, striking outcrop; the two families seemed to have some sort of a symbiotic relationship. The Tarahumara lived in a wall-less thatched hut with a sleeping loft that was on another level of earthiness from the Muñozes' adobe farmhouse and was far more exposed to the elements. I wondered how they made it through the winter. Other Tarahumara live in walled-in overhangs and in stone-walled huts with grooved beams for runoff, which are laid next to each other for roofs. Not surprisingly, they have a lot of respiratory problems.

Maybe Chalo himself took it. He admired it greatly, couldn't take his eyes off it. I had bought the knife on Key Largo and knew I would never find one again I liked as much, but what was this theft compared to the theft of these people's land, culture, and soul committed by my fellow gringos? *Já era,* as the Brazilians say. It was history. I came to accept the loss of my favorite knife as a kind of tax for being white and First World, a member of the privileged class.

Delicately, that afternoon (I didn't notice the knife was missing till the following morning), I had steered the conversation to drugs. The young man from Urique seemed to know a lot about them. He said that the Cerro Colorado Canyon was a big center of poppy production, but the army had just swept through and wiped out many of the fields. I stole a glance at Chalo, who looked sheepish having been caught in his lie, with "the parakeet fluttering in his mouth," then I took out my notebook; the young man was the first good source I'd run into on the trip. But when he saw the notebook, he suddenly became very nervous and said he had to be going, and picking up a little tote bag with his things, he up and split. The daughter laughed. "He's a grower and a *burro,* a runner" she explained. I had ruined his visit, and he had walked five hours to see his sweetheart.

We didn't talk anymore about drugs, because I realized that the Muñozes could have had a few *plantíos,* patches, on the back forty themselves. They certainly didn't see anything wrong with growing the stuff. They didn't seem to understand how a plant could be illegal.

The trail into the Barranca de Urique, which we started down after the unfortunate knife incident, was *muy trabajosa,* as Chalo put it. The canyon is as vast as the Grand, but much lusher, smothered on this, the sunny, side with teeming jungle. For the better part of the morning, we descended the *faldas,* or skirts, of the plateau, laboriously traversing out to projecting remnants of weathered strata and doubling back across treacherous gullies. We saw lots of beautiful butterflies, among them a superb, giant swallowtail, black with purple lunules and orange ocelli, probably the dark male form of *Pterourus alexiares garcia.*

Butterflies, including undoubtedly forms still unknown to science, are among the numerous nonhuman victims of the Mexican Attorney General's Office's eradication campaign in the Sierra Madre, wiped out by the withering herbicide paraquat sprayed from the Federales' helicopters.

We overtook a group of men and women making their way down to the canyon with some sort of bundles. *Mucho chutama por aqui?* I asked one of them casually.

Oh yes. There's lots of poppy around here, he said. Want to buy some?

Late in the afternoon we waded the muddy torrent of the Urique River, which went up to my chest as I led the mule. The other group all got into a rusty box and pulled themselves over the river on a cable. When we reached the town of Urique, one of the most squalid holes I'd seen in some time, in contrast to colorfully decaying, still-picturesque Batopilas, there, smiling and waving from a doorway, was the Muñoz girl's boyfriend.

The drug violence in the Sierra Madre escalated in the years that followed. In March 1994 *traficantes* killed fifteen Tarahumara in the municipality of Urique. When the traditional governor protested, his brother was killed, his seventy-year-old mother was beaten, and he himself was hanged, but survived. By then the Colombianization of Mexico, as some were calling it, was well under way. Much of the government—up to the highest levels, both federal and state—was corrupted with drug money. In 1993 the second-highest man in the Mexican Catholic Church was gunned down in Guadalajara by hitmen in the Tijuana drug cartel, in what was initially thought to be a case of mistaken identity, but it later turned out that the archbishop was in fact part of the entourage of the rival drug lord that hitmen were gunning for. This was followed in 1994 by the assassinations of the ruling party's presidential candidate and secretary general, on the orders, it was rumored, of the president himself and with the apparent collaboration of the head of the gulf drug cartel, Juan Garcia Abrego. No one was quite sure what Abrego looked like, but the FBI put him on its ten-most-wanted list. His cartel alone was estimated to gross twenty billion dollars a year transshipping Colombian cocaine, and there were two others. (Abrego was apprehended and extradited to the United States in 1996, where he is behind bars, as is the former president's brother, Raúl Salinas, who received millions of dollars of payoffs from Abrego.)

The Pacific cartel was based in Culiacán, which I visited in 1988. I had become interested in the drug wars—the question of who was to blame, the producers or the consumers, whether young North Americans' insatiable appetite for drugs was destroying Latin America or the drug lords were cynically sacrificing the youth of North America for the huge profits to be reaped from making these highs available. The drugs wars had begun with the 1985 torture-murder in Guadalajara of Enrique "Kiki" Camarena. Three years later, it was an election year in the States, and congressional candidates eager to demonstrate a strong stand on drugs had been flinging accusations from their side of the border that Mexico wasn't doing anything about the problem, that its eradication campaign was riddled with corruption, which infuriated the honest Mexican agents who were risking their lives in the fields against *traficantes* armed with sophisticated weapons of North American manufacture, while cases of flagrant dereliction in their ranks kept surfacing often enough to give the accusations credence.

The attorney general's Permanent Campaign for the Eradication of Narcotics (or *estupefaciantes,* stupefiers, as they are called in Spanish) had been taking considerable and not entirely undeserved flak, so I was invited to go out with some of its agents in Culiacán and see what a good job they were doing. The Pacific cartel derives most of its income from marijuana and opium poppy grown in the Sierra Madre, while the bread and butter of the Gulf and Tijuana is transshipped cocaine. The *narcotraficantes* of Culiacán have their own patron saint, Jesus Malverde, a Robin Hood–like bandit who earlier in the century relieved *ricos* of their money and gave it to the poor, and they supposedly go to his chapel in the city and pray, "Malverde, increase the gringos' craving. Allow us to harvest the grass and make great bunches of silver coin."

I was met at the airport by two agents of the Federal Judicial Police, the enforcement arm of the Attorney General's Office. Soon we were speeding through the desert in a V-8 Silverado, *ranchera* music blaring over the radio, a walkie-talkie and a holstered sawed-off shotgun next to the stick shift, and a buxom woman whose cotton dress was riding way up her thighs in the passenger seat. The agent at the wheel was a pockmarked man whose blunt, reptilian demeanor reminded me of something a government minister in Mexico City had told me: "There are two things we do with our social deviants. We put them in prison, or we recruit them for the Federales." I asked the agent what his name was, and he said, completely in earnest, Ernesto Fonseca. I realized that my leg was being pulled. Ernesto Fonseca was one of the drug lords who was in prison for the murder of Kiki Camarena.

I asked "Fonseca" if the people who grow the marijuana and poppy have any idea of the damage they are doing to young minds on *el otro lado,* that a hundred thousand Americans were projected to overdose on heroin that year. "They don't," he said. "They're just campesinos. Some guy they have never seen before comes and gives them the seeds and says, 'I'll be back in three months.' The marijuana goes for about twenty dollars a kilo in the sierra. By the time it reaches Culiacán it's worth two hundred dollars, and once it has crossed the border its street value is around two thousand."

I was taken to meet a *burro,* who delivers the harvested product from the *sembrador,* the grower, to the *financiero,* the backer. The *burro* had just been picked up in an outlying village. The interview took place before the *comandante* of the State Judicial Police. Camarena had been killed by officers of this agency hired by the *traficantes.* The agency was eager to show that it was taking the eradication campaign seriously, while respecting human rights. "As you can see, he hasn't been *golpeado,* slapped around," the *comandante* assured me. "There isn't a mark on him."

The *burro,* a Mexican mestizo, was twenty-four. His story was this: "A man from Tijuana came to my *pueblito* and offered me five hundred thousand pesos to pick up some poppy. It had already been bought. The transfer took place in an arroyo, but on my way back I ran into an army roadblock. They searched me and found the stuff. Now I will go to prison. But I am poor. I have a wife, but no kids. What can I do?" He claimed it was the first time he'd ever done anything like this and that he had no idea what the stuff was for. The *comandante* smiled appreciatively at this lie.

The Federales sent me up in a helicopter combing the sierra for illegal *plantíos* of marijuana. "*Alla!* There's one." The pilot pointed down to a small clearing in the *monte,* the dense coastal thorn scrub, and brought the chopper down until we were hanging right over dozens of rows of bushy plants, close enough to make out their unmistakable jagged, palmately cleft foliage. "*Muy gorditos,*" he observed. "Fat little ones, aren't they?"

There are two theories about how marijuana, an Old World narcotic, medicinal plant and fiber plant (hemp), was introduced to Mexico. Either hemp was brought over in 1550 because its fibers could be spun into rope and cloth, by a soldier named Francisco Cuadrado, who had fought with Cortés, or it came from the Philippines on the Manila galleon. There was a woman named Maria Juana who peddled joints in Acapulco in the nineteenth century. Its euphoric properties were not lost on slaves who recognized the plant as the *kif* they had smoked in North Africa. *Kif* is the Moroccan word for cannabis (in fact, *grifa*, one of the Mexican slang words for cannabis, is derived from *kif*). A man in the eradication campaign told me that the first pothead in the Americas may have been none other than Cabeza de Vaca's companion Estéban. The slaves may have turned on other members of the underclass. Indians drifting into the Spanish towns may have picked up the practice and taken it back to their villages. A new high, guys. It's not hard to imagine such a diffusion.

In New Spain, not only several species of hallucinogenic mushrooms, but also the sacred peyote, morning glory seeds, datura, and mescal beans *(Sophora secundiflora)*, had been in ceremonial use for centuries. The missionaries did their best to suppress them, and a number of tribes, submitting to the ban on these substances, adopted cannabis as their new "intermediary with the gods." The Otomi of the central plateau used it to intercede with the Virgin Mary; the Tepehuano of the Sierra Madre Occidental substituted it for peyote; and it was known as *tutzu* to the Cuicatec, *macusi* to the Huichol, and *hapiscotl* to the Seri. A man now in the movie business, who used to be a marijuana grower, told me about a potent variety known as Popo Red that certain Indians cultivate just below the snowfields on the slopes of the volcano Popocatepetl. When the plants flower, the Indians yank them up and thrust their roots into the snow, which sends a shock of resin up to the buds, increasing their potency. Then the plants, for good measure, are crucified. This man told me he used to fly shipments of Popo Red in a small plane to the Hopi Reservation, and in the early seventies he had sixty acres of it under cultivation in Beverly Hills. It was from Popo Red that he claims to have developed the potent modern seedless strain, sinsemilla.

There were many Spanish names for cannabis as well, including *santa rosa, hierba de santa rosa, juanita, mariguana,* and *rosa maria.* Cannabis was a standard folk remedy for fatigue, asthma, and rheumatic pain. It was used to accelerate the heartbeat, as a relaxant and an antivampiric. Old women in the back mountain valleys of northern New Mexico still smoke *mota,* as it is called in Mexico and the Hispanic Southwest (from *la motivador,* the motivator) on porches; herbalists in the isolated mountain villages of northern New Mexico prescribe it smoked, chewed, or drunk as tea for protection against witches. At any given moment, a significant percentage of rural *nuevomejicanos,* not to mention Chicanos in L.A. and all over the Southwest, are probably sitting around on an old car seat on the porch, maybe, getting wasted, or, in their own language, *se poniendo locos,* or in even more choice slang, *se poniendo mas pedo que la chingada,* making themselves more shit-faced than the fucked one. Some mix their *mota* with *punche mexicano,* desert tobacco.

As in many parts of the world, *mota* became associated with violence, irresponsibility, and antisocial behavior, with *nuevomejicano* cutting and shooting. Haniel Long, an Anglo writer who was part of the Santa Fe group that included Oliver LaFarge and Erna Fergusson, wrote in his 1941 book, *Piñon Country,* "marijuana is a drug which introduces what is unforeseeable or unaccountable into situations. This is the way marijuana works, producing violent changes of mood, then terrible happenings." But many noncriminals smoke *mota* simply to get high. One Chicano artist told me he had been a daily user for thirty years. "This *mota* has good creep," he told me, passing me a joint of $260-an-ounce sinsemilla grown in the North Valley of Albuquerque. "It creeps up on you. It has cruise-control creep, cruise creep." There were several grades of *mota,* he explained: "bud" was the best; "shake," from the lower leaves, was the lowest; and "bud-shake" was a mix of the two. Cannabis, I learned, is equally widespread in the Anglo and Native American communities of the Southwest. It's hardly even considered a drug, an Anglo woman told me. Joints are passed around as casually as cans of beer. A Navajo smoker told me that the Native American term for cannabis is *pagee,* a Lakota word meaning "that grass over there."

During the end of the last century, as detribalized Indians migrated to cities and were absorbed into the mestizo population, their use of cannabis and the indigenous hallucinogens became more widely known. People began to experience the plants' effects outside of their controlled ritual and contemplative contexts, and cannabis, particularly, became associated with marginals and crime. During the Mexican Revolution, Indian battalions toked up on cannabis to steel themselves for battle. But this was nothing new. The word "assassin" comes from "hashish." Hit men in the Arab world supposedly smoked it before going to work because it blunted moral responsibility. It was in the black and Chicano and Native American subcultures that the beatniks, the pioneer Other-questing dissidents of Anglo-America, comparing themselves to the young aristocrats at the end of Rome they read about in Spengler who were no longer interested in what was happening in Rome and became interested in what was happening on the fringes of the empire, first encountered marijuana, mushrooms, peyote, and other mind-expanding drugs that would acquire new sacramental and political significance in the countercultural revolution of the sixties, as the Beats segued into the next, numerically much more significant wave of dissident Other questers, my coming-of-age con-temporaries—the hippies.

According to the Mexican Attorney General's Office, the opium poppy was introduced to Mexico during the Second World War by the American Department of War, which had asked the Mexicans to grow it so there would be a supply of morphine for the wounded GIs (the United States was cut off from its traditional Asian poppy sources). But there were a lot of Chinese in Mexico and well-established opium dens on the U.S. border in the late nineteenth century. There was a den in Tombstone, Arizona, for instance, at the time of the gunfight at the O.K. Corral in 1881. Liquor was not the only poison in the Wild West, and not a few gunslingers and upstanding citizens were junkies.

The poppy itself was native to the Near and Middle East and was introduced to China by European traders, especially those in the British East India Company, for commercial reasons, in exchange for silks and spices, to create an addicted labor force that would keep pro-ducing these things. The Chinese were extremely receptive to it. By 1867 an estimated seven hundred million Chinese had been deliber-ately addicted to the "demon flower." That year 50,550 pounds of opium were shipped to California to feed the habit of sixty thousand coolies working on the western frontier, mainly on the railroads. So the stuff was around well before World War II.

And now, in 1988, an estimated hundred thousand Americans, most of them inner-city blacks, were going to OD on heroin. Thirty million Americans, 15 percent of the population, were smoking, snorting, or shooting up drugs, and the curve was rising. They were spending $150 billion a year on drugs, half again the Mexican foreign debt. "This is an obscenity," an official in the Attorney General's Office in Mexico City had told me. Eight million pounds of marijuana annually were being flown, floated, or walked over the border. Half the heroin con-sumed in the States was thought to have been processed from *chutama* grown in Sierra Madre. *Chutama* is a Tepehuano word meaning gum or resin.

A Friend of the Indians

Few dared to stand up to the *traficantes* because it was suicide. But one man—Edwin Bustillos—had dedicated himself to stopping the violence and devastation the drug trade and lumber companies, many of which are in league with the drug lords, had brought to the sierra. Bustillos was Tarahumara on his mother's side, and he was the founder and director of a grass-roots human-rights and environmental organization called CASMAC (the Spanish name translates to "Advisory Council for the Sierra Madre"). I returned to the sierra in the fall of 1994 to learn about his work. By then the Sierra Madre Occidental had become one of the most productive drug-growing areas on the planet, after Myanmar's (formerly Burma) Golden Triangle. In the previous twelve months, the *traficantes* had tried to kill Bustillos three times, but there he was—or what was left of him—in the crowd that had come to Chihuahua Airport to meet my plane from Mexico City. His most conspicuous disfigurement, as he stepped forth, was a sightless, white left eye. But it had been injured when he was a child and had nothing to do with his personal war against the *traficantes*.

The way the thirty-eight-year-old Bustillos was bent over like an old man, however, was the result of spinal damage and broken ribs he had suffered the previous April, when a three-ton truck came up from behind on the road to Guachochi, one of the big trading centers in the Sierra Madre Occidental and forced his Ford Bronco over a three-hundred-foot embankment. Bustillos had been hurled from his vehicle and rushed by friends to a hospital, where he underwent hours of surgery on his crushed left arm, but he would never regain full use of it.

His skull had nearly mended from an incident on Christmas Day, 1993, when five men—two of whom he claims he recognized as off-duty police officers—pulled him out of his car near his home in Aguas

Azuls, beat him senseless, and left him for dead by the road. Bustillos would later become convinced that the attack was ordered by Ismael Diaz Carillos, the municipal president of Guachochi. A board member of a local bank, Carillos was widely believed to have laundered millions of dollars for the Fontes cartel, a drug organization that Bustillos suspected was also involved in the illegal logging that has defaced much of the Sierra Madre.

And speaking of the devil, there was Carillos himself, surrounded by three gold-festooned bodyguards, standing no more than thirty feet from us. They had come in on the same plane.

"That is the man who tried to kill me," Bustillos muttered, glaring at Carillos with his one good eye.

This was a man with a mission, I thought as we drove into Chihuahua City. He had no wife or children, no attachments. Clearly the prospect of an early, violent death was no more of a deterrent than it was for the masked, pipe-smoking Subcomandante Marcos, who had organized and long exploited and marginalized Maya of Chiapas into the Zapatista Liberation Army and was rumored to be an ex-priest. Why are you doing this? I asked Edwin.

"Because I feel I can be useful to my land and my people, and because I think the objective of being on this earth is to be useful. But," he quickly added, "I am *not* religious."

"Bustillos" is a common name in the sierra, especially around Guachochi. Edwin's great-grandfather had been the wealthiest landowner in the *municipio* before the revolution. Not only his many offspring, but the numerous Tarahumara he had working for him, took his name, the way African slaves in the South were given their owner's name. Edwin didn't know the family history very well, because he and his father had not spoken in a long time. Last September, one of his relatives, a policeman by the name of Alonso Bustillos, had actually fired some shots over his house during the night. "Some of the Bustillos are my worst enemies," Edwin told me.

After the revolution the Bustilloses' latifundio was nationalized, and they became like any other mestizo family. Edwin's father was a saddle maker, and he had a ranch and a little store in Aguas Azuls, forty-five minutes from Guachochi. Edwin went to the local school, and it was his maternal grandmother who bought him books and pencils and encouraged his studies. His father was angry when he won a scholarship to high school in Guachochi and even angrier when he won a scholarship to the university in Mexico City. His father wanted his son on the ranch, but Edwin balked at the whole macho cowboy trip. He had other plans.

At the university Edwin became politicized. Several classmates were now doing similar human-rights work with the Maya in Chiapas. The government of India, which was making a study of the Tarahumara's medicinal plants, took him under its wing, setting him up in a house with a pool and a tennis court and a car. Invited everywhere, he made friends in high places, and when he graduated, in 1986, he could have had an important government post in Mexico City, but he decided to go back to the sierra. He got hired by a lumber company, which opened his eyes to the abuses that were going on in the backcountry. The loggers were just coming in and clear-cutting and killing anyone who didn't like it.

After a year of this, he quit and traveled all over Mexico for a year, doing forestry and ethnographic research, then the government of India sent him to New York City to study English for a year at Columbia. Returning in 1990, he went to work for the National Institute of Indian Affairs (INI), Mexico's equivalent of the BIA. He worked in remote, violent communities like Coloradas de la Viergem, Baborigame, and Morelos, where the Tarahumara and their neighbors, the Tepehuano, were being forced to grow drugs and were having their land taken from them.

Edwin started a campaign of what an anthropologist colleague described as "ethnic recuperation," trying to restore the Tarahumara's traditional territories and system of authority, which had been replaced by Mexican institutions—the *ejido,* or common lands, and the *municipio*—controlled by the local mestizos usually on the payroll of the *traficantes.* He would get the Tarahumara in a rejuvenated community to declare that they didn't want any more drugs grown on their land, and he would get its leaders to show him where the *plantíos,* the poppy and pot fields, were. Then he would bring in the federal police to destroy the plants.

Drug eradication is the job of the federal police, but the army often lends a hand. The Federales and the soldiers had been coming in and arresting the *sembradores,* the small, usually coerced, growers—so the Indians were being persecuted by the *narcos* and by the persecutors of the *narcos*—but they never got the *cabezas* who were behind the operation, and they seldom got the big plantations because they didn't know where they were, and half of what the army ripped up, by Bustillos's estimate, didn't get burned. A well-placed source in the capital told me that the army and the party (PRI) have a deal: the army can have the drug trade as long as it stays out of politics. A few months earlier, there had been an embarrassing shoot-out in Veracruz between the Federales and army troops defending one of the big drug lords. Not that the Federales don't require careful supervision as well. The last delegate of the Attorney General's Office, who commanded the federal police in Chihuahua, complained that her men only lasted a few months in the field before they were corrupted by the *traficantes*.

The temptations for being less than conscientious are pretty irresistible. A kilo of marijuana is worth two hundred kilos of corn to a Tarahumara grower, two hundred dollars to a mestizo in the sierra, and five hundred in Chihuahua City; in the States an ounce of Mexican weed goes for around two hundred dollars. The escalating return on poppies is even more impressive. Each seedpod, lanced on a sunny day, oozes three to five grams of sticky white opium gum. A Tarahumara can harvest two or three hundred grams a day, which is worth a hundred thousand pesos or so—thirty bucks—but he is usually paid in goods, clothes, corn, or liquor, if he is paid at all. In the sierra a kilo of raw opium goes for five thousand dollars. Seven kilos, mixed with chemicals in the laboratories in the sierra or down in the city of Cuauhtémoc, makes one kilo of heroin, which is worth anywhere from eighty to five hundred thousand dollars north of the border. So when a bust coordinated by Bustillos wiped out twenty-five acres of *chutama* in the sierra, that was roughly a million dollars the *traficantes* weren't going to be making.

After two years and two months, INI asked for Edwin's resignation "because I was trying to help the Indians stand up against the *traficantes*," he explained. So Bustillos had to find other sources of support. He hooked up with Randy Gingrich, a conservationist with the Arizona Rain Forest Action Network, who helped him write some grant proposals, and in November 1992, with funding from groups like the Santa Fe–based Forest Guardians, USAID's Biodiversity Program, and the Wallace Genetic Foundation, he founded CASMAC. There are hundreds of grass-roots advocacy groups like CASMAC in Mexico—three hundred in Chiapas alone, another three hundred in Oaxaca, sixty in Guerrero, forty in Veracruz. But CASMAC had North American funding and was unusually well equipped and effective.

Bustillos started getting calls ten times in the night. "Edwin, take care of yourself, because you're in danger." "What are you helping those lazy Indians for? You can make more money with us." Fifteen months ago, driving out of Coloradas de la Viergem, he found a pickup blocking the way and several of the Fontes gang—the most violent *traficantes* in the sierra—leaning on it, drinking beer. They taunted him and invited him to fight. Edwin sat quietly with his gun at his side, and after forty-five minutes they let him through.

CASMAC's headquarters was on a quiet, upscale residential street in Chihuahua City and boasted a copy machine, several computers, and several four-wheel-drive rigs. From there Edwin and his staff, which included two anthropologists and his sister Adaeli, worked on projects ranging from biodynamic agriculture to saving the endangered *guacamaya,* or thick-billed parrot. CASMAC had coordinated meetings between indigenous leaders and the Chihuahua legislature that led to an amendment in the state constitution recognizing the Indians' autochthonous territories and governmental structure, their rights to perform their ceremonies, to practice their traditional medicine, and to be educated in their own tongue. It had halted two illegal logging operations, helped settle land claims, and, working with U.S. environmental groups, had stopped a ninety-million-dollar World Bank road-building project that would have enabled timber companies to cut four billion board feet from more than twenty million acres in the Sierra Madre.

But mostly, and most urgently, the CASMAC staff was focusing on basic human rights, and it was getting no help in this highly dangerous work. "No foundations are interested in helping communities that are being torn up by the drug war break out of the exploitation and dependency cycle," Gingrich complained. It was easier to get funding to study the endangered military macaw.

Before we headed up into the sierra, Edwin thought it would be good for me to talk to Agustín and Rojelio Fontes, two of the biggest killers in the sierra, who were in the Chihuahua penitentiary. Agustín had killed seventeen Tarahumara, one of them the traditional governor of Coloradas de la Viergem, who had objected to the illegal logging of the ancestral forest. Rojelio had been the chief liaison between Artemio Fontes, the cartel's cacique, and his cousin Lauro Molina, who distributed most of the product from the southern sierra through Culiacán. His arrest was more significant than Agustín's, which was probably why the *comandante* of the penitentiary denied that he had him.

"Who told you Agustín and Rojelio Fontes are in here?" he asked, looking over the documents supporting my claim to be "the international press from New York." I said, lying, High officials in Mexico City. "How would they know?" he asked. There was also an article about them in the States, I added. "Why would they write about them in the States?" the *comandante* probed. Because there's a lot of interest in what happens down here, I said with a winning smile. Look, I went on. I just want to talk to some *traficantes.* Get their point of view. Again, the *comandante* asked how I had heard about these prisoners.

He eventually admitted to having Agustín and said he had no problem with my talking to him as long as the conversation was taped (an invasion of privacy that I later learned was technically illegal but commonplace in Mexico's prisons). He handed a recorder to his *subco-*

mandante, who escorted us to the visitors' room. The *subcomandante* and I got talking about the *narcocultivo. Es muy verde la sierra*—there's a lot of green stuff up there—he said.

Agustín Fontes appeared in shorts, sneakers, and a tank top, having just been pumping iron. He was a virile twenty-three-year-old man, five-foot-ten, with black hair. *Buenas tardes,* I said, and he reciprocated with a look of mocking indifference.

"How they treating you in here?"

"Not bad."

"This is a pretty civilized pen. You get conjugal visits?"

"Every third day."

"TV in your own cell?"

"*Sí.*"

"How long you going to be in here?"

"Ten years with good behavior."

"But didn't you kill another inmate a few weeks ago?"

"Yes. He pulled a knife on me, so I took a board and beat him to death." (It was actually the other way around, according to Bustillos: the other inmate had the board; Agustín had the knife and stabbed him fifteen times. But Fontes successfully pleaded self-defense before the prison officials, so the incident wasn't going to increase his time.)

"Why did he attack you?"

"It was an old family problem."

Fontes's veracity quotient was not real high. He denied being from Coloradas de la Viergem and claimed he had no involvement with drug trafficking. "It's bad for people. A lot get killed."

"Didn't you kill seventeen yourself?"

"That's what they say. But they were because of old family problems and had nothing to do with drugs. I raised cattle and did a little prospecting, but I had nothing to do with drugs."

"Aren't you Artemio Fontes's nephew?"

"They say I am, but I don't know him. I killed the *pistolero* Marco Antonio Aruportio, who thought I was the same Fontes."

We weren't getting very far, maybe because the *subcomandante* was holding the tape recorder up to Fontes's face. "You can't talk because of this thing, right?" I suggested. "If you say anything about Artemio, he will have you killed."

"Yes."

"Even in here there are people who could do it."

"True."

It was obvious to me now that the corrections system, too, was enmeshed with the cartel, another corrupted cog in the machine. How else was Artemio Fontes going to know what Agustín said unless the *comandante* gave him the tape?

"One last question. Are you in favor of legalization? Wouldn't it diminish the violence if everybody could grow *mota* and *chutama* as freely as corn?"

"*Quien sabe?* Who knows?"

One of the eight drug lords now operating in the Sierra Madre Occidental, Artemio Fontes was the son in a large family of mestizo hillbillies with an unsavory history of gunslinging and internecine feuds. Artemio got his start in the drug trade in Coloradas de la Viergem twenty-nine years ago and now lived in ostentatious impunity in a guarded mansion in Chihuahua City. The Fonteses and their "cowboys" didn't just kill you; there was usually a sadistic twist. Like the five men who accosted Edwin's uncle, Moises Bustillos, as he was walking to the Tarahumara community of Yoquivo the previous July. A screwdriver was forced into Moises's arms, legs, ankles, and groin, and he was buried alive and left there. Four days later he was found almost dead and was able to identify the assailants as associates of Angel Fontes, aka El Towi (the Child), Artemio's second-in-command.

The PGR—the Attorney General's Office—had put out a warrant for Artemio, but when federal police agents tried to arrest him, he came out of his mansion in his bathrobe and slippers and produced a letter of general amnesty, signed by a federal judge, that granted him immunity from prosecution. On the way to ask the federal prosecutor in Chihuahua, Alonso Jardí, how this had happened, we passed a mural depicting an apple with a bite out of it and a black horizontal line through it, with the caption, *La mordida es la corrupción.* That, in a nutshell, was what had happened. The judge had been unable to resist taking a bite out of the apple.

"Artemio's *amparo definitivo* was given by Abelina Morales Guzmán, a corrupt judge in third district," explained Jardí. "We have a problem with judges letting people go. Our investigation was ready, but Guzmán said it was weak. The permeability of *narcotrafico* is very strong."

"How much of the political structure is corrupted?"

"I don't know, but it's *alto.*"

"How many of the crops are you getting?"

"In August we eradicated six hundred acres. It was the best month in the PGR's history. We are getting maybe fifty percent."

"How many of the *cabezas* are you getting?"

"The web of contractors and subcontractors is very hard to disentangle. The higher they are, the harder it is to get them. I don't think we are getting more than three percent of the top ones." Unofficially, the PGR, at Edwin's urging, is no longer prosecuting the Indian *sembradores*.

The U.S. Drug Enforcement Agency (DEA) also works with the PGR, but clandestinely and only to a limited extent, because of Mexico's sensitivity about sovereignty. Edwin had worked once with the DEA, but he had problems with the agency because it had a different agenda: it was focusing on higher-volume but less violent competitors of the Fontes cartel. A few years back, Edwin had told the DEA about a connection with the Denver police. The DEA had busted the Fontes middleman who was running the drugs up to Denver, but had then let him go with a hundred-thousand-dollar fine. That was the last time Edwin had worked with the agency.

Jardí showed Edwin a deposition he had just received from a twelve-year-old Tarahumara girl from the village of Wachamuchi who had been raped by *traficantes*. "A corrupt local magistrate didn't accept the deposition because he said there was no doctor's certificate confirming that she was raped. The girl didn't know she needed one, but there is no doctor in Wachamuchi anyway, and the local prosecutor doesn't have the balls to do anything about it, so we are getting into the case," he explained. Murder and rape are state offenses, but the state police were notoriously lax. One of Artemio Fontes's brothers had been a state police *comandante* and had been gunned down by the army while defending a plane full of marijuana.

"The only way to get rid of the violence and the permeation of corruption is legalization," Jardí said. "It's hard to help the Indians because they have few options. This is their cash crop. They have no other way to make money." Edwin told me about a young Tarahumara who came into his father's store in Aguas Azules one morning with two big marijuana plants that he wanted to trade. He didn't understand that there was anything wrong with having grown them or bringing them in to trade.

Edwin decided to take the Jeep Wagoneer, even though its suspension was shot, and it lurched down the pike like a motorboat in a choppy sea. We passed the adobe slums of Chihuahua City and, outside the city of Cuauhtémoc, giant Mennonite farms—shimmering fields of grain, orderly rows of pear trees draped with black hail screens.

As we rose into the sierra, the roofs became pitched to handle snow, and pines checked in. The Sierra Madre is estimated to contain about two-thirds of the standing timber in Mexico. There is little evidence of severe deforestation, but in recent years logging companies have been forcing new roads into remote settlements and cutting the last old-growth stands where Tarahumara families forage for wild berries and nuts and shamans gather ceremonial herbs. In 1994, Mexico's department of agriculture estimates, as many as 300 million board feet of timber were cut in the sierra. Nearly 20 percent of the timber was sold to the United States as plywood, pulp, or paper. In the most severely deforested parts of the region, the overcutting has resulted in soil erosion, habitat destruction, watershed damage, and the extinction or endangerment of species. The spraying of the backcountry with paraquat, moreover, has contaminated local water supplies and plant life, presenting particular hazards for the Tarahumara, who eat more than 220 wild plant species and use another 300 for medicinal purposes.

Winding up hairpin turns, we kept passing canvas-backed army trucks, some of which, Edwin suspected, may have contained confiscated marijuana plants. He estimated that half of the cannabis that the army is supposed to burn on the spot ends up being sold in the States. "The general of the army in this state hates me," Edwin confided.

Driving past a column of swirling dust, which Tarahumara believe contains a soul in transit, we reached Creel. We saw a few women in kerchiefs and voluminous skirts and men with white untucked shirts and sashes and headbands woven in geometric designs, both sexes shod in tire-tread sandals or huaraches. But most were dressed in jeans and down jackets, like the mestizos, now that winter was setting in. Edwin said you couldn't tell a Christian from a *gentile* by what he or she was wearing. The streets were full of young German backpackers soaking up the primitive Indianness of it all.

This time Father Verplancken, a Jesuit who had been in the Tarahumara since 1952, whom I had missed in '86 and '88, was there, but he was late for a meeting and said he could give me exactly five minutes of his time. The takes on Father Verplancken were conflicting. North American anthropologists whose studies of the Tarahumara he had helped set up spoke highly of him, but INI's state delegate to Chihuahua described him as a "chameleon. He wants to be on the good side of God and the Devil."

Father Verplancken claimed he didn't know who Edwin was, even though Edwin said some Danes had made a video of them being interviewed together. Perhaps this was because Edwin had accused Verplancken of fabricating the terrible drought that the sierra was supposed to have been in the throes of, of scouring Tarahumara communities for sick kids to fill his hospital beds, then getting the international media to publicize the disaster so foundation money would come pouring in, and he could buy a new fleet of Suburbans. A few weeks earlier, *The New York Times*'s Anthony de Palma had written, "On the surface, the drought is not easily recognized. The Tarahumara's slopes are still green with pine trees. However, the evidence that something has gone very wrong was evident [*sic*] at St. Theresa's pediatric ward." Father Verplancken told me this year's corn harvest was "zero to thirty percent," but Edwin pointed out that there had been no problem with the drug harvest, "and the *narcos* plant in the most difficult places." Others agreed that the drought was sensationalized and had various theories about who might have also been in on the scam: (1) the state government, which was hoping to get emergency funds from Mexico City; (2) PRI, the ruling party, which wanted PAN, the opposition party, which had carried the state elections, to look as if it were doing nothing; or (3) the bishop of Guachochi, who was raising money for a new church. CASMAC itself had received 254 tons of food from the States and from rich people in Mexico City, which Edwin was planning to distribute to forty-five communities. "But they should have had this food in April and May—the dry months, when there are always deaths from hunger." My impression coincided with Edwin's. The arroyos were running. It didn't look like the drought was all it had been cracked up to be.

Edwin had a low opinion of the Church in Chihuahua. The diocese had purged its liberation theologists—priests who might have helped the Indians organize against the *traficantes*—in the seventies. The remaining men of the cloth were "not compromised with social struggles," as one man put it. Edwin even knew of one padre who was a drug dealer. Edwin was in touch with the Zapatistas, but in his view the only thing an armed insurrection would accomplish for the Tarahumara would be to get more of them killed. So his strategy was "to get what I can from the system, and to make it work."

We spent the night in Aboreachic, a relatively undisturbed community with a school whose children kept playfully approaching and fleeing the strange *chabochi*. The traditional governor, Petronillo Bustillos Gonzales, who took the bronze for the marathon in the 1988 Olympics, informed me that "Aboreachic" means "Lots of Juniper" and that it was drug-free. There were four hundred families living in thirty-five small valleys. "I talk to the people on Sundays, tell them to behave well and not plant *mota* or *chutama* because these things make you crazy, and the people are in agreement." But an anthropologist later told me that twelve- to fifteen-year-old kids around Aboreachic, whose role models are the *traficantes,* were addicted to pot and cocaine and were shooting up heroin.

Three hours by foot, the governor told us, was a hot spring with some old caves with a lot of bones and ruins. This was possibly a Tubare site. The Tubare, who are thought to be extinct, were neighbors of the Tarahumara. Carl Lumholtz, exploring a possible historic connection between the Arizona Cliff Dwellers and the Tarahumara, encountered what were thought to be the last eight Tubare families a hundred years ago, but deep in a canyon in the *municipio* of Morelos, south of us, Edwin told me he found an old Tubare couple a few years ago—possibly the last of the tribe. The woman had been accused of cannibalizing a Tarahumara girl. There may be other remnant groups in this vast wilderness. A new group called the Masculai was discovered in 1985, and there are rumors of a fugitive band of Apache—periodic sightings of Indians with turned-up shoes, long, straight hair, and sashed white homespun blouses. Twenty to thirty Chiricahua Apache— Geronimo's subtribe—are known to have held out in the northern part of the Sierra Madre until the 1930s, when their leader, Juan or Bigfoot, was killed by a posse of local ranchers. The more recent sightings, the anthropologist Jerome Levi, who did his doctorate on the *gentiles,* told me, are probably Yaqui, who dress similarly. "It's amazing that there are still people romping around in loincloths just a few hundred miles south of the border," Levi mused.

Everyone from Aboreachic was going to Guachochi for the Yumari Festival. "There will be *muchos compañeros,* and we will dance the Matachines," said the governor, who was wearing his best cowboy hat, with a gold band, like all the other men crammed into the flatbed truck that departed from Aboreachic the following morning. Yumari lasted three days and was the big blowout of the year. First, there were thanksgiving dances for the harvest, then dances for rain.

As we approached Guachochi, elegant stone walls defining the *estancias* of *traficantes* began to line the road. Guachochi is a hot, dusty, ugly town of twenty-two thousand people, plus a large population of mangy pariah dogs. There are no tourists. Edwin took me to the Hotel Melina, which had been built with opium money. The owner had left the country. He was not a bad person, Edwin told me. In fact he provided the Tarahumara who grew drugs for him with schools, clinics, and other services the government was supposed to provide, but didn't. "I'm not against all *traficantes,*" he said, "just the violent ones."

The Yumari celebration was happening in a big open field across the road from a school. Throngs of Tarahumara were gathered around huge, crackling bonfires. Some were brewing *tesguina,* the corn hooch, in huge vats. At each bonfire, two files of men wearing helmets decked with colored streamers were shuffling to simple, two-chord jigs played by a pair of men on homemade fiddles and a third on guitar. This was the Tarahumara version of the Matachines—a far more tame one than the Matachines the Pueblos of Santo Domingo had put on for Christopher Columbus XXII. The dancers were all men, and they seemed oddly inhibited, even repressed. The women sat motionless in their shawls, staring off into space, zoning for hours at a time. There were a couple of beautiful *negras,* Tarahumara women with slave blood. "The women are saying nothing because if they talk they will miss the ceremony," Edwin explained. I sat on a log, taking in the insistent rhythms that a dancer in shell-decorated leggings was stamping out in the dust with his tire-tread sandals. After a few hours, as I settled into the scene, I began to slip into Tarahumara time, into a cosmos in which maps and clocks are of little use, where the physical plane is not what is really happening.

Edwin introduced me to a half-dozen refugees from Coloradas de la Viergem standing in the field. It was difficult to draw them out—such was their ingrained shyness, not to mention suspicion, of *chabochi*—but as they spoke of their home, the picture that emerged was of a place truly gripped by terror. Only a handful of Tarahumara remained in Coloradas, the majority having relocated to larger Indian communities like Baborigame and Guachochi.

One of the refugees, a young man in jeans and a cowboy hat, was Jesús Martínez Chaparro, the president of the Coloradas *ejido.* The previous president had been killed last March 28 by Fontes cowboys who were harassing his two-year-old niece, and Chaparro himself had been sleeping in the forest; his wife brought him food. "If someone wants to be a leader of the indigenous people, they will kill him," he said. Edwin indicated a mestizo who was watching the dancing. "That is Henrique Seballos, one of the Fonteses' field operators. His son just killed a Tarahumara on Glorious Saturday, because the man complained that drugs had been planted on his land. That brings the death toll in Coloradas up to thirty-nine."

I wanted to meet some of the most traditional Tarahumara, the *gentiles.* There were none at the Yumari Festival because they did not know how to dance the Matachines, which had been introduced by the missionaries. (Of course the Tarahumara had, over time, infused the pageant with meanings of their own.)

If you want to meet some *gentiles,* Edwin said, you have to go to them. Poring over maps, we decided that the best place for me to visit was Piño Gordo. It was relatively safe. No one had been killed there this year. As its name (Fat Pine) suggested, there were still some stands of old-growth ponderosas, and it was so remote that it had been left alone by the padres. There were only two ways to get there: to walk sixty miles or to drive for twenty hours in a four-wheel drive. These were as pure, uncontaminated Tarahumara as one could hope to find.

The sixty-mile walk (which the Piño Gordians did in one day) entailed crossing the Barranca de Sinforosa, the largest and deepest canyon in the system. I decided to do it. Edwin bowed out, due to back problems from the latest assassination attempt. He said he would go around with a car and meet me there. He arranged for one of his body-guards, Alonso Garcia, and his father, Manoel, who knew the way more or less, to go with me. What if we ran into some *traficantes?* I asked.

"Alonso will have a nine-millimeter pistol," Edwin said.

"Won't they think I'm the CIA or the DEA?" I asked. Edwin said that could be a problem.

"I know," I said. "I'll pretend I'm some out-to-lunch gringo journalist covering the drought. Or better still, I'll pretend I'm a drug-loving American tourist, a *gringo estupefacto.* I'll clap them on the back and say, 'Hey man, I really like your product.' "

The next evening, at a quarter past six, Alonso, Manoel, and I, and Manoel's male cross between a horse and a burro (and therefore not a mule), whom he called El Macho, descended into the barranca from the Cumbre (pinnacle) de Sinforosa. The trail was steep and loose, and I kept doing involuntary splits and dodging needle-sharp, eye-level spikes of maguey. We got as far as a shelf known as La Mesita, built a fire, and lay in the darkness munching burritos and listening to the howls of an animal Manoel identified as *el tlalquachi.* He said it was a little gray-and-white-striped cat with a hairless tail. I wondered if it was an ocelot, a margay, a bobcat, or a jaguarundi, all of which inhabit the sierra. There are also three big cats: the *tigre,* or jaguar, which prowls the canyon floors; the *león,* or puma, which prowls the sierra; and one that lives way up in the mountains and is known as the *onza;* Piño Gordo is one of its reported locales. The *onza* is said to be more aggressive and vicious than the other two, and the local people are really scared of it. It has been reported in the sierra for two hundred years. The German scientist Helmet Heller hypothesized that it might be the North American cheetah, common in the Pleistocene and known only from fossils and thought to have been extinct for ten thousand years. Finally, in 1987, an *onza* was shot in the southern sierra. It was the same tan color as the puma, but slightly smaller and not as bulky or big pawed.

"Its legs were much longer, and its body was more gracile and slender, more like a cheetah's," Richard Greenwell, the secretary of the Tucson-based International Society of Crypto-Zoologists, which investigates reports of folkloric creatures like Yeti, Bigfoot, Nessie, and the *onza,* told me. "It had faint horizontal lines on its 'wrists'—the inside of its front legs—which had never been seen on a puma. But mitochondrial DNA and electrophoresis studies, which are not a hundred percent reliable, suggest that we are dealing with a new subspecies of puma, an altitudinal variant. The mystery is what is a sprinter, built for the plains, doing in high mountains? Maybe other cats took over its niche and drove it up there."

The Sierra Madre abounds with natural-history mysteries. Like what was this *tlalquachi?* A *mapache* is a raccoon, but my guess is that this was a *tlalcoyote,* a Mexican badger, and either I misheard Manoel, or that is the name for badger in that part of the sierra. The hair of the *tlalcoyote* is sought for shaving brushes.

Alonso threw another oak fagot on the fire, and the subject turned to drugs. "What do you Americans do with all the marijuana they take out of here?" Manoel asked.

"We roll it into cigarettes and smoke it."

"But they take tons and tons."

I said I was turned on to cannabis in the sixties, and still took a puff now and then, and was really distressed that this plant, whose effect on me, at least, was to open windows of the mind, and which had been such an integral part of the countercultural peace-and-love ethos, should be hurting the Tarahumara and other Mexicans, even getting them killed. That was what was tragic and criminal, not *mota* itself, which I maintained to Manoel and Alonso was no more harmful than beer, and much more interesting.

The obvious solution was to legalize cannabis, I went on, regardless of its merits or demerits. *Chutama* was another question. But it would be political suicide for any American congressman to propose such a bill. Legalization would only happen if the entire hemisphere agreed on it.

"And what about the *traficantes?*" Manoel asked. "Don't tell me they are going to sit by and watch their incredibly profitable business go down the tubes."

"Maybe they'll go along with it," INI's delegate had suggested in Guachochi, "if you let them put the money they have already made into legitimate enterprises. Then they wouldn't have to go through such elaborate lengths to launder their money and invest it in other people's names, they wouldn't have to worry about being busted or rubbed out, and they wouldn't have the blood of so many Indians on their hands." Oddly enough, the delegate went on, in Mexico growing cannabis is illegal, and so is harvesting it or having it on you, but there is no law against smoking it. "So we are already halfway there," he had said with a laugh.

In the middle of the night, it started to rain, the first rain in three months, and we took shelter in a cave. The next morning the trail had been wetted down and was easier going as we jigged down to the canyon floor, where there were prickly-pear and pitahaya cacti the size of trees, and cattle were feasting on the tasty orange fruit of *vainora* trees. The rattlesnakes had retired to their dens a month ago, Manoel told me. Like many life-forms, these "fiery little animals with castanets on their tails," as one of the early conquistadores described them, experienced a tremendous evolutionary radiation as the Sierra Madre rose up. In some locales five species—black-tailed, ridge-nosed, twinspot, Mojave, and rock—have been found living together. Manoel said that a small, gray, woolly, pincushion cactus clinging to a boulder was peyote, but this was one of the five nonhallucinogenic species the Tarahumara call peyote, not *Lophophora williamsii*, the one with the psychotropic alkaloids that they get down in the Chihuahuan Desert.

The Tarahumara's peyote rituals are the most complicated and carefully guarded part of their culture. Only a few *chabochi* have participated in them. Peyote is used to cure illness and madness, to bring rain and a good harvest. It is widely feared for the ability of shamans under its influence to see what is happening to other people's souls, and for its use by sorcerers to harm or even kill. It is also used to influence the outcome of the *rajalipame* relay races.

We swam across the Río Verde, and as we were making our way up the other side of the barranca, it started to rain hard, so we took shelter in a cave with a spring and a beautiful view across the majestic gorge. We built a fire and hung our clothes to dry around it. Manoel produced some coffee, and we brewed it in his tin cup and waited until the rain stopped and a rainbow appeared. From where we sat, we could see that a crop had recently been harvested on the steep slope below the cave. Manoel said it was a local family's *chutama* patch. I was sorry to have missed the spectacle of a poppy field in its full profusion, the showy, five-petaled flowers in white, pink, carmine, or purple bloom. By now the locals would have run with their ball of opium gum across the canyon to Guachochi and traded it for sacks of corn to see them through the winter. To whatever extent the drought had been exaggerated, the corn harvest had been poor this year, Manoel said, and the only way for many Tarahumara to survive was by growing a little *mota* and *chutama* on the side.

As plumes of steam licked up the *arroyitos* and curled around the *faldas* of the eroded plateau, we hit the trail again, passing a stand of beautiful, unfamiliar conifers with long, droopy, light-green needles that Manoel said were called sad pines. After a couple of hours we made it up to the sierra and walked along a ledge overlooking a spectacular hidden valley with cornfields and a log cabin a thousand feet below. Every so often a twisted red tree with flaky bark—one of the sierra's four kinds of madrone—would appear under the pines (often with a wispy golden globular epiphyte, known as *muerdago,* in its branches) like a gratuitous bit of chinoiserie. The Tarahumara make full use of these trees. They eat their red berries, treat kidney ailments with their bark and flowers, and make balls for the *rajalipame* game from their wood.

We met a woman who was sitting at a fire under a lean-to and watching goats, and she let her son, who had a horrible sore on his cheek, take us to the Cumbre de los Duraznos, where some *traficantes* had put in a landing strip. There was no place to stay, and it was getting dark, so we kept walking and just made it to a little hut that belonged to a Tarahumara named Francisco Ramos and his wife, Maria, who invited us to spend the night with them in the six-by-six-foot space they called home. Both Francisco and Maria had the same congenital abnormality, a right clubfoot, suggesting, given the high frequency of intrafamily marriage among the Tarahumara, that they were cousins.

All Francisco and Maria had to eat—all they ever had to eat, most of the time—were scrawny three-inch-long ears of corn. They and their little boy, who was naked from the waist down, were themselves stunted corn-fed constructs. Francisco and Maria had lost another son to gastroenteritis and a daughter to tuberculosis. Tiny Maria, kneeling in a corner and rocking back and forth, was grinding untoasted white kernels on a slab metate into a gruel called *yorike.* Edwin had catalogued something like three hundred ways the Tarahumara have of eating corn. Each traditional district, he said, has its special ways.

As we huddled in the hut, with blackened pots and filthy clothing hanging from the ceiling, it began to rain torrentially. The roof leaked, and water soon spread across half the dirt floor. All Francisco had to do was berm the open side of the shed to divert the water, but it was clear he wasn't going to do this; our hosts were happy to let nature take its course. We produced a tin of sardines, an avocado, some tortillas, and some marshmallows, and the six of us had a feast. The Ramoses insisted that I sleep in the mud-and-wattle room that made up the rest of their home. I nodded off among hundreds of ears of corn, while the others stayed in the shed, laughing through the storm.

The next morning, really motoring, we made Piño Gordo by eleven, but no Edwin. When is he coming? I asked his associate, Gumercindo Torres. *Quien sabe?* he said. Torres was another refugee from Coloradas de la Viergem, a tough, thirty-one-year-old hombre whose body was pocked with the scars of bullet wounds. Among other responsibilities, he was the de facto doctor of Piño Gordo, dispensing tetracycline and other wonder drugs when the ministrations of the shaman appeared to be doing no good. His Tarahumara wife, Paula Vrieto, was a teacher at the school just below their house.

There was a pastoral and wholesomely alpine atmosphere to this sparse settlement of thirteen families nestled in a small valley. Piño Gordo had been completely isolated until 1990, when a timber company called Impulsora Forestal du Durango put in a road to within fourteen miles without consulting the village and then tried to charge the locals the equivalent of a hundred thousand dollars for it, triple the going price for such a project. Impulsora said it was willing to be compensated in trees. With CASMAC's help, the people of the community took Impulsora to court in Chihuahua City. The judge ruled that they didn't have to pay for a road they had never asked for. They subsequently decided that they didn't want any of their forest logged, legally or otherwise, and declared their woodland a preserve. Randy Gingrich was putting together a network of similarly created forest reserves, totaling a hundred thousand acres, that would run almost all the way to the border. "This is our ultimate goal," he explained, "to turn human-rights disasters into conservation gains."

Impulsora Forestal was the same company that was cutting the largest continuous stand of primary forest in the sierra, near Coloradas de la Viergem, and was the subject of an ongoing government investigation into alleged links with the Fontes cartel; the company has an office on Park Avenue. Certainly the advantages of such an association would be numerous for a drug operation: new logging roads would make it easier to remove the harvested crops, the timber trucks would provide a camouflaged mode of transport, the logging crews would serve as a standing army of enforcers to keep the local indigenous population in line, and the company would provide a legitimate enterprise for laundering money.

Lately the *ejido* of Piño Gordo had become divided because the *traficantes* had allegedly managed to corrupt one of the local Tarahumara leaders, Raul Aguirre, paying him to persuade fellow Indians in a nearby settlement to grow opium poppies in exchange for alcohol. A new airstrip had even been built to transport the harvested opium gum. "They gave Raul a house in Chihuahua City," Edwin had told me earlier. "He is destroying his people."

Last May, *pistoleros* of a female rancher *traficante* who lives close by allegedly killed five Tarahumara and rustled seventy head of cattle. Now this woman was threatening violence if the people of Piño Gordo didn't let her build a road into their forests. (She has since been arrested and sentenced to prison.)

That afternoon Edwin appeared with his companion Lupe, the handsome and beautiful seven-souled son of a famous shaman, early in the afternoon. Last summer Edwin had taken Lupe to the United Nations conference on human rights in Geneva. There was a confusion at the airport when the customs man asked Edwin, in English, if he was bringing in any "spirits," and Edwin said no, and the customs man looked in his suitcase and found a bottle of tequila. As we sat around the woodstove in Gumercindo and Paula's kitchen, Paula cooked tortillas, and Gumercindo related the incident that had forced him to leave Coloradas.

On December 12, 1993, Torres and his brother Luis, the local traditional governor, who opposed growing drugs, were dancing the Matachines in the Coloradas church. About thirty men, and more than a hundred women, were packed inside. Agustín Fontes and four other cowboys were heard joking outside the church.

At about 9 p.m. Agustín and another *pistolero* burst into the church, while the others barred the door so no one could escape. Once inside, the two men started shooting into the air with AK-47 rifles. A few seconds later, Fontes grabbed Luis Torres by his T-shirt and whispered in his ear. Then he shot Luis eight times at point-blank range in the chest, pumping two or three slugs into his arms and legs for good measure. Luis Torres died on the spot. The other assailant proceeded to gun down Gumercindo as he was moving along the wall of the church. He was hit in both shoulders and in one of his hips. After he fell, the man fired one last shot at his head, and then the two *pistoleros* fled, thinking that they had surely killed the Torres brothers. But as it turned out, the last bullet had only grazed Gumercindo's scalp.

After treatments by Tarahumara shamans and Mexican doctors, Gumercindo had fled to the relative safety of Piño Gordo. Edwin eventually convinced the federal police to escort him to Coloradas, where he persuaded 110 eyewitnesses to walk fourteen hours to the town of Baborigame and offer depositions that ultimately resulted in Agustín's arrest.

Gumercindo's eyes burned with anger as he told his story. He would have loved to get his hands on Agustín Fontes, but Fontes was in the Chihuahua pen, convicted of the murder of his brother and awaiting trial for sixteen other murders. "A few days before Agustín was arrested," said Gumercindo, "people in town told me that they heard him boasting, 'How pretty it is getting money for killing Indian authorities, and how easy it is.' "

Edwin explained that he had taken the Scottsdale, only to discover that it wouldn't go into four-wheel drive, and the road, muddy from the rain, had been almost impassable. He and Lupe had had to walk the last ten miles of it, which was why they were late. Soon the traditional leader of Piño Gordo, Agustín Ramos, came walking down the hill, and we talked about the problems of the community. Agustín was one of Piño Gordo's three shamans. One specialized in peyote, the other in medicinal plants, and Agustín was the expert on interpreting dreams and locating errant souls.

"Is it better that the modern world has come to Piño Gordo?" I asked Agustín.

"It would have been better if there were no *chabochi*," he replied, "but now that they are here, we must come to some agreement."

"Have you ever used peyote to find answers to your problems with the *traficantes?*" I asked. Edwin later said this was an excellent question, but Agustín would never tell me. "You cannot ask a direct question like that and expect an answer. It would take two months to find that out."

All Agustín would say was "Peyote is not for modern problems."

Piño Gordo was ninety miles from the nearest paved road, which we reached nine hours later, after much pushing of the Scottsdale and placing of rocks and branches under its wheels, and threading a maze of little roads that finally came out at a grungy little place called Hiervitas; it would have been impossible to find the way back to Piño Gordo unless you already knew it. We crashed in a truckers' flophouse and the next day descended from the sierra into a vista of polka-dot mesas and *quebradas,* or ravines, which looked a lot like New Mexico, except that way below there was a golden savanna studded with flat-topped oaks, which looked like Africa.

As we neared the *municipio* of Balleza, we passed, to the right side of the road, a crashed DC-7, upended and lying on its nose. This was one of the four cargo planes in which, from 1988 to 1991, tons of cocaine had been flown up from Bolivia. From there pilots for the Fontes had flown the coke in small planes to Las Vegas or Denver, sometimes throwing in grass or heroin from the sierra, or the stuff was driven over the border in lumber trucks. The transshipment of cocaine is where the big money is. The municipal president of Balleza, whose nickname was El Guante, the Glove, had personally overseen the operation, which ended when the army sabotaged the landing strip, causing the front wheel of the plane to break off. The last shipment was supposed to contain three tons of coke, but only three hundred pounds were recovered.

We reached Parral, where Edwin put me and Lupe on a bus to Chihuahua. Edwin was continuing to Baborigame, where one of his promoters, a Tepehuano Indian named Guadalupe Rivas, was in hiding after two Fontes cowboys had tried to kill him. Winged in the shoulder, Rivas had killed one of the assassins with his knife. A few days later, Fontes cowboys had gunned down a police captain and tried to blow up the municipal police station. "It looks like the Fonteses may be hanging themselves," Edwin said. From Baborigame Edwin was picking up an escort of five federal policemen, going to see what was doing in Coloradas de la Viergem.

"Hey Edwin," I called to him as he was walking toward the Scottsdale, and he spun around.

"Watch your back."

He gave a grim little smile.

As of this writing, Edwin is still alive and, with the help of an article I wrote about him for *Outside* magazine, he got on the shortlist for a human-rights award from the Robert F. Kennedy Center, which he didn't win, but he was awarded a Goldman environmental award that pumped fifty thousand dollars into CASMAC.

Spreading the Word

ost of the other *chichimecos* were more reducible than the Tarahumara. Like the other Mexican tribes, they were already a conquered people, and they submitted docilely to the Spaniards, who were, on the whole, a lot nicer to them than the Aztecs had been. The missionaries were able to tap deep wells of native meekness and devotion. Indian and Christian ritual calendars combined to produce a rich year of fiestas, pilgrimages to holy sites, an ongoing pageant of devotion found in few parts of Christendom.

Within a few years of contact, most of the *chichimecos* had been converted from "savages" to "self-conscious children of God." They were civilized *gentes de razón*, rational beings in the Enlightenment sense; they wore clothes (and were what are known in the Amazon today as shirt Indians), spoke a little Spanish, were Christian, or almost. Within a few generations they would be fully assimilated campesinos who had lost their language and culture. Of the original forty-five tribes of the Greater Southwest whom the missionaries contacted and identified by name (and every one of the names was a misnomer, starting with the term "Indian"), only twenty-five are left.

By the eighteenth century, an estimated 70 percent of the Indians of New Spain were still living in their traditional way; almost all the rest were mestizo, Indians who had crossed and backcrossed with Spaniards and African slaves. The Spaniards, themselves a mixed people, a blend of a dozen or so ethnic strains ranging from Visigoth to Moor, had fewer hang-ups about miscegenation than the English did, and instead of killing off or relocating the Native American population, as happened in the British colonies, they absorbed it or, perhaps more accurately, were absorbed by it, which explains partly why Latin America is less "developed." The absorption process slowed them down. Not that mixing with the natives was a deliberate part of the program. There were damn few Spanish women in the colony.

More than a hundred terms arose for different racial types in New Spain. A *coyote* was a Spanish-and-Indian half-caste, the most common mix. It retains the meaning of "mestizo" in *nuevomejicano* today. A mulatto, or *café-con-leche,* was the child of an African mother by a Spanish father; a *lobo* (wolf) was Indian and black (the term had a pejorative connotation like "nigger"); a *castizo* was Spanish and *coyote* and often looked so much like a criollo, a "pure" Spaniard, that he could pass as one; a *saltapa'tras* was someone who had "jumped backward" and turned out darker than both his parents; a *notiendiendo* (literally, "I don't understand you") was an undecipherable mix. *Morenos* were dark-skinned Moorish North African–Arab–blacks; in Brazil *moreno* means simply dark-skinned rather than completely black African, that is, 90 percent of the population. *Trigeños* were more olive-skinned Mediterranean.

While the racial differences became increasingly blurred, the prejudices died harder. The many-tiered colonial caste system was in the end racially determined. The whiter and more criollo you were, the higher your status. Typical of the prevailing attitudes was a report from the Jesuit father Ignaz A. Pfefferkorn, who spent from 1756 to 1767 as a missionary on the northern frontier in Sonora. He claimed that the local *coyotes* were "not as brown" and were on the whole more intelligent, stable, enterprising, and lively than the pure Indians. The mulattos were "generally not trustworthy," while the *lobos* were the ugliest of all, of "evil disposition, fierce and crafty" to boot.

The North Beckons Again

The line of the northern frontier of New Spain was shaped like a hand whose fingers pointed upward.* It crept up haltingly, working its way around pockets of resistance like the Tarahumara, sometimes drawing back when a local uprising flared up. Ultimately it would reach southern Utah and Colorado and along the Pacific Coast as far up as Vancouver, and its spread from east to west would be some two thousand miles. The northern borderlands would embrace an area of roughly 960,000 square miles—a good deal larger than all of Western Europe.

There were three main thrusts: one east, into Texas; one up the Pacific Coast, into California; and one up the middle, into Cíbola. For forty years after Coronado returned empty-handed from Cíbola, no European set foot in the region; no one capitalized on the significant contribution the expedition had made to knowledge of what lay to the far north. News of Alarcón's discovery that Baja California was a peninsula for some reason did not register with the cartographers in Europe, and it remained an island on most maps through the seventeenth century, until Father Kino rediscovered its connection to the mainland in 1700. Kino began to suspect the connection after the chief of the Cocomaricopas, one of the Colorado River Yuman tribes, sent him twenty blue abalone shells of a type not found in the gulf. He reasoned correctly that the Cocomaricopas must have had some way of

---

* I was just savoring this image. Not bad, old boy. It's this kind of writing that makes history live. Then I realized that I was not the author of it (though the second sentence about the hand creeping up haltingly and drawing back is my imaginative catching the ball and carrying it downfield). I had appropriated it mentally and begun to think of it as my own, when in fact it was the New Mexico historian John Kessell who shared it with me in a conversation in 1986. It was a beautiful case of unconscious theft, to which I can only respond by sheepishly recycling a remark by Victor A. Kover, a lawyer specializing in First Amendment cases: "Ultimately all history is based on the history of others."

getting to the Pacific, on the "opposite coast" of Baja, which must therefore be a peninsula.

The maps of this period reveal how much of the New World was still terra incognita. Sanson's map of 1650 has the hemisphere plunging off into nothingness beyond "Cíbola" and "Florida." Beginning in 1561, some chroniclers refer to the vague northern lands Coronado had explored as the "Kingdom of New Mexico," even though no new Mexico had been discovered.

De Soto's even more disastrous quest for the Seven Cities confirmed Coronado's conclusion that there was nothing up there worth bothering with, hardly even enough Indians worth the trouble of subjugating or saving. What got Spain interested in the north again was yet another geographic fantasy—the nonexistent Strait of Anian. European geographers couldn't believe there was no way of getting from the Atlantic to the Pacific for the entire length of the North, Central, and South American landmass, that nature could have been so inconsiderate of human interest. In 1578 the English privateer Francis Drake threaded his ship, the *Golden Hind,* through the Strait of Magellan, then made his way up the Pacific coast, plundering Spanish ports and galleons, and the next that they heard of him he was back in England. Spanish intelligence, trying to track his movements, couldn't believe that he had struck out across the Pacific and circumnavigated the globe; he must have found a northern passage to the Atlantic and returned through the long-sought Strait of Anian. Suddenly, on the strength of this erroneous assumption, the far north of New Spain became important again, this time for strategic reasons. We must get up there and control the strait before the British do, King Philip II's advisers told him.

It was to locate the strait and find the best site along it for a presidio that a small reconnaissance party under Father August Rodriguez— three Franciscans, nine solders, sixteen Indian auxiliaries—set out in 1581 from a little place in the province of Coahuila called San Bartolomé—at the time one of the northernmost outposts of the viceroyalty—followed the Conchos River to its meeting with the Rio Grande, and went up into Pueblo country. No one there could direct them to the strait or even provide a lead. After several fruitless months the soldiers decided to go back. The friars stayed to save the Indians and were all martyred. One was killed by Tano Pueblos, another by Tiwas.

The following year a small expedition led by the wealthy Zacatecan António de Espejo came to prospect for minerals under the pretext of rescuing the friars. Striking out west from the Rio Grande, he stopped at Hawikuh, where the old men regaled him with their reminiscences of the battle with Coronado, then he continued through Hopi country to the Verde River of central Arizona, where he picked up some promising silver samples and rumors about a lake of gold. He estimated the native population of the Kingdom of New Mexico to be 250,000.

By this time interest in the north had been rekindled, despite the inability of anyone to find the strait, and several men were under consideration for the royal patent to conquer and settle the region. Exploration and colonization in Spain's colonies were strictly controlled by the authorities; freelance efforts were not tolerated. Even the missionaries were on a tight leash. There was a precept against their knowing anything about mining, for instance. So the unauthorized initiative of Gaspar Castaño de Sosa, the lieutenant governor of the province of Nuevo León, was not appreciated. He set out for New Mexico in 1590 with 170 colonists and was arrested by soldiers who caught up with him at Taos and escorted him out of the area.

I would like at this point to beg off telling the entire history of colonial New Mexico, my original intention, and to quote instead the UCLA librarian and eminent Southwest scholar Lawrence Clarke Powell: "Although I know that Cabeza de Vaca came first, I am unable to name his followers in their proper order: Coronado, Vargas, Oñate, Mogollon, Alvarado, Anza and Kino, Marcos de Niza—the music of their names is quite enough for me."

I'll do just one more of these caballeros, Juan de Oñate. Another rich Zacatecan and a well-connected one, Oñate won the patent to colonize Nuevo Mexico in 1598. His wife was a granddaughter of Cortés; his father, Cristobal, had governed Nueva Galicia during Coronado's absence and had later been one of three partners who discovered silver in Zacatecas. The Oñates were Basques. Much of the commerce on the northern frontier was controlled by Basque entrepreneurs. They developed mines and ranches. Sheepherding in Nevada is dominated by Basques to this day.

Don Juan was cut in the brutal Guzmán mold. The wounds Coronado had inflicted on the Pueblos fifty years earlier might have healed if he had not opened them again. He was also, as many of his *compadres* seem to have been, in the habit of flogging himself as a means of atoning for his violence to others. One of Oñate's captains describes how the first Holy Week in New Mexico was celebrated:

> The soldiers with cruel scourges beat their backs unmercifully until the camp ran crimson with their blood. The humble Franciscan friars, barefoot and clothed in cruel thorny girdles, devoutly chanted their doleful hymns, praying for the

forgiveness of their sins. Don Juan, unknown to anyone except me, went to a secluded spot where he cruelly scourged himself, mingling bitter tears with the blood which flowed from his many wounds.

On April 30, 1598, at a pueblo twenty-five miles north of present-day Santa Fe, Don Juan formally took possession of New Mexico in the name of the king, and construction of its first capital, San Juan de los Caballeros, began. From there he sent out parties to explore and exact allegiance and tribute. One party went west to look for the South Sea (later called the Sea of Cortés or the Gulf of California) which Oñate had heard was full of pearls and offered a shipping route to Peru; apparently unaware of the distances involved, Oñate was hoping to establish a close trading relationship between the two colonies. The Spaniards never made it to the gulf, but they met some Mojaves who told them about the great Lake of Copella, whose natives wore gold bracelets, and about a rich island of bald-headed men ruled by fat women with big feet, hard by some other people who slept underwater at night. The information was duly passed on to the authorities in Mexico City. No one seems to have had any trouble believing it.

The Indians came to dread these little detachments with lances and harquebuses and curved helmets, these somber files of iron-clad menace. The Navajo called them *nakai,* those who go around in groups, or travelers; the Tewans called them *quanko,* simply, iron (literally, malleable rock) and also used a long phrase meaning purveyors of mischief, wreakers of havoc, destroyers of things, both of which terms are still in use. Oñate tried to recruit 200 soldiers, but only got 129, and these were mercenaries of distressingly low moral character.

The main body of the expedition, led by Oñate himself, reached the fabulous citadel of Acoma at the end of October and was cordially welcomed with corn, turkey, and water for the horses. According to Peter Nabokov's *The Architecture of Acoma Pueblo,* the People, as the Acoma call themselves, emerged at a place called Shipap (the Pan-Puebloan *sipapu*), sprouting from deep within the earth, and were brought to life, quickened by rain, the same way the buried seed of a corn plant is germinated by a downpour seeping into the earth. They were guided through a sequence of villages by Iatiky, "mother of all Indians," and the Corn Mother, who with her sister was nursed in darkness by Tsichtinako, "Thought Woman." The mesa is shaped like the "head" of a perfectly kerneled ear of corn. The pueblo has been there since at least 1200. Ward Mindge, who has written a history of the Acoma nation, told me there are traces of raised causeways on the valley floor leading to the mesa, which suggests that it could have been at one time an island in a lake, like the floating city of Moctezuma, since smothered by Mexico City.

Perhaps not understanding what they were getting into, the Acoma agreed to become royal vassals. Oñate had his harquebusiers fire a salute "to the wonder and terror of all the savages." The elders invited Oñate into the kiva to seal the agreement in a sacred ceremony. Oñate looked down into the dark pit and, thinking they had some kind of treachery in mind, refused to go. The insult simmered in the Acoma's hearts, or something else touched them off, and on the first day of December they killed Oñate's nephew and all but five of a party of about thirty caballeros following the main expedition. One of them escaped by leaping off the butte into the sand four hundred feet below.

In January the nephew's brother, Sergeant Major Vicente de Zaldívar, returned with seventy soldiers to avenge his death. After three days of fighting (in which Santiago reportedly materialized, riding a white horse with a spear in his hand, killing infidels "like the whirlwind," as Ramón Gutiérrez writes, at his side "a maiden of most wondrous beauty, presumably the Virgin Mary"), twelve Spaniards and eight hundred of Acoma's estimated six thousand citizens were dead. Eight girls from the pueblo were taken off to Mexico; all males of age twenty-five or more had one foot cut off and were sentenced to twenty years of servitude; and the right hands of two visiting Hopi were amputated as a warning to their people. Then the pueblo was torched and leveled to the ground.

The People and their culture lay shattered until 1629, when a Oaxacan priest named Juan Ramirez persuaded them to pick up pieces of their lives and rebuild the pueblo, but this time with a mission as its centerpiece. According to legend, Ramirez caught a baby accidentally dropped off the butte. Because of Ramirez's truly Christian kindness, the Gospel had more penetrance at Acoma than it did at the Zuñi or the Hopi villages.

The pueblo has had the Spanish form of civil government, with a frequently rotating governor, *alcalde, topil, fiscal,* and other officers, since 1620. Behind this is the real government, the ancient theocracy, with a head cacique and other religious leaders. There are thirteen surviving clans. The Antelope clan meets behind the church, in which there are hidden idols. Many of the Acoma are Christians in the real sense, but a lot of other stuff is going on; the old religion is still alive.

Recently the pueblo and Jemez Pueblo have come under fire from animal-rights protectionists for a sacrificial rite they perform at the Feast of Saint John the Baptist, on June 24, in which horsemen compete to uproot a rooster that has been buried up to the neck, often getting just the head and sending blood spurting around the plaza. The roots of the rooster pull are in medieval Spain, where it was a fertility rite, the rooster's blood moistening the earth, symbolically fertilizing it to make it fruitful.

One of the most important Acoma rituals is the little pony dance, which happens only every seven years. People approach the spirit representative who is mounted on a stick horse and whisper to him and walk away with tears streaming down their faces. "It's a very solemn thing," Mindge told me. In the thirties an anthropologist named Leslie White collected many of the esoteric rituals and ceremonial secrets, including the details of the pony dance, by taking his informants to an Albuquerque hotel room and loosening their tongues with liquor. "The Acoma want to round up and burn every copy of White's book, that's how strongly they feel," Mindge told me.

"There's been a lot of cultural loss in the last twenty years," he went on. "Vets have returned from all over the world with their outlook changed. Many can't even speak Keresan." With the mines in the vicinity shut down, local work opportunities are limited, and many of the four to five thousand Acoma work in Albuquerque, which is a little over an hour away. The proximity of this big city imperils their culture, and there's been a problem with a neighboring rancher named Gottlieb, an environmentalist named Paul Robinson, who works with the tribe, told me. "Horace Springs, which pours out fifty gallons a minute, drains the malpais on the Gottlieb ranch and is less than a hundred yards off the reservation. This is the only flowing stream in the area, and since time immemorial the Acoma have been using it for mitzvahlike bathing rituals. Water was given to the People by Father Sun at emergence, along with sky, fire, and corn, but they don't control this major discharge point; they only get second hit. Until eight years ago raw sewage, including floating turds, was discharged by the city of Grants into the San José River, which flows past Horace Springs, but the Acoma sued successfully to upgrade what could be put into the San José, so now the water is okay for drinking or swimming."

Such encroachments, along with the memory of the bloodiest, most traumatic contact of any of the Pueblos, have resulted in a rise in traditionalism and xenophobia in recent years. There's a problem of who is an Acoma. Some tribes admit those who are as little as one-eighth (that is, one great-grandparent belonged to the tribe), but the Acoma are reluctant to let their blood run that thin. Privacy is a big issue. "One way to close the door is to ask about religion," Mindge told me.

The first time I visited Acoma was the summer of '86, when I was following the advance of the northern frontier of New Spain. Now there's a road to the citadel. It's a postmodern experience, as Nabokov puts it, but there are no wells or electricity up there. The modern world has not yet overwhelmed the feeling of deep antiquity verging on time-lessness, the sense of having always been there (Mindge's translation of what "Acoma" means), that imbues the pueblo. Its importance is now mainly ceremonial. Only fifty or so elders live there. The other Acoma are scattered over the valley floor, or they live in Acomita, a new community twenty miles away, right off I-40.

I drove up with a busload of tourists. Our guide was a young Acoma woman who sat beside the driver, reading a paperback called *The Coming of the Quantum Cats,* until we reached the top and it was time to start the tour. She was not friendly, not a people person, at least with us, but proud and aloof. She led us out to the edge of the butte past several sacred golden eagles tethered to a roof, and we took in the view to the east. Milton's word "emparadised" came to mind; the Acoma were emparadised on their mesa. There was another butte on the valley floor, which she said was called Enchanted Mesa. The People used to live there, but one day a "raging rain" washed away the steps up to it. A young girl and her grandmother were stranded on top. Rather than suffer a slow death from thirst and starvation, they jumped.

We continued along a narrow alley smelling of piñon smoke that led between mud-and-straw walls with timbers protruding from them. Old women sat in doorways behind tables of white-slipped pottery, freshly baked fry bread, and peach tarts. The place was at once earthy and unearthly.

In the middle of the mesa stands the mission of San Estéban del Rey, built from 1629 on, destroyed during the Pueblo Revolt of 1680, and rebuilt from 1700 on. It is the largest and one of the finest examples of early Franciscan architecture in New Mexico. Our guide pointed up to a cluster of ancient bells in its open belfry that had been brought from Spain via Mexico. One was traded for ten children, who were taken off as house servants. There was a small fenced cemetery in front of the church. The earth to bury the dead there was brought up by women carrying baskets balanced on their heads, the same way they trans-ported earthen ollas. The interior of the church is a vast, cool nave with a dirt floor. The adobe walls are sixty feet high and four feet thick. Forty-foot pine vegas, or ceiling beams, brought from the San Mateo

Mountains, forty miles away, on the shoulders of Acoma men, carry the roof. According to legend, the vegas were not allowed to touch the ground during their journey. Several small windows below the roof provide the only light. The centerpieces of the altar are a wonder-working *bulto,* or painted wooden statue, of Saint Stephen, which is taken out of its niche and paraded on his feast day, and an iconlike painting, or *retablo,* of Saint Joseph with the Christ Child, presented by the Spanish king Carlos II. When there had been no rain, the Acoma would have taken Saint Joseph down to their fields at Acomita, and the rain would start to fall. They would have rain when there was no rain in all the country, and they would have crops when their neighbors the Lagunas had none. The Lagunas kept pleading with the Acoma to lease them the *retablo.* At last the Acoma relented. But then the Lagunas refused to give it back. Not until blood was shed and the Acoma had taken the Lagunas to the Supreme Court was it returned, in 1856.

So much I learned from the tour.

Five years later, one of the first things I did after settling in in Albuquerque was to take the family out to Acoma. After an hour on the desert steppe, we saw signs along the interstate: GENERICS NEXT EXIT. WINSTONS NEXT EXIT. ACOMA EXIT NOW. We parked at the cultural center below the citadel and hastened to catch the bus that was about to leave. A polka rock band playing in front of the center was taking a break. "Boy he's nervous," I heard the bloated bass player remark as I tried to hustle everyone into the bus.

Having been in Tibet a few months earlier, I was struck by how Tibetan Acoma seemed: the women sitting in front of turquoise and silver wares, the mangy dogs, the slab walls, the glimpses of the barren, breathtaking plateau at the end of zigzagging alleys, the soaring choughs. Rosette, my wife, stood at the edge of the butte and exclaimed, "Nature speaks here." She got talking with an old woman who was selling some pots etched with busy black lines, and the woman said that her goal in life was to make people happy and to leave the world a better place.

It was Labor Day, and the elders were having a procession. One old man paraded the cane that Lincoln had presented, two others bore the *bulto,* the statue, of Saint Stephen. Something very meaningful seemed to be going on underneath the procession that was making its way down a dusty alley.

The last time I visited, with a photographer friend from back east, we walked up to the citadel on the old path through the crack, and when we reached the top, the same woman who had been my guide five years before was waiting for us. "You're not allowed to do that!" she yelled out. She reminded me of the Intourist guides in Russia in 1979, before glasnost, who kept saying every time I looked behind a door I wasn't supposed to, "*Nelzya!* It is forbidden!" The atmosphere was very repressive, like "Moscow on the eve of the purges," as Edmund Wilson had found Zuñi in 1947. My own attempts to get to know the Acoma were rebuffed. The writer-historian of the pueblo stood me up for lunch in Albuquerque. I tried to arrange an interchange through the All-Indian Pueblo Council. What do you want to know? the Acoma representative asked. Basic things, to start with, I said, like the meaning of *estruda* or *kashdura* or whatever the word for "Spaniard" is. (I had heard two versions, but neither informant knew what his or her version meant.) "We don't give out that kind of information for nothing," he said. "We're wise to you guys." And he came out with this rap about royalties and cultural property rights. I said, "No thanks. I'm a great believer in the free exchange of information."

Zaldívar, the same sergeant major who laid waste to Acoma in January 1599, the following July led twenty-five men to conquer the seven easternmost pueblos, one of the largest population centers, with some ten thousand people. Three of the pueblos were Tompiro, four Tiwa, two were variously called Jumano, Humano, Xumano, or Rayado— the last meaning "Striped People," because they had a stripe tattooed or painted on or above their noses. These people lived on the edge of the Plains—the Plains were just over the mountains—and they did a lot of trading with the buffalo-hunting Kiowa Apache. It was so dry where they lived that they saved their urine to mix with adobe. Their existence as sedentary agriculturalists was precarious in the extreme, and they had nothing to spare.

Riding into one pueblo, Zaldívar demanded tribute—the cotton blankets that the women wove and tortillas. The people offered him stones. Some months later Oñate himself returned in force to punish them for their insolence. He set fire to the pueblo, his harquebusiers picked off five or six people on the rooftops; two of the more bellicose men were hanged. When his interpreter protested, he was hanged, too.

In time, the seven pueblos were pacified, five missions and two *visitas* were set up among them, a vigorous campaign to stomp out their religion was undertaken, and there were frequent levies of piñon nuts, buffalo skins and jerky, and cotton blankets. One blanket levy, a captain reported, left "the women stark naked, holding their children to their breasts." Tompiro bearers were forced to carry salt from a salt lake in the vicinity down to El Paso del Norte, where they were often enslaved and put to work in the Parral silver mines. The salt was used in the patio process of silver smelting. It was one of the four riches Oñate managed to turn up in New Mexico. The other three were pearls, buffalo hides, and cotton blankets.

The eastern pueblos were unable to withstand these pressures. Between 1600 and 1660, the population of the largest pueblo, Gran Quivira, dropped from 3,000 to 1,000, probably because of introduced diseases, measles and smallpox being the likeliest candidates. Another 450 died during a drought in 1668. In 1672, perhaps driven out by Apache, the surviving Gran Quivirans abandoned the pueblo and scattered to parts unknown.

Oñate's dreams of founding a new colony, with himself as viceroy, were short-lived. Returning at the end of November 1601 to San Gabriel (his new capital, across the Rio Grande from San Juan de los Caballeros) from a three-month sally into the Plains, he found the place practically deserted. The twelve Franciscans (a deliberate echo of the twelve "apostles" in on the conquest of Mexico), appalled by the atrocities perpetrated on the Indians and their women by the soldiers, had talked the colonists into giving up. The colonists, who had suffered an unusually harsh winter and shortages of food the year before, had agreed, and all but a handful had departed south for Sonora. Oñate had them brought back and sentenced them all to death as deserters, then he realized he had no such authority over them; they were not soldiers under his command, slaves, or savages, but his own countrymen who had come of their own free will.

News traveled through the Franciscan grapevine across the Atlantic and finally reached the ears of King Philip III, who gave the order five years later for all further exploration in the kingdom of New Mexico to cease and for Oñate to present himself at Mexico City immediately. On the way down, his party was attacked by Indians, and Don Juan's son Cristobal was killed. Don Juan's luck had run out. He was charged with thirty offenses and convicted of twelve of them, including maltreatment of the Indians and failure to report wealth accumulated on the Plains—the latter a groundless charge, as there was no wealth on the Plains, at least of the kind the Spaniards were looking for. The same charge had been made against Coronado.

The Diffusion of Horses

on Juan's legacy went beyond the death and hatred he sowed in New Mexico. His expedition is thought to have introduced the horse into the Southwest. Scholars of the question are now quite sure that Coronado was not involved; only two of the 558 horses that set out from Compostela in 1540 were mares. "No hidalgo would deign to ride a mare," J. Frank Dobie explains in his book *The Mustangs*. "Spanish men boasted of their *huevos* (testicles), as a source of virility. The ideal Spanish horses had *huevos* also." Dobie dismisses as a "pretty legend" the theory that one of Coronado's stallions met up on the Plains with one of the lost mares of the de Soto expedition and mated with her, as some have proposed. "If another fable had placed Adam in Asia and Eve in Africa, the chances of mating would have been about as high."

By contrast, a hundred mares and colts, in addition to seven hundred stallions and mules, went on the Oñate expedition.

The Spanish horses were a far cry from the wild species of *Pliohippus* and *Equus* that had died out in the Americas ten thousand years earlier. They were basically barbs brought to Spain by the Moors, with varying doses of Arabian blood—the horse of the North African desert, bred for endurance, adapted to dryness, with a coat as variable as a cat's. Pure Arabians are solid colored: chestnut, bay, sorrel, roan, gray, *tostado* (dun). Barbs are splotched, dappled, calico, piebald, or painted; and the two breeds eventually blended to produce what Dobie characterizes as the "hammer-headed, ram-nosed, ewe-necked, goat-withered, cat-hammed, sore-backed, hard-mouthed, mean-natured, brown-tailed bronco of the West."

At first the Indians didn't know what to make of the Spaniards' horses. Some Indians thought that the horse and the rider were one being. Some called the horses "big dogs" and "monsters" and rubbed horse sweat on themselves in the hope of acquiring the animal's magic. Soon they learned that horses were mortal and aimed their arrows at them, because demounted, the Spaniards lost much of their edge in battle. The Indians discovered that horse flesh is tasty. But still they were wary of the beasts. António Espejo, Oñate's predecessor, would have been set upon in the night by warlike Indians near Jerome, Arizona, in 1583, had the Indians not been frightened off by the neighing of the horses.

The Crypto-Jews

n 1630 Fray Estan de Perca, the *custos,* or agent, of the Inquisition in New Mexico, began a nine-year investigation of the moral state of the *intendencia,* the colonial administration. He found rampant corruption among both soldiers and priests and widespread evidence of bigamy, adultery, and witchcraft. One man was brought before the Inquisition for no other reason except that his father had never said he was not a Jew.*

The initial function of the Holy Office in New Spain was to enforce orthodox conduct and belief in the recently converted Indian population. Later this was delegated to the friars; each prelacy had its own torture implements, stocks, leg irons, and infrastructure for dealing with backsliders. The office also dealt with *judaizantes* and Moriscos—lapsed Jewish and Moorish converts, of which the Church was fairly tolerant until the Counter-Reformation of 1580. It policed minor infractions, like blasphemous language, cards, and gambling. One man who was brought up before it had broken out in buboes of tertiary syphilis, had said God did not have power to cure illness, had spat on some holy images, and had done some unspecified dirty things with crucifixes. Other crimes: posing as a priest, bigamy, polygamy, clerical heresy, concubinage, desecration of a church, eating meat on Friday, failure to attend church, paganism, performing Jewish rites, reading prohibited books, human or animal sacrifice, sexual immorality, solicitation of women at the confessional, sorcery and occult art, treason, usury. A man in Michoacán in 1537 had hung *ristras* of chile to sun-

* The sources for the following discussion include *The Mexican Inquisition of the Sixteenth Century,* by Richard Greenleaf; France V. Scholes, "Church and State in Mew Mexico," *New Mexico Historical Review* XI, no. 4 (Oct. 1936), 297–325; Mary Elizabeth Perry and Ann J. Cruz, eds., *Cultural Encounters: The Impact of the Inquisition in Spain and the New World* (Univ. of California Pr., 1991); *A History of the Jews in New Mexico* (Univ. of New Mexico Pr., 1990).

dry on the arms of an outdoor cross. Native healers and shamans were persecuted for using hallucinogens like *pipiltzintzin* and performing human and animal sacrifice. Protestants, known as *luteranos* and *extrangeros,* like one Robert Tomson, were forced to wear *sambenitos,* penitential garments, for three years. So was a nun, for reading a treatise by a "Cathusian" advocating that man could achieve perfection by simply observing the Ten Commandments. Other punishments included burning at the stake; confiscation of property; excommunication; being forbidden firearms or horses; pilgrimage; public humiliation; service in a sweatshop; spiritual penance; tongue piercing; torture by rack, by water (the *submarina,* aka *la pileta,* whereby the head is submerged, preferably in a turd-filled toilet bowl, still a favorite interrogation technique of the Federales and of Paraguayan, Brazilian, and other Latin American constabularies), and other means; horsehair shirts; whipping.

In 1580 Spain took over Portugal, sending a wave of educated Portuguese Jews in flight to the Indies. There was a flowering of the Catholic faith in Mexico, which precipitated a crackdown. *Limpiezas de sangre,* pedigree checks, were made of those suspected of having hidden Jewish blood and of being "crypto-Jews," only pretending to be Catholic, for which there were several terms: *converso,* Marrano (literally, filthy pig), and *cimarrón* (the term also applied to the Tarahumara *gentiles*). As Richard Greenleaf writes in his book *The Mexican Inquisition of the Sixteenth Century,* "Investigation in depth into the Inquisition Archives leads one to believe that there were more Protestants and Jews in Mexico than is generally supposed. Only a small number came before the Holy Office." If you kept a low profile and went about your business and did not bring notoriety to yourself, you didn't usually come to the Inquisitors' attention. But in a 1528 auto-da-fé two Jews were burned at the stake in Mexico City for heresy. Between 1589 and 1596, the Holy Office prosecuted almost two hundred *judaizantes* for observing Yom Kippur. The worst years of persecution were 1585 to 1601 (when silver boomed; then the climate became tolerant again) and 1642 to 1649 (when there was a new crackdown on Portuguese in the colony after the duke of Bragança freed Portugal from Spain in 1640). One *converso* explained his circumcision as "due to an early infirmity I had in those parts." Another tried to explain it away as "the mischief of women." (Catholics at this point in time weren't generally circumcised.)

Many *conversos* made their way to the northern frontier. The illegal 1590 *entrada* of Gaspar Castaño de Sosa seems to have been a quest for religious freedom, much as the Mormons' trek to Utah under

Brigham Young would be three centuries later. The names of de Sosa's *compañeros*—Rodrìguez, Nieto, Carvajal, Díaz, Hernandez, and Pérez—are the same as those on Inquisition rosters. The expedition was arrested by soldiers of the viceroy and taken back down to Mexico.

How many crypto-Jews came to the northern frontier to escape persecution after the de Sosa expedition there is no way of knowing. Henry J. Tobias, who has studied the *conversos* of New Mexico, believes few could have escaped the elaborate screening, the background checks, the *limpiezas de sangre,* colonists went through. Families with certain surnames were banned from emigrating to the *intendencia,* such as "Carvajal," after the martyrdom in 1596 of Luis de Carvajal the Younger, one of the most learned Judaizers.

Even after the Inquisition finally shut down in 1820, crypto-Jews in New Mexico were still reluctant to reveal themselves because their land grants might have been open to question. Some intermarried and became among the most pious Catholics, while holding on to vestiges of Judaism, such as lighting candles on Friday, their descendants in time not even knowing why they did it except that it was a family tradition. Another scholar, Martin Cohen, writes that there is "no evidence that any Jew ... reached New Spain during the sixteenth century, and scant evidence for the balance of the colonial period." No one, in any case, was ever convicted of being a Jew in New Mexico. One governor, Lopez de Mendocino, was accused of Judaic practice, but the charge was dismissed as political assassination.

However, in the past few years, many *nuevomejicanos* have been discovering or finally owning up to Jewish heritage. A Dutch film crew was shooting a documentary on the *conversos* while we were living in Albuquerque. I knew the saga of the persecuted Sephardic Jews who fled to Pernambuco, Brazil, in the early 1500s, and then were persecuted and fled again to New York City, where they founded the city's first synagogue, on Central Park West. I knew that much of the Brazilian intelligentsia is of old submerged Jewish ancestry, and a Brazilian writer friend from the northeastern state of Ceará told me that her father had a gold watch engraved with the Lion of Judah that had been passed down to him and that she was beginning to suspect that she was Jewish. The Argentine fabulist Jorge Luis Borges was a *converso.* So I wasn't surprised, having written a book on genealogy and kinship systems, and knowing that six generations back each of us already has 126 ancestors, to hear people saying that every old *nuevomejicano* family has a hidden Sephardic line. This wasn't what people like Senator Tom Benavides wanted to hear, who considered themselves blue-blooded *peninsular,* pure criollo Español, untainted by any Indian or Marrano blood, espousing what one scholar sardonically describes as the "airlift from Castile" theory.

I began to realize that there is no single Hispanic New Mexican, but a variety of types, a number of ways of seeing oneself: Chicano, criollo, *cholo* (a Chicano, like "dude" in current Anglo slang), *converso.* The *conversos* also fit into another category. They were another of these persecuted hermetic southwestern groups, like the Penitentes, like the Pueblos, who kept alive their ceremonies in the darkness of their kivas. Jewishness being matrilineal, the mothers kept the faith alive. The female lines were more hidden. Some never told or would admit to being Jewish to their children and yet taught them Ladino, the Sephardic Yiddish that is largely *siglo del oro* (Golden Century) Cervantean Castilian. "Ladino" means having a mastery of Spanish, as in *es ladino en el idioma.* This remarkable saga of mother love, of cultural tenacity, is just being pieced together. In one family, the kid plays with a spinner known as a dreidel used in celebration of Hanukkah. Another family eats *pan de semita,* kosher Passover pastry, during Lent. A man comes to a seder in Taos with a Talmud that's been in his family for three hundred years. Others cover mirrors, cut clothes, or smear themselves with ashes when there's a death in the family, not understanding why. For some, it was a shock to discover that they were one of the Matadores de Cristo, the Killers of Christ, and that Christ, in their family's belief, was not the Messiah.

Within a few days of our arrival in Albuquerque, I learned of the existence of the *conversos* from the real estate woman who rented us the beige mock adobe on La Hacienda Drive. It wasn't hard to find them, she told me. There were plenty of them around, and they were reembracing their faith and being welcomed in the synagogues as long-lost brothers and sisters, like the Falasha of Ethiopia whose emigration to Israel I'd written about a few months earlier. The Falasha, however, may not be Jews at all but Christians who, due to a schism in the Ethiopian Orthodox Church in the thirteenth century, removed the Christ from their Christianity, becoming de facto Jews of a sort while retaining much of their Christian liturgy.

Through Tonantzin, the traditional peoples' advocacy group, I got to know Nicásio Romero, a sculptor and ceramicist who was also the president of the New Mexico Acequia Association. About a thousand acequias, or irrigation ditches, survive from colonial times, and each is a self-governing micro-jurisdiction. Nicásio and his wife, Jane, née Stein, an artist originally from Brooklyn, live in the Rio Arriba at a bend of the Pecos River called El Ancón, the Elbow. One morning

Nicásio and I were sitting around with his mellow neighbor, Joe García, a wrangler who breaks horses. Nicásio and Joe both consider themselves Chicanos. One of Nicásio's grandmothers was a Hopi medicine woman. One of Joe's great-grandfathers was a Comanche *genízaro* (a captive brought up in a Mexican household), who was forced to be a scout for the army, and his maternal great-grandfather was a San Ildefonso Pueblo. At the moment, Joe told me, he and his wife, Celina, were taking care of two black runaways, twelve and thirteen, from Houston. The two boys had decided to take off and see what the world outside the ghetto was all about. "I just put them on their first horses," Joe told me. "You should hear their slang. Do you know what they call pussy? Tuna. Here it's the fruit of the prickly pear. It used to be ginch or poontang."

Celina is a *converso*. Her full name is Celina Rael de García. "Rael" as in "Israel." A beautiful woman and a dynamic activist, she'd had a longtime involvement in the militant Chicano group the Alianza, trying to get back land of La Raza ripped off by Anglo lawyers and the National Forest Service. Her sister in Dallas, Anna Rael de Ley, recently reconverted to Judaism. "She went for it," Celina told me. "She's been written up in magazines." "Celina's sister never felt healthy as a Catholic," Joe told me. "A lot who discover their roots are going all the way." Celina and Anna's mother would never admit she was Jewish. Nicásio knows a man named Aaron whose mother, Ruth, only opened up to Jane, herself an Austrian Jew, that she was Jewish after they'd known each other for eight years. The family name was Chavez. They didn't eat pork. "They weren't even that crypto," Nicásio continued. "Archuleta Chavez became a rabbi. It's just surfacing after all these years."

I called up Anna Rael in Dallas, where she teaches school. "In 1710 we had a relative named Ysrael," she explained. "A place-name surname like 'Madrid' or, in Germany, 'Berlin' is the first sign you could be Jewish. The Inquisition wound down in New Mexico in the 1820s, after Mexican independence. But even after that, the *conversos* were in danger. They lived in secrecy in isolated little mountain villages, like Villenueva, and minded their own business. I grew up in Santa Fe and didn't know what I was till high school, when I started reading Jewish books. I was attracted to it. I found that our family had some of the same customs. My paternal grandmother, who lived on a farm, always questioned what I'd been eating when I arrived. She said it was forbidden to mix milk and meat, and at Easter we always had these hard bread-type things, and we cleaned out the cupboard and lined it with paper. Father, when he butchered a lamb or a sheep, always prayed before he removed the sciatic nerve. I asked him why he did that, and he said, 'I don't know. That's the way we've always done it.' Mother lit candles on Friday, and she didn't know why either. Everybody in our neighborhood in Santa Fe did it. My grandparents told me, 'Whatever we do in this house, don't tell anybody. It's not anybody's business.' In parochial school I began to have questions about the Catholic religion. How could they say that this man [Jesus Christ] was it when other men and women did great things? The nuns were mean. A whole lot of other things kinda started to fit in. I went down to Puerto Vallarta, Mexico, for vacation. At a restaurant I gave my name Rael, and the waiter asked if I was Jewish. My brother really looks Jewish. I brought a little Star of David pin to school, and a fellow teacher who was Jewish asked if I was, too. I read Joyce's *Ulysses*. Blum was an outcast, and I could identify with him."

Anna and a friend went to a graveyard in Galisteo where both their ancestors who had died in the late 1800s were buried, and they found a lot of Stars of David on the headstones. "I'm still going through the conversion process," she told me. "There are many others like me. We're finding each other. Some embrace it; some deny it and say there's just no possibility. As I started learning the customs, I felt kind of relieved, as if I'd finally found my place. I asked my dad, and he says we might be, and Mom says no. But why does Mom know these Ladino Passover songs?"

I heard about a *converso* named Ernie Orona who works at the Freeway Liquor Store, right under I-25 in Albuquerque. Orona looks to be in his late forties. He has a handlebar mustache and an Einstein-like daftness about him. I'm not expecting a man of such erudition, but in a few minutes we are *batendo papo,* palavering away in Brazilian slang. He owns the place, and he seems to do a brisk business. Right now, it's quitting time, so he's real busy cashing paychecks, taking care of his regular clientele of bums and winos, who are known in *nuevomejicano* as *borrachos,* letting one guy have an eighty-five-cent jar of coffee for a quarter, advancing a six-pack of beer to another on credit, switching easily from "Right on, brother" (to a black customer) to *"Gracias amigos"* and talking to me beween transactions. Orona did a tour for the Peace Corps in the Colombian Amazon and is working on a novel he plans to call *Nowhere, New Mexico*. Interesting guy.

"I suspected from an early age I was Jewish," he tells me. "My grandfather Elauterio Sanchez, I eventually found out, belonged to an old Sephardic family that came to New Mexico right after the *reconquista* in 1704. He had some prayers that he never said in public. My mother passed on Ladino to me, but to this day she refuses to admit that she is Sephardic Jewish. She married a Basque. I think there was a conspiracy on the part of the mothers to protect us that lasted for centuries. Jaramillos, Carvajal, Sanchez—any of the families that have been noticeably active in New Mexico over the years are at least part Jewish. The psyche of Old New Mexico is different because of the fact that we Marranos were hidden, like the Penitentes. I'm trying to convey in my novel what it's really like to be one of these bowlegged, cross-eyed, pinheaded, isolated, undereducated Old New Mexicans who missed out on the Industrial Revolution." A bleary-eyed *nuevo-mejicano* enters the store. "Here's another one," Orona says, lowering his voice, "a half-dilapidated hidalgo."

The man leaves, and he continues his story. "Ladino is the Spanish that was spoken in 1492 when the Sephardics were kicked out. In modern Castilian you say, 'Lo vi.' 'I saw it.' But in Ladino it's 'Lo vide.' There's considerable overlap with the Cervantes Spanish spoken by non-*converso* Old New Mexicans, but every once in a while you get a really archaic expression, the way Kentucky hillbillies speak Eliza-bethan English and Afro-Brazilians in Bahia speak purer Ibo than the Ibo. Seven or eight percent of the Old New Mexicans speak Ladino. Most of them have Sephardic in them and don't know it. I could always tell two kinds of people in New Mexico, the Old New Mexi-cans and the *mexicanos*. Chicanismo is the post-Woodstock urban street ideologues trying to get back to their ethnic roots. The Old New Mexicans never got into it, but their kids did. All of us from Old New Mexico knew we were different from mainstream Latinos but couldn't identify what it was. I put it together when I saw Latin America in the Peace Corps. The Old New Mexico psyche is very different from main-stream Latino, because of the *converso* hidden culture. It's still very European."

Seventeenth-Century New Mexico

The Spanish ascendancy as the dominant Western power was already over by 1580, and by the time Oñate was taken down to Mexico in chains, Spain was on the wane. The British had taken control of the seas, and with their privateers intercepting much of the bullion from the New World, they were recycling the blood and sweat of Indians into their own coffers and imperial agendas. The deeply religious, half-mad, probably syphilitic Spanish king Philip II retreated into his enormous palace in Madrid and refused to have anything to do with the ideas and technological advances that were creating modern Europe (as was explained to me by the brilliant, etiolated official chronicler of Mexico City, Guillermo Tovar y de Teresa, who himself had the blood of *le tout* viceregal New Spain in his veins). He was followed by a series of incapable Hapsburgs, and instead of having a Reformation, a Renaissance, and an Enlightenment during the late sixteenth, seventeenth, and eighteenth centuries, Spain remained locked into a course of inexorable stagnation and decline. The empire was in disarray everywhere. Little Castile had bitten off far more than she could chew. Remote territories like New Mexico, which existed mainly for humanitarian reasons—for the salvation of heathen souls—and weren't self-supporting, and were a drain on the royal treasury, were left more or less to fend for themselves.

It took six months to get to Mexico City, and there was a chronic shortage of specie in the *intendencia*. The only regular contact with civilization was the caravan that came up on average every three years with wine, windowpanes, paper, silks from the Manila galleon, chocolate for sweets and mole (the rich chocolate-chile sauce for chicken), wedding dresses, manufactured goods from Puebla, bullets, china, books (which were greedily devoured by those who could read), perfume, and other luxuries to keep the few Iberian women happy. By the time the goods reached *el fin del mundo,* as one colonist described New Mexico, they had been taxed many times over and were exorbitantly expensive.

The isolation led to boredom and heavy infidelity. The women sought herbs, powders, and other potions from the Indians to lure back their philandering husbands, pastes to apply to their men's bodies to heighten the pleasure of intercourse. One was made of mashed worms cooked with *atolé,* or corn gruel. While their husbands were off with other women, priests seduced wives by persuading them that if they were going to sleep with anyone, it was less sinful to sleep with a man of God. The priests took liberties with the beautiful, giving Pueblo women as well. Ramón Gutiérrez, sifting through the parish records and other primary documents of viceregal New Mexico, finds all kinds of hanky-panky. "Because sanctity and sex were so closely related in the Pueblo world, it was common for men and women to give their bodies to persons they deemed holy, in order to partake of their supernatural power," he writes, and many an unscrupulous priest took advantage of this belief. With typically earthy humor, the Pueblos called those who submitted to baptism Wet Heads. The term, Gutiérrez told me, was in time extended to all the Spaniards.

The first Franciscans to come to San Juan Pueblo found the people praying to their kachinas for relief from a withering drought. Soon after their arrival, it started to pour, and after a few days the rising floodwaters threatened to wipe out the pueblo, but after a few waves of the cross by the Brown Robes, the rain miraculously stopped. Among the Hopi, a Brown Robe placed the cross and smeared some mud and spittle over the eyelids of a blind boy and said *Epheta,* and the boy's sight was restored. The Hopi thought at first that the priests were potent Inside Chiefs, in close contact with the forces of the cosmos, but it didn't take long for the Hopi to see through their juju.

The priests seem to have been into either gratification or mortification of the flesh, which, in the latter case, Gutiérrez writes, "had to be tamed, punished . . . and repressed with devout and continuous prayer, with flagellations, vigils, fasts and abstinences from food and drink." If you really succeeded in achieving self-mortification, you might get stigmata like Saint Francis. If you absolutely had to fornicate, it should not be done from behind, "doggie style," but with the man on top—which is how the term "missionary style" originated. For some of the Brown Robes, the Pueblo dances with fathers and daughters, the Hopi fellating snakes, sticking the wriggling serpents in their mouths, were an incredible turn-on. In 1638 the Taos Pueblos complained that Fray Nicolas Hidalgo "twisted [the penis of one of them] so much that it broke in half," leaving him without the head of his member. Others grabbed the testicles of reluctant converts.

Whipped for "lewd" dancing, their idols smashed, keeping their kiva secrets alive, as the *conversos* did, the Pueblos were converted by force, but in the end Christianity became more than a veneer; many became genuinely devout Christians. "Why did we accept Christianity?" Dave Riley, a Laguna Pueblo asked. "That's a big question that no one has really addressed." Part of the answer, surely, is that not all of the priests were the kinky perverts Gutiérrez makes them out to be. There were good priests and bad priests. Some, like the Oaxacan Juan Ramirez, who spearheaded the reconstruction of Acoma, were behind the Indians and the mestizos.

The miscegenation of male Spaniards and female Indians produced a cultural *mestizaje* and syncretism of the negative aspects and applications of spiritual energy. New World and Old World fears of sorcery fed on each other. Both derived from a common source—the same Holarctic Paleolithic culture that had been generalized in Eurasia and had traversed the Bering Strait. The Christian notion of Satan was the one thing indigenous southwesterners could most easily relate to. The demons of the native shamanism dovetailed with those about in Extremadura. The *nuevomejicanos,* huddled in isolated *poblaciónes*— mountain villages, outlying missions, and fortified settlements called *placitas* (when Santa Fe became New Mexico's third capital, in 1610, there were no more than three thousand colonists in the entire Rio Arriba)—were as afraid of *los difuntos* as the Navajo and Apache were of the ghosts of their dead.

It's hard to say who was more paranoid. The Acoma used quartz crystals, which they believed gave them second sight, to divine the identity of the sorcerers among them. Zuñi, Isleta, Nambe, and San Ildefonso Pueblos lost some of their most prominent citizens during witch hunts in the nineteenth century. Convergences included the Hispano *brujas,* who sally forth at night in the form of coyotes, wolves, cats, or owls, like the Navajo skinwalkers. The owl is the messenger of death for Tarahumara and Navajo, but it also makes Old *nuevomejicanos* uneasy.

One morning Nicásio Romero and I were heading out to his barn on the Pecos River when we spotted a great horned owl sitting high in a huge old cottonwood tree. Nicásio said the owl hunted mice in the open loft and often waited out the daylight from that perch. It sat motionless as a branch stump, its ears retracted, its neck tucked in, its body bands blending with the light bark. The only part of it that was discernibly animate was its yellow, narrowed eyes, which watched our every move.

Later in the day, Nicásio and I drove past the *población* of El Tecalote, the Owl, on the freeway. "El Tecalote is supposed to be a witch village," he told me, "to have more *brujas* per capita than any other village in the Rio Arriba, but the people I know from there are pretty mellow. A lot of midwives and people who know herbs live in El Tecalote. My grandmother was a Hano Hopi from First Mesa [the Hano are a Tewan group that joined the Hopi around 1700]. She was trilingual. She spoke Hopi, Tewa, and English and was an herbalist, an *arbulária*, with healing powers especially for intestinal problems and fever, and a *partera*, a midwife. My mother gained much knowledge of herbal *remedios* from her. If the treatment goes right, you're a *curandera*, if not you're a *bruja*. The line between *curandera* and *bruja* is sometimes not that clear."

What other plants do the *arbulárias* use? I asked. "*Mota* is used as an herbal and smoked, drunk, or chewed to keep witches at bay. The dope culture in Old New Mexico goes way back. My grandfather used to smoke it. Another old *remedio* is *cachana*—weird, slow-burning roots from Mexico. You inhale the smoke and get an incredible rush. *Oshá* [*Ligusticum porteri*, a panacea in the parsley family] roots are chewed as a potent medicinal like ginseng. Others are *hierba del manso, dela negrita, de la vivera, imortal, romero* [rosemary], *colita de ratón*. Oregano and horehound grow wild. We hang out strings of garlic to ward off vampires. There are counteractive herbs for impotence and for *bruja* spells. Many of our practices are not that different from those in rural Rumania."

Other convergences between Old and New World black-arts traditions include the *mal genio* or *mal ojo*, evil eye, a powerful glance from a *bruja* that can drain you of your strength. Children are especially vulnerable. Navajo burn or shoot effigies of people they wish evil to or break their porcelain or other precious possessions. Rural Rio Arribeños paint the doors and windowsills of their houses turquoise to ward off witches—the color of the Virgin Mary's serape, but this is also a Moorish tradition. Indians wear turquoise talismans for the same purpose. To this day houses in remote *poblaciónes* come under supernatural assault, as Marc Simmons reports in his book, *Witchcraft in Old New Mexico*.

"The belief in the existence of La Llorona, the Wailing Woman, is still strong," Nicásio went on. "She's always there, hovering. We were told as kids that if we misbehaved we would hear her, and I did hear her once when I was seven. She cries for you, reinforces your guilt complexes. It's really you that are crying. When you see her, she's always cloaked in a black or white veil. Sometimes she flies. Another function she has, which may be Aztec or Moorish in origin, is to find lost children. I heard La Llorona in an alley in Mountainair, where I grew up, just as it was getting dark. I was coming back from the movies and was halfway down an alley. There was no way to get away. You talk about breaking the hundred-yard dash! When I got home, I buried myself under the blankets. It was the saddest, shrillest, most piercing cry you ever heard. It cut right through your heart."

Motorcycle cops patroling Albuquerque's open, cement-lined ditches, which are like half pipes when there's no water in them and are great for skateboarding, warn kids about La Llorona, the water witch, the ditch witch, who will sweep them away in a flash flood. According to *Crosswinds,* a Santa Fe alternative paper:

> La Llorona (Weeping Woman) is a legend who haunts the country streams of all Hispanic lands. The legend probably originated in Greece with Medea, who murdered her children. La Llorona, according to legend, drowned her children and is doomed to search for eternity, calling and crying along rivers, ditches, and arroyos. As a result, mothers warn their children never to go near the running waters at night.

El Hombre Largo, another folkloric supernatural being, stalks in Santa Fe, and every village has its miracle and its stories of inexplicable occurrences, of "witch lights"—luminescent fireballs dancing on distant ridges and so on. Perhaps the most amazing occurrences were the apparitions of the profoundly religious Franciscan nun Maria de Agreda. Too frail for missionary work in New Spain, Maria de Agreda remained in a convent in Spain. There, for three years, beginning in 1620, when she was eighteen, repressing and redirecting her sexuality and going into frequent trances, she received the divine gift of ecstasy and levitation. "Other nuns would lift her veil to glimpse the pale radiance of her face in ecstasy, or position Maria in levitation where outsiders could peek through the grillwork of the convent and blow to make her weightless body sway," the historian of viceregal New Mexico, John Kessel, told me. (Kessel gave me a monograph he had written but not yet published called "The Broken Triangle: Maria de Agreda, Franciscans, and Jumanos"; I first read about her in Paul Horgan's *Great River.*)

Stories of her sudden appearance in remote uncatechized Indian villages of New Mexico began to reach Spain. One report had her seen and heard preaching the Gospel in four widely distant pueblos at the same time. She was reported to have been slain with arrows once by Jumano and twice by Colorado River tribes, left for dead, and to have come back to life and vanished into the air. These reports were investigated by the Inquisition—female natures being regarded as weaker and more susceptible, it was always possible these acts could be deceptions of the devil—and the Inquisitors confirmed her ability to bilocate, to be in two places at once, to transport her spiritual essence, which then projected her physical likeness, wherever it was needed. There are similar stories about great lamas of old Tibet and their mastery of teleportation.

Revolt

As the seventeenth century wore on, the Pueblos grew increasingly restive under the Spanish yoke. The people of Jemez and Taos killed their priests in 1623 and 1631. The Zuñi decapitated and scalped their fathers, Friars Francisco de Letrado and Martín de Arvide, and cut off their hands and feet as trophies. The horses and the slave raids of the Spaniards had by then upset the fragile peace the Pueblos had been struggling to maintain with the Band People on their fringes. Pueblo men were expected to help defend the colony against the attacks of the Navajo and the Apache and were often forced to join the Spaniards in offensives against them. As a result, the Band People, by the seventeenth century, began fresh onslaughts on the Pueblos, who were caught in the middle. The Zuñi had to abandon six of their pueblos and collect into a single one; the Jumano had to clear out entirely. It became impossible to go out and work in the fields and for the male head of each household to keep coming up with the annual tribute of one *fanega* (2.58 bushels) of wheat that the Spaniards demanded, and the Pueblos began to starve. On top of this, entire communities were being wiped out by a strange pestilence that could only have come from the Wreakers of Destruction—smallpox. Beginning in 1663, there was a six-year drought that left Pueblos "lying dead along the roads, in the ravines, and in huts," according to one account. A census of the Pueblos conducted the following year counted only 20,181 souls. In 1630 the missionaries had boasted of converting 80,000.

For all these disruptions of the Pueblos' relationships with their nomadic neighbors and with the forces of nature, the Spaniards were to blame. By forbidding them to practice their religion, to perform the propitiatory rites that were necessary to maintain the balance of nature, to bring the very sun up into the sky each morning, the Spaniards were clearly precipitating cosmic disaster. The Indians tried to keep up the rites in secret. They went underground. They compartmentalized, were Christians on Sunday and Pueblos the rest of the time. The friars kept banning their dances and railing against their polygamy and promiscuity and their satanic orgies and flogging any Pueblo caught conducting heathen rites and confiscating their "idols," their kachina dolls and masks and other sacred objects, and burning them in great bonfires, but it was all to no avail. The Pueblos kept making new dolls and masks, and the friars weren't astute enough to dislodge the Pueblos from the center of their universe, the pueblo itself (although several were wiped out, and there was a lot of moving around and relocating of village sites). They didn't understand that the pueblo was the central shrine, and in the darkness of the kivas the Pueblos managed to keep the old ways alive to a remarkable degree, even to this day.

The Pueblos were also waiting for the right moment to make the Spaniards pay for the liberties they had taken with Pueblo women, who were "well-made and modest," in one chronicler's description. Particularly eye-catching were the virgins, the unmarried girls, who "go nude until they take husbands, because they say that if they do anything wrong then it will be seen and so they do not do it." Not only soldiers, settlers, and colonial officials, but even priests, consumed by temptation, had relations with the "sinks of iniquity," as one friar described the women. Known "sinks" had their hair shorn as fornicators.

Tension mounted, and the Spanish settlements on the Rio Arriba became like islands in a sea of increasingly hostile Indians. It became obvious to Pueblo elders that if the people were to survive, the Spaniards had to go. In 1640 a plot involving members of Jemez, Isleta, Alameda, San Felípe, and Cochiti Pueblos was discovered, the ringleaders were hanged, and the other conspirators were sold into slavery. Ten years later, a plan for a general insurrection was hatched at Taos Pueblo. It was circulated on deerskins, but the Hopi refused to participate, and it never got off the ground. During the famine of the 1660s, the entire *intendencia* threatened to blow. In 1672 the Jumano of Ab'o Pueblo stripped their father, Pedro Avila y Ayala; put a rope around his neck; flogged him to a bloody pulp; and finished him off with tomahawks. His naked body was found clutching a cross and an image of Blessed Virgin Mary. At his feet lay three lambs with their throats slit. "The message was unequivocal," Gutiérrez writes. In 1673 the Pueblos began to openly perform prohibited dances, "making offerings to their gods and begging them to return. The medicine men worked feverishly, placing hexes on the Christians and trying to steal their hearts. Apparently their magic worked. In 1675 alone, Indian witchcraft was blamed for sending

seven friars and three settlers to their graves." That year, when 47 of
their leaders were flogged for witchcraft, idolatry, or the promotion of
idolatry, the Pueblos reached the breaking point. The 25,000 to 30,000
Indians in the Rio Grande drainage, including Apache and disaffected
genízaro, mestizo, mulatto, and Moorish servants, rose up against the
2,350 Spaniards and staged the most successful native revolt the New
World has ever seen. (The next most successful one is the ongoing insurrection of the five Mayan groups in Chiapas, Mexico, who call themselves the Zapatista Liberation Army.)

The purpose of the revolt was primarily religious: to restore the spiritual balance with the forces of nature and fellow beings necessary for
the preservation of the Pueblo peoples. Every one of the seventy-odd
pueblos except that of the Piro, who weren't notified, was involved in
its careful planning. Its leaders were Popé of San Juan Pueblo (the
name may mean "Ripe Squash"; to this day in the Rio Arriba, if you
want to compliment someone for being slick or sagacious, you can say
Es muy Popé); Francisco El Ollita, war chief of San Ildefonso; Luis
Tupatu of Picuris; the great Keresan leader Antonio Malacate; and El
Saca. Several mixed-bloods, notably the mulatto Domingo Naranjo,
were in on it.* The conspirators would meet after midnight on the
feast day of a particular pueblo, when they had an excuse for being

---

* Peter Nabokov's *Indian Running* begins as a journal of the Tricentennial Run of 1980 com-
memorating the spreading of the instructions about the revolt, and it evolves into a broad survey of running in the native Americas. Nabokov retained a single custom as his focus. For
Nabokov, the project became "an object lesson in what can happen when you track down a
seemingly isolated or minimal feature of American Indian life. A whole system unfolds before
your eyes." The main reason for running was, of course, the need to get messages from one
community to another. But in Wisconsin there were messenger monks who ran, were celibate,
carried special bowls and spoons, and sound like the Tibetan trance runners, or lamas *lung-
gom-pa,* who were allegedly able to become airborne. So does the last of the old-time Chemehuevi ceremonial runners, a quiet twenty-year-old by the name of Rat Penis who one morning
in the 1920s, Nabokov writes,

> left his friends at Cottonwood Island, in Nevada, and said he was going to the mouth of
> the Gila River, in southern Arizona. He didn't want anyone else along, but when he was
> out of sight, the others began tracking him. Beyond the nearby dune his stride changed.
> The tracks [Nabokov's source, the anthropologist Carobeth Laird, reports] "looked as
> if he had been just staggering along, taking giant steps, his feet touching the ground at
> long, irregular intervals, leaving prints that became further and further apart and lighter
> and lighter in the sand."

Some runners enlisted a spirit helper or dream helper, datura or a talisman, strong wild
trance-inducing tobacco, or swallowed biting ants in their effort to leave the ground. A young
Hopi runner in 1903 took a message 72 miles and came back with an answer in thirty-six
hours. Another ran from Tuba City to Flagstaff and back—156 miles—in less than twenty-four
hours with news of Navajo renegades. The Hopi Tewans "run for rain." Nabokov found that
running messages was more than just a job. It had a consciousness-raising purpose. Running
"outside the message," the runner seems to undergo a deeper transformation, performing Aris-
totle's definition of motion as, in Nabokov's words, "the mode in which the future belongs to
the present . . . the joint presence of potentiality and actuality," until finally "he becomes the
message."

together. They bided their time until 1680, just before the big triennial caravan from Mexico was due, when the colony was low on everything, then they sealed off Santa Fe, stationing guards to intercept anyone who tried to escape or go for help.

Meanwhile runners from Red Willow (Taos) spread the word to the other pueblos, carrying knotted yucca cords for counting down the days and deerskins with a pictograph explaining that everyone should strike together on the day of the August new moon, the ripe corn moon. The revolt had all the earmarks of a revitalization movement, like the Ghost Dance that the Paiute of southern Utah started doing in 1889. The Pueblo Revolt was similarly atavistic, primordialistic, messianic, millenarian. Let the ancestors get us out of this and put our culture back on track. The ancestors will only be happy when all the Wet Heads have been killed or driven from the land, Popé preached. It will be like the time of emergence. A woman for every Spaniard killed.

Two days before the full moon, two runners from Tesuque Pueblo, Nicolas Catua and Pedro Omtua, were captured by Spanish soldiers and taken to Santa Fe, where under torture they revealed that a letter from the Indian lieutenant of someone called Poseyemu had been sent around threatening death and destruction to any pueblo that didn't take part in the rebellion. This lieutenant, they said, was tall and black, with large yellow eyes. The Spaniards took Poseyemu to be the devil. Other rebels later interrogated in Santa Fe revealed that Poseyemu was "he who strews the morning dew," and that he lived far to the north, where Moctezuma had come from. Moctezuma was a culture hero for the Pueblos. He taught them how to build their multistoried, many-roomed mud houses and their kivas, then went down to Mexico City and founded the Aztec empire. His eponymous descendant was defeated by Cortés. In many Pueblo legends, Moctezuma and Poseyemu are one and the same. Sometimes Poseyemu is also identified with Christ, whose Second Coming is imminent. Poseyemu is coming back to save the Pueblos from the Spaniards, just as today certain tribes of the Upper Amazon are waiting for "the Inca" to reappear and take them back to the time before the whites came into their world and ruined it. Some scholars think that the tall, black, yellow-eyed lieutenant may have been the mulatto Domingo Naranjo, cleverly passing himself off as Poseyemu's prophet.

Word of the runners' capture reached the people of Tesuque, and they jumped the gun on the revolt. Their priest, Fray Juan Pió, watching as they painted their faces red, said, "What is this, children, are you mad? Do not disturb yourselves; I will help you and will die a thousand deaths for you," and with that, writes Gutiérrez, "a shower of arrows pierced his breast." The other priest, Father Hidalgo, barely escaped to Santa Fe with news of what had happened. Other pueblos ordered all Wet Heads to leave. The most dedicated priests stayed and were martyred. Twenty-one of the thirty-three Franciscans in the territory were killed. One, Fray Juan de Escalona, had prophesied the revolt a decade earlier. All told, four hundred Spaniards lost their lives. Acoma threw their priest, Fray Lucas de Maldonado, off the mesa.

Those who escaped barricaded themselves in Santa Fe. The Pueblos cut off the town's water supply, the Agua Fria, and waited, then they torched the town, and as it burned they mockingly sang Latin liturgies. On the eleventh day of the revolt, Antonio de Otermin, the governor of the colony, gave the order for everyone to head south. The fugitive Wet Heads trudged through scenes of destruction, past bodies in missions and *estancias* along the river. "If the Pueblos had been warlike, they could have attacked the helpless, thirsty, and bedraggled Spaniards," the ethnohistorian and Jemez Pueblo Joe S. Sandos writes of the exodus. "But as their purpose appeared to become a reality, the Pueblos only observed the Spaniards moving out. And once the Spaniards were gone, every object and relic of the Spanish era was destroyed."

The Border/Frontera

Scalded, the spread-fingered hand of New Spain's northern frontier drew back to El Paso del Norte, at the bend of the Río Bravo, and there the colonists regrouped. Some left the frontier altogether. For twelve years the Pueblos had their purged ancestral homeland to themselves. But the new dispensation was a short and a disappointing one, a last taste of freedom from European contamination. It did not live up to Popé's buildup. It wasn't at all like the time of emergence and became more like one of the half-made countries of postcolonial Africa, with a would-be dictator rushing into the power vacuum. Popé declared himself king of the Pueblos, and eliminating his rivals, he soon began to demand even greater tribute than the Wet Heads had. As with so many revolutionaries, power began to act on him as he strolled in the ruined arcades of Santa Fe, and assuming gubernatorial airs, he became increasingly a burlesque of Otermin. But the Pueblos weren't ready to unite under a central authority. Without a common enemy to bring them together, ancestral differences reasserted themselves. The famine and epidemics that they had blamed on the Spaniards continued to plague them, and the Navajo, in equally dire straits, with no one else to prey on, started raiding the Pueblos again. The ancestral gods deserted them. Already, the Pueblos were in a different place. They couldn't get together, and they couldn't go back to the way it was. The cosmos was irrevocably tainted.

Three hundred and six years later, having caught the train at Creel and descended from the Sierra Madre to Chihuahua City and continued north in a succession of pickups and buses, I reached El Paso del Norte, now the twin cities of El Paso, Texas, and Ciudad Juárez, Chihuahua. In Chihuahua City I had seen the bullet-riddled black Dodge Brothers sedan in which Doroteo Arango, better known as Pancho Villa, caught sixteen slugs at 8:30 a.m. on July 20, 1923, in a fusillade ordered by President Adolfo de la Huerta, who wanted to go another term, even though it was prohibited by the constitution. Villa had vowed that if de la Huerta was "reelected," there would be another revolution. Villa had lived in exile in El Paso for several years with Luz Corral, one of the twenty-six women who considered themselves his wife; it was from there that he crossed the Rio Grande and, in a series of eight remarkable victories, ushered in the second Mexican Revolution. Blondie, as Villa called Corral, was rumored to be still alive somewhere in Juárez, but I wasn't able to find her because, as I later learned from her moving memoir, *Pancho Villa an Intimacy* [*sic*], she had in fact been dead for five years, having passed on the sixth of July 1981 at the age of eighty-nine. "I loved Villa with all my heart, loved him as he was, fierce and violent like the streams from the mountains," she reflects in the memoir, penned when she was fifty-nine. "Let them [who accuse him] consider the humble origin of his life, the hardships of his lonely, hunted youth in the midst of a hypocritical, selfish world, his generous, stubborn fight for freedom and his life in constant peril; and let them tell me if his existence, complex and tortured, is not the genuine reflection of the life of the Mexicans during the years of their fateful Revolution."

Juárez/El Paso is one of the paired, mutually predatory cities along the 1,952-mile-long border. The others, starting at the Pacific and proceeding east, are Tijuana/San Diego, Mexicali/Calexico, the two Nogaleses, Nuevo Laredo/Laredo, and Matamoros/Brownsville.

I drove to Tijuana with a friend from San Diego in 1976; this was my very first foray into Latin America. I don't recall seeing such a visually violent cultural and economic clash in all my subsequent travels. The two worlds ran up against each other right at the seven-foot chain-link fence. On the Mexican side was "the worst hellhole on earth," as a recent sheriff of San Diego referred to Tijuana, or as Ovid Demaris describes it in his novel *Poso del Mundo,* "the toughest, roughest, gaudiest, filthiest, loudest—the most larcenous, vicious, predacious—the wickedest border town of them all. It is all border towns wrapped into one smelly reefer and freaked out on its compulsion to 'skin the gringo.' No border town hates the gringo with the intensity of Tijuana, and no border town does a better job of separating him from his bankroll." Today something like three million people are spread out along Greater Tijuana's fifty miles of fence and in the thirty-odd canyons of the Tijuana River drainage, many living in shacks sided with flattened cardboard boxes. (In January 1993, tens of thousands of these ramshackle dwellings were washed away or carpeted with mud after twelve days of heavy rain, temporarily checking Tijuana's chaotic, uncontrolled growth.) The streets seethe with life, people grazing at taco stands, guys *comiendo moscas,* whistling at *chicas.* The American side, *el otro lado,* is clean, open, empty desert until you get to San Diego, whose streets are in much better repair but they are dead. If Mexicans have their "labyrinth of solitude," a different loneliness—the price of progress—quickly takes over.

The multilane customs booths at Tijuana have been compared to a giant starting barrier at a dog track, but far more duck La Migra and enter illegally, as *mojados,* or wetbacks (literally, wet ones; having just talked about Wet Heads, we now have a water-based pejorative for a category of Latinos). How many nobody knows, because those who get caught are only a drop in the bucket; maybe a couple million a year, most, but by no means not all, of them Mexicans. Now, ten years later, after virtually my first visit to Tijuana, every male under thirty I had been meeting en route to Juárez had been to *el otro lado.* Sneaking over the border seemed an almost-obligatory rite of passage.

As with any life-cycle initiation, there had to be an element of danger, the possibility that one might not make it. An armed patrol of neo-Nazis had just been arrested in the desert outside of El Paso for harassing a group of Mexicans who had come in. The border was dangerous for everybody. At the Big Bend in Texas, a party of Anglos rafting down the Rio Grande in a rubber raft had come under fire from a sniper on the Mexican side, and several had been killed.

Juárez/El Paso in 1986 was much less jarring than Tijuana/San Diego had been ten years earlier. The transition was more blurred, and the blurring, the merging of the two worlds, continues. With 1.5 million residents and a large floating population, Juárez has big shopping malls and suburban subdivisions just like the ones in El Paso; parts of the city are completely *agringolado,* Americanized, and thousands of its citizens commute to jobs in El Paso, some with work permits, some without. (Those lacking permits wait by the fence for their employers to pick them up; if La Migra is around, the employer keeps going and swings back later.)

Many big companies—Ford, General Motors, RCA, Zenith, Westinghouse—ship their raw materials to plants they have in Juárez known as *maquiladoras,* where, because there are no unions and safety and environmental codes are laxer, the materials can be assembled far more cheaply. The finished products—carburetors, chain saws, TVs, washing machines, computer disks, shirts, underwear, dollhouses, false teeth—are brought back in and taxed only the value of the labor. With a huge and growing pool of Mexicans and Central Americans willing to work for three or four dollars a day, squatter camps without plumbing or electricity are shooting up in the desert out of town. Because labor costs were much lower than in Hong Kong or Malaysia, Volkswagen, Nissan, and Sony were getting in on the deal by the early nineties. Some envisioned a high-tech industrial zone rivaling Taiwan, South Korea, or the southern Chinese economic zone of Shen Zhen—a golden age for the border. In anticipation of the signing of the North American Free Trade Agreement (NAFTA) in November 1993, the Tijuana, central, and Gulf drug cartels were already starting that spring to set up factories, warehouses, and trucking companies and to buy up *maquiladoras* and other legitimate companies in Juárez as fronts to exploit the flood of transborder commerce and the relaxation of border controls. But the following year the Mexican miracle unraveled.

On New Year's Day, when NAFTA went into effect, the Zapatistas struck in the south, and the ancient grievances of the long-exploited and marginalized Indians and campesinos, which two revolutions had failed to redress, surfaced again. As the year progressed, the ruling party's presidential candidate and then its secretary-general were assassinated, exposing the moral bankruptcy of the political system and massive drug corruption at the highest levels of government. That December, foreign investors panicked and, after several hours of frantic mouse clicking, transferred out the millions of dollars they had been pouring into the country, and the peso crashed. The *frontera* remains in squalid limbo, a virtual third country that, as Tom Miller writes in his book *On the Border,* "does not adhere to the economic, ethical, political, or cultural standards of either country" and, since the 1850s, when the boundary was first established, has been "a place where every conceivable form of illicit activity is condoned."

Even if the savage-capitalist vision of the border had come to pass, for whom would it have been a golden age? Certainly not for those who work in the *maquiladora* zone, which has the lowest wages in the New World next to Haiti and a much higher accidental-finger-loss rate than American plants, for instance, while those that remain—the hands of assembly-line workers, seamstresses, chicken packers, and so on, which are required to perform rapid repetitive motion all day long—frequently end up crippled with carpal tunnel syndrome. The citizens of Tijuana, Juárez, and the other Mexican border cities also suffer the effects of millions of gallons of toxic chemicals from American plants that are trucked over the border and are promptly dumped into the local sewers. In one recent case *maquiladora* effluent including the compound THC seeped into groundwater back on the American side and contaminated the wells of two Arizona trailer parks.

Exposure to solvent may be responsible for a recent cluster of anencephaly and spina bifida in heavily polluted Brownsville/Matamoros. In three months three babies there were born without brains. Such people are victims of environmental racism, on which I attended a conference in Albuquerque in the fall of 1991. Albuquerque is probably the most ethnically aware place in the Southwest and indeed the world, where the understanding of social injustice is most sophisticated and refined. You would think that environment knows no color, but, in fact, an activist named Irene Reyna explained, people of color—Latinos, African Americans, Asians—suffer from not only racial but environmental discrimination. The concept was first advanced in a 1978 study of silicosis among black miners called *Toxic Waste and Race*. In Albuquerque, she claimed, the Environmental Protection Agency is "one of our most racist institutions," selectively policing toxic dumps, so that in the Valley, where Chicanos, blacks, and other dark-skinned poor live, 20 public and 450 private wells are contaminated by leaking underground petroleum storage tanks and septic tanks and improperly stored or disposed of industrial chemicals, including carcinogenic benzene, xylene, and toluene, while the water in the white neighborhoods on the Heights is clean. "The Southwest is an internal colony of companies that are looking for cheap ways to produce goods," Reyna, who belonged to a solidarity group called the Fuerza Unida, continued. "New Mexico is basically a colony of the military-industrial complex. Many of the most toxic chemicals from these activities are shipped to Mexico in unmarked containers, and that's premeditated murder. We view the border as a political fiction. This is our same family regardless, and we must all come together to fight the notion that people are expendable."

By lifting duties on American goods and enhancing Mexico's manufacturing capabilities, letting Mexico finally have its own indigenous auto industry, for instance, NAFTA was supposed to have reduced the flow of illegal aliens, but the bottoming out of the Mexican economy has in fact sent a new wave of desperate *mojados*. Maria, a Mexican woman who came once a week to our rental on La Hacienda Drive and would clean up a storm, softly singing *ranchera* tunes, told us she had been wading across the Rio Grande on the outskirts of Juárez, even though there was *mucho molesta de las chiquitas,* many women are raped. During one three-week stretch, she didn't come, and when she finally appeared, she had a baby with her. It was her sister's, who had been killed in a car crash in Chihuahua. She had gone and gotten the baby and waded across the Rio Grande with it.

Walking down Juárez's Avenida Siete de Septembre, I flipped a hundred pesos into the voluminous skirts of a blank-faced Tarahumara woman sitting on the sidewalk in native dress with her little daughter, and she gave me back a slight alteration of her mask, a flicker of recognition. A vivacious young woman in tight slacks, with her navel exposed and her bosom busting out of her blouse, smiled invitingly. Like the other border towns, Juárez performs the function of sin city for visiting gringos. Many a Texas boy has lost his virginity in Juárez. The women come up from the distressed republics of Central America for the greenbacks they can make in the brothels, which are open for business twenty-four hours a day.

Outside the *feira*, the tourist bazaar, a sombreroed mariachi band serenaded a party of Texans, an assortment of vendors came and went dangling their wares, while a row of unshaven, unfazed taxi drivers sat on the hoods of their cars. I asked one of the drivers how much to the dump. The Juárez municipal dump—acres and acres of garbage with vultures and women and children picking over it—is impressive even by Latin American standards, and I was told it was not to be missed. The driver, perceiving I was a gringo, said twenty dollars. I said how about five, but he refused to come down. So I asked him if he knew where I could find some coyotes, who are also known as *polleros* (like the "chicken train" I rode up into the Sierra Madre), and *pasadores*, ferriers (over the river). He said a bunch of them usually hung out in the Plaza de la Reforma. Their clients are not only known as *mojados* and *juareños* but as *espaldas* (backs or shoulders, that is, people who ride on them) and *surumatos* (people from the south).

Running aliens is profitable business. Increasing numbers of those who cross—currently an estimated 5 percent—are what the U.S. Immigration and Naturalization Service, La Migra, calls OTMs (Other Than Mexicans) from more than sixty countries. Some begin their journeys as far away as Rio, New Delhi, Belgrade, and Istanbul. One route starts in Fujian Province, China, and goes through Hong Kong; the price for safe arrival in the States via *la frontera* is thirty grand. There's a steady stream of Guatemalans, Hondurans, Nicaraguans, and Salvadorans like the ones who died hideously of desert thirst on the way to Why. Central Americans have to pass another *frontera*, the Mexico-Guatemala border. Three hundred a day, trying to cross the Shuciate River on rafts and other ways, are apprehended by the

Mexican Migra, and an estimated fifteen hundred get through. "This is a social problem beyond our ability to control," an exasperated official in Gubernación, the ministry that deals with foreigners, complained in Mexico City. "A country like ours must view its border as a strategic point of control and simply cannot permit people to enter and exit at will, without any respect for our territorial security."

The brothels on that *frontera,* too, are full of Central American girls trying to make enough money to pay a coyote to get them past the next barrier, the Rio Grande. Even as far north as Chicago, La Migra has found Central American girls forced to work as bar girls and prostitutes to pay off their coyote, and many Asian girls and boys are in servitude to the Chinese gangs that brought them over, some for as many as ten years. The border imposes all kinds of degradation.

When I got to the Plaza de la Reforma, a matinee of *The Treasure of the Amazon* was just letting out, and a dozen young couples clinging in amorous melancholia joined the milling crowd. In a tent two doctors were on day twelve of a hunger strike to protest the recent elections in which PRI claimed to have swept all fourteen seats in the Chihuahua state legislature and sixty-five of the state's sixty-seven mayoralties. An old man on a bench was more philosophical. "When is an election not rigged?" he observed.

I asked him if he knew where I could find a coyote. He was a little hard of hearing and thought I was looking for peyote. When he understood, he said, "A *camioneta* [a little truck] stops there every twenty minutes," and motioned with his eyes to a corner of the plaza. "It will take you to a place where you can get across, and it only costs seventy pesos. Coyotes are a lot more expensive, and they're dangerous. They take your money, and then they don't take you over. They hide you in a car trunk and drive you to a place where you wade across. Somebody is supposed to meet you on the other side, but lots of times nobody shows. Many are cheated."

Now looking at me hard, he said, "But what do you need a coyote for anyway? With your face and your color you can go right over the bridge. If you really need to slip in, my niece is married to a taxi driver. He may be able to help you." I said I had heard there were coyotes here in the plaza, and the old man said, "See those guys under the statue? They're probably coyotes."

The statue was of Benito Juárez, whom a plaque on the pedestal described as the reformer, benefactor, and liberator of the Americas. I approached the men. "What do you need a coyote for?" one of them asked. "Aren't you American?"

"Yes, but I have problems," I said. "I need a coyote."

"How many did you kill?" he asked, laughing, and he suggested I try the shoe-shines at the bridge. Alien smuggling wasn't his line at all—so I gave them a try. One of them said he had a friend who was a *pasador*. "He knows where there's a hole in the fence, scouts from a rise to make sure the coast is clear, then he takes you across on his shoulders, and from there you run for it. He only charges a thousand pesos. Coyotes charge a lot more. They take you to a certain place for two, three, five hundred dollars. See that guy over there?" The guy was leaning against a streetlight. "He's a coyote, but he's a *cholo malo,* a bandido, a *ratero.* He smokes dope. He's no good."

I went over to the coyote. He said, "Anybody can go to El Paso, but I have a car on the other side. Right in El Paso. And I know how to avoid La Migra by driving up into the sierra."

We got down to business. "How much to Wichita?" I asked.

"Which Wichita?" he countered. "Wichita, Kansas, or Wichita Falls, Texas? Kansas is four hundred and fifty bucks. Texas is three hundred and fifty. Albuquerque is three hundred and fifty. Phoenix, four hundred; Tucson, four hundred. For two bucks, I take you across the river. For twenty, I take you to the center of El Paso.

"Of course you could hop a freight," the coyote went on, "but there's no guarantee you'll make it." That summer eighteen aliens and two coyotes had been found dead in a sealed boxcar in Sierra Blanca, Texas, ninety miles east of El Paso. They had suffocated in the estimated 120-degree heat. Some had gone into convulsions, others had bled from their noses into their mouths, and they were all in an advanced state of dehydration. There was only one survivor, who had poked a hole in the floor with a spike and gulped air through it. The group, he explained, had hopped a Missouri-Pacific freight train, headed for Fort Worth, at El Paso and had been inadvertently locked in by a security man. The train experienced mechanical difficulties and was delayed for hours on a side track at Sierra Blanca. No one was around to hear them screaming for help and frantically beating the boxcar's walls.

In the end I recalled I had a family and decided to forgo the wetback experience. A month earlier *The New York Times* had reported, "Law-enforcement officials say that almost every day they find the bodies of shooting victims in the bushes or floating in the Rio Grande, some of them immigrants robbed while trying to cross the border, some of them victims of smuggling deals that went wrong. The officers say, furthermore, that they are frequently caught in battles with drug and weapon traffickers using machine guns." I ended up taking a cab right over the main bridge to El Paso. It would have been a stupid way to go.

I refer the reader to Ted Conover, who penetrated the cutthroat subterranean world of the coyotes and published a book by that name a
year after my cop-out, and to the movie *El Norte,* which portrays the
harrowing odyssey of a young Salvadoran couple.

I asked the driver, who was licensed to make trips to El Paso, to stop
in the middle of the bridge, and we looked down to the Río Bravo, as
he called it. It was unusually high, higher than it had supposedly been
in forty years, too high to wade, and dangerous to swim. Several
would-be *mojados* had drowned in it the week before, the driver told
me. "It's a problem without end," he said. Apprehensions had been
way down lately, to around three hundred a day from the usual eight
hundred; the river was stemming the tide of illegals far more effectively
than La Migra.

Nevertheless, in 1986, a dozen Mexicans had made it to the American side in a small inflatable rubber raft, beached on the bank below
them, and they were waiting for a green border patrol cruiser, just visible behind some railroad boxcars, to leave. Several dozen people on
the Mexican side of the river were watching the cat-and-mouse game,
waiting interestedly to see the outcome. "The patrol car can't wait
there forever," my driver went on. "Maybe one of them will sacrifice
himself, and the others will make a run for it."

The man at the customs booth leaned down and ascertained that I
was Anglo. "Sure is nice to be back home," I said, and he waved me
through without even asking for my documents. We pulled into the
railroad yard and saw that the patrol car had backup, a green van with
a wire cage in back. The motor was running, an Anglo in border patrol
uniform was at the wheel, sharing a sandwich with a sexy Hispanic
woman in tight jeans and waiting to nab anyone who got past the first
line of defense.

The next few blocks were full of young Hispanos, moving stealthily
through the streets in Reeboks. It was impossible to tell who were
mojados and who were Chicanos without checking their IDs, and if
the subject didn't have any ID and you detained him and he turned out
to be legal, he could sue you for violating his rights. So La Migra was
in a bit of a bind.

The Water Rights of La Raza

Cruising the backcountry of the Chicano homeland one morning six years later, in 1992, Nicásio Romero and I dropped in on Michael Coca, a bearded, brooding artist and water-rights activist whose place was very funky, with derelict cars and stacks of tires and lumber in the yard and the word CUNT spelled in big white block letters against a sage-spattered hillock. Michael was building what he called a retrofit, encasing his existing house in a new one. "I grew up in Los Alamos, Bomb City," he told me. "I was a product of American acculturation. I was indoctrinated with the revisionist history of the dominating class. I really thought George Washington was the father of our country, and that Boston was the center of the universe. But New Mexico is not the U.S., and it isn't Mexico either. It's another country. People who are dead are still voting around here, still on the tax rolls. The going price for a vote is a half-pint of port or seven dollars. The winos love Election Day. My grandfather had a general store–bar–dance hall–rooming houses a couple of villages from here. People came in wagons to dance on Saturday night, with the kids sleeping under the benches."

On the way back to Nicásio's, he taught me a few choice Chicano-ismos, the way Spanish is handled by hipsters and lowriders in places like Española, the capital of Rio Arriba County. *Que huvo le ese vato?* "Wha's happenin' bro?" *Onde la tiras ese?* "Where you goin' man?" *Vamos en mi rienfla.* "Let's go for a cruise in my car." *No te aguites.* "No hassle." *Y la huisa?* "Where's the chick?" As the kids lost their Spanish in junior high, they started speaking Spanglish. What's that guy doin' *con la vata* [with his chick]? The real heavies, the warlords, the leaders of the *pachucos,* the guys in El Burque (Albuquerque) who wore zoot suits and rumbled with chains and switchblades and became extinct in the seventies, or rather evolved into modern gang members, were called *cholos*. When they wanted to dance, they said, *Vamos a chanclar*. "Let's boogie." *Los chanclos* are high-heeled dancing shoes. *El mero pendejo* is the real stupe. *Mero* is Chicano for *mas*. *Entre verde e seco*, "between green and dry," that is, good times and bad, is a way of answering, How's it going? A guy comes home late, and his wife asks him, *Con quien estavas andando, pendejo?* "Who were you out with, numbnuts?" and he tells her, *Tu no mas xanei*. "There's nobody else, honey. I love you and only you." Other Spanglish words: *bequenpaura*, baking powder; *chite*, shit; *chanza*, perhaps; *sobrechuses*, overshoes; *taite*, tight, stingy; *yonque*, junk. In the Rio Arriba there are subtle differences in inflection and vocabulary from town to town and valley to valley. *Safau* is dense, out of it, and *safau a la verga* is completely out of it, dense to the max (*la verga* is penis). A *gringo salado* is a scum-sucking gringo.

The use of *chingolés*, fuck words, is a fine art in the Southwest. Some examples: *que jodido*, fucking A. *Estoi mas pedo que la chingada*, I'm drunker than fuck. *Es mui chingón, huevón*, or *jodón*, he's radical, awesome, bogus, a hot shit. *Es una ruca mui chingona*, she's a hot chick.

The Romeros have a beautiful spread. An acequia, which Nicásio has lined with rocks, runs through the backyard, and by lifting a metal drop gate he can divert it to capillaries and water his tomatoes. As the president of the New Mexico Acequia Association, Nicásio is not only involved in maintaining the thousand or so ditches in the state and protecting the water rights of their traditional *parciantes*, or communal users, he is also compiling their history. New Mexico has the oldest irrigation system in the country, he told me. Some of the ditches are three hundred years old. "Water is life for the Indians and the Chicanos. You can't separate the people from their water. It's their soul." We walked across the fertile bottomland below his house to the bank of the Pecos River, from which his acequia draws. The river here is about the size of the Jordan's headwaters, observed Nicásio, who had been to Israel one time. In May of 1984 a blizzard of monarch butterflies migrating back up from Mexico swept through the valley. "You couldn't even walk 'cause you'd squoosh them. Sometimes you see a sandhill crane drinking at the stock pond."

Back east, a river this size—twenty or thirty feet wide—would hardly even be considered a river, but the Pecos is one of the few rivers in New Mexico that run full-time, and its water-rights situation is typically complicated and multitiered. There are basically five claims on the water that runs past the Romeros' house: (1) Local users like the Romeros share their three-mile-long ditch with thirteen or fourteen other *parciantes*. (2) The city of Las Vegas, downstream, is trying to get even more of the Pecos's flow than it is already entitled to by invoking something called the Pueblo Water Rights, which say that as a city gets bigger, its water rights increase proportionally. This doctrine was allegedly invoked on a river in Los Angeles County, California, in the 1870s and is supposed to take precedence over even the prior-appropriative rights that apply throughout most of the West, but it is now regarded as having been made up and sold to the courts by a lawyer-historian named John Dwinell. In the 1970s the city of San Fernando tried to invoke it, and after 180 days of trial, the court said no. Nicásio told me that Las Vegas already took the water from the people on the Gallinas, one of the Pecos's main tributaries, so they had to move down to Las Vegas, where the city sells their water back to them. (3) The state of Texas, way downstream, isn't getting the quota it's entitled to according to a 1949 compact and has successfully sued New Mexico for fourteen million dollars' worth of shortfalls. There is pressure on the New Mexico state engineer to retire junior rights on the upper Pecos and tributaries like the Gallinas, where there are thirty ditches whose *parciantes'* rights go back to the 1823 San Miguel grant, but fifteen will be retired because they haven't flowed in more than four years, and the law says if you haven't used your water in four years, it can be taken from you. Nicásio and Michael Coca are trying to motivate the old Hispano families to get their abandoned but still-unappropriated ditches flowing again before they lose them. "There is a need of *nosotros* to strengthen our water rights," Coca said. (4) Environmental groups like the Sierra Club and the Audubon Society are having a showdown with the longtime *parciantes* because the environmentalists are lobbying for a guaranteed minimum "in-stream flow" to ensure the health of the river and of its aquatic life. In dry years they want "in-stream flow" to have priority over the rights of water users. "We kept shooting them down in the state legislature," Nicásio told me. "Now there's a dialogue." (5) Storrs Reservoir, which since 1900 has been entitled to the Pecos's *sobrante,* or flood, waters, but according to Nicásio has been taking more than this, thus depriving the *parciantes* of their fair share.

"There's all kinds of chicanery in American water law," he went on, "that Anglo lawyers have been pulling on *nosotros* for decades, like transferring water rights. You can buy up rights upstream and transfer them downstream, or even from another tributary in the same basin. There's an out-of-state company that's been buying old farmers' water rights on the Pecos and transferring them to a spot about thirty miles upstream, which is the only way they can get water to a golf-course condo development they want to build on land that used to belong to the old Hollywood cowboy actress Greer Garson."

Nicásio's wrangler neighbor, Joe García, told me about a convention center upstream that has been dumping raw sewage and cleaning fluid into the river. A friend of Joe's who worked for the center was fired for reporting it. Joe is the *mayordomo,* the administrator, of his and Nicásio's ditch. "Every time there's an emission, you find a water-quality-control expert that's been bribed," he complained. Also, lead washing into the Pecos from an old mine upstream periodically results in massive trout die-offs.

A similar mess exists on every band of moving freshwater in the state. Just on the Gallinas, Michael Coca told me, there were fifteen hundred names in the state engineer's adjudication suit and five hundred actual water users. It was the second time since 1933 that the *parciantes* had been forced into court to adjudicate their water rights. The old land grant had a board of trustees who were bandidos, he said, and sold the rights to speculators until they were so whittled down the people on the Gallinas had to move to Las Vegas. "We can argue that the ditches were abandoned because the water has been illegally diverted by the city by the same sort of unscrupulous judges who have been ruling against us ever since the United States came in here," seethed Coca.

The main event each spring in the Rio Arriba is the opening of the acequias. There's something joyous and reassuring about the narrow channels, flowing through backyards. The acequias are lifelines culturally, too; like Robert Frost's Vermont stone walls, good ditches make good neighbors. On the day the ditches are to be opened, the *mayordomo* walks with a rod called a *vara* marking off sections, and when he gives the word, the men of the village jump in with shovels and clean out the winter's accumulation of debris: rocks, willow branches, beaver dams. The women bring food—*posole,* frijoles, tortillas, *biscochitas.* The event is half work, half fiesta, like a barn raising, as much an affirmation of culture and community as the spring branding of the calves is for the cowboys to the east. My old school buddy Don tells me that each spring, when the water is let out of the acequia he shares in Coyote (he has moved back up from Santa Fe), there are trout flopping in the alfalfa fields.

The Two Charlies

ut when the *parciantes* on the same ditch aren't getting along, it can be a problem, especially when the rift is along ethnic lines. In Mimbres, down in the lower left-hand corner of the state, two old men, both named Charlie, one Texan and the other *nuevomejicano,* had been feuding over access to their common ditch for four years. David Lujan of Tonantzin invited me to fly down with him for a "grass-roots show of support" for Charlie and the other Mimbreños who he said were being squeezed out by Texan ranchers, many of whom were absentee owners. The state engineer, who adjudicates water rights, was also planning to be there. Our plane and pilot were provided by an Anglo environmental support group called Light Hawk. The other passengers were Nicásio, Michael Coca, and a water-rights activist named Denise Lamb.

Western water law is based on Spanish water law, which in turn derives from Moorish law. It is appropriative rather than riparian. English water law is riparian. It prevails in the East and entitles you to the water that flows along or through your land. But Spanish water law gives you entailed rights only to your groundwater. You can divert the water that runs along or through your land for domestic use, but not for irrigation or to power a mill, unless you make a separate claim. In Moab, Utah, for instance, an Anglo artist friend told me she had several springs on her land, but she wasn't legally entitled to use their water until she "proved them up." This involved giving notice in the local newspaper for ninety days that she intended to lay claim on them, in case there was anyone with a prior claim. According to Spanish law, whoever taps the water first gets to use it. "Prior use" can be chronological, or it can mean upstream. This has led to legal situations of tremendous complexity on the Colorado and the Rio Grande, as distant cities and private water companies serving them keep up-streaming each other.

The doctrine of "first in time, first in use" is not only Spanish-Moorish, but is indebted to mining law, where the sources of the ore and of the water to separate it are often distant from each other. Another point is that not all of the Southwest is under prior appropriation. Texas is riparian, and California is mixed. But in general, in arid regions one inevitably gets into moving water. The ethical basis of the doctrine is that a river system drains a vast area, and all the people in the drainage, not just those who live along the river, should be entitled to it.

The first Spaniards used many of the same techniques that the Indians had developed. Locating by a perennial stream, they threw up a crude blockage dam, diverting water into the adjacent floodplain by gravity feed or into ditches that watered the fields by percolation. More elaborate acequias were lined with stone or adobe to reduce seepage. Laterals were run off the main ditch, or *acequia madre*. The water was returned to the river or bled off the flooded fields by *sangrías*, outlet channels, to avoid buildup of salts. Eventually, more substantial dams of stone and mortar were put in, and devices like the *malacate*, or windlass hoist, which was basically a wheel with buckets, were installed to raise water up a riverbank to a field (in this case, the wheel was moved by the current) or to remove water from a flooded mine (in this case, the wheel was fitted to gears turned by a donkey). Windlass hoists are still used in Tibet. I saw one turning outside Lhasa in 1990.

The Mimbres (Willow) River rises in southeastern New Mexico's Gila wilderness and disappears into sand fifty miles south of Deming. It was along this drainage that the Mimbres subculture of the Mogollon turned out its exquisite pottery around the turn of the millennium. We flew down at the end of September 1991, and passing over one bone-dry arroyo after another from several thousand feet in the air, we could see clearly what a miraculous and precious commodity water is in this part of the world and its dramatic imprint on the land, how the runoff of brief torrents had cut veins, gashes, rills, and dendritic fans in small mounds of sand and clay and even in large massifs; how the arroyos started from nothing, a few branching crevices halfway up a hillside, and kept gradually enlarging into *cañoncitos, cañónes,* and finally barrancas; and all due to this "prayer," as the Navajo call it, this *navala,* or life-giving liquid essence, as the Hopi call it, that had materialized from the air and carved the land, but was at this time of year no longer there.

We landed in Silver City, the site of several atrocities after gold was found up in the Gila wilderness. Here Mangas Colorado and other leaders of the Gila Apache were invited to a great peace banquet, seated at the table, and blown away with grapeshot from a concealed cannon. The band had been persistently hostile since the broken promises of the Spaniards. In one of their raids, which received nationwide attention, on March 28, 1883, little Johnny McComas, son of a judge, was kidnapped, and his parents killed. Rumors of his survival persisted as late as 1938, when an archaeological expedition in Mexico discovered an alleged lost tribe of Apache that had supposedly escaped over the border at the time of Geronimo's capture in 1888. Its leader was red haired and blue eyed.

The WPA guide to New Mexico offers this vignette of Silver City in full boom:

> [As in] most western mining towns, soft-handed gamblers in wide-brimmed black hats, frock coats, and diamond-studded cravats presided at gaming tables. Cowboys strode up to the bar in high-heeled boots and demanded shots of red-eye, bug juice, or mescal for themselves and companions from Shady Lane. If their demands were not supplied immediately, they shot out the lights, the bar mirror, and any other attractive target, then they turned over the roulette tables.

In this century, the metallurgic appetites of the gringos turned to copper. The exploitation of local *nuevomejicanos* who worked in the huge open-pit mine out of town during the Depression inspired the powerful film *Salt of the Earth,* commissioned in the thirties by the Mine, Mill, and Smelter Workers Union. (The action, which has all the grimness of *Grapes of Wrath,* centers around a woman named Luz and her husband, who works in the mine of "Zinctown, U.S.A." The couple lives in a shack without plumbing and is hopelessly in hock to the company store. "At least the flowers are ours," Luz muses proudly. Her one extravagance, a phonograph bought on the installment plan, is repo'd. Her husband is working so hard he forgets her saint's day. There are five accidents a week in the mine because the big, beefy white guys have accelerated the conveyor belts to increase production. Finally the mine workers strike. After they are arrested, the women offer to take over the picket line, which is a problem for the men's machismo. Luz goes to jail, and her incarceration makes her increasingly militant. . . .)

We passed mountainous slag heaps as we drove up, in a caravan of funky cars, over the mountains to the higher, greener Mimbres Valley.

"This is the sort of dispute that up to World War Two would have been resolved with lever-action Winchesters," Nicásio observed.

"Now it's resolved with lever-action lawyers." The antagonist we had come to support was Charlie Norrero, a seventy-four-year-old full of life and fun whose great-grandfather, a Mexican of Italian descent (his one surviving document said he was born in Geneva, but Charlie was pretty sure this was a mistake for "Genova") came up from Mexico in the 1870s. Charlie wasn't of old *nuevomejicano* stock; he was a completely Americanized *mexicano*. He grew Bartlett pears, and his orchard was irrigated by an acequia that ran off the Mimbres and that he was the *mayordomo* of. The other three *parciantes* on the *llano* ditch, as it was called, were Anglo "proxies," caretakers for absentee owners in Texas who "have no respect for our traditional historical rights." Charlie needed to go across the land of one of them, Charlie E. Disert, to repair the diversion dam that had washed out in a spring flood, so he could get the water off the river into the ditch, but Disert, who was the same age as Norrero, wouldn't unlock his gate. Charlie N. showed us a letter he'd gotten from Charlie D. It said: "Charlie, you do not have any rights on my property therefore I am not going to supply you with a right of way." It was a culture clash. Disert, it seemed, was thinking like a Texan, in riparian terms, that the rights to the water automatically went with the land. He didn't appreciate the communal nature of the acequia relationship.

The competition for the Mimbres's water was typically intense. Many of the *mexicanos* whose people came up with Charlie N.'s great-grandfather had never gotten around to proving up their rights, so they had to let the water go because others downstream had priority dates. "A lot of *parciantes* sit back and let it happen to them and bitch about it when it's over," Charlie explained. In times of shortage, everybody had to stop irrigating and let the water go to the livestock. In another case, Charlie's young neighbor Dennis Chavez claimed he had lost the ability to irrigate his twenty-one acres because a Texan upstream had whisked off through an underground culvert the sixteen acre-feet he was entitled to. Dennis showed me Mason jars full of the different kinds of beans he had grown on his land last year: protein-rich Anasazi beans, speckled beans, fava beans, Aztec white beans, Hopi yellow beans, scarlet runner beans, Hopi red pinto beans. A short, feisty man in his early twenties, Dennis was not going to sit back and let it happen. He talked tough and had a gun cabinet full of high-powered hunting rifles. His position was "We're occupied Latin America." Denise Lamb, who was of Irish descent and had lived for many years in Chimayo, where she was the only Anglo on her ditch, found a lot of similarities between the *nuevomejicanos* and the Irish: "They're both proud, oppressed colonial people with a rebellious streak." In the

Southwest, she said, water is the currency, the way salt is in Tibet and in the tropics. The people put the same energy into the elusive fluid that New Yorkers put into money.

That evening Dennis's wife put out a great spread in the community hall where Charlie and all the *mexicano* friends and neighbors on the river gathered to plot strategy for the public meeting the next morning. Before the meeting, we held hands in a circle outside the church, and David Lujan led us in prayer. Then we went into the community hall. The meeting was very polarized, with the big, beefy white guys on one side of the room and small dark-skinned *nosotros,* with a few Anglo sympathizers like Denise and me, on the other. It reminded me of the polarization in the Brazilian Amazon state of Acre between the big, beefy white *fazendeiros,* or ranchers, from the state of Acre, and the small dark-skinned *seringueiros,* or rubber tappers, that I'd written about two years before. My role was to be the media, the public conscience that senses there's an injustice going on here and could thus provide *nosotros* with a little leverage and counterintimidation. David introduced me, without any forewarning, as *The New York Times.* I rolled my eyes, and the Texans looked nervous. After the meeting, they gathered around their pickups on one side of the parking lot, and the *mexicanos* gathered around their pickups on the other, and when the Texans finally drove off, Dennis Chavez shook his fist at them. That boy's going to get himself killed, like Chico Mendes, I said to Nicásio, and Nicásio said, "They won't kill him; they'll squeeze him out."

I went over and talked to Charlie Disert before he left. He was less spry and youthful than Norrera. The whole thing seemed to be getting to him. Brushing a wasp off my shoulder as a gesture of friendship (into which I read, What are you doing with those wetbacks? Why aren't you with us?), he said he had no objections about talking with me "unless you're an ecologist." Then he asked how to spell my name (read, Russian, eh? You one of them Commies?). "I have no objection with Charlie," he told me, his voice trembling with emotion. "He is the reincarnation of his grandpa. Talk to his Mexican neighbors. I don't hate anybody for race. The problem is Charlie's different. Ask Rudy Dominguez [a *mexicano*]. He won't talk to me. He drives up and down the road and dims his lights so he can see what we're doing. I don't know what bothers him. He doesn't need to go through my land. There's another way upstream to get access to the diversion dam that's shorter."

I went back over to the *mexicanos* and said, "This Disert doesn't seem to be such a bad guy. I think he's ready to talk. The whole business seems to be taking its toll on him." Chavez and Norrera said no way, David was furious at me for even talking to him, and Pedro, a big, sweet, *sincero mexicano*, explained, "He's real neighborly, especially when he's about to screw you."

The state engineer, Eluid Martinez, had flown in that morning, and after the meeting was over, he gave his opinion of the proceedings: "The individual is not allowing access to a ditch heading, and he just doesn't give a damn about the other water users in the system, and unless the dam is repaired, nobody will have water in this ditch. Blocking access to a ditch is a criminal misdemeanor, but the district attorney puts such relatively minor and local-impact cases on the back burner. The state engineer has no jurisdiction, so what I'm saying is I can't do anything about it; I can't force Charlie Disert to give Charlie Norrero access to the dam. Water users have the right of access and even of condemnation if a guy isn't allowing access. The state should be able to go after the violator, but its hands are tied. Disert's attitude is 'Go ahead, sue me.' The water users should be able to get along with each other because if the state steps in, their power will be diminished." He finished by offering his services as "a catalyst to bring people together."

Later, Martinez and I sat and talked. Calm, lanky, sensitive, cerebral, an artist who made *bultos* and stained-glass windows and lithographs of traditional subjects, Martinez was sympathetic to his fellow Hispanos, but he also had to represent the state's interest in all this. The Mimbres, he told me, was a small river with lots of small conflicts. "There are thirty acequias, with ethnic lines drawn on each of them. These are not old *nuevomejicano* ditches, but *mexicano* ones, put in between 1880 and 1890, so they don't have treaty problems. The 1848 Treaty of Guadalupe Hidalgo, or of Mesilla, as Mexicans call it, that was signed in Mexico was different from the one signed by Congress. In the latter, article 15 was eliminated. It says words to the effect that Mexico passes over these lands to the United States, but the United States must recognize the sovereignty of the Indians and the existing land grants and water rights. These grants and rights, however, have to be proven—an expensive legal process whose outcome isn't guaranteed and that made millionaires out of nineteenth-century Anglo lawyers, who ended up with title to 80 percent of the old Spanish grants as their commission. David was considering taking the United States to the UN for its numerous article 15 violations in New Mexico.

"Actually," Martinez went on, "the copper mine is whisking off much of the Mimbres's flow before it even gets to San Lorenzo [where the two Charlies live], and the Texans and the *mexicanos* are fighting for scraps."

It was bad here; people were opening the gates at night and stealing water out of turn and putting padlocks on their gates, and the padlocks were being blown off, so they were putting on more padlocks, triple padlocks. On top of everything, the Mimbres was home to the endangered Chihuahuan chub, to ensure whose survival the U.S. Fish and Wildlife Service had severed twenty-four acre-feet from the landowners' water rights.

Martinez said the mess on the Mimbres was only one of seventeen suits in the state; 65 percent of the state's water is under adjudication. "A lot of rivers have some customary form of apportionment worked out for times of shortage that has never been written down, and these are the type of things that need to be sorted out. The first on the list is the Aamodt case, which has been going on for twenty years and has still not been resolved. It is between the members of Nambe Pueblo, above Santa Fe, and the Anglo and Chicano water users downstream on the Nambe River. If you took the first-in-time, first-in-right doctrine literally," Martinez pointed out, "everything would belong to the Indians, and this is obviously not acceptable. The way the Anglo water lawyers get around this is by arguing that the prehistoric Indians were largely nomadic and should only be entitled to what they historically used. Twelve adjudications involving eighteen tribes and twenty thousand people are pending. The problems on the Mimbres are relatively self-contained, so they are not a priority compared to the Indian-rights and interstate problems on other rivers. New Mexico's water is governed by four water-law systems—Spanish, Mexican, federal, and Indian—but the state's basic position is that the waters of the state belong to the state, and individual rights are subject to forfeiture. Before 1963, forfeiture was automatic if there had not been 'beneficial use' for four years, since then the state engineer must give notice of one year to a party who is not exercising his rights.

"Eventually you're going to see meters at every diversion," Martinez continued. "The Colorado already has them. Phoenix and Tucson are sitting on depleting aquifers, and they've finally gotten some relief with the completion of the Central Arizona Project's aqueduct, which delivers the share of the Colorado River they're entitled to by the Colorado Compact. But this will spell trouble for California, which has been drawing 5.8 million acre-feet from the Colorado, including Phoenix's and Tucson's hitherto unused share. Now it will have to cut back to its 4.4 million acre-foot entitlement, which means it will have to turn to in-state retirement of agricultural water and to desalinization to make up the shortfall. New Mexico's water-supply problems are not as acute. The Rio Grande aquifer, which supplies

Albuquerque, is continuously recharged by the Rio Grande, but there are water-quality problems that are larger than perceived, including arsenic from natural deposits and radioactive waste from Los Alamos entering the system. Water in New Mexico is not a problem. This year, in fact, has been a banner year. All reservoirs are full to record capacity. It's the right to use it that's a problem, and since the 1850s the state's surface water has been entirely appropriated."

Driving us down to the airport, Charlie Norrera told us how Charlie Disert had used the same lawyer in Silver City, Wayne Woodbury, to draw up their deeds and water rights, then Disert had used Woodbury to challenge Norrera's rights. "At the trial, Wayne, now representing only Disert, asked me, 'Are you using your water efficiently?'

"I asked him, 'What do you mean?'

" 'Are you using it when it's your turn?'

" 'When my plants need water, I water them,' I said. 'Otherwise I let the water go on down.'

" 'Well, that's not efficiently,' Wayne said.

"So I said, 'With the court's permission, can I have a glass of water?' The bailiff returned with a big glass. I took a little sip. The judge said, 'Aren't you going to drink the rest?'

" 'No, I'm not thirsty,' I said, and I passed the glass to Wayne. 'Here you drink the rest. It's yours. This is my water, and I'm giving it to you.'

" 'Are you crazy?' Wayne said. 'I'm not thirsty.'

" 'You have to drink it,' I said. 'You asked if I was using my water efficiently. If you're forced to keep drinking when you don't need to, what's going to happen? You're going to get diarrhea. Well it's the same with my plants. That's why I don't water them unless they need it.' "

El Tigre

few days after crossing the border at Ciudad Juárez, continuing to wend my way north with the Hispanic frontier, now in a rental car in 1986, I dropped in on J. B. Jackson, pioneer scholar of the American landscape, particularly the roadside landscape, and author of *The Westward Moving House,* whose course I had audited at Harvard fifteen years earlier. His own house, which he had built south of Santa Fe, was a big, beautiful, East-type, architecturally-in-tune-with-the-grand-tradition, unsouthwestern dream house, which I now got the feeling was sort of an embarrassment. He was living in a little funky adobe in front of the property, pumping gas at a local station, and, last I heard, cleaning people's yards for nothing except the insights into the American domestic landscape he thus derived; having embraced at first intellectually the vernacular and the fellahin funkiness that had seemed so quaint and intriguing, he had finally ended up part of it. It was a process that many transplanted easterners I have met in the Southwest seem to have undergone. To eastern eyes, it may seem like cultural devolution, but cultural devolution, the actor Dennis Hopper, who lived for many years as a wild man in Taos, told me, is what this part of the world is all about.

I found Jackson dressed in a black leather motorcycle jacket and boots, a small, frail old man with liver-spotted skin and a cultivated eastern accent (these things are hard to get rid of). His Harley Davidson, on which he still took off on field trips, was parked out front.

New Mexico, Jackson told me, was basically a depressed expastoral landscape, aptly named the Land of Enchantment, a beautiful but unhappy place that kept experiencing boom-and-bust cycles. He cited the copper, uranium, Texas oil, and natural-gas bubbles, the promise of dry farming that had been wiped out by the Depression; the bursting of the weapons-lab and military-base bubble was still a few years in the future. "The difference with New Mexico is that this is a projection of Catholic, not of Protestant, Europe," Jackson reflected. "It's picturesque but not perceived as important for the country, and it isn't self-supporting anymore. It exists on federal money. Arizona, with its high-tech irrigation crops and its influx of rich from the coast, is a different story. Here the role of the mother is crucial. She spoils her sons so they feel they can't leave. She chops the wood; the boys do nothing. A chance comes for them to go to Albuquerque or Denver and make something of themselves, but at the last moment the car isn't in shape, or they find some other excuse for staying."

The next day I passed, north of Santa Fe, the town of Nambe, where my long-lost great aunt, Olga de Hartmann, had spent her last years. After some difficulty, I had finally tracked her down in 1980. Nobody in the family had talked to her in twenty years; she had been more or less excommunicated. It had been my third visit to New Mexico, a quick overnight shot. I still had no interest as yet in the Southwest per se. I was on a different errand, writing my fifth book, which was about my family. My paternal grandfather's sister, Aunt Olga had been one of the first disciples of the Georgian mystic G. I. Gurdjieff. On the eve of the Russian Revolution, she and her husband, Thomas de Hartmann, had fled Russia with Gurdjieff over the Caucasus Mountains. Thomas de Hartmann was a young composer of such promise that the Tsar, it was said, personally exempted him from fighting in World War I after attending one of his ballets. Gurdjieff, the de Hartmanns, and other followers, including the terminally ill novelist Katherine Mansfield, took over an old priory in Fontainebleau, outside Paris. Gurdjieff got Thomas, who was only there because of Olga, to compose music for his "movements," which required different parts of the body to move in unrelated ways, like a child patting his head and rubbing his stomach at the same time.

Later, Gurdjieff and the de Hartmanns came to the States. Olga's brother, Leo Shoumatoff, my grandfather, was already there with his wife, the former Elizabeth Avinoff, and her brother André. The Avinoffs were devoutly Russian Orthodox and would have no truck with Gurdjieff. After my grandfather died, in 1928, Olga attempted to hit my grandmother up for twenty thousand rubles, which she claimed her brother had lent her before the revolution, and it was this move that got her drummed out of the family. She wrote a book called *Our Life with Mr. Gurdjieff* and became something of a cult figure in occult circles, where she was known as Madame de Hartmann. Because of chronic bronchitis, she ended up in Nambe, a latter-day lunger, where a new generation of Gurdjieffians gathered around her. The cult was controlling. One practitioner, the novelist John Nichols recalls, was forced to leave his wife and give up playing ice hockey. Another Gurdjieff scene arose in Phoenix around another of his early disciples, Madame de Saltzmann, and included the Frank Lloyd Wrights.

By the time I found Aunt Olga, she was ninety-six and not well. Thomas had died years earlier, and she was living with a much younger companion named Pete Colgrove up the road from the duke and duchess of Bedford and down the road from Nambe Pueblo. The house needed repair and was modest by eastern standards, the only ones I had.

"She has good days and bad days, but she very much wants to see you," Colgrove told me, and he showed me into her bedroom. Aunt Olga had wasted away to almost nothing, but her face was still almost frighteningly compelling. She spoke mostly French. We looked through the childhood chapters of her unpublished autobiography, titled "What For?" She showed me photos of the family's summer place in Karelia, since returned to Finland, and explained why she believed her grandfather was a morganatic son of Kaiser Wilhelm I by a Polish woman named Labounsky. We took a drive along the Nambe River, which was crowded with tamarisk and Russian olive. Both species were introduced to the Southwest for erosion control and have become an ecological disaster, outcompeting the native species (tamarisk is yet another part of the Southwest's North African legacy, introduced by the Moors to Spain and brought over from there). It was early May, and the desert was subtly in bloom. We drove over the Rio Grande, which was unusually high. "We haven't been here in three years," Colgrove reflected, and Aunt Olga said, "*Il est joli, le petit pont.*"

Later, I drove up to the pueblo by myself. Nobody seemed to be around, or at least I couldn't get a rise out of anybody. The community seemed hermetically sealed, like a cryptic desert form. I had no idea about the Aamodt suit, the bitter feud between the pueblo and downstream Anglo water users. If the violaceous violence of the vast desert vista, with its juniper-spattered, bristle-basted hillocks, had any impact on me, I have no record or memory.

Continuing north with the radio on (back in 1986), I caught something about the Jicarilla Apache Detoxification Center, then reached Española, the capital of Rio Arriba County. The whole town, pretty much, is Chicano, except for the occasional turbaned Anglo Sikh riding a bike or Black Muslim, who have communes out of town. There's a lot of vintage roadside kitsch: a potted green-neon cactus in a front window; a hand-lettered JUMBO BURGER sign; the billboard with an 800 number for the Virgin Mary; another one with a woman holding up a baby, captioned LIFE'S PRECIOUS GIFT OUR SACRED TRUST. Ansel Adams's famous photograph, *Moon over Hernandez,* was taken just out of town. On Saturday night red-bandannaed lowriders cruise in '55 modified Chevy (hard *ch*) coups and other vintage bombers with small steering wheels (the joke is so they can drive with handcuffs on), maybe a plastic Jesus on the dash, the suspension so low they're just about scraping the ground. The lowriders cruise abreast and so slow it can take an hour to get through town.

Española jokes are a favorite New Mexico genre. Example: What do cow patties and Española cheerleaders have in common? The older they get, the easier they are to pick up. What did the Española fireman call his two sons? JosA and JosB. What do you call a three-piece suit in Española? A defendant. As Nicásio put it, "Española's pretty intense, pretty dead end."

I had *pico de gallo* and fajitas at the Paraguas restaurant, Luis and Francisco Atensio, proprietors. The Atensios came up with Vargas (Captain General Diego de Vargas Zapata Lujan Ponce de León y Contreras, who reconquered and recolonized New Mexico in 1692). They started out twenty-five years ago with a taco stand. The young Chicana waitress, hearing I'd come up from Mexico, said, "Isn't it neat down there? When I go to Mexico, I feel like an American."

The road northwest to Tierra Amarilla leads deep into Spanish Appalachia, isolated mountain *poblaciónes* where the old people still speak the Castilian of three centuries ago, mixed with the speech of Andalusians, Asturians, Basques, and Galicians, with occasional borrow words from Nahuatl or Rio Grande Pueblo—very different from the Chicano Spanglish of Española or El Burque: "to sell" is the obsolete *mercander;* "where are you going" the floridly polite *donde usted es iyendo; pelilludo* pertains to a donkey or a horse with only one functional testicle. Much of the surrounding land has been transferred to local political bosses in return for favors such as getting sons out of prison; it's debatable whether the *nuevomejicanos* have been screwed over more by their own *patrón* system or by the Anglo lawyers who verfied title to the old land grants in return for a chunk of the acreage.

A historic marker. Drive-up history. These are always edifying. Here passed the trail forged by Fray Luis de Escalante from Santa Fe to

Monterey, California, in 1776 through the red-rock desert of southern Utah, where a town and a river bear his name, and where Everett Ruess disappeared, and where at the end of his first term, in 1996, Bill Clinton would declare the 1.7 million-acre Grand Staircase/Escalante National Monument.

I pick up a young *marijuanito* and give him a lift to Abiquiu, the *genízaro* buffer town where Georgia O'Keeffe lived and painted, her last, nearly blind years taken care of by a young hippie drifter named Juan Hamilton, who wouldn't let anybody see her and who inherited most of her paintings. The buffer-town concept was borrowed from the Ottoman Empire, where mercenaries were used by the Turks for protection and labor and often adopted Turkish culture, and have been compared to the strategic hamlets of Vietnam. The *genízaros* were captive Indians—Apache, Navajo, Ute, Comanche—who were to keep the *intendencia* from being overrun by still-hostile ones. The historian Benito Cordova has called the *genízaros* "living land bridges between two cultures," and he estimates that at one time as much as one-third of New Mexico's population was *genízaro*. After 1740 there was friction between Abiquiu's *genízaros* and their colonial masters, who accused them of apostasy and witchcraft. With Mexican independence, Abiquiu was left to its own devices, and it became a hotbed of the Penitente sect.

By the time I reached Coyote, a few towns later, the feeling of being in a foreign country was quite intense. It was here, in fact, in 1966, that a charismatic man named Reies Lopez Tixerina had declared a local Chicano republic and organized a secession movement. El Tigre, as his followers called him, was living in retirement in a fenced-off compound just off the road. I asked for him there but was told he was in Israel, shooting a movie on his life. I went up to the mesa where my old school buddy Don and his wife Katie had homesteaded, but their adobe was abandoned, so I left a note on the door.

The Spanish colonial approach to real estate, which Tixerina wanted to restore, emphasized the communal rather than the individual, fee-simple type of ownership prevalent in the English colonies (although the Anglos, too, had their commons). Large tracts were set aside as *ejidos,* multipurpose common lands. The 1848 Treaty of Guadalupe Hidalgo, which defined the terms of the transfer of the annexed Mexican territory to the United States at the conclusion of the Mexican War, protected "all property belonging to Mexicans." But it was unclear, or so Congress claimed, about the *ejidos.* Many slipped into the hands of

Anglo ranchers, eastern investors, or were declared national forest, which was at first a formality, as the local Hispanos were allowed to continue grazing their stock on them. Congress's argument was that the *ejidos,* belonging to no single individual, had been the property of the national government of first Spain, then of Mexico, and therefore they now belonged to the United States government.

Another major bone of contention was the old land grants, or *mercedes.* The heirs of the grantees had to prove ownership, which provided a field day for lawyers, who verified claims in return for part of the property. By 1904 80 percent of all *mercedes* were in Anglo hands. All kinds of scams were used to get land, similar to what is known in Brazil as *grilagem:* you buy ten acres and go to the town clerk and register a thousand. (Brazilians tend to be cavalier about zeros, partly because their currency is always adding or losing them.) Ripping off Mexican land was a time-honored practice, dating back to Jim Bowie of the Alamo and the knife, who, after running slaves in Louisiana with the pirate Jean Laffite, in 1834 began to acquire eleven-league land grants in Texas by inducing a prospective settler to apply for a grant and then buying it himself, until he had personally amassed seven hundred thousand acres. The whole Texas revolution, which I once heard described at a rodeo in Amarillo as "claiming our American heritage," can also be seen as a land grab that precipitated one of the biggest and most spectacular rip-offs of all times—the northern two-thirds of Mexico, following which there were innumerable small rip-offs, many of which have undoubtedly still not come to light. One morning at the offices of Tonantzin, for example, David Lujan showed me a case, near Roswell, New Mexico, where an Anglo rancher had bought twenty-seven acres from a *mexicano* and registered them as thirty.

A gargantuan real estate hoax was nearly pulled off by the Confederate veteran, onetime St. Louis streetcar conductor, and subscription agent for the San Francisco *Examiner* James Addison Reavis, who drifted out to Arizona about 1880. Reavis fabricated a lineage to one Don Nemecio Silva de Peralta de la Córdoba, who had been given the title Barón de los Colorados and a huge *merced* in 1748 by Ferdinand VI of Spain. The parcel was a rectangle three hundred by a hundred miles, which included Phoenix in its northwestern corner and extended to Silver City, New Mexico, in its southeastern corner. Reavis claimed to have obtained title to the grant from a conveniently dead eastern mine developer who had allegedly got it from an impoverished descendant of the baron, a campesino named Miguel Peralta, who in fact never existed. To strengthen his case, he later married a Mexican orphan and by forging birth records for her in California made it look as if she were "the last of the Peraltas." After prominent lawyers upheld his claim, people in the rectangle panicked and paid Reavis for quitclaim deeds to their homes, farms, mines, and even schools. The Southern Pacific Railroad forked over fifty thousand dollars for its right-of-way. The Silver King Mine coughed up twenty-five thousand for mineral rights. Reavis bought homes in St. Louis, Washington, Madrid, and Chihuahua and lived like a king until 1895, when the scam was finally exposed, and he went to prison.

No one profited more from phase two of the American annexation—the gobbling up of the *mercedes*—than the Santa Fe Ring, a cartel of lawyers, judges, merchants, and local politicos, Republicans mostly, with links to Republican-era Washington and prominent lawyers, public servants, and bankers in New York, Philadelphia, and Providence. By 1880, 70 percent of New Mexico's old grants belonged to lawyers, most of whom belonged to the Ring. Thomas Benton Catron, another Confederate who drifted out after the Civil War, became the largest landowner in the country. He eventually acquired two million acres, some through a judicious marriage, and was a partner in four million more. One of his properties, the six-hundred-thousand-acre Tierra Amarilla grant, north of Coyote, Catron obtained in return for getting a rich *haciendero* named Francisco Martinez acquitted on a murder charge. Five hundred thousand acres of his holdings were former *ejidos*.

Resistance to the gringo usurpers began almost at once. In 1847 Mexican nationalists with allies from Taos Pueblo started an insurrection in Taos. The wife of the territorial governor, Charles Bent, was raped in front of him, then he was beheaded or scalped (there are two versions of this), and his head or scalp was joyfully paraded on a pole. Another group, the Mano Negro, or Black Hand, ran Coyote for more than thirty years after the Apache cleared out. It and Las Goras Blancas, the White Hoods, went out at night cutting the gringo ranchers' wire fences. In 1929 Arthur Mamby, an Anglo developer who wanted to turn Taos into an international spa and acquired nearly the entire Antonio Martinez land grant, was found beheaded, although some claim the body wasn't his. Ethnic tensions in Taos are still high.

Even before the Mexican War, there was a prophecy that a great number of people would come "laughing" from the East and take the *nuevomejicanos'* land from them, but then a leader would come, also from the East, and send these people "crying" back to where they had come from. During the sixties, the civil-rights movement and countercultural disaffection with the American mainstream helped provoke a rise in Mexican American ethnic self-awareness. The young generation began proudly calling themselves Chicanos, formerly a disparaging term. They spoke of La Raza, the way the Navajo called themselves Diné, the People. Some talked about a mythic lost homeland called Aztlan, which was like Ethiopia to the Rastafarians of Jamaica. The Rio Arriba Hispanos were ripe for a revitalization movement of their own. But they needed a leader, a Quetzalcoatl, a Poseyemu, Popé-Christ figure, a Martin Luther King, a Cesar Chavez.

Around this time the National Forest Service began to award large lumbering and mining contracts to out-of-state Anglo corporations and to phase out the free-use permits to local Hispanos that gave them the right to gather firewood and graze their cattle on their ancestors' land, further inflaming bitterness that had been simmering since 1846 when New Mexico became an American territory. The longed-for messianic figure appeared in the person of Reies Lopez Tixerina. Tixerina came from the east—he was born in Texas in 1923 or 1926, so he fulfilled the prophesy (one recalls how Quetzalcoatl was expected from the east by the Aztecs as well). Tixerina had little formal education and spent his early years as an orphaned migrant laborer following the crops, picking cotton in Texas, beets in Colorado, sometimes, he later claimed, reduced to foraging in garbage cans for something to eat. Later he joined the Assembly of God, but he fell out with the Church because, he explained, it was taking money from the poor, and it should have been the other way around.

During his wanderings, Tixerina became convinced that the suffering of La Raza resulted from the loss of its land. One of his great-grandfathers had in fact been cheated out of his land and murdered by Anglos. He spent six years in Mexico studying the old colonial land grants, then in 1963 he returned to New Mexico and founded the Alianza Federal de las Mercedes.

By July 1966 the Alianza had twenty thousand members. Many of the Hispanos accepted Tixerina as the Messiah, and he identified with the role. "The poor sucker thinks he's Moses come again," one local Anglo observed. His followers would come up to him and kiss his feet at Alianza meetings, and Tixerina claimed—like Joseph Smith, the founder of the Church of Latter-Day Saints, and many southwestern Indian leaders—to receive guidance, "revelations," in his dreams. He preached that the world was coming to an end and that it would be followed by a millennium in which no land would be owned individually, just as in the days of the old *mercedes*. His followers weren't worried when he went to prison because they thought he would be able to walk through the walls.

That October, in 1966, Tixerina and militant Aliancistas occupied Echo Amphitheater in the Carson National Forest, north of Coyote, which had been part of the five-hundred-thousand-acre San Joaquin del Rio Chama grant, and declared it the Republic of San Joaquin, electing as mayor a descendant of the original grantees and "arresting" two park rangers for trepassing. The state police moved in and arrested Tixerina and several of his followers on charges of assault and battery and expropriation of government property. Playing to the media, with a national forum now, Tixerina spoke against "American imperialism." He claimed that because the old *mercedes* were independent city-states, the sons of the old Hispano families were being drafted and sent to Vietnam illegally. He talked about issuing visas to "foreigners" who wanted to visit the republic. He talked revolution and liberation. "Fidel Castro has what he has because of his guts," he said. "Castro put the gringos off his island, and we can do the same." (With the selective memory typical of ethnic causes, the Chicanos made no mention that their ancestors had wrested the land from Navajo, Apache, Pueblos, and other indigenous peoples.)

Through the fall and the following spring, unrest in the Rio Arriba mounted. The homes, barns, and haystacks of Anglo ranchers were torched; their ditches and fences wrecked; their water tanks shot up; their cattle rustled. Tixerina, released by the police, scheduled a mass meeting in Coyote for June 3, 1967. Fearing an insurrection, the district attorney of Rio Arriba County, Alfonso Sanchez, forbade the Alianza to assemble, and on the night of the second he arrested twelve of its leaders (Tixerina was not among them). On the seventh Tixerina made a citizen's arrest of Sanchez for violating his constitutional right to assemble. Twenty armed Aliancistas broke into the Tierra Amarilla jail, shot and seriously wounded a policeman and a jailer, beat up two other policemen, and busted out the prisoners. It was the frontier again. La Raza had taken the law into its own hands to redress long-standing injuries.

The wounded jailer, Eulogio Salazar, identified Tixerina as the man who had shot him, and the governor, ordering what would become the largest manhunt in New Mexico history, deployed a massive force. Four hundred National Guardsmen and two hundred state troopers, assisted by cattle-brand inspectors and various other law-enforcement agents and backed up by two antiaircraft open-turreted "duster" tanks, helicopters, and artillery, stormed into the village of Canjili, where Tixerina was rumored to be holed up, but there was no trace of him. A tip led to his arrest in Albuquerque two weeks later. Tixerina was cleared of the charges stemming from the jailbreak, but he served two years for the Echo Amphitheater incident. Suffering from poor health, he was paroled in 1971 on condition that he no longer hold office in the Alianza. By then the movement had lost steam. Tixerina kept trying to get a court to hear the land grant issue, but none would take it on. After one last try in 1979, he gave up and turned to writing his memoirs. The trip to Israel was apparently not a positive experience; since then Tixerina has become obsessed with "the world Communist Jewish conspiracy." Despite this rap, he still has followers, but "he is not the leader of the movement," an activist in the new wave that is fighting for the return of the *mercedes* told me in 1992. As Tixerina himself said recently, "I slowed down because I was getting ahead of God." The latest news (February 1994) is that all the buildings in his compound in Coyote have burned to the ground. But the chief suspect is an enemy of his son.

There's a big split in the movement, this activist told me. Others are doing the work that Tixerina is no longer doing, like Amador Flores, who owned 18 acres across the road from a ski resort that had been proposed in Tierra Amarilla and for twenty years had paid back taxes on another 500 acres that were originally part of the Tierra Amarilla grant but that the resort's developers claimed were theirs. So in 1988 Flores barricaded himself with guns, and several Vietnam vets joined him and dug ditches. Finally he settled for 210 acres and the return of another 15,000 as common land. This is the first part of a *merced* that has ever been returned. Only one grant, in Chilili, New Mexico, was never transferred or broken up, and it remains intact.

The End of the Road

At last I reached San Luis Río Colorado, the northern-most extant Hispanic settlement in the New World and the oldest town in the state, as a sign in white-washed boulders proclaimed from a hillside. Settled by Mexicans in 1851, three years after Mexico had lost its northernmost Internal Provinces (as the northern borderlands of New Spain were known after 1776), San Luis sits at 7,565 feet on cold desert steppe with high peaks looming on three sides, some with tongues and flecks of snow lingering on their upper slopes even now, at the height of summer. San Luis Valley is the largest alpine valley in world, and under it is the largest untapped aquifer in the West, a liquid gold mine with an esti-mated 2 billion acre-feet that has not surprisingly inspired yet another bitter water-rights battle. This one is reminiscent of John Nichols's novel *The Milagro Beanfield War*. Thirsty cities in the American West are willing to pay $7,000 for an acre-foot of water, so the aquifer is in theory worth $14 trillion. A billionaire from Vancouver named Sam Belzer founded the American Water Company, which bought up 143,000 acres in the valley and planned to build a 45-mile pipeline that would deliver 25,000 to 200,000 acre-feet of the water a year to a river that flows to Denver and generate annual gross revenues of $175 million to $1.4 billion. This was being fought tooth and nail by the local Hispanos of the valley.

San Luis's claim to being the northernmost extension of the Spanish frontier is actually rather suspect. In Alamosa, north of San Luis, a party of Ute on their way to Washington in 1868 passed several Mexicans who had been lynched on a telegraph line as a warning to any of their kind who were thinking of settling farther north. But Leadville, north of Alamosa, has a substantial Hispanic population, not to mention the Mexican barrios, some of considerable vintage, in Denver. But I was tired of traveling and was prepared to accept San Luis as the symbolic end of the line.

It could have been a depressed town in Montana, except that there was a restaurant called El Patio that served a tasty indigenous sopapilla—beans, beef, onions, and lettuce rolled in fry bread and smothered with green chile and melted cheese—and a Hispanic Culture Center with a diorama of the original plaza, old photographs and costumes, the butterfly and beetle collection of San Luis's beloved Theatine father Bernard Roger, who had died the week before. A booklet explaining the exhibits began, "The Hispanic population [of San Luis] . . . has made a decision, for good or bad, to languish culturally in the past, while the rest of the world has eagerly embraced progress in its headlong flight to a destiny yet to be determined." The community had hesitantly made only "the most obvious and necessary contacts" with the "dominant culture" and had retained a proud, local outlook. To its nine hundred residents, this valley, not the United States, was *el país,* their country. Their ancestors had carried corn from the field in carts with large, "almost round" wooden wheels to be ground by hand on metates. Dario Galleos opened the first store in 1854 with $452 worth of merchandise. On his second buying expedition, he was attacked by Indians. Ute, Kiowa, Comanche, and Navajo also lived in the valley. The existence of a store was in some ways unfortunate, the brochure continued, because it created a cash economy and made *la gente,* the people, consumers of the encroaching Anglo culture.

The first homes in San Luis were jacales, rows of upright poles slathered with adobe. Later, clay, sand, straw, and water were mushed together in shallow pits by the feet of livestock, poured into wet wooden molds, and sun-dried into forty-pound bricks, which were stacked in double rows for walls. Courtship "in the early days" had a rigid procedure: young members of the opposite sex weren't even allowed to speak unless a *dueña,* a chaperone, was present. If the girl's family wasn't interested in the young man's proposal, or *pedimento,* he would "get the calabash": a pumpkin would be placed outside his parents' house.

This was not a wealthy town. San Luis's original Sangre de Cristo land grant had been sold five times for taxes. In 1960 *Forbes* magazine bought a large chunk of it. It and other slick magazines in the East advertised acreage in an upscale residential and vacation complex called Wagoncreek. But even so, the brochure went on, "change has been slow to come."

I decided to celebrate the end of my journey with a haircut. The barber of San Luis, Ernest (he had dropped the *o* as a concession to the dominant culture) Sanchez, was running for commissioner of Costilla

County; in the window there was a poster of him wearing a Stetson. "Our heritage is disintegrating slowly, you might say, due to the fact that our children don't want to speak Spanish," he told me sadly as he pinned the striped sheet around my neck. "In another generation, when these grow up, that'll be it. They don't teach Spanish in the schools. I try teaching it to my kids, but there is no interest. What are you going to do? The big necessity isn't there."

He asked how I wanted the back of my hair—square-blocked or tapered. I said square-blocked, thinking of the famous scene in *The Treasure of the Sierra Madre,* where the barber's chair spins to reveal the naked back of Bogart/J. Fred Dobbs's neck.

Five years later, a few days after arriving in Albuquerque, we were driving around, checking the place out, and I suddenly decided to swerve into a Burger King on San Mateo and sideswiped a Pinto I hadn't seen coming up in the right lane behind my Explorer. I got out, as did the driver, a small man, named Marvin Ortiz, with a genial, humorous face reminiscent of the Chicano comedian Cheech Marin's, and we hugged. "Oh man. Whew. Oh man, oh man. Wow, whew," he kept saying. We traded phone numbers and discussed whether to get the police involved. The fifty-cent-sized dent I'd put into his Pinto wouldn't even be covered by his five-hundred-dollar deductible. My dent, a long streak in the passenger door, was more serious, but it was my fault, although legally, I pointed out, he was responsible because he had been behind me, and even though I failed to signal, he was supposed to have braked, and if we reported the accident, both of our insurances are going to go up, and I really don't want to bring in the police, so why don't we just let it go?

Ortiz just stood there, shook up, wondering what to do. "It could have been bad," he said. "I thought you were drunk. But I can see you're a nice guy." The longer he stood there, considering the options, the more suspicious he became, but at last, not sure he wasn't going to regret it, still wondering whether he was getting screwed, he hugged me again and drove away.

The whole exchange—Marvin's humanity, he was a beautiful guy; his switch from warmth to wariness; the fact that I, the generic Anglo, had been the aggressor, the one who cut him off—had subtle ethnohistoric resonances. It was as if the accident were not an isolated incident, but something taking place in the context of a long history of conflict. And this is sadly true, I would venture to say, of most ethnic interactions in the Southwest.

Part Three

A Changing of the Guard

A s Spain was losing control of the Americas, a new type of European—blond, blue eyed, Aryan—began to trickle into the Internal Provinces of New Spain, the far northern outliers of Catholic-Moorish-Latin Europe. The Texanos and *nuevomejicanos* called them *americanos,* which would be corrupted into *bilagaana* by the Navajo, *melika* by the Zuñi, and *meligan* by the O'odham.*

They also called them gringos, according to one derivation because the unofficial theme song of the Anglo colonists who seceded from Mexico and declared Texas a republic in 1835 was "Green Grow the Lilacs." Others claim "gringo" comes from the French *dégringolade,* meaning downfall or tumble. Others say it's a corruption of the swearword *chingado,* fucked one. The dictionary of Velasquez Wehtsen defines "gringo" as "someone who doesn't speak the language intelligibly or with a good accent." But the term was already in circulation by the eighteenth century; one 1787 dictionary of Castilian has it as a perversion of *griego,* Greek, meaning any foreigner (the same sort of expansion *germanos,* or German, has undergone in modern Greek). The term has a derogatory edge, like *mzungu,* the Swahili word for white (literally, exploiter), or *gallo,* the Somali word for white (literally, camel), but it is not as derogatory as *gavacho,* or *gabacho,* from the French *gavache,* for a southern Frenchman, a *nuevomejicanismo* applied to the French Canadian voyageurs and trappers.

The Apache called the gringos "pale eyes" (which Hollywood changed to "paleface"). To the Acoma, they were "gray eyes," to the Tewans *kepi,* "red necks"; the Jicarilla word for the britches they wore meant "buttocks bags." Narbona, the Navajo leader who was chosen

* Cf. the Somalis' *maraika.*

to work out a peaceful settlement with the *bilagaana* and who was
shot in the back by Colonel John M. Washington's men in 1849, when
he was eighty-three, called them "the new men." In the Southwest
today, everybody calls them Anglos, a term that embraces anyone of
northern European stock.

The first Anglos to appear on the eastern horizon tended to be big,
beefy, braggadocian types—larger-than-life, self-creating legends like
Paul Bunyan and Mike Fink, who boasted "I can outrun, outhop,
throw down, drag out, and lick any man in the country. I'm a Salt
River roarer, I am. I love the 'wimming,' and I'm chock full of fight."
Perhaps these frontiersmen needed to inflate themselves to feel that
they mattered in the endless wilderness west of the Mississippi. They
had broken away, these Anglos, from the ancestral hold of northern
Europe and belonged to a hot new culture that was making itself up as
it went along, a culture that was on a roll, rolling over the Alleghenies,
pouring through Cumberland Gap, flooding into the Mississippi Valley, swarming over the Plains, "claiming our American heritage," as
the emcee at a rodeo in Amarillo I attended put it, until the young
republic had fulfilled its "manifest destiny" and the Stars and Stripes
flew "from sea to shining sea." The cold cultures of the Indians and the
Spaniards, frozen in what Paul Horgan has called "a fixed, traditional
present," were no match for them, and by midcentury the Spaniards
had gone from being conquistadores to being *conquistados* and had
joined the ranks of the superseded Indians.

The Anglos brought with them a mind-set that had not been seen in
these parts before: the analytic curiosity of the Enlightenment. Nature
was to be dissected, collected, categorized, catalogued, manipulated,
and conquered, rather than respected and revered and let be. It was in
this spirit that President Thomas Jefferson, in 1804, sent the Lewis and
Clark expedition up the Missouri River, to see if it offered water communication to the Pacific and, if it didn't, to find the most direct water
route across the continent "for the purpose of commerce." All observations, Jefferson instructed, were "to be taken with great pains and
accuracy, to be entered distinctly & intelligibly for others as well as
yourself . . . & put into the care of the most trustworthy of your atten-
dants, to guard by multiplying them, against the accidental losses to
which they will be exposed." The expeditionaries were to inform
themselves about minerals and new species, about "the Rio Bravo,
which runs into the gulph of Mexico, and the North River, or Rio Colorado, which runs into the gulph of California." But the lasting contribution of the journals, which were brought back to civilization in tin

boxes two years later, was more literary and mythopoeic than scientific. "To a nation with no commonly sung mystique of the State or of the Race or of the empire, no national literature, no *Iliad* or *Chanson de Roland* or *Kalevala*—these uneven, fragmented, and unpolished journals offered the equivalent of a national poem, a magnificent epic for an unfinished nation," writes the Americanist Frank Bergon.

Three years after Lewis and Clark set out, Zebulon Pike, the leader of another intelligence-gathering expedition, was captured by Spanish soldiers in southern Colorado and taken in chains down to Chihuahua. His voluminous notes on the natural history and culture and military strength of New Spain, collected over a year of captivity (Pike finally talked himself out of prison by offering to start a smallpox-eradication campaign), were smuggled out in gun barrels. Published in 1810, they became an overnight sensation.

From 1807 to 1821 the western border of American Louisiana was closed; the authorities in New Spain were threatened by Americans' goods and ideas. But this border was vague and undefined. At one point, Spanish and American troops clashed in what is now Nebraska. But already by then, predominantly French Canadian traders known as Commancheros (who had been supplying guns to the Comanche to destabilize the Spanish since before the Louisiana Purchase) would occasionally show up in Taos, and Anglo and French Canadian trappers were making their way into New Mexico along its eastern drainage in search of the lighter-skinned, slightly smaller, desert river beaver. The vogue back east for beaver hats would last until 1835, when the animals were pretty much trapped out and the burgeoning China trade brought silk hats into fashion. The trails they blazed were, with the ancient Indian paths and trade routes of the Aztec *pochtecas,* the forerunners of wagon trails and modern interstates.

Some of the trappers came down the rivers in buffalo-skin coracles known as bull boats, but more often they traveled on foot, with pack trains, their personal articles in buckskin "possible bags." Rugged cusses like Peg Leg Smith and Uncle Dick Wooton would follow the Gila and the San Juan and other tributaries of the Colorado, harvesting the seemingly boundless abundance of bears, mink, and foxes, the idea of extinction years from occurring to anyone. The trapper James Ohio Pattie claimed to have seen two hundred grizzly bears in a single day along the Arkansas; but according to the historian Bernard Fontana, 60 to 70 percent of his memoir is sensational hyperbole. The mountain-man memoir was part of the frontier genre, which flourished after the West was wrested from Mexico.

Pattie spent six years in the southwestern wilderness, including a stretch as an Indian captive. He was a survivor of the Miguel Ribodoux party, which was massacred by "Papago" (Fontana says they would have been Yavapai). His comrades "were literally cut to pieces, and fragments of their bodies were scattered in every direction." Later, Pattie came upon some Mojave roasting some of his other companions. "On the 30th . . . we found the man that the Indians had killed. They had cut him in quarters, after the fashion of butchers. His head, with his hat on, was stuck on a stake. It was full of arrows, which they had probably discharged into it, as they danced around it. We gathered up the parts of the body, and buried them." The arrows were tipped with poison made from rattlesnakes tormented in a pit into striking at an antelope or deer liver, mixed with the blood of a woman. How much cannibalism actually went on in the Southwest is now hotly debated. Missing from these accounts are the atrocities committed by the Anglos. Scalping was commonly practiced by both sides. Pattie himself admits to cutting up Indians and hanging their body parts in trees as a warning not to mess with him.

Once a year the trappers and mountain men would converge on Taos for a big blowout. The annual sprees of Old Bill Williams, when he descended on civilization with his pelts and whooped it up until the money was gone, were legendary. Like many a frontier marksman, Williams was unable to hold his long-barreled flintlock steady and shot with a "double wobble," sweeping across the target and squeezing the trigger just as it lined up with the muzzle. After the beaver market bottomed out, the trappers became guides for wagon trains or surveying expeditions. In 1848 Williams guided John Charles Frémont's disastrous fourth expedition in search of a railroad route through the Rockies. The party was immobilized by a blizzard. Eleven of the thirty-five men starved to death. Emergency cannibalism is suspected to have taken place. In the spring Williams returned to retrieve some abandoned equipment and was massacred by Ute.

The former trapper Jedediah Smith met a similar fate. In 1831 he set out for Santa Fe from Independence, Missouri, with twenty-three wagons and eighty-five men. Deviating from the usual route, the caravan struck out into the waterless waste west of Dodge City between the Arkansas and the Cimarron Rivers. After three days, the animals were giving out, and the men, semidelirious from desert thirst, began to wander off in small groups. Alone, Smith finally reached the dry channel of the Cimarron, dug a hole in the sand, and, after it had filled with water, plunged his head into it. While he was thus cooling off, several Comanche crept up, spooked his horse with a mirror and blanket, and jumped him. Smith had allegedly killed two Comanche with a single pistol ball five years earlier (this was before the invention of repeaters). But this time they got him.

No one embodied the American rugged-individual prototype or played a more prominent role in the successive phases of the nineteenth-century frontier, or personified the spirit of manifest destiny more perfectly, inheriting the frontiersman mantle of Boone and Crockett, than Christopher "Kit" Carson. Physically, Carson was unimpressive—five feet, six inches; barrel-chested; with shoulder-length red hair, steady blue eyes, and an almost-girlish voice. Born in Kentucky, he was apprenticed to a saddler, and at the age of sixteen, he ran away and joined a wagon train heading out on the Santa Fe Trail. After he recovered horses stolen from a trapper named Ribodoux, Ribodoux took him under his wing, and for the next twelve years he was a trapper. In 1837 he married an Arapaho woman named Singing Grass, then a Cheyenne woman, then Josefa, the kid sister of Maria Ignacia, the wife of Charles Bent, the trader who became the governor of the newly annexed New Mexico territory. Josefa was there, in Taos, on January 19, 1847, when her sister was gang-raped before Bent's eyes and he himself was scalped or beheaded by Mexican and Pueblo insurgents. She died in 1868 at the age of forty while giving birth to her eighth child. A month later, Carson died with blood gushing from his mouth. His last words: "Doctor. *Compadre*. Adios."

Though illiterate, Carson was conversant in Spanish, French, and eight Indian tongues. In 1842, at the age of thirty-three, he went with John Charles Frémont to map the Oregon Trail. Later, he was a scout with General Stephen Watts Kearny's Army of the West. Though he could scarcely write his own name, he became a dime-novel hero in his own lifetime, harassed by celebrity seekers. "The paperbacks took him up," Milo Milton Quaife, the editor of his autobiography, writes, "and before long a wholly imaginary superman had taken shape in the public mind, while the real [Kit Carson], still in the prime of life and with half his career before him, was pursuing his unostentatious course of life in the remote American Southwest."

The Navajo called him Rope Thrower, because in 1863 he captured as many of them as he could—about eight thousand—and marched them down to Bosque Redondo, where they spent five years in detention. Many sickened and died there from eating maggoty tins of beans and other spoiled rations and from drinking the bitter alkali water of the Pecos, or convinced that Changing Woman had deserted them, sank into despair and lost the will to live. Venereal diseases, smallpox, chicken pox, and pneumonia carried off about a quarter of them. Nine hundred escaped. The survivors were allowed to return to a 90-percent-reduced Dinetah (later increased fivefold to its present size). They gave up raiding, and their numbers grew quickly. Rope Thrower died the year of their release and did not live to see their astonishing recovery.

Changing Notions of the Frontier

n 1819 the secretary of war John C. Calhoun appointed Major Stephen H. Long to lead a scientific expedition into the unexplored country between the Mississippi River and the Rockies. Long got no farther west than northeastern New Mexico, but this didn't stop him from labeling the region "the Great American Desert"—a slogan, as my Navajo friend Tom would call it, that would deter Anglo migration into the Southwest for the next three decades.

But even so, within months of Mexico's independence, Anglo traders were setting out from Franklin, Missouri, for Santa Fe. The following year, 1821, one of them, William Becknell, gathered a crowd in Franklin and poured out a sackful of silver Mexican pesos before it to dramatize the money to be made from commerce with Mexico. After the Mexican War, this trade route became the migratory route known as the Santa Fe Trail. Many of the emigrants were fourth- or fifth-generation pioneers. The first generation had poured over the Appalachians after the American Revolution, the next into the Mississippi Valley, the next onto the Plains. This wave took on the Great American Desert.

The frontier was a safety valve. Until 1890 and even after that, even now, one could always head west and start anew. Fresh arrivals from Europe would come to work in the factories of the East, and after they had earned their stake, they would head out west, and new immigrants would arrive to take their place. For many the East was just a stopping-off point. Those who already had their stake didn't even stop, but joined the wagon trains of older pioneer stock.

Frontiers are conquered in stages. In the Amazon today, much as was the case in the Southwest a century and a half ago, the first wave is known as *desbravadores*. They hunt and trap jungle cats—the jaguar and the ocelot—for their skins, have Indians working for them, are often half Indian themselves. Then come the *garimpeiros,* the prospectors—marginals for whom the urban centers back in the civilized part of the country have nothing to offer. The *garimpeiros* massacre the Indians. Then come the cowboys and the ranchers with their herds of cattle, and *pistoleiros* with John Wesley Hardin mustaches who pattern themselves after the Wild West gunslingers in the *bangybangys*—the old Hollywood-western reruns on Brazilian television. They are followed by agriculture and industry, if it gets that far.

Comparing the American expansion to that of Rome and Spain, the historians Henry Steele Commager and Richard Brandon Morris point out that "no other nation had ever expanded so rapidly, or expanded so far without putting an intolerable strain upon the existing political and economic fabric." What they find most impressive "is the ease, the simplicity, and the seeming inevitability of the whole process." The slow westward movement of the frontier line seemed as natural as the shadow of a cloud. The vast landscape it passed over is evoked by Wallace Stegner thus:

> The plains lay out between their swinging rivers, spring-green and summer-brown, treeless except for the belts of cottonwood along water, deserted except for coyotes, an occasional shanty, the ungathered bones of the buffalo, domed by a great bowl sky that filled and overflowed with dramatic weathers. . . . Beyond the plains went the wrinkled spine of the continent, range after range, bare granite, black spruce, gold aspen on the autumn slopes, timbered valleys. . . . Beyond those mountains and plateaus . . . the veritable and incontrovertible desert stretched across salt flat and dead lake bottom and barren range after barren range to the Sierra where the West ended and California began.

In his book *America's Frontier Heritage,* the historian Ray Allen Billington analyzes several hundred travel accounts of eighteenth- and nineteenth-century Europeans, who found the American frontiersman, on the whole, to be "wasteful, democratic, and inquisitive." Life on the frontier was hard; there was no leisure, no time for cultural creativity, and the western pioneer tended to be anti-intellectual and materialistic and to play his games "with a grim determination to have fun" and to win. He had little attachment to place or family tradition. In anthropological jargon, he was neolocal: each generation moved farther west, reinventing itself, searching for new space, more freedom. Traditional class distinctions were meaningless on the frontier, but the settlers tended to be belligerently nationalistic and ready to magnify minor incidents into war.

The "frontier hypothesis" elaborated in 1893 by Frederick Jackson Turner in his seminal essay "The Significance of the Frontier in Western History" postulated the "formation of a composite nationality" in the "crucible of the frontier." This dominated scholarly thinking for decades. Modern scholars are inclined to reject Turner's notion that the frontier era was over by 1890, when the U.S. Census Bureau announced that the frontier, as a line, no longer existed; to them it's still going on, and the main thing about it is its violence.

The death, in 1836, of 189 Anglo-American immigrants to Texas, trapped by thousands of Mexican soldiers in an eighteenth-century Franciscan mission called the Alamo, became a central frontier creation myth. The slogan "Remember the Alamo" came to evoke the American settlers' struggle against tyranny and replaced "*Santiago y a elles*" as the battle cry of the new conquistadores in the Mexican War, which the incident eventually escalated into. But few elements of the Alamo myth prove to be grounded in historical reality. Davy Crockett never wore a coonskin cap and, according to recent research, hid under a bed throughout the fighting and tried to surrender rather than fight to the death. William Travis, the commander of the besieged Americans, whose desperate letters appealed for reinforcements "in the name of Liberty, of patriotism & everything dear to the American character," was half mad from venereal disease and the mercury he was drinking to cure it and "never issued his legendary challenge for the brave to join him across his sword-drawn line in the dirt," a 1993 *New York Times* article reported. Jim Bowie was a land speculator who "stole a hoard of silver and gold from Apaches he had butchered and hid it in a well on the Alamo's grounds." General Sam Houston, who "was at least wise enough not to send reinforcements," was an opium addict. A new wave of Chicano revisionists have recast the Alamo, like Columbus, as a symbol of Anglo imperialism and racism.

In the typical pattern of the conqueror, Mexicans were depicted in American tracts of the day, like G. N. Allen's 1847 *Mexican Treacheries and Cruelties,* as a savage mongrel race that butchered the helpless and mutilated the dead.

Typical of the negative stereotyping were the remarks of a traveler named Rufus Sage in 1846:

> There are no people on the continent of America . . . more miserable in condition or despicable in morals than the mongrel race inhabiting New Mexico. Next to the squalid appearance of its inhabitants, the first thing that arrests the attention of the traveler on entering a Mexican settlement, is the

uninviting mud walls that form the rude hovels which consti-
tute its dwellings . . . [whose] inmates . . . at nightfall . . .
stow themselves away promiscuously upon the ground or in
narrow bins, and snooze their rounds despite the swarms of
noxious vermin that infest them.

Crossings

The Santa Fe Trail went two thousand miles across the Plains. In places like Glorieta Pass, on its last leg, southeast of Santa Fe, the earth is still scored with wagon ruts. Working on the emigrant trains was an entry-level position for aspiring young frontiersmen like sixteen-year-old Kit Carson. Most of the crossings went without major mishaps, but the one described in *The Santa Fe Trail to California 1849–1852: The Journal and Drawings of H.M.T. Powell* was full of incidents. There is no information about who Powell was, exactly, or what eventually became of him. Two sketchbooks filled with drawings were purchased from Powell descendants, whose "present whereabouts are unknown," their editor, Douglas S. Watson, wrote in 1941. "The years that have elapsed have drawn a curtain."

Of the company Powell left Greenville, North Carolina, with on April 3, 1849, to make their fortunes in the California goldfields, three of the eleven died of cholera on the way. Scarcely had cholera taken Isaac W. Carter, of Concord, New Hampshire, age thirty-five, when George Ferguson "was taken with violent retchings," Powell reports. Bull Creek, Missouri: "The road today seemed like a lengthened cemetery. The mounds of graves of the emigrants thrown up at intervals on either side of the road and the bones and remains of cattle and mules strewn in all directions was but a dismal sight." On to the Plains: "From the absence of timber the Prairie has the almost boundless appearance that I anticipated." Powell gives a note for "my dear wife" to a wagon train headed the other way. Dr. Park gets cholera. Powell himself gets it. Dr. Burchard tells him to prepare and drink a decoction of black-oak bark. The company joins up with some South Carolinians and Germans, bringing the combined total now to forty-eight men. "Duty has sent me here, and duty shall carry me forward," Powell continues. The train arrives in Santa Fe, "a miserable hole; gambling and drinking in all directions." It leaves Santa Fe on July 24 and doesn't reach San Diego until December. So abundant is the wildlife—turkeys, grizzly bears, antelope, and so on—that the company can live off the land without supplement. Powell shoots an animal he calls a Mexican lion, bags a bear and wounds two others, and blows the head off a large rattlesnake. A mule, stumbling on "a perfect den of rattlers," is bitten and dies "in a very short while." (The frontier therapy for rattlesnake bite was excise, suck, plug with gunpowder, and hope for the best.)

Powell makes note of "singularly variegated" grasshoppers. "Mr. Felder's gun accidentally went off. It was loaded with buckshot and many of them passed through Mr. Coy's wagon in which Mrs. Coy was at the time getting some flour. This is the tenth accidental discharge of a gun since leaving. . . . Truly we ought to be thankful for a protecting Providence, for a more careless, heedless set I think I never knew." There is an altercation in the adjacent Berry's train: Gadson stabs Wiginton with a bowie knife, and Wiginton dies. A jury is picked from Powell's train, and Gadson is sentenced to fifty lashes and expelled from the train.

The Mexican men, he reports, wear leather trousers with untucked shirts, the women chemises over colored skirts, "a mere petticoat with a deep flounce, the eternal 'rebozo,' blue-and-white-spotted with a little fringe at the end, and with their faces daubed over, either with poke juice or a mixture of flour and water. The houses have little penthouses over their windows with mica stuck in roughly for glass." The company catches "a great many catfish, up to 20 lbs.," in the Rio Grande del Norte. They vote to take in McSwain's wagons, bringing the total to thirty-two, with seventy men, "besides which there are 4 coloured men." September 17: "Rufus Turner went up to the top of the mountain to the right of the pass and found at the highest peak an Indian fire still burning and heard a noise beyond, as if one was going down on the other side through the bushes." At noon they camp on the other side of the Continental Divide and find a human skull. Tubac, near Tucson, had been sacked by Apache "two months since," and three or four women had been killed. "The wolves last night were more than usually noisy. I could not sleep for their constant howling." On November 20 Powell is nearly mugged by three Pima who steal a large bag of his clothes. He saves himself by laughing and rattling on and keeping them in good humor as he walks back to camp. Like most of the other prospectors, Powell has no luck at the goldfields and returns home by sea. He has been gone two years and has nothing to show for it.

. . .

The most riveting example of the wagon-train genre was *Captivity of the Oatman Girls,* by the Reverend R. B. Stratton, an instant best-seller in 1857, comparable to Pears Paul Read's *Alive* in modern times. Already by this time, events on the frontier were being imaged back to civilization almost immediately, almost as they happened, the only lag being the time it took to write them up, set the type, and distribute the publication. *Captivity* purported to be the unembellished memoir, as told to Reverend Stratton, of Olive Oatman, the only survivor of a family of nine that was massacred on the trail by "Apache" (actually Yavapai) in 1851. Olive was ransomed five years later from Mojave, to whom she had been sold. They had tatooed her chin with black lines, pricked with a very sharp stick dipped in the juice of a certain weed that grew on riverbanks mixed with the powder of a certain blue stone, which she would have for the rest of her life.

The Oatmans were attacked eighty miles from Fort Yuma, at the confluence of the Gila and the Colorado, on February 18, 1851. This was still Mexican territory; the Gadsden Purchase, which would move the border down to its present location, was two years off. The Oatmans were Brewsterites, dissident Mormons who had repudiated Brigham Young, decided that Young had led the persecuted Saints from Illinois to the wrong place, that the valley of Great Salt Lake where Young founded his Kingdom of Deseret was not, in fact, the promised land. Their leader, James C. Brewster, claimed to have deduced from the book of Esdras that "in the land of California, shall my people find refuge from the evils and troubles that afflict the nations of the earth: there they shall have peace, and enjoy all the blessings that those that remain faithful shall receive." In that land "the kingdom of righteousness shall be built up . . . there shall none be poor, neither shall there be any that are rich." (Which is not exactly the way Los Angeles, with entire municipalities of multimillion-dollar homes and of ghettos exploding into self-trashing rage, turned out.)

The fifty-two Brewsterites set out from Independence, Missouri, on August 9, 1850. At Santa Fe, thirty-two of them, including Brewster himself, took the northern route. Royce Oatman and several other families chose the southern route, which went down the Rio Grande Valley, passing through Socorro, Santa Cruz, and Tucson. So many horses and stock were made off with that the Wilders and the Kellys decided not to push on to the mouth of the Colorado, and the Oatmans proceeded alone; Royce was confident in his ability to deal with the Indians on the basis of their common humanity.

The Old Santa Fe Trail, along the Gila River, was littered with the graves of emigrants and prospectors. Olive/Stratton muses:

> Monuments! monuments, blood-written, of these uncounted miseries, that will survive the longest lived of those most recently escaped, are inscribed upon the bleached and bleaching bones of our common humanity and nationality; are written upon the rude graves of our countrymen and kin, that strew these highways of death; written upon the mouldering timbers of decaying vehicles of transport; written in blood that now beats and pulsates in the veins of solitary and scathed survivors, as well as in the stain of kindred blood that still preserves its tale-telling, unbleached hue, upon scattered grass-plots, and Sahara sand mounds.

The Oatmans pass through this surreal, Bosch-like landscape with a mounting sense of foreboding: "It seemed . . . that the dark wing of some terrible calamity was spread over us, and casting the shadows of evil ominously and thickly upon our path."

The family makes camp on an "elevated, narrow tableland" overlooking the Gila. Just after sundown, nineteen "Apache" approach leisurely, professing friendship, like the ragged bandidos who behead Bogart's Dobbs in *The Treasure of the Sierra Madre*. As Royce converses with them in "the Mexican tongue," the lingua franca of the frontier, slowly he realizes that he and his family are going to be massacred. "The blood rushed to my father's face . . . a death-like paleness . . . spread over his countenance. . . . He succeeded, however, in controlling the jerking of his muscles and his mental agitations, so as to tell us, in mild and composed accents, 'not to fear; the Indians would not harm us.' "

Incredibly, Olive's brother Lorenzo, who was clubbed unconscious and left for dead, comes to and staggers to Fort Yuma with the help of some friendly "Pimole" (Pima?) Indians. Olive and her little sister Mary are taken captive, and after a year with the Yavapai they are sold to the Mojave, who march them two hundred miles in three days to a village of unimaginable "filth and degradation." Their captors' "mode of dress, (but little dress they had!) was needlessly and shockingly indecent." They ate "worms, grasshoppers, reptiles, *all flesh*," and "for whole days . . . would those stout, robust, lazy lumps of a degraded humanity lounge in the sun or by the gurgling spring." They were "utterly without skill or art in any useful calling" except for "the rudimentary flood-plain agriculture" with which they grew a few crops. "Had the industry and skill of the least informed of our agriculturalists been applied to this Mohave valley, it might have been made as productive and fruitful a spot as any I ever saw."

The girls witnessed "unmitigated cruelties which are sometimes perpetrated by them under the sanction of their barbaric beliefs." They watched Cocopa captives killed so they could be slaves of a dying father in the hereafter and the sacrifice of prisoners to avenge the death of fellow warriors. Runners, whom Olive calls " 'criers,' bore messages to and from friendly tribes." Gradually they "became more lenient and merciful" toward the girls and began to ask all sorts of questions—"if the whites possessed the other big world on the east of the Atlantic; if there were any Indians there"; how women were treated; if a man was allowed more than one wife. Olive told them "of the well-founded belief . . . that the stars above us were peopled by human beings," at which "they scoffed; if the stars were inhabited, the people would drop out, and hence they knew that this was a lie." As for the notion that the earth performs a complete revolution on its axis every twenty-four hours and travels around the sun every year, "upon this they said we were just like all the Americanos, big liars, and seemed to think that our parents had begun young with us to learn us so perfectly the art of falsehood so early. But still we could see . . . by their astonishment . . . they were not wholly unbelieving."

The Mojave told the girls that an "evil spirit" reigned among the whites and was leading them to destruction. "You whites, continued they, have forsaken nature and want to possess the earth, but you will not be able." Their myth for how the races came to be separated had biblical resonances: "There once was a flood in ancient time that covered all the world but that mountain [which was visible from the village], and all the present races then were merged in one family, and this family was saved from the general deluge by getting upon that mountain." Everyone in the family was red except for the progenitor of the whites, who stole and was punished by being turned white. His part of the family went north, taking all the cattle. They were known as the Hiccos, the dishonest whites. "They said the Hiccos . . . would lose their cattle yet; that this thieving would turn upon themselves."

Mary eventually died among the Mojave, but Olive was ransomed and returned to her world. But with her tattooed chin and her equally indelible memories, she would never fit in. Despite rumors that she had left behind two children whose father was the chief's son, the Los Angeles *Star* reported two weeks after her deliverance that "she has not been made a wife . . . and her defenceless situation [was entirely respected during her residence among the Indians]." Stratton himself marveled: "Let it be written . . . to stand out before those whose duty and position it shall be, within a few years, in the American Council of State, to deliberate and legislate upon the best method to dispose of those fast waning tribes; that *one of our own race, in tender years, committed wholly to their power, passed a five-years' captivity among these savages without falling under those baser propensities which rave, and rage, and consume, with the fury and fatality of a pestilence, among themselves.*" Olive was either eleven or thirteen at the time of her capture, but Stratton made her fourteen, perhaps to enhance the sex appeal of the narrative, the pioneering anthropologist A. L. Kroeber theorized.

Route 66

Commissioned in 1926, Route 66 was cobbled together from old wagon routes and Indian pathways, and by the midthirties it was drivable for its entire length, 2,448 miles from Chicago to Los Angeles. Okies, like the Joad family, fled the Dust Bowl on the Mother Road, as John Steinbeck dubbed the two-lane bituminous track, and headed west for the truck farms of California. It became a boon for crows and other carrion feeders and spawned the age of motor tourism. Families would pile into touring cars—Buicks, Cords, La Salles, Lincoln Zephyrs—with canvas water bags slung on the bumpers in case the radiator overheated, and would hit the road, cruising past billboards that proclaimed the efficacy of Alka-Seltzer or Bromo Seltzer for the dyspeptic, of Coca-Cola for the thirsty, of Burma Shave for the unshaven, stopping for flocks of sheep tended by old Navajo women, pulling into a tourist trap that boasted a den of live rattlesnakes. The children would push coins through the wire mesh, which the snakes would just let bounce off them.

I drove back and forth across the country on Route 66 with my dog Willie in 1970 and 1971. Then there was a gap of twenty years—until I set out for Albuquerque with my family from our home in upstate New York in the wake of Hurricane Bob and the toppling of Gorbachev. By then Route 66 had been superseded by I-40 and four other interstates. The biggest roadside attraction along I-40 was the row of ten classic Cadillacs half buried, at the angle of the Great Pyramid, with tail fins upthrust, at Stanley Marsh's Cadillac Ranch in Amarillo. The models range from '46 to '64. Marsh told me he wanted them to look as if they had been planted by members of some high civilization. The Cadillacs face west. As a teenager, Marsh dreamed of driving west on Route 66 to Las Vegas and breaking the bank, or of going to Hollywood and becoming a movie star.

Marsh's brother was a friend of mine back east, and the following spring I drove from Albuquerque to Amarillo to visit him. He had said he would introduce me to some cowboys. "You'll have to drink with them and fuck with them for at least a month before you can begin to understand what they're all about," he warned. Heading east on I-40, I passed Zuzax, New Mexico, filing it away for the next Geography game. There was already a billboard in Moriarty for the Big Texan, Amarillo's biggest restaurant, which offers a free seventy-two-ounce steak if you can eat it in an hour. On past Pastura and Colonias, where monumental pivot spraying systems, also known as circle systems, with hundreds of yards of perforated pipe on giant spokes that can be rolled back and forth, were irrigating peanut and cotton fields. Some mineral inside a mesa that resembled a slice of parsley-spattered meat loaf had brought a little boomtown called Cuervo into brief existence at its base. The mesa was riddled with abandoned tunnels belching tan slag heaps creased with dendritic rills. Cuervo was still partially inhabited, but Endee, where I stopped for gas, appeared to be 100 percent dead, a ghost town. The gas pumps were hooded, the R had dropped off the sign for its bar, the café-motel was closed, the Endee apartments were boarded up. The town had been in a slump for decades. The WPA guide to New Mexico, written during the Depression, describes Endee, population 350, as "a sunbaked ruin of delapidated shacks and frame buildings." It had been "a blow-off town for the cowpunchers in the early days of its existence. In its heyday, the town had regular Sunday morning burials for those who had been too slow on the draw. It is said that in preparation for their reception, a trench was dug each Saturday on the edge of town."

I pulled into motel-rich Tucumcari (whose *a* is long, I learned, as in "corral," pronounced "corr-ALE," or "calves," pronounced "caves"). For years Harry Garrison, who was never a working cowboy, would greet the train, wearing pearl-handled six-guns, and invite passengers to his café, Harry's Lunch. Then he would take them to Boot Hill Cemetery in the nearby hamlet of Montoya, which (the WPA guide explains) was "distinguished from others in that decent folk, who died in their beds as a result of so-called natural causes, were laid away in 'hallowed ground,' while those whose trigger-fingers were a trifle sluggish, or who felt the ire and the bullets of an enraged citizenry, were grudgingly flung with their boots on into a pit beside others who had suffered violent deaths."

Suddenly overcome by a hankering to play golf, I asked the attendant at the Circle K convenience store if there was a course in town, and he said, "You bet." I stopped a girl on the street and asked her,

"Where's the golf course?" Perhaps affected by the blinding, brick-baking noon heat, she answered, apologetically, "I probably know, but I just can't remember." At last I found it, at the end of town—the Mesa Country Club Municipal Golf Course, $5.25 all day. I teed off with two local men who didn't introduce themselves, but I found out one's name soon enough, when he chastised himself after missing an easy putt on the first green: "Wayne, you wimp." It was so hot I remember nothing about the round except for the small sticker someone had affixed to the eleventh ball washer. It said VIETNAM VETS NOT FONDA JANE.

A billboard proclaimed Tucumcari to be the GATEWAY TO THE SOUTHWEST, but the naturalist Joseph Wood Krutch proposed that the Southwest actually begins about sixty miles to the east, where the plain of Texas, "dryish but undramatic," gives way to "red, eroded sand-stone and . . . cactus . . . the first real desert." But Stanley Marsh considers the Texas Panhandle more part of the Southwest than of Texas, and my own position is that the eastern edge of the Southwest is actu-ally much farther east. The line would appear to pass through Mount Vernon, Missouri, where the University of Missouri College of Agri-culture has its Southwest Research Center. Right down the road, no more than a minute east, is (or was, the last time I passed through) the Mid-America Dental, Hearing and Visual Center.

I reached the place Krutch must have been talking about, where the interstate ascends to the vast tableland of the Texas Panhandle known variously as the High Plains, the Southern Plains, and the Staked Plain (Llano Estacado, supposedly because early Spanish explorers pounded stakes at intervals so they could retrace their way). The earth here is so flat you can see that it is actually curved. Endless freight trains accen-tuated the horizontality, more lengths of irrigation pipe on huge wheels receded to the vanishing point, grain elevators stood on the horizon like giant idols or conning towers, Aermotor windmills twirled in the oceanic short-grass. On the radio of my pickup, the actor Ricardo Montalban was doing a spot for the New Mexico Tourist Board about the Indian known as the Turk who led Coronado and his men on a final wild-goose chase across the Plains to a rich kingdom to the east called Quivira, where even the common people supposedly ate off plates of gold. *Un poquito mas allá,* just a little farther, he kept tell-ing the Spaniards as he guided them across the Texas and Oklahoma Panhandles.

This was the area Captain R. B. Marcy dubbed "the great Sahara of North America" in an 1849 report. On the High Plains, the distance between water can be eighty miles. There is little relief, apart from the dramatic gash of Palo Duro Canyon, where the Red River rises and the Comanche had one of their major encampments. The Comanche would return to the canyon from a raid in Mexico triumphantly, with bananas and parrot feathers. But in 1874 Colonel Ronald McKenzie drove off and killed their pony herd, which was almost two thousand strong, and marched the stunned Comanche to a reservation in Oklahoma. By then caravans of prairie schooners and Conestogas were rolling across the Plains, and buffalo hunters were taking as many as a hundred skins a day; "floating outfits" of "hands" would go out for a year at a time. After the Plains were cleared of buffalo and Indians, cattle were moved in, and the range was fenced with barbed wire.

The stench of thousands of cattle in the feed yard at Wildorado, just west of Amarillo, was detectable even at seventy miles an hour. Then Stanley Marsh's Cadillacs, painted baby blue, hove into view.

The Wizard of Amarillo

I found Stanley, a jovial, rubicund fifty-four-year-old, playing croquet in his office, which took up the entire top floor of the Team Bank Tower, the tallest building in town, soon to be the First Bank Tower (Team Bank having been one of the notorious recently failed savings and loans). The building's name had changed a dozen times since Stanley had been up there, monitoring Amarillo and the world. One large, sunny room was totally given over to croquet. The hoops were chrome. A stuffed pig surveyed the pitch. The decor of the other rooms was dominated by dozens of eight-foot-high canoe paddles Stanley had bought in New Guinea and shipped back home. A wall of his office was taken up with television sets tuned to all three stations, one of which, KVII-TV, an ABC affiliate, he owns. "We broadcast to more jackrabbits and cacti than any other station in the country," he told me.

Stanley was a connoisseur of the local news. This week the top story in Amarillo was the murder in a park of a four-year-old girl by a twenty-six-year-old drifter who had rented a room from the girl's parents three weeks earlier. "He didn't look like the type," Stanley told me. "First, he put her body in an ice chest, then he threw it into a dipsy Dumpster, where the police found it. This could have happened to anybody, so it's a big story. The first criterion for watching news around here is, Am I safe? No food poisoning, no rabid dogs, floods; job's okay; family's fine. Then what's happening in the world? Shall Princess Di have a nose job? Thank God for the royal family.

"Amarillo averages one fatal a day," Stanley went on, "usually a car accident. There are a hundred and forty thousand people here now, but it isn't a city because we don't have any drive-by shootings. The Texas Panhandle is kind of like Uruguay, and Amarillo is the capital of it. We make no finished products except for atomic bombs, which we are the only source of,* but I feel like everything that comes in and out of here I should get a percentage of. My secret ambition is to persuade the Panhandle to secede, and I would become its dictator."

Amarillo (named for the yellow flowers that bloom on the banks of its creek in spring) was an insignificant cow town and buffalo-hide depot (the roof and partitions of its first hotel were made of buffalo hides, which were in much more plentiful supply than lumber) until it became the junction of two railroad lines in 1874, whereupon it boomed. It had a whole street of whorehouses. Bankers and aristocrats from London and Edinburgh bought up much of the Panhandle and created vast cattle kingdoms. Oil was discovered in the Panhandle in 1922, natural gas four years later, but it didn't have any value until 1943, when German U-boats were sinking oil barges that left Galveston, and an overland route for the oil was needed, and a big pipeline was opened to St. Louis that could deliver the natural gas, too. "Natural gas is real efficient if millions of people are together," Stanley explained. It made his father, Stanley Junior, a fortune. Stanley I, a bookkeeper, came from Ohio via Coalgate, Oklahoma, and arrived in Amarillo in 1926. Stanley Junior acquired for a song a lot of the acreage overlying the Haugoton-Anadarko Basin, which is the largest natural-gas field in the world. This had enabled Stanley III to devote himself to being a character, and as one of his friends told me, he worked hard at it. Stanley the sought-after judge in local wrestling matches; Stanley in *Esquire* some years back, dressed in a black-and-white-large-checked shirt and suit, sitting in an identically checked chair in the middle of an identically checked floor.

Stanley drove me out to see his environmental sculpture, *Floating Mesa,* whose subversive intent was to do away with museums: a mesa with a thick strip of canvas wrapped around its entire girth so that the mesa seemed to be suspended in the sky. A monument known as *The Grave of the Unknown Pet,* on a dirt road way out in the middle of the prairie, was appreciated only by prairie dogs and prickly pears; several miles down the road a white marble head and two legs lay in short-grass with a plaque quoting Shelley's "Ozymandias":

> I met a traveller from an antique land
> Who said: 'Two vast and trunkless legs
> Stand in the desert. Near them, on the sand,
> Half sunk, a shattered visage lies, whose frown,

---

* Many of the people who assemble or, more recently, disassemble nuclear warheads at Amarillo's Pantex plant are millenarian fundamentalists and are the subject of a book by A. G. Mojtabai called *Blessed Assurance.*

> And wrinkled lip, and sneer of cold command,
> Tell that its sculptor well those passions read
> Which yet survive, stamped on these lifeless things,
> The hand that mocked them and the heart that fed.

The plaque explains that the famous poet passed here in 1810 on a horseback trek over the Great Plains with Leigh Hunt and his wife, Mary Wollstonecraft Shelley (which is, of course, total bull).

"We own as far as you can see—two hundred square miles—because Wendy's ancestor invented barbed wire a hundred and fifteen years ago," Stanley mused. Wendy is Stanley's wife, who is active in the arts and is the honorary French consul of Amarillo. "Her ancestor Joseph Farwell Glidden was, you'd better say, one of the inventors of barbed wire," he went on. "Glidden's daughter married Wendy's grandfather, who bought this spread, Frying Pan Ranch. Barbed wire has been around since the Middle Ages, but spot-welding tines to two twisted strands of wire was Glidden's idea. He got it from the welded wire frames of beaver hats and took out the patent. But he and the inventor of a slightly different form of barbed wire, Jacob Haish, became entangled in suits that went on for years, draining the incomes of both. And there were several others with versions that went nowhere financially."

The impact of barbed wire on the frontier cannot be exaggerated. Walter Prescott Webb has a full discussion of it in his history of the Plains. Barbed wire brought down the cattle kingdoms, converting open, free range into big-pasture country, on which blooded stock replaced the longhorn steer introduced by the Mexicans, and it put an end to the long drive. During the severe winter of 1884, thousands of antelope, deer, and buffalo expired along the Great Panhandle Drift Fence, a three-strander stretching two hundred miles, trying to get to the grass in the Canadian River drainage on the other side. Big-time ranchers fenced out little legitimate owners, which led to the fence-cutter wars of Texas, Wyoming, and New Mexico. "Millions of feet of barbed wire were cut, twisted, and rendered useless," writes Harry Sinclair Drago in *The Great Range Wars*. Two groups of militant *nuevomejicanos,* Las Goras Blancas and Mano Negro, went around at night cutting Anglos' (that is, Texas ranchers', for the most part) fences. In 1889 nocturnal saboteurs snipped El Cintillo del Diablo, the Devil's Hatband, which two Britons, William Rawlins and Frank Quarrel, had strung around the old San Miguel land grant. There's an expression in the Rio Arriba, *Quando vino alambre, vino el hambre* (When barbed wire came, so did hunger).

Barbed wire did in the nomadic life of buffalo, antelope, Indians, and trail drivers. It sectioned off the unlimited space that had been the essential quality of the frontier. Mother Earth was now cut up into ever-diminishing parcels that the Anglos were under the illusion they possessed.

There is a museum in MacLean, Texas, devoted to "devil rope," with the world's foremost barbed-wire scholar, Delbert True, in residence. Some barbed-wire buffs call themselves "barbarians." More than seven thousand varieties have been identified, among them Mack's twist, ribbon wire, Beer-Eaton's cross-over barb, Billing's simple 4-point, Glidden's 4-point, "H" bar 2 point, Corsican clip, Upham's snail barb, Brotherton's flat barb, Havenhill's arrowpoint, and Huffman's parallel. A recent issue of *The Barbed Wire Collector*, which comes out monthly, carried a letter from a husband-wife team of collectors who call themselves the Prickly Pair, and another from Marvin NcNeely of Hameson, Missouri, relating how he found a piece of rare Crowell wire in a half-collapsed barn, "layed up behind the old oak poles, which the old barn was built from."

After dinner with a couple who, like the Marshes, belonged to the incestuous group of two hundred Amarilloans who "matter," Stanley mused, "We are of pioneer English stock, and we don't know the names of our great-grandfathers. We could have been Turks; we could have been Croatian. We know nothing about Spanish land grants, Mexicans, Chinese, Japs, Indians. I look at Spanish architecture and Mexican food as hyphenated 'southwestern.' The real Southwest was shooting the buffalo and taming the Indians to make it safe for settlers, manifest destiny chasing the Spanish and the Mexicans out, putting up fences, building railroads."

Stanley continued: "The settlement here started with the Homestead Act for veterans of the Civil War. The offer of free land was advertised in Europe and cleaned out the slums of New York. But even though Amarillo goes back only four generations, it has more heritage and more continuity than most places. Your granddaddy started all the banks," he said to his guest, and to his wife, "*Your* granddaddy was the first doctor. He delivered my dad. My granddaddy made a fortune in natural gas. Wendy's ancestor invented barbed wire. There's continuity, although there's nothing here. As in the rest of rural America, there's no sense of being anonymous. You're careful not to be rude to people because you know you're going to see them tomorrow. We haven't been here for very long, and we didn't have much schooling, and nobody wrote it down, so we don't really know what happened. So we made it up."

Among the Cowboys

esides being a character, Stanley is "practiced at receiving easterners," in the description of Jane Kramer, whose book, *The Last Cowboy*, explored the relationship between one of Amarillo's new breed of college-educated cattleman— a friend of Stanley, actually—and his ranch hands. This man breaks his word after shaking on a deal, demonstrating his contempt for the way things had always been done. This was in 1977, and there was a lot of resentment about how the new cattleman, with his concern about dollars and cents, was killing the old cowboy way of life on the range. It had become more economical to shoot the steers full of hormones and keep them in feed yards, standing in their own shit, than to turn them loose on the prairie.

Between Amarillo and Las Vegas, New Mexico, there are still a number of very large working ranches with working cowboys. Stanley's brother Michael told me about an heir to the Phillips 66 fortune who runs the family ranch near Las Vegas. "He rejected the world of oil and money, and everybody loves him," Michael explained. "These sort of people made a choice to lead this kind of life and not become urban. They can go to Paris, and do, but not very often. What they do is get up at five o'clock in the morning. Being hunters, they really understand conservation. They want there to be twenty thousand quail every year."

Stanley introduced me to Jay O'Brien, a major cattleman, and his wife, Lucy. "Jay went to Yale. He's a smart-ass," Stanley explained. "He's all business." Or as one of Jay's hands put it, "He works his mind and his butt off." Jay and Lucy took me to a working-cowboy rodeo. Hands from fourteen ranches that belonged to the old families—including Corsino, XL, Bell, Fork Bitter Creek, and Frying Pan— were competing. Among them were Jim Bob Walton, Pecos Hagler,

Burl and Monty Holler, Chris Craft, Rick Furnish, Boots Blasingame, Tommy Thunderbird, and the former world champion Tubby Thompson. A color guard of mounted cowgirls bearing the Coors beer, Lone Star State, and American flags kicked off the evening. The events included steer and calf roping (the former around the neck, the latter around the legs), mugging (wrestling an animal to the ground and tying three of its legs together), team penning (cutting out a heifer), bronc riding ("You just try and keep your ass on," Jay explained). "Did you see the move that horse had on him?" a friend of the O'Briens asked after a beautiful gray mustang, a "blue" from an Indian reservation in Alberta, bucked Monty Cluck twelve feet and pawed him above the right eye. Jay introduced his foreman, an English-literature and biology major from Virginia, who had been to graduate school in animal science—a modern cowboy.

"Some people herd with four-wheelers these days," Jay told me, as the awards—saddles and spittoons—were being presented. "But without the horse, there is no cowboy, and the mounted cowboy is still irreplaceable. He isn't going to vanish anytime soon. A lot of this country we run is so rough.

"Generalizations don't work any more with cowboys than with anyone else," he continued. "Some are drifters. It's very valuable to have someone who sticks because he cares for the ranch as if he owned it. Sometimes there are repeated generations, like Monty Holler: his dad was on the ranch. But I don't think you'd get much out of him. You'd have to draw out every word." The women in the stands were chicly dressed in designer jeans and jewelry, and the men all had Stetsons and boots, just like the ranchers I met at a cattle auction in the Amazonian state of Acre in 1989. Beside the stands, a two-year-old toddler was twirling a rope.

Sunday morning, Jay and I drove out to his ranch in a Silverado with a phone. We stopped at Taco Bell (which was decorated with Armando Piña's smoothly professional postromantic paintings of Indian women with pots) to pick up some sixteen-ounce Thirstbusters of Diet Coke. There were a lot of false storefronts in downtown Amarillo. Like Albuquerque, this was a drive-up society—food, fuel, cash, booze, a last look at a departed loved one, could all be done from your car—but it was more vintage, with American classics like the Double Dip drive-in, Doug's Bar B. Q., and Feferman's Army Navy store.

"My grandfather put together eighty thousand acres in New Mexico," Jay told me, "and he was just a cowhand. But he lost them in the Depression, so I understand land lust and loss, the sense of stability that land gives you, even though the ownership that any of us has is limited. A lot of ranches out here have been overgrazed. Their owners are one or two generations from the original entrepreneur, and they're not making money because they own the land free and clear and they don't have to. They're not running the ranch as a business, seeing the land as a renewable resource that must be carefully managed. If you have this attachment, if you own, you're less likely to overgraze. To me there's no greater high than turning a place around, buying land—getting the asset—and making it work and improving it, feeling connected to a working landscape, having some honest love of the land.

"The land in the West has always represented opportunity," Jay went on. "It's been a safety valve for people. I sometimes wonder whether Kennedy started the space program just to compete with the Russians, or whether he also did it to extend the frontier, all the land in the West having been spoken for. Americans aren't used to restricted opportunity. It doesn't sit well." Which reminded me of an Arizona politician's comment on the spectacular wheeling and dealing of Charles Keating, the savings-and-loan king, which had just landed him in jail: "We don't stymie individuals here."

At the rodeo Jay had introduced me to Nina Blivens, whose son was his partner on one ranch he was working. Nina's father had been a close friend of General Phil Sheridan, who arranged elaborate military-escorted buffalo hunts, and of "Colonel" Charles Goodnight, who invented the chuck wagon and pioneered the Goodnight Trail to Denver. Nina's grandfather, an Englishman named Wadsworth, acquired almost a million acres, including the Palo Duro Canyon, and started the Perpetual Motion Ranch, so named because the cattle were run around a conical mountain, low in the winter, high in the summer. Another big English rancher named Rowe went down on the *Titanic*. Jay started leasing land, then acquiring it. "I re–put together Rowe from the heirs, who sold me forty-five thousand acres," he told me.

The going price for rangeland was $125 to $175 an acre with water rights. The water is pumped up from the Ogallala aquifer, two to four hundred feet down, which had seemed inexhaustible in 1914, when a booster of irrigated agriculture named Zenas Black wrote, "For hundreds of years this water has been flowing under the plains on its way to the Gulf and mankind knew it not. Now that this subterranean pipe-line is being tapped, the plainsmen claim that they have the nearest ideal system of agriculture on earth." Pumping began in earnest in the fifties and soon turned Lubbock into the cotton capital of the world. Sorghum was the next-biggest crop. But the aquifer's recharge rate was so slow—one-twentieth to half an inch per year—that the historian W. Eugene Hollon already cautioned in 1961, "Here on the

Llano Estacado, man has conquered nature by tapping the underground water supply for irrigation. But he has also sowed the seeds of ultimate destruction of this region as a great agricultural center. For several years water has been taken from the subsurface at an alarming rate." By 1970 5.5 million acres were under irrigation, and 45,000 wells were pumping up water from the aquifer; in 1930 there had only been 179. Feedlot cattle raising had boomed: three million head were on lots, their feeding coordinated by computer. But the drawdown was so severe that according to one prediction the aquifer would be sucked dry in thirty or forty years. By the end of the seventies, however, the rise in the cost of fossil fuel had raised the cost of pumping and bought the aquifer, and the region, a little time.

Jay explained the modern scientific approach to raising cattle: "What you're doing is converting cellulose to protein, and the more you move cattle, the less weight they gain. It takes a while for cattle on the range to sort out their social order and to get comfortable at a water hole. We graze them on grama and buffalo grass for eighteen months. To bring one seed cow with her calf to weaning, it takes eight months and fifteen to thirty acres of pasture. Then we take them to the feedlot, where they eat corn and milo [sorghum]. Within a hundred miles of Amarillo are twenty-five percent of the feed cattle, the finished beef, in the country."

Jay had Black Angus, tan Hereford, and Charolais crosses on eighty thousand acres. I asked why he didn't raise buffalo instead of these exotic strains, and he explained that "the rear end of the buffalo has no meat. Its hindquarters, where the best cuts are, are cat hammed."

He pointed out how much more flowering yucca was in the highway's right-of-way than was over the fence, where some steers were grazing. "Cattle love yucca," he said. "They eat it like candy. Yucca flowers are high in protein. Cowboys call it soapweed." We passed the Canadian River's breaks, where the capstone had been broken by the water—it was May 17, and the river was already down to an interbraided trickle—and turned into the EXO Ranch. Jay said that sixteen years ago, when he first leased the ranch, he laid off a third of the range the first year. "Studies show that grazed land does better if it is periodically rested," he explained. "But this was a big investment, because we were leasing every acre."

The High Plains were in blazing bloom. Jay took out a field guide he had in his glove compartment; he was teaching himself the wildflowers. We waded out into a field with slowly rocking oil pumpjacks interspersed among rashes and splashes of yellow goldenrod, evening primrose, orange caliche mallow, tandy aster, a mint called coast germander, Indian blanket, wild gourd, plains verbena, locoweed, low *Astragalus mollisimus,* white poppy, Lambert's crazy weed. Just as in the Sonoran Desert, 1992 was a banner year for wildflowers in Texas. "I'm just flabbergasted by the yucca. The term 'riot of color' honestly at times applies."

Alan, the EXO's foreman, gave me a mounted tour of the ranch the next day. We set out at 7 a.m. The Plains were alive with birds and were wrapped in a thick, wet mist that quickly burned off to blue sky. We rode past a calf pen. "We're a yearling, or stocker, operation," Alan explained. "There are only a few breeders left. These calves came in from Lake Okeechobee, Florida, yesterday. It's a three-day ride. We're keeping them here on feed and watching them real closely, doctoring them and vaccinating them and sorting out the sick ones. They've been without food for thirty-six hours, so you have to get their rumen healthy again. We'll pasture them till November, then put them in a winter-wheat pasture through March, then they'll be finished off in the feedlot, then they'll be processed."

We talked about cowboys. Alan said, "There are all sorts of cowboys, just like everybody. I feel it's a dwindling art. There's not a lotta young kids coming up that want to do this, and with technology and stuff there's not as many required. But still you gotta get on the horse and work the cattle. There used to be bachelor camps and drifters—true misogynists, who loved their horse more than any woman—but no more." Alan had a rope on his saddle, but he didn't use it much. "We don't stress the animals with rope; we keep them in line with our horses. A horse that can sort and push animals into a pen is important, and it's a beautiful thing to watch." There were regional differences in roping techniques, Alan explained as we ambled along. "Some cowboys dally: they wrap the end of the rope around the saddle horn after they've thrown it. Others tie on before. If you dally, it's safer because if it gets hung up you can let go. But you could lose the rope."

Alan was thirty-two, with a thick black mustache and the hair under his black hat already gray and a deep red face, almost purple, from the sun. His family had been cowboys four generations. He'd been brought up by his grandfather and had gone right into cowboying. "It's what I always wanted to do," he said. I asked why. "'Cause you're dealing with nature. You're dealing with what God made. I mean I don't know how to explain, it's a feeling you get when you're on top of a rise or look out at all these soapweed blossoms, or when you're cutting out a cow, and it's trying to get back in the herd, and your horse does just what he was born to do; you have nothin' to do with it; you're just sitting up there. There's something out here. . . . We don't have a lot of faith in preachers with their fire and brimstone. We're alone a lot, but never lonely. Most of us would prefer it. It's more like pragmatism, an appreciation of the rightness of it.

"Tom Blasingame [who had competed at the rodeo] said one time, 'A cowboy's a cowboy 'cause of horses. If you take away the horse, there is no cowboy.' We don't necessarily like the cows, but we love our horses. But if a heifer is having a calf, and she's in trouble in the middle of the night, we go out and help and stay with them. You develop a fondness for all life just watching baby calves playing.

"We have six horses apiece. Like humans, some are better suited for different things. Some horses excel at sorting [also known as cutting], others at roping. Some have endurance; others have a lot of go to them. A young horse is just like a child: any habits it acquires are your fault. A rodeo is man and horse on display. You take pleasure in another person's horse being quality. Cowboys are not competitive. A cowboy never tells another cowboy he screwed up. Talking about this is abnormal. You don't run it right in front of a man. And your word is your bond."

There was a strict taboo, Alan continued, against crossing in front of somebody. "If a cowboy wants to talk to another cowboy, and he has to pass a third cowboy, he has to go around behind him. Otherwise he is shunned. You learn not to go in front of somebody by the time you're nine. If you've got a guy who says he's a cowboy—if he's carrying a rope and advertising that he's a hand and he does that—you know he's not. He's broken his word. It's not only etiquette; it's disrespect for my knowledge and ability. It's an insult, insinuating I don't know what I'm doing. When you got a poser like that, you don't talk to him, and he kinda just fades out. You put him cleaning stalls or fencing. I'll never tell him what he did wrong unless he asks. Most of these guys learn from their dad or uncle. It's something you jiss git instilled in you. You've got to earn the respect, and once you earn it, you expect it.

"Cowboys are not owners," he continued. "But in my mind I own as much of this place as the Bivinses or the O'Briens do. I own a piece of everywhere I've been." Alan had been EXO's foreman for the last eight years. I pointed out that the European notion of ownership was alien to the Indians, and Alan said, "They must have had some sense of ownership, otherwise they wouldn't have fought the settlers so hard."

We rode along in silence, and after a while Alan resumed his exposition. "There's little verbal communication driving the herd; cowboys don't communicate verbally, plus the next hand may be half a mile away. You have to have a certain instinct to ride fifty head that'll tell you which cow is going to take off, and that has nothing to do with how you dress and talk.

"You can tell where the herd is from how the horses are facing. And another rule is never turn your butt to the herd. You never know when a cow could run out. I've worked with people who aren't athletic enough to keep their horses facing the cows, and it eats me up.

"There's a lot of observation in cowboying," he went on. "You look for a grass with a blue tint—bluestem grama grass—because cattle do best on it. You study manure—how beady it is, or how green—which tells you when it's time to move the cows. You see when it's starting to rain. It all boils down to rain, like everywhere else in the Southwest—and to management of what God's growing.

"Considering everywhere around you, you feel a oneness. Topping out on a ridge, and you haven't seen anybody in forty-five minutes, and you're not even five minutes apart—that's the oneness. If your partner doesn't show after a while, you got to find him because this job can git you killed. You git a feeling of the dynamics, the flow of the herd, which is poetry in motion, like a school of minnows or a flock of birds, of its pecking order and its territoriality. They imprint on a water hole, and even if it's dry, they'll stay there until they almost dehydrate. Cows have to eat three percent of their body weight a day, so you got to keep 'em busy. The grass is sixty-seventy percent moisture."

I picked up some of the lingo: a real cowboy is "real western" or "real punchy" (as in "cowpuncher"; a punch is the metal prod used to drive cattle into railroad stock cars), while a "poser" is a cowboy wanna-be, who dresses the part.* Alan had chosen a gentle "plug" for me to ride after I explained that my lifelong saddle time probably totaled no more than three days.

We checked one of the thirty-eight windmills on the ranch that services all but two of its "fairly dependable" water tanks. It was an Aermotor. To turn it off, you pulled the tail from perpendicular to parallel to the ground. A perpendicular tail keeps the wheel into the wind. A really strong wind can blow a tail off, which is why Alan had to check them periodically.

The windmill was invented in the East, but it was mainly used on the Plains. The first windmill, the Halladay Standard, based on the principle of the self-furling sail, came out in 1853.† Other approaches included umbrella mills, vaneless mills, post mills, tower mills, horizontal mills, ones with wooden blades. Ariel, Empire, Jumbo, Battle-axe, Dempster, and self-oiling jobs like the Leffel Iron Wind Engine

---

* See also Ramon F. Adams's *Western Words: A Dictionary of the American West,* University of Oklahoma Press, Norman, 1968.
† My source is T. Lindsay Baker's *Field Guide to American Windmills,* University of Oklahoma Press, Norman, 1985.

were among the competing brands, but Aermotor was the biggest. By the 1870s windmills were all metal. They supplied water to homes and even entire towns, but domestic use is in steep decline, and these days they're mainly used for cattle tanks. Many stand in rusting ruin, symbols of a bygone era. The windmill may come back, wind being the cleanest and least complicated way to generate electricity. There is already a stand of aeroelectric windmills at Altamont Pass, in California, and Steve Baer, a solar-energy pioneer in Corrales, New Mexico, believes that they are the wave of the future, that before long they will be supplying at least 10 percent of the Southwest's power needs. Baer lives on a ridge and has a windmill beside his house. "You grow to love the sound of it creaking," he told me.

A red-tailed hawk swooped down into a stand of prickly pears in a "wasty" moonscape. "He's got something," Alan said. Two hundred paces away, a pronghorn antelope was staring at us intently with bulging eyes that could pick up movement four miles away. It was a doe (lacking the buck's black facial markings)—a heifer, as Alan called her. "She should have already dropped her kid by now. If you see a heifer alone you know something's wrong." We stood watching this magnificent creature—perhaps the largest wild animal left in the Southwest and the fastest in the New World (and one of the fastest on the planet), capable of twenty-foot leaps and bursts of speed of up to seventy miles an hour. They needed such speed to outrun the gray wolves that preyed on them but were killed off, like the buffalo and the grizzly bear, by trigger-happy *americanos*. Coronado and his men, as they were led across the oceanic Llano Estacado, or High Plains, by the Turk, saw innumerable herds of them.

The pronghorn is not a true antelope, like the gazelle, but the last representative of its own unique family, the Antilocaprids. Until the Pleistocene extinctions ten thousand years ago, there were thirteen genera of Antilocaprids. Pronghorns once ranged from southern Canada to the plateaus of Mexico and from the Mississippi to the Gulf Coast. Performing epic migrations across the entire West, they probably exceeded the buffalo in numbers. The prime wild game, the prize trophy for "dudes" (as the cowboys called eastern or European city boys, like Teddy Roosevelt, Lord Dunraven, and Grand Duke Alexis of Russia),* by 1902 their numbers had shrunk in fifty years from an estimated thirty or forty million to twenty thousand.

---

* For a Hollywood treatment of the titled European big-game hunters, see the 1968 movie *Shalako,* starring Sean Connery and Brigitte Bardot—a period piece in its own right.

In 1908 William T. Hornaday, the chief taxonomist at the American Museum of Natural History, went to the Sierra de Piñacate, just below the Arizona border, with Dr. D. T. MacDougal, the creator of the Desert Botanical Laboratory in Tucson. MacDougal had never shot a pronghorn and was desperate to bag one. While examining the vegetation in a crater that was "Grand!" like "Vesuvius in the desert," they spotted "a bunch of antelope" who

> jauntily walked out upon the ash field and began to feed. As they nibbled, they slowly walked straight toward us. The original distance of half a mile narrowed very slowly . . . after a long and rather tiresome interval the herd had reached within about three hundred yards of the hunters . . . and their rifles rang out. One of the bucks was seen to fall and struggle violently upon the ground. . . . The other five pranced wildly about, undecided what to do. . . . More firing, shot after shot, in quick succession. Then the unwounded five antelopes divined the source of the alarm, headed due south, and in single file scudded away like the wind. To our horror the wounded buck then got upon his feet and ran after the herd, on three legs.

The naturalists took off on their horses but never caught up with the wounded buck. Instead a "locoed coyote" walked twenty paces in front of them. "I could have blown the animal to bits, but somehow he seemed a little out of sorts, and 'off colour' physically. . . . No promenader ever walked more leisurely than he, and with the outrageous contempt of a drum-major he completely ignored man and horses, save for one contemptuous glance."

I saw my first pronghorn one morning in 1986 as I was driving through Lincoln County, New Mexico—Billy the Kid country—along a sage-studded plateau that was almost as deserted as it had been in Coronado's day. I must have gone thirty miles without meeting a car. The only warm-blooded life I saw was a pronghorn that had somehow gotten trapped between the wire fences on either side of the highway. It kept veering frantically from one fence to the other as I cruised behind it. I drove it for several miles at around forty miles an hour. Finally it found a spot where it wriggled under the wire and trotted off with evident relief into the open range. Six years later, on several occasions, driving through the grasslands east of the Sangre de Cristo Range, I saw young "bachelor herds." The bucks' snouts were masked with black, and their tawny necks had horizontal white ruptive bands. They were sitting Sphinx-like and facing different directions, like covered wagons. The longer I stayed in the Southwest, the more antelope

I saw. They are, to me, an indicator species showing that there is still something left of the region's natural life.

I asked Alan if he had ever worked with any New Mexican *vaqueros*. He said he had, and they had the same outlook and were often even more skilled than Anglos. The American cowboy who rapidly became such a symbol of our culture is basically a revamped *vaquero* (and the cowboys in the Amazon are *vaqueiros* come home again, a backcross of the American cowboy whose Stetsons, denim, and six-guns were transmitted by Brazilian westerns). The longhorn steer, the sheep, and the mustangs that roam the Southwest's grasslands and sagebrush steppe are of Spanish provenance, as are the wheat, barley, alfalfa, and other grains that they feed on, which were introduced by the Jesuit father Kino and his associates.

"In perfecting the methods of ranching in the Interior Provinces, Spanish and Indian *vaqueros* drew heavily on Spanish techniques brought to Mexico and adapted them as they made their way northward," Odie B. Faulk writes in his history of the Southwest, *Land of Many Frontiers*. "The process evolved almost all of the techniques and paraphernalia associated with the cowboy complex of the American post–Civil War period"—a broad-brimmed sombrero to shade the eyes from the blazing sun, a bandanna to protect the nose and mouth from dust, *chaparajos* (chaps) to ward off thorns, pointed boots suited to the stirrup, the spurs with big two-inch rowels; a lariat (*la reata*) for roping, a saddle with a horn for dallying a rope (very different from the type used by Englishmen), a hackamore (*jaquima*), or rope without a metal bit. The branding of livestock dated from the Roman era and had come to the New World by way of Spain; it was not in common use in England or in English colonies. The rounding up of livestock from an unfenced range became a standard procedure in the Southwest, quite distinct from the fence-pastured methods employed on the East Coast. A lot of mexicanismos became stock lingo in the Hollywood western: "vamoose" (from *vamanos*), *adios amigos*, "pronto," "desperado" (a simplification of *desesperado* and easier for the American tongue), "hombre," not to mention "ranch," "rodeo," "corral," and topographic terms like "arroyo," "mesa," "rincon," "malpais," "bajada," and so on.

According to this school of thought, the American cowboy is a re-invention, a borrow. Another school emphasizes his southern roots.* The white and black cowboys who came to Texas in fact brought with them a long heritage of open-range cattle herding, reaching back to

---

* See Terry G. Jordan's *Trails to Texas: Southern Roots of Western Cattle Ranching*, Lincoln, Neb.: UNBP, 1981.

colonial South Carolina. Branding styles, the use of cow dogs, and range burning all trace to the Carolina seaboard. "Buckaroo" may not derive from *vaquero* but from the Gullah word *buckra*. Texas was a melting pot. The cowboy yodel came from Switzerland. The sub-Saharan country of Gambia, which provided many of America's slaves, had nomadic cattle keepers and yodeling traditions of its own, and some may have acquired riding skills from Arabs.

Others argue that the cowboy was created by the aridity of the High Plains. It was too dry for sodbusting; grazing was the only productive use of such land, so the tillers who emigrated from the Midwest became cattle keepers. The Plains historian Walter Prescott Webb leans more toward the market-accessibility model. In regions that are far from markets, the least intensive type of agriculture—running cattle—takes hold.

Whatever its roots, the most amazing thing is how the craft of cowboying has only been around for about 120 years, as the Texas novelist Larry McMurtry points out, and "has been in decline for at least half that time, and has never involved very many people, yet its potency in the American myth is unrivaled." The core element of the myth is the cowboy's independence, and "in the increasingly suburbanized American environment even to think about the pastoral brings a kind of uplift," McMurtry maintains. Cowboys, moreover, are, like the Bedouin, superb workmen—alert, humorous, and subtle. The real cowboy is short on words, courtly, tough as rawhide on the outside, soft as a cow's nuzzle on the inside. He loved a woman once twenty years ago and never got over it. The hat varies. Some have a tall, bullet-headed crown like the arm of a saguaro. His six-gun is a "piece." And Jane Kramer writes,

> The farming settlers of our folklore, rattling across the prairie in Conestoga wagons with their hearty, bonneted wives and broods of children, their chests of pots and pans and quilts, their plows and oxen, shared a republican dream of modest property and the rules and rhythms of domestic law. But the cowboy carried no baggage. Like the frontier, he had no past and no history. He dropped into the country's fantasies mysterious and alone, the way the Virginian arrived one day in his Wyoming town—by right, and not for any reason that he cared to give. With his gun and his horse and his open range, he followed the rules and rhythms of unwritten law and took counsel from his own conscience.

The Chicano cowboy takes himself less seriously. There's an expression in New Mexico, *Mejor cowboy que cagao* (Better to be a cowboy than to have shit in your pants.) A Chicano friend told me that "I have always found cowboys to be extremely feminine, with their high-heeled boots, tight pants, and colorful scarves."

Alan and I reached an oasislike dimple in the prairie known as Bootlegger Springs. Two families, the Romeros and the Sandovals, had come in 1875 from New Mexico in Civil War–surplus Conestogas and settled here. The Sandovals had run ten thousand sheep on the south side of the Canadian River, which was just over the rise, and had homesteaded here at the springs until 1890 when, perhaps driven out or bought out by Anglos, they went back where they came from. In those days Tascosa, now a section of suburban Amarillo, was the most famous blow-off town in the Panhandle. All the famous badmen and their nemeses—Billy the Kid, Bat Masterson, Frank James, Pat Garrett—patronized its saloons and its girls. Alan pointed out a *toscadillo*, a wild turkey. "The way we think isn't something you can shut off," he said. "It's not like being a welder, which I was for twelve years. You don't go home and keep thinking about welding. This isn't my job; it's my life. They actually pay me to do this, maybe not as much as folks in town."

He recited a couplet by the cowboy poet Baxter Black: " 'She's a cow and I'm a cowboy / and I guess that says it all,' " then he commented: "But you don't get attached to cows the way you do to land or horses. Some I get to know and respect 'cause they challenge me, and you feel good when you see them getting fat. But you don't *love* them. I don't feel bad about sending yearlings to their death every fall. That's what they're made for. God said go and subdue the earth. We're not doing this for the cattle."

Alan and his wife had three children. The oldest was ten. None of them had ever been to school. His distrust of politics was total: "I don't think the government can do anything right."

Jay O'Brien gets to his office in downtown Amarillo at five every morning and snaps on his computer, on which he keeps track of twenty-five thousand head of cattle in different places and their estimated daily gain on pasture, wheat, or feed yard, so he can determine things like whether the grass is drying and it's time to bring these cows to the feed yard and establish the cost of gain and the estimated break-even price should he sell out; cattle are a very liquid commodity. He computes the sale history of all the cattle he has ever owned so he can do sorts by buyer, feed yard, ranch, or time of year placed or purchased and decide whether to hedge on a futures contract or sell it or buy it back. "I'm not a soothsayer, I'm a historian," he explains. But most mornings, before he gets down to business, and before anyone else has arrived, he boots up his novel, which is about modern cowboys and cattlemen, and works on it for an hour or two.

As with the Indians (maybe this is a characteristic of cultures in decline), there are traditionalists and progressives among cowboys. If Jay O'Brien was a progressive, Bobby Boston was a traditionalist. He was, in one of his friends' descriptions, "a gentleman cowboy with the cowboy attitude," a man's man, a Marlboro man, as charismatic as Kris Kristofferson and much admired for his slow delivery. He had eaten the seventy-two-ounce steak at the Big Texan in an hour twice. Bobby had lost his ranch because, some said, he wasn't interested in modernizing or running it as a business and ran a traditional labor-intensive operation and had more cowboys on the payroll than he really needed, just to keep them going. And who bought it? Jay. Everybody said I had to go down to Clarendon and talk to Bobby Boston.

A picturesque town of white clapboard Victorians an hour south of Amarillo, Clarendon was founded a bit earlier, in 1878, by a Methodist minister. Liquor was forbidden, and you had to hang your gun in the hardware store upon arrival. Titled Englishmen owned big ranches outside of town, and the first settlers included Ivy League graduates. The JA Ranch, owned by "Colonel" Charles Goodnight in partnership with the Adairs, who were Irish noblemen and financiers and the forebears of Ninia Bivins, was more than a million acres, one of the largest in the world. Nearly all the land around was English owned. The Rowe brothers, who went down with the *Titanic,* had another big ranch.

Bobby Boston took me to the Bronco Cafe for chicken-fried steak. A black man in overalls was telling jokes, cracking up two crackers who were sitting at the counter. Race relations in the Panhandle, where there are only 9,000 blacks out of a population of 250,000, seemed to be extremely retrograde, as if the Civil War, let alone the civil-rights movement, had never happened. The blacks in Clarendon lived in a "Colored Town" across the tracks, in shacks with yards of bare, swept earth, with the old people sitting outside in the yards and shooting the breeze, just as in Africa. The Amarillo Country Club still refused to let in blacks, as a result of which it had lost the Ben Hogan Tournament, a Junior PGA event. "They told us we had to let in a black, and we told them, 'Who needs the Ben Hogan anyway?' " a member told me.

"Cowboying is the last profession in the modern world you spend in nature," Bobby observed. "In the old days you might have been out two, three months at a time. The expression 'on the wagon' comes from the chuck wagon that the cowboys ate from when they were out on the range. That's how they sobered up, how they dried out. But now it takes a hell of a lot less cowboys than it used to, and a lot of the old ranches that had oil income are looking more and more at cattle as a business. The big change now is that all the cowboy wives work, 'cause the pay is so low, and many of them make more than their husbands."

A couple of years back, Bobby had a dude ranch. His main clientele was Germans—middle-class mechanics and such—who belonged to cowboy clubs and were steeped in cowboy lore, knew the old trails and everything. "I'd put the Krauts in boots and jeans and take them out to a chuck wagon on old plugs that were on their last stop to the glue factory," recalled Bobby. "They slept in bedrolls in tepees. One time we ran into a rattler. I drew my six-gun, and one of the Krauts begged me to let him shoot it, so I did. He was ecstatic. 'That was one of my two goals in life,' he said after he had blown the snake away. I asked him what the other one was, and he said sheepishly, 'To sleep with a black woman.' "

I drove out to Jay's other ranch, the Swamp, and found his foreman, Pecos Hagler, standing with blood all over his hands and arms in a corral littered with hundreds of pairs of bull balls. "You don't want to shake my hand," he told me. With an electric prod, he was maneuvering three-to-five-month-old calves one at a time into a hydraulic clamp known as a calf cradle. After an initial terrible bellow, the clamp would close, and the calf would pipe down, the breath having been squeezed out of him, and Pecos would reach down with a knife and castrate him, then he would brand the calf with an electric branding iron, dehorn him, give him a worm shot, and turn him loose. Calf testicles, known as mountain oysters, are considered a delicacy; they are served at the Big Texan. But Pecos said that "after four hundred pairs, you get kind of sick of them."

Pecos had been born and raised on a ranch in Coleman, six hundred miles south. He was twenty-four and had a college degree in ranch management. "It's fading away," he said of his profession, "but I don't think it's ever going to fade plumb out. There's very few of the old cowboys and a lot of the new. To me that's what's playing out. But you know everybody has to adjust to something one way or other, and I been real lucky."

Late in the afternoon we drove around the ranch in Pecos's pickup, checking the salt licks and seeing if any of the calves had gotten themselves stuck in a thicket or into other trouble. This aspect of the cowboy's work, usually performed after everything else has been done, is called prowling. "Each pasture has a name," he explained. "This is Three-Tree Pasture, named for Three-Tree Creek down there. There's Initial Rock, River, Horse, Locust Pasture, Troublesome Pasture 'cause it's hard to get the cattle out, McCormick Pasture after the man that used to own it, Noname Pasture 'cause they couldn't think of a name.

"Wildflowers are pretty, ain't they?" Pecos remarked a little farther on, and still farther he recited the southwestern refrain: "We need rain. The grass needs a drink of water. The old-timers say that when a turtle is crawling uphill, it's gonna rain." Then he resumed, "The only downfall in cowboying is that it don't pay. It costs the shit out of us just to operate. Damn clothes is so high. Saddle's over a thousand, a rope is twenty-five, and you wear out one a month." (Jay dismissed the complaints about the low pay: "Why doesn't a ski instructor make money? 'Cause it's fun.")

I asked Pecos whether he would be upset if a black married his sister, and he said, "That would be a problem. We'd have us a necktie social. But I don't think I'd have to deal with it. My sister's got more smarts than that."

Horrace McClelland, Bobby's second cousin, was seventy-six and had been a cowboy "just about all my life except for four years in the army"; his family on both sides were cowboys. He took me out to some sandy country, which Bobby and his brother Jinks were leasing and running nine hundred head on, to check on some recently foaled colts.

"Looks like it might rain," I observed, and Horrace said, "Good chance. We can always use rain.

"For thirty years we used to put a wagon out in the spring and come back in the fall. We'd go a couple of months without coming to town. Then we'd come in and get chuck, get a haircut, get civilly [a new word to me, meaning "civilized"]. A good cowboy's hard to find these days, especially in the younger generations. They're smarter than we were, got more schooling. There's a lot more mesquite on the range than when I was a kid 'cause there's nobody to keep it down, and there's gittin' to be a lot of wild hogs. There used to be a lot of wolves. Old 'Colonel' Goodnight gave a fifty-dollar bounty for 'em. I saw one's head that my daddy killed.

"Bobby breeds cutting horses," Horrace went on, "and I take care of sixteen mares. Nine of 'em just had colts, and a couple of more are pregnant. Bobby helps a lot of us down-and-out old-timers. I had both legs broke by a horse falling on me. I've had some ribs broke, a shoulder knocked down. I had another horse get knocked out from under me by lightning. It's a lonesome old job, but I don't know; there's something fascinating about it. Riding a good horse in sandy country, sniffing the good old fresh air—there's nothing to me like riding a good horse. I never did live in town. Town was never a place for me."

He reminisced about the Dust Bowl thirties. "There was a big duster on May 12, 1933. It blotted out the sun in Washington, D.C., I heard, and deposited a red film on the decks of ships hundreds of miles out in the Atlantic. There were big old balls of dust. My daddy sold his calves. It broke a lot of people."

Horrace confirmed what Alan had said about the taboo against riding in front of somebody. "If you did that, somebody roped you and jerked you off your horse," he told me. "Now you jiss don't have cowboys like you used to. You couldn't stake a horse or take a crap within a hundred yards of the wagon, and if you broke wind under the flier they laid you over the wagon tongue and shapped you [another new term: whipped you with chaps]. They'd take your hide off. I got shapped once after I broke wind under the flier. I didn't intend to, but with all those beans . . ."

Another convergence besides the traditionalist-progressive cleavage, I reflected: all three of the Southwest's cultures go in for ritual flogging to inculcate novices. Other convergences: traditional spring branding, where all the neighbors come and help you drag your calves to the fire and sear their rumps with your logo, is half work, half fiesta, like the annual cleaning of the ditches on the Rio Arriba. The cowboys seem to have their own equivalent of *hozho,* the Navajo's "walking in beauty."

On the way back to Amarillo, I stopped to observe a vast prairie-dog town. Its denizens were standing on their haunches, gathered like village gossips. They have no private holes; there is no ownership of holes, the novelist John Nichols, who takes a keen interest in natural history, pointed out one morning as we came across a town on the steppe outside Taos. Each marmot, which is actually a barking ground squirrel, only lives about fifteen months, but the society is highly organized, not to mention reproductively dynamic. Their social groups are called coteries, and their towns can cover sixty acres.

Back in Albuquerque, on the Ladera Golf Course, I sliced my ball one afternoon into a blinding desert of almost pure-white sand, and only when I had gotten within twenty yards of it did I realize that a dozen spotted ground squirrels were standing frozen erect, with their front paws hanging over their chests, each of them facing away from me at a slight angle. Eight inches tall, they were like miniature prairie dogs. The ground-squirrel tribe is omnivorous, preying on kangaroo rats, lizards, grasshoppers, and beetles as well as munching seeds, grass, and cacti. Under extreme heat loads, antelope ground squirrels drool. According to the naturalist Peggy Larson, "The moisture which wets the fur of its chest provides evaporative cooling at a lower metabolic cost than the alternative of panting."

As for the sexual mores of cowboys: I asked Bobby Boston whether the practice known in Arkansas as buttfucking, and fairly common throughout the rural South, occurred at all on the range, and he said, "I've heard of guys in Hedley fucking pigs. A lot of teenagers have screwed heifers, but they won't admit it. Cowboys slept together in bedrolls, but I never heard of a single queer."

Bestiality is not unknown among Navajo sheepherders either, I was told, but once the word gets out that a particular sheepherder is into it, nobody will buy his sheep. The Chicano expression *chingando la borega* has already been noted; presumably it has some physical basis. So this is another custom the three cultures have in common.

Tombstone

The heyday of the cowboy was from 1860 to 1890. "Cow-punching, as an occupation, attracted an unfortunate breed of men," William W. Savage writes in his book *Cowboy Life: Reconstructing an American Myth*. The majority of the cowboys were Civil War vets or adolescents orphaned by the war with no business aptitude or schooling or entrée for much else. "With the beginning of the long drives, first to railheads in Missouri and Kansas and later to feeding grounds in Wyoming and Montana, the cowboy life seemed to offer adventure and an opportunity to go somewhere, anywhere," Savage explains. Not a few of the vets had witnessed and participated in massive carnage in the war and were inured to violence.

The imaging of the cowboy and the creation of "America's most potent myth" began almost immediately. There was nothing inherently more colorful about the American cowboy than his counterpart in Australia or the leather-helmeted, leather-skinned, dust-bitten indigenous *vaqueiro* of northeastern Brazil. He just happened to belong to a hot young culture that needed myths and had the means to make them. The first media that celebrated the cowboy life and the cowboy ethos of courage, honor, chivalry, and individualism included the dime novel, Buffalo Bill's traveling Wild West Show, and the genre fiction of Owen Wister and Emerson Hough. Theodore Roosevelt wrote several very popular books about the West, extolling the strenuous outdoor life. An early lunger, Roosevelt, beginning with a trip to the Badlands of South Dakota in 1883, when he was twenty-five, attacked the West with zest and reinvented himself on the frontier as a man of action. By the 1920s the cowboy culture had become frozen in a fixed, traditional present like the Indian and the Hispanic cultures, and cowboys began to reflect nostalgically and self-consciously on it the way Indians nowadays talk about spirituality and Mother Earth.

The relocation of the fledgling movie industry from New Rochelle, New York, to Los Angeles in the twenties because the taxes were lower and the sunlight was stronger (this was before the development of artificial lighting, and strong natural light was needed to illuminate the sets) was a tremendous boon for a mythopoeic tradition that was already fifty years old. The filmmakers took the material that was at hand and created the Hollywood western, a genre that is still evolving; the spring of 1994 saw the appearance of not one, but two, new movies about Wyatt Earp and the gunfight at the O.K. Corral. You could choose your Wyatt from two box-office hunks—Kevin Costner or Val Kilmer.

As a boy in suburban Westchester County in the fifties, I was nurtured on the cowboy myth. I had a complete Hopalong Cassidy outfit with six-guns that fired caps, and I rarely missed an episode of *Gunsmoke, Rawhide, Bonanza,* or *Death Valley Days.* So potent was the myth that the actor Ronald Reagan, who played the good guy in dozens of Hollywood westerns, was able to parlay it to the presidency, as Theodore Roosevelt had in a different way early in the century. Today the myth's hold on the American mind is no longer so strong, but in 1988 I took my sons, eight and nine, horseback riding in Mexico and was astounded when they mounted, reared up their horses, put them through some fancy moves, and headed down the trail at an expert trot. "Boys, I happen to know this is only the second time in your life you've been on a horse," I said. "Where did you learn to ride like that?" Nick, the younger, said, "Television."

There are two epicenters of the myth in the Southwest: Lincoln County, New Mexico, and Tombstone, Arizona. Lincoln County was where William H. Bonney, aka Billy the Kid, spent most of his short, violent life. Far more extraordinary than its events or the Kid himself—who, according to one scholar, had "the i.q. of a semi-retarded fourteen-year-old" and was "a real ugly adenoidal adolescent," five-foot-five, with a long chin pressed flat on his neck—is the interest they continue to inspire. In the fall of 1992, Kid scholars took over a whole hotel in Ruidoso, New Mexico, and traded Bonneyana for several days. As one of them told me, "The Kid still rides." As a popular-culture icon, he has attained the status and the epistemological complexity of Dracula, Mickey Mouse, and Elvis.

Each generation has reinvented the Kid in novels and movies, comic books, plays, and ballets, according to its own view of American society. Stephen Tatum traces the process in his book *Inventing Billy the Kid.* Originally, the Kid was seen as the embodiment of frontier savagery, whose death reaffirmed the benevolent course of American

history, but by 1920 he had become a symbol of nostalgia for the freedom and the wildness of the Old West. By the fifties he had been variously recast: in one metamorphosis, he was the champion of the
underdog, a Robin Hood/Che Guevara type who took sides with the
natives and the settlers against ruthless cattlemen, a heroic outlaw
recycling the ill-gotten money of the big-time bandidos. Already during his life he had been a hero to the local Mexicans, and as such he
remains of interest to Chicano intellectuals. "I can't understand it,"
complained the governor of New Mexico (and author of *Ben Hur*),
Lew Wallace, to whom the Kid gave himself up in 1878. "He seems to
be the idol of the Spanish Americans. At night, they gather about the
jail and actually serenade the young thug who is guilty of a score of
crimes."

In another metamorphosis, the Kid was a misfit, a fugitive, an out-
sider, alienated from and disillusioned with a system that was corrupt,
self-righteous, hypocritical, and unfair in a Wild West that was a
metaphor of the modern world, in which "law and justice were second cousins not on speaking terms," as Tatum puts it. In Sam Peckin-
pah's movie *Pat Garrett and Billy the Kid,* Lincoln County is a world
of closing options and diminishing individual freedom. The range is
being fenced in, and the Kid is an outlaw on the run who has no more
place in the new West than his contemporary Geronimo (who was
himself the subject of two movies, each with a different revisionist
take on his character and motives, in 1993). Other Kids of recent
years paint him as the most notorious desperado the West ever bred,
who killed anywhere from four to forty people, a frontier killer without a cause who gunned people down mercilessly, just to see them
kick, and as a daring, generous-hearted symbol of "the undying anar-
chy in the heart of every man."

I mentioned earlier the pronghorn antelope caught in the right-of-
way that I drove for several miles with my rented car when I was touring Lincoln County in 1986, until he finally slipped under the fence.
Boxed in, cornered, the frantically darting antelope evoked in my mind
inevitable comparisons with the Kid on the run. The historical Kid,
born in Brooklyn in 1859 or 1862, is mostly a mystery, an early example of the reinvented easterner. In 1877 there were several levels of conflict in Lincoln County. On one level, it was an English-Irish feud,
projected onto and played out on the American frontier between the
Irish Murphy Gang, connected with Thomas B. Catron's Santa Fe
Ring, and the entourage of the British cattle baron John Chisum. There
was also a financial rivalry between the First National Bank of Santa
Fe and Lincoln County Bank. The Kid surfaces as a hand of the British

shopkeeper John H. Tunstall, a newcomer who challenges Murphy's monopoly on the army's beef contracts—thousands of head of cattle and the hay and corn to feed them to provision the Ninth Regiment of U.S. Cavalry. Tunstall is bumped off on February 18, 1878, by a Murphyist posse under Sheriff William Brady. The Kid joins a posse, called the Regulators, that gives Brady his just deserts on April 6, and the Kid goes on the lam. Through the fall of 1878, he runs stolen horses to Old Tascosa, the lawless predecessor of Amarillo. He surrenders to Wallace the following March 17, but escapes from prison and forms a gang. Pat Garrett becomes sheriff. The Kid gives him the slip repeatedly, is finally caught, but he escapes again, this time killing two guards. Garrett takes off on his trail and finally, on a tip, ambushes him two months later in his long johns in his room at Pete Maxwell's inn in the Tularosa. The Kid is eighteen or twenty-one years old. These are the bare bones of his bio. Everything else is open to interpretation.

There is also an underlying conflict between the usurping gringos and the local Mexicans. The county seat, Lincoln, was originally Las Placitas del Rio Bonito. The new name was less than ten years old. The Kid moved easily among the Mexicans and dated their raven-haired daughters. Lincoln today is a town totally dedicated to the memory of itself. The velvet-grassed, juniper-dotted valley in which the town sits is still, aptly, named Bonito. There's still a lot of indigenous violence in the county. The murder rate in Roswell is double the nation's. I saw the bullet holes the Kid made in the stairwell of the county courthouse during his second escape. Garrett had captured him at Stinking Spring, and he had been brought to Lincoln to await hanging in two weeks. Garrett was off in White Oak picking up the lumber for the scaffold and had left the Kid with two guards, James Bell and Bob Ollinger. The Kid is alone upstairs in a specially constructed cell, his hands and legs manacled. He waits for Ollinger to go across the street for dinner, then asks Bell if he can go to the privy, where Sam Corbet, Tunstall's former clerk, has left him a gun. The Kid returns and blows away Bell at the top of the stairs, gets Ollinger's double-barreled shotgun and blows him away from a window. "If those shots hadn't been fired, none of this would be here," a docent said of the museum that the courthouse, lovingly frozen at the moment of the double murder, as if the Kid and his guards had just stepped out, had been turned into.

There were only three Earpologists—scholars of Wyatt Earp and the events leading up to the renowned gunfight at the O.K. Corral—in 1985; Earp's field was less crowded with scholars than the Kid's, closer to the number of rival Hopi prophets. One of the Earpologists, whose name was Glenn Boyer, took a shine to me and my family. "Wyatt's niece was like a mother to me," he told me. "When she died, I took it on as a quest to straighten out the picture. Stuart Lake [who wrote the best-known biography of Earp] made a Boy Scout out of a profane frontier gambler who was scrupulously honest with those he wasn't gambling with.

"This was really a political and economic fight between on the one hand the old territorial Democrats who controlled the sheriff, Johnny Behan, and backed a group of rustlers known as the Cowboy Gang," Boyer explained, "and on the other a group of wealthy Republicans who wanted domestic tranquillity and were too scared to take care of the rowdy 'cowboy element' themselves. Earp drifted into Tombstone from Dodge City with a reputation as a peace officer and the Republicans hired him to do a 'range cleanup.'" Frank Waters, in his book *The Earp Brothers of Tombstone,* characterizes Earp as

> an itinerant saloonkeeper, cardsharp, gunman, bigamist, church deacon, policeman, bunco artist, and a supreme confidence man. . . . A lifelong exhibitionist ridiculed alike by members of his own family, neighbors, contemporaries, and the public press, he lived his last years in poverty, still vainly trying to find someone to publicize his life, and died [in a trailer court in Los Angeles in 1929] two years before his fictitious biography [Stuart Lake's] recast him in the role of America's most famous frontier marshal.

Boyer edited and embellished the memoir of Earp's wife, Josephine. "A voluptuous eighteen-year-old with huge lambent brown eyes," as he describes her (a provocative photograph survives of her nude from the waist up with a filmy robe painted over to cover her breasts), Josephine Marcus had run away from home in San Francisco with a traveling troupe performing *H.M.S. Pinafore,* which blew into Tombstone in the fall of 1879. The dark-haired Jewish beauty initially took up with Johnny Behan, who was in cahoots with the Clanton boys and would become Wyatt's archenemy. She performed in variety shows at a dive called the Bird Cage, which had cubicles where you could draw the curtain and get special attention from the girls. While prostitution was never her main, steady profession, Josephine was, in Boyer's description, a "four-pistol," who gave "payment in kind." Eventually, she took up with Wyatt, and they stayed together until he died. He was thirty-two when they met, with a flaring handlebar mustache that seemed almost pasted on, and was already married to a woman who would kill herself after he left her.

Tombstone at the time of these events was a silver boomtown only a year old. The 1878 discovery of a rich vein in the sagebrush by a miner named Ed Schieffelin had catapulted it into existence. It started as a few thousand tents, and very quickly, as lumber came in on wagons, it acquired a two-and-a-half-story Grand Hotel and ten saloons. Within six months the population had shot from zero to ten thousand, and there were two papers, the *Epitaph* and the *Nugget,* whose versions of the news seldom agreed. The Oriental Saloon, tended by pigtailed Chinese, had faro tables and an opium parlor in the back room. Many of the crazed Civil War vets were addicted to opium or its derivative, morphine. The Chinese had been addicted to opium by the British East India Company to force them to produce silk, and by the time Chinese coolies were brought to the American West, mainly to build the railroads, there were seven million addicts. Many of the coolies managed to work free to become launderers, grocers, owners of restaurants, whorehouses, and gambling dens. Chinese monte was popular with the Apache. Sometimes "Chinks" were harassed by rowdies. As their piece of the western action became increasingly significant, the so-called Tong Wars broke out between the Chinese in California and Arizona.

Like the town in Gabriel García Márquez's *One Hundred Years of Solitude,* or Xapuri, where Chico Mendes was gunned down by Amazonian *pistoleiros,* who are the last emanation of the western gunslinger tradition, Tombstone, when it was brought out from its stark isolation into the world's attention, had universal resonances. The gunfight became, like Mendes's murder, a morality play enacted before the world, and its protagonists archetypes of good and evil.

The town attracted a vibrant cast of characters. John Clum, the first mayor and the editor of the *Epitaph,* was a retired Apache agent, much respected by the Chiricahua; he had brought in Geronimo (who later bolted down to the Sierra Madre) in 1877. Doc Holliday, who joined Wyatt in the gunfight, "had got his prefix as a dentist," as Boyer put it, but in recent years "he had been drilling more people than teeth," and his legend preceded him. A galloping consumptive and an alcoholic, with the lugubriously drooping walrus mustache sported by many of his ilk, Doc was a notoriously poor shot, but fearless. He had popped a rustler in Dodge City who was about to shoot Wyatt in the back, and they had been bosom buddies ever since. When Holliday finally died in a sanatorium in Glenwood Springs, Colorado, Wyatt eulogized him thus: "Doc was a dentist whom necessity had made a gambler; a gentleman whom disease had made a frontier vagabond; a philosopher whom life had made a caustic wit; a long, lean ashe-blonde fellow nearly dead with consumption and at the same time the most skilful gambler and the nerviest, speediest, deadliest man with a six-gun I ever knew."

Tombstone's reputation for violence, for being a place that dished up "a dead man for breakfast every morning," was exaggerated. In the year John Clum was mayor, there were only three murders within the city limits. Your life was no more in danger in Tombstone than it was in Schenectady, if you behaved yourself. Not everybody wore a gun. In fact, there was a sizable contingent of civilized, educated citizens that included the young Reverend Endicott Peabody, who later became the legendary headmaster of Groton, an exclusive prep school in Massachusetts. Of blue-blooded Bostonian stock, Peabody came to minister to Tombstone's Episcopalian congregation in January, three months after the gunfight; the previous minister had not worked out. He was only twenty-two, fresh out of the seminary, and in love with his cousin Frances, whom he would marry. The verdict on "Cotty," as his friends called him, was that he was okay—down-to-earth, absolutely square, and aboveboard and not at all a snob. When he left in July, people were sorry to see him go. He played baseball and joined the high-stakes poker game with the managers of the mine. Sometimes there was a thousand dollars in the pot. He preached sermons about the evils of cattle rustling and carousing, and in no time he had whipped up the finest choir in the territory. When the Tombstone Musical Society decided to put on *H.M.S. Pinafore* as a fund-raiser for the church, he went around to the saloons passing a plate for production money. The sunsets, he wrotes Frances, were "simply exquisite, most brilliant and painting the many ridged hills with every conceivable colour. . . . It is then that one likes Arizona better than at any other time."

Cotty and most everybody who came to Tombstone arrived on the Benson stage, which another passenger, John Gray, on his way to California in 1880, described thus: "That day's stage [from the town of Benson] will always live in my memory—but not for its beauty spots. Jammed like sardines on the hard leather seats of an old-time leather-spring coach, [we crept] much of the way through miles of alkali dust that the wheels rolled up of which we received the full benefit." In March 1881 the Cowboy Gang held up the Benson stage. The *Nugget,* which was anti-Earp and controlled by the Irish territorial Democrats, said it was Doc Holliday who did it.

In December 1883, five desperadoes entered the general store in Bisbee, south of Tombstone, and three men and a woman were wantonly killed. One of the killers, John Heath, was lynched on a telephone pole in Tombstone. The coroner's report read: "I find that the deceased died of emphysema of the lungs which might have been caused by strangulation, self-inflicted or otherwise." Four months later the other four were hanged in a two-story tent erected for the occasion. The sheriff had invitations to the "necktie party" printed up, and the *Epitaph*'s account was headlined DANCING ON AIR and blurbed: "The Bisbee Bandits atone for their crimes on the scaffold; an ignominious but well-met fate bravely met; the 'final launch into eternity' successfully accomplished by Sheriff Ward."

The following May 25, a drunk Mexican set a fire that razed the center of town. Deputy Sheriff Phillips was against lynching him, but told the *Epitaph:* "I really think that an example of frontier justice with the next white murderer would be a good thing—for the place is full of desperadoes who hold the lives of others and themselves very cheap."

Glenn Boyer told us that the gunfight didn't take place at the O.K. Corral at all (where it is now reenacted every half hour by animated dummies representing the participants), but at a livery stable a couple of buildings up the street. "And they didn't stand there when the initial shooting broke out; they took cover, as is correctly depicted by the classic movie about the gunfight, with Burt Lancaster as Wyatt and Kirk Douglas as Doc. The movies that have gunfighters standing and drawing and firing, or handing over their gun butt first, then twirling it and firing, are bullshit. Wyatt was not this flashy gunman, like some quickdraw artists who drew and cocked with the left hand and pulled the trigger in one blurred motion. The thing about Wyatt that was intimidating was his cool. He was tall, deadpan, and calculating, and he would wait for the other guy to fire and miss a couple of times, then slowly draw a bead on the guy with his special twelve-inch barrel, and fire."

Boyer took us to a beautiful ranch in a better-watered, high valley out of town, where the boys and I shot his six-gun. "The first self-contained cartridge appeared in 1860," he told us. "The Colt Peacemaker came out in '72, but Wild Bill Hickok used cap and ball up to the 1880s. He was a real shootist. The frontier Colt was single action. You had to cock it with your thumb each time you fired. With practice you can learn to draw, cock, and fire in single motion. It's effective at one hundred yards if you raise it to your eyes and sight your target and hold it steady with both hands. From fifteen paces it's pretty easy to hit with. A Colt .44 duel was from twenty paces. The duelers stood back to back, then each took ten paces. Only there weren't any duels like this, nor did the gunfighters have to stand and beat each other to the draw. The gun battles were more impromptu. Those with sense used shotguns and went more for accuracy than speed. You aim for the belly button if you're in it for real. Each time you cock, you lose your sight fixture."

Boyer fired a couple of rounds into the trunk of a saguaro and passed the gun to me. The spiteful whine of a ricochet informed me that I had missed. "I shoot a few rounds every day to keep my chops up," Boyer told me. "A frontier Colt has considerable recoil, and you can develop a built-in flinch that will make you miss."

The house on La Hacienda Drive we rented six years later, in 1991, was in an older dream section of Albuquerque. The neighbors were all elderly Anglos who had been living there since the fifties. Their windows were always blinded, and we didn't meet our next-door neighbors, an elderly couple originally from Arkansas who lived thirty feet away, until we'd been there several months. Across the street was a twenty-four-hour supermarket. Banking, Chinese food, a gourmet supermarket, dentists, and insurance were all in walking distance; it was a five-minute drive to golf and a twenty-minute drive to ski slopes. I'd never lived anywhere so convenient.

One night we were watching television in the living room, and right in front of the house, a police car with flashing bar lights pulled over a windowless white van. Backup quickly arrived. Two Hispanics were ordered out of the van and were frisked, spread-eagle against the side of the van. One of the cops told me that they were looking for two men who had been pulling a series of burglaries in the neighborhood. A month later I saw the same van with the same two men cruise slowly past the house, and my paranoia increased after a dark-skinned man in a red sedan stopped across the street late in the afternoon three days in a row and just sat there for half an hour, as if he were staking us out. (I finally accosted him, and it turned out he was a Hindu from Calcutta on his way home from work, who had pulled off busy Carlisle Avenue to meditate on a quiet side street.)

I decided I'd better get me a piece, a shooting iron. I went down to a gun shop on Central Avenue and discussed my security needs with a macho guy with a mustache at the counter. He said what I needed was a semiautomatic with stopping power. He recommended a nine millimeter. You keep it in your bed table, and if you hear a prowler, you shove in the clip and *blam!* Could I live for the rest of my life with having killed somebody? I wondered. But suppose somebody broke in? I had to defend my family. So I bought it.

A few days later I drove out to the desert with my boys and stood a Coke bottle on the sand and squeezed off a whole clip trying to hit it from twenty feet, but I didn't hit it once. When I got home, I put the gun in my bed table and never looked at it again until we were about to leave nine months later, and I sold it back to the guy with the mustache, who gave me half of what I'd paid for it.

From Tombstone we drove to torrid Yuma, where we picked up a brochure titled *Where's Your Sense of Yuma?* and visited the Arizona Territorial Prison, which had been turned into a museum. The worst offenders, who had been found guilty of opium use, adultery, or selling liquor to an Indian, were put into a pit known as the Snake's Den. Three-finger Jack Laustennau, a burly Rumanian labor agitator and one of the most violent and vicious of the incorrigibles, who started a riot in the prison, died after two years in the Snake's Den, apparently of rage at his confinement. John Ray did five years for a "crime against nature"; Lee Soon a year for forgery, after which he was deported to China. Eleven of the inmates were polygamists; these would be Mormons. One was convicted of incest, another of attempted abortion. There were rustlers; one train robber; Buckskin Frank Leslie, a bartender at the Oriental Bar, who killed the jealous husband of the winsome Mary Galeen; and a bunch of Indians. George Dwyer was a victim of the opium habit and was caught smuggling in morphine. You were allowed to have one toothpick. That was the day of ivory toothpicks elegantly manipulated and sometimes secured on a fine gold chain.

John Mason Jeffrey writes in *Adobe and Iron,* a history of prison, "Elana Estrada, lacking self-discipline at a moment of crisis when betrayed by her boy friend, was not satisfied with his death. She might have gotten away with killing him, but she went too far. Elana cut out his heart. Worse, she slammed it in his face. This disturbed her peers, and Elana wound up for a short stay at the Old Pen." The deputy superintendent was none other than Earp's nemesis, Johnny Behan.

Pearl Heart, with her partner Joe Boot, pulled the last stagecoach robbery in Arizona, on May 30, 1899. In prison, she built up a large following, which she tried to capitalize on, after she was released, by becoming an actress. After this failed, she married a rancher and spent the rest of her days peacefully in the central part of the state. I submit a poem she wrote about the holdup as an early example of southwestern imaging, of self-promotion in its innocence:

> The sun was brightly shining on a pleasant afternoon
> My partner speaking lightly said the stage will be here soon
> We saw it coming around the bend and called to them to
>   halt

And to their pockets we attended, if they got hurt it was
    their fault
While the birds were sweetly singing, and the men stood up
    in line
And the silver softly ringing as it touched this palm of mine
There we took away their money, but left them enough to
    eat
And the men looked so funny as they vaulted to their seats.
Then up the road we galloped, through a canyon we did
    pass,
Over the Mountains we went swiftly, trying to find our
    horses grass
Past the station we boldly went now along the riverside
And our horses being spent of course we had to hide
On the night we would travel, in the daytime try and rest
And thrown [sic] ourselves on the gravel, to sleep we
    would try our best
And as our horses were staying, looking for some hay or
    grain,
On the road the posse was tramping, looking for us all in
    vain,
One more day they would not have got us, but my horse
    got sore and thin,
And my partner was a mean ass, so Billy Truman roped us
    in
Thirty years my partner got, and I was given five
He seemed contented with his lot, and I am still alive

Desert Utopias

t was the dream of all Americans, Goethe said, to escape from the European past and build a new society. Few of the early pioneer groups were more successful at realizing their dream than the Latter-Day Saints, or Mormons, who walked across the Plains, dragging their possessions in carts, and founded their earthly Zion, the Kingdom of Deseret, in the valley of Great Salt Lake, Utah. Their utopian experiment can be seen in the light of several traditions. Like the *conversos,* the Mormons were fugitives from religious persecution. They became, like the Hohokam, a communitarian irrigation society, in which individuality was submerged. At the same time, the historian Ralph Barton Perry argues, they remained quintessentially American: "Mormonism was a sort of Americanism in miniature; in its republicanism, its emphasis on compact in both church and polity, its association of piety with conquest and adventures, its sense of destiny, its resourcefulness and capacity for organization."

The founder of the Church of Jesus Christ of Latter-Day Saints, Joseph Smith, grew up in upstate New York during the first half of the nineteenth century, in what his biographer, Fawn M. Brodie, describes as a "religiously fecund atmosphere." Among the prophets one could choose from were Ann Lee, the mother of the American Shakers, who called herself the reincarnated Christ, whirled dervishlike, spoke in tongues, and was reputed to indulge in promiscuous debauchery and to practice infanticide; Jemima Wilkins, who proclaimed herself "the Christ" and "the Universal Friend" and posthumously appointed as her chief aide the prophet Elijah; William Miller, as a result of whose prediction that Jesus would visit earth and usher in the millennium in March 1843, thousands auctioned off their property and bought ascension robes (although Miller lost face after 1845, when after several recalculations Christ had still failed to appear, his Adventists,

Brodie writes, are "still an aggressive sect"); John Humphrey Noyes, founder of the Oneida community, who preached that the millennium had already begun. Faith healers and circuit-rider evangelists went from town to town, "preaching in great open-air camp meetings where silent, lonely frontiersmen gathered to sing and shout. The Revivalists knew their hell intimately—its geography, its climate, its vital statistics—and painted the sinner's fate so hideously that shuddering crowds surged forward to the bushel-box altars to be born again." Some were seized with "the jerks"; others, seized with "the barks," went crawling on all fours and vocalizing like dogs.

Young Joseph Smith of Palmyra couldn't decide which prophet to go with, and retiring to the woods, he had the first of a series of encounters with an angel named Moroni, who told him that there was no true church of Christ upon the earth, and that he should join none of them. In 1827 Moroni presented the twenty-two-year-old Smith with two golden tablets containing, in what Smith called "reformed Egyptian" hieroglyphs, the story of the lost tribe of Lehigh, who had fled Israel to avoid being conquered by the Babylonians and traveled by barge to South America, where they divided into two groups—the Nephites, a "fair and delightsome people," who were farmers and temple builders, and the Lamanites, "wild and ferocious, and a blood-thirsty people." In a.d. 420 the Nephites and the Lamanites, having gradually moved north, fought to the death in the valley of Cumora, near what became Palmyra. This great battle explained the burial mounds in the vicinity, which had fascinated Smith and which are thought by archaeologists to have been left by certain Upper Mississippian Indians who, well before the arrival of Europeans, had a festival of the dead in which they exhumed the bones of recent ancestors and reburied them all together. The Lamanites won the battle, but their descendants, the Indians, were blighted with dark skin for turning away from the Lord (the same belief that was used, not only by the Mormons, but by the cutting-edge ethnologists of the day, to explain the dark skin of the otherwise European-looking North African "Hamites").

Smith translated the story on the tablets into English with the aid of some "spectacle-like instruments," also received from Moroni, which enabled him to penetrate the meaning of the hieroglyphs, and it became known as the Book of Mormon; Mormon was a Nephite prophet who had condensed the history of his people into the form on which it appeared on the tablets.

The details of the religion were disclosed to Smith in "revelations" in the years that followed. Heaven had three levels, the terrestrial, the telestial, and the celestial. One of the revelations concerned "the new and strange doctrine of Baptism for the Dead." Smith declared that certain sacraments, or "proxy ordinances," had to be performed so those who had lived before the founding of his church could be posthumously admitted to the highest level, the celestial. Since then it has been the responsibility of every Mormon to trace his ancestors and to perform the sacraments for them and ultimately for everybody who ever lived, and one of the church's central activities has been to collect the names of the dead and to perform these sacraments for them. Of the 69 to 110 billion people thought to have existed since the appearance of humans, the names of 6 to 7 billion are thought to survive, preserved by various societies around the world, and the Mormons have gathered about a billion and a half—by far the world's greatest genealogical archive and the closest thing to a primary record of the human family that exists. The names, computerized and, when possible, lineage linked, are stored in a bombproof vault in a canyon outside of Salt Lake City.

I came into contact with the Mormons through their International Genealogical Index (IGI), which makes the processed names available to the public. I was writing a book on my own family, and the IGI turned up a whole Finnish side of it that no one had known existed. The more I learned about the operation—that Mormon genealogists are going around tape-recording pedigrees chanted by chieftains on remote atolls in Oceania and microfilming pilgrim rosters at the Hindu shrine in Hardwar, India, which go back centuries—the more fascinated I became, so much so that I ended up writing what began as an article about it that gradually expanded into a book-length panoramic history of kinship that occupied me from 1983 to 1984; I called it *The Mountain of Names.*

The Church, one gathered, was a bit retrograde in its attitudes toward women, blacks, and homosexuals, but my relations with its genealogical wing were warm and positive. Up till then, the only Mormon I had known was a lapsed one (or jack Mormon, as they're called),* whose grandfather had invented agricultural machinery with the help of visions. Opinion on the Mormons seemed to be divided. The writer Alex Haley, who shared their interest in roots, had nothing but good to say about them, and the explorer and ethnographer Richard Francis Burton, who visited thirteen-year-old Salt Lake City in 1860, wrote up his favorable impressions in a book called *The City of*

---

* "Jack" can refer to the male of certain species, as in "jackrabbit" and "jackass," but this meaning for "jack" I haven't been able to track down.

the Saints. Burton found the Mormon wives "exceedingly pretty and attractive, supreme in their domesticity and motherhood" and a refreshing contrast to "a certain type of British and American woman" who was "petted and spoiled ... set upon an uncomfortable and unnatural eminence, aggravated by a highly nervous temperament, small cerebellum, constitutional frigidity, and extreme delicacy of fibre." Burton approved of the Mormon practice of polygamy, which owed its existence to another of Smith's revelations. Burton offered as a "physiological defense" of polygamy that it abolished prostitution, concubinage, celibacy, and infanticide. His study of society in the Middle East, Africa, and the Orient, he explained, had led him to believe that "man is by nature polygamic, whereas woman, as a rule, is monogamic, and polyandrous only when tired of her lover. The man loves the woman, but the love of the woman is for the love of the man." Others, like Edmund Wilson, felt the religion was basically a fraud, something Joseph Smith had made up as he went along rather than the natural accretion by a society of moral values and wisdom.

Whatever the genesis of their beliefs, the Mormons not only survived, unlike most of the sects that appeared at that time in American history, they went on to establish a virtual theocracy in Utah and to become one of the nation's healthiest (thanks to revelations about the ills of alcohol, coffee, and tobacco), most fertile, most cohesive, and most prosperous enclaves, with assets of billions of dollars from tithing, the 10 percent of his or her income that each Saint must contribute, and some thirty thousand missionaries abroad in the world.

In 1830 Smith had only six followers. The reception to his Book of Mormon was generally hostile, so he moved west to Ohio, where the Church prospered for a while, but then, under renewed attack, he moved west again in 1837, to Missouri, where he was driven by mobs eastward to Illinois and founded the city of Nauvoo on a bluff projecting into the Mississippi. The Latter-Day Gospel, with its promise of salvation and new life in a virgin land, fared better in Europe, connecting with slum dwellers and the industrial underclass. By 1844 there were fifteen thousand Saints. That year Smith, who had been informally taking women in "spirit marriage," including the wives of his followers, unbeknownst to them, made official his revelation about polygamy. On June 27 of that year, Smith and his brother were killed by a mob of irate monogamists.

The equally remarkable Brigham Young became the new president of the Quorum of the Twelve Apostles. Young decided the Saints had to move again, to the most remote part of the West, where they could practice their religion in peace, and that he would be their Moses. He studied John Frémont's journals and *The Emigrant Guide to Oregon and California,* and in the summer of 1847, a year and a half after they had crossed the Mississippi, he led 144 Saints over the Wasatch Range and down into the valley of Great Salt Lake and declared that this was the place, the promised land. The pioneers dammed what is now called City Creek, one of the streams rushing down from the mountains, torched the sagebrush, and hastily planted some crops. Thus began what the historian Ray Allen Billington describes as "one of the most successful cooperative experiments in all history." Young built a mansion for himself and his twenty-seven wives, which he called the Beehive House, and the following year he proclaimed the Kingdom of Deseret ("Deseret" being reformed Egyptian for "Honeybee," whose selfless industry every good Saint strived to emulate).

The main irrigation ditch came off Big Cottonwood Creek, and its water was further distributed by laterals. The bishops assigned work proportionately to the water that would be used and set up a rotation system for drawing it. Later, elected "water masters" decided the apportionment of the precious fluid throughout the burgeoning theo-democracy. Soon more than eleven thousand acres were under irrigation, and there were more than nine hundred applicants to use them. Lots were cast for the land abutting the ditches, "as Israel did in days of old," Young explained. Ten acres were given to mechanics and artisans, and twenty-, forty-, and eighty-acre lots were given to farmers. But Young departed from the English concept of riparian water rights, declaring that there would be no private ownership of the streams that came out of the canyons, and that the water diverted to the rows of crops should be returned to the streams, if possible, in undiminished volume. As Marc Reisner writes,

> The Mormons attacked the desert full-bore, flooded it, subverted its dreadful indifference—moralized it—until they had made a Mesopotamia in America between the valleys of the Green River and the middle Snake. Fifty-six years after the first earth was turned beside City Creek, the Mormons had six million acres under full or partial irrigation in several states. In that year—1902—the United States government launched its own irrigation program, based on Mormon experience, guided by Mormon laws, run largely by Mormons. The agency responsible for it, the U.S. Bureau of Reclamation, would build the highest and largest dams in the world in rivers few believed could be controlled—the Colorado, the Sacramento, the Columbia, and the lower Snake—and run aqueducts for hundreds of miles across deserts and over mountains and through the Continental Divide in order

to irrigate more millions of acres and provide water and power to a population equal to that of Italy.

Already by 1848 there were forty-one irrigation districts in the state.

The cooperation and cohesion required to keep the water flowing and the ditches in repair and to make the desert blossom fostered what Donald Worster describes in his book *Rivers of Empire* as "a world view of permanent subordination" that was very different from the individualism of the nomadic pastoralists—the Band People and the cowboys. The Mormon lifestyle wasn't for everyone, and some bolted and hit the Outlaw Trail, like Robert Lee Parker, aka Butch Cassidy, and his Wild Bunch. And those who remained piously in the fold weren't without their own streak of endemic violence, stemming from persecution trauma and cultish control trips. In 1857, 120 settlers on the California-bound Fancher train were massacred under the instructions of a zealot named John Doyle Lee, who was Brigham Young's adopted son and had nineteen wives of his own. The settlers, who were mostly from Arkansas, had called Lee's wives whores, and Lee called down a "blood atonement" on them, not only for this insult, but for all the atrocities the Saints had suffered at the hands of the Gentiles, going back to the murder of Smith.

In a few years Salt Lake City had become a thriving human colony. The Tabernacle, shaped like a huge, flipped-over, halved egg, was completed in 1867. Its ellipsoid vaulted roof had unusual acoustics, the better to display the vocal virtuosity of the Tabernacle Choir and the tone of its eleven-thousand-pipe organ. One afternoon in the summer of 1983, I sat in the VIP gallery with two fidgety men in their thirties and an old man, who turned out to be William Casey, then director of the CIA, and his Secret Service guards. The Central Intelligence Agency and the Federal Bureau of Investigation recruit heavily from the Saints, who make ideal operatives because they are extremely patriotic and have an aptitude for surveillance technology. Obedience to "the law of the land" dates to the Woodruff Manifesto of 1890, when the church, after years of persecution, reluctantly abandoned its core doctrine of plural marriage. Utah was admitted to the union in 1896 on condition that polygamy be "forever banned" by its state constitution. But not everyone was prepared to "put up all his wives but one." Die-hard polygamists fled to Wyoming, Oregon, Idaho, New Mexico, Chihuahua, and Alberta.

Having more than one spouse at once is a third-degree felony in Utah, but as many as forty thousand of its residents—fundamentalists who do not recognize the divine origin of the Woodruff Manifesto—

may be members of multiple-parent households, as they are called. On December 1, 1982, Roy Potter, a policeman in Murray, a suburb of Salt Lake City, was dismissed from the force after a complaint was lodged that he was living with two women. Potter, who subsequently took a third wife, argued unsuccessfully that the practice of plural marriage was a theological necessity for him, without which he could not secure salvation or exaltation, and was thus protected by the First Amendment. Plural marriage and cohabitation became illegal in the United States with the Morrill Act of 1892. The act was challenged by George Reynolds, Brigham Young's secretary, who had several wives, but the Supreme Court ruled that "polygamy has always been odious among the northern and western nations of Europe." This was not true, in fact: Christian monogamy was not imposed until A.D. 600, by Gregory the Great, and both kinds of polygamy—polygyny and polyandry—flourished among the Celtic and Germanic tribes. Nevertheless, Reynolds was sentenced to a year and a half in prison.

In 1986 I visited Mennonite and dissident polygamous Mormon communities in the vicinity of Nueva Casas Grandes, Chihuahua. The Mennonites, like those who have a colony in the Chaco of northern Paraguay, speak German and Spanish and drive around in horse-drawn buggies and make cheddar cheese. At the colony of El Capulín I bought a postcard of three young women dressed in bonnets, black dresses, and black shoes, whose caption read "*Menonitas: muchachas bonitas.*" This group had arrived in Chihuahua from Canada in 1921. They picked up a hundred thousand acres at $8.25 per. A shopkeeper in Nueva Casas Grandes told me that the Mennonites were scrupulously honest; one time a boy who had stolen a ball came back a few days later and paid for it. They marry among themselves, and some of the women don't even speak Spanish, he went on. Just about their only concessions to the industrial age are electric-generated tractors with iron wheels. I asked two men in bib overalls if they were allowed to marry their first cousins, and they both answered at once. One said yes, the other no. Unlike the Mormons, the Mennonites are allowed to smoke and drink a little, but if they get drunk, they are punished.

The Mormon presence in Mexico dates to 1874, when Brigham Young sent missionaries who founded eight colonies in Chihuahua and Sonora. Before long, they had a hundred thousand acres under irrigation. One canal was twenty-four miles long. After the Woodruff Manifesto, they were joined by dissident polygamists. The governor of Chihuahua tried to expel them, but his order was overturned by President Porfirio Díaz. At the outbreak of the Mexican Revolution, some women and children were killed, and the rest were evacuated to tent cities in El Paso and Douglas, Arizona. Seven years later, one-fourth of them returned and revived five of the colonies. Today only two remain—Colonia Juárez and Colonia Dublán, and there are fewer than five hundred pure Anglo descendants of the original colonists. Many of the children have married Mexicans, and three out of four inhabitants are dusky, mestizo *Mormones morenitos*. "The Mormons have brought us much progress," a Chihuahuan told me.

Colonia Juárez was the birthplace of the politician George Romney. It was a flourishing enclave of imported America, frozen in the fifties, with two-story brick houses and fruit orchards (Bartlett pears and several types of delicious apples; Pancho Villa had been a customer), whose wholesomeness was becoming eroded by *narcotrafico;* dealers, some of them wayward Saints, were building big houses in the neighborhood. When I got there, a falling rain had just turned to hail, and a little girl was catching the stones in her hands. I called on the town's doctor, Le Roy Hatch, who had a satellite dish in his yard with a deer browsing in a pine forest painted on it. Dr. Hatch had lost his two wives and a son in a car accident the year before and was alone now.

He told me about the Le Baron boys, who had brought shame to the Mexican contingent. The three brothers* were descended from the grandson of one of Joseph Smith's bodyguards, who was excommunicated for polygamy and took his wives to Colonia Juárez. Joel F. Le Baron challenged the validity of the Mormon priesthood and, claiming to be God's anointed, to have been called by God to set his house in order, founded his own church. Ervil M. Le Baron, a big, tall, good-looking bruiser, served in his older brother's church for ten years, then, claiming to be God's legal administrator, with the power over life and death, and branding all who opposed him as criminals, he went off and founded Colonia Le Baron. Colonia Le Baron was like Jonestown, the doctor told me. Ervil had about two hundred followers, and "they had to be nude 'cause the clothes they were gonna use in the hereafter weren't the clothes they had here." The prime target of his wrath was his brother's church, the Church of the Firstborn of the Fullness of Times. Joel's colony, Los Molinos, in Baja California, was attacked. People were killed, homes burned. The youngest brother, Verlan M. Le Baron, who sided with Joel, wrote a book called *The Le Baron Story,* which was published by a vanity press in Lubbock, Texas (the dedication: "with special thanks to my wife Charlotte. Also with gratitude to my wife Elizabeth"). Joel was killed in 1972, and Ervil masterminded

---

* Actually, there were a lot more than that. There were two other brothers, Ben and Wesley, and three sisters, Lucinda, Alma, and Esther, but they don't figure in the story.

perhaps twenty other killings throughout Mexico and the West, including those of his daughter Rebecca; a seven-foot defected follower named Dean Grover, who was shot dead in Natural City, California, by one of Ervil's wives, Vanda White (who was sentenced to life imprisonment in 1977); Dr. Rulon C. Allred, the head of the second-largest group of fundamentalists, who was gunned down while attending a patient in Murray, Utah. Ervil threatened Lyndon Johnson, Richard Nixon, Jimmy Carter, Walter Mondale, Billy Graham, and the president of the Mormon church, Spenser Wooley Kimball. He was finally picked up by the FBI in Oaxaca and taken over the border at Laredo and was found dead in a stateside prison in 1981, possibly after having made a suicide pact with one of his thirteen wives.

THE COMMUNES OF THE SIXTIES

The countercultural revolution of the 1960s produced a shorter-lived and less coherent spurt of utopian activity in the Southwest than the Mormons'. Much of it was centered around Taos and in the surrounding Sangre de Cristo Mountains. In 1969 there were twenty-seven communes in the vicinity. The hippies and the local Hispanos did not, by and large, hit it off. Four years later, only four communes were still going. The Hog Farm disbanded, and New Buffalo, where there was a lot of experimentation with peyote, is now a bed-and-breakfast. After the communes broke up, many of their members stayed on. As William de Buys writes in his history of the Sangre de Cristo Range,

> The flowering of the counterculture had a lasting effect in the southern Sangres, for it brought Anglos permanently into communities where none had lived before. Today at least one or two Anglo families live in virtually every mountain village and many of them possess the same qualities of hardiness, self-reliance, and inventiveness that characterized the homesteaders of a hundred years ago. In some villages they have won the respect and friendship of their Hispanic neighbors. In others, relations are more often strained and tense.

Today gray-haired ex-hippies are an important force in New Mexico politics and tinge the cultural landscape in many interesting and positive ways. They are an important counterbalance to the conservative redneck element.

Quite a few communes were scattered in the Rio Arriba in 1986. There was a group of turbaned Anglo Sikhs outside of Española, and another one of Black Muslims from the Virgin Islands outside of Abiquiu.

A Santa Fe man told me about a militant lesbian commune called Arf, up in the hills near Nambe. "They're armed with guns and bows and arrows, and they're very antiman," he warned, "an ugly little group that has it in for everybody." I had a special interest in all-female societies, having written a book that traces the historical basis for the legends about a tribe of women warriors for whom the Amazon River is named. I followed a dirt road up to the top of a ridge, where there was a row of pickups. A woman named Sunflower, with tangles of hair sprouting from her chin, was unloading groceries from the back of one of the trucks. From there a path went down into a deep forested canyon. "I wouldn't go down there without an invitation if I was you," she said in a menacing tone, and went down the path. Another woman arrived in a pickup. She wasn't a member of the commune, she was just house-sitting for one of its members and was more friendly. She offered to go down and see if anybody was interested in talking to me. After a while, a woman with long, straight blond hair in a long skirt and a loose Indian-print blouse, braless and reeking of patchouli—very six-ties—came up the path to get a bag of cement out of her pickup. Her name was Riverbend. The commune had been going for ten years, she told me. There were ten members, two with children. One was her twelve-year-old girl, with whom she juggled at shopping malls for bread. The commune was called Arf because there were a lot of dogs—"at least two per person," Riverbend went on.

"The lifestyle is primitive. We cook over an open fire and get water from the brook. The land binds us together. We're not open to men, not even to visitors, unless they're okayed by the whole commune, like if somebody's dad wanted to visit. Men's energy is too much. Every-body's pretty fed up with the outside world."

I asked if male dogs were allowed; she said as long as they were fixed. Riverbend herself had been there a year; you had to have stayed a year, to have seen the four seasons through, before you could build a house, which she was now in the process of doing. She had come from a commune in California "that was getting pretty wild in the sense that everybody was growing dope. I was looking for something more spiritual. This is it. We celebrate the equinox and the solstice. Last night the hills were all dressed in rainbows. Down the road there's a community of monks [the Sangre de Cristo Center of Chris-tian Studies, a retreat for Catholic brothers of the De La Salle order]. We bump into each other at the waterfall. But we're not celibate like them; we're lesbians. Below them are some old Hispano families. In the spring we all get together to clean out the irrigation ditch. It takes three or four days. It's a wonderful way to meet your neighbors. It crosses all boundaries."

Over the Memorial Day weekend, six years later, my Albuquerque golf buddy Patrick Markwith took me and our boys (Patrick has two sons, too) up to El Rito, deep in the mountains of the Rio Arriba, to 160 acres of forested canyon known as the Cañada del Potrero that belonged to a guy named Terry, where Patrick had lived for a year around the time I had my psychotropic first encounter with the Grand Canyon. Terry's land wasn't a formal commune; he was just generous about letting people live there. Terry was still there. Everyone else had split long ago, leaving the ruins of their jerry-built dwellings scattered among the ponderosa pines and the Douglas firs: Naomi's hogan, David's hobbit house, Victor the Cosmic Cowboy's plastic dome up on the ridge. "A lot of [substance] abuse took place in this canyon," Patrick reminisced. "One of Terry's high-school buddies spent a week out in the woods, tripping on [mu]shrooms, and when he came back, he had blossomed." The place we slept in still had a mouse-chewed collection of the classic psychedelic texts: Steven Gaskin's *Monday Night Classes,* Baba Ram Dass's *Be Here Now,* Alan Watts's *The Joyous Cosmology.* This place should be on the National Historic Register as a sixties ruin, I told Terry.

A *potrero* is a horse corral. Rustlers used to hide their horses in the canyon. Exploring the canyon, we came upon meadows of lupine, some kind of grosbeak I had never seen before, with a stripe on the back of its head (a black-headed grosbeak). A lone bald eagle was patroling the ridge, and we spotted a large bear poking around in a stand of aspens—not a grizzly, but a cinnamon (a reddish-brown phase of the black bear). "They say if you gotta outrun a bear, run downhill, because its front legs are shorter," Patrick counseled us.

THE BACA PROJECT

Over the Colorado–New Mexico border, in Crestone, to the northeast, a more upscale utopian experiment was flourishing—the Baca Project, where a woman named Hannah Strong was trying to bring together the world's five great religious traditions on a spectacular property overlooking the San Luis Valley. Strong, whose husband, Maurice, organized the 1992 Earth Summit in Rio de Janeiro, claims that there are higher vibrational energies on the land than at Chartres,

Stonehenge, Lhasa, or Machu Picchu. A self-styled visionary, she believes that in a few years the world's population will shrink to four hundred million as a result of environmental degradation, that "AIDS is nothing compared to what is coming." And so she was donating the property—part of the five-hundred-thousand-acre land grant made by King Ferdinand to some deserving subjects named Baca—as a refuge, a sort of Shambala (a place in Tibet where Buddhists believe their sacred texts and their tradition will survive the Dark Age), where the world's religious wisdom and the seeds of its flora can be stored, a "dream corridor" where "ancient souls" can be reborn.

Her husband, a Canadian financier who had his eye on the untapped two billion acre-foot San Luis aquifer, bought the land sight unseen as part of a much larger purchase. Soon after Hannah arrived to take a look at it, an old cowboy came up to her and said, "I've been waiting for you." He described a vision he had had of a woman who looked like her coming and gathering all the world's religions at the Baca, which had been a vision-quest site for the Ute. Hannah went up on the land and fasted and meditated and observed for three days and decided to create a place where the Old West meets the New Age, as one visitor described it. Tibetan Buddhists of the Kagiupa order have built a stupa on sixty acres consecrated by their late head, the sixteenth Karmapa. A Hindu temple, a Zen monastery, a Carmelite monastery, a Taoist retreat, a Jewish mystical center, and a Sufi center are in various stages of development. The Dalai Lama, Lakota shamans, Penitentes, and assorted Rockefellers are regular visitors.

BIOSPHERE 2

The New York Times called Biosphere 2 "a utopian planet-in-a-bottle." I first heard about it in 1987 from a botanist who specializes in the Amazon, who told me he was involved in designing a miniature rain forest, one of the five biomes in a 3.15-acre terrarium that was being built in the desert outside of Tucson, in which eight people were going to be sealed for two years.

A few days before "closure," I went to meet the Biosphereans before they became incommunicado. Biosphere 2 was out in Oracle, past some retirement communities (adult miniutopias of the American dream, in a sense, whose residents were blissfully golfing away the last chapter of their lives). The terrarium itself, a tiered, flat-topped glass structure, resembling a ziggurat or a Mayan temple and surrounded by subsidiary structures—a quarantine station, greenhouses, mission con-

trol, an "insectary"—was perched on a ridge with a sweeping view of
the twenty-five-hundred-acre Sun Ranch. Formerly the winter home of
the countess of Suffolk, the property had been acquired by Ed Bass, the
second son of the fifth-wealthiest man in the country. Bass's great-
uncle, a Fort Worth saloon keeper by the name of Sid Richardson, had
discovered the Keystone oil field in west Texas, which was where the
money came from. Bass also owned a rain forest in Puerto Rico, a
solar-powered hotel in Kathmandu, and a five-hundred-thousand-acre
ranch in Australia and was a supporter of big environmental projects.

Biosphere 2 was the brainchild of Bass's old friend from the sixties
John Allen, who had run a commune in New Mexico called the Synergia Ranch. Its members, including the young millionaire Bass, were
stripped of their bourgeois propping; given new names like Firefly,
Green, Honey, and Valentine; and put through a process of draconian
reinvention. Allen was a powerful personality, into Gurdjieffian control and ego shattering, and he tore Bass's moneyed arrogance to
shreds. Synergia Ranch was an intense scene—the quest for the Other
taken to new extremes. Allen and a beat poet named Johnny Dolphin
directed a Theater of All Possibilities. Believing that Western civilization was dead, Allen became increasingly interested in desert survival-
ism and what he called ecotechnics, and in leaving the planet and
starting a new community in outer space, and Bass fell under his spell.

The press, which had initially been enthusiastic about Biosphere 2,
caught wind of the strange doings at Synergia Ranch in the sixties.
Critics began to complain that the whole thing was not science as
much as theater, whose real intent was to make money—a sort of *Star
Trek* theme park. Tourists would come in buses and would pay $11.95
a head to see the Biosphereans at work through the glass and would
drop another twenty at the Biosphere Café on T-shirts, mugs, or other
souvenirs. More affluent visitors could take a room at the Inn at the
Biosphere; an ecologically sound golf course, with no pesticides and
watered with treated effluent, was planned. John Allen explained to
the critics that Biosphere 2 wasn't about "approach-traditional" science, which made the scientists who had been hired as consultants nervous and, the more they saw their expert advice not being taken, bitter;
it was about the race of technology against decay, about preparing to
take off for the new frontier, as Kennedy called space. Steve Baer, the
Albuquerque-based solar-energy pioneer, pointed out that the Biosphere wasn't really self-contained because gas-powered air conditioners were being used to offset the passive-solar-heat gain, while they
could have simply used louvers to block the sunlight and chill the
ocean; the technology to have kept it self-contained and save

air-conditioning costs existed. He criticized "the constant encourage-
ment of more artificiality" that the project represented. "Let them take
off in spaceships while they still have faith in technology," he told me.

I was greeted at mission control by Sabrina, the Biosphere's flak person; the closure had attracted a media feeding frenzy, and we were
being done in batches. I was shown around with a safari-jacketed correspondent for *CBS News*. Access to the Biosphereans was limited.
"Right now closure's coming up and it's probably not a real good time
to talk to them," Sabrina explained. There had been a last-minute
replacement for one Biospherean who turned out to be allergic to
sorghum and rye. John Allen was "not talking to the press; he's a
genius, but he doesn't have the gift of translating his thoughts into
nomenclature," Sabrina went on. The biosphere concept was invented
by the maverick Russian academician Vladimir Ivanovich Vernadsky
(1863–1945), she told me, and was revived during the sixties; the
space race and the threat of nuclear holocaust gave the idea of creating
habitats for the moon and Mars a boost. The planning for Biosphere 2
began in 1984. (Biosphere 1 is, of course, the planet Earth.)

Walking in the desert, we passed an antinuclear warrior kachina, a
religious sculpture by the Santa Fe artist Tony Pryce from nuclear
bomb parts he had scavenged from Los Alamos. Several rappellers
were lowering themselves down the pyramid on ropes, testing seals.
The visuals were great. Some Tibetan lamas in full ritual regalia were
coming to bless the Biosphereans, Sabrina told us as we entered the
double submarine door. I asked about the outside natural-gas energy
that was being used to chill and heat the pipes that controlled the air-
conditioning, and she pointed out that earth isn't self-contained either;
the atmosphere receives regular infusions of cosmic dust. The important point was that all of Biosphere 2's energy came from the sun. Nor
would the Biosphereans be cut off from developments in the outside
world; a satellite dish beamed the six o'clock news and the other fare
of dozens of channels to TVs in the Human Habitat section, which was
quite cushy. There was some concern about a possible buildup of toxic
gases from rugs and foam padding, particularly in the Command
Room.

The Biosphereans, in orange jumpsuits, looked very *Star Trek,* particularly one bullet-headed sixty-eight-year-old. None of them had
completed higher scientific degrees, but they were all photogenic. The
women were very attractive. Jayne Poynter, the vibrant, enthusiastic
entomologist, said about 250 species of insects were being sealed off
with them: five kinds of bees, heliconian and pipe-vine swallowtail
butterflies to pollinate the flowers in the twenty thousand square-foot

rain forest; termites, ants, Puerto Rican and Spanish cockroaches, and other detritivores would break down the compost. Spiders had volunteered from the desert and multiplied prolifically. Two hundred grasshoppers had been introduced last week to feed the toads, lizards, and frogs; and other beneficial insects—ladybird beetles, lacewings, and Formosan parasitic wasps—were part of the mix. "The populations will be on their own, unless there is a plague, then we will have to move in and manage them," explained Poynter.

Mark Nelson, another of the Biosphereans, said, "This is the chance of a lifetime, a historic step—the first clone of the earth, the birth of comparative planetology, and the dawn of comparative biospherics. The reason the Gaia debate goes on about whether the earth behaves as a single organism is because we have no other time line or evolutionary track to compare."

Mark took us into the intensive agriculture biome, which had a half-acre rice paddy, papayas, bananas, lam-lam beans, peanuts, sweet potatoes, and enough coffee for one cup per week for each of them. A few of the Biosphereans were unhappy with this. Elephant grass was being intercropped with high-protein lucaena for the stock (rapidly reproducing bush babies, African pygmy goats, and Ossabaw feral swine). A pond was covered with a floating mat of azolla for the tilapia fish to eat, and the tilapias' droppings would be used to fertilize the crops. "The operative principle of this system is that there is no waste. Waste is a resource. You can't disappear anything. The amount of water, for instance, is fixed, and we'll be drinking recycled waste water, collecting it from condensate on glass or in the air," Nelson explained.

"This is like *Brave New World*," he went on. "They laughed at Columbus, too. People doing something innovative always encounter malice. The flat-earthers are really caustic, but this is tremendous theater. I've been locked in worse playpens; ask my parents. This isn't pure science, but who cares? It's a working theory, and let's see what happens. Nothing ventured. . . ."

All the Biosphereans were single and free to form whatever relationships they wanted to, as long as they practiced birth control. They came from different countries—England and Belgium. Each had different strengths. One had been a tool-and-die maker and was very handy in the machine shop. There was a chef, a dentist, and several musicians. Mark had grown up in Brooklyn and arrived at Synergia Ranch in 1969, having done premed and philosophy at Dartmouth, followed by "the usual"—taxi driver, social worker, court reporter. The ranch was windblown, overgrazed, and desertified, and Nelson studied with Hopi dry farmers and with Michael Evanari, the grand old man of Israeli desert research, and gradually created an oasis, supplying a ten-acre orchard with drip irrigation, harnessing flash floods and runoff. The Biosphereans would spend about four hours a day as subsistence farmers, harvesting and processing their food; leisure time would transpire in the Human Habitat, working out in a little gym, jamming in the music room, watching one of the 250 movies in the video library.

Biosphere 2 was interesting from many angles. It would shed light on the minimum critical size ecosystems need to have to remain viable, on the effects of inbreeding and genetic bottlenecking, on the effects upon the crew of being isolated and confined but on view, like zoo animals, on what sort of fissioning and dominance hierarchy develops in a closed arena. Commercializable technology might come out of it—air purifiers that scrub out trace gases, soil-bed reactors, and so on. "Ed's plan is to get up to positive cash flow," explained Stanley F. Buchthal, a New York–based consultant on the financial aspects, "through tourism—we project six hundred a day by the end of next year—and merchandising of patents and intellectual property rights. We have taken out several dozen worldwide patents in certain technologies like wastewater management and are in discussion with several countries that are interested in having a clone of Biosphere 2 and duplicating our experiments. Kansai, the General Electric of Japan, already has its totally electric Kansai Science City, and it may want to do a biosphere. In two years there will be an international space university on the site, and a space camp for children that will be like an ecological Epcot. We'll be selling books, videos, puzzles, and board games. We're gonna do movies—animation and licensing off the animation. We have video conferencing and global broadcast capabilities within the closed site. There are many different sides to this and ways to make money."

A few weeks later Jayne Poynter lost the tip of a finger and had to be briefly evacuated. "But this is not considered breaking closure," Sabrina assured me. Several scientific consultants disassociated themselves, complaining that closure was broken repeatedly, and the data were hopelessly corrupted, and the whole thing was a complete travesty, but Thomas Lovejoy of the Smithsonian, who remained with the project, said to me, "The scientific jury is still out on this and will probably be out for some time. Somehow the science got lost in this multifaceted hundred-and-fifty-million-dollar scientific-educational-commercial venture. Bass now calls himself an 'ecopreneur.' The project needs a scientific director who will develop, monitor, and coordinate the science. But even if everything dissolves into a pool of slime, it will still be scientifically interesting."

The geneticist David Suzuki was of the opinion that "the effort and money invested in Biosphere 2 is of little scientific value and merely adds to the widespread public impression, created in the nuclear-apocalypse survivalist environment, that we are in control and can create our own livable environment. That's what's killing the planet."

Rumors of a secret tunnel leading to a nearby Circle K convenience store, that the Biosphereans were sneaking out for pizza every night, were belied by the observable fact that all were dramatically losing weight, on the order of forty pounds, between 8 and 15 percent of their body weight.

By January 1993, scientists were mystified by a 28 percent drop in the oxygen within the Biosphere. Arrangements were made to pump in pure oxygen should the eight inhabitants begin to languish. The oxygen level was now the equivalent of being at twelve thousand feet above sea level. Four of the Biospহereans were put on an altitude-sickness drug. What was happening to the abundance of oxygen produced by the plants during photosynthesis? the scientists wondered. Rust binds oxygen to steel, but the Biosphere was stainless steel throughout, so oxidation couldn't be a factor. Maybe the oxygen was being taken into the soil through respiration. Finally the cause was discovered: an explosive growth of oxygen-eating bacteria in the peat, compost, and other organic material. When the oxygen level reached the equivalent of fourteen thousand feet, liquid oxygen was injected as vapor through a sealed port, saving the Biosphereans but further compromising the data.

A year later, at the fourteen-month point, I spoke by phone with the ranking scientist, Abigail Alling, inside the Biosphere. She sounded genuinely glad to talk with someone new. "We're beginning to realize the oscillation factor, the difficulties of people living together closely and maintaining a healthy profile in these kinds of conditions, as in space and Antarctica. Not all is roses. There are ups and downs, and we are experiencing that. I'm open to extensive information exchange with people on the outside, but I'm lucky to have close friends in here. A couple were friends before, and I have one new friend in here, which is very nice and unexpected.

"Being in here gives you a real sense of the future," she went on. "If you have a broken pipe that needs PVC glue, you think twice because PVC is toxic when released into the air. You have to be aware. Every person in here has had to adjust and participate and become more waste conscious and more intelligently involved with the world. We brew banana wine, and once a month we have a big feast and just sit around and eat. You need to bask in pleasure and instinctiveness, which is something I never thought about in my prior culture because I was overstimulated. I never realized the importance of food and partying." I learned later that Alling had left a four-year-old daughter on the outside.

The insects were not doing very well, she went on, because some local birds—a thrasher and a couple of sparrows—sneaked in before closure and had a field day and finally died from overeating.

The Biosphereans accomplished their mission by September 1993 and came out. By the following spring, Bass and the emerged Biosphereans had bitterly fallen out. Bass had taken legal action to remove half a dozen of the top management team, charging them with gross, deliberate mismanagement of funds and personnel, while they, claiming he owed them money, had hired their own lawyers. Mark Nelson, one of the casualties, said that "Ed Bass has moved in like big Texas money always moves in. It's a revolution that is rude, crude, and semifascistic. The project was on the verge of becoming a success and making some money, and he tried to grab it all."

One night Abigail Alling and her new friend, fellow-former-Biospherean Mark Van Thillow, crept up to the Biosphere and broke five seals and a pane of glass, letting in air from the outside and corrupting the experiment yet again. They denied it was sabotage and claimed they did it to protect their replacements, the next generation of Biosphereans, for whom any mechanical failure, without Van Thillow's knowledge of the life-support systems, could prove fatal. The latest news is that Bass has handed the Biosphere over to Harvard and Columbia, to scientists with the credentials and experience to take advantage of the facility and get some real science done.

SANTA TERESA

This is a more down-to-earth utopia, taking up sixty-four thousand acres on both sides of the Mexican border, just over the Franklin Mountains, the next valley west from El Paso. The developer, Charlie Crowder, planned to create a new, nonexploitative twin city, a new port of entry like Juárez/El Paso or the two Nogaleses. There would be twelve *maquiladora*-type assembly plants, but—this was the twist— they would be on the American side of the border. Everything would be made in the United States, and the Mexicans would come over and work in them. Santa Teresa was now, in the words of the Dallas *Morning News,* "a dream bordering on reality." CROWDER SEES UTOPIA, *Business Week* bugled.

I lunched with Crowder at the Santa Teresa Golf Club. Outside, golfers were flailing away in swimming hundred-degree heat. "Golf courses are amenities for land fraud," Crowder observed. "The ideal course is twenty-five yards wide and ninety miles long. On this one, we don't care who your grandfather was. You'll find the president of the largest corporation playing with a plumber. My dream is to have a course whose holes are staggered along either side of the border." Crowder's house was eight hundred feet from the first tee, and he commuted the three hundred yards to his office in the clubhouse in a Mercedes. He put in the two eighteen-hole tracks in 1973 to 1974 with the help of Lee Trevino, sold them to Trevino in 1975, then bought them back three years later. Trevino, now one of the most colorful and successful players on the Senior Tour, had grown up in Dallas, but being Hispanic he was unable to play in the private clubs.

Also joining us were Luis Roberto Camacho, a member of one of northern Chihuahua's most august families; Frank Getman, a Texas businessman; and New Mexico state senator Tom Benavides, whom I had met during the visit of Christopher Columbus XXII.

The senator said we were in a period of reviving ties between Old and New Mexico. Aeromexico was talking about a new route to Albuquerque, and a New Mexican delegation was in discussion with Pemex, the Mexican oil and gas monopoly, about selling it some fossil fuel.

Crowder was one of the Southwest's major operators. "I belong to the frontier tradition," he told me. "I've had experience with disaster and success, and I've learned to recognize them both for the impostors that they are." Born in the Ozarks in 1932, Crowder hitchhiked west at the age of thirteen. He picked apples in Colorado and eventually became a contractor, building irrigation ditches, erosion-control fences, stock ponds, and dirt mountain roads. In the late forties he was building roads for seismographic crews on the Jicarilla Apache Reservation. "I became the leading brush eradicator in New Mexico," he told me. "My brothers and I cleared three hundred thousand acres in Lincoln County with an anchor chain stretched between two tractors, ripping out cedar and piñon to create range." He did a stretch as a private eye in Albuquerque, investigating arson, murder, and embezzlement. He swapped land with the Bureau of Land Management—the hundred-thousand-acre Cañon de San Diego, up north, near Jemez, for instance, for three hundred thousand acres of grazing land in the southern part of the state.

"In the early sixties I became acquainted with Teofoilo Barunda, the governor of Chihuahua," he went on. Barunda got him interested in the possibilities of Mexico. "Mexico," Crowder argued, "is our new defense department. It will defend us against the brutal eroding of our world market position." Realizing that Ciudad Juárez was one of the fastest-growing cities in the world—a million and a half souls and counting—and that a third of all the manufacturing in Mexico was done there, he began to think of creating a new community that would be a conduit for trade, commerce, and technology. "Texans understand the importance of trade with Mexico, even though they don't respect Mexicans; there isn't a single Hispanic in the El Paso Country Club," he continued. "It does $9.7 billion a year in sales to Mexico, and Mexico does $13 million a year in sales to Texas." But the trade with New Mexico was almost negligible.

" 'Bring us your most menial tasks, and we let you in with machinery and ideas,' Barunda told me. 'This will increase your markets, and we will industrialize and become an equal trading partner. We need each other.' " So Crowder traded his grazing land for what would become the easternmost port of entry in New Mexico.

Crowder started with five thousand acres, eighteen hundred of which belonged to the old Santa Teresa land grant. It is illegal for foreigners to own land in Mexico, but there were bilateral treaties, and Crowder was able to work out an understanding. In 1985 he came out with his border plan. "I have never looked on this as my project," he said. "It was bigger than I was before I was born."

Luis Roberto Camacho was a civil engineer, and he had been a major player when Chihuahua took off in the late sixties. "I designed Antonio Bermudez Park, the largest industrial park on earth, paved the city without federal or state funds, built nineteen plants, put in the natural-gas system, built the airport and the country club," he told me in fluent English. "I became an industrialist. I had the largest agribusiness, with two hundred and forty thousand pear and forty thousand pecan trees irrigated from eleven dams. It was the most beautiful ranch in Mexico, with fifteen thousand acres. But then I had a problem with my wife and I took off. Two years later I came back and put in the sewer and the water system, wells, aqueducts, pumping plants in the valley of Juárez. Below the city the valley had been ruined by dumping of raw sewage; the wells were contaminated with all sorts of poisonous materials."

The great thing about Santa Teresa, Senator Benavides pointed out, was that you would be starting with a clean slate and could avoid making the same mistakes, like pollution or putting the railroad or the warehouses in the middle of town. "I visualize Santa Teresa as New Mexico's gateway to Latin America and Spain and our mutual culture."

Frank Getman said, "I'm going to cover New Mexico with human dung. I'm getting treated waste from New York City and applying it to the soil in Sierra County. I'm going to cover New Mexico with good old shit. Our senators have been shooting it for so long."

The population of Santa Teresa was currently a couple of thousand, which Crowder predicted would expand to 100,000 to 150,000 in the next fifteen to twenty years. "There's enough water for a hundred years," he assured me. "The first thing I did was the most comprehensive and scientific water-well field-development project in the history of the Southwest, and damned if I didn't hit oil, too. We already have a ten-and-a-half-million-dollar fiber-optics plant here. We've got Foamex which does the seats for the Ford plant in Chihuahua. We have a hospital, a substance-abuse center, and a community college. We have Reuben's Prepared Foods, which makes fish sticks and controlled-meat patties for fast-food companies like McDonald's and Hardee's. We'll be bringing cattle over the border, dipping them, and processing them. People equate New Mexico and west Texas as primitive podunk places, but there's a trillion dollars business in the Rio Grande corridor for anybody that's willing to share research and development."

After lunch Crowder took me to his office and showed me a map of the corridor stuck with pins that explained what he was talking about. "There's a new generation of composite airplanes lighter than fiberglass but stronger than steel. There are the labs—Los Alamos, Phillips, Sandia, the Technet Center for Explosive Technology Research. We are the center of the universe in the highest technology, and all this is available to manufacturers. Research and development is labor-intensive, and our friends in Mexico help with that. We don't use the words 'cheap labor.' "

But that was what was turning the Chihuahua border into "the Hong Kong of the twenty-first century," as an El Paso realtor put it. Electric and garment companies were flocking to the border. There were already two thousand *maquiladoras* and seventy-five of the *Fortune* magazine's top five hundred companies, including General Motors, Ford, IBM, GE, Chrysler, and Texaco, had assembly plants. The hourly wage for a *maquilador* was $2.01. In Korea $4.65, in Singapore $3.66.

Santa Teresa's twin city would be called San Jieronimo. It would provide "high-density, low-cost, generous-sized worker units within walking distance of all mechanics-of-life requirements, and of the plants on the U.S. side. How can you be efficient if you wake up with no plumbing, walk through a slum to work, and worry about your grandmother's safety?" Crowder asked.

His utopia was still a little raw. There was a Mexican strip with a pawnbroker offering cash loans of up to $350, a junkyard, a flophouse called the Papagayo Apartments. Signs for future businesses and medical offices had been planted in the vast, empty creosote flats. If it hung in there for another twenty years, if the Mexican economy recovered and NAFTA got back on track, if the water held out, if it wasn't done in by unforeseeable macroeconomic, political, climatic, or other developments, if it was meant to be, perhaps Santa Teresa might in time become another Tucson; perhaps not.

Oases

uman life in the arid Southwest is enclaved, sited according to the availability of water. My prowls in the region essentially consisted of enclave hopping: from the Tarahumara to the polygamous Mormons, from the Pueblos to the large urban oasis of Albuquerque, the lesbian commune of Arf, the fantasy bubble of Santa Fe, the ghetto paradise of Havasu Canyon, the top-secret nuclear weapons laboratory at Los Alamos. Each enclave has evolved, in its isolation, its own distinctive subculture, its own cosmos, and even the most isolated rancho, *rancheria,* or *población* has by now, of course, been touched by the modern world.

The most beautiful oasis in all the Southwest is Havasu Canyon, a branch of Grand Canyon, where the Havasupai live. The Havasupai are the "tall people" one of Coronado's reconnaissance parties was told about by the Hopi, but they weren't contacted until 1776, by the Franciscan Fray Francisco Garcés (who was killed five years later by Mojave on the left bank of the Colorado). The tribe presently numbers about six hundred and is a "different part of the native mix," as a man who helps it deal with its environmental problems explains. Linguistically, the Havasupai belong to the Yuman group, with the other Pai— the Yavapai and the Hualapai. The society is ostensibly matriarchal (no truly matriarchal society, with women ruling men, has ever been found, but some of the best Havasupai leaders have been women).

Until the late nineteenth century the Havasupai had almost no material culture. They preserved nothing from the past. Death was oblivion. They had no formal clans, only an extensive web of kinship that embraced the whole village. They were a happy-go-lucky people, like African Pygmies, content to be loosely related by multiple consanguinity. They grew goatees and tattooed one another's faces elaborately with cactus tines. They tipped their arrows in datura juice, scorpion poison, and other noxious substances and used barrel cacti and prickly pears for target practice. They ate tunas of the prickly pear (which, since the arrival of candy, have gone unharvested), but their most important plant was the banana yucca, whose fruit they roasted or sun-dried and stored or brewed into a nectarlike drink, whose leaves they soaked and pounded, separating the long inner fibers, and twisted into cordage or wove into sleeping mats and brush shelters. Their subsistence pattern was what anthropologists call transhumance, involving seasonal migration to different elevations and life zones. After the growing season was over, they came up on the canyon rim and hunted and collected, especially piñon nuts. Come spring, they moved back down into the lush, Shangri-la-like Havasu Canyon and planted squash, corn, melons, and other crops on its floor. Their name, Havsuw 'Baaja, means the "People of the Blue-Green Water," after the river that cascades through the canyon. An anthropologist named John Martin lived with them for a year in the sixties and wrote a dissertation on them. "Do you know what most of them were thinking about?" he asked me. "Ass. I thought it was something mystical."

In 1889 the Paiute of southern Utah started doing a new dance called the Ghost Dance. It grew into a messianic anti-Anglo revitalization movement that spread east to the Plains tribes and down to the Pai, including the Havasupai. The purpose of the dance was to try to turn back the clock. Its basic premise was that the dead would soon return, white men were going to disappear, and game would again be plentiful, as in the days of yore. Members of the cult were told that they would be impervious to bullets.*

The Havasupai Ghost Dancers danced around a central pole, which they climbed and clung to until they were exhausted, then they would slip down and report that they had been visiting with the dead. But the

---

* There were a number of parallels to the Ghost Dance in Africa, beginning in the 1850s with the Xhosa, South Africa's most sophisticated nation, who, after fifty years of disastrous wars and British betrayals, killed all their cattle and destroyed their food stocks at the urging of prophets who rose among them promising that if they did these things a supernatural agent would restore everything tenfold, and the white man would be expelled from the land he had stolen. Thousands of Xhosa starved to death. In 1910 Queen Muhumuza of the Kigezi district of Uganda deceived her followers that she would tap supernatural powers that would turn the bullets of the *bazungu*, the whites, into water. Similarly in Madagascar, participants in the Rebellion of the Spears (La Rébellion des Sagaies) of 1947 were assured that their sorcerers possessed magic so that the French guns would shoot only water, while the Simbas in Zaire during the sixties and the followers of Alice Lakwena in Uganda during the eighties were given a magic oil to smear on their bodies that was supposed to make them invulnerable to flying lead. Lakwena herself was struck by a bullet and remains in prison in Kenya. Currently, a rebel group called the Mai Mai is at large in eastern Zaire. The Mai Mai wear metal water faucets around their necks, which they believe protect them from bullets, and they won't let anybody touch them lest they lose their power.

dead did not return to help them, and those who had visited with the dead in time died themselves, and the cult died with them.

Things began to fall apart for the Havasupai in 1905, when President Theodore Roosevelt told them they were going to have to make way for a national park. In 1913 they swore allegiance to the United States in return for an American flag, which opened the door for the National Park Service to take the land up on the South Rim, where they roamed half the year. This land was called Coyote Tail because it was full of spruces that reminded the Havasupai of coyote tails. Having acquired it by eminent domain, incorporating it into a "park for all Americans," the park service eagerly awaited the disappearance of the last Havasupai so it could get the spectacularly picturesque canyon as well. From the journal of a park service employee around this time:

> The barefoot women and filthy children were quite friendly but the lazy, filthy bucks would have been insolent had I been alone . . . the children filled sacks with snow to melt for drinking purposes. To be sure they didn't waste any of it in washing themselves. . . . [The Havasupai] are held in low esteem by all other Indian tribes and never marry outside of their own people. . . . This last fragment will pass away within a few years and all trace will be lost. . . . It is a people looking backward down the years with no thought of the morrow. . . . Not many morrows for that doomed tribe.

Stuck down in the canyon year-round, the Havasupai were ravaged by flu epidemics and on several occasions were nearly wiped out by the spring snowmelt or summer torrents. After they signed away the mineral rights to tens of thousands of acres, not understanding what they had done, the floods in the canyon posed the additional danger of radioactive contamination from thirty-some uranium mines up along its rims.

A familiar pattern of cultural degradation ensued as this century wore on. Government agencies kept whittling away the Havasupai's shrinking land base. They abandoned their traditional subsistence pattern and, surviving on soda, stale beans, and coffee lowered into the canyon by cable, grew up bloated and diabetic. The children were taken out of the canyon after second grade for schooling, and their families disintegrated. Around 1970 hippies tripping in the Grand Canyon turned them on to marijuana. Patches of "sacred weed" (cannabis) started appearing in side canyons. The subadult generation, like the Hopi, got into reggae in a big way in 1975 (the Zuñi were more drawn to heavy metal), growing dreadlocks and staying stoned most of the time. The songs about going home to a lost homeland, to the way things used to be, resonated. Rastafarianism became the new revitalization movement. Navajo like my friend Tom call the Havasupai black Indians, and Havasu Canyon Little Jamaica. That year the tribe sued successfully to get some of its land on the rim back and was awarded three million dollars in damages to boot. Suddenly there was plenty of money to buy dope and to bring hot reggae bands up from Jamaica. One white guy brought down a pound of dope, and the young heads of the tribe took the dope and turned him over to the tribal police. In 1987 a young white woman on assignment for *Reggae Beat* was kidnapped by a drunken chief.

This was two years after I went down to the canyon with my family, which was like, as Tom puts it, "going down to the fourth level. You see all this water, start smelling all this vegetation." But if it was Eden, it was a spoiled Eden, like Tahiti or Negril, Jamaica—part paradise, part ghetto. Our boys, five and six, dashed down the switchbacks from Hualapai Hilltop, where we left the car. It was eight miles down to the village of Supai. The trail followed a draw with occasional clear algae-rimmed pools from the last rain. Spadefoot tadpoles were swimming in the pools. They were most vulnerable to ravens, a girl who caught up with us at Crystal Cataract Creek told us. She was returning from Gallup with her Hopi girlfriend. Several boys on horses, naked from the waist up, with long, flowing black hair cinched by red bandannas, trotted briskly by. They were superb riders, one with their mounts. One of them told me about his cannabis patch and how he and his friends sometimes ate jimsonweed "to see what happens."

Next morning we hang out at the 196-foot waterfall that plunges from a ledge of redwall limestone into stepped clear blue-green pools, some of them twenty feet deep, with minnows cruising on the bottom, rimmed with travertine (calcium carbonate precipitating from the water, coating leaves, twigs, and other debris on the edges of the pools, and hardening). In the woods downstream, there is a campground where young budget travelers from Europe, mostly, have pitched their tents. A few weeks earlier, an Australian girl was raped in the woods. There were several tourist rapes on the trail a few years ago, the missionary told us yesterday. Large four-wing dragonflies and red-spotted purple butterflies with iridescent blue hind wings cruise among wild celery and cattails tipped with two-and-a-half-foot, brown, sausage-like spikes. I chew several of the long yellow stringbeanlike pods trembling on a honey mesquite bush until their sweetness is gone and spit out the tasteless quids. An orange danaid, not a monarch, but a more semitropical queen, coasts over a bed of (introduced) watercress. Under roots dripping down the bank, an arresting black-and-white-banded snake, a little constrictor even of rattlers, pleased to meet you bro king snake.

By noon the pools are filled with tourists coptered in for the day. A real desecration. A bloated young longhair on a rock gives us the hairy eyeball, as if his eyes were daggers. My wife in her bathing suit is uneasy. Just as when we ride out next morning and are followed by two short, stocky guys who have no waists, like bears. We have hired three mounts from a guy named Beamus Oqualla, whom we found in the village watching his mother-in-law's TV. She bought a used dish in Las Vegas. Beamus looks and acts thirty-five but is only twenty-three. He seems completely reliable, a 100 percent *sincero,* unlike the wasted freaks behind us. He takes my oldest boy, André; I take Nick. In October, Beamus tells me, he's going up to the rim to hunt mustangs in the sage-and-juniper prairie. He'll stay up there through March picking piñon nuts, then he'll bring down the horses and get them nice and fat for summer and plant corn, squash, melons, and tomatoes at Peach Springs. As we say our goodbyes at the car, he invites me to "come back and we'll chase the wild ones." I've always meant to take him up, but one thing or another has gotten in the way.

We follow the tribal cop car with two disorderlies in back who are going to the cooler.

Eight years later, I am trying to retrieve that brief visit. I thumb through my little stack of books on the tribe. One is called *Havsuw 'Baaja: People of the Blue-Green Water* and is by Stephen Hirst, who lived with the Havasupai for a decade as an adviser to the tribal council and really got down with them. The book is published by the tribe and is a beautiful and illuminating portrait of one of the Southwest's native cultures. I learn from it that whites are *hay gu.* Hirst tells how a Havasupai named Clark Jack took his wife, Ethel, to spend the winter of 1942 to 1943 at the place where she grew up with her grandfather, which was about to be appropriated by the park:

> Ethel became gravely ill after her stay at the Place Below the Spruce trees and began to sink despairingly week by week. Her father called the healer Allen Akaba to help her, and four times Allen Akaba came to her to sing and take the sorrow and sickness from her soul. On the fourth visit he placed an eagle feather in her hair and said he could do no more. That night Ethel felt she must die and began to slip away. While she

was unconscious that night she heard horses coming up the canyon from the falls. Soon she saw two horses arrive and stand outside the house, a sorrel and a beautiful, slim gray horse. Her father went out to them and soon called her to come out and mount the gray. She asked weakly how she could do that. He told her she must come out to the horses by herself and told her to walk slowly and she could make it. She found she could rise then, and when she reached the gray it knelt like a cow so she could mount it. Then it stood.

Her father held the horse while he gave her last-minute instructions. He gave her a quirt but told her just to hold it and not to touch the horse with it or say anything to the horse, for it knew where to take her. He told her she would never be ill again and released the horse. Ethel says the horse rose into the air and began to travel through the sky toward the east. Before long she could see a place below with many houses and lights. Grass and trees grew everywhere. Never had she seen such a place. She says it appeared that she was seeing it through a bird's eye as she descended. Then she was standing among the trees in a wonderful place, smiling. Then her dream ended, and she awoke in her father's house in Havasu Canyon. She remembers she felt reborn.

Another gemlike oasis that the Indians picked up on is the Cochise stronghold, in the Dragoon Mountains, east of Tucson. The Dragoons are a highly eroded porphyry formation with a lot of hiding places—canyons, arroyos, crevices, box canyons, rincons, canyon defiles—where the Apache could hide and, playing with acoustics, throw off pursuing the U.S. Cavalry. Cochise, born in 1812, 1815, 1823, or 1824, was the great leader of a band of Chiricahua, who became the implacable enemy of the Cavalry because of an incident known as the Bascom Affair at Apache Pass, about thirty miles east of the Dragoons. This was one of the band's seasonal hideouts—a lush haven for all kinds of life, we realized when we cased it a few days after coming out of Havasu Canyon. A bobcat with one of her young crossed the road and disappeared into a thicket, followed by a deer a hundred yards on. Down to the left, a perennial stream purled among syacamore pines, Mexican piñons, Arizona cypresses, sixty-five-foot-tall alligator junipers (so named for their rectangular-plated, deeply furrowed bark), and assorted hardwoods—tall silverleaf oaks, tomey oaks, Arizona white oaks whose limbs were deformed by mistletoe, pointleaf manzanitas whose berries resemble small apples and are relished by bears, birds, and javelinas. In this ambrosial microclimate the band had everything it needed. The Chiricahua ate mesquite pods and sun-dried the fleshy fruits of banana and mountain yuccas, grinding them into small cakes that helped see them through winter. They brewed a beverage from the fuzzy red fruit of the skunkbush, a nonpoisonous relative of poison ivy. Wait-a-minute, or catclaw, acacia was an excellent honey-producing plant. The cabbagelike bases of the wispy-stalked sotols had sap with high sugar content. (Sotol is fermented in Mexico to produce an alcoholic beverage of that name.) Cracks in the rock were crammed with cliff-brake ferns; cane cholla, or tassajo; canyon grape; prickly pear with bristly figlike red tunas; coral-bean bushes whose scarlet seeds the Chiricahua wore as charms; sacahuiste, or bear grass. Hawks, vultures, and an eagle soared over tilted, segmented pillars and spires of lemon-yellow porphyry, spattered with lime-green lichen and intruded by weathered domes of stronghold granite.

We sat at a picnic table with eighty-year-old Dick Shaw, a local cowboy, who regaled us with Cochise stories. One was about how President Grant got tired of the attrition Cochise was causing and sent Thomas Jeffords to make peace with him. Jeffords had been trying to resurrect the main service of the Pony Express, sixteen of whose riders had been killed by Indians, and had learned the Apache smoke code. Riding into the Dragoons, he sent up "one man comes in peace," then he sat down, fired up his pipe, and waited. Before long a voice behind him asked in Spanish (which was still the lingua franca of the frontier), "What do you want?"

"I just want to talk to you," Jeffords replied.

"Unbuckle your gun," the voice said, and Jeffords did so and said, "If we don't come to an agreement, I expect to leave here alive." A three-day conference ensued. From then on the Pony Express had a Chiricahua escort through their country. They rode parallel to it, just out of sight, to make sure it wasn't attacked by other Indians. "The Apache were the epitome of freedom," Shaw told us.

Cochise's principal wife was Dos-teh-seh, the daughter of Mangas Colorados, and she was said to have had the gift of the power; the life force of the universe would suddenly come upon her, without the help of sacred plants or a vision quest. John Gregory Bourke, the author of *On the Border with Crook,* about the campaign to bring in Geronimo, met Cochise and describes him as

> a fine looking Indian of about fifty winters, straight as a rush—six feet in stature, deep chested, roman nosed, black eyes, firm mouth, a kindly and even somewhat melancholy expression tempering the determined look of his countenance. He seemed much more neat than the other wild

Indians I have seen and his manners were very gentle. There
was neither in speech or action any of the bluster characteristic of his race.

This was in 1872, when Cochise "expressed his own earnest desire for
peace."

The Bascom Affair was set off by an 1860 Apache raid during which
an eleven-year-old, half-Irish, half-Mexican boy named Mickey Free
was taken captive. Cochise was suspected, but he was innocent,
although he had participated in other depredations. In January 1861,
Second Lieutenant George Nicholas Bascom was sent to Apache Pass
with fifty-four men to recover the boy. When Cochise appeared with
his wife and son and two nephews to deliver some wood to the soldiers, Bascom held them hostage for the return of the boy, but Cochise
cut through the tent with a knife and escaped, and he took hostages to
secure the release of the others. The bluecoats released Cochise's wife
and child, but hanged his nephews. Cochise retaliated by killing his
captives and then went on the warpath, vowing to kill all whites in Arizona. At that time, the Butterfield Trail, which was the transcontinen-
tal route for mail and stages, was in Confederate territory. (The route
was later moved north, through Nebraska and Wyoming.) Cochise
made a pact with Jeffords to protect the traffic on it, but remained hostile to all other whites until 1872, when he and his people were given
the Dragoons and the Chiricahua Mountains, to the east, for their
homeland. He died two years later.

Cochise is now a county; the Apache is a car, along with the
Comanche and the Navajo; "Geronimo" is what paratroopers cry
when they jump from planes; and English is the lingua franca of the
Southwest: what Navajo called a ramada a few generations back is
now an "arbor." Converting the Indians to counties and cars was the
final step in the Anglos' onslaught, in a process traced by Gerald D.
Nash's book *The American West in the Twentieth Century: A Short
History of an Urban Oasis*. Starting in 1898 and over the next three-
quarters of a century, forty million Americans and at least eight million
foreigners poured across the Mississippi, bringing eastern culture, con-
ceptions of social and ethnic status, the American faith in science and
technology, a desire for material gain, and a rapacious attitude toward
the exploitation of natural resources. "Their supreme confidence in the
superiority of their values led them to look somewhat askance at existing cultures in the region," writes Nash, "those of the Indians, Spanish-
Americans, and Mexicans." Even those trying to escape the European

mind-set and to reinvent themselves brought it with them and ended up reproducing and imposing it.

Between 1898 and the start of World War II, Nash argues, the West was like a colony of the East. The war liberated the West and ushered in the progressive era, in which the West became the pacesetter. But even earlier, between 1895 and 1905, there was a wave of wealthy and intelligent newcomers, with civic vision, enterprise, talent, intellect— "boosters" who arrived not in covered wagons but in Pullman cars and founded chambers of commerce. They included lungers—consumptives and asthmatics.

From 1905 to the First World War, retirees from the Midwest poured in. They didn't want the big-city life, they didn't want to live in apartments but in houses, and re-created cities that were sprawling versions of the small towns where they had spent their productive years. The proliferation of these modern urban oases was made possible by a number of technological strides. A billion-dollar citrus industry blossomed in California, thanks to the refrigerator car and to irrigation systems that employed the deep-well, oil-fired pump to bring up groundwater.

From 1912 on, the motorcar ushered in the era of long-distance travel. Automobile clubs were formed; lobbies for paved roads descended on Washington. The West became the playground of America and, with the opening of the Panama Canal and the closing of the frontier, increasingly independent of the East. Grand hotels went up, like the Brown Palace in Denver and—the grandest, with 750 rooms— the Coronado in San Diego. The railroads built spurs to the spectacular national parks, the colorful Indians and Hispanics. Well-dressed, superbly trained waitresses and tour guides known as Harvey Girls took visitors around. The Harvey Girls occupied, in Nash's estimation, "as exalted a place in the mythology of American womanhood as airline stewardesses of a later age. Many of them married leading citizens of the West."

From the twenties on, 96 percent of the westward migration was to cities, particularly to Los Angeles. Runaways, con men, mystics, freaks, mental outlaws, aspiring movie stars and starlets, and others— a high proportion of whom were over forty-five, many bringing midwestern biases and attitudes—came to L.A. Some spilled over the mountains into Denver, Salt Lake City, Phoenix, Albuquerque. The cafeteria—a large self-service restaurant that was, according to Nash, a twentieth-century version of the Wild West saloon—made its first appearance in Los Angeles in 1912. It was well suited to older, mobile, rootless people of lower-middle-class rural background. Cafeterias were friendlier, less formal, and cheaper eating places than regular restaurants, and soon they became the hub of social life for the over-fifty, transplanted midwesterners, many of whom were "dries" and eschewed bars. "The informality of the cafeterias was especially appealing to ex-farmers or small townsmen, for in the twenties many cafeterias exhibited all the aspects of an indoor picnic," Nash writes. Cemeteries and other businesses catering to the dead flourished. The unusual attention devoted to pets and their care was a reflection of the large number of childless people.

Los Angeles became the world's first city on wheels, and from it high-speed multilane roads known as freeways shot off in every direction. Suburbanization and real estate speculation on the "Los Angeles pattern" created collections of villages knit by the automobile that were essentially Los Angeles clones in Albuquerque, Phoenix, Tucson, El Paso. In 1936 the California architect Cliff May unveiled the low-slung, one-story "ranch house," which became the quintessential suburban residence. Its features included a family room or den and a patio for outdoor entertaining.

But there was considerable social malaise in the new suburbs. People on the same block were often complete strangers. Loneliness, divorce, delinquency, high suicide and murder rates, susceptibility to cults, evangelists and faith healers, were common aspects of this hollow, transplanted existence. Shopping centers geared to car customers displaced downtown pedestrian shopping districts. Fast-food joints, gas stations, tourist courts, motor courts, and other plebeian establishments to serve the multitudes multiplied. The first gas station, a gas tank on a farm wagon parked at a corner, appeared in Los Angeles in 1909. The hamburger, a spin-off of the car culture, was big in California by 1930. The broiled or fried low-quality ground-beef sandwich had been introduced to America by German vendors at the Louisiana Exposition of 1903; sailors in Hamburg had adapted the Finnish and Estonian practice of eating the red meat raw. The hamburger spawned the roadside drive-in and created a big new market for Plains cattle.

By the twenties the West was getting forty million tourists a year. Most came by car. The rich came to experience "life on the range," to ride horses and dress up in western duds at dude ranches. The post-frontier population derived much of its income from imaging the West that had been. Dying forms of Native American art, many of which had been banned by the Franciscans—weavings, pottery, jewelry, basketwork, kachinas now devoid of religious significance—were revived to sell to the tourists.

Then came the Depression, and the dizzy progress the West had been experiencing ground to a halt. In Oregon, apples were left rotting on trees; sheep were driven over cliffs because it cost more to ship them than what they could be sold for; meanwhile, millions of Americans were starving. Only movies survived. During nine of the years between 1929 and 1939, there was below-average rainfall on the Great Plains. The drought was cumulative, creating severe dust storms by 1935, and in the years that followed, plagues of grasshoppers, which ate everything, filled the sky. Okies poured into California's Central Valley under the illusion that jobs were waiting. In 1939, the California legislature enacted a law prohibiting indigents from entering the state, and for the next two years, until the Supreme Court declared the law unconstitutional, the state police turned back travelers unable to give evidence of property or wealth.

A recent evolutionary development in the urban oasis is the emergence of ethnic and economic "mafias." In Los Angeles, for instance, the largest oasis and the prototype for the Southwest, a Philippino mafia controls health-care services; a Chinese mafia is big in real estate and import-export; Koreans are also big in real estate and in mom-and-pop stores; Salvadorans have many of the restaurants, along with Mexicans; anything to do with car repairs or landscaping is usually Mexican; Haitians drive the cabs; Chicanos have thousands of small businesses and own a big part of the city, especially East L.A.; African Americans have integrated into the white corporate world or remain in the ghetto underclass. The future and the entrepreneurial energy of the oases are increasingly in the hands of immigrants, as is the case with North American cities in general.

Watering the Oases

During the twenties, Los Angeles added a hundred thousand new residents a year to its population of two million or so, straining the water supply. The Owens River was diverted; scientific and occult rainmakers and Indian medicine men were consulted. Rainmaking had come a long way since the sixteenth century, when French and Italian adherents of the concussion theory, believing that thunder produced rain, attempted to jar and wring precipitation from the skies by firing cannons and pealing church bells. But it was, and still is, an imprecise science. The Dyrenforth expedition of 1892 attempted to make rain by exploding charges from the ground and from balloons. The Australian rain doctor, con man, and gambler Frank Melbourne charged $150 to $500, releasing chemicals previously unknown to science at fairs and promising results in three days. He picked his rain dates according to the weather forecasts in popular almanacs.

The modern approach to rainmaking is weather modification by cloud seeding. There was a lot of talk about it during the drought years of the eighties; since then there has been less. But a spokesman for the Bureau of Land Management's Project Skywater remained enthusiastic about cloud seeding, which he told me is "the only viable alternative we have for increasing water in the West. Increasing the snowpack has many unique and attractive features and is the most cost-effective way of securing extra water. It doesn't require major, permanent construction; you do it as you need it. What you do," he explained, "is seed winter orographic storms to increase the amount of snow on the high mountainous watersheds. There's a potential for a ten-to-fifteen-percent increase in the West's water supply. The annual potential for water augmentation of the Upper Colorado Basin is 1.4 million acre-feet; of the Lower Basin, three hundred thousand. This would augment the economy by $136.6 million annually from hydroelectric and energy production, $54.9 million from salinity reduction, and $48.5 million from additional water supplies."

The way cloud seeding works, the spokesman explained, is that "supercooled droplets form supercooled clouds as moist air flows over mountain barriers. If the droplets freeze, they fall as snow. If their concentration is too low for precipitation, you seed the clouds with dry ice and/or silver-iodide crystals; you fly into a storm center with a turbo-prop jet and inject silver iodide into the clouds to increase their efficiency." The pilot cloud-seeding project took place on the Mogollon Rim in 1987. Nine years before that, ten propane-fueled generators sprayed silver-iodide crystals along fifty miles of the San Gabriel Mountains and were so effective at increasing cloud efficiency that they were blamed for severe storms, floods, landslides, twenty deaths, and forty-three million dollars of damage.

But most of the water for the Southwest's urban oases comes from rivers, especially from the Colorado. The Colorado Compact, signed in 1922 between the seven states that draw its water, decreed that half of its flow must pass through Lees Ferry, Arizona (downstream from Glen Canyon and above the Grand Canyon; for many years the main crossing of the central Colorado, Lee's Ferry was run by the same John Doyle Lee who had organized the Mountain Meadows Massacre of 1857 until his execution by a firing squad twenty years later), to be shared by Nevada, Arizona, and California. Colorado was entitled to 52 percent of the remainder, and the rest was shared with the other Upper Basin states—Wyoming, Utah, and New Mexico.

In 1928 construction began on the Boulder Dam, later renamed the Hoover Dam, below Grand Canyon. Four diversion tunnels were blasted through a box canyon. Workers were killed by falling rocks, explosives, electrocution, heat prostration. Some days it was so hot you could almost fry an egg on the bare rock. Whores operated from shacks, and the unemployed camped nearby, waiting for someone to die. At its completion in 1935, the dam was the largest in the world, a multistate water reserve that provided irrigation for the vast truck farms in the Imperial Valley, augmented Los Angeles's supply, and generated hydropower for the entire Southwest. "The first of the world's truly great dams," as Marc Reisner describes it, the Hoover Dam "rose in the depths of the Depression and carried America's spirits with it," and it would give engineers confidence to dam the Columbia, the Volga, the Paraná, the Nile, the Zambezi.

The Colorado is not even one of the world's twenty-five largest rivers. Its annual discharge, for the purposes of the Colorado Compact, was calculated at 17.5 million acre-feet, but this figure was the product of eighteen years of imprecise measurement, during which the river had "gone on a binge" three out of every four years; the actual volume is more like 15 million. During the drought years of the thirties, it dropped down to about 10 million. About 2 million evaporate each year from all the reservoirs on the main stem and its tributaries. Close to 40 million are stored in reservoirs in the Lower Basin such as Lake Havasu, Theodore Roosevelt Lake, Apache Lake, Bartlett Dam and San Carlos Reservoir, and Lake Mead, the largest artificial body of water on earth, which holds 28 million. Of the 8.75 million that have to pass through Lees Ferry, 4.4 million are allotted to California, which by 1930 already had almost 6 million people. Arizona gets 2.8 million, Nevada only 300,000, and Mexico is supposed to get a million and a half.

But Arizona wasn't prepared to put in the expensive water-moving infrastructure to make full use of its entitlement until 1992. Until this happened, California "borrowed" the unused surplus, constructing an aqueduct that provided Los Angeles with another 700,000, and Phoenix relied for its water on the Salt River, a tributary of the Gila, one of the Colorado's main feeders. In the 1890s Phoenix experienced a severe drought, and water was so scarce that armed men patroled the canals, some of them revived from the Hohokam system, that fed the emerging city. At least a third of the 200,000 acres of irrigated farm-land "was forced out of cultivation," Jay J. Wagoner writes, "livestock died, orchards became like firewood, and families packed up and left." When the rain finally came, it fell in buckets, washing out the brush diversion dam on the Salt and compounding the disaster. A large storage dam on the Salt that would provide a dependable water supply was obviously needed.

There was a good site where Tonto Creek came in, except that it was remote, requiring 112 miles of access road. In 1901 the Salt's flow was down to 800 miner's inches (a miner's inch is roughly 11.5 gallons per minute passing a given point), and after a settlement was reached with local farmers and eleven water companies, who had prior water rights on the river, construction of what was to be the world's highest dam began in 1903. The construction town of Roosevelt, now under Roosevelt Lake, created by the Roosevelt Dam, was unusually tame and orderly. No saloons, gambling halls, or houses of ill repute were allowed on the main street. Men outnumbered women three to one, and to avoid fights at the dance hall, each man was given a tag. Numbers one through twenty got the first dance, one through forty the next, and so on. The dam took five years to complete. One of the seventeen men who died during its construction was the German-born Indian scout Al Siebert, who was trying to save some Apache under his supervision from a rock slide. Siebert had served under Generals Crook, Stoneman, and Miles in the Geronimo and other campaigns. Working with Hualapai allies, he was considered relatively successful at keeping the Apache in line because, as he explained, "When I tell 'em I'm going to kill 'em, I do it, and when I tell 'em I'm their friend, they know it." Now, with the frontier era over, he and his Apache friends had no choice but to work for the technology that was destroying it—a final humiliation, dealing the coup de grâce to their way of life themselves.

The Salt River Project eventually provided Phoenix with 2.3 million acre-feet, which was the Salt's historical flow. California argued that since this water was being diverted from the Colorado, it should be deducted from Arizona's entitlement, and in 1952 began construction on yet another aqueduct. But Arizona took California to the Supreme Court, which upheld Arizona's right to 2.8 million acre-feet from the Upper Basin, ruling that the Salt was an internal state river and its diverted flow should not be deducted from the entitlement. As a result of this dispute, the Central Arizona Project (CAP), to finally make use of the state's entitlement and deliver it to Phoenix and Tucson, was born. The project was incredibly expensive: the Bridge Canyon Dam alone, at the point where the Colorado was to be diverted, cost a billion dollars. The aqueduct was built in three segments, each with a different name, totaling 336 miles. It starts at Lake Havasu and ends 14 miles south of Tucson. Fourteen pumping stations lift the water a total of 3,000 feet, and for every hundred units of energy required to lift the water, only seventy-five can be recovered by hydroelectric generation on the way down. So this muddy water from the Colorado ends up costing farmers around Tucson $135 an acre-foot, while they can buy clean, pure groundwater from the aquifer for $30. But the aqueduct has taken some of the pressure off the aquifers, helped solve the groundwater overdraft problem. Eventually, when all systems are online, it will deliver 1.5 million acre-feet.

But as a result of the CAP, southern California, which had been using 5.8 million acre-feet under the "use it or lose it" principle, now has to cut back to its 4.4 million entitlement and is desperately casting about for new sources of water. Hardest hit is San Diego. The last I heard, San Diego was looking to buy 500,000 acre-feet a year of Colorado River water from a private company called the Galloway Group, which was planning to build a dam in the Upper Basin. This was a legally acceptable way—by invoking the law of prior appropriation—of getting around the restrictions on the Colorado water available to California.

Flying into Phoenix in 1985 with my family to begin research on my "hydrohistory," I find myself sitting next to a man from Nebraska who is going to Lake Havasu to save his daughter's marriage to a mechanic. We can see from the air how the city was sited where the Salt and the Verde Rivers flow into the Gila, and open, concrete-lined canals distribute water from the two tributaries, which provide 60 percent of Phoenix's supply.

"Sure are a lot of swimming pools down there," observes the Nebraskan. Appended to condos, in pie-shaped lots behind ranch houses, from the air they look like bathtubs. There are also dozens of golf courses (as of 1993 there were 108 and counting) in the Valley of the Sun that collectively use enough water to "replicate a rainforest," according to an article in the hard-hitting, since-defunct Tucson-based City magazine. Greens and fairways are as thirsty as cotton, requiring 5 acre-feet a year per acre, "but look at the upside," a booster of Arizona golf countered. "The 7.6 million rounds of golf played in Arizona annually bring the state eight hundred million dollars, and it's a clean industry. The water is piped over from the Colorado, hundreds of miles to the West. The Sonoran Desert wasn't going to get it anyway. If anything, these courses are taking water from the ones in San Diego County, which depends on a downstream diversion and has been on severe water rations for the last few years."

The swimming pools are in many cases probably more totemic than functional—symbols of the fifties' good life the way the Jacuzzi became the dolce vita statement of the eighties. I wonder how many swims they actually get—and each of them loses about an inch a day to evaporation. Today probably a lot more, because on this August 6, it's 120 degrees in the shade. It's so hot people fear to venture out-of-doors. One man, I hear over the radio of our taxi, was found this morning on the street, dead of apparent dehydration. Phoenix has slowed down like a city in the North hit by a blizzard. There have been record demands on electricity for air conditioners; the schools have let out early; the matinees at the movie houses are packed; boysenberries are cooking right on their branches; planes are running ninety minutes late. (In the summer of '91 it will be so hot Phoenix airport will close because of the danger of incoming planes skidding on the melted tarmac.) "This is just like Baghdad," our taxi driver, an Iraqi, tells us.

Forest fires are breaking out all over the West. The heat is like a hair dryer blowing in your face, like a microwave oven.

Few cities have such vast horizontality as "the blob that ate Arizona," as Edward Abbey describes Phoenix. During the winter inversion, the blob is enveloped in smog, most of it vehicular in origin. We drive past a subdivision, glimpsing multilevel gambrel roofs of red and Gatorade-green tiles over a high wall. A sign out front proclaims: LUXURY GOLF COURSE LIVING AT L'ELYSEE.

The groundwater in the Valley of the Sun, developers soon discovered, was close to the surface, in the root zone, but since the forties it has been going down in some places six to eight feet a year, and now it is three hundred feet down. Most of the pumping has been from deep wells for irrigation; during World War II the federal government put pressure on Phoenix to produce crops. With progressive overdraft of groundwater, there has been land subsidence. One spot in the suburb of Florence has subsided twelve feet.

We've taken a condo for a few days at a development called Fountain Hills, which boasts the world's tallest fountain. The fountain is in the *Guinness Book of World Records*. Every fifteen minutes, daily, starting at 10 a.m., it sends up into the clear blue, water-sucking Arizona sky a snow-white, 560-foot jet of recycled irrigation water, which is more than three times as high as Old Faithful and five feet higher than the Washington Monument. The man who thought up this insolent symbol of man transcending his environment is Robert McCullough Sr. of the chain-saw family. McCullough also brought the original London Bridge to Lake Havasu City. Lake Havasu was created so Robert McCullough could test his outboard motors, his flak person tells me. He hired C. V. Wood, the theme-park specialist who did Disneyland, to build a tourist attraction around the bridge.

In 1980, the tenth anniversary of Fountain Hills, the population was about fifty-five hundred and was almost exclusively midwestern. The initial appeal was to retirees, but now young professionals are the target market, and the lots are going fast. The development also has a connection with White Castle burgers, which were started in Chicago by McCullough's father. Two hundred thousand of these burgers a day are eaten nationwide. The White Castle burger franchise at Fountain Hills does a brisk business and helps the midwesterners feel at home.

I shoot a round of golf with two young longhaired Pima who work as hod carriers for the construction company that is building the homes. The land Fountains Hills is on belonged to their tribe. Mike Villapondo ("See—I even got a modern last name," he ribs me) is married to a Hopi from Second Mesa. He can't speak Pima, but his buddy Delmar speaks a little. Both have excellent hand-to-eye coordination. Delmar tells me the Pima used to play a game called *tokka,* which consisted of knocking around a braided leather ball with a tamarack stick, so golf isn't foreign to him at all.

The flak person tells me that the Fountain Hills groundwater is the underflow of the Verde River—or at least no one can prove that it isn't—and is thus appropriable. But the Salt River Project claims right to the water and is also pumping it from a deep well below Roosevelt Dam. "The future of the Fountain Hills pump water is clouded," he says. I wonder how much of this situation has been alleviated by the subsequent arrival to Phoenix of hundreds of thousands of acre-feet of Colorado River water.

The following fall of 1986, a woman in Denver alerted me to a situation on the South Platte River, where the Denver Water Company was planning to build a dam that would flood a beautiful mountain canyon and wipe out a rare subspecies of butterfly known as the Pawnee montane skipper, whose only known habitat is in the canyon. The environmental-impact assessment for the proposed dam had kept four hundred people working full-time for two years. It still wasn't finished and had already cost a staggering $36.6 million. I remembered being impressed twenty years earlier that the main form of recreation for Denver's retirees seemed to be watering their lawns. I had driven down Pennsylvania Avenue late one afternoon, and dozens of old people were out in front of the houses, directing streams from handheld hoses. At the time, I hadn't realized the environmental implications of this.

Denver depends mainly on Colorado water, and getting it there, so the city could get its share of the state's entitlement, had required incredible feats of engineering. The Continental Divide had to be bored through, and the water shot through tunnels and flumes, down sophisticated canals, from one drainage to another. But even with the longest water tunnel in the world, the Harold D. Roberts Tunnel, these "transmountain diversions" were not sufficient, according to the Denver Water Company's calculations of the city's projected water needs. Denver lies east of the Front Range, in the Rockies' rain shadow. It gets only fifteen inches a year, and there had been explosive growth in its suburbs; a rash of condo subdivisions had gone up to house the employees and families of the area's big defense industry and other federal agencies. The architecture of the condos and the malls that serviced them harked back to Colorado's mining towns, the regional counterpart of New Mexico's ersatz-pueblo, Kansas's ersatz–grain-elevator, and Vermont's ersatz–country store, condo–mall architecture. Others were attracted by the close-to-year-round recreational facilities, and in the last few years Denver had enjoyed a boom, becoming the hub of the High Plains and the Rocky Mountain region.

I drove out to the canyon. It had a beautiful dam site, where it became very narrow. There were three other dams on the South Platte already. Did Denver really need to sacrifice this beautiful mountain valley for another one, to keep its lawns and golf courses green? Was this another example of the Army Corps of Engineers reclamation mania that has ruined some of the West's pristine watersheds? But on the other hand, did the problem really require a thirty-six-million-dollar environmental-impact statement? The butterfly itself, I discovered, was small and drab olive-orange, with a wingspan of less than an inch. So well camouflaged was it as it zipped from one nectar plant to another that you could hardly even see it. The dam would wipe out most of the subspecies, which boasted only several thousand individuals. A local bighorn sheep herd would also be adversely affected by the project, and the reduced flow of the South Platte would affect birds way downstream in Nebraska, such as the whooping and the sandhill cranes, the locally endangered interior least tern, and the locally threatened piping plover. Denver would get another ninety-eight thousand acre-feet, but even fish in rivers on the Rockies west slope would be impacted by the diversion, such as the endangered bonytail chub, the humpback chub, the Colorado squawfish, and the state-endangered but not federally listed razorback sucker in the Colorado River. It was to spell out these and other repercussions through the ecosystem that the impact statement's millions of words and elaborate charts were devoted.

I scrambled up a rill-streaked slope of loose, orange nuggets too fine and firm to be called scree, but not organically developed enough to be soil, with Scott Ellis, a young ecologist with the firm that was overseeing the statement. Ellis called the nuggets Grape-Nuts. The vanilla odor of ponderosa pine mingled with the pungence of fringed sage. A goshawk was hovering over the sunny, south-facing slope. Grasshoppers were crepitating—snapping wings to attract mates—among Plains prickly pears. Ellis pointed out one of the skippers—a barely visible female on a spike of blue grama grass. "All right! I think's she's going to oviposit," he exclaimed. "This has only been seen a few times. Come on, baby." The females produce 560 to 1,000 big pearly-white eggs during their brief lifetime. We watched and waited, but no egg. "Damn! That's what's so frustrating," Ellis continued. "They sit and flit around all day and nothing happens."

In the end, the dam was shot down, but the butterfly had nothing to do with it. It was listed as threatened but not endangered and was not the deciding factor. The Environmental Protection Agency got involved and made the call, and President Bush backed its ruling that the water company's estimates were inflated and that the canyon was too beautiful to lose, and this stretch of the South Platte was declared a Category One Wild and Scenic River. Already in 1984, each Denverite was using an average of 221 gallons of water a day. As I drove around between appointments the following afternoon, wherever I looked, fans of fine spray were arcing slowly over glistening greenswards; jets were spurting, flicking in revolutions. One biologist had argued that if Denver's Kentucky-bluegrass lawns were replaced with native buffalo grass, that alone would have obviated the need for the dam.

Albuquerque: Our Oasis for a While

The decision to spend the 1991–92 academic year in Albuquerque was typically last minute. I had friends in Tucson and knew only one couple in this friendly, laid-back oasis of five hundred thousand that sprawls from the base of the Sandia Mountains to the other side of the Rio Grande. But at the end of July the University of New Mexico invited me to be a visiting scholar in its department of communications. It was a loose appointment. There were no teaching responsibilities, no money or housing, but I did get a pass to the libraries and membership to the university's two magnificent golf courses at the reduced faculty rate. All I had to do was give the Earth Day speech.

Before we set out, over the phone I attempted to rent a "faculty-preferred" house, with four bedrooms, two VCRs, and a gardener who came once a week, from an elderly academic couple who were taking a sabbatical in India for a year. The real estate broker who was handling the listing was named Sandra. She had a German accent and was all business, and she said no pets. So we reluctantly agreed to leave our dog with the people who were renting our house in upstate New York. Sandra said the owners would prefer no children either, but I said I had two boys, and they were coming; there was no play there. I brought Sandra down from sixteen to twelve hundred a month, and we made a verbal agreement, but a few hours later she called back to say she had run a credit report on me and learned that over the past couple of years I had let several car payments go for more than thirty days, so she was sorry, but the deal was off. I offered to pay the whole eight months' rent up front, but it was still no go. "You don't have a credit-worthy profile," Sandra explained.

So we hit Albuquerque completely cold, blowing into town like microscopic airborne eggs of fairy shrimp from some distant evaporated rain puddle, tumbling in like airy tops of tumbleweed, or perhaps more germanely, we rode in like latter-day pioneers in a red Ford Explorer utility wagon and a Chevy Cheyenne truck instead of a Conestoga or a prairie wagon—having been sucked west for three days along inter-states by the slipstreams of eighteen-wheel semis; Nick and I were in the truck and André and my wife were in the Explorer. We kept in touch by CB radio.

We started out renting one of the Executive Suites, right off I-25—two bedrooms, bar with fridge, TV, but no cooking facilities, sixty-five dollars a day—and put our stuff in a self-storage space up the road. A few days later, I read in the Albuquerque *Journal* a customer at this same self-storage place smelled a putrid odor coming from under the door of one of the other spaces and called the police, who came and broke the lock. Inside were the bloated remains of a man who had driven in with his car and left it running and died of asphyxiation. It was a puzzling case: it couldn't be called suicide, because someone had locked the man in the storage space from the outside, nor could it be considered murder, because he presumably could have turned off the engine. Perhaps it was an assisted suicide.

By this late date, with the fall term about to start, the good rentals were gone. The best place we could find was a two-bedroom apart-ment on Jefferson Avenue in a funky old mansion that had been stuc-coed over to look like an adobe—"chocolate sauced," as a Santa Fe friend describes the process—and was now surrounded by two-story low-rent apartment buildings. The rent was very reasonable—three sixty a month. The living room had a window with a fine view of San-dia Peak to work from. And most important, the address was in the district of what was said to be the best middle school in Albuquerque, Jefferson, so we took it and entered the boys.

The following night, at Furr's Cafeteria (four bucks, all you can eat), we met the man who would become Nick's soccer coach. Soccer is very big in Albuquerque. It is a way for parents to keep tabs on their kids, and for the kids it is either soccer or hanging out at the mall and maybe ending up in a gang. There aren't many choices for a teenager in El Burque. A hundred thousand Albuquerqueans—one out of every five—are said to belong to a gang. Many of them own handguns and semiautomatic assault rifles, and the police are nervously aware that if they all joined forces, they could take over the city. Luckily they prefer to fight among themselves. In the fall of 1991 there was a ten-thirty curfew in the South Valley and out at Rio Rancho, the most gang-infested parts of town.

Every week or so a drive-by shooting would be written up in the city's two papers, the *Journal* and the *Tribune*. "Drive-by shootings are part of gang life," explained Clarence "Pee Wee" Kennedy, a young black in the Bloods gang who was arrested for having popped Dominique Velasquez of the Crips in front of the Lotaburger on Coors Boulevard. "It was wrong, but when you're in a gang that kind of stuff happens."

The drive-by-shooting phenomenon should probably also be placed in the context of the drive-up culture. Money, booze, food, a last look at a departed loved one—most of the basic human needs can be taken care of from your car in El Burque.

Jefferson was the least gang-ridden middle school in the Albuquerque system. Nevertheless, the previous April, Evangeline Martinez, fourteen, had stabbed a fellow Jefferson student, thirteen-year-old Joalla Moares, once in the heart in a parking lot after school. (She was later acquitted of murder charges on the ground of self-defense.) There were two relatively benign gangs at the school, the Skaters and the Lowriders, and no one was under any pressure to join either of them. The girlfriends of the Lowriders wore skyscraper hairdos and were known as *cholas*. "They travel in flocks," André told me, "and block the halls and if you even nick them they say, 'Hey. Get out of my way. Watch where you goin', or I get my boyfren' to bea' you up.'"

A young woman from Las Cruces and her longhaired rock-musician boyfriend rented the apartment below. This was just "a pit stop," she told me. Central Avenue, the staging area for drifters who had just blown into town, the guns and gals street, where black girls in tight leather miniskirts blew kisses at you as you drove by and scientists laid off from military labs brought their guns and VCRs to pawn, was just a few blocks away. The hard-core homeless slept in the cemetery along Yale. On April 26, Kenneth Merriman, a wheelchair-ridden Vietnam vet who lived with his wife and four kids in the Park East Mobile Home Park, off Central, claimed he heard screams in the abandoned Villa In Motel, and he found twenty-six-year-old Brian Lucero sodomizing a three-year-old kid and nearly beat Lucero to death with a baseball bat. The prosecutor said he wouldn't have brought charges against Merriman even if he had killed Lucero.

Across the street from the Circle K on Central, where I picked up my morning paper, was the Heights Beauty College, in whose parking lot late one morning that fall a pretty, aspiring beautician, Cathy Griego, was allegedly kidnapped and killed by a drifter named Derel Wayne Brown. Her body was found in a ravine near Tigre Canyon, out of town. A few weeks later, right in the next block over from our apartment, the police gunned down a man who had violated his parole in Lubbock as he sneaked out the back door with a toy Uzi, which they said they thought was real.

All this was a little too close for comfort, so after a month we upgraded to the beige stucco pseudoadobe on La Hacienda Drive, a quiet street in the university section. I converted the large family room in the back of the house into my study and soon settled into a civilized routine, writing in the morning and hitting the links in the afternoon. Around eleven the postman, whose name was Luis Baca, brought the mail. A Baca cut my hair; another Baca had fixed my phone line. "You Bacas have this place sewed up," I kidded Luis.

I stopped reading *The New York Times*—an important break from the East—and instead took out a subscription to the *Journal*. The longer I stayed in the oasis, the more its news took precedent over the world's. Some random items:

• Great Plains Insurance, who covers our vehicles, collapses and is seized by the state of Nebraska, leaving a trail of bad debts and frustrated policy holders, and thousands of unreimbursed auto-repair and hospital bills.

• Twelve hundred starlings are mysteriously murdered by the pesticide Starlicide. The starling is a varmint, so the local Fish and Wildlife people are not looking deeply into it. If the birds had been bald eagles, it would have been another thing.

• Mayor Luis Saavedra is under investigation for diverting funds from the Technical and Vocational Institute. Former Belen city manager Bonifacio "Bonnie" Lopez is convicted of six counts of embezzling more than two hundred grand of city funds. There are rogue cops, a renegade sheriff, a ninja bank robber who turns out to be a cop; another cop is suspended for forcing a Mexican national he pulled over for a traffic violation to perform oral sex on him.

• Tom Sanders of Santa Clara Pueblo, to the north, is convicted of killing his girlfriend Christine Torres's husband, Roberto, for his life insurance, so they can open a nightclub. "This is as cold a murder as I've ever seen," says the prosecutor. "I mean this thing was polar."

• Deborah Jane Martinez, depressed at her brother's death, stabs her twelve-year-old son to death for playing Nintendo after the funeral, which she sees as an act of disrespect, and is now on suicide watch.

• Two Laotian refugee girls drown at Elephant Butte Reservoir, two hours south, by Truth or Consequences. A third, fourteen-year-old Amphonepeth Chaleunponh, is still clinging to life. The three girls held hands; one of them stepped off a ledge and pulled the other two under. None of them could swim. Two to three hundred Laotian refugees live in Albuquerque.

Off the family room, there was a patio where between stints at the computer screen I would pace or practice my golf swing or set out a jar of sun tea—water with tea bags for the sun to brew. The patio became for me, like the mud walls of Georgia O'Keeffe's Ghost Ranch, a microcosm of the Southwest, a template on which the sun's daily drama played out. A limited number of life-forms made it over the neighbor's wall, many of them attracted to the lilac bush, in one of whose branches I found one morning a dead, two-inch-long, black-and-white beetle.

When the lilacs bloomed that spring, half a dozen painted-lady butterflies came to take nectar from the blossoms. The painted-lady hatch in the Southwest that year was the largest anyone could remember. You'd drive in the desert and dozens of these ornate cosmopolites would be plastered on the windshield. Oregon juncos, and house finches of a color phase I had not seen before—with yellow flanks and the rest salmon pink—would come to the halved three-liter plastic Pepsi bottle I hung upside down and filled with sunflower seeds. An occasional blue-throated hummingbird would zip in for a moment, then buzz off. Inky-cap mushrooms sprouted in the cracks of the concrete. I picked them and sautéed them in butter.

Often, when I was written out, I'd drive over to the university's North Golf Course. My rounds were always elucidating. I had no control over whom I'd be teeing off with, and my partners were a random sampling of Duke City golfers that cut across culture, color, class, age, sex, and tribe. Sometimes I'd hook up with Wayne, who had visited the oasis from Kansas thirty-four years ago and had fallen under its spell and been there ever since. Many had similar stories. One man, headed for Los Angeles on the interstate, had been having a fight with his wife. He had hit her, then full of remorse and thinking, Nothing is worth this, he pulled into Albuquerque; this was twenty years ago, and they were still there. Another, an artist, had been passing through, and his paintings blew off the roof of his car. Another's car had broken down in 1973. He had taken what he thought would be a temporary job to pay for the repair. He was still with the same company, but now its president. Once they had stopped in Albuquerque, people had a way of staying. This is what is known in New Mexico as being enchanted.

Albuquerque is big enough that there are things to do. You can learn to tango at the local Arthur Murray studio or take in a lecture on bat-sexing techniques at the university, but the atmosphere remains that of a "big hick town that has become a city but doesn't want to admit it," as Patrick Markwith, a builder who became my main golf buddy, put it. Over the years Patrick had done work on just about every street in the city. He was constantly running into former employers and greeting them with questions like "How's the door hanging?" One time the two of us were stopped at a railroad crossing, and as the train sped by, Patrick saluted it with a hearty, "Hello America."

Albuquerque is an island. Beyond the city limits, the desert lies out there like the sea. Nothing but "the outback," as Patrick calls it, for hundreds of miles. Flying in at night, one can suddenly see the lights of the oasis appear on the other side of the Rio Grande, with the major boulevards traced by green streaks of neon. The carpet of glittering lights ends at the river; it is like coming into the Florida Gold Coast from the sea.

As tolerant and ethnically aware as El Burque is, it has not escaped ethnic and economic stratification. Like Kinshasa, Bujumbura, and other cities in Africa, it has a *ville,* where the whites and some successful nonwhites live, and a *cité* for the poor Chicanos and blacks, and some whites, only here they are known as the Heights and the Valley. In the Heights you can fill your car with gas, then pay; but in the Valley, you have to pay first. The social strata, in the typical American pattern, conforms to the geologic strata (unlike Rio de Janeiro, for instance, where the slums are in hills, and the poorest people have the best views, if nothing else) and nicely illustrates the concept of environmental racism: wells in the Valley are contaminated with petroleum compounds, solvents, nitrates, and so on, but in the Heights the water is good because it isn't drawn from the Rio Grande aquifer; it comes down from the Sandias. One afternoon I walked up to an arroyo above the city, at the foot of Sandia Peak, whose bed fell in tiers of saturated, slushy "Grape-Nuts." Water oozed out of every other tier and disappeared again. The runoff from this and other arroyos was carried down to the Heights in the concrete-lined Embudo Channel, which was empty. A straw-hatted Mexican, probably a *mojado,* was walking in it. The *Journal* ran a story about how the great-grandfather of four-year-old Ashley Rubio, who had been swept away by the swift, icy Arenal Canal, was suing four government agencies for failing to mend the hole in the fence that she had crawled through.

The average Duke City resident consumes 240 gallons of water a day (compare this with Tucson's 160 and Las Vegas's 360; the Albuquerque figure counts industrial and commercial consumption, including golf course irrigation, but the other cities' figures do not). The Rio

Grande at this point is what is known as an abrading stream, constantly precipitating sediment and shifting its channel. Modern Albuquerque sprang up in 1880 in what was known as the yazoo, an ancient abandoned channel that had sprouted a cottonwood bosquet. Despite being continuously recharged by the river, the Rio Grande aquifer is going down four or five feet a year. It may be contaminated with radioactive waste from the Los Alamos Laboratory, far upstream.

Patrick calls the Heights Nosebleed Country. The politics there, on balance, are "slightly to the right of Attila the Hun." In the subdivision of Sandia Heights, right under the mountain, everything "has to be the Southwest look," a real estate woman explained. Sometimes on a Sunday afternoon, we would go look at houses. We'd walk through Prestige Homes' latest creation at Pinnacle Estates. Around this time, a couple posing as prospective home buyers was ripping off credit cards and jewelry when the real estate woman's back was turned. Even smoother was the con man Steve Byers, who posed as an attorney, a home buyer, or a car buyer to get cash, jewelry, credit cards, and cars, and, changing into a three-piece suit for his arraignment, talked his way out of the Sandoval County Judicial Complex and continued his spree, occasionally taunting the police from a pay phone.

Architecturally, Albuquerque must be one of the most undistinguished cities in the modern world. Some of the houses in Glenwood Heights, which Patrick calls Big Macs, with thick-shingled mansard roofs, French windows, solaria overlooking pools, and central vacuums, attained extravagant, almost-surreal levels of mainstream kitsch. Neighbors in the Heights could go for years without meeting each other. Sometimes the throwing together of transplants resulted in an ugly ethnocultural clash. Relations between the Danielses and the Restanis, for instance, deteriorated when the Restanis' adopted son, Jason, said to the Danielses' son, as they were playing in the sandbox, "Let's kill your mom." Forty-four-year-old Vittorio Restani was a Vietnam vet who had relocated from Long Island; Marc Daniels an award-winning teacher in the Albuquerque public-school system. After this comment, the Danielses wouldn't let their boy play with Jason, and the Restanis took offense. According to the Danielses, the Restanis poisoned their lilacs, punctured the radiator of their truck, and stole their firewood. Sometimes Kari Daniels would see Vittorio standing in the window staring at her and pointing his first finger like a gun. One day Vittorio offered a colleague at the post office named Tiny five hundred dollars to kill Kari Daniels and another hundred to beat up her husband. "They'll be easy patterns. They're pretty much John Doe

Americans," he told Tiny, but the trouble was, Tiny was an undercover agent who was working for the post office to root out bad employees, and he turned Vittorio in.

There are a few striking exceptions to the unexciting architecture, like the home of Bart Prince, a maverick disciple of Bruce Goff and one of America's most daring designers. His home mixes cornball science fiction, surrealism, and weird Orientalism to produce an individualism without historical precedent that he calls organicism and looks like a giant bug or an interplanetary way station, which is all the more bizarre in its surroundings of ranch-house and adobe nonentities.

Steve and Holly Baer's house on a ridge in Corrales, a suburb in the North Valley, was an eccentric honeycomb configuration of geodesic pods. "The aluminum skin is like a moth when it's overcast, but it blazes with movement and color under an active sky," Baer explained. In addition to the changeable metal surface, the house was rigged with "skylids" and "sunbenders" he had designed. The skylids were on the south solar face and could be closed with pulleys at night and when it was cold. Baer is often described as "the spiritual father of passive solar energy," and his workshop, Zomeworks, a friend told me, is "a mecca for all sorts of Gyro Gearloose types. He always has a product to save the world, and he's always just breaking even." Baer was developing new applications for photovoltaic systems, like a twelve-volt photovoltaic fence charger to keep cattle from straying, another system for melting the ice on stock tanks. He had rigged a remote ranch in the Ladron Mountains with a system that made it totally energy independent. Photovoltaic cells generated electricity and pumped the well water, solar cookers prepared the food. The cost was fourteen thousand dollars.

"The general conception is that unless there's a scorekeeping system," he explained, "unless it goes through a pipe or over a wire, it isn't energy, but everything is really already solar. We're solar. What energy do you think enabled you to walk in here from the parking lot? And in a sense we run on water. Our movements use it up." Baer was also working on harnessing night-sky radiation, the flip side of solar energy, as a means of cooling air. "When you take a reading on the top of your car, it's twenty-five degrees Fahrenheit cooler than the air, because the heat is radiating into the sky. You could use this radiation to cool batteries down and store them underground in the desert or to maintain chilling ponds on your roof. This technology has been completely neglected."

The most common form of air cooling in the Southwest remains the swamp cooler. It uses much less electricity than air-conditioning, and practically every house in Albuquerque has one. Without the swamp cooler, the modern way of life, quite simply, would not have been possible in the desert. One morning Patrick and I went up on the roof at La Hacienda and took a look at our unit. A cubical structure, it sat on the flat roof and had a characteristic hum and a smell of slightly mildewed moisture. Inside there was a pan of water, maintained at a steady level by water pumped up through a copper pipe (or, in other coolers, plastic line). The water dribbled down and was distributed over cooler pads on the sides, and a blower pulled in air, which was refrigerated by the cooler pads and blown down into the house.

Baer was developing a swamp cooler that would run off photovoltaic cells.

As October progressed, tumbleweed heads in the outlying steppe died, snapped off their stems, and were buffeted into the oasis. Road crews with pitchforks and trucks would have to clear the exit ramps on the interstates that were choked with them. And with the tumbleweed, in cold, gray, prewinter overcast, came human drifters. We could see them standing right at the corner of Carlisle and Constitution, a hundred yards from our house, and when I stepped out of the bank, two Mexicans with bedrolls asked for a handout. I gave them a dollar, and one of them said, "Bless you, sir. You have a kind heart." I was often accosted by drifters in the huge parking lot of the supermarket—an itinerant Hopi silversmith-kachina carver, Anglo burnouts in cowboy hats and boots.

The airy balls of tumbleweed resembled rolling brains and were another of the Southwest's emblematic organisms, like the saguaro and sagebrush, the roadrunner, the coyote, and the sidewinder. Tumbleweed is any plant that breaks loose from its stem and blows around in the wind. These tumbleweeds are also known as Russian thistles and include several species of *Salsola,* in the goosefoot family, which includes spinach and beets. They are native to Europe and Asia and are partial to sandy seashores. In England they are known as prickly saltwort, and their sodium-rich ashes are used to make soap and glass. In Russian they're called *salinka* or *perikati polye* (roll-across-the-field). They are thought to have been introduced by Mennonite emigrants to southern Kansas in the late 1880s with shipments of Kharkov wheat from the Ukraine. The *Salsolas* have two alkaloids, and salsoline hydrochloride, synthesized from them, is used as a sedative to relieve blood pressure. The Apache soon discovered that in the spring they could eat the young green shoots when they were two inches high, before they produced spines. There was a bar in Albuquerque called Tumbleweed that featured live bands like Sidewinder. We brought in a big tumbleweed from the desert on the top of our car for our Christmas tree.

The university's basketball team, the Lobos, lost again, this time 94 to 17 to Fresno State. The losing Lobos are part of Albuquerque mythology. Joke: The son says to the judge, "I don't want to live with Dad 'cause he beats me." The judge asks: "How about Mom?" "She beats me too." "Well what about your grandparents?" "They beat me too." "Well who do you want to live with?" "The Lobos, 'cause they never beat anybody."

One night I went to see the Dukes, a farm team of the Dodgers, with one of the city's most prominent chiropractors and our sons, who had become friends through playing on the same Peewee ice hockey team. The ballpark was small and intimate, the evening glorious; this was Albuquerque at its finest. The batter would hit a long, high drive that would fall two feet short of clearing the left-field fence; the shortstop would dive for a sizzling grounder and miss it by a hair. That's why they weren't in the majors: a difference of a split second, a couple of inches.

Chiropractors, an Albuquerque art dealer told me, "are the aristocracy of the Sunbelt. They all go to Scottsdale, Arizona, and pay sixty-five hundred dollars apiece for a four-day seminar on how to maximize their profits. The basic idea is that you partition your office into as many rooms as you can and schedule your patients fifteen minutes apart. You come in and give the patient three minutes of TLC—how are you feeling today? etcetera—then you put them on the machine and plug into their insurance. At forty dollars a patient, and let's say twelve rooms, that's forty-eight patients an hour times forty hours a week—seventy-six thousand eight hundred dollars. Not bad for a week's take."

This chiropractor had a Mercedes with a phone and a television and lived in one of the Heights's most surreal subdivisions, with its own golf course undulating among close-packed homes of prodigious square footage. A complete spinal manipulation, he told me, took only twelve minutes, and there were a lot of lonely people—the worried well, he called them—who came to him because they needed physical contact. "The attitude of mainstream medicine is give 'em a pill or cut it out," he said. "If you've got a pinched nerve or a pulled muscle or your back is out, there's really nothing they can do for you. That's where we come in." Like the drunk-driver, personal-injury, and "split-igation" lawyers, rival chiropractors had billboards on the interstate.

The first thing that struck me in Albuquerque, where the houses and trees are low and unprepossessing, was the sky, the unobstructed visibility, which I came to call the Vasta Vista. Like many others before me, I found the openness and the light, the colors of the sky and the weathered naked land beneath it, to have a wonderfully soothing and therapeutic effect, once I got used to them. They activated the contemplative recesses of the brain and were the most special thing about the Southwest. From the city's Heights, you could see all the way out to Mount Taylor, the sacred southeastern corner of Navajo land, seventy miles west. But you didn't have to have an expensive piece of real estate in the Heights to get the view. It was there for everyone, and it was free—the Vasta Vista por Todos—and something beautiful was always happening in it.

For someone like me, coming from the hemmed-in, forested East, it took a while to adjust to the scale. Sometimes as I drove around in my car, skimming the pavement, I would feel strangely light-headed. Even Albuquerque itself seemed slightly unreal. There was a hallucinational edge to its everyday reality. This sensation was not unusual for an easterner. The critic Edmund Wilson, for instance, noted "a strange sense of unreality in the West that makes human existence appear hollow." He was writing about Los Angeles in 1932, but he could have been describing Albuquerque now. Wilson attributed the hollowness to the effects of the climate and the landscape, not the tacky, soul-robbing convenience, the blah samsara of the modern culture, whose chimeric, impoverished incarnation in Albuquerque I called, after my Navajo friend Tom's typology, Sloganworld. One day as I got on the interstate I passed a bearded drifter panhandling on the ramp. He was holding up a poster with a portrait of himself, captioned FACE OF THE HOMELESS, which for some reason I misread as HOME OF THE FACELESS.

For the first month, when we lived in the funky old adobe mansion that had been split up into apartments, I did my writing at a second-story window that looked out on the spectacular west flank of Sandia (Watermelon) Peak. I got to know its many moods. From afar, framed. I watched cloud banks curl over the peak like giant, crashing waves, sunsets that turned its five-thousand-foot granite wall luminous, juicy-watermelon orange-pink, and its talus slopes a subtly iridescent purple.

Volcanic sunsets flaming in high, flowing altostratus meadows and turning the sky between the clouds sometimes green, sometimes a color between apricot and gray, were a daily occurrence. The sun would drop quickly behind the volcanoes, and thick, pitch-black night would envelop the oasis, then tens of thousands of lights would go on.

Some mornings a low layer of cloud would linger in the valley as over a lake, penetrated only by the small thicket of downtown commercial towers, making them seem like a dream city. By eleven the layer would be baked off, as if it had been sucked away by the invisible Zuñi spirit Cloud Swallower. During the summer minimonsoon there was an afternoon cumulus buildup. Momentous meteorologic exchanges took place between the mountain and the valley. On March 2 it was snowing in the Sandias. The peak was wrapped in clouds. My son was up there snowboarding on ninety inches of powder. But the valley was a sunny, sixty degrees, and I played golf. Next day the cold came down into the valley. Several days of crackling dryness just above freezing ensued, with static electricity flying from hair or brushed clothing. Several times I was caught on the golf course by a hailstorm. Within minutes, the fairways would turn white, covered with marble-sized ice balls. One time a twosome playing right behind my wife was hit by lightning. They had taken shelter from a shower under a Chinese elm. One was thrown twenty feet. Apart from a cracked rib, he was more shook up than anything. The other player, who had put his back to the tree, was taken away in a coma.

Sometimes lightning would strike way out in the desert, leaving a decaying phosphorous version of itself for a second or two and illuminating dark skeins of precipitation under clouds. Sometimes a lavender-edged line of darkness overhead would glower over a mesa, backlit with creamy white. Each day would bring a slightly different drama of light. Sometimes, in the late afternoon, the cedar tree in our driveway would become sun-haloed or, as my friend Patrick put it, "light-frosted," which gave it several minutes of intense singularity. As N. Scott Momaday, the Kiowa writer, remarks, "All things are isolate in the plains." Once, I pulled up right before a bristling yucca at the edge of a parking lot, just as the sunset was trapped and trembling in its spikes. A few days later, at the same time of day, I drove up to the same yucca again, but nothing happened. Objects are always unpredictably lighting up here and there in the Vasta Vista.

Fantase

The drive up to Santa Fe from Albuquerque on the autobahn, as Patrick calls the freeway, takes about fifty minutes and is spectacular. At Cochiti you go up an eroded grade known as the Bajada to a juniper-dotted shelf under the Sangre de Cristos, and there it lies—"Fantase," Patrick calls it, "the land of the tragically hip." Others call it, less charitably, Santafake. My old school buddy Don, who builds, paints, and blows the sax there, describes it as "a high-end scene." It's for the aristocrats and the tourists, for management, while Albuquerque is the working town, the industrial area. The two will never conurbate, grow together like the myriad municipalities of Los Angeles, because of the Indian pueblos between them, but there's talk of a ninety-mile-an-hour bullet-train-rapid-rail link, like the Rapido between Florence and Rome.

Three flags have flown over Santa Fe's Palacio Real since 1610. Now Santa Fe is the trendsetting imaging center of the Southwest, where the men have ponytails and the women are done out to soft-western perfection. The flavor of Santa Fe has not changed as much as it has evolved since 1927, when it was caught by the writer Emily Hahn. Hahn was working as a Harvey Girl, taking tourists out on the Indian Detour to see the pueblos and the quaint Hispanic villages of the Rio Arriba. Santa Fe, she wrote in a memoir years later,

> was not merely my state of mind. It was really an interesting place—possibly the only town of its kind anywhere. You couldn't dismiss it as a resort for pleasure seekers, because it was also the state capital, as well as a refuge favored by doctors for tuberculosis cases. Santa Fe was a mecca for American Indian experts, being a living museum of Mexican and Indian culture. These differences didn't leap at once to the eye—I doubt if my Detour dudes saw them—but Santa Fe

was a rich, rare city to live in. Strolling around the plaza at lunchtime on an idle day, I would pause every few steps to chatter with friends—an English girl training to be a vet, a hopeful t.b. case, a sculptor, a curio dealer, an archaeologist, a millionaire in search of something to do. They all dressed the same, too, in Levis, boots, and bandanas. It was the holiday uniform—the Santa Fe uniform. Nobody could have told the difference in people's social strata. Santa Fe had a way of mixing them up.

Sixty-five years later, Indian women were still selling turquoise-and-silver jewelry under the arcade in the plaza, the terminus of both the Camino Real from Chihuahua and the Santa Fe Trail from Independence. I tried to imagine, as I strolled through it, what the plaza was like when the Oñate expedition approached Santa Fe in 1692. It had been in Pueblo hands for twelve years, since the revolt. Columns of smoke were rising in the distance. "The palace was partly a ruin, partly a pueblo," writes Paul Horgan:

> All Spanish furnishings had been burned. Rooms had been added, and battlements. Other communal dwellings had been built until there were four, with cells for a thousand people. The church on the plaza and Saint Michael's across the creek were open to the sky. Their doors were long since burned. Cattle and sheep were corraled within the charred walls of the churches. The plaza was bare of all but refuse. Spanish trees had been hauled out by the roots, Spanish flower beds dug up, orchards were ruined and fields where once wheat and melons grew, grapes and other products of Spain, were long since ravaged. . . . Dogs and turkeys wandered freely in the plaza dust. The city was neither pure pueblo nor Spanish capital, but a heap of occupied ruins of both kinds of life.

But now the plaza has been "chocolate sauced, Necco Wafered," in the description of an interior decorator married to a natural-gas heir from Amarillo who had moved to Santa Fe and was occupying himself by reading the literature of the world. There was a store that sold high-quality African art and another with masks from New Guinea. A fire-engine-red London cab, driven by a Jamaican in dreadlocks, was waiting for a fare. Two alert buppies, black yuppies, were checking out the scene, trying to decide, Is this cool, or is this not cool? I walked into Ortega's Turquoise Mesa, just off the plaza, and discussed with a saleswoman what I needed to get with it sartorially, head to foot. To start with, she said, I needed a concho belt, with tooled silver disks. She recommended a "ranger set" buckle, which had two keepers. I could wear the concho belt instead of a cummerbund with a tuxedo. Then I needed a bola tie, and a chunky bracelet with a lot of large stones, an oilcloth "duster" raincoat, with a flap over the shoulder such as was worn on the range, and then, obviously, a silver money clip. Then cowboy boots and a silver bootstrap with liberty dimes or buffalo nickels on one boot, a simple chambray work shirt, and a black felt cowboy hat. A leather vest, she suggested, would go with the boots. For a dude to be properly outfitted would run a couple of grand, maybe thirty-five hundred.

For a woman, it was more. She'd need a crushed-velvet skirt, pleated and tiered, for $250. Her concho belt would run anywhere from $300 to $3,000, with $1,500 the average. The saleswoman showed me an extremely pretty one, encrusted with stones, by a local designer for $2,700. A woman would need earrings, bracelets, and a necklace. "This massive necklace, with multiple strands and lots of fetishes and stones, is very Southwest," she explained. "A lot of women enjoy big dangle earrings with stones. A modest pair runs anywhere from three hundred and fifty to six hundred. The blouse could be embroidered cotton or *embroudé*. She could wear a flat black gaucho hat with a silver band and boots with a silver strap on one, like the man."

How would you describe this style? I asked. "It's a takeoff; I mean a mix between Spanish and Indian influence," explained the saleswoman. "White folks just pick what they want. There are some who say, 'This won't translate well in Boston,' but a lot of affluent tourists want that southwestern charm and buy the whole ensemble. Fashionwise, it's taken off in the last two, three years, although right now it's kind of slow. I fell into it myself with the whole hippie thing."

The mix of Santa Fe today consists of ever-fewer Hispanics; there are only a few Hispanic barrios left. "The real estate is so inflated our kids can't afford it. I'm glad I knew Santa Fe when it was still real," a woman of the venerable Baca clan, who had been born there in 1908, told me. The natives are being driven out by trust-fund hippies and movie stars. Santa Fe is the sort of place to which the sons and daughters of well-to-do capitalists in the East and Texas gravitate. "The theory of the dumbest son has a simplicity that has always appealed to me," the journalist Calvin Trillin wrote in a 1982 *New Yorker* piece called "Thy Neighbor's Roof," about an architectural dispute in the historically zoned old part of town. "I suspect that a theory closer to the truth would be the theory of the son or daughter Who Didn't Fit In—didn't fit in because of being uninterested in business or being artistic or sickly or eccentric or dumb or not dumb enough to devote their lives to a family bank."

The houses in Old Santa Fe, the historic district in the old part of town, can only be in the Old Santa Fe style, also known as Spanish-Indian Revival or Pueblo Revival. Their walls must be adobe, and their roofs must be flat. Brick coping along the top of the walls—a touch known as territorial—is permissible. Narrow streets weave among the adobes like "a drunk Mexican," someone once observed. The historic-styles ordinance was written in 1957 by Oliver La Farge, the anthropologist and writer who celebrated the Navajo in such books as *Laughing Boy* and who was a luminary of the Santa Fe cultural scene that included Erna Ferguson and Haniel Long. The ordinance "doesn't demand mockery," Trillin wrote, "but it does encourage mockery." The dispute he focused on was over the portholed, vaulted "Coney Island Texas Gothic" roof of a radiologist named Maurice Weisberg. Weisberg had bought his lot in the historic district from his neighbor, Jesse Merlan. Both were originally from New York, but Merlan was a serious aficionado of the southwestern look, one of those transplanted Anglos who abound in Santa Fe and who avidly collect Navajo rugs, Pueblo pots, and Hopi kachinas and hang the obligatory red-chile-pod *ristras* on their patio. Merlan, according to Trillin, "implies chumminess with the Giscard d'Estaings and thinks his santos are more authentic than his neighbors," and he complained not only that Weisberg's roof violated the ordinance, but that lights from the portholes shot up into the sky, "causing him sleeplessness and great distress." Among the characteristics of Santa Fe's transplanted-Anglo scene, Trillin identified "a tendency to refer casually to one's precise arrival date in town as a way of establishing rank, a willingness to drop an important name now and then as a way of indicating that all ties to the cultural and financial capitals back East have not been severed, a commitment to some artistic or literary project that seems to take a long time to complete, and a belief that Texans in large numbers are the equivalent of Visigoths in large numbers."

The current crop of Santa Fe intellectuals includes the anthropologist Alfonso Ortiz, who edited the southwestern volumes of the *Handbook of North American Indians,* and the novelist Evan S. Connell. Peter Nabokov, the ethnologist-writer whose father, Nicholas, was a composer and the author of *Bagazh,* grew up there and was a young reporter for the Santa Fe *New Mexican.* "Santa Fe is a little village," he recalls. "It was a great place to be a punk journalist." Growing numbers of movie actors have settled there, like Gene Hackman, Mickey Rourke, and Val Kilmer; Robert Redford and Oprah Winfrey have houses in Tesuque, north of town. More and more people who are sick of Los Angeles are spending two weeks in Santa Fe and flying to L.A. for a day or two to do the business they can't do by phone or fax. There's a sizable gay community and an active Tibetan-Buddhist scene, with a resident lama. There are "people who have money who are boring," as my wife called them, relocated easterners with limited capacity or interest in reinvention, old-line WASPs from Greenwich who hang southwestern landscapes instead of horse-and-hounds prints in their living rooms but are otherwise pretty much status quo. Canyon Road, where many of the art galleries are, is like Provincetown. "You have to look behind the purple and pink coyotes to find the real Southwest," Kenneth Canfield, a gallery owner, told me.

With a little digging, real art, real people, real music, and real food can be found without much difficulty. In 1981 the journalist Lee Eisenberg wrote of Santa Fe: "You've always dreamed of living there—the great good place where everything is going to be different. You're too late for Aspen, Key West is too crowded. But don't give up. We've asked around and checked the maps. There's still a chance you can make it to Santa Fe." The city offers dozens of bookstores; thousands of acres to hike, climb, and fish in; skiing; opera; lots of single people; more women than men "drawing alimony, selling real estate, opening boutiques, working in the ubiquitous galleries." There were local characters, like the sexagenerian Winnie Beasley, who bombed around on a motorcycle with her companion riding in a sidecar with breasts painted on it. But since then, Santa Fe, too, has been discovered. If one were looking for a place where "everything is going to be different," one would do better to check out San Miguel de Allende, down in Mexico.

Not much actual adobe is going up in Santa Fe anymore. The vega, or projecting roof beam, ends are increasingly not wood, but Styrofoam, Patrick told me; the siding is wood frame with AIS (asphalt-impregnated sheeting) sprayed with celotex foam, then stuccoed.

Some of Santa Fe's most prominent citizens, I was told by reliable sources, got their start dealing drugs, and there continues to be major money laundering through galleries, ski resorts, and hotels. Everybody seemed to know about a murder in one leading citizen's past that he seemed to have gotten away with, how years back he had offed a young couple in Mexico who crossed him on a drug deal and made it look like an accident.

One evening we drove up to Santa Fe for a dinner that Gerald and Kathleen Peters were having in honor of the actor Dennis Hopper and the writer William Burroughs. Gerry Peters is a controversial figure in Santa Fe. "He bought up the real estate around the plaza, drove out the locals, and leases it to people from Carmel," one woman told me.

Kathleen ran a gallery and was having a show of violent images by Hopper and Burroughs. Hopper, who for many years was a wild man in Taos and was now living in Venice, California, made it to the dinner, but the octogenarian Burroughs remained in Lawrence, Kansas. The party was in the De la Peña house, which started as a four-room adobe built by a Mexican sergeant in 1824 and had gone through many renovations and expansions, the latest by the Peterses in 1987; it was featured in that month's *Architectural Digest*. On the walls were nine of Georgia O'Keeffe's most famous paintings, including *Jimson Weed* and *Petunia No. 2*. The guests were extremely hip. The grub and the music a man was making on a piano were very subtle. No drugs were taken, drugs being passé. It was all too hip for words. Hopper had a red-dyed crew cut for his latest movie role, and at the dinner table he laid a heavy rap about "cultural devolution," which in his view is the central process that is going on in the Southwest.

The Imaging of the Southwest

The Southwest is now in what might be described as the advanced replica stage. Coronado is a huge shopping center in Albuquerque; Cíbola a ski run at Sandia Peak. Its emblematic organisms include the coyote, roadrunner, sidewinder, saguaro cactus, sagebrush, and tumbleweed. The coexistence of the ersatz frontier and the actual frontier, and of the Native American, Hispanic, and Anglo cultures, makes it all very complicated. Academic attention is now largely directed at the ersatz frontier, at the imaging process. In the winter of 1990 the *Journal of the Southwest* put out a special issue called *Inventing the Southwest*. "Invention," and "re-invention," have been the big buzzwords in academic circles for the last couple of years. Inventing Billy the Kid, inventing the Indian.

Santa Fe is the capital of the ersatz Southwest. "Now we pretend love for the brutal desert from our air-conditioned and watered environment, make romantic figures of ancient cliff dwellers and conquistadors, and dote on 'strands of Native American culture,' " observes Kathy Cone, editor of the *Workbook*, a quarterly journal on social and environmental issues in the Southwest. "Instead of real people, real conflict, real pain and drama; instead of an honest mix of 'great natural beauty' and 'abundant human ugliness,' we get images of the region with the rough edges smoothed, the unattractive prettified, the colloquial gentrified, and with this romanticized subject matter conveyed in the soft-focus pastel images found in the bad paintings that fill Santa Fe's tourist art galleries."

The first images for Anglo consumption were transmitted by expeditionary artists, naturalists, and journal keepers dispatched to the terra incognita west of the Mississippi early in the nineteenth century. As with the chronicles of the Spanish explorers, these images are full of distortion and bias, projection and revisionism, conscious and unconscious.

Beginning with Lewis and Clark, making their way up the snag-infested Missouri, keeping a sharp lookout for everything, collecting birds unknown to science, like Lewis's woodpecker and Clark's nuthatch. The image of the wilderness they brought home was that of a new Eden: "The whole face of the country was covered with herds of Buffaloe, Elk & Antelopes . . . so gentle that we pass near them while feeding, without appearing to excite any alarm among them and when we attract their attention, they frequently approach us more nearly to discover what we are." But as Frank Bergon writes, "The real snake in the garden hideously follows the explorers themselves. . . . In the slaughtering of the animals and the proprietary glances toward the land and native people, we get sad glimpses of the coming dark side of American imperialism."

George Catlin spent eight years among the horse tribes of the Plains in the 1830s and immortalized their final years as free-roaming nomads. The son of a Pennsylvania woman who had been abducted by Indians, he perceived his subjects as people, not as savages, and his images transcended the romantic or negative stereotypes that most of his contemporaries bought into, like Alfred Jacob Miller's soft-toned, sentimental watercolors of mountain men in the Rockies setting traps and trading with Indians at the annual rendezvous. Catlin died penniless. His paintings were seized by creditors. Many were destroyed by fire, water, mice, and insects.

Stephen H. Long's 1819 description of the Plains as "the Great American Desert" (the Spaniards' "great despoblado") acted as an effective deterrent to settlement and conquest of the Southwest until it was overridden by another slogan, "manifest destiny." The phrase was coined in 1845 by John O'Sullivan, the editor of the *Democratic Review*. It was "our manifest destiny," O'Sullivan argued, "to overspread the continent allotted by Providence for the free development of our yearly multiplying millions." The wonderfully iterative, energizing phrase was the Anglo equivalent of the conquistadores' "*Santiago y a elles.*" It set you in motion, gave you marching orders. Fill 'er up with manifest destiny. All aboard the manifest destiny special. It was perhaps the conceptual progenitor of another slogan that would become very important in the securing of the West for the dominant culture—eminent domain.

As President Polk sold Congress and the media on his expansionist program, the unappetizing image of a Great American Desert was replaced by luscious visions, like this one conjured by the *Illinois State Register:* "Shall this garden of beauty be suffered to lie dormant in its wild and useless luxuriance? . . . myriads of enterprising Americans would flock to its rich and inviting prairies; the hum of Anglo-American industry would be heard in its valleys; cities would rise upon its plains and seacoast, and the resources and wealth of the nation be increased in an incalculable degree."

The seven million Mexicans—"a wretched people; wretched in their origin, history, and character," preached the Reverend Theodore Parker, a Unitarian minister, in Boston—would have to yield to what the *American Review* hailed as "a superior population, insensibly oozing into [their] territories, changing [their] customs, and out-living, out-trading, exterminating [their] weaker blood." The New York *Herald* editorialized that it was the duty of "the universal Yankee nation" to "regenerate and disenthrall the people of Mexico" and "our destiny to civilize that beautiful country." Venturesome farmers began to see that the notion that the Plains and the lands to the west were a pathless, waterless Sahara was poppycock.

After the Mexican cession, Richard H. Kern served as the artist on four major mapping and scientific expeditions in the far Southwest, from 1848 to 1853. He provided the first detailed images of the Navajo, the Zuñi, the Pueblos, the Pai, and the Mojave, of the Canyon de Chelly and the Camino Real, but in 1853, while on John W. Gunnison's expedition, surveying the thirty-eighth parallel, he was murdered by Pahvant Indians in Utah. Mormons later recovered his cap, his bloodstone ring, and his mutilated body. Kern was only thirty-two, but in his brief, compressed life he had already become a superior draftsman and aquarellist, an observant ethnographer, and an accomplished linguist. He rendered pretty much what was there, but "perhaps because he held them in contempt and did not regard them as exotic," the historian David J. Weber speculates, "Kern, like other expeditionary artists, did not draw Mexicans except as staffage elements," ciphers wrapped in ponchos and leaning against buildings, in stark contrast to his lovingly detailed renditions of the Indians. Nor did he attempt to capture the vivid colors of the desert, rendering it in brown, green, and blue; the colors would have to wait for O'Keeffe. The observations in Kern's journals today seem appallingly racist, like this one on a "Yamapai" (probably Havasupai) couple. They were, he wrote, "extraordinary-looking objects—small in stature—the old man with a remnant of red paint on his idiotic face and no covering but the breech clout. The woman was a disgusting looking beast. Any mop was well combed in comparison to her hair and the upper part of her face was painted black. She had on the remnant of a Navajo blanket and altogether they approached more the Ourang Outang than any of the genus homo I have seen." Kern seems to have been prepared for his

violent end, judging from a letter he wrote to the widow of a good
friend:

> Life is but a journey. On we travel mid mirth and woe. Time
> flies along and will not wait or linger on the way. Or as a
> stream . . . rushing with impetuosity into the great Ocean of
> Death. . . . Our circle of light increases, only to be surrounded
> by a greater circumference of darkness. Death claims all for
> his here—he anoints innocence in its playfulness, youth in its
> panting ambition, manhood in maturity, and old age in
> decrepitude, resting on crutches and waiting his approach.

In 1849 John Woodhouse Audubon, John James's youngest son, set
out from New York City for the California goldfields. The thirty-six-
year-old Audubon *fils* was gone two years. He took the Mexican route
through newly won Texas, crossing into Chihuahua at Brownsville/
Matamoros—a good choice except for cholera, which claimed the lives
of ten of his companions at Rio Grande City, and for the hostility they
kept encountering from Mexicans. Audubon's journal, too, is full of
sketches and digs at the local wogs. At Cerro Gordo, Sonora, "a miserable den of vagabonds with nothing to support it but its petty garrison of a hundred and five cavalry mounted on mules . . . we were
hooted and shouted at as we passed through, and called 'Gringoes.' "
At El Valle he danced the fandango "with some quite good-looking
senhoritas." He encountered some "Tarimari" Indians and three
Frenchmen who had been in Trinidad, selling mescal liquor to the
natives, so long they had almost forgotten their language. Audubon
asked the Frenchmen why they were staying and was told because of
the love of gold. Have you found it? No, one of them explained, but
we cannot return without it. On the way to California, Audubon met
numerous other casualties of what he took to be environmentally
determined cultural devolution:

> Many of all nations who, lured by the stories of fortunes eas-
> ily made, come to this part of the earth and grow more and
> more lazy and indolent, until they have become unfit for the
> active, energetic industry requisite in happier and more
> enlightened portions of the world. The people here simply
> vegetate; many of them drink, and are depraved in many
> ways. Some seem happy with their Mexican wives, who,
> however, are neither as handsome nor as clever as quadroons.

But "nature," Audubon noted, "is beautiful at every turn, now in
bird and beast, then in tree and flower, then in rock and rill." He saw
a caracara, or Brazilian eagle, large flocks of yellow troupials, and,
ascending the Colorado River to some Papago villages, came upon "a

little waterhole filled with animalculae," a dry wash "which Penny-packer called a 'thunder-shower river,' " a female rattlesnake, with nine young in her nest—"beautiful little creatures about a foot long; they had great courage, and coiled and struck with fury at anything placed near them." Reaching the goldfields at last, Audubon tagged along with the prospectors, more interested in the mores (or lack thereof) of their "mushroom towns," than in the metal they all were there for.

Whig connections got John R. Bartlett appointed "boundary commissioner," charged with resurveying the Mexican-American borderline after the 1848 Treaty of Guadalupe Hidalgo. On the official Disturnell map, El Paso had ended up thirty-four miles north and over a hundred miles east of where it actually was. A bookish bibliophile, etymologist, and amateur ethnologist who had compiled a dictionary of American English, Bartlett welcomed the respite from his sedentary life and the opportunity to meet some Indians in the flesh. His topographical work was rendered irrelevant by the Gadsden Purchase, which changed the border again a few years later; it was his sumptuous, two-volume *Personal Narrative of Explorations,* illustrated with his own fine water-colors, which ranks with such classics as the narratives of John Frémont, Francis Parkman, and Josiah Gregg, that ended up being Bartlett's lasting contribution. As the historian Jay J. Wagoner writes, "for many a hammock reader at Saratoga and Newport it opened up an exciting America and helped create an image of the exotic West."

Bartlett became involved in the efforts to get a pretty fourteen-year-old Mexican girl named Inez Gonzales back to her family in Santa Cruz, Sonora. Inez had been rescued from New Mexican traders who had traded for her with Apache; she had been kidnapped by Apache the year before. She struck Bartlett as "quite young, artless, and interesting in appearance, prepossessing in manners, and by her deportment gave evidence that she had been carefully brought up," and he deemed it his duty to "extend over her the protection of the laws of the United States" and see that she got home. Inez's joyous return sparked "one perpetual fandango" that lasted several weeks, but a year later Bartlett found her living in a dilapidated hut in the small presidio of Tubac with a Captain Gomez. She was no longer sweet and innocent.

By 1855 the acquisition of northern Mexico had sparked a new age of discovery. The *Washington National Intelligencer* wrote:

At no period since the days of Columbus and Cortez has
the thirst for exploration been more active and universal
than now. One by one the outposts of barbarism are stormed
and carried, which when once established can never be
retaken . . . [and explorers] are gradually closing around the
yet unconquered mysteries of the globe. Modern exploration
is intelligent, and its results are therefore positive and permanent. The traveller no longer wanders bewildered in a cloud
of fables prepared to see marvels, and but too ready to create
them. He tests every step of his way by the sure light of science and his pioneer trail becomes a plain and easy path to
those who follow. The pencil, the compass, the barometer,
and the sextant are his aids; and by these helps and appliances
his single brain achieves results now which it would once
have required an armed force to win.

Glorious careers in western exploration were available with the
Army Corps of Topographical Engineers, created in 1838, which
became, in the words of the historian William H. Goetzmann, "a central institution of Manifest Destiny" and the "department of public
works for the West." It was responsible for putting in the modern
infrastructure—roads, railroads, bridges, harbors—and had a multiple
character. Its field agents were at once military men, naturalists, and
scientists, and they took note of every road, path, river, creek, hill, forest, and village, and these images and specimens—whatever was shot,
picked, dug up, measured, or noted down—were sent back to Washington. Nothing was too tribal, local, or circumscribed to escape attention—the habits of a mountaintop bumblebee, a gesture of sign
language.

The first topographical expeditions had been guided by mountain
men. As late as 1806, hope was still entertained that the Missouri-
Columbia route would "facilitate a water transit to Cathay," Goetzmann writes, "thereby shrinking the continent in human terms."
Alexander von Humboldt's 1811 Carte Général du Royaume de la
Nouvelle Espagne combined the data of Escalante and other Spanish
explorers on the Colorado, Gila, and Rio Grande with Zebulon Pike's
and was surprisingly accurate. But nothing compared to the thirteen
massive volumes of the Pacific Railroad Reports, which the Army
Corps put out under the direction of John Frémont, its most famous
topographical engineer, whose 1842 expedition was the most significant reconnaissance since Lewis and Clark's and gave Frémont the
stature to run for president and to eventually become the first senator
of California. The reports constituted (this is Goetzmann again) "an
American encyclopedia of western experience" and exhibited "all the

strengths and weaknesses of the cosmic approach to science" embodied by Humboldt. Three volumes were devoted to zoology. Extraordinarily detailed drawings of the plants were made by John Torrey and Asa Gray, the great botanists of the day. All that was lacking was a Darwin to provide a theoretical overview.

John Wesley Powell, who in 1873 led the first expedition to the last unknown region in the continental United States—the headwaters of the Colorado River and the Grand Canyon—was another visionary figure in Southwest imaging. A conchologist and professor of geology at Wesleyan University who had lost an arm at Shiloh, Powell had made the first systematic collection of the river shells of the Mississippi. The canyon "will give the best geological cross-section on the continent," he argued in lectures to raise money for the expedition. At that time geologic thinking was still dominated by catastrophism, which postulated a single great upheaval as opposed to a longer process in which landforms were shaped by the forces of rain, wind, earthquakes, and volcanic eruptions. The notion that the Grand Canyon was a product of erosion wasn't accepted by even the eminent earth scientists at Yale. The best-known set of images of the canyon were those of Baron F. W. von Eglottstein, who had accompanied the Ives expedition of 1857 as artist and topographer. They were fascinating from an imaging point of view: ignoring the stratigraphy, wildly exaggerating the narrowness and the height of the walls, they gave the folks back east their preconceived notion of what the Big Canyon must look like. Even Thomas Moran, the artist who accompanied Powell, blurred and distorted the literal visual scene before him at will. His painting from a spectacular prospect called the Transept, for instance, was "painted from careful observation," Wallace Stegner writes, "but it is realistic only in details where it chooses to be." Moran had learned to blur from Turner; he proceeded from facts but attempted to transcend them, believing that the artist's business was "to produce for the spectator of his pictures the impression produced by nature on himself . . . I place no value upon literal transcripts from nature. My personal scope is not realistic; all my tendencies are toward idealization . . . topography in art is valueless." The canyon would not be rendered with scientific precision until the almost-photographic drawings of William Henry Holmes, who accompanied the Hayden Survey through the rest of that decade.

Powell and his companions shot the Colorado in canvas-covered dories, unraveling the mysteries of the rocks, discovering fossil sharks' teeth embedded in the flank of Mount Goat, running aground on sand-bars, swamping, losing instruments, assimilating and mentally appro-priating the landscape, bestowing Anglo names on passing projections and cascades: Gunnison Butte, Moran Point, Pilling Cascade (after his secretary), and the more literary canyon of Lodore, Aquarius Plateau, Vermilion Cliffs. Captain Clarence E. Dutton, his right-hand man, was more highbrow in his nomenclature: Ottoman Amphitheater, Hindoo Amphitheater, the Temples of Osiris and Isis, the Transept, the Clois-ters, Point Sublime. Spray from the rapids got into everything. Food moldered, beans sprouted, and there were cockroaches "on every front."

While the theory of uniformitarianism, recognizing the earth's sur-face as a series of strata laid down over a long period of time, which Powell and a handful of other maverick geologists espoused, had got Darwin thinking along evolutionary lines, Powell rejected the way Darwinism made man seem like a pawn of evolutionary forces. "In his view," Stegner writes, "man escaped the prison in which all other life was held, because he could apply intelligence and will to his environ-ment and bend it." The running of the Colorado early in his career became symbolic of his later activities. Like Theodore Roosevelt, Pow-ell was an explorer who, in the historian Bernard de Voto's words, "embraced the code of action." He was an "eminently magnetic man" (Stegner) who could work his charm equally on squaws and war-riors, university presidents and editors, and who could make himself understood.

The best writing in his *Exploration of the Colorado River and Its Canyons* is descriptive: "Below is the cañon through which the Col-orado runs. We can trace its course for miles, and at points catch glimpses of the river . . . wherever we look there is but a wilderness of rocks; deep gorges, where the rivers are lost below cliffs and towers and pinnacles; and ten thousand strangely carved forms in every direc-tion; and beyond them, mountains blending in with the clouds." At times the style becomes gauzy and sensational; Powell's use of the pathetic fallacy ("the slumber of the chasm is disturbed," and so on) and other devices is so exuberant that at times he appears to be "romancing with facts" (Stegner again). But the report reshaped the science of physiography. "Nature abhors a mountain," he observed, and he identified three kinds of slowly erosive drainage: antecedent, consequent, and superimposed.

The Vasta Vista began to act on Dutton. His system began to accept it and to see it as it was. He found the Plateau Province—the slowly ris-ing, deeply dissected, and in places eaten away and only vestigial Colorado Plateau, from which the Colorado had carved the canyon, "a great innovation in modern ideas of scenery." Its colors were, he observed,

> the very ones he [the lover of nature] had learned to shun as tawdry and bizarre. . . . But time would bring a gradual change. Some day he would suddenly become conscious that outlines which at first seemed harsh and trivial have grace and meaning; that forms which seem grotesque are full of dignity; that magnitudes which had added enormity to coarseness have become replete with strength and even majesty; that colors which had been esteemed unrefined, immodest, and glaring, are as expressive, tender, changeful, and capacious of effects as any others.

In 1877 Powell published his farsighted *Report on the Arid Lands of the United States, with a More Detailed Account of the Lands of Utah*, a remarkable monograph on the Plains west of the hundredth meridian. This was the so-called Great American Desert, where thousands of dryland farmers were trying to eke out a living from the soil— "this complex, misunderstood two fifths of the continental United States," Stegner writes,

> where men had come before law arrived, and where before there were adequate maps there were warring interests, white against Indian, cattleman against sheepman and both against nester, open range notions against the use of the newly invented barbed wire, Gentile against Mormon, land rights against water rights, appropriation rights to water against riparian rights to water, legitimate small settler against speculator and land-grabber. The public domain . . . [whose] only unity [was] the unity of little rain.

Powell realized that individual initiative was not sufficient to break the wilderness beyond the hundredth meridian and that water was its true wealth. Foreseeing the danger inherent in the western concept of appropriative rights, that water companies could sew up the rights and set up exploitative monopolies in which small independent homesteaders could become virtual debt peons, he proposed self-governing irrigation districts that were more along the communitarian Mormon model, each with nine farmers, and no farm more than eighty acres. But this flew in the face of rugged individualism, of robber barons, cattle barons, and other vested interests, and was quickly shot down in Washington.

Toward the end of his life, Powell turned from geology to ethnology. His work on the linguistic families of the North American tribes for the Bureau of Ethnology became, in 1907, five years after his death, the *Handbook of American Indians.* In Powell's final years, using data gathered by assistants as building blocks for a synthetic cultural history of mankind that would embrace all speculations men have made to understand and explain phenomena, his mind took off in increasingly abstruse and esoteric directions, until at last he lost everybody.

The Reverend R. B. Stratton, in his 1857 best-seller, *Captivity of the Oatman Girls,* speaks of "sketches and delineations in this volume . . . touching the region lying to the West and the Southwest." This, as well as I can determine, is the first identification of "the Southwest" as a region. The first aficionado and celebrant of the Southwest (who credits himself with thus "christening" the region) was a young journalist named Charles Fletcher Lummis, who crossed the region while walking from Ohio to California in the early 1880s. Lummis lived among the San Isleta Pueblos, chronicled General George Crook's campaign against Geronimo, took part in archaeological digs, collected Mexican-American folklore, provided glowing descriptions of the Grand Canyon and other wonders in such books as *Some Strange Corners of Our Country* and *The Land of Poco Tiempo.* In *Mesa, Cañon, and Pueblo,* one of his later books, published in 1925, Lummis writes:

> For nearly forty years I have been writing of the nearly million square miles which include New Mexico, Arizona, southern California and adjoining parts of Colorado, Utah, Texas, and northern Mexico—an area to which I was first to apply, over a third of a century ago, the generic christening by which it is now commonly known—THE SOUTHWEST. My books were the first to make widely known most of the marvels of that incomparable Wonderland.

The subtitle of *Some Strange Corners of Our Country,* which appeared in 1906, is *The Wonderland of the Southwest.* Lummis really pitches the region in this work. He complains about the "unpatriotic slighting of our country," how every year thousands of Americans go abroad to see "scenery infinitely inferior to their own." They go to Oberammergau for the Passion Play, which is nothing compared to Penitentes of New Mexico, whose "ignorant fanatics" perform real, "flesh and blood crucifixion." You want snake charmers? Lummis continues. Go to the Moqui (Hopi) snake dance. Everybody's heard how Australian Bushmen are experts with the boomerang, but how many Americans are aware that thousands of aborigines—Pueblo Indians—annually kill thousands of rabbits with "magic clubs"?

The marketing of the Southwest as a tourist destination for Americans began with the completion of the Atchison, Topeka, and Santa Fe Railroad to Albuquerque and on down to Rincon, New Mexico, in 1880. The railroad's dynamic head of restoration, Fred Harvey, realized that the scenery was there, and the only thing keeping the tourists from coming in droves was the food on the train and at the stops. So he set up a chain of Harvey Houses, with uniformed Harvey Girls, at places like the Grand Canyon. Harvey also figured New Mexico would have more appeal if it was sanitized a little, disassociated from the lazy-bum *corrupto* image of Mexico and presented as a quaint pocket of Spain, and he prevailed on the locals to think of themselves, not as Mexicans, but as Spaniards.

Harvey was helped by the Taos art colony, a group of eastern health seekers and children of wealth who gravitated to Taos in the twenties, where they began to affect a bohemian Indianism, growing ponytails, wearing Indian duds, and so on. With Harvey's sponsorship, these artists began to produce sentimental canvases with Indians wrapped in serapes gazing down from ledges into gaping canyons and cowpunchers chowing down around crackling campfires. The Indians found themselves being "museumized," frozen in an "ethnographic pastoral," turned into figures of what the University of Arizona cultural anthropologist Barbara Babcock calls "banana republic imperialist nostalgia." "All colonial discourse entails the objectification and aestheticization of the dominated," Babcock writes, and she adds that "in the business of commodifying the Other, racist and sexist gestures frequently compound each other." Examples of this process include Laura Gilpin's photograph of the Navajo Madonna for the 1940 WPA guide to New Mexico and the images of Pueblo women carrying jugs of water on their heads that became one early cliché of southwestern art, going back to the olla maidens of Santo Domingo in the 1848 Emory report.

At the same time that Harvey was buying work from the Taos art colony, the architect John Gaw Meem began to design wildly romantic Spanish Pueblo Revival houses in Santa Fe, with deliberately battered corners and other atmospheric touches, as getaways for rich easterners, and Arthur Mamby, northern New Mexico's first developer (who was later found beheaded, if the body was his), boasted that he was going to turn Taos into an international spa.

"I want something extremely informal that will let us amuse ourselves with old ways and old things," said a wealthy East Coast

woman who commissioned a Meem house. "But may heaven preserve
it from looking arty." In Arizona the influence was more Spanish.
There were three waves: Mission Revival, which began around 1900
and featured mission tile, arched windows, and scalloped gables; Spanish Colonial Revival, which appeared in 1915 and, according to the
architectural critic Lawrence Cheek,

> supposedly recalled the grand life of the dons who had ruled
> colonial California from pink haciendas with gracefully
> rhythmic loggias, tiled domes and Islamic courtyards. A
> lovely image—and pure flimflam, a fantasia spun over a foun-
> dation of myth. Neither that architecture nor that lifestyle
> ever existed in what is now the United States.

The third, "now in profuse bloom," Cheek continues,

> doesn't have a name. Two possibilities, suggested by archi-
> tects, reek of scorn: "Taco Deco" and "Mariachi Moderne."
> Developers lean to the warmer but vague Southwestern/
> Mediterranean or to simply "Spanish." I have tried "Spanish
> Colonial Revival Revival," but editors always think it's a
> typing mistake. The other day someone suggested "refried
> architecture," which I rather like. It's brief, it implies both
> revivalism and a Mexican connection, and it is not nec-
> essarily catty, although it could be if the project at hand war-
> rants it.

And so an imaginary southwestern landscape, with an emblematic
flora and fauna, useful to developers and the travel industry, was created. The landscape kept evolving as hundreds of Hollywood westerns
were filmed in it; it has been in what one gallery owner describes as "a
purple and pink coyote phase" since 1984. By now the Southwest has
lent its name to thousands of companies and products. There is a
southwestern cuisine, southwestern furniture and dress, all of which
are big in New York. Southwestern scholarship is a thriving industry.
Scores of books and papers on southwestern subjects are published
every year. Almost every aspect of the region has been quantified.
There is a field guide to the windmills; a book devoted to the early
underground mine lamps of Arizona, another to the *Dogs of the Conquest;* a recent study of the Navajo code talkers; a book on women and
cars, recognizing that women in the Southwest spend just as much time
behind the wheel as, if not more than, men do. Billy the Kid is still very
big. Currently the coyote (in Navajo and rancher circles), Columbus
(in Native American circles), and manifest destiny (in historical circles)
are out. We've heard the conquerors' versions; now we're getting the
victims' and the women's side of the story. The dark side of the west-

ward "realization" is being examined, and the hip thing in southwestern studies is retracing the creation of the ersatz Southwest, whose capital, whose imaging and replication center, is Santa Fe. New Mexico, a gay publicist who had recently moved from Los Angeles to Albuquerque told me, is "a state of mind." (This same phrase I caught on TV the other day, applied to Arizona in a commercial for Arizona Jeans.)

The Southwest today is in an era of increasingly refined self-caricature. You have the real and the virtual playing off each other, Navajo driving Navajos. Mazda has come out with three new models of Navajo, to keep up with the Apache, the Comanche, the Coyote, the Cherokee, and the new Zia edition of the Ford F-150 truck. You have the lavender pots and the pink-and-purple paintings with coyotes—the California stuff, which appeals to and is bought by Californians. You have the real stuff—the "genuine reservation pawn"—old wristwatches with heavy turquoise-and-silver bands, and so on. You have the road stuff—Indian dolls, drums, Southwest-style candles, rattlesnake-skin belts and hatbands, bullhorn whips, kachina dolls, moccasins, postcards of jackalopes, fur-bearing trout, sliced geodes. Along Interstate 10, between Deming and Lordsburg, New Mexico, there are tons of rocks and relics and objets de kitsch and soon-to-be kitsch.

After pumping some gas at a convenience store in Alamogordo, New Mexico, I went in to pay. On the counter by the register was some primo kitsch: a brown plastic flying saucer shaped like a cow patty and called a Chip-Chucker—"the original Old West throwing disc." An Indian Weather Rock, consisting of a small rock hanging from a stick on a rawhide thong. The base had a chart:

IF ROCK IS	WEATHER IS
wet	rainy
moving	windy
cool	cold
hard to see	foggy
casting shadow	sunny

I probably should have bought the Indian Weather Rock on the spot; it could only have increased in value. But I said to myself, I'll be coming back this way in a couple of days, and I'll get it then. Of course, I never did. As my buddy Patrick says, "Things slide in the Land of Mañana."

Four Tucsons

During the Spanish and Mexican periods, Tucson was the northernmost outpost of saguaro-studded Alta Pimeria. Its population got up to a thousand at one point, but in 1852, when it passed into American hands, it was down to three hundred, and John R. Bartlett, the boundary commissioner, found it in a state of near siege by Apache. "The houses of Tucson are all adobe," he wrote, "and the majority are in a state of ruin. No attention seems to be given to repair, but as soon as a dwelling becomes uninhabitable it is deserted." Tucson now sprawls over almost fifty miles of desert floor. Retirement condo villages with names like Kachina Hills are eating up the desert, which is becoming like Florida's Gold Coast without the ocean. Tucson's winters are warmer than Albuquerque's, so it gets many more "snowbirds"—drifters who set up their tents in parks and augment the crime statistics dramatically. The atmosphere is different from Albuquerque's—more Mexican— and Tucson is more relaxed than Santa Fe, where people don't dress as much as they costume. The oasis is lusher and more tropical.

While the Pueblo Revolt of 1680 left the Franciscan frontier in shambles, the Jesuit frontier expanded into southern Arizona, largely due to the remarkable missionary Father Eusebio Kino. It was he who established the first European presence in the Bac-Tucson Valley. Born in the Tyrolean Alps in 1645, Kino was about to embark on a university career in mathematics when he came down with a nearly fatal illness. He vowed if he recovered to dedicate his life to overseas missionary work for the Society of Jesus, and this is what happened. Requesting India, he was posted instead to the godforsaken northern frontier of New Spain. In 1687 he began a twenty-four-year career in Alta Pimeria, a region of some thirty thousand Rancheria People belonging to four related tribes—Pima, Soba, Sobapuri, Papago (now called O'odham)—that is basically consonant with the Sonoran Desert.

In his own way, Kino was a protoliberation theologist, as concerned with improving earthly status as with securing a heavenly reward for obedient subjects of God and crown. He taught not only the Gospel but how to grow cabbage, lettuce, leeks, lentils, chickpeas, garlic, mint, watermelon, oranges, peaches, apricots, sugarcane, figs, quinces, pomegranates, and other Castilian and neotropical vegetables and fruits from distant corners of the Spanish empire. He brought sheep and cattle—the long-horned steer of Spain, which could go for sixty days without water and adapted admirably to the desert—and converted the Pimans from gatherers and rudimentary agriculturalists into ranchers. When he traveled to minister to his flock, he took no intimidating military escort, only a few Indian guides and droves of horses and cattle to distribute. His personal requirements were minimal; he was more Franciscan than the Franciscans. He slept on his horse's sweat blanket and owned only two coarse shirts. Once colleagues found him in church whipping himself mercilessly. The Indians recognized that he was a highly evolved soul, an inside chief, and though they would rise up from time to time and kill his compatriots and fellow padres, poison their water or shoot them full of arrows, they let Father Kino come and go in peace.

Twice a year Father Kino mounted a major desert expedition and was gone for months touring his *visitas,* mediating conflicts and straightening out problems that had inevitably arisen since his last call. He produced the first accurate maps of the region, which dispelled once and for all the myth that California was an island, and his maps of the *tinajas* (tanks) and springs were not surpassed until 1922, by Kirk Bryan's and E. Meinzer's *Routes to Desert Watering Places in the Papago Country, Arizona.* He "discovered" Casa Grande, the great Hohokam ruin on the Gila River, and wondered who lived there. "The casa grande is a four-story building, as large as a castle and equal to the largest church in these lands," he wrote. "It is said that the ancestors of Moctezuma deserted and depopulated it, and, beset by the neighboring Apaches, left for the east . . . , and that from there they turned toward the south and southwest, [and] finally founded the great city and court of Mexico." Not only did Father Kino produce several important astronomical treatises, he also picked up several stories about apparitions of a lady in blue, possibly the bilocating nun, Maria de Agreda, along the Gila.

Establishing a chain of missions and *visitas* up into the Bac-Tucson Valley, Father Kino soon had two or three thousand freshly contacted

Pima growing corn, beans, calabashes, melons, and cotton along ditches they had run off the Santa Cruz River. The Indians took him up a flat-topped mountain where a huge white stone had been planted in the ground: "Conjecturing that it might be some idol which the heathen Indians worshiped, we used force and pulled up the stone, which was embedded in the soil a third of a *vara,* leaving a round hole." On the way down, a gale-force wind arose, knocking everyone to the ground. Only when several of the Indians returned and put the stone back in the hole did the wind stop.

In the fertile, well-watered valley, Father Kino built a beautiful church, San Xavier del Bac, the White Dove of the Desert, which still stands, an island of simpler, slower, more gracious, more Mexican-Indian-fellah time (like the Pueblo suburbs of Albuquerque), on the outskirts of modern Tucson with its freeways and subdivisions and monumental shopping malls and Mariachi Moderne adult golf communities. In the plaza, O'odham women cook popovers and enchiladas over mesquite fires under brush ramadas. Thousands of pilgrims, some arriving on foot in penance or thanksgiving from all over Catholic America, come to pin little effigies of afflicted body parts, known as *milagros,* to the recumbent statue of Saint Francis in the basilica.

In the spring of 1992, with the surrounding desert in glorious bloom, I attended an eight o'clock mass at San Xavier del Bac with Bernard Fontana, the ethnographer of record of the Tohono O'odham, who has lived for many years right off the plaza. A gentle, generous soul without a bad thought for anybody, Bunny doesn't permit more than a few sentences, his or yours, to pass without an explosion of laughter.

The service was drenched with water symbolism. Quoting the Scripture, "O let all who thirst / Let them come to the water," the padre gave a sermon about Jacob's well, where Jesus asked for a drink of water from a Samaritan woman, which was like drinking with an untouchable. He mentioned how most of the O'odham place-names had to do with H_2O: Whirling Water, Bitter Well, White Well, Covered Wells, Standing Water, Cave Water. By asking for water from her, Jesus broke down racism. There is water in the desert, he preached, but it must be worked for. Green grass grows for everyone; the living water flows under the surface. A woman publicly offered a *milagro* and a prayer that her two sons stop fighting. After the service, Bunny told me that the Jesuits were less coercive than the Franciscans. "They let the Indians build their own chapels and conduct rituals that must have meant something quite different." Father Kino's successors were not as compassionate as he. In 1750 the Pima, sick of being whipped for backsliding and angry over the loss of some of their best land, rose up and tried to stage a repeat of the Pueblo Revolt. But after three months and the deaths of several hundred settlers, they were persuaded to return to their villages. Sixteen years later, politics in Europe accomplished what they had been unable to. The Jesuit infrastructure in Pimeria Alta was dismantled, the entire Society of Jesus expelled from the New World, partly because the Jesuits in Paraguay were interfering with the exploitation of the Guarani Indians and partly because the Marquis de Pombal, who had influence in both the Spanish and Portuguese courts, had it in for them because they stood in the way of the Enlightenment. The Franciscans took over the northwestern frontier, but the momentum of acculturation was lost.

Whenever one of my prowling loops took me to Tuscon, I'd visit Tom, an old Anglo (actually Irish-American) buddy from the East, who was living in a funky little adobe in a paloverde-choked vacant lot behind one of the big hotels. The entrance was in back, and I'd wade through automotive detritus—a Volkswagen bus and two sedans up on blocks, waiting for the right part or for Tom to get the energy to tackle them— and other *junque.* In a previous life, Tom had been a stockbroker who commuted to Wall Street from a house in northern Westchester and belonged to the local country club—the whole suburban number—but in the late seventies, he had a belated sixties awakening and discovered mescaline. His marriage exploded, and he built himself a shack in the local woods; he had gotten off the modern grid right in the suburbs. Then he drifted out to Tucson, where his wife had gone with the kids, and there he underwent a ten-year process of cultural devolution. Now the transformation was complete: he had shucked the East and was happy as a clam—a mellow, middle-aged guy who "did a little prospecting" to pay the rent and occasionally helped the Christic Institute bring Salvadorans and other asylum-worthy aliens up over the border. With his handlebar mustache and broad-brimmed hat, he didn't look like a prospector, he *was* a prospector. His family and friends back east had written him off as a gone case, living in this Mexican squalor, but in fact Tom had simply "become real," as my Navajo friend Sally would have put it. The last time I saw him he'd just come back from the Nevada desert, where he'd been probing for drilling sites with electric currents—an offshoot of Nevada nuclear-weapons technology—sulfide ores act as capacitators, he explained. When he got back, he'd found his place burglarized.

Tom barbecued some chicken on mesquite coals, and we stayed up late drinking mescal in the moonlight with a handsome Mexican woman he was seeing. He kept a long-barreled .22 revolver handy in case the burglars returned.

Next morning I drove past a bus stop where a teenage Latino couple was clinging and making out passionately between licks of frozen yogurt, past a driving range with big nets to keep passing cars from being hit by errant hooks. I pulled up at a light beside a yellow Volkswagen bug with black antennae—one of Truly Nolen, the exterminator's, mobile units. The housing in Tucson has a lot of turnover, and Truly Nolen is prospering because the first thing every new owner does is fumigate. I pulled into Roz Spicer's driveway in the old Fort Lowell District, which is another island of Old Mexican Tucson in an anonymous sea of Mariachi Moderne subdivisions, strips, and offices. Roz came out, an attractive, seventyish woman wearing a beret and smoking a cigarette in a black holder. Her husband, Ed, who had been dead twelve years, wrote *Cycles of Conquest,* one of the seminal books on the Southwest, and was the ethnographer of record of the Yaqui who came up to Tucson during the Porfiriata, the administration of Porfirio Díaz, having been driven off their fertile lands on the Yaqui River by genocide and the damming of the river upstream. The Spicers had moved out here in 1948, when it was still rural, made their own adobes, and built the house together. Roz took me into the book-lined office where Ed had worked. It looked on the patio garden, where sunlight was flowing through fragrant blossom-dripping boughs. A lot of the barrio was still more or less intact desert, but humans had been active in it for a thousand years, so it was a beautiful microcosm of the Southwest. All the layers were there: Hohokam canals, which had been revived by Mormons; an old fort with a parade ground, where cavalry had drilled and a band had practiced until 1886, when the capture of Geronimo had put it out of business; it was finally abandoned in 1900. Then campesinos from Sonora and Baja had moved in and founded the *rancheria* of El Fuerte, a cluster of modest adobes and huts where the Tanque Verde and the Pantano flow into each other, becoming the Rillito. In recent years the barrio had become gentrified by Anglo aficionados, who had kept their construction discreet and in keeping with the flavor of the neighborhood, and everyone had banded together and fought to get it declared a historic district, so it wouldn't be overrun. We walked down a dirt street called El Callejon lined with adobes that looked like a village in northern Sonora. The people living on it were descended from the original families and still cooked on woodstoves, collecting honey mesquite from the adjacent bosquet and preparing traditional dishes like frijoles, tortillas, *menudo, calabacitas,* and tamales. Roz pointed out how the walls of some of the adobes extended above the flat roofs, forming parapets—a feature of the Sonoran Ranch style; the walls of Santa Fe–style adobes curve at their meeting with the flat roofs without differentiation. The Rillito ran pretty strong after a good rain, Roz told me. In the local lingo, the slashing summer monsoon rains are *chubascos;* the gentle, pattering winter rains are *aquipatas.*

Loew's Ventana, an elegant golf resort and residential community in the high desert at the foot of the Santa Clara Mountains, voted number five out of a hundred mainland resorts that year (1992) by the readers of *Condé Nast Traveler,* was high-end Mariachi Moderne— one of the more seductive examples of what Roz called "a different value system." Diversifying from the source of their initial fortune, a chain of movie theaters, the Loew family had bought one-third of CBS and all of the Giants and done this place right. The two courses, the Mountain Course and the Canyon Course, both designed by Tom Fabio, were like tossing seas, undulating Daliesque pools of gleaming green in the desert, which was in full spring blaze the morning I slipped into a shotgun scramble with three food brokers who were attending a convention at the resort. The errant Ultra of Dale from Dallas, who provisioned Albuquerque with its Tropicana orange juice, Chicken of the Sea tuna, and Clorox, struck the arm of a saguaro with a squamous *thok.* Dale said something he shouldn't have, which prompted one of his partners to chide him, "Now, now! Profanity in the presence of the cacti." Players were requested to take a stroke and drop rather than go into the desert after their balls, where they could be bitten by diamondback or Mojave rattlesnakes.

"If you don't like this," Dale said, embracing the riotous bloom with his arms, "there has to be something wrong with you." The ocotillos were tipped with crimson streamers; tubes of red or yellow petals—bristly, waxy, crawling with ants—had burst out on pricklypear and barrel cacti, blazing meadows of mustard, poppy, and mallow carpeted the desert floor.

Here and there in the cactus forest poked lavish Moorish, California Mission, Sonoran Ranch, Taco Deco, and Pueblo Revival homes in various stages of construction. "I wonder what they're going for," I said to Dale, and he said, "If you have to ask, you can't afford 'em."

A Soul Reading in Phoenix

Phoenix: "the Blob That Came to Arizona" (Edward Abbey). "A potent vision of empire in the desert" (Peter Wiley and Robert Gottlieb). A renegade capitalist and developer's dream come true. A woman who had just moved from Phoenix and was cutting my hair a few months back in Lake Placid called it "the New Jersey of the Southwest, plain yogurt—only yogurt has a living culture. Motorcycle gangs—Hells Angels, Diablos—were taking over the neighborhood where I lived," she went on. "Nobody I met there was actually from Phoenix. Everybody was from someplace else. It was weird—all these people packing guns like a modern-day Wild West. Nobody knew each other and they didn't have to. You could easily get into being a bad person, and I almost did. Because everybody came from someplace else, and they weren't such good people to begin with. I was there when the pope came," she went on. On August 26, 1992, the pope celebrated mass with tens of thousands in the desert outside. The temperature was well over a hundred, and several dozen were hospitalized with dehydration; a few died.

The last time I was in Phoenix, the Arizona State Tourist Office was running a statewide contest for a new slogan, to replace the rather lame existing one: "If you knew it, you'd do it." The office's director explained that he was looking for something "people will really latch onto and that will be picked up all over the world," like "I love New York" or "Land of Enchantment" (the title of a book by Lilian Whiting, it replaced the "Sunshine State" as New Mexico's slogan in 1934).

Maybe Arizona's slogan should be "We don't stymie individualism here." This was uttered by Republican senator Jan Brewer on the occasion of the arrest of Charles H. Keating Jr., an upstanding Phoenician and the principal architect of the savings-and-loan collapse, which ended up costing taxpayers $2.5 billion. In their book *Empires in the*

Sun: The Rise of the New American West, Wiley and Gottlieb describe
Phoenix as a place where "myriads of individuals and companies [are]
involved in outrageous, often illegal activities, especially land fraud."
After tourism, land fraud is the number two industry in the state. The
growth of the city's population has been explosive—from 160,000 in
1950 to 1.2 million in the late seventies—and as the city took off, there
was a dramatic rise in gangsterism, gambling, prostitution, municipal
graft and corruption, which had already been rife from the city's beginning. In 1988, Governor Evan Mecham was impeached after he pro-
voked a national boycott of Arizona by opposing a state holiday for
the Reverend Martin Luther King. In 1991, the FBI videotaped seven
state legislators taking money in a Phoenix motel room from an agent
posing as a casino middleman. Former governor Bruce Babbit told *60*
Minutes that he wouldn't have been surprised if half the state legislature was on the take. "Anything that purports to be business is not to
be critically examined," he complained. "State government exists for
the purpose of facilitating business deals." In 1995, Governor Fife
Symington, an enthusiastic free-marketeer and great-grandson of the
Pittsburgh robber baron Henry Clay Frick, filed for Chapter 7 bankruptcy to protect himself from $24 million he owed seventy-five credi-
tors as a result of thirteen failed development projects in the eighties,
and he is now under investigation by a grand jury.

The murder of Don Bolles, an investigative reporter with the Arizona *Republic,* had already exposed some of the dark underbelly of the
Arizona boom. On June 2, 1976, Bolles cranked up his Datsun and
was blown to smithereens. He had been investigating links between
organized crime, the Phoenix dog track, a company called Emprise,
and a man named Bradley Funk, who was a crony of Senator Barry
Goldwater. He was also looking into kickbacks on fat mining, electric
energy, and government contracts on the Navajo Reservation; he had
been fleshing out a complex, slimy web that, as Lake Headley and
William Hoffman assert in their book, *Loud and Clear,* seemed to go
right up to the governor. A lot of people wanted him out of the way.

The Goldwater brothers, Bob and Barry, were major power brokers
in Arizona for forty years. Their grandfather Goldwasser had come
from Poland during the gold rush. "Big Mike," as he became known
on the frontier, peddled supplies to Indians, soldiers, farmers, and miners at the Colorado River outpost of La Paz. One of his sons started a
general store in Phoenix that eventually grew into the huge, Macy's-
like Goldwater's department store. Barry was born in the lap of luxury,
"in a log cabin equipped with a golf course, a pool table, and a swimming pool," he liked to tell people. His brother was a founder of the

La Costa Country Club near San Clemente, California, along with the former Cleveland mobster Moe Dalitz and the convicted embezzler C. Arnholt Smith. He had a three-thousand-acre ranch northwest of Phoenix that employed illegal Mexicans for five dollars a day minus food. The braceros lived in hovels made of orange crates, screened from view by black plastic sheets, and were prey to tuberculosis, lice, scabies, impetigo, and flu.

During his thirty years as a Republican senator from Arizona, Barry Goldwater revitalized the right and once even ran for president. His national career was launched with a five-thousand-dollar contribution from the racketeer Willie Bioff, who was a friend of Gus Greenbaum and ended up being blown up by a bomb. Greenbaum worked for Meyer Lansky and Bugsy Siegel, ran the horse-track wire in Phoenix, and operated the Flamingo and the Riviera hotel casinos in Las Vegas, where the Goldwater brothers stayed gratis. He and his wife were found one day on their living-room floor in Phoenix with their throats slit. Goldwater was also close to Moe Dalitz, who got backing from Lansky so he could open a Goldwater's in Las Vegas.

Goldwater got on well with the Mormons, and he had a special place in his heart for the Navajo, whom he had befriended in his early years. In fact, he named the sprawling house he built in 1957 on nine and a half acres in the Phoenix suburb of Paradise Valley Be-Nun-I-Kin, "House on Top of the Hill," and the Navajo called Goldwater Chischilly, "Curling Hair." "The Indians make more sense of nature than white men do," he told the journalist Burton Bernstein. "They accept and use it, even if they can't explain it. They go up in the mountains and sit there and watch the gods walk through the trees. I used to run a trading post in Navajo country, so I know them well. They don't respect the white man. There's nothing to respect, when you really get down to it."

But in the Hopi-Navajo land dispute of 1974, Goldwater voted for the Hopi, because he couldn't control the Navajo tribal chairman Peter MacDonald. Black Mesa, a tremendous outcrop of coal shale, was awarded to the Hopi, who, with Goldwater's engineering, leased the mining rights to Black Mesa to the Peabody Coal Company. John Harvey Adamson, one of the men convicted for blowing up Bolles, testified in 1977 that he discussed with an associate of Funk the idea of also planting a bomb in MacDonald's office or, alternatively, in the office of Tony Lincoln, the local Bureau of Indian Affairs director, and then having the bomb found, so it would look as if MacDonald had put it there, and martial law would be declared on the reservation, with Lincoln, a Goldwater protégé, in charge.

But Goldwater had a different strategy for getting rid of MacDonald. In 1975 he had the General Accounting Office audit tribal operations, and all kinds of irregularities implicating MacDonald were uncovered, which led to his removal. "I used to think Goldwater was a straight shooter," Mike Stuhff, a Las Vegas lawyer who did civil-rights work on the reservation in the seventies told me. "But if he fell off the edge of the Grand Canyon in a drunken stupor, he'd be looking for something to steal on the way down and somebody to blame it on. Does that encapsulate my feelings?"

Phoenix is not known for its tolerance, although it has the ethnic diversity of any metropolis. Anti-Oriental sentiment—a feature of the West since coolies were brought in to build the railroads—is on the rise. Groups like the Liberty Lobby and the Confederates Hammerskins preach that the worldwide Jewish conspiracy is importing Asians to miscegenate with the white race. On August 10, 1991, at a Buddhist monastery outside of Phoenix, six monks, a seventy-year-old nun, a novice, and a layman—all Thai—were forced to kneel and were killed, one by one, with a small-caliber bullet to the head. It was the largest mass murder in Arizona history. The killers wore latex gloves, and they stole two CD players, a camera, and two rings and carved the word BLOOD on a wall of the temple. A month later five men from a high-crime neighborhood in Tucson were arrested. But the following month they were released, and two teenagers linked to the crime by their rifles were arrested, but they, too, were released, claiming that their confessions had been coerced. In September 1995, an Amtrak train speeding through the desert west of Phoenix was derailed by a group calling itself the Sons of the Gestapo. A porter was killed, and nineteen passengers were seriously injured.

I cruised a large mall that was truly multicultural: an Egyptian family manned a taco stand, Indians from India with stockings on their heads milled with *cholas* in hairnets and blacks with their pants falling down. Then I drove past Papago Plaza and a subdivision called Sincuidado and got on the Hohokam Expressway. Out in the desert I saw a regal horned lizard, which with its bristling collar of neck armor looked like a miniature dinosaur. The state reptile of Arizona is the ridge-nosed rattlesnake, "but voters might be forgiven if they occasionally confuse the reptile with some of their politicians, who have been slithering past the law since the days of congressman Charles Poston, the father of Arizona," *Time* magazine quipped.

Forty-fourth Street could be anywhere in urban America but for the palms that mark it as somewhere in the Sunbelt. A store window advertised a sex nutrition special. Next door were Dental Arts and

Avalon Realty, itself for lease by Lou Branco Realty. After some looking, I found a little office, like a dentist's, whose waiting room had a
glass cabinet with—instead of dentures and oral-hygiene implements—quartz and amethyst crystals on display. A little man who
looked like a dentist came out and greeted me. His name was Frank
Alper. I had booked a "soul-life reading" with him a few weeks earlier.
His secretary had made me precharge a deposit for it to the Church of
Tzaddi on my Mastercard. The soul-life reading was $125; a soul heal-
ing and activation was $150; a complete life profile was $300. "Some
are legit and some aren't," a disciple of Alper's had told me. Alper, she
said, was very low profile, but was one of the real heavies in New Age
thinking. He had come up with—or channeled—the concept of the
walk-in.

The term "walk-in" can have various meanings. The window of an
Albuquerque barber shop, for instance, had a sign that said, WALK-INS
WELCOME. In Cold War espionage lingo, a "walk-in" was an opposition agent who defected or offered himself for recruitment. But Alper
was the first to apply the term to someone who believes that he has
been taken over by an alien soul, inhabited by an extraterrestrial.
There was a large colony of walk-ins in Sedona, two hours north.
"Sedona is one of the most physically gorgeous places on earth,
with its different-colored strata, and it's very peaceful, but there's too
much ego there," Alper told me. "I don't bother with people in Sedona
anymore."

Alper came to Phoenix from the Garment District twenty years ago,
and he retains a Brooklyn accent. "I was called here," he explained.
"Arizona is the Aquarius State, and Phoenix is the Scorpion City. It has
the same ancient spiritual energies as the Middle East and Egypt.
Phoenix is the solar-plexus chakra of the earth. It has energies that
push you into facing yourself. People come here to cleanse themselves,
to clean out their past garbage so they can get to a new level and finish
their life cycle. This usually takes one to two years. Some really
go through hell. Then they move out. But twenty-five percent end up
staying."

Alper told me that he himself was a walk-in and was able to con-
sciously channel his alien soul, whose name was Adamis. "The soul
enters the fetus at conception, but sometimes it is rejected, like a transplanted organ. Sometimes the soul has a more highly evolved frequency of energy, and it is very difficult to find a woman whose energy
is high enough to bring it into this world. When soul rejection occurs,
another soul, one that is compatible, offers to help, and it stays
through childhood, normally until the age of five to twelve. When it

leaves, it takes no energy or life experience, it leaves everything there, and the higher soul enters. At that precise one-millionth of a second—when the switch of souls occurs—that is walking-in. But the consciousness personality is not aware that anything has happened.

"After you die," Alper continued, "your conscious persona never exists again, but your soul goes up to heaven and remains as pure energy for fifteen or twenty years before entering another living fetus."

"So you're basically talking about reincarnation?" I asked.

"Yes. But we don't believe that humans evolve through grasshoppers, ants, etcetera. Your soul has always been a human soul. But it has sojourned on many planets. One astronomer certified that there are about three hundred billion planets in our galaxy, and about three hundred billion galaxies. One hundred million planets in our galaxy can house human life. The planets are at various stages of evolution. We're about in the middle. This is like the first year of high school. Most souls come here. The average soul incarnates on earth between forty-eight and seventy-two times, then it goes to a higher dimension."

The purpose of the soul-life reading is to get in touch with your previous "expressions" and find out what sort of a soul you are, or is in you now. "Maybe you're driven to try to make money, and you can't," Alper explained, "because in a previous life you had money and misused it. The purpose of the past is just to understand it and let it go. There is no failure, only different levels of success." So few people were compatible with their walk-ins that they often became alcoholics or committed suicide. But "to be a catalyst—a Hitler or a JFK—you have to have an alien soul," he maintained.

Alper showed me into his office and had me lie down on an examining table and close my eyes. Then he placed his hand on my hand and gradually moved it down my body, touching my chakras, until he got to the lower abdomen. The next stop was my groin. I held my breath, and the voice of Adamis began to speak the King's English in a professorial British accent with slight traces of Brooklyn. "You are not a walk-in," Adamis told me. "Your mother's energies were high enough for you to enter at conception. You are a service soul here on this planet earth. Exactly 327,834,424,642 years ago God created your soul—a trinity of vibrations: male, female, and love expressions. Within each soul one vibration is dominant, and your most powerful frequency is love."

I had been incarnated thousands of times, Adamis continued. My soul had had three expressions in the ancient kingdom of Lemuria, and three in the temple of a certain priest in Atlantis—and had sometimes remained for long periods in pure spirit. In 71,248 B.C. my soul had requested to descend to earth for sixty-seven expressions, and this was the sixty-seventh. "You shall walk in this lifetime until your work is done," he told me. "Then you will exist for one thousand six hundred years as pure spirit, helping other souls, then you will leave this galaxy for a higher one. It's not a coincidence that you write, that you scribe the word, that your travels have taken you to many areas of this world, that you have gained a certain reputation for credibility. You are here to be detached from other people, to stand alone but to open your heart chakra so that others can experience the light. When you and your soul blend together, the true writing will commence." He urged me to "meditate semiregularly with your eyes open, and if it will be of assistance to you, here is a vibration correlation to the language of your soul—not a soul name—Rotana."*

Alper's walk-ins are no more outlandish than the *actual* aliens that are sighted in the Southwest with some frequency, the most famous one at Roswell, New Mexico, on July 3, 1947, when a rancher named Mac Brazel came across the wreckage of what appeared to be an alien spacecraft. Four days later, the bodies of four extraterrestrials were allegedly discovered a few miles away. But on July 8, the U.S. Army and Air Force cordoned off the area and removed the physical evidence—all the debris and the bodies. The foreman of the ranch said he had seen a pasture littered with debris over three-quarters of a mile long and two or three hundred feet wide. The debris was some lightweight metallic material, pieces of soft thin wire, I beams of paperlike brown parchment inscribed with geometric symbols. According to a group of university archaeologists who had been digging in the vicinity and had happened on the bodies, they were "not human." They were small with large, pear-shaped heads, skinny arms and legs, and no hair, and they had on formfitting gray suits of a metal-like material, without buttons or zippers. An officer in the 509th Bomb Group warned the archaeologists that it was their patriotic duty not to talk about what they had seen to anyone. Scoffers say it was a weather bal-

---

*The walk-in belief system is quite similar to that of the Heaven's Gate cult, whose members tried to accelerate their souls' passage to a "new level" by committing collective suicide at Rancho Santa Fe, California, in March 1997. My wife and I with another couple golfed at Rancho Santa Fe at the end of 1991. My write-up of the visit was one of many sections of the original manuscript that have not made it into the book. By some definitions, San Diego County is part of the Southwest. It was certainly having serious Southwestern water problems. Rancho Santa Fe is an older, second-level vision of California dolce vita, which struck us at the time, in its conservative yet rootless and empty materialism, as quite unreal. In hindsight it seems another entirely appropriate place to have wanted to take off from.

loon or, in a recent version, a top-secret balloon for monitoring nuclear tests, and that the glyphs and the bodies were like the mermaids and the monsters reported by the early Spaniards, but since all the evidence seems to have disappeared, the jury is still out on whatever it was that came down at Roswell.

The Walk-Ins of Sedona

Sedona was the name of postmaster Karl Schnebly's wife. The Hopi name for Sedona meant "Blossoming Flower," I was told by a Mexican Indian who took me into its canyons. The Hopi have a legend, he said, that "when California breaks off the ocean will come back, and Sedona will once again become beachfront property." In 1985, passing through Sedona, I had tried to make contact with a Hopi prophet named White Bear, but was unable to get past his Anglo entourage. There are several rival Hopi prophets, each with their protective Anglo intermediaries.

The spectacular red-rock country of Sedona and of Oak Creek Canyon, just to the north, was immortalized by Zane Grey, the son of a Zanesville, Ohio, dentist and a major southwestern image maker who wrote sixty western romances, which were made into sixty-eight movies starting in 1956 and are full of hard-riding cowboys, villainous desperadoes, stoic Indians, and wholesome frontier girls. Grey took his pen name from a great-grandfather, Ebenezer Grey, who had been a revolutionary hero. Like Karl May (1842–1912, German author of seventy westerns celebrating the exploits of a sort of proto-Schwarzenegger named Old Shatterhand, who could knock out bison with his bare hands, and his sidekick and blood brother, a young, proto-Tonto Mescalero chief named Winetou), he was influenced by Darwin and Spenser, and "he paints a picture of a stern environment where the struggle to survive and the elimination of the unfit are immutable laws," Candace C. Kant writes. "The harshness of the land was the vehicle through which the process of natural selection occurred and [it created] a particular breed of men and women who were strong, fit, and pure." Very Teddy Roosevelt, very Hemingway, very Marlboro Man. Grey was strongly influenced by Roosevelt's romanticization of life on the range, and he went west during Roosevelt's administration. He was also influenced by Turner's thesis, which he studied in college, that America's democratic principles could be traced to the existence of a frontier, and he "made the West the repository of American values," Kant continues. "No other writer placed the West so squarely in the forefront of his work"—until the mantle passed to Louis L'Amour. His cowboys lived according to the code of the West and rode with their ladies across the purple sage into the sunset.

The high point of Grey's popularity was from 1917 to 1924. Cracks were beginning to appear in the veneer of western civilization. Americans, disillusioned by the horror of the First World War, looked back to the golden age of nationalism, reform, conservatism, environmentalism, faith in technology, individualism, and buoyant optimism embodied by Teddy Roosevelt earlier in the century, and Grey simplistically celebrated these values, while at the same time eyeing with suspicion the monopolies and the huge corporations that he felt had duped the American people into entering the war, and that he could see were beginning to spread their greedy tentacles into the pristine western landscape.

It was interesting how the same landscape could evoke such diametrically different responses, I thought as, driving north up I-17, I passed a turn-off for Deadman's Wash and another for a place called Bloody Basin—names from the frontier days, Zane Grey names. The perception of the Amazon had gone through a similar evolution, from Green Hell to the Emerald Forest. In Grey's day the purpose of the red-rock country had been to forge true grit; it had been a sort of proto–Virtual West, in which treachery lurked at every turn. Now, in phase two, it had been aestheticized and draped in gauze. Its purpose was to heal. People went out and did "color work," focusing on the blue sky for mental clarity, on the tan of the Coconino sandstone, on the various shades of green—the light green of the leafing-out spring foliage, the darker-green stubble of the junipers among the needles and spires—to get a leg up on worries like death or money.

If the fiction of Grey had idealized the Anglo-Americans, now Anglo wanna-bes seek the sacred wisdom of the Indians. Grey hadn't known what to make of the Jazz Age and had been utterly horrified by the flappers. I wondered what he would have made of the fuzzy-wuzzy New Age freaks who had taken over Sedona, how he would have reacted to all the "hooey," as an abstract painter who had been wintering there since the forties described it. A few years ago, *48 Hours* had a segment about a New Age realtor in Sedona, who had her clients sit in a circle around a crystal on a pendulum on the living-room floor of the house she was showing. If the crystal swung the right way, they were meant to have it.

There is a turnoff of Interstate 17 for Arcosanti, a futuristic community that is the brainchild of Paolo Soleri, a disaffected disciple of Frank Lloyd Wright, and that supports itself with the sale of wind chimes. The members live in a cluster of cubic modules with overvaulting arches out in stark, four-thousand-foot desert. Soleri's idea is that urban sprawl should be reorganized in dense configurations according to the principles of "archology," his fusion of architecture and ecology. "I believe in urban intensity, and I'm here in the middle of nowhere," he said in an interview. One of his plans has a million and a half people living and working in a hivelike "envelope" three times the height of the Empire State Building but only a mile and a half wide. Skeptics see threatening overtones for human privacy.

I skipped Prescott, which has a sizable retired CIA colony and which an Arizona friend described as "incredible white bread—no drunk Indians or Mexicans. No bikers or hippies. The law comes down real quick on such elements." In 1987 the computerized financial records of the town vanished. All expenditures, revenues, and accounts were inexplicably erased, showing a balance of zero, a chagrined mayor reported to the town council.

The tourist facade of Sedona was tackier than Santa Fe's. It was more like Taos's, only mellower and cuter. There was a Hathaway shirt outlet, a craft market like the one in Guadalajara, and the familiar purple-and-pink coyote stuff in the galleries, sometimes with a New Age touch, like the howling coyote would be on an amethyst stand. Behind the facade, the town was polarized—but not ethnically, the way Taos is. Here the clash was subcultural, among persuasions of Anglo: the New Age against the modern age, the environmentalists against the developers, the people who were trying to turn Sedona into Beverly Hills against the vision questers, with a few cowboys thrown in. But the developers were on hold. This was not the eighties, and resorts like L'Auberge were in the throes of financial reorganizations; Poco Diablo was being refurbished and sold as a time-share; some Swiss had bought the Sedona Golf and Tennis Club, and now it was back up for sale, as were Enchantment and Takalapaki. There was also a relict population of cowboys, who were doing the Zane Grey Virtual West number. I met a real punchy cowboy named Jim. He dressed the part and exuded the ethic, the quiet-spoken courtliness. He was a practitioner of the discipline and, it turned out, a reinventee, originally from Brooklyn. Like William Bonney.

I had lunch at a Burger King window framing a mesa vista that would have been almost impossible to photograph or paint without its becoming an instant cliché, then I wandered over to Crystal Castle Books, where I'd been told to ask for a woman named Xiayon, who was a walk-in. She used to be called Loupard. No one in the bookstore knew her by either of those names, but a woman there told me, "People around here change their spiritual names so often you can't keep track of them. But don't worry, finding a walk-in isn't going to be a problem. Every other person in Sedona is a walk-in." This was the thesis of a book called *E.T. 101,* whose coauthors, Saviza and Silarra, I noticed in the acknowledgments, were friends of Xiayon. We're all extraterrestrials, and the main function of the walk-in is "to assist ground crew members to awaken to their true identity." Saviza and Silarra kept referring to "mission control"—the same lingo as the Biosphereans. The woman in the store said she found the walk-ins "rather soulless, because they're borrowing somebody else's body and don't have much heart-chakra energy. I believe in them, but I stay away from them." She added that the "walk-in group" was doing a lot of the chemical hallucinogen Ecstasy.

But the main importance of Sedona is not that it's a mecca for walk-ins anyway; it's the "vortexes" in the surrounding canyons. Sedona is one of the special places on earth, the woman in the store told me, where the ethereal imprint of pyramids holds down energy, and these power spots are known as vortexes. To demonstrate what she was talking about, she suggested I take a vortex tour. This was easily arranged. That very hour I left the store in the company of a handsome young Indian with streaming black hair, named Rajelio. Rajelio was Purepecha, a Mexican tribe from the state of Michoacán descended from the Tarascans, whose empire had neighbored the Aztec's. But he had grown up in Chicago. "My family was Catholicized and Hispanicized, so I went on a journey of rediscovery of my Indian roots," he told me. "As a child I had many mystical experiences, which forced me to study and do research on ancient wisdom, but it was getting more expensive all the time because I was living in California. The prices here are much cheaper.

"The first time I came here, five years ago, my middle chakras vibrated when I saw that rock formation," Rajelio said, stopping at a wall of eroded towers that looked to him like the Council of Elders. "One of the elders had X-ray vision and saw right through me, and guided me to the realization that I should work in a shamanic way, healing the land and awakening people." Rajelio did hikes, "real powerful" overnights, sweats, ceremonies with drumming, and guided meditation. He had been initiated into Tibetan Buddhism and Eastern transcendental metaphysics. "The physical appearance is an illusion of form," he explained. "Basically it is atoms and molecules vibrating, the same as the sun and the moon and the stars. There's more space than matter, and so it is with the physical plane. In reality we are living in a sea of light."

Rajelio (who had been born Rogerio; he had grafted his new, spiritual name from the Egyptian sun god Ra and the Greek word for "sun") took me out to this small, low mesa surrounded by spectacular canyon walls like Tsipin or Acoma, composed of the same geologic sequence as the Grand Canyon: red sandstone capped by yellow limestone like frosting or snow, capped with black lava, the strata deeply slashed into gorges and suggestive pillars and needles. The Russians, in 1973, photographing the earth's energy field from a satellite, found the earth to be a faceted crystal, made up of a dodecahedron and an icosahedron, Rajelio told me. "It's like you take a picture of the energy of a leaf and cut off a section of the perimeter, and the piece that's missing will appear as a phantom image," he explained.

"This is part of a very large, balanced vortex," he continued, embracing 360 stunning degrees of red-rock canyon land. "God is a spiral vortex, and in a sacred land the mountains have a power of silence about them, and that silence can bring you back to your own silence, to the ancient wisdom of the power of the silence of all-knowingness that is within us." He suggested we "sit in peace" for a while.

I noticed that we were not alone. A middle-aged Anglo woman was sitting with her back against a tree, her eyes closed in bliss, her feet shod in intricately beaded knee-length white doeskin moccasins that must have cost hundreds of dollars. "Trees are alive and have been known to have sacred effects," Rajelio whispered. We grooved on the bristling spines of a mescal rosette, which trapped the light hallucinationally.

Then a jeep drove up and a middle-aged veteran of the sixties, with graying long hair, came out and started chanting like an Indian and striking an expensive drum as he walked around a medicine ring, a circle of stones in the center of the mesa. His eyes had the glazed, watery look of someone who has just fired up a joint. Then another jeep, this one from Red Rock Jeep Tours, arrived, followed by another and another, and about twenty tourists got out to take in the ceremony. The old hippie stepped up his Indian routine, but he had as much heart in it as a burnt-out male stripper. "It's all relative," Rajelio said, noticing my arched eyebrow, "who's real and who isn't. The guy's just trying to make a living."

The Puzzling Death of Leroy Jackson

Tony Hillerman is probably the most prominent producer of southwestern images working today. His Navajo are keenly intelligent, grounded, with good hearts and senses of humor—pretty much the way I have found the Navajo I know. He puts the People in a good light without romanticizing them and writes about them with love and respect, so I was surprised that the Navajo I spoke with had a low opinion of him. Ray Morgan didn't think Hillerman was accurate or that he was doing any good for the Navajo, but was just "out for himself"; he heard that Hillerman was giving tours of Chaco Canyon for a thousand dollars a head. My friend Tom said, "Hillerman is exploitation fantasy, an eighth of a hundredth of a hairline of what we're about. He doesn't know what he's talking about, and he's got nothing to back him up." But cries of exploitation had been going up since Laura Gilpin's photograph of the Navajo Madonna in the thirties. I thought he had done a lot to introduce Anglos to the People and their culture. A white man depicting Indians is obviously tricky business. If you present them in a glowing light, you are accused of romanticizing them. If you bring out anything negative, you win their enmity. Either way, if your book makes any money, you are exploiting them, guilty of "cultural imperialism," the charge leveled at Paul Simon, who collaborated with South African musicians on his *Graceland* album. Robert Redford had made a movie of Hillerman's *Dark Wind,* but the Hopi were so upset at some of the scenes, which showed drug dealing on the mesas and a kachina dancer having his mask torn off, that it was never released.

Hillerman's mysteries seem to be accurate in a fundamental way. They pick up on a basic quality of Navajo country: it *is* mysterious, perhaps because the culture recognizes levels of reality unfamiliar to the Western mind, particularly in its relationship with evil, which is omnipresent, part of everyday life, not down in some underworld.

In the summer of 1993 an "unexplained respiratory distress syndrome" broke out in the Four Corners area. IN NAVAJO LAND OF MYSTERIES ONE CARRIES A DEADLY ILLNESS, The New York Times reported on June 5. By November, by which time forty-five cases, twenty-seven of them fatal, had been reported, the cause of the syndrome was announced: a new strain of hanta virus, spread in the urine, feces, and saliva of deer mice. But my friend Sally wasn't sure this was the real cause. "We've lived with these rodents forever," she told me. "We do our thing, and they do their thing. Most of the people who died were young adults, born around the time those mines and power plants started being built, twenty years ago. Maybe they were born with this thing. The sun is not like it was before. It's brighter, and it hurts. The water, the air, have so much stuff in them, it's not safe to even sleep outside. It probably has to do with something in the air, and they're not telling us. Maybe it's from the missiles in Utah."

That fall Nicásio Romero sent me a clip about a mysterious Navajo death that seemed right out of Hillerman. At 4:20 p.m. on October 9, 1993, Officer Ted Ulibari of the New Mexico State Police smashed the driver's window of a white '90 Dodge van parked, with the doors locked and the windows curtained, at the Brazos Bluff Lookout along Highway 64 and was greeted by a nauseating smell. Lying in the backseat, covered with a heavy purple blanket, was the badly decomposed body of a Navajo environmental activist named Leroy Jackson, who had been missing for eight days and had been dead about that long. An autopsy performed in Albuquerque found traces of Valium and marijuana and a possibly lethal level of methadone. Because there were no indicators of foul play, such as bruises or trauma to the body, the cause of death was ruled an accidental methadone overdose. But Jackson's family and friends remained convinced that he was the victim of a sophisticated hit. His efforts to save the last extensive forest on the Navajo Reservation had not only made him enemies among his own people, he was becoming a threat to the entire American logging industry. In a few days after he disappeared he had been due to testify in Washington on behalf of the endangered Mexican spotted owl, as a result of which thousands of acres of forest in the Southwest would have been declared critical habitat and would have become off-limits to chain-saw crews.

When I arrived in Albuquerque the following January, the case was still open. A Santa Fe–based conservation group called Forest Guardians, which had worked with Jackson and was frustrated with what it considered to be the laxity of the police investigation, had hired its own private investigator, but "quite frankly, we have not found out what happened," its executive director, Sam Hitt, told me.

Sally's kid sister Louise was involved in Diné CARE, the environmental group that Leroy had helped found (for Diné Citizens Against Ruining the Environment), so I drove out to Big Mountain to see if she would come with me when I went to talk to Leroy's widow and colleagues. I pulled into her mother's outfit. Alice gave me a little smile; she knew that I'd been trying to get her grandson Clayton out of Leavenworth. Louise's husband, George Crittenden, was working on his pickup. He had a red bandanna around his head and a walkie-talkie with which he was monitoring the traffic in and out of Big Mountain, and on the front seat was a revolver. George was a Cherokee; he was named for a Major Crittenden who had marched his people on the Trail of Tears to Oklahoma the century before. There were a bunch of unrelated Cherokee Crittendens, he told me; they'd been named in batches. George had been a security guard with AIM and had come to Big Mountain in 1974, when it looked as if there would be a showdown like the one at Wounded Knee the year before, and there he had met Louise. They'd gotten together and had some kids, and he'd been at Big Mountain ever since. It turned out that George had been working with Leroy Jackson to develop less destructive alternatives to logging. He regarded Leroy as "one of the best people I met in all my life," and he had no doubts that Leroy was murdered. "The tribal government is the biggest bunch of redneck Indians," he told me. "They don't give a fuck about their own kind, and Leroy was digging deep into their shit. He was getting the goods on important people. Heads were going to roll. They must have hired someone good to do him. Someone with surgical gloves."

A Pueblo activist in Albuquerque told me, "All these Indian leaders are selling out right and left. The tribal governments are like Third World dictatorships operating under the guise of sovereignty. They have their own goon squads who keep everybody in line by fear and intimidation." She mentioned Peter "Big Mac" MacDonald, the tribal chairman twice convicted of corruption. His successor, Leonard Haskie, was indicted by a federal grand jury in 1994 for taking bribes of nearly forty thousand dollars from two logging companies.

"You can bet Big Mac knows what went down," George said. Mac-Donald was in prison, but George was sure that most Navajo would vote him back in if he ever ran again for tribal chairman. "All they want is a well fifty feet away. Almost nobody would choose to live the way we do out here—with no traffic or television to distract you from everything you're supposed to be."

Championing the environment in this part of the world was a dangerous calling, especially if you were an Indian. George told me about "a Navajo woman who was fighting an airport they wanted to put in in Chinle, and her trailer was shot up," and about a Navajo employee for Peabody Coal who had been trying to enforce the company's own environmental regulations and had been told "if you don't watch it, you'll wind up like Leroy Jackson." This was three weeks after Leroy's death.

George and I drove up to Tom's hogan to see if he was there, and he was. Tom belongs to the same clan as Leroy Jackson, Waters Flow Together, but he hadn't met him until a year ago, at a Senate hearing about using the American Indian Religious Freedom Act of 1978 to protect sacred sites. Both Tom and George ended up driving with me to Tsaile, where Leroy's widow, Adella Begay, and their three children lived.

On the way George pointed out a goshawk hovering over a greasewood flat. "Bad news for rabbits, man." We passed the mine at Black Mesa, where the coal-bearing shale is being gouged out of the earth by the dragline with a bucket big enough to hold forty people, then crushed and flushed down 273 miles to the Mojave power plant in Laughlin, Nevada, with three million gallons a day pumped from the Navajo aquifer—the most obscene rape of fossil water in the desert Southwest. Tom invited me to the Big Mountain spring gathering, in the third week of April. They were all going to moon the mine, take down their pants and stand in a line, and on each of their butts there would be a letter, spelling GIVE A HOOT DON'T POLLUTE. George said: "Peabody has Wackenutt rent-a-cops to make sure nobody sabotages the slurry line. They used to be cops but were busted for butchering people, likely indigenous people. I wouldn't be surprised if one of them did Leroy."

Leroy was born in 1946 in Shiprock, New Mexico. His first three decades were sadly typical of the twentieth-century Native American experience. His father took off before he was a year old. His mother, Jane, who later married a *bilagaana* named Popovich, was a dealer in Navajo weavings and jewelry and had a drinking problem. Her three children were bounced between grandparents, traditional sheepherders who taught them the Navajo Way, and Dickensian Indian boarding schools run by missionaries who did their best to disabuse them of their religion, culture, and language. After graduating from high school in Flagstaff and briefly studying electronics in Dallas, Leroy received his draft notice and was shipped to Vietnam as a Green Beret. He didn't talk much about what happened over there, how many yellow brothers he had to kill for Uncle Sam. His tour was cut short by a dishonorable discharge for repeated drunkenness and disorderliness. For the next ten years, he lived in the streets of Phoenix, Albuquerque, and Los Angeles, sleeping in Salvation Army Dumpsters, in and out of the cooler for public intoxication. At some point, while he was living in Oakland, California, he married a white woman. They had two daughters. One lives in Sacramento, estranged from her Navajo-ness, and has found Jesus. The other OD'd in her teens at an Indian boarding school in Phoenix.

When he was thirty, Leroy woke up on the floor of a Salt Lake City jail cell and asked himself, What am I doing here? From then on, he never took another drink. A Pawnee named Big Elk got him into treatment. He got a job, counseling at a local Indian drug and alcohol rehabilitation clinic, and one day he met a lovely Navajo nursing student at the University of Utah named Adella Begay. Adella, on her part, was taken by this five-foot-eight thirty-year-old with high cheekbones and rugged good looks who spoke so seriously and movingly. They got married in 1977. As is the Navajo custom, he went to live among her people, in Tsaile. He went back to school, studying mechanical engineering, and worked for eighteen months at the San Juan power plant. But "Leroy was a rebel," Sam Hitt told me. "He couldn't live under the confines of a nine-to-five life." So he quit and became a trader of Indian crafts. Dealing mainly in Navajo blankets, which fascinated him (they are not only works of art, but visual records of the People's history, encoded in horizontal bands of zigzags, diamonds, and stripes), he traveled around, sometimes as far as Oregon, buying and selling and living out of his van. This seminomadic life was much more to his liking.

Through the Begays and their cousins the Redhouses, who lived traditionally, Jackson reembraced the Navajo Way and became what his mother, who gave up alcohol for Christian fundamentalism in 1964 and now lives in Phoenix, called a reconstructed Indian. The Begays had a summer sheep camp in the Chuska Mountains, above Tsaile, and Jackson started going there and participating in ceremonies with local elders who worshiped the forest. The hexagonal hogan sat in a natural meadow surrounded by aromatic two- or three-hundred-year-old "yellow-belly" ponderosa pines, which the elders called the grandfather trees. In the spring of 1991, Jackson went up to the camp. It had been a while since his last visit, and to his horror he found that the grandfather trees had all been cut, and all that remained of the forest was a bleak, mutilated vista of oozing stumps and stacked slash. The elders had long been deeply upset by the logging in the Chuskas, but they couldn't speak enough English to make themselves heard, and the problem hadn't gotten much attention because of all the other horrendous environmental problems on the rez.

A petite, poised woman in her thirties, Adella Begay lived in modern housing—one of several identical ranch houses built on a circular cul-de-sac. We arrived just as she was leaving for work. She's the head nurse at Tsaile's Indian Health Clinic. The kids—seventeen, six, and five—had already left for school. Adella said to feel free to visit the summer camp. But as for her own participation, she said, "I loved my husband very much. I talked to a lot of reporters, and they twisted what I said and took it out of context, and I'm kind of burnt out on them." She had asked Lori Goodman, a cofounder of Diné CARE, to "do the interview." Lori told us that the police had just released the van and its contents to Adella the day before. Obviously she needed to be alone, so we drove out to the camp. George had been there the summer before, and he knew the way.

The hogan sat in a grassy meadow at the foot of Roof Butte. It was a beautiful spot. "This place is sacred for the family," George explained. "A lot of ceremony is done here, and a lot of people are buried here." The only big ponderosas that remained in the surrounding forest were snags—standing dead trees—and culls, marked with three stripes of blue paint to identify their rotten interiors. "That is what most logging executives are—culls—rotten from the inside out," George said.

"The last time I saw Leroy, he was leaning on that tree, talking to some loggers," he went on. "We were trying to get them interested in permaculture." He showed me a swale he had dug perpendicular to the slope, so it would catch the runoff, and you could grow crops in it—a traditional arid-land farming technique and the main strategy of permaculture. George was applying for grants from the Patagonia company and Ben and Jerry's ice cream so he could introduce the science to communities on the reservation. "Leroy was advocating not bulldozers but people power, sustainable agriculture, erosion control, watershed management, appropriate housing and technology—community development in the true sense, with everything working to feed something else and hardly any waste. I walked around in these woods, planning where to run my swales, and I don't know what he was doing, but I found Leroy's tracks all over the place. He wore pointed cowboy boots."

Lori Goodman lived up in Durango, Colorado, three hours north. Durango was one of the famous wide-open towns of the Wild West and the northern limit of the Southwest, according to one scheme (this version runs from Durango, Colorado, to Durango, Mexico, and Las Vegas, Nevada, to Las Vegas, New Mexico). It had been in a slump for most of the twentieth century, surviving mainly on tourism and the abundant snow that falls in the surrounding Rockies, but in the last few years had been discovered by New Yorkers and the Hollywood crowd. Big money was moving in and driving up the real estate. But behind this new facade, it was still, like Taos, raw frontier. "It don't take long to go through this town, unless you cross wires with the rednecks," George said.

We checked into a cheap motel at the far end of town, half of whose neon sign was on the blink, and called Lori, who gave us a rendezvous at a Chinese restaurant. Lori was married to an Anglo doctor and was, like Adella, a refined intelligence, fluent in the ways of the modern world; as Sam Hitt described them, "we're talking upper-crust Navajo here."

Adella had asked her not to talk about the "personal stuff." "Right now we're under a lot of pressure to complete what Leroy started," Lori explained. "We'd like to know what happened, but we don't want to dwell on it. It will come out. We just want to be with Adella and her wishes."

When Jackson hooked up with Lori, she had just won a grass-roots battle to stop a forty-million-dollar hazardous-waste incinerator and toxic dump in the rural Navajo community of Dilkin, Colorado. They joined forces with a third activist, Earl Tulley, who was continuing the work of Larry Casuse, trying to clean up Gallup. Jackson had finally found an outlet for his abundant physical energy and his untapped leadership talents. In the two years that remained to him, he would accomplish tremendous things. "He was always frustrated with us because we weren't doing enough," Earl Tulley recalled. "He was going full blast, and we couldn't keep pace. It was like he was on a marathon. He knew he had a destination to meet." In fact, Jackson was a long-distance runner. He ran to recharge himself and burn off energy. Tom found he couldn't keep up with him even when he was walking; he had to take two steps to Leroy's every one.

"By the time I knew him, Leroy was extraordinarily articulate and informed in economic and biological issues," Sam Hitt told me. "But more than anything, he was a riveting speaker in Navajo. He had discovered these roots he never knew he had. Like Alex Haley, he had experienced a rebirth, and this gave him power. Adella was fascinated with this power. Jackson had been there, he had an understanding of the informal support systems you need to stay alive on the street, and he brought all these qualities to the environmental struggle, street smarts, a warm, personal manner, an unusual empathy for his fellow man, a great sense of humor—the Navajo humor, full of nuance—a survivor's refusal to back down or give up, a distrust of anything that comes down from the authorities, and an uncanny ability to probe the bureaucratic facade."

"Leroy was right on the case," Lori told us. "He knew their tricks." The logging in the Chuskas was being done by a tribal enterprise called Navajo Forest Products Industries (NFPI). Since the early sixties, they had been, in Sam's description, "cutting like banshees." Forty trucks a day had been rolling out of the Chuskas to the NFPI's mill in the little community of Navajo. The annual harvest was forty million board feet (a board foot is twelve inches by twelve inches by one inch thick). Most of this was old-growth ponderosa pine, a high-quality wood used for moldings and trim. A mature tree can fetch as much as a thousand dollars. And yet NFPI was millions of dollars in the red. Was this due to mismanagement, Jackson wondered, or were individuals skimming the profits? It certainly wouldn't be the first time a tribal enterprise had been plundered.

NFPI's board consisted of five Navajo and four whites, who all hailed from the Pacific Northwest and belonged to the traditional "forest management" school of logging, which basically regards the forest as an industrial tree farm. It was their philosophy—that old stands are susceptible to fire, insects, and disease and should be replaced as quickly as possible with plantations of thrifty young trees—that was denuding the Chuskas, because the second half of the program, the reforestation, wasn't being followed through on. Disgruntled loggers and millworkers complained to Jackson of being laid off without notice and of having their worker-safety program dismantled as a money-saving move, while high-salaried non-Navajo managers and board members held their meetings at posh resorts off the reservation.

It was the responsibility of BIA's area office in Gallup to ensure that NFPI complied with federal environmental law, and it didn't take much digging before Jackson found out that the logging had been going on for years without ever being subject to the National Environmental Policy and Water Acts. Timber sales had repeatedly been concluded without an environmental-impact assessment ever being done. The BIA had simply signed off that the logging would have no effect on local human activities, and instead of enforcing the mandatory two-month waiting period for appeals to the sale, the chain saws generally went to work immediately. The laws against cutting beside a stream or on slopes of forty degrees or more were repeatedly ignored, and the best-grade lumber, from the grandfather trees, was sold at less than half market price.

When Jackson confronted the BIA, NFPI, and the tribal council with all these irregularities and demanded an independent audit of the entire operation as well as an examination of the relationship between the mill and outside logging interests, "he started making people real uncomfortable," Lori continued. Jim Carter, the BIA's *bilagaana* Gallup area director, whom Sam Hitt described as "the chief prince of darkness," threatened Jackson with his own medicine. According to Lori, he said, " 'I'm going to report you to the IRS. You couldn't be doing this for free.' The guy couldn't believe Leroy was defending the forest because we were being cheated out of our culture. Twice he offered to pay Leroy off. Leroy told him, 'It's not 1492 anymore.' He had a way with words."

Jim Carter's side of the story, which I got a few days later, was, not surprisingly, quite different. "Leroy was pretending the trees were sacred so he could create an issue that would enable him to run for office," he told me, while Diné CARE was basically "a front for Forest Guardians [a white environmental group], which is trying to get its foot in the door on an Indian reservation." The incident in question took place at a public meeting, where "Leroy was pleading poor and saying that the tribe should hire him because he needed money to carry on his quest—a peculiar request. But Mr. Jackson dressed well, and poor people making money selling a few Indian trinkets don't have the money to jet to Washington [as Leroy had done to bad-mouth Carter to his superiors]. So I asked, Who paid him? Where did Diné CARE get its money? He said from something called the Tide Foundation, which I guess is one of the many liberal groups that throw money at Indian causes."

The tribal council hemmed and hawed about the audit, and it was only after Leroy's death, on November 16, with national network television filming the proceedings, that it agreed to it. The audit had supposedly been completed and was expected to be released momentarily. "Hopefully, unless it's a whitewash, there will be an inkling of something," Lori said. "There has obviously been intertwined corruption.

It's just a matter of somebody letting go. All you have to do is target one person so he spills the beans."

Now that he had boned up on environmental law, Leroy started using it as a weapon to challenge upcoming timber sales. In 1983 the tribe and the BIA had adopted a ten-year forest-management plan that divided the Chuskas and the adjacent Defiance Plateau into sixty-three timber-cutting compartments. In 1992 he filed an appeal to stop the logging in the Whiskey Creek–Ugly Valley area, in which four compartments with a total of 23.6 million board feet were at stake, on the grounds that the BIA had allowed it to proceed without an environmental-impact state-ment, contrary to its own regulations. As soon as the appeal was received, the logging was supposed to be suspended for thirty days, but instead the NFPI kept its loggers cutting twenty-four hours a day, under arc lights. So Jackson had to seek a temporary restraining order from the federal district court in Albuquerque, which suspended the logging for ten days. When this happened, the loggers hung effigies of Jackson from their rigs. Jackson was upset by this and by having to go to federal court to settle a dispute with his own people. He knew how scarce jobs were, that there is 35 percent unemployment on the reservation. Eventually, his actions would put 120 of his fellow Navajo out of work, and this tore him up. His hair went gray, and the paralyzing migraines he had suffered from since childhood came with increasing frequency. "But he believed in what he was doing," Lori went on, "and he really put him-self on the line."

Leroy's objection to the logging was essentially spiritual. As his mentor, the longtime Navajo activist John Redhouse explains, "The entire Chuskas are a male deity. They are the complement and supple-ment of Black Mesa, which is the female deity. Both of these interior mountains are part of the Navajo hogan, if you will, and provide har-mony and balance that are essential for the survival of the People." As Jackson testified to the Senate Select Committee on Indian Affairs in February 1993, only one of the compartments in the Chuskas had been surveyed for sacred sites, and many of the places where the traditional healers made offerings and gathered sage, bucktail, and other medici-nal herbs were being destroyed. These places, he argued, were pro-tected not only by the American Indian Religious Freedom Act but, because of their cultural importance, by the National Historic Preser-vation Act as well. But it was the Mexican spotted owl that became, improbably, Leroy's most potent ally.

As of 1990, only 2,160 Mexican spotted owls were known to be in existence. A southwestern subspecies of the same spotted owl that proved the nemesis of the Pacific Northwest's timber industry, *Strix occidentalis lucida* made the endangered species list on March 16, 1993, and was immediately recruited in the battle to save the Chuskas, one of its main habitats. That spring the Tonitsa timber sale, with roughly thirty-two million board feet of old-growth ponderosa at stake, came up for review. The "logging cartel," as Sam Hitt called it, was forced to come down to eighteen million board feet to accommodate the owl. "I told Leroy we were going to win this battle on the wings of the owl," Sam, whose Forest Guardians were providing legal and technical support, told me. "He didn't want to hear that, because of the power of the owl. The owl for Navajo is a living presence of everything dark and powerful and beyond human control. It is a messenger of death and other big change. Leroy was quite leery of its potential to do harm. He said, 'Sure we can win on the wings of the owl, but when we take that genie out of the bottle, what are we going to do?' Looking back on it, I think he may have been foreseeing his own death."

John Redhouse, however, maintains that the owl is "not necessarily bad. It's part of the creation and was put there to alert you about bad things like NFPI and overlogging and other threats to the sacred mountain. It's a cultural and environmental indicator, a warning that you'd better get your act together."

Tom said that the owl "is there to tell your family some ceremonies need to be performed. He's only bad if you don't do a protection ceremony. He's like an omen on yourself that you're not listening."

But the bottom line is that if an owl hoots near a Navajo house, the family interprets it to mean that somebody is going to die. This belief is held not only by Navajo, but by Pueblos, Tarahumara, Rwandan Tutsi, and many other traditional peoples around the world.

With the timber industry depressed in the Northwest, thanks in no small degree to the northern spotted owl, and the eastern slopes of the Cascades, once bristling with ponderosa, pretty much logged out, there was growing interest in southwestern Indian lands as a new source of timber. The BIA had been notoriously lax about enforcing environmental regulations, but now Jackson was starting to cramp their style, and this new owl had come into the fray. Sam recalled, "I was constantly getting calls from consultants for lumber companies asking, 'Are you going to war over the owl down there?' "

Another timber sale, Big Water, for twenty-seven million board feet, came up, and Jackson got nine million of it set aside for the owl. This was starting to affect the bank accounts of people like Henry Nez, one of two contract loggers for NFPI. Nez, a Navajo, had been operating in the red even before Jackson came on the scene, and, according to

Sam Hitt, Leroy's legal plays cut his income in half. On September 28, three days before Jackson left on his fatal business trip to Taos, Nez said at a public meeting that if Jackson continued to challenge the timber sales, there would be violence similar to what had happened in February 1989 when chairman Peter MacDonald was placed on administrative leave, and his supporters, wielding baseball bats, clashed with the tribal police at Window Rock and two people were killed. But Henry Nez, Sam told me, is "a pretty Neanderthal guy. It's hard to imagine him concocting a sophisticated murder plot. If anything, he's the fall guy, maybe part of the team." (I tried to get Nez's side of the story, but Ed Richards, NFPI's manager, told me his phone was disconnected because he hadn't been working for quite a while, and he lived seventy-five miles from the mill and would be very difficult to get hold of.)

Jimmie Bitsui, one of NFPI's Navajo board members, also made an oblique threat several weeks before Nez's. He told Brenda Norrel, a longtime *bilagaana* correspondent on Navajo affairs for the AP and local papers who had been giving Leroy and his struggle a lot of favorable publicity, "Tell Leroy and Diné CARE somebody's going to get hurt." Brenda had never seen Bitsui so angry, and "I knew he was serious," she told me, "because I was told the same thing in 1987 by a board member of the Window Rock school system, whose budget had a quarter-of-a-million-dollar discrepancy that I was investigating, and that night I came home to find two people in a car waiting for me outside my house. I pulled out fast, and for a long time after that I slept with a sawed-off shotgun."

New Times, a monthly magazine published in Phoenix, reported that Jackson also received threatening late-night phone calls. According to Earl Tulley, he dimissed the threats as "catcalls" and joked that if he was done in, the police would have plenty of suspects. Earl asked if he was afraid driving around by himself, as he kept doing, and he said, "I'm so much out in the open, anybody could get me. But what I am really afraid of is that somebody's going to put something into my drink, so I never drink anything that I'm offered."

That summer, the logging cartel counterattacked with a petition to the U.S. Fish and Wildlife Service by the tribal council that the Navajo nation be exempted from the Endangered Species Act on the ground that it was a sovereign nation and had the right to determine its own environmental policy. Big bucks were at stake: if the exemption was granted, it would give the timber industry relatively unrestricted access to the reservation's forests.

Jackson got his hands on an August 1 memo to Fish and Wildlife's regional director in Albuquerque from the BIA's area directors in Phoenix, Gallup, and Albuquerque:

> As you are no doubt aware, the issue of whether tribal lands can or should be included in a designation of critical habitat for the Mexican Spotted Owl . . . is a very important one for the tribes in the Southwest. In this case, not only are issues of sovereignty, self-governance, and economic development involved, but cultural and religious issues are also entwined as well since the owl is held in low esteem by the Navajos, Apache, and many Pueblo people.

When Jackson read this last bit, he hit the ceiling. On September 23, he fired off a nine-point letter to the same regional director. "Should there be any doubt in your mind, the BIA officials who composed this letter DO NOT write on behalf of traditional people, but rather on behalf of the tribal governments which have embraced a model of economic development that is foreign to our traditional culture." The assertion that the owl is held in low esteem by Navajo, the letter continued, was "just plain false and an insult to our philosophy." Jackson explained that the owl did have a "negative" connotation in Navajo culture, but negative as opposed to the positive characteristics of other creatures, in the sense of aggressive, male, and self-protective. Owl feathers, he pointed out, were used in several Protection Way ceremonies and adorned the war cap, enhancing the warrior's aggressiveness.

What makes Jackson's colleagues really suspicious are not only the strong local and national motives for taking him out, but the timing: on October 6 he was going to Washington to tell lawyers at the Department of Interior's Solicitor General's Office that the tribal council was lying about the owl and to present evidence of all the other malfeasance he had uncovered. According to one theory, it was not his imminent blowing the whistle on mismanagement and corruption that got him killed, but his calling the tribal council liars on religious matters that could not be countenanced. According to another theory, which I heard from several sources but didn't put much stock in, he was done in by traditionalists who were upset with him for revealing religious secrets about the owl and specifics about ceremonies and sacred sites. "He stepped on some sensitive toes," a Pueblo environmentalist told me. "I'm not surprised he was killed. Leroy was out there in the limelight all by himself. When a single individual on the reservation sticks his neck out like that, you can bet it will be chopped off. I learned real early if you get into this work, you got to be damn careful."

But none of Leroy's family or associates in the struggle believed he was killed by his own people or by others in the logging cartel. Although they couldn't yet explain how, they were all convinced the perpetrator was "the corporates." Lori believed "the mining interests" were behind it. Why would they care about Jackson? I asked.

"Because he was setting a precedent for every company that's operating on tribal land without an environmental-impact statement. What he was doing resonated far beyond the Navajo Reservation."

Lori felt sure he had been trapped. "It was definitely somebody he knew" who was paid to do him, she said. And according to her, it wasn't the methadone that killed him. The methadone was forcibly introduced, or maybe someone slipped him a methadone mickey without his knowing it to make him look like a druggie and discredit the movement.

So what did kill him then?

"There's drugs that metabolize within forty-eight hours," she said. "You can inject a person with air."

"There are sophisticated ways of offing a person and allowing for decomposition to cover it up," John Redhouse mused. "You can inject somebody under a fingernail, and it wouldn't show up in an autopsy."

George agreed with Lori. "He was grabbed by someone he knew. He wouldn't have let them take him without a struggle. Now all you got to do is think like a cop and figure out what asshole did it."

"We live in a sophisticated era," Earl Tulley told me. "If we can change from a man to a woman and create life in a test tube, we can kill somebody and make it look like an accident. My theory about accidents is that there are none. Leroy's life ended because of what he believed. If he'd stuck to engineering or trading arts and crafts, he'd still be alive. But once you start defending something, it takes on a life of its own, and sometimes a life has to be lost before the issue can be settled."

That was one school of thought. Another held that Jackson was a suicide. "He was under a lot of stress. The last two, three months he wasn't his old, upbeat self," Brenda Norrel recalled. Late on the morning of October 1, he stopped in at Steve Eich's gallery in Taos to pay an eight-hundred-dollar IOU. Eich's wife, Cindy, recalls that he was "much less friendly than usual." He kept staring off into space, as if bothered by something. She wondered if he might be having one of his headaches. The Pueblo environmentalist didn't rule out suicide. "What if he came to the conclusion that the odds were impossibly stacked against him?" she mused. "His own people were coming down on him. He wasn't going to save the Chuskas. What if he said fuck it?"

But his relatives and associates didn't think this was a possibility. He had too much to live for, they told me. He was really psyched about going to Washington. He had already put in the foundation for a solar house he was going to build up at the summer camp, and he had just bought fifty head of four-horned *churro* sheep, which are prized possessions among the Diné. He had so much going on.

One thing was for sure: a lot of people weren't telling everything they knew. Adella's gag order had spread another layer of mystification over her husband's death. None of the people George and Tom and I went to see were exactly forthcoming. "Doesn't it bother you how Adella and Lori were unwilling to talk about the details of the case?" Tom said as I dropped the two of them off at their hogans. "Doesn't it make you think they've been threatened or paid off? Or maybe they're starting to figure things out, and they don't want to talk till they do."

The next day the Albuquerque *Journal* and the Santa Fe *New Mexican* both ran stories that provided a far less conspiratorial explanation for Adella and Lori's reticence: the state police had found in the engine compartment of Leroy's van (the hump between the two front seats) a bottle of antihistamines prescribed to him by a drugstore in Shiprock. There were no pills in the bottle, but there was a residue of pink liquid that turned out to be methadone. In Rinconada, south of Taos, Leroy had spent a couple of nights with an Anglo trader named Mark Marcus, who, according to Sam, had a seventeen-year history of methadone use. So Marcus could have given Jackson some meth for his migraines; Adella had said he was out of his prescription medication, Valium and Tylenol III with codeine. So he could have OD'd on the stuff after all.

This didn't look good for the cause. But there were still serious problems with the accidental-overdose hypothesis. The white '90 Dodge van with Leroy's body was found on October 9 parked in plain sight, with its windows curtained, at a scenic overlook along the road that goes over the mountains from Tres Piedras to Tierra Amarilla. Jackson was last seen by the owner of a convenience store at about five-thirty on September 30. The next day Steve Martinez, a Santa Fe optometrist who had driven up to hike in the mountains and usually left his car at the same Brazos Bluff Overlook, found the van there, so he parked elsewhere. But on the fourth of October, Jimmy Martinez (no relation to Steve), a tow-truck operator from Chama, cruised Route 64 looking for business—deer hunting had just begun, and there were a lot of drunk Texans with thirty-ought-sixes on the road—and he swore the van wasn't there. When Jackson didn't come back to

Tsaile the next day for his plane tickets to Washington, Adella, who had been worried since his failure to show up at Shiprock on the second, knew something was very wrong. That day—the fifth—David Lang, an Anglo doctor she works with at the clinic, drove back and forth on Route 64 looking for him, and he, too, was adamant that the van wasn't at the overlook. "Maybe it was foggy, and he failed to see it," Sam Hitt mused. "But this stretches the imagination.

"It could have been there all the time, but Rio Arriba County is the second- or third-poorest in the state. Abandoned vehicles are quickly stripped of their tires and batteries. Plus hunters were cruising all the time with their CBs, and it's hard to believe one of them wouldn't have reported something unusual like a van that had been sitting there for several days. And if the van wasn't there, where was it? There has to be a second party, but who? Why was it left there? It's a very special spot, a majestic scene, overlooking the Brazos cliffs, which are sacred to the Ute. Tony Hillerman has a description of it in one of his books. Is there some message in this we aren't getting?"

I had breakfast with Earl Tulley at the Navajo Nation Inn, where the tribal council and the logging cartel take their meals and seal their deals, but it was Saturday, and I hadn't been able to reach any of them. Their numbers were all unlisted. Most Navajo who have phones, in fact, don't seem to be listed, which is perhaps an index of the society's paranoia. I tried some other numbers I'd been given, but either they weren't any good, or when someone did answer, he or she could tell from my voice I was Anglo and gave me the runaround. "You're not going to get anything from them anyway," Earl told me. "They'll just tell you he OD'd." But I needed to hear the other side of the story. Dexter Gill, the *bilagaana* forest manager for the Navajo nation from 1982 to May 1993, who now runs a little bookstore called the Howling Coyote in Gallup, gave it to me.

Gill suggested we meet at Baggett's 76, a truck stop on the edge of town. He was an earnest, square-jawed man of fifty-one, originally from Cortez, Colorado, dressed in jeans and cowboy boots with silver-and-turquoise bands on his watch and cowboy hat.

"I've been in forestry thirty years," he began. "I came to work for the tribe right after the ten-year management plan, which was written on five hundred thousand acres of accessible forest. The plan was to harvest forty million board feet a year, then drop to thirty-five million. Much of the forest is overmature ponderosa, which is dying faster than it's growing. There's a lot of cull—trees that have already rotted. The annual mortality is twelve, fifteen million board feet. From a total forest-management standpoint, you've got to get the old stuff out of there. So we targeted the so-called grandfather trees, which is how the conflict started, because they're the most sacred ones.

"When I first met Leroy, he was just a mouthpiece. He didn't have the ability or understanding to do much. His wife was basically the brains behind that pair. She's sharp—misdirected but sharp. Jackson started raising a ruckus about how NFPI is trampling over our sacred trees, and when he got a whole compartment thrown out of the Whiskey Creek–Ugly Valley sale, that put the mill under the gun. It needs thirty-five million board feet a year to survive. Suddenly a whole lot of sacred sites were being defined because they didn't want us to do logging, and I got my hackles up. Then they started bitching about the owl. Other compartments were thrown out because of that cotton-picking little bugger. It's not endangered—hell, it's an invader! If it's true that it prefers dense second growth, we've created more habitat for it. It wouldn't be so bad if you were dealing with an environmental community you could sit down and talk with, but with types like Leroy there's no compromise. They're selfish. They want to go to any part of the forest at any time and see what they want to see. 'It's got to be perfect for me at all times.' This is . . . utopian, and it's just a local example of what's taking place nationally: pseudoenvironmental groups screwing up tribal people by trying to use Indian culture as a springboard to buy into preservation philosophy rather than good management."

One of the things Jackson turned up was that Gill had paid a computer analyst from Northern Arizona University (NAU) in Flagstaff twenty-one thousand dollars for a three-day presentation of a multiple-use model of the Chuskas he had worked up. Such models, Gill explained, were "cutting-edge means of making decisions." Leroy's objections to it, Gill told me, were a case of "the black box syndrome. When you have something people don't understand, they say, 'Dexter and NAU are conspiring to ruin our forest.'

"I wasn't surprised by the medical examiner's finding," he went on. "Leroy was irrational. You'd explain something to him, and he couldn't understand it. The guy went to Taos and found an old buddy and got some goodies and overdosed himself. I know the timing looks terrible, but there was no foul play. I don't know any logger who would go to that length, and as for 'corporate interests'—there are none." (This was definitely not true of the oil and mining operations on the rez, which are leased to "corporates" and which were, as Lori Goodman pointed out, threatened by Leroy's insistence on compliance with federal environmental law, which many of them were violating. For instance, Peabody Coal's 273-mile-long slurry line from Black Mesa to Laughlin had been operating for seventeen years without a permit from the Office of Surface Mining. And while NFPI is intra-tribal, corporations were harvesting Navajo timber on the Defiance Plateau and in southern Utah.)

"I'll tell you my first reaction, when I heard he was dead," Gill said, lowering his voice. "Skinwalker. I believe that stuff. It's real. The dark side. You can hire a skinwalker so someone dies of 'natural' or uniden-tified causes, or something no one can explain happens. Look what happened to the three teenagers who rolled the three drunk Navajo in Farmington in 1974.

"But most probably the guy OD'd," he went on. "Most of us feel they use corporate America as a martyr system to further their cause. However he died, it has to look like it was in the throes of protecting the land. 'Remember Leroy.'

"Our only screwup has been in the lack of effort in reforestation. But we're imperfect people operating with imperfect knowledge. And what's the choice? Go back to caves and wear loincloths? But then we'd have to kill animals."

"The bottle in the engine compartment looks pretty bad," I said to Sam Hitt. I was sitting in his office in Santa Fe, in the same chair Jackson had sat in, sometimes for hours, when he and Sam got going about the struggle. On a table was a stack of bumper stickers that said STUMPS DON'T LIE.

"The police found it more than a month ago," Hitt said. "I don't know why they didn't tell anybody about it. But they didn't find the pills—we did, last week when they turned the van over to us. Our investigator was going through a stack of blankets and a couple of dozen loose pills—the missing antihistamines—fell out."

That changed the picture, since it seemed unlikely that Jackson would have chucked out prescription pills that he had paid money for. Now there was a possibility that someone could have planted the methadone to make it look as if Jackson had taken it. "Was the bottle dusted?" I asked.

"The police say they dusted everything, but they didn't come up with a single identifiable print, not even Leroy's. We have a lot of prob-lems with their investigation. They didn't do standard things like photograph the crime scene. Their excuse was that their crime unit was tied up investigating a high-profile son-father homicide in Española. We interviewed a lot of people they should have talked to, but didn't. They haven't talked to anybody on the rez or looked into the whole threat question."

Was there any chance the police themselves were involved?

"You'd have to be really paranoid to think that," Hitt said. "I don't think you understand the level of incompetence we're talking about here. Our New Mexico state troopers are just incredibly dense, untrained, and lax. They couldn't possibly have engineered such a cover-up. But I do think there was an element of racism. They won't tell you this, but their reaction when they found Leroy was probably, 'Well, what have we here? A dead Indian.' Whites die of some disease or foul play, but Indians sometimes just die, as if they have power over their life and death, and many die drunk, so there's a tendency for the police not to investigate an Indian's death as thoroughly as they would if it was one of their own. Plus the van had Arizona plates. Not only was Leroy an Indian, he was out of state."

We reviewed Jackson's last week.

September 28. Leaves Tsaile, attends forest task force meeting in Shiprock, visits friends in Albuquerque and Santa Fe, stays with Mark Marcus in Rinconada, seventeen miles south of Taos. This is basically a business trip. Jackson is gathering Navajo textiles on consignment for a trade show in Chicago. He wasn't a good businessman—he often acted as a middleman for Anglo traders and was taken advantage of—but he loved the trading world, in which IOUs were respected, and the web of friendship reminded him of his life on the street. There are unsubstantiated rumors of a second person in the van. Jackson's trading buddies have not been forthcoming.

According to Hitt, Mark Marcus was "sleazebag city. You've never seen such a down-and-out junkie, or such a rat hole like the place he lives in. We found out (which was news to the police) that he has a prior arrest—for heroin possession in Thailand in the early seventies. Anybody who can manage a habit that long is a survivor, but the guy is constitutionally incapable of telling the truth." In an earlier conversation Hitt had told me "we don't feel Mark's a suspect or the girl"— Mark's "fiancée" Francesca Lorrimer. "The girl was into marijuana and coke." (In fact she was doing time in Missouri for possession of twenty-seventy pounds of marijuana and a phial of methadone, which she said she got from her boyfriend.) Hitt's reasons for not suspecting Mark were that "junkies don't share or party the way marijuana smokers do. Furthermore it's not clear the methadone dose was lethal.

It looks like borderline or lower end, but it could have had a synergistic effect with the Valium. The police suggest he took it for a migraine, but he didn't complain of one his last day [but what about Cindy Eich's observation at her husband's gallery, which Leroy left at two-thirty?]. I've seen Leroy with migraines. Adella says he would have consulted her before taking something like methadone. Methadone is not an effective painkiller. It's a downer. It's widely available on the street in Taos. You can make it in your kitchen. Was he taking it to get high? That doesn't sound like Leroy. How could he have been so articulate, how could he have assembled such a body of information about the logging cartel? As for the marijuana, everybody says he didn't touch the stuff. There was so little in his system it could have been second-hand, from passive inhalation."

But something had happened to change Hitt's mind about Marcus. Now he told me, "My biggest question is, was Mark Marcus paid to kill Leroy Jackson? One key is Francesca. She's getting out of prison on February twenty-eighth and has indicated that she wants to tell the truth, but our investigator hasn't been able to talk to her alone. The only thing she's said so far is that Leroy got stoned on marijuana that Friday afternoon [contradicting ubiquitous testimony that he was not a cannabis smoker]. The other key is Adella. She knows more about Leroy's drug use than she's saying." Hitt said he'd just found out some "explosive stuff" that was "drug related," but he wasn't comfortable talking about it until he spoke with Adella. "This is a complex human being," he went on. "Not a saint or a sinner, but somewhere in between. This man had a lot of power, and the power was good and evil. He could go between two worlds. He went through the walls we live behind. I still love him, and I miss him desperately, and the movement is not the same without him, but he had a dark side."

The twenty-ninth is an active trading day for Jackson at Taos Pueblo, which is celebrating the Fiesta de San Geronimo. Sam hasn't learned where he spent that night, but the next night he's back at Marcus's. The next day—Friday—he leaves. "We have everything down except the three-hour period between two-thirty and five-thirty, when he stops at the convenience store in Tres Piedras. That afternoon Adella says he called and said he was out of Valium and to bring some to Shiprock, where they were meeting the next day. From the convenience store he calls a friend he has some beads for at the Ute Mountain Casino, near Cortez, Colorado, and says he'll be there around eleven p.m. The woman at the store remembers that he was very friendly and outgoing. He buys a snack and some pop and takes off.

That's the last time he's seen alive, and that's where the mystery begins."

Officer Ted Ulibari, who found Jackson in a semifetal position with his shoes off and a heavy blanket completely draped over him (Adella said he sometimes pulled off the road to ride out a migraine, but not like that) was not allowed to talk about the case, nor was detective Noi Galvano, who was conducting the investigation out of Farmington. Major Frank Taylor, with the state police Office of Professional Standards and Internal Affairs in Santa Fe, was handling the press, so I dropped in on him. "All indications are that it was an accidental death," he told me. "The case is still open. The private investigator says he has information pertinent to it, and other people in the wool business are starting to come out of the woodwork, but so far nothing has been provided to change the course of the investigation."

I brought up the pills that were thrown out among Leroy's blankets. Major Taylor was intrigued. This was the first he had heard of them. Why didn't the police find them? I asked.

"There was a lot of items in the van," he said, "including a six-to-eight-foot burlap bag that was full of wool. I guess he lived out of it.

"It's a very complex case," he continued. "We have information that he was possibly murdered, but everything we have factually developed gives the appearance he took the methadone himself. According to his wife the deceased was known to take nonprescription medication of various types when he had a severe headache and didn't have his usual prescribed medicine. There is no indication that force was utilized, and if someone wanted to kill a person with methadone, he would have given him a lot more."

"If you think methadone is what killed him, why haven't you brought any charges against Mark Marcus?"

"Marcus is the leading person we're looking at. But we can't indict him on just suspicions alone," Major Taylor explained.

He admitted the cause of death could have been something other than methadone intoxication and that "a lot of things disappear after forty-eight hours," including crack cocaine and insulin, which Sam said had been implicated in the deaths of several other Indians. He also agreed that the van would probably have been vandalized if it had sat there for nine days. "The biggest problem we have is from October first to October ninth. What happened in between we have not been able to develop."

Why did Officer Ulibari break into the van? I asked. Because he had seen it sitting there for several days?

"No. Because the police were notified that it was there by the Civil Air Patrol, which was helping in the search. One of their planes spotted it."

Why, if the van was at the overlook all the time, and an all-points bulletin for it went out on October second, didn't the state police see it there before?

"I don't know," Major Taylor said a little testily, "because there is no record of any police officer cruising Route Sixty-four or passing that spot between October first and October ninth, or of whether the van was seen there or not."

Why weren't any pictures taken at the scene? Isn't this standard in a case of unattended death?

"Our office didn't take any pictures because we thought the Office of the Medical Examiner did."

What about the blood that (a confidential source told Sam) was all over the backseat and the front seat as well, and according to Sergeant Joe Mascarenas (who told this to the Washington *Post*) on one of the outside door handles?

"There was no blood on the outside," Major Taylor assured me, "and the only blood inside the van was a pool on his pillow that was released through his nose by decomposition."

What if you got a tip that he was killed by somebody in Arizona?

"That's beyond our jurisdiction, but if information was developed that there was a conspiracy of any type, we would call in the proper authorities. If it was on the reservation, that would be the FBI. We need somebody to come forth and give us more information. Because it's considered an accidental death, it hasn't even been on *Crimestoppers* [a television program that offers rewards for unsolved crimes]. Sure there's some very questionable stuff that happened, but until we get something concrete, we can't proceed."

This was similar to the position of Dr. Patricia MacFeeley, who performed the autopsy. I had heard from Sam and others that because Jackson was a Navajo, and the Navajo want to get their dead into the ground as soon as possible and with minimal cutting, the autopsy had been an abbreviated one: only a visual examination for foul play and toxicology; no blood analysis. But Dr. MacFeeley assured me that Jackson was given a full autopsy. "It was not a quickie," she told me. "We knew we did not have a cause of death. He had a full screen that would have picked up all the most commonly abused substances and the most generally prescribed drugs, and this is all we came up with." The marijuana could have been secondhand, the Valium was within "therapeutic levels," and the methadone was "at the low threshold of toxicity." The Valium, she said, was not enough to be significant and wouldn't have acted synergistically. "People don't usually die of Valium. It's a fairly safe drug. You can be taking it for a long time, and it won't kill you. Methadone tolerance varies considerably. This was enough to kill someone who wasn't a user, or even a user who hadn't taken the stuff in some time. To have had that level on board he would had to have taken it before he died."

If someone had wanted to kill him with methadone, wouldn't they have given him more? This was a "reasonable argument," Dr. MacFeeley said. There was no evidence he was subdued, not enough heart disease to kill him, no tumors or ruptured aneurysm. The signs of respiratory arrest were sufficiently masked by decomposition that you couldn't tell for sure if the lungs or the heart had gone first, but "it looked like the kind of death you get with a narcotic," she said, and she stood by her finding. No one had informed her at the time of the autopsy that there were strong motives for killing him, but even if they had, she wouldn't have done anything differently.

Is it possible that something else that had already broken down by the time you got the body could have been the cause of death?

"Hundreds of things that our tests wouldn't have picked up would have worked," she said. "But methadone within toxic range was on board. We have a cause. But we've always been open. We're still available to do more tests, but unless someone comes forth with specific information on a specific substance, we don't want to use up our specimens, and if something really unusual came up, we could exhume him, and some toxicology tests could still be done. It *is* a mystery. But we have a lot of amazing stories that aren't this high profile that are of concern to the families, and it's often the families who prove to be the least objective."

I had an introduction to a burnt-out hippie woman in Taos named Dune, who was a friend of Mark Marcus. Up to this point Marcus had not been cooperative with anybody. Dune's apartment, in a one-story adobe in the old part of town, behind the tourist facade, was beyond squalor. Plastic bags overflowing with garbage crowded the back entrance, a TV that no one was watching was on in the living room, and strung out people kept emerging from or disappearing into the bedrooms. Years of shooting hard drugs had made Dune look like an old woman, but she was only in her early forties. Her brain was fried, but she was still a compassionate person, and she still made sense, in her own way.

"In my soul I feel it was murder," she told me as we sat at the kitchen table, drinking coffee. "I think somebody made him drink the methadone to set Mark up. Mark's been in the hard-core scene all his life, but he's a real nice guy. He couldn't have possibly done anything like that. So was Leroy. I only brushed shoulders with him twenty times, and I never even saw him smoke a joint, although he was often in the company of people smoking. He was always intent and business-like. It must have been someone who knew that Leroy was hanging with Mark. There's been many murders in this town swept under the rug the last couple of years because [here she mentioned one of the town's officials], who runs the place, is a coke smuggler himself and has his own hit squad. Five, six years ago two brothers up at Taos Pueblo died on the same day, and they never found out what killed them. It could have been the hanta virus; it could have been something else. They had an Indian autopsy. Last year my neighbor, Ellen Hafner, was murdered in her house, and that wasn't solved. Also last year two people were dissolved by being thrown off the bridge into the Rio Grande Gorge. They call it the seven-second flight. In fact we're all living in fear of our lives. Last summer I let this guy Rory, who was living in his van, stay in the house, and he turned out to be real bad news. He was into snuff flicks and had made a movie of killing his wife. I tried to get him to leave, but he wouldn't, and on July 5 he killed my ex-husband and made a movie of it. The police know this guy did it, but he's still at large. He could show up at any moment." Taos seemed to be a place where finding someone to do your killing for you wouldn't be a problem.

We talked about methadone. "What methadone does is it gives me a real up so I get my house cleaned. It would be my drug of choice," Dune confessed.

Is it possible to spike someone's drink with methadone without their knowing it? I asked.

"The stuff tastes like shit, but I suppose it would be possible," Dune said. But her own theory was that someone threatened to kill him if he didn't drink the methadone, then gave him a whiff of cyanide.

Dune rang Mark and said, "I'm here with this guy who writes about mysteriously muffed ecology types," then she passed me the phone. Mark said, "I can't talk. Here that?" Every few seconds there was a click. "I'm being tapped." Suppose I come down to Rinconada? I suggested. He hesitated and finally said okay.

Mark's directions—the only chain-link fence in Rinconada—were succinct. The front door was opened by an old Hispanic woman. Her husband, who was now blind, Mark would explain, had blown away six men back in the twenties who had been balling her at the peyote orgies of Mabel Dodge Luhan. During his lengthy incarceration he had been the warden's chauffeur. Having no children, they had sold Mark the lot in back, and he had built a long barnlike structure on it. The front half was where he did his silversmithing: concho belts, buckles, and other southwestern pieces. It was quality work. Years ago, in Baltimore, he had gone to dentistry school, but had been busted for pot. He and Francesca and her nine-year-old daughter lived in back. I wouldn't have exactly called it a rat hole—that description was more apt for Dune's apartment—but it was definitely funky, and Mark, a bearded, wired, frazzled guy about Dune's age, was definitely hard-core. But after hanging out with him for two hours, I realized that he also possessed a certain sweetness. At first he didn't quite know what to do with me, so he kept showing me things. He showed me a cardboard box full of sherds of prehistoric pottery he had found picking over Anasazi ruins in the vicinity. "This is what me and Leroy were all about," he said. He showed me another cardboard box full of bonds, blue-chip stocks, and dividends made out to Francesca (who was still in prison in Missouri). "My fiancée is the heir to the *Saturday Evening Post*," he told me. "The Lorrimers are *Who's Who in America*. You don't want to scum her family in any way."

There was a pool table, so I proposed we shoot a game of eight ball. After we had knocked the balls around for a while, Mark began to open up. "This was Leroy's home away from his wife," he began. "She wants to make a martyr out of him. It seems she wants to fuck me, and I've only been trying to protect his memory. Believe me, I'd love for him to have been murdered. I loved the guy. But I don't think that's the way he went. He died of natural causes or suicide, and I don't give a fuck what anybody says.

"The last time he showed up here, he was very depressed," Mark went on. "He had a lot on him. I think he was ripped because his parents were getting divorced or something. He had a big bottle of pills on him—enough pills to last a lifetime. Francesca and I were worried, and we called Adella, and she was frantic. She said, 'You didn't give him

Valium, did you?' I don't think he died of drugs, because he was on top of his drugs. He was no beginner. He didn't experiment. He didn't touch pot, although he bought pot to trade for jewelry. He did occasionally smoke heroin with tinfoil, but his drugs of choice were Valium and Tylenol III with codeine. He took them for five years. He never exceeded the prescribed dosage, but read between the lines: it's progressive. You keep taking the stuff until your life falls apart. I think he fucked up on those pills. Something gave out. Maybe an aneurysm broke loose [but MacFeeley says no]. His level of addictiveness was way too high for a little bit of methadone to kill him.

"I keep getting these calls. 'Indian killer,' the person says, then hangs up. I think of the magnitude of what Adella has to cover up and of poor Leroy: that's not the way he wants to be remembered. But I either got to call him an addict, or they put me away. I'm caught between a rock and a hard place. Either I look bad, or he looks bad, and I want it over. If telling the truth is what it takes, let's do it. *I didn't kill no fucking Indian!*"

I called Leroy's mother, Jane Y. Popovich, in Phoenix. "Yes, I am getting divorced from Popovich, my husband of twenty-five years, but that wouldn't have bothered Leroy," she told me. "Popovich was the only man I know who Leroy didn't get along with. About a year ago Leroy came to see me, and Popovich ran him off. Leroy wasn't depressed. That's another lie. He was really looking forward to going to Washington. I seen him when he was depressed. *I'm* very depressed about all the trash that's being put out about my son. We all knew he was taking the Valium, but Leroy was not a drug addict, so he must have been forced to take that methadone or been given it in a drink. Leroy had a very sound mind, and he just did not do things without thinking. His work and his family were very important. He appreciated them, and he was excited about what he was doing, always talking about it. I talked to some of his buddies in Taos, and they said he was pretty normal and happy like, talking all the time like he usually did. He wasn't a depressed man. What would he be depressed about?"

"Mark Marcus was pretty convincing," I said to John Nichols. Best known for *The Milagro Beanfield War* (which Robert Redford made into a movie), Nichols is another important southwestern image maker. The anthropologist Bernard Fontana observes that the unromantic views of the Southwest Nichols and Edward Abbey present have paradoxically "added to its mystique, and . . . have . . . become a part of a romantic image of the Southwest." Nichols and I were driving out to Tres Piedras to talk to Barbara Kozart, the woman at the convenience store, the last person to see Leroy alive. Route 64 was closed for the winter from there to Tierra Amarilla, so there was no way of getting to the Brazos Bluff Overlook unless we rented a snowmobile, which didn't seem worth the trouble, because Nichols knew the spot and said, as everybody else did, that any vehicle parked there would have been completely visible.

"But Mark lost a little credibility when he said he'd never even tried methadone," I continued. "Sam Hitt says he's been on it for seventeen years. I'm also not sure I believe he really blew out Barry Serafin's windshield with a 410 Intimidator [as he said he had done when Serafin came to interview him with an ABC crew]. As Sam says, he's a fascinating guy who drew Leroy into his crazy world. Sam also says he's a dope pusher and is known for getting teenagers involved in smack, and he wouldn't put it past Marcus to be involved in some sort of a plot. I'm not sure what I think. Sam argues that Mark and Francesca were around until early in the morning of October second, when they drove to Missouri for her sentencing hearing, so he could have given Leroy some methadone for the road on the afternoon of the first. But why would Leroy have wanted to take methadone if, as Mark claims, he had a big bottle of Valium and if, as the autopsy shows, whether this bottle existed or not, he had Valium in his system?" The Valium, by the way, has not been found. Nor has a small antique cradle board that Mark claims Leroy bought at the Fiesta de San Geronimo, nor has Leroy's jewelry suitcase. Mark suggested talking to a Ute named Buffalo, who was with Leroy in Taos and was going to catch a ride with him to the Ute casino in Cortez, Colorado, where Leroy was going to drop off some beads and was planning to spend the night before meeting Adella in Shiprock the next morning. But Buffalo ended up staying in Taos. Sam's PI tracked him down, and he didn't have much to say.

"But let's assume Mark did give Leroy some methadone—not to kill him, but for his migraines—and that Leroy took it and pulled over and OD'd that evening," I said. "Then you still have the problem of where the van was on the fourth and the fifth, when two witnesses swear it wasn't there."

Nichols pointed out that "it's common in the drug culture that if somebody OD's, you get him out of there." That's another theory: Jackson was partying with some friends and OD'd and they freaked out because they knew they were looking at wrongful-death charges at the very least, and they ultimately drove the van to the overlook and left if there on or around the ninth (Mark and Francesca have an alibi because by then they were in Missouri; presumably they and Leroy said their goodbyes on the first). That would work except for Steve Martinez's testimony that the van was there on the second. And the missing cradle board, pill bottle, and jewelry case, plus the way the pills were dumped out among the blankets, are still very fishy and point to the involvement of some other party. But that could have been the police, posthumously tampering with the evidence. Or somebody could have ripped off the missing items while the van sat for ten days in a garage in Chama, before the police got around to investigating it, and somebody could have planted the methadone in the glove compartment as "extra proof," as Brenda Norrel put it—like O.J.'s glove on the walkway at Rockingham.

Nichols's opinion of the police wasn't much higher than Sam Hitt's. "When police fuck up badly, I get suspicious," he remarked, then he brought up the famous Karen Silkwood case. An employee at the Kerr McGee nuclear power plant in Oklahoma, Karen was on her way, on November 13, 1974, to give a *New York Times* reporter documents which she thought showed that Kerr McGee had been knowingly irradiating its employees with plutonium, including herself, and also covertly selling plutonium to Israel in violation of the Nuclear Nonproliferation Act, when her car was run off the road into a culvert. She was found slumped over the wheel, dead. "By the time the state police got there, the car had been picked clean," Nichols went on. "Then it turned out the police had been bugging her house. I was working with Danny Sheehan of the Christic Institute on a script about the aftermath of the Silkwood case that would have brought all this out." But Karen's father agreed to a million-dollar settlement from Kerr McGee after her estate had won a $10 million jury verdict on its negligence claim. The judge threw out a separate claim for conspiracy to violate Silkwood's civil rights, however. "So there was no trial, no denouement, no catharsis, and we couldn't get anybody to make the movie."

"Regardless of how he died, Leroy was a brave man," I said. "He knew his life was in danger, but he didn't back off, and whether or not he was hooked on Valium is ultimately irrelevant, except that it's important for people to realize that environmentalists are as human as the rest of us, and in many cases considerably more tormented. Dian Fossey took a variety of downers and often drank herself to sleep. Being close to nature doesn't necessarily make you Saint Francis. And the possibility of a drug dependency doesn't mean Leroy couldn't have been murdered either. What we need to know is more about these drugs."

Several pharmacologists and experts on substance abuse at McGill University and the Harvard Medical School found the possibility of a

Valium addiction in a former alcoholic not at all surprising: Valium and alcohol are both central-nervous-system depressants; they satisfy the cravings of the same dopamine, serotonin, and norepinephrine receptors. But methadone belongs to another class of drug, Mark Pelino, the president of the American Methadone Treatment Association in New York, explained. It's a synthetic narcotic analgesic and is mainly used in the treatment of opioid addiction, to prevent heroin addicts from going into withdrawal, for instance, or to keep them off heroin by entering them in a long-term methadone maintenance program. It's also used to alleviate the pain of dying cancer patients, and Pelino said it would have worked for a migraine, but there were better drugs for that, such as codeine and Percocet. The methadone high is like the heroin high, but it's smoother and longer lasting. It kicks in after about forty-five minutes and one hit—the drug is taken orally, often dissolved in orange juice or some other liquid—and can last twenty-four to thirty-six hours. You don't get as high as you do on heroin, but you don't crash so badly either; you feel "calm and very much at peace with the world," Pelino explained, so some druggies actually prefer methadone.

The chat with Pelino produced three additional revelations: you *could* slip someone a methadone mickey, particularly someone who had never tasted it before, if you masked the bitterness by mixing it with sugar; mixing methadone with marijuana and Valium could have a synergistic effect "for sure" (which MacFeeley has since admitted is true); and a non-narcotic-tolerant person taking methadone for the first time could die from a dose as low as ten milligrams or even lower. "It depends on the individual," Pelino explained. (I ran this past MacFeeley, who said that the actual dose Leroy took was not determinable, only the blood level, which supported Pelino's hypothesis.)

So this brings us back to the voluntary ingestion/overdose scenario, and I've already gone over the problems with that. Pelino said if you were going to kill somebody there were much better drugs to use than methadone, such as fentanyl, which is more potent, quicker acting, and has quicker renal clearance.

There is a methadone scene in Taos, so the source of Leroy's methadone could have been any number of people besides Mark Marcus. There are also coke, smack, and crack scenes, and marijuana use is so widespread that it's hardly even regarded as a drug. "As a friend of mine puts it, 'Taos ain't for amateurs,' " John Nichols told me. "Its setting is absolutely magical, it's supposed to be one of the seven or eight sacred centers on the planet, but it's really a dark little place. People come here full of starry-eyed New Age idealism, jumping up and down like April lambs, and get bashed flat—robbed, raped, murdered, real quick. I can't tell you how many times I've seen this happen. The racial and economic disparities here are enormous. You've got a big upswing of rich Californians moving in in the last five years and buying up the old adobes and the picturesque spreads of the local Chicanos, who feel like Palestinians, like second-class citizens in their own land, and you've got the Indians who have been living out at the pueblo for a thousand years, who feel museumized. It's a society that's going through a kind of collapse, a situation with a lot of tension, especially at the lower end of the spectrum, where three impoverished groups—freaks, Chicanos, and Native Americans—are pitted against each other, and there's a lot of drugs, drinking, and violence."

This was Leroy Jackson's world, I reflected—a complex and volatile mix—a bunch of cosmologies to juggle. The clientele in the diner next to the convenience store in Tres Piedras, where Nichols and I found Barbara Kozart, was typically eclectic. At one table sat two muscle-bound gays in jeans and work shirts. One had a toy poodle on his lap; the other had an accent that sounded Australian and seemed to be extremely put out about something. At the next table there were two old Chicanos, and next to them sat an Anglo woman and a Sequamish Indian (Chief Seattle's tribe) by the name of Thomas One Wolf, who seemed to be the woman's spiritual mentor. When One Wolf heard us talking about Leroy, he said he'd been apprenticed as a child to a Navajo *hosteen,* or medicine man, and that if Jackson had been on drugs, he would have gone to a medicine man and had the Enemy Way and Protection Way ceremonies. "There's a whole lot more to this, and his medicine man would know," One Wolf said. "What I'm hearing is not somebody from the big rez, but an out-world touch."

Barbara told us that when she saw Jackson's picture in the paper, she recognized him instantly as the man who had come into the store nine days earlier. "I don't know why this person touched me," she said. "I didn't even know him. But I remember the white van pulling up. He waited for about a minute before getting out. There was no one with him. Then he went to the phone booth and made a call." A check of Leroy's Sprint-card bill by Sam's PI confirms that this was the call he made to the woman at the Ute casino, telling her he'd be there in a couple of hours.

"Then he came in," Barbara continued. "I can tell when somebody's on drugs, and he was definitely not on anything. He teased me, 'How come these cookies are three for a dollar, when I can get them for seventy-five cents back home?' Then he left and drove away up the road into the mountains.

"My personal opinion is that the investigation was very shoddy," she told us. "Some of the officers around here are unbelievably lax. They just treated him like another dead Indian. But that overlook is not where the man died. He was killed elsewhere."

Brenda Norrel, the AP stringer, was clearly shaken by the whole business. Her reaction reminded me a lot of Barbara Kozart's. "I met Leroy in February 1992," she began. "He breezed into the Crystal chapter house and told me, 'I'm taking on the timber cutters.' I'd been on the rez for thirteen years—I was married to a Navajo—and I'd never heard anybody talk like that. He had this crazy, fun-loving nature. We became instant friends, like brother and sister, and I can tell you: Leroy did not use drugs. He was a health nut."

That's what the actor River Phoenix was supposed to be, I pointed out, but then he OD'd and turned out to be riddled with drugs. And Leroy was hanging with some hard-core druggies in Taos.

"That doesn't mean a thing," Brenda countered. "I have all kinds of friends, including druggies. That doesn't mean I'm one myself."

I observed that Leroy could have shown different sides to different people, like the characters in the movie *Rashomon*. Leroy on the rez or with his family could have been a different person from Leroy on the road—that's common enough. Brenda admitted this was possible, then she returned to her train of thought. "The danger of having all kinds of friends is that they can be bought," she said. "Maybe one of them just asked him for a ride. Maybe it happened as simply as that."

I told her that I had spent an evening with Mark Marcus, and I wasn't convinced that he was involved. Brenda asked me, anxiously, what he looked like. "Was he an emaciated, anorexic Hispanic with a goatee and a high receding hair line?"

No, I said. He was emaciated, all right, but he was an Anglo, and he had a full beard and head of hair.

"Let me explain that question," Brenda said. "I'm not a psychic or weirdo, I'm an AP reporter, and I don't normally have dreams or premonitions, but the week before Leroy left, I returned late at night to the place in Window Rock where I was staying, and there was this black car with black-tinted windows parked across the street. I couldn't see who was inside. The next day I dreamed about this emaciated Hispanic, then the Monday after Leroy's body was found, I *saw* him at a session of the Navajo tribal council. He was sitting alone and didn't talk to anybody. This guy didn't belong here. He looked like a Chicano from Española. I followed him out to his car. It was the black car with black-tinted windows. The plates were New Mexico [Window Rock is just over the Arizona border]. He drove off before I could get down the numbers. Then five days later—on Friday—I passed the car on the road, coming into Window Rock from the east. This time it didn't have any plates at all."

Creepy, I said.

"The day after Leroy was found, I had another dream," Brenda went on. "I saw the back of somebody's head, and I knew that one of my friends had died, but I didn't know who. I didn't even know Leroy was missing. I believe there's a spirit after death, and that Leroy's been trying to communicate to me, to tell me to get out of here. 'You don't know who you're dealing with, Brenda. I didn't.' "

It has been four years now since Leroy turned up dead. The case is still open, but the police investigation is inactive. Francesca did not shed any light on Mark Marcus's role when she got out of prison, as Sam Hitt had hoped. "We may have to live without ever knowing what happened," he told me. There is no resolution, no vindication, no happy ending. Which is the big difference between this case and the mysteries of Hillerman.

The following spring, someone sent me a clip about another tribal environmentalist who had possibly met with foul play. Forty-two-year-old, half-Pima, half-Zuñi Fred Walking Badger had rallied opposition to reckless pesticide use on the Gila River Reservatiion, in the low desert between Phoenix and Tucson. The downwind drift from crop-dusted cotton fields leased to non-Indian farmers was killing the gardens of Pima and Maricopa who lived on the reservation. They were afraid to eat the wildlife (quail, rabbit, duck) and worried their drinking water was contaminated. On May 21 Walking Badger set out to run a brief errand near the town of Sacaton with a twenty-six-year-old Pima named Aaron Leland Rivers. They never returned. On June 10 Walking Badger's car was found burned in the desert, but there was no trace of either of them. Walking Badger left four children; his wife was pregnant with their fifth child. He had had a drinking problem in the past, but this is not believed to have figured in his disappearance. Rivers left behind two children and a fiancée he was to marry in December.

New Orders for the Mesa of Doom

The Anglo presence in the Southwest has always been tied to war. First the Mexicans, then the Navajo, and finally the Apache, were defeated militarily. Theodore Roosevelt captures the imperialistic spirit of Americanism that motivated these campaigns in his 1886 "magnum opus," as he proudly called it, *The Winning of the West*:

> The most ultimately righteous of all wars is a war with savages, though it is apt to be also the most terrible and inhuman. The rude, fierce settler who drove the savage from the land lays all civilized mankind under a debt to him. American and Indian, Boer and Zulu, Cossack and Tartar, New Zealander and Maori—in each case the victory, horrible though many of his deeds are, has laid deep the foundations for the future greatness of a mighty people . . . it is of incalculable importance that America, Australia, and Siberia should pass out of the hands of their red, black, and yellow aboriginal owners, and become the heritage of the dominant world races.

After Arizona and New Mexico were pacified, Anglo civilization mushroomed in the Rio Grande Valley, mainly thanks to World War II. The frontier fort gave way to the top-secret military laboratory, where the capability to obliterate an entire city with a chain reaction of imploding atoms was developed. Weapons of undreamed-of destructiveness were tried out in the remote desert. Trillions of dollars were spent until a nuclear arsenal capable of taking out every human being behind the Iron Curtain was in place.

Albuquerque got a big lift from the war. In 1940 it was still a slow-paced southwestern mud town, threatening to slide back into the Depression. But the bombing of Pearl Harbor turned its fortunes, pumping millions into the local economy. While the war was on, of course, austerity measures were imposed. Gas was rationed, so everyone had to walk. Only 122 automobile tires were allocated for the entire city in 1942. By 1944, cigarettes, matches, sugar, coffee, canned goods, meat, shoes, fresh vegetables, and nylon stockings were all but unobtainable. Businessmen and politicians congregated at the Rex Billiards. A complete dinner at the Liberty Cafe and Cocktail Lounge cost fifty cents. When the war was over and gas became available again, more and more people got in the habit of eating in their cars and patronized places like Blair's modernistic drive-in. There is still a drive-in diner on South Central where miniskirted waitresses on roller skates bring your order to the car. Trailer courts, trailer camps, and gas stations proliferated. There was an army base east of town, the U.S. Army Air Corps Advance Flying School. But it was still a small town. Everybody knew one another.

After the war, the downtown blossomed in glass, chrome, and neon, a Woolworth's with a hundred feet of display windows sprouted on Central and Fourth, and Albuquerque never looked back. The pace of construction stepped up to a home a day. Factories started manufacturing things like pontoons for amphibious planes and autopilot gyroscopes. Postwar Albuquerque became the fastest-growing city in the country, mushrooming from 45,000 before the war to 262,000 by 1960, to 481,000 in 1992. Each of the eventually sixty-two thousand defense-related jobs in New Mexico created an additional estimated two civilian jobs—and yet New Mexico remained one of the poorest states in the country.

The desert Southwest was ideal for testing weapons because of vast, empty (of humans, that is) spaces and the secrecy they afforded. You could shoot a missile up to Nevada and be pretty confident of not hitting anything significant if it missed its target. One errant German V-2 (twenty-five were brought over and tested after the war) crashed in the foothills outside of Alamogordo, east of the White Sands Missile Range; other strays came down south of Ciudad Juárez, north of Holloman, west of Albuquerque. No one was hurt. In Nevada there is still a top-secret testing facility known as Dreamland, which you won't find on any civilian map. It was there that the Stealth Bomber was developed.

Between 1951 and 1963, 126 secret aboveground nuclear tests were conducted in the Nevada desert. Several thousand Americans died from their radioactive fallout. There were three types of victim: civilian workers at the test sites; soldiers within a few miles of ground zero, where the bombs went off; and rural Mormons living to the east, in southern Utah, downwind of the explosions—the so-called down-winders. They died, prematurely and grotesquely, from thirteen varieties of cancer.

The most unfortunate victims were the Mormons, who just happened to be living in the wrong place. They were even encouraged to go out and watch the fallout clouds pass overhead and "participate in a moment of history." A top-secret Atomic Energy Commission (AEC) memo dismissed them in sinister gobbledygook as a "low-use segment of the population." The blasts were allegedly scheduled when the wind was blowing east, so the clouds would miss more populous Las Vegas, and President Eisenhower is said to have told his advisers that he had no objections if a few thousand people had to be sacrificed in the interests of national security. The irony was that the Mormons had become, since their repudiation of the doctrine of plural marriage, among America's most law-abiding citizens. They had come to believe that the American government and the Constitution were divinely inspired and that the "letter of the law" must be obeyed without question.

Beginning in 1983, New York–based photographer Carole Gallagher spent ten years interviewing and photographing dozens of the test victims. Renting a basement apartment from two polygamous widows in St. George, Utah, Gallagher "dropped out of life as I had known it," she subsequently related. To win the trust of the xenophobic Mormons, she wore long skirts and modest blouses and got the New York out of her voice. Many of the victims were already in the last stages of their cancers. The government hoped their stories would die with them, but Gallagher presented them in a book, with wrenching photographs, called *American Ground Zero: The Secret Nuclear War.*

The effects of the fallout were first noticed among the sheep, who had "beta burns" on their mouths and in their alimentary canals and intestines. The pregnant ewes began to miscarry with alarming frequency, and some of the lambs were born with their hearts beating outside their chests. The Atomic Energy Commission assured the shepherds that these problems were due to "mismanagement, malnutrition, and perhaps poisonous plants on the range."

Reports showing clear linkages between radiation and cancer and chromosome damage to humans exposed to the blasts were suppressed. Women with hair loss and severe skin wounds came to the Public Health Service and were clinically diagnosed as "neurotic" and suffering from "housewife syndrome." Isaac Nelson rushed into the bathroom when he heard his wife, Oleta, shrieking. She had been combing her beautiful, long, raven-black hair, and "half her hair was layin' in the wash basin."

The son of Ken Pratty, a movie stuntman, was born with a massive hole in the middle of his face.

When Grace Swartzbaugh's husband, who had worked at the test site, died in 1969, "his whole insides . . . just looked like a big bowl of solid Jell-O," as she described them. A few days later, she claimed, two men came, flashing AEC badges, and burned all the papers in his desk, so she couldn't prove he had ever worked there and would have nothing to submit in litigation.

Multiple myeloma (cancer of the bone marrow) had whittled Herman Hagen, a pipe fitter at the test site, down from 277 to 98 pounds when Gallagher interviewed him in 1986. "Right to the end, Herman Hagen maintained that the Test Site 'paid the best salary in the state, outside of organized crime,'" she writes. "When I suggested that it might actually be organized crime, the laughter that shook his disintegrating bones soon changed into a grimace of pain."

In 1990, after a lengthy legal battle, President Bush finally signed the Radiation Compensation Exposure Act, which established a fund to compensate the victims. But for many it was too late. They were already dead or irreversibly, terminally metastasized.

The desert is also a great place for disposing of obsolete matériel. South of Tucson, on the way into Davis-Monthan Air Base, thousands of no-longer-serviceable airplanes are parked in the desert—belly-landed B-52s, the old A-12 blackbirds that the CIA used to fly, practically every craft in the air force or navy inventory has made it there at one time or other—waiting to be stripped for parts, for "final disposal," or other instructions. Down the road is the Titan-missile launching pad, which was on twenty-four-hour alert for nineteen years, until 1983, and is now a museum that attracts nineteen thousand visitors a year. The Titan II had a range of five thousand miles, the heaviest payload, and was the largest missile the United States ever built. It was replaced by the smaller, more accurate Minuteman.

The desert around Fort Wingate, on the edge of the Navajo Rez, is filled with mounds of obsolete ammunition. The fort was originally a cavalry post whose purpose was to keep an eye on the Navajo after their release from Bosque Redondo. In this century it was converted to an ordnance depot, due to the proximity of the railroad. Some of the ammo there goes back to the First World War.

Currently, thousands of Cold War nuclear warheads are being dismantled, in concert with ones in the former Soviet Union, at the Pantex plant in Amarillo, Texas, where many of them were assembled, and their grapefruit-sized plutonium "pits" (other terms for the pit are the primary and the physics package) are being stored at the Pantex plant. The local populace is not overjoyed about this.

Several things conspired to make New Mexico particularly useful for the war effort: its uranium-rich Grants Mineral Belt, vast empty stretches of desert in the lower part of the state where bombs could be exploded, and, up above the Rio Grande between Santa Fe and Española, a remote mesa called Los Alamos that was perfect for clandestine research. It was chosen in 1943 as the site of the Manhattan Project, which produced Little Boy and Fat Man, the atomic bombs that destroyed Hiroshima and Nagasaki, because Robert J. Oppenheimer, the physicist who was put in charge of the project, had hiked across the mesa in his teens and remembered how beautiful it was. Six thousand scientists and military personnel—"the greatest collection of eggheads ever assembled," in the words of General Leslie Groves, the project's military director—were sequestered there, in a hastily erected compound that did not officially exist. In Santa Fe, forty miles south, it was known by a post office box. No one knew what had been happening up there until the war ended a few weeks after the bombings.

The project took over the buildings and grounds of the Los Alamos Ranch School, an expensive boarding school whose mission was to make rugged hombres out of soft rich boys from the Midwest and the East. The director, A. J. Connell, a homosexual who disguised his orientation under cowboy machismo, was in the habit of surprising his "gibbons," as he called the students, in the act of masturbation. The boys wore short khaki shorts and kerchiefs like Boy Scouts and slept out on screen porches even in winter. The school produced two distinguished writers, both gay: Gore Vidal and William S. Burroughs. Burroughs spent his three years there (he left in 1931, at age seventeen) target shooting and throwing knives at fence posts. He nearly OD'd on chloral nitrate and fell hopelessly in love with a schoolmate. "It was no accident that I went to the Los Alamos Ranch School where they couldn't wait to make the atom bomb and drop it on the Yellow Peril," he reflected years later. Burroughs saw the bomb as a watershed event, in which America lost its innocence and made a pact with the devil, selling its soul for undreamed-of power. Thenceforth the individual was powerless against state control, manipulated by unknown forces, in constant fear of instant annihilation. As Burroughs's biographer, Ted Morgan, writes,

Through his attendance at the Los Alamos Ranch School, Burroughs felt personally connected to the dropping of the bomb. Connell's eviction was a parable for the age. The idyllic Ranch School, an outpost of the pastoral dream, which trained boys in the values of capitalist leadership, was commandeered by a government agency for a team of foreign-born scientists who gave away their secrets of mass destruction to the generals and the politicians, wrecking the America the school represented.

In only twenty-seven months, the bomb was put together from little more than theoretical notions of what atomic fission was capable of, and two bombs were dropped, killing 150,000 Japanese. Los Alamos's mission was supposed to be over. It was only meant to be a temporary installation, but the Cold War and the arms race prolonged its existence. In the decades that followed, four trillion dollars' worth (according to a study by the Brookings Institute) of progressively lethal and efficient nuclear weapons that were never used were designed there, and a town, a lovely subalpine suburb, eventually with its own golf course and ski mountain, grew up around the Los Alamos National Laboratory (LANL). But underneath the facade of all-American normalcy that it struggled to maintain, it was a very strange place. Of all the enclaves in the Southwest, it was perhaps the most bizarre and secretive, in a state of strenuous self-denial, plagued by a host of environmental, medical, and psychological problems, real and imagined—alleged brain-tumor clusters, elevated suicide, divorce, and spousal-battery curves.

With the end of the Cold War in 1989, the "nuclear weapons complex," consisting of thirteen facilities around the country, was being radically downsized. So far Los Alamos had survived closure, but the labbies lived in fear that they would lose their funding or even be terminated, and there were bitter debates within LANL, with the Department of Energy (DOE) to which it belonged, and with Congress as to its future mission. By 1995 it looked as if the military-research boom, the latest in the Land of Enchantment's long list of boom-and-bust cycles, was going the way of the copper boom, the uranium boom, the oil and natural-gas booms. The cones, as the nuclear scientists were called, had enjoyed a pleasant, pork-lined ride for half a century, but now, maybe, Los Alamos was running out of energy, its time was up, and maybe in a few decades it would become another New Mexican ghost town. Maybe in time it would even come to resemble the Anasazi ruins that litter the seductively beautiful Pajarito Plateau, which the mesa is part of (like Tsipin, which my old school buddy Don took me to). There are several huge, long-abandoned ceremonial centers right on LANL's forty-three-square-mile grounds. Reduced by time and the elements to skeletal floor plans, with a few slivers of wall still standing here and there, they look startlingly like the photographs of the charred remnants of Hiroshima and Nagasaki.

On Sunday, August 6, 1995—the fiftieth anniversary of the bombing of Hiroshima—I drove up State Route 4, the detour off the highway from Santa Fe to Española to the Hill—Los Alamosans' low-key name for their town. Overhead loomed the spurs of the dramatically eroded Pajarito Plateau, which was created, aptly enough, by the violent explosion of a volcanic caldera 1.2 million years ago. Fallout spewed as far away as Kansas, and a glowing ash flow oozed down, gradually cooling and hardening into the plateau's top layer—800 to 1,300 feet of porous white volcanic tuff. In the millennia that followed, the plateau was whittled down to the five slender finger mesas and the deep intervening canyons that are now taken up by LANL's seventy-four technical areas (TAs) and the commercial and residential districts of Los Alamos. The canyons drain into the Rio Grande—a matter of concern because each flash flood washes radionuclides from various spills that much closer to the drinking supplies of Santa Fe and Albuquerque. Along the intermittent creeks in the canyons, *alamos*—cottonwoods—grow. "Los Alamos" is a strange name choice because piñon and ponderosa pine predominate overwhelmingly on the Hill.

Men with close-cropped hair were jogging along the road—soldiers keeping themselves combat ready and creeps, as the intelligence types who surveil the lab population are called. The Hill did not reek of evil as far as I could detect. Its architecture was singularly drab and rather seedy government issue. The shopping center, devoid of southwestern flourishes, boasted the usual doughnut shop, dry cleaner, auto-parts store. The residential district was mostly no-nonsense, barrackslike duplexes that hadn't been built to last fifty years and, having passed into private hands, were peeling and in various states of disrepair. Perched on the rim of North Mesa, overlooking the golf course, were some fancy California-style homes, where the LANL's managers—the high priests, as some call them—lived. But the Hill's general tone was relentlessly low-key. This was a place that did not want to draw attention to itself, to the fact that it "may be the country's wealthiest and most erudite company town," in *Forbes* magazine's description. The TAs were particularly well camouflaged. You couldn't tell from the road or through the trees that anything out of the ordinary was going on behind their barbed-wire fences, which were posted at intervals with small yellow signs citing the penalty for entering, removing, or destroying government property. The only obviously heavy-duty installation was TA-55, the nation's only remaining fully operative plutonium facility. It had high walls with guard towers and triple-redundant fencing topped with razor wire and looked like a little Fort Knox or a small maximum-security prison.

A small, intent vigil, with about thirty people sitting in a circle, was in progress beside concrete-lined Ashley Pond, in the park at the heart of the original Ranch School/Manhattan Project complex. Some were meditating with their eyes closed; every so often one of them would share his or her thoughts. Among them were Mary Risley, a silver-haired pacifist with the Los Alamos Study Group, which tries to monitor LANL's activities and to hold it accountable for the radiation it has leaked into the surrounding desert; a Santa Fe poet in drag; two anthropologists studying the nuclear lab cultures here and at Livermore, California; and several repentant scientists who had worked in LANL's top-secret weapons group. Ed Grothus, the town's lone white-haired dissident, its Socrates, who had once proposed to the Los Alamos County Council that its name be changed to Buchenwald II, was spreading luminaria (sand-filled brown paper bags containing candles) out on a nearby grassy knoll so they spelled ONE BOMB IS TOO MANY. Crazy Ed, as everyone called him, had worked for LANL until 1969 and since then had been collecting salvage from it—gizmos and buzzers from the age of Sputnik—and selling it to movie studios, metal sculptors, and mad scientists.

I talked briefly with Crazy Ed, but he seemed distracted, off on his own trip, and was hard to corner. Perhaps this was his way of dealing with the community's animosity, or perhaps he had, in fact, been driven a little crazy by his inability to change the world. "There aren't any people here like me," he told me. "I arrived in 1949 and put in twenty years as a machinist in the weapons group, making better bombs. The Vietnam War was a turning point in my life. I just decided to do something else, so I started selling surplus. The labs are rich troves of everything. My first acquisition was six hundred pairs of khaki shorts, which I sold to a reform school. I have vitriolic enemies who have tried to close my business, but my roots are too deep in the surplus business to leave.

"The lab society is a self-selected, incestuous culture," Grothus reflected. "It is thrice screened. First, in order to go to work there, you have to agree with the mission, to persuade yourself that these weapons are necessary to save the world. Second, you have to have a Ph.D., a topflight scientific mind, and training. Third, you have to have a Q-clearance, or a Ku Klux clearance, as I call it. If you slept with a Communist [like Oppenheimer, who lost his clearance in the McCarthy years], if you read the wrong books, belonged to the wrong clubs, inhaled, you can forget about working at Los Alamos."

The protesters seemed to be about as welcome as lepers. Three local kids walked quickly by, one of them whispering, "Don't make eye contact." Earlier in the afternoon, someone had shown up in a sick T-shirt with a mushroom cloud, captioned MADE IN AMERICA, TESTED IN JAPAN. A senior at the high school named Joel Younger had set up a one-man counterdemonstration with a banner celebrating the FIFTY YEARS OF FREEDOM the bomb had brought. Joel's father was one of LANL's high priests, in charge of Russian Collaborations—helping the former Communists dismantle their missiles and making sure their plutonium and their laid-off weapon designers didn't fall into the wrong hands, such as Saddam Hussein's. Younger *fils* was wearing his ROTC uniform when I interviewed him at his home a few days later; he was so straight and blond, blue-eyed Aryan that at first it was a little creepy. A few months earlier, he had swayed the Los Alamos County Council to vote against allocating a plot for a proposed memorial for the children of Hiroshima and Nagasaki who were killed by the Manhattan Project's bombs. I asked what his objection had been to the monument, and he said, "I told the county council, 'We don't need the statue. We have the bomb and the flag, and that's peace enough.'"

Three days later I drove over Omega Bridge, which spans Omega Gorge. Down in the gorge were the Omega Reactor, shut down in 1991 and discovered to have been leaking tritium into the aquifer beneath it for years, and the Omega Lab, where on May 21, 1946, a physicist named Louis Slotin was performing a "crit test," lowering two halves of a beryllium sphere that would convert a plutonium pit to a critical state, when the screwdriver that kept them from touching slipped, the assembly went supercritical, and a blue glow lit the room for less than a millisecond, during which Slotin received a lethal dose of gamma and neutron radiation; he died nine days later. The accident is harrowingly portrayed, with John Cusack as Slotin, in the movie *Fat Man and Little Boy*, and is one of the few cases of injurious radiation the lab admits to. Another scientist in the room, Allen Kline, was diagnosed at the time with radiation sickness, but when he later tried to get his medical and dosage records from the lab so he could obtain compensation, he found that they had disappeared. Not until 1984 were they discovered by a graduate student doing a master's on radiation issues.

This was Nagasaki Day, and even less was happening at Ashley Pond—just Crazy Ed keeping his lonely vigil, as he had been doing for years. The American public was far more worked up about the sudden death of Jerry Garcia that day; that evening two hundred people with candles and offerings of joints and flowers would spontaneously materialize at Roosevelt Park in Albuquerque. Nagasaki had always played second fiddle to Hiroshima, and not many people seemed to remember or care about either of them. Most Americans weren't even born in 1945. I recalled an op-ed piece in *The New York Times* a few months back titled "A Nation of Nitwits" that reported the results of a countrywide survey: most of the respondents thought the bombing of Japan was ordered by JFK.

Omega Bridge leads from the Los Alamos town site to TA-3, LANL's administrative headquarters and also the scene of a lot of the research, which is conducted in the windowless interiors of such buildings as the Advanced Computer Laboratory, Chemical and Metallurgical Research, Cryogenics, and CNLS Technical Research. Here also are support facilities like the Badge Office, the Industria! Agreements Office, and the Wellness Center. I hung a left onto Pajarito Road, following a blue Volvo station wagon with a large galvanized cage in back—not your ordinary dog cage—but a LANL flak man assured me no animal research was being done there. I pulled up to the Public Affairs Building, and soon I was sitting with Sid Hecker, LANL's fifth director.

Trim, slight, gray haired, a big mountain biker like many Los Alamosans, Hecker was a plutonium metallurgist. He'd been at the lab twenty years, director for the last nine. Mary Risley describes him as "a really nice man who views his role as a shepherd who is supposed to look after his flock's jobs." He came across as clearheaded, caring, fatherly—a scientist with unusually good communication skills. "I came here not because I was interested in the bomb, but in the metal," he explained. "Plutonium is the most fascinating of materials. Most metals have just one crystalline structure, but Pu can adopt six different ones at ambient pressure, each of which has a different behavior and can make Pu act like glass or aluminum, just like that, with little change of temperature or adding other elements.

"But I believed it was important for this country to be strong from my personal background, so I had no problem being drawn into nuclear weapons," Hecker continued. "You see, I was born in Poland, of Austrian parents, and grew up in Bosnia. My father was drafted into the German army and was sent to the Russian front. So I had an appreciation of what war does to families and was willing to do my part to keep this country free. In what other country could a person with such a background have become the head of a lab like this?"

Hecker traced the evolution of man's ability to kill ever-larger numbers of his own kind from the invention of the crossbow in the twelfth century to gunpowder in the sixteenth century to high explosives by Alfred Nobel, mustard and nerve gas by World War I. "From 1.5 million war-related deaths in the sixteenth century, we had eighty-six million in the first half of the twentieth, fifty-five million in World War Two alone. The atomic bomb changed all this," he argued: since Hiroshima there had been a mere seventeen million. "As Oppenheimer put it, 'The atomic bomb was the turn of the screw. It has made the prospect of future war unendurable. It has led us up those last few steps to the mountain pass; and beyond there is a different country.' "

Now that the chances of a third world war erupting seemed slight, what was the future of the lab? I asked, and Hecker said, "If it doesn't have a compelling national mission, you can't justify such a facility. The Second World War was very compelling, then came the Cold War. Now we must live with the legacy of the bomb. Now the mission is to bring the arsenal down while maintaining its deterrent effect, to help the country run its engines in reverse while keeping weapons out of the wrong hands. The key step to proliferation is getting hold of nuclear materials. Once you have them, it is frightfully easy to make a weapon. Between us and Russia we have two hundred metric tons of weapons-grade plutonium and a thousand of uranium, and another hundred tons, globally, are in civilian hands. These materials have ten million times the energy content of coal. If we could extract energy from them for the world's electric grid, burn up most of the world supply of weapons-capable material to light up the world, without creating waste and environmental problems, by transmuting the materials into something benign—by feeding them through a field of neutrons made by an accelerator like the electron-scattering research accelerator we already have here—that would be a compelling mission for the lab. But we need to keep attracting good scientists and to keep at the forefront of computer technology, which we couldn't do without the defense budget."

At that time, LANL's annual budget was about a billion dollars, of which roughly 20 percent was for environmental restoration and waste management, and 25 percent—under heavy fire from Congress—for non-defense-related research. The rest, plus unknown "black-budget" contributions from the Departments of Energy and Defense and the CIA, was for keeping the world free, or fattening the bank accounts of defense contractors and research scientists, depending on one's take. Hecker had worked hard with New Mexico senators Domenici and Bingaman to move the lab over from weapons work to technology transfer—cooperative research-and-development contracts with the private sector, especially high-tech companies in the Rio Grande corridor—in 1989, when it seemed in danger of collapsing. He was proud of the non-defense-related science it was doing—computer-generated mapping of the human genome, of the ocean, of the brain, for instance; using lasers to unclot coronary arteries, to shrink swollen prostate glands, to measure the air pollution in Mexico City; new ion-beam archival-storage technology enabling twelve pentabytes of information, the equivalent of ten thousand floppy disks, to be inscribed on an inch-long tungsten or stainless-steel pin; acoustic-resonance spectroscopy, originally developed to ascertain the contents of warheads, but also useful in checking eggs for salmonella or surveying the bridges in Korea after the recent earthquake; modeling internal-combustion engines so that someday cars could get eighty miles to the gallon. Chaos theory, the microwave oven, Velcro, much of the development of the computer, and, most recently, the discovery that the phantomlike particles known as neutrinos may have a trace of mass, which could revolutionize physics and cosmology, all came out of research done at LANL.

But the lab's mission was in flux. The Gingrich Congress had said the CRADAS (cooperative research-and-development agreements) smacked of "industrial policy" and had cut back all funding that was not defense related. The new mission was now supposed to be "stock-pile stewardship"—making sure the remaining weapons in the reduced post–Cold War arsenal worked, and keeping the knowledge to make new ones alive—and "remediation": the lab was bidding for the contract to clean up the radiotoxic sites throughout the nuclear weapons complex, which no one so far seemed to know how to do. It seemed ironic that, in a desperate effort to stay alive, LANL should now be vying for the opportunity to clean up its own messes.

But who could say what was really going on up on the Hill? The activities of LANL have always been veiled with layers of secrecy. It was entirely possible that a new generation of nuclear weapons was surreptitiously in development, and that not even the cones, who are given their top-secret Q-clearance on a need-to-know basis, who are only allowed to know about the particular piece of the puzzle they are working on, in other words, were aware of it. Even though there wasn't any enemy of the free world out there at the moment, except China, the designers had to keep their chops up. A lot of people were interested in seeing that the work continued.

I had breakfast at the Los Alamos Inn with John Hopkins, a former associate director of nuclear weapons development who had been recommended as "an articulate weapons person."

"When I came here, in 1955, there wasn't a great deal of soul-searching about the morality of nuclear weapons, but there was a little concern about fallout," recalled the sixty-seven-year-old Hopkins, who had short white hair and a short-sleeved white shirt and epitomized the neutral, rational, disembodied scientist so much in evidence in Los Alamos. "A test in the Pacific had irradiated a Japanese fishing boat, the *Lucky Dragon,* and a number of Marshall Islanders. But I worked with accelerator-induced radiation for twenty years, and I'm still here. I'll bet you can't find a single Los Alamosan, whether he is happy or unhappy with his life, who says he has an identifiable negative effect from radiation, apart from a few fatal accidents early on. If you used the statistics alone, you might even conclude that plutonium is good for you."

I asked about the silhouettes of Hiroshima victims left on walls several miles from ground zero. Hopkins explained that the blinding flash of the blast cast the victims' shadows on the wall and burned around them, much as the legs of a deck chair would be imprinted into your deck if the sun stayed still and didn't move across the sky. "And seconds later the victims were"—I searched for the right word—"vaporized? Incinerated? Thermoradiated?"

"How about burnt to a crisp?" Hopkins suggested, and then he giggled—not maliciously, I don't think, but nervously. It was more of a dissociative giggle than an uncompassionate one, like the off-color joke a surgeon might make about the anesthetized patient he is cutting up. Noticing my wince, Hopkins quickly caught himself and told me about a series of interviews PBS had conducted with surviving Soviet leaders of the Stalin and Khrushchev eras. "Everything the hawks said about the Russians' intentions were true. They were going full blast on the hydrogen bomb while we were still debating it. They manipulated the peace movement in the U.S. So nuclear weapons did play a positive role in preserving world stability, and they will play a different one in the future. They will remain in the arsenals of the superpowers—the U.S., Britain, France, China, Russia—and some others like Israel, India, and Pakistan, who we think have a small handful of nuclear weapons, which deters hostilities. It is clear how deterrence works when two adversaries are facing off, but not so clear when several are locked in a balance-of-power situation. If a country or a subnational element wants weapons bad enough and has money, like the oil countries, sooner or later it is going to get them, and we're not going to give ours up as long as other countries have them. So places like Los Alamos will continue to work on them. The Cold War generation is not appropriate because changes from aging, remanufacture, or storage problems could make them unreliable. I think we should make two or three thousand very simple and reliable new ones with lower yields, the way England makes Rolls-Royces and Japan Toyotas."

Hopkins's concerns about the stockpile were echoed by James Mercer-Smith, the deputy director of Nuclear Weapons Technology. Mercer-Smith was about forty and a lot less buttoned-down than Hopkins. I would have pegged him for a TV producer. He had a way with words, unlike some of his colleagues, who were incapable of explaining what they were doing in terms intelligible to me. The interview took place, as did Hecker's, in a windowless room in the Public Affairs Building. Mercer-Smith compared himself to "the witch in Grimm—my job is to scare you into being good" and quoted LANL's third director, Harold Agnew, recommending that every few years the leaders of the world should have to strip to their skivvies and feel the heat of a nuclear blast from twenty miles away to remind them of their awesome responsibility. "These materials tend to degrade over time," he explained. "The decay rate of tritium, for instance, which is required for our weapons to operate, is 5.5 percent a year, and plutonium, being sensitive to the slightest change, has long-term compatibility problems. And if you don't have confidence in your stockpile, you have no credibility." Then he thought of an image to bring his point home. "I got a deal for you. You're going back east, right? How'd you like to fly out of Albuquerque in a 707 that hasn't been started in twenty-five years?"

A lot of LANL's budget—no one knows just how much—is used not for science, but surveillance and intelligence gathering, maintaining the veil of secrecy, securing stashes of "the product" worldwide, and neutralizing situations that might result in "yield." Bob Kelly, who was in charge of nonproliferation and emergency response, was amiably evasive when I probed about what rogue states, terrorists, or other subnational elements—Mexican drug lords? the Montana Militia?—LANL was worried about making a play for its plutonium. He was equally vague about the measures being taken to protect the research from industrial and other espionage. "I'm not aware of any breaches since Klaus Fuchs [the German scientist who kept Stalin continuously informed about the progress of the Manhattan Project]," he told me. "None of the technicians who work with materials is ever allowed to be alone with them, and as they leave the area they are monitored several ways, to see if they have picked up any metal or radiation. When something is really important, we compartmentalize and do things a little different." The cones were pretty much on the honor system; they had already been carefully screened ideologically, psychologically, and otherwise before they were given access to classified areas. There were surprisingly frequent nuclear threats to the United States, Kelly continued, but they were generally low quality, "the scribblings of a psychotic." He claimed his nuclear bomb squad could be anywhere in the world in a matter of hours in the event of an accident or a terrorist threat, and that the security of LANL was not his main concern, which was Iraq; three West German scientists had already sold out to Saddam Hussein, whose billion-dollar nuclear weapons program had thankfully so far failed to produce a bomb. "This is a hard target, a test bed for security," he assured me. "The guys who make concrete and rebar for us are very happy, and if a yellow Ryder truck shows up, we have a pretty good idea what's in it [thanks to technology like acoustic-resonance spectroscopy and the light-detection and -ranging lasar (LIDAR)]."

Four Pueblo nations, San Ildefonso, Jemez, Santa Clara, and Cochiti, surround LANL. The most directly impacted is P'o-woge, Where the Water Runs Through, known to the outside world by its Spanish name, San Ildefonso. The ancestors of the San Ildefonsans, whose ruins I had already encountered at Tsipin, originally lived on the Pajarito Plateau, which includes the site of LANL, but moved down to the Rio Grande Valley during a prolonged drought in the thirteenth century. Several thousand of their ruins, among them the large ceremonial complexes, lie within the fenced-off technical areas, a matter of great resentment for the San Ildefonsans, as well as the fact that some radioactivity may be migrating into their sacred area, down the canyons, and through the deep aquifer, and that the elk they hunt and eat are picking up radionuclides from grazing in hot areas. There is a more basic friction between the Pueblo and the Hill—between a traditional culture with a land-based religion, which venerates sacred shrines scattered throughout the landscape, and a modern one that worships technology at the altar of the atom and whose creed is the laws of physics.

The history of San Ildefonso's contact with Europeans, first Spaniards, then Anglos, has been typically traumatic. By 1793 half the pueblo had been wiped out by smallpox. The influenza epidemic of 1918 rained more death. Virtually every able-bodied man went off to fight in the Second World War, and many didn't come back. For centuries the Franciscans had tried to disabuse them of their horticultural mysticism; then anthropologists, tourists, and wanna-bes had pried into what was left of their culture. When Pueblo vets went to college on the GI bill after World War II and discovered how many of their esoteric ceremonies had been published in minute detail in the bulletins of the Bureau of American Ethnology, the Pueblos threw up what the anthropologist and San Juan Pueblo Alfonso Ortiz has called the adobe curtain. So I knew I was going to take a certain amount of generic abuse just for being "Anglo" (even though I don't have a drop of Anglo-Saxon blood) when I went to see Gilbert Sanchez, a former governor of the pueblo who was now the director of its environmental program.

The previous January the DOE had approved giving each of the pueblos $150,000 a year to hire staff and buy equipment so they could independently monitor their environmental impact from the lab, which Mary Risley complained had stifled those who had been speaking out. Three of the four governors were lab employees on leave, and many people from the pueblos work there, so the Pueblos are in the same bite-the-hand-that-feeds you bind vis-à-vis LANL as the local Chicanos are.

"We lost 1.6 million acres of our aboriginal holding in 1905 when Teddy Roosevelt signed the National Forest Act, and it has been dwindling ever since," Gilbert Sanchez, a genial man of about fifty, told me. "Now it's down to sixty thousand acres. Of the six hundred and nineteen pueblos that existed when the Europeans came, only nineteen survive. Up on the mesa we had lost forty-nine thousand acres to Spanish settlers. In the thirties we were trying to buy back this Ramon Vigil grant, which includes twenty-two hundred of our cultural sites and encompasses the totality of LANL. But then Oppenheimer came and told us he needed the land to create weaponry to end all war, and that on completion of the Manhattan Project the land would revert to the tribe. But all we've gotten back so far is seven hundred and ninety-nine acres, which are known as the Sacred Area."

I asked if there was any chance of visiting the Sacred Area, and Sanchez said, "No, we can't do that. Sorry." What about going out with one of the guys who is taking the samples? No to that too. "The plateau is the central part of our religious activities," he told me. "Since 1943, when they built the chain-link fences, our people haven't been able to go in, and there have been no ceremonies." I asked what the nature of the ceremonies, the beliefs about the plateau, were, and Sanchez said he couldn't talk about them. It wouldn't be possible to go out with or talk to a traditionalist either. "They're protected by our government. We don't give out their identities. We learned our lesson.

"The longer you prolong confrontation," he observed, "the higher your GNP grows. Until this country learns to live with a peacetime budget and economy, there ain't gonna be no way in the world we're gonna be able to sustain man's time on earth. We're in a catch-22. No matter how big the bomb is, whether we use it or never use it, the by-product or the end product is going to destroy us; either we will be killed instantaneously or over a long period of time by the residue from development. And for what? National security? When your population is no longer capable of producing intelligent life-forms where are you going to be at?"

The golf course at the Los Alamos Country Club is an unusually pleasant, nonthreatening track. Yellow sulphur and painted-lady butterflies were taking nectar from Indian paintbrushes and other wildflowers in the rough on the afternoon I played it with Grant Slade, who grew up in Los Alamos in the early fifties. "The city was completely sealed off," he recalled. "You had to show a pass at a gate guarded by a tank to get in. My father had the dairy concession for the facility. It was an idyllic childhood. I caddied and knew every cave and cliff. Sometimes we would be awakened at four in the morning by an incredible ruckus. Bears—big cinnamons [a color phase of black bear] were rummaging in the garbage. The only problem was the constant fear of the red peril. Los Alamos was obviously the first place the Russians were going to hit if all-out nuclear war broke out. We were constantly having drills and having to duck under our desks." Grant was a Boy Scout, and the troop met in Fuller Hall, one of the old Ranch School buildings, with vertical-log, white-chinked jacal walls, which is still the social center of the town, where important lectures, concerts, and receptions are held. When he was ten, one of Grant's scoutmasters made a pass at him on a field trip, and he ran off into the woods. The laboratory's security apparatus launched a manhunt for him, including helicopters, which he eluded for two days.

The lab community had three strata: the longhairs (now known as cones), the plumbers (the technicians), and the creeps. In addition there were locals like Joe Gonzales, whose family had run sheep on the mesa. After the war, having fought on nine European battlefields and been wounded repeatedly, Gonzales went to work for the Zia

Company, which had the maintenance, waste-disposal, and snow-removal contract for LANL. Gonzales didn't think much of his Anglo bosses, the scientists. They made him feel like a second-class citizen in his own homeland. "I used to drive for the scientists, and they didn't know shit from shinola," he told me. "They got too much mice and rats in their head that just go round and round. The ex-Nazi rocket scientists were real racists. One time we held our foreman over a hot sludge pool and threatened to throw him in until he wet his pants and begged for mercy."

The cones had their own subdivisions: Germans, Jews, Mormons, and so on. The inner circle, the priesthood, were the weapons designers. "The labbies looked down on people in town who didn't work at the lab," said a Los Alamosan whose parents had been schoolteachers. "They were the Brahmins."

Everyone believed he was on a heroic mission, saving the human race from itself and keeping the world free. No one admitted to having qualms, at least publicly, but there were an alarming number of suicides. One night in the early seventies, Tom Roberts, a research scientist at the Cryogenics Lab and a state representative, put a plastic bag over his head and filled it with helium; another scientist hanged himself by a bootlace in Aspen, another by a light cord in San Jose; a chemist who had made some comments to Sam Barthel, an employee in the Safety Department, about the moral implications of weapons work was found by Barthel asphyxiated by a sweeper hose he had tied to his car exhaust; and there were two other apparent moral-qualms suicides in the late seventies, one a prominent weapons scientist who left a note saying he didn't want to do this anymore.

Outwardly, statistically, Los Alamos County, which consists almost entirely of Los Alamos and a satellite suburb called White Rock, is impressive by national, and even more by New Mexican, standards. It boasts the lowest unemployment rate in the country, the highest per capita income, the highest proportion of Ph.D.s, the highest ratio of high-school graduates who go on to college, the most National Merit Scholars, the most heavily patronized public library, and, curiously, the most churches (forty-nine) for a town of its size (nineteen thousand).

But not all the kids at the high school are successes. Some are anorexic; drug use is on the rise; some are into heavy metal and even Satanism. Michael Coca, the Chicano artist and water-rights activist I visited with Nicásio Romero, grew up in Bomb City, as he calls it, in the fifties. "My father was one of the carpenters who built Los Alamos. He had been a master sergeant in the Army Air Corps. I call him Archie Bunker de la Raza. Our parents didn't speak Spanish to us. We lived there like white middle-class Anglos until I got out of high school in 1962. At the time we were fairly oblivious to what was going on, living on the mesa in a semiutopian situation, no unemployment, no old people, no crime. We didn't experience racism too much, though some with more Hispanic-sounding names I know for a fact did. We had the best education system in the state. It was the only federally funded one. We had art in all twelve grades. By the time I got out of high school I had had three years of mechanical drawing and one year of architectural design and had designed a couple of houses. But in 1960 two of my dad's best friends were killed. They were milling high explosives, and the detonator went off. He had to ID their bodies. I couldn't relate to people getting killed in Japan because I wasn't there, but I could relate to this, and I became an antinuclear activist.

"It was a dead town in the early fifties," Coca recalled. "It was cop-heavy, and the lab security cruised around in pickups with M-16s. I still hate to go up there, I feel really uncomfortable and paranoid. A couple of us weren't as straight thinking as most of our classmates, and we became kind of like James Dean–type guys, into Buddy Holly, rock and roll, and chasing girls. We would sit around drinking beer in the woods and arguing. 'Hey man the stuff that's going on here is bullshit, and you're going along with it.' I'm just waiting for the people of Bomb City to wake up to what they're doing. There's enough intellectual knowledge up there to turn around the whole state of New Mexico in five years."

The proliferation of churches, the odd coupling of churchiness and weaponry, of science and religion—does this reflect a need for guilt atonement? I asked John Hopkins, and he said, "That has nothing to do with it. Because a hundred thousand people die in cars every year, are the people who make them killers? In the beginning, when Los Alamos was a closed town, the churches played a big role, because all the entertainment was self-generated. The community started from scratch. By 1955 there were two hundred clubs—chess, debating, fly tying, quilting, folk dancing, rock climbing. Most of them met in churches. The churches were the only entertainment."

The Los Alamos *Monitor* takes up a little building on D.P. Road. Across the street there used to be a trailer park that was built right on top of a radioactive dump site. Evelyn Vigil, the *Monitor*'s editor, told me, as we sat in her office, that the site is now covered with asphalt, "which stops alpha rays, but the asphalt is beginning to crack. I'm worried what this means." At the end of D.P. Road is the original hot dump, which is still, an environmentalist at the lab claims, "really hot" and is now being monitored by honeybees, who concentrate the radionuclides in their honey. Up the street are the small but lively Living Water and New Testament Baptist Churches. A lot of the lab's technicians are fundamentalists from the South, as are the people who assembled and are now dismantling the Cold War arsenal at the Pantex plant in Amarillo, Texas. One of the anthropologists I met at the Hiroshima Day vigil explained that fundamentalists are attracted to this type of work because "they want to be right there when the end comes."

The cones and the old Manhattan Project people went to the Unitarian church, Evelyn Vigil told me. "There was a brouhaha last Christmas about kids donating food to 'the Christmas lady.' The Jews objected, and some received anti-Semitic threats." She told me about a controversial mural painted by students at the high school in which one of the subjects' fingers appeared to be making the white-supremacist gesture, and about the equally controversial Church of Our Lady of the Woods, a Wicca coven some of the labbies belong to that was into "nature worship and being good witches and has caused untold sleepless nights for the fundamentalists." Then there was "this ardent creationist named Baumgartner who is a geologist at the lab, of all things, and doesn't accept that the world is more than six thousand years old. He tried to get evolutionism taken out of the education system but was shot down because the school board wanted solid science."

There's a lot of talk about the Mormons taking over the place. Al Shapolia, a laid-off Jewish labbie now said to be working at the Radio Shack in Española, unsuccessfully sued the lab, alleging that he had been discriminated against by his Mormon boss. Someone sprayed graffiti on the concrete dividers along the highway coming up to the Hill alleging AVERAGE MORMON RAISE 14% AVERAGE NON-MORMON RAISE 3%, but it's since been covered with silver paint. The deputy director, heads of personnel and the purchasing department, and the chief lobbyist, said to be the power behind the throne, are all Latter-Day Saints. "They're always a little weird," said a man who had put in almost three decades at the lab until his department was phased out. "They have this wide-eyed look, and they hang together. Many of them are brilliant, but I had one incompetent wacko Mormon working for me. They do have special access because we had a disagreement, and he went right to the deputy director, which backfired because he was sent for psychological evaluation and was diagnosed with paranoid tendencies.

"There's a green conference room in the weapons complex," the former labbie went on. "One day I tried to reserve it and was told I couldn't have it on Thursdays between twelve and one because the

Mormons use it for their prayer meeting. That church business was being conducted on government premises, that there were prayer meetings in the war room, shocked me. There are rumors that the Mormons want to become a nuclear power in their own right, which are tongue in cheek, of course, but food for thought, because the Mormons do have a strong in with the nuclear weapons complex."

By 1962, when Charles Barnett came to the lab as an environmental physicist, Los Alamos seemed to be metamorphosing from *Ozzie and Harriet* to *Peyton Place*. "It was a real insiders' club," he recalled. "A lot of partying, drinking, and wife swapping was going on. There was a bar called the Office. The labbies would call their wives and say, 'I can't come home; I'm at the Office.' Stanislav Uloff, the Polish mathematician who was the coinventor of the Super [the hydrogen bomb], felt Los Alamos was so sterile he and some friends started a coffeehouse called the Café of the High Ideals."

One of Barnett's friends was Judy Blume, the teenage-fiction writer. Blume was married to a labbie "until she freaked out about what was going on up there." In the seventies she wrote a steamy novel for adults called *Wifey* about the sexual fantasies and adulterous affair of a bored suburban housewife, set in Plainfield, New Jersey, but said to be based on Los Alamos.

The cutisms and inside jokes became a little wearing for Barnett. Inside the security area there was a low-ceilinged stairwell with a sign that said WATCH YOUR CONE. The units in which the power of a detonation is measured are called shakes—of a little bomb's tail.

Los Alamos is frequently accused of being in deep denial of its horrible raison d'être. Hugh Gusterston, an MIT anthropologist studying the nuclear lab cultures at Los Alamos and Livermore, California, whom I met at the vigil, maintained that "denial is a culturally and politically biased term. The weapons makers could just as easily say that the peaceniks are in denial of what would happen if there weren't any nuclear weapons." Gusterston said he had yet to meet a weapons person who was tortured about what he was doing (although some over the years certainly were). There are an inordinate number of shrinks in Los Alamos and in Santa Fe who treat Los Alamosans, but the weapons scientists rarely see them because it would jeopardize their clearance. The patients tend to be their wives and children and scientists in nonweapons research. I was interested in talking to a Jungian analyst because of the Jungian concept of the shadow, the dark side that every individual and every community has, the unpleasant negative part that we don't want to look at and project onto others.

"There must be a big shadow in this town," I observed to Dr. Alicia Lauritzen, a Jungian whose father had worked on the Manhattan Project and who shrinks a lot of Los Alamosans. Dr. Lauritzen told me about an exhibit called "The Artistry of Dreams" that showcased the work of Los Alamosan artists a few years back. Among the works that were hung was a weaving of bodies being chopped up. "But it was taken down because the community didn't want any nightmares on the wall. Yet it is creating the ultimate nightmare. On the external level Los Alamos is very neat, but there is a lot of dark shadow material that is not talked about. Teenagers are acting out a lot of the repression."

I asked whether the reports of teenage Satanism could be the shadow expressing itself, and Dr. Lauritzen said very possibly. Even more suggestive was an incident in 1994, when some teenagers planted a homemade bomb, consisting of a Coke bottle containing gunpowder and some bullets, in the park on LANL's central administrative boulevard and ignited the fuse, which fizzled. Hugh Gusterston interpreted this as classic "Oedipal emulation. Dad doesn't get to have all the fun."

"The labbies have this lily-white appearance," Dr. Lauritzen went on, "because if they show anything else they don't get clearance. The scientists here have a stacked deck. They have developed their left brain, their linear, pragmatic, technological side at the expense of their right-brain, intuitive, compensatorial anima. This has made them smart and brilliant, but lopsided, and has made for a lot of marital problems."

I remarked how Santa Fe seems to hate having this horrible karma and toxicity in its backyard. Its mayor, Debbie Jaramillo, had recently branded Los Alamos "an island of paranoia and privilege" and suggested it should employ more Hispanics and people of color in management. Dr. Lauritzen believed it was "synchronicitous" that artsy, New Age, bohemian Santa Fe should have a "totally linear and pragmatic" community for a neighbor, and proposed that Santa Fe and Los Alamos were each other's shadows. "Santa Fe carries a lot of Los Alamos's undeveloped dark side. Los Alamosans put Santa Feans down as sexually wanton New Age airheads, while Santa Feans see Los Alamosans as stuffy, conservative, uncreative types who don't flow with life. Jung says to have something so archetypically opposite, so yin-yang, is synchronicitous.

"Los Alamos is mostly white patriarchal workaholics," Dr. Lauritzen went on. "Women in the lab complain of being diminished. Managers deal with people in a way that is not psychologically advanced. Management was supposed to have announced eleven hundred layoffs, but it has just delayed the announcement for a month and refuses to reveal who the people are, and everybody is on pins and needles. The heart mode is not stressed up there, which is in itself indicative of the shadow. How long can you be a computer? How many breakthroughs can you make? No brownie points are given up there for having a good marriage or becoming more self-aware.

"I think Los Alamos is our entire culture's collective shadow," she argued. "Fifty percent of the lab is still working on plutonium and weapons research. Think about the origin of the word 'plutonium': Who is Pluto? The god of the underworld, of death. That something like LANL exists, that we as a culture allow this multi-billion-dollar industry dedicated to death to exist, and nobody is doing anything about it, suggests to me that Los Alamos is our collective shadow."

Robert Weiss, a Santa Fe therapist, was treating an Españolan named Jonathan Garcia, who had put in fourteen years at LANL as a heavy-equipment operator, hauling and disposing of radioactive waste. Garcia was suffering from depression because he had leukemia and painful sores in his mouth from host-virus disease, which his compromised immune system was unable to fight off. He was depressed because he couldn't work and because he knew he was going to die soon; his former coworkers had been dropping like flies in the past couple of years. One morning I drove up to the Hill with Garcia and his wife, Jeanette. He showed me TA-54, also known as Area G, the hot dump, where he buried, by his estimate, seventy to eighty thousand barrels of plutonium- or uranium-contaminated sludge. "I was stationed at the hot dump from 1976 to 1988," the feisty little red-haired forty-four-year-old, whose nickname was Colorado, told me. "I ran bulldozers, scrapers, backhoes, bobcats, loaders, cherry pickers. Two times a week they locked us in the hot dump to dispose of what had accumulated. I buried monkeys, pigs, cows, dogs, elk, that had been dissected and monitored. They even said I buried some human parts. I covered the drums under a foot and a half of earth or dropped them into eight-by-eight culverts. Lots of times the covers would come off or the drums would get crushed under the weight of the dozer, and the sludge would splash all over the place, but I wore nothing special, just white coveralls and a T-shirt. They told us it was low level and wouldn't harm us unless we held it in our hands or took a bite out of it. But probably always we had a doubt in our minds working around all this junk that something might happen."

The sludge, Garcia went on, was like "tortilla dough, but yellow. Some of it came in cardboard boxes. I'd pick it up on the treads. My mechanic, Willie Romero, used to work on my bulldozer all the time. He was diagnosed with cancer in March and died in May. He was breathing all these fumes from welding. Jesus Gutiérrez, who used to haul Dumpsters to the hot dump—he was diagnosed with cancer in May and died in July. Armando War, a pipe fitter, got some kind of leukemia which is different from mine. Five people I know who worked up there died different deaths in one week."

LANL spokesmen flatly denied that anyone at the lab had ever suffered negative effects from exposure to nuclear materials apart from the fatalities years ago. "Our health and safety record is as good as an insurance company's," John Gustafson, one of its flak men, assured me. Garcia was unable to hold LANL responsible for his leukemia because of the terms of a fifty-thousand-dollar settlement he signed two years back, but he was testifying for three of his buddies who were suing the lab for health problems they claimed arose from their work. If he ever decided to return to court in his own behalf, he would have trouble proving his case because, he claimed, "I went to get my records, and I found that they didn't correspond to what I had done there at all."

Gustafson claimed it was impossible for the waste-disposal workers to have picked up undetected doses of radiation because they all wore dosimeters, but Jonathan said he had only worn his off and on, and, in any case, it wouldn't have picked up all the different kinds of radiation he was exposed to over the years. His therapist faxed a list of seventeen of Jonathan's former coworkers who had died prematurely of leukemia or other cancers or had cancer or other serious illnesses they believed came from handling radiotoxic waste.

Bill Atha, an epidemiologist with the New Mexico state health department, studied an apparent cluster of brain tumors in Los Alamos that was uncovered by an independent environmental monitor and caused panic a few years ago. People started worrying not only about their health, but about their property values. The DOE delegated $400,000 to study the problem and came up with the reassuring conclusion that, as Atha told me, "There was in fact a small excess of brain cancer in the mid- to late eighties, but what we were seeing was probably random fluctuation. That's one of the great liabilities of working with small areas. But in the course of our brain cancer survey we found a fourfold increase in thyroid cancer, a pattern that really jumped out. I've never seen anything like it in this or any other county. Ionizing radiation at moderate levels can give you thyroid cancer, especially in childhood. We've been looking at everything, but the short of it is that so far we don't have an explanation."

Atha also noted that there were ten suicides in Los Alamos between 1991 and 1993, 43 percent above the national rate. "Does that mean anything?" he asked. "It's definitely a high-pressure situation up there. One-third of the adult males have Ph.D.'s. Slackers are not tolerated."

Tyler Mercier, the man who brought to light the eleven brain tumor deaths, remains unconvinced that they were just the result of "random fluctuation." "I am a sculptor with a degree in engineering and a technical and mathematical background," he told me. "My wife works in the lab's computer group. On January 31, 1990, a group of people from Santa Fe and Taos requested that a credible person do independent environmental monitoring of the lab, and I was an acceptable candidate to LANL because I had always been a big booster of the lab and was trained by it until May, when we had three dosimeters set up around town. The first results were ready in July, and they indicated, to my shock, the lab had been understating its radiation emissions and its background radiation. A physicist at the lab, who refused to go public, told me, 'Perhaps these findings explain why there is an unusual number of brain tumors in my neighborhood.' This was in the Western Area, adjacent to the CMR [Chemical and Metallurgical Research] Building, which is responsible for ninety percent of the lab's plutonium emissions. Most of the housing was built in 1947, some of it over old toxic dumps. There were eleven brain tumor deaths in a population of one thousand over a period of five years in the late eighties, when one or two would have been expected. Most of the victims were housewives who stayed home and got exposed.

"Seven days after I made the tumor cluster public, our house burned down," Mercier went on. "I had been threatened by someone at the lab who said, 'In this work people who make a fuss have their houses burned down.' There was never an adequate investigation, and I find it an uncomfortably frightening coincidence, particularly after learning that a scientist at Livermore named Goffman had his house burn the day after he changed boats on the dangers of atmospheric testing, and that the same thing happened to four elders on the Marshall Islands after they complained about increasing rates of thyroid cancer among their people. Karen Silkwood was dosed with radiation in the midseventies, and she came to Los Alamos with her boyfriend for dosimetry, and within twenty-four hours she was killed. It's mighty interesting how people have accidents when they criticize the nuclear industry."

There are enough skeletons in LANL's closet to make one wonder whether William Burroughs's paranoia about the state, and Tyler Mercier's about LANL, aren't well founded. Between 1945 and 1947, for instance, eighteen people were injected with "the product" (the word "plutonium" was still classified) to see how it reacted in the body. These subjects were not told the nature of the experiment, never gave informed consent to it, and were identified only by numbers until Eileen Welsome of the Albuquerque *Tribune* tracked down the identities of five of them five decades later, in 1993, for which she won a Pulitzer Prize. Most of them were injected at a hospital in Rochester, New York, but the plutonium was provided by LANL, and the urine, blood, and stools of these unwitting human guinea pigs were analyzed by its scientists. All suffered in the usual horrible ways. The last surviving plutonium patient, a retired black railroad porter named Elmer Allen, died in 1991.

The only major suit by an employee LANL has lost was that brought by David Nochumson, its Harvard-educated air-quality coordinator, who was ordered to have psychological testing and was demoted after publicly disclosing that emissions data were falsified and he was asked not to do things properly. Nochumson sued for harassment and was awarded one hundred thousand dollars, but his wife meanwhile died of brain cancer, and he was living in Santa Fe and was said to be a wreck. Gustafson dismissed Nochumson as "one of those people who is having job performance problems and turns to whistle-blowing for protection. Noch was in charge of bringing the stack monitoring program into compliance with the new 1990 provisions of the Clean Air Act, and there was severe friction with his manager. He came up with a Ferrari of a plan we couldn't afford, and we asked him to come up with a cheaper, scaled-down plan. He interpreted this as harassment and filed suit claiming that he was being prevented from doing his job. Technically Noch is really good, but he's a prickly character."

Tyler Mercier testified at Nochumson's suit. He suspected the Hill's dramatic levels of thyroid cancer were caused by radioactive iodine 131 discharged by three reactor meltdowns in the sixties, whose details are still classified, that he found out about from the Centers for Disease Control. As for the brain tumors, Gilbert Sanchez offered a different diagnosis: excessive cerebration. "They think too much up there."

At Ashley Pond I chatted with Mary Risley, the antinuclear activist with the Los Alamos Study Group. Fifty-three, she looked like Joan Baez and emanated the same fearless, uncompromising probity. When the conversation turned to something that really burned her up, her voice would become shrill. Her great-grandfather, a shell-shocked Union Army vet, had settled in Mesilla, downstate, and she had grown up in Roswell, the daughter of a lieutenant general in the marines, so she understood the military mentality.

Area G, she said, was so contaminated that all the trees there had to be scraped from the surface because their roots would bring up radionuclides and transpire them into the air. "They can't have any trees there for twenty-five thousand years, the time of toxicity for plutonium."

Mary explained that since the first atomic bombs, seventy thousand nuclear weapons had been produced in this country at a cost equaling the national debt. "The culture of LANL has always had unlimited resources," Mary seethed. "The 1992 Motorola report found that it cost three hundred sixty-five thousand dollars to support each technical staff member of the lab, as opposed to one hundred sixty thousand dollars at the Bell Lab. Every question has to be a major research problem, and because nuclear research labs don't share, everything is started anew."

A few days later, Sam Hitt, the Santa Fe environmentalist, who had been watching and wondering about LANL since the fifties, shared his take on the place: "At the bottom it's pork. There isn't any nuclear threat out there. What the lab is really worried about is being able to continue sucking the tit of the military-industrial-congressional complex, to keep the priesthood alive and relevant seeming in a changing world. I can imagine the Mayan hierarchy in the jungle having the same line. Look at our pyramids. But this is an insulated priesthood that denies reality and has created the recipe for its own destruction. I can't imagine it will be around much longer."

Hugh Gusterston's book on nuclear lab cultures has chapters on the denial question, he told me, the effect of secrecy on marriage, the labbies' relationship with their bodies, and, most intriguing, "My thesis is that the nuclear test is the core ritual through which the community affirms itself. The weapons designer is the elite within the lab. He has to study others' explosions for five years before he gets to do his own. Rituals, as the pioneer anthropologist Bronislaw Malinowski proposed, are attempts to deal with anxious situations where pragmatic human control is limited or nonexistent—death, crop failures, plague, etcetera. The test is the way the designer affirms control of his weapon, the only way he can find out if it works and does what he thinks it will do. But now this core ritual is banned, so if you are a designer, what are you living for?"

Gusterston's impression that the designers were getting antsy under the comprehensive ban on nuclear testing that had been in effect since the fall of 1992 and looked as if it wouldn't be lifted anytime soon was confirmed by John Hopkins—not so much by what he said, as the way he said it—as we sat in the restaurant of the Los Alamos Inn. We were talking about DAHRT, LANL'S controversial $124 million dual-axis radiographic hydrotest facility. "Some people have suggested that the true intent of DAHRT," I said, "is not to make sure the existing stockpile remains viable, but to design new weapons." Hopkins assured me, "It is of no use in developing new weapons if we can't test." Then he added, gritting his teeth, obviously very agitated, "And the president has said we can't test."

And I thought I detected a twinge of nostalgia as James Mercer-Smith told me about his last detonation at the Nevada Test Site, a few years back. "The last thing I did there was not particularly big, but it was the third- or fourth-largest earthquake in the world that week—four point something. You could feel the earth shake from twenty miles."

I went to Ed Grothus's salvage company, the Black Hole, to soak up the once-state-of-the-art technology the lab had spun out over the years. The "nuclear waste," as Grothus called it, was housed in an A-frame that used to be the Missouri Synod Lutheran Church and in a small adjacent former supermarket (the Shop 'n Cart), which had gone under ten years before. The big stuff was out in the parking lot. The neighbors kept threatening to sue. Crazy Ed wasn't around, but an old hippie associate I'll call, honoring his request, Don't Quote Me, with long gray hair in a ponytail and a thick Long Island accent, gave me the tour. "This here is the happening part of a laser beam," he explained. "Here is a thermonuclear pump with the power supply ready to go. You can make your own Jack Daniel's with this here fermenter." A gizmo with dials and knobs labeled CAVITY RELIEF CONTROL shared a shelf with a vial of molecular sieves. Strainage control panels jockeyed for space with synchronicitous and stepping motors and control units. Out in the parking lot was a million-dollar solar-cell system from the Reagan years. Don't Quote Me claimed it had been cranked up once and "after it reached its four hundred fifty degrees Fahrenheit and they saw it worked, they put it out for salvage."

"What do you want for this?" I asked. It was a big red metal sign that said in white caps DO NOT GO BEYOND THIS POINT FOR MORE INFORMATION CONTACT GROUP AMX-15 OFFICE.

"Make me an offer," Don't Quote Me proposed.

A Look Behind the Curtain

n May of 1992, as our sojourn in Albuquerque was drawing to a close, I contracted with a travel magazine to write an article on the subject of "culturally correct tourism in the tribal Southwest," which would enable us to make a last tour and visit some of the native nations I still hadn't gotten to; there are nineteen in Arizona and twenty-two in New Mexico. I particularly wanted to take a last crack at breaking through to the Hopi. The article ended up being rejected. I felt kind of proud when I found out why: its tone was, my editor explained, "militantly antitourist from start to finish, which is somewhat self-defeating in a travel magazine."

This time my wife came with me, which was a great help, because wherever we went, the native people reacted to her as a vibrant tribal woman. "He was okay, but his wife was great" was the feedback I got on our visit to the White River Apache, for instance. Up to this point, I still hadn't made much headway with Hopi. The man I had particularly wanted to meet, a religious leader from the village of Shongopovi, the oldest and most conservative of the thirteen Hopi villages, had stood me up on a previous appointment. But this time he was there. He met us at the cultural center on Second Mesa, of which Peter Nabokov writes:

> These tourist depots serve a cunning function for Indian communities concerned about cultural privacy. It might not have been a conscious item in their planning, but they provide buffer zones for absorbing, directing, or deflecting the insistent curiosity of outsiders. They apportion degrees of cultural goods and information, from native-made and signed crafts for sale to the casual tourist, to books and tips for the aficionados who want to attend a specific ceremony. As

checkpoints between cultural worlds, they help to put access back under Indian control.

As the three of us sat drinking coffee, a busload of French tourists trooped in. Several of the men were wearing blue souvenir U.S. Cavalry caps. "Wow," said the man from Shongopovi. "That's like if I went to Paris with a toy guillotine."

As we drove down to Shongopovi, the man explained that Hopi xenophobia was on the rise because the mesas were under siege. Peabody Coal was sucking the water out from under them. Sacred springs were going dry, and Moenkopi Wash (which means "Wash That Flows Continuously"), along whose banks the Hopi grew most of their corn, had become an intermittent stream. The Hopi Reservation was a little island within the vast Navajo Rez, and the Hopi felt surrounded by their ancient enemies, whose word for them translates to "Skull Bashers." Recently some Arabian horses in Keams Canyon had been stolen and eaten; the Navajo were still raiding. The young Hopi were being seduced by reggae and heavy metal and drugs. One clan, in particular, was bringing in "booze, rock, and chaos," the man said. (Rosette had found a sexually explicit inscription in the ladies' room of the culture center, which was either evidence of this disintegration or a confirmation of Ramón Gutiérrez's claim that the Pueblos were a healthily unrepressed, sex-positive culture. It said, "I like to fuck someone with a big long dick it feels so good when he's moving it between the lips of my vagina ooh.") The movie of Hillerman's *Dark Wind* had shown a murder taking place during the holiest *wuwuchin* ceremony and a kachina dancer being demasked. It was like "a movie of the pope taking a shit," the man told us. On top of this, Marvel Comics had put out a comic book that had Killer Kachinas wielding chain saws and meat cleavers. All dances and ceremonies had been closed in protest, and six villages had withdrawn recognition of the tribal council, so it could no longer raise a quorum. The breakaway communities felt that the council had been created to sign away the Hopi's natural resources, and they had reembraced the old, undemocratic theocracy of the *kikmongwi,* the religious elders.

Shongopovi was a cluster of slab and cinder-block houses perched on a mesa. Its feeling was, like Acoma's, very Tibetan: the eaten-away brown flatness of the Colorado Plateau, with the snow-covered San Francisco Peaks far in the distance; the rude stone architecture; and the round, wrinkled faces of the old women were all evocative of that distant land. The Hopi have perhaps the most rarefied existence of any southwestern tribe, attempting to orchestrate through complex prayers and rituals a harmonious and fruitful interaction between the sun, water, and their corn plants.

We went down to the man's house and sat talking with his wife, a Navajo woman who worked in Tuba City as an infectious-disease control officer, distributing a brochure on AIDS that said, "You can't get AIDS from hearing too much about it. You can get AIDS from silence. There were five million Indians in the U.S. when Columbus came over. Now there are 1.6 million. We can't afford to lose any more people." The Hopi word for "AIDS" is *bayao,* the woman told us, the same for any disease or scourge; for the Hopi who fought in the First World War, the *bayao* they had to worry about was mustard gas. The Navajo call AIDS *asii ye na ghaa ya ool da,* "attacks your defense mechanism." "I think AIDS is man-made," the man said, "to weed out the undesirables, the blacks and the gays, the people with the least defenses."

He told us that the details of the kachinas in the Marvel Comics could only have come from someone in Shongopovi. "There is a traitor in our midst who is selling out our culture for money. It could be my brother, my uncle, my father," he said. "This is the most traditional stronghold, the only village that still does the full ceremonial cycle of twelve seasons." He had been so preoccupied with political problems that his previous wife, a Hopi woman, had left him. His new wife wasn't accepted. The people of Shongopovi called her Here She Comes Again. "This isn't even our house," the woman complained. "It belongs to his sister. We could be kicked out anytime." The man lamented how young Hopi were stealing sacred paraphernalia from altars and selling it to "desert rats" to raise money for drugs or booze, and the paraphernalia was ending up on someone's dining-room table in Los Angeles. Particularly horrible was the disappearance from Shongopovi in 1977 of the *dalaudumsi,* a doll-like idol that was necessary for men's society initiations. For five years no one had been able to proceed from the Third to the Fourth World. "We're stymied," the man said grimly.

At last I get behind the adobe curtain, I thought as we drove down from the village, and what is there? Not a whole lot at this point. To me the most interesting Hopi concept is that of *koyaanisqatsi,* which is the opposite of the Navajo's *hozho.* It means "everything is crazy, haywire, the world is out of joint"—the modern condition, my modus operandi, in other words. Like the time in Albuquerque my wife came out of an exam she'd been up all night studying for, and her car had been towed. The composer Philip Glass did the score for a movie called *Koyaanisqatsi.* The movie starts on the Hopi mesas with images of serenity, peaceful horizontal nature, the plateau segueing to the ocean, with calmly flashing waves, then it gets louder and faster, with city traffic, sidewalks seething with rushing people.

Rosette and I drove up to Walpi, the most picturesque and frequently painted and photographed of the villages, with ancient slab dwellings straggling along a knife-edged mesa spur that rises three or four hundred feet from the plains below. Here Major John Wesley Powell took a break from his descent on the Colorado and, climbing up the canyon walls, spent two days trading, acquiring artifacts for his ethnological collection. He witnessed the snake dance, performed by men in loincloths who "with little feather-tipped wands . . . herd all the snakes in a great mass of writhing, hissing, rattling serpents" and finally release them. We took a tour conducted by a poised, pretty young Hopi woman, along with a couple from New York City. The woman was a public-school teacher, and her husband sold floors; they were coming from Las Vegas, where he had attended a convention, and were wending their way to Phoenix, doing a little tourism on the way. "Honey, when you have these ceremonies it's coed, right?" the woman asked.

Our guide was a little nonplussed by the woman's upfrontness. "Not really," she said. "Usually only the men go down in the kivas." She explained how the kachinas are ancestors and how the masked dancers dance themselves into a trance, until they become kachinas, and how the kachinas' home is a kiva on San Francisco Peaks. Every February the kachinas come to the mesas, bringing the clouds with them, and they go back home to the mountain in July.

I stopped to talk with two old women, great old gals, golden oldies (as a woman who came to our house on La Hacienda Drive to make sure we registered to vote had described herself). They were like a slapstick routine. One had on a pair of big Miami Beach sunglasses, and the other was selling a carved wooden kachina with long hair and beard that symbolized the rain streaming down from the belly of the clouds, sending down their *navala* (liquid essence) at planting time, which had been the subject of a dance just last week. She wanted thirty dollars for it. I said I wished I had the money; it was beautiful. She pointed out the cornfields in the distance, down on the plain, and said, "I used to walk down to them. Now I can't, so I'm everybody's grandmother." I bought a postcard from the other woman for a dollar, and she said, "Oh goody, now I can buy my friend a pop, and I'm real glad about it."

I drifted back to the tour. The woman from New York was saying, "The kachinas are ancestors. Keep going. I love it." Then noticing the frown on our guide's face, she said, "I see you're not comfortable talking about this." The two of them walked out to the end of the spur and talked for five minutes, at the end of which the woman from New York returned, visibly moved, blown away.

"It's so interesting to see the commonalities," the woman told me as we returned to our cars. "But we can't do that. We might find we liked each other, and that would ruin everything."

Epilogue: I Bring My Shadow to Big Mountain

As we drove down the steep, curving road from Walpi, suddenly a huge raven appeared, hovering in the air maybe twenty feet above the windshield, with its wings outspread, four feet from tip to tip. After it had gotten my attention, the raven scooped the air with its right wing and did a complete flip, like a swimmer executing a racing turn, except that it ended up exactly as it had been, hovering there again with its wings outspread—almost mockingly, it seemed. Then it banked like an F-86 and shot off into the distance until it became a tiny black speck and finally disappeared altogether. All this happened in a few seconds—so fast that my wife, sitting beside me, her mind elsewhere, didn't even notice the raven, and I didn't tell her about its sudden appearance and the amazing flip it did in the air because I was trying to process them myself. It felt as if they were meant for my eyes only, as if the raven were trying to tell me something.

Consulting the ornithological literature, I discovered that the raven had performed what is known as a full roll. Ravens are known for their acrobatic flight. Dirk Van Buren, an authority on the species, rejects the hypothesis that their aerial acrobatics are a form of "social display," and finding no relationship between them and courtship, concludes that they are apparently "useless . . . play," except for the possibility of their serving as "an indicator of overall vigor and foraging potential." Van Buren had witnessed far more complicated moves: "an Immelmann turn in reverse," and a "sequence that included six half rolls, two full rolls, and two double-rolls."

I began to wonder whether this lone, somersaulting raven, righting itself after momentary turbulence, were a vision of some sort, a message to someone who had done his share of *koyaanisqatsic* twisting in the wind, especially in the last few years. It was intriguing and suggestive that back east we happened to live at the foot of a mountain called Big Crow, for the black birds that nest on its cliffs. The birds are actually ravens. We don't have much to do with them. They do their thing; we do ours. Occasionally we hear their garrulous chatter, or one sweeps by on a gust of wind.

So perhaps the message was, You didn't have to come all the way to Arizona to see a raven; you have them in your own backyard. Or as T. S. Eliot puts it in "Little Gidding":

> We shall not cease from exploration
> And the end of all our exploring
> Will be to arrive where we started
> And know the place for the first time.

I had known this, intellectually, years ago. The year I saw the Grand Canyon, 1970, I was writing lyrics like:

> I met an old man in a canyon
> Who lived underneath a waterfall
> And he told me the truth is
> There isn't any truth at all . . .

and

> I was walking down a stream
> When I came across an elf
> He said what do you think you see in me
> That you don't see in yourself?
> I been walking this world ten thousand years
> And you can see for yourself
> How it appears . . .

So I knew that there was no reason to go anywhere. But there was also no reason not to go, and I was too restless to live my quest in one place. In the years that followed, I traveled to many places—Madagascar, Tibet, the Amazon—in search of the Other. I had to live my quest, and even though I eventually realized that it was misframed, a wild-goose chase in some respects, I wouldn't have missed it for the world. But after a certain number of stamps in my passport, after devoting twenty years to my futile quest, the far reaches of the globe ceased to be exotic. I saw that behind their plumage and their mascara, people are pretty much the same everywhere, at whatever stage of culture they find themselves: they have the same intellectual and emotional range, the same fear of dying and capacity for lying, the same balance of good and evil. Of course there are indelible, identity-defining cultural and environmental differences among groups and individuals, and it is unquestionable that important things, especially the spiritual connection with nature, have been destroyed by the advances of modern technology. But it is also clear that spiritually deprived moderns tend to put traditional peoples like Indians or Tibetans on a pedestal, when they are human, too, and have their shadow side, like everybody. In Jungian terms, the Other is your shadow, the part of yourself you don't want to deal with and project onto others. Europeans, as they conquered the world, projected their own violence onto the "savages" they were colonizing. Later they romanticized them as noble savages with unpolluted minds, uncontaminated by their own venality, unwarped by the modern ego. But this was also a projection of the Other—in a more positive form, but a projection all the same. Neither the Other nor the self who is projecting it exists independently. That is elementary Buddhism.

Perhaps I could have saved myself twenty years of wandering if I had studied the teachings of Buddha in my midtwenties, but I had to discover the truth of what he called *shunyata,* or emptiness, for myself. I had to go through the process of discovery, and in a way the process was the goal.

With the realization that there is no Other, my quest was over. When precisely this happened, I can't put my finger on, because it wasn't a sudden epiphany; the disillusionment was cumulative; but our visit with the religious leader in Shongopovi was certainly a climactic event. And when I stopped projecting spiritual expectations and other things onto the Indians I met, I found that the problems I had been having interacting with them improved dramatically. I had given a lot of thought to what the Wall, as I called it—Alfonso Ortiz's adobe curtain—is made up of. The first layer of the Wall is negative stereotyping by the dominant culture, to enable colonial policy to proceed. The anthropologist Keith Basso, for instance, gives a scathing characterization of this layer in his chapter on the Western Apache for the *Handbook of North American Indians:*

> Of the hundreds of peoples that lived and flourished in native North America, few have been so consistently misrepresented as the Apacheans of Arizona and New Mexico. Glorified by novelists, sensationalized by historians, and distorted beyond credulity by commercial film makers, the popular image of "the Apache"—a brutish, terrifying semihuman bent upon wanton death and destruction—is almost entirely a product of irresponsible caricature and exaggeration. Indeed there can be little doubt that the Apache has been transformed from a native American into an American legend, the fanciful and fallacious creation of a non-Indian citizenry whose inability

to recognize the massive treachery of ethnic and cultural stereotypes has been matched only by its willingness to sustain and inflate them.

In fact, Basso goes on to point out, as with the Pueblos, there are a number of distinct Apache groups, "each characterized by a unique constellation of cultural features." Similarly, the Nigerian Kwame Anthony Appiah writes in his book *In My Father's House,* "the very category of the Negro is at the root a European product: for the 'whites' invented the negros in order to dominate them . . . whatever Africans share, we do not have a common traditional culture, common language, a common religious or conceptual vocabularly . . . we do not even belong to a common race."

The next layer is the understandable xenophobia of the Indians themselves, their own negative stereotyping of people like me. "They are seeing you as a white, not as who you are," my wife remarked after I had been cold-shouldered at one of the pueblos. Like many Americans, I was a generic, cultural Anglo who didn't in fact have a drop of Anglo-American blood, my Russian grandparents having landed on these shores because of a revolution in their country in 1917. I felt not that much more at home in the dominant Anglo culture than an African American or a Native American, which is perhaps why I was so strongly attracted to non-European cultures, so fascinated with the Other. And now I was being cast as one of the oppressors. I began to feel what it was like to be stereotyped.

As part of the research for my ill-fated article on "Culturally Correct Tourism in the Tribal Southwest," I had met in Albuquerque with a group of Pueblos and Navajo to discuss their problems with tourists.

"One thing I resent is the way we're all lumped together as 'Indians,' when we're as different as Arabs and Israelis, Italians and Danes, Englishmen and Irishmen, New Yorkers and Texans," a Navajo woman told me.

"When tourists come to our dances, they're in the way; they're always interrupting," a man from Jemez Pueblo complained. "They should be quiet and observe. Don't take the best seats. Wear proper attire. We put on good stuff when we come to Albuquerque."

What about picture taking? I asked.

"We don't allow it, sketching, video filming, or tape-recording," he told me.

But other tribes do, I said. In those places, the photographer should obviously always ask first, right?

"Yeah, but then they come up to you and say, 'Hey can my wife take a picture of me standing next to you?' which really bugs me," a Navajo complained.

A man from Taos, the most heavily visited pueblo, told us about how some tourists hold up their cameras to its windows and squeeze off a frame without having any idea what's inside.

"They think they're going to the zoo," another woman added. "We get these disappointed Germans asking, 'Where are the feathers? How come you aren't living in tepees?' "

"They think we're flies in amber or something," said another man, "but we go to the supermarket and watch TV just like them. We just want to be treated like people."

"Don't ask questions," a third woman implored. " 'What is that for? Why do you wear that? What does that mean?' Just step back and bite the bullet. Don't try to understand us in one day. You Americans are looking for instant religious satisfaction, like instant mashed potatoes. But it's a lifetime thing. We live it every day."

"Do you have any special word for 'tourist'?" There I was, doing just what the woman had said not to do: asking a question.

"I call them moon children," a Navajo told me. "They must have come from the moon because they have no respect for the earth, and they're so pale."

The final, subtlest layer of the Wall is what the ethnographer Peter Nabokov described to me as "your own impatience barrier. And once you break through it and enter their time, you begin to hear the opera of the cosmos."

In the middle of February 1996, I got a call from a filmmaker in London who said he was making a documentary on the honeypots, the women who were used and abused by the KGB to seduce Western embassy personnel into surrendering intelligence. His name was Jamie Doran, and he explained that he had worked for many years as a producer for BBC and was now an independent. He was particularly interested in the story of Clayton Lonetree and Violetta Seina and was wondering if I would take him out to Big Mountain and get Clayton's family to do a traditional ceremonial for him that he could film for the end of the movie. The last I heard, Clayton was still in Fort Leavenworth. He had been eligible for immediate parole since November 1993, but nothing was happening.

Jamie sounded sincere, concerned, and legitimate. He had an engaging brogue, having grown up half Irish in Glasgow, and I, having the highest regard for the BBC, was ready to be of help. It just so happened that I was about to hand in a long magazine piece and would be able to take off for a few days. The idea of seeing my friends at Big Mountain and helping to direct some more media attention to Clayton, who was languishing in prison, all but forgotten, was appealing, especially if I was going to be paid for it. After negotiating a consultant's fee, I called Sally in Tuba City.

The last time Sally and I had spoken was in the summer. I had been talking with William Kunstler, Clayton's original lawyer, who was thinking about getting back into the case because it was now clear that the CIA operatives whose deaths Clayton had been blamed for had been betrayed by the CIA's own Aldrich Ames. Sally said she wasn't crazy about Kunstler's getting involved again, because he had rejected a plea bargain that would have gotten Clayton a much lighter sentence and used the case to rail against the military-industrial complex, but in any event Kunstler had died that fall, and nothing came of it.

I started telling Sally about Jamie and how we wanted to come out to Big Mountain, and she interrupted me. "Guess what—Clayton's getting out!" All she knew was that he was being released on the twenty-eighth, after nine years and three months of imprisonment. It had all happened very suddenly. She had only heard a week ago. She had no idea why the Marine Corps had finally decided to free him. Sally was flying out to Fort Leavenworth to meet him, then he was coming to Big Mountain. She had hired a *hataali*, a singer, to do a four-day-long Beauty Way ceremony to cleanse Clayton of all that he had been through. "I wish I'd done it before he went into the service," Sally told me. "Maybe then none of this would have happened. I wanted to do it, but Clayton said he was going to be fine and not to worry, there was no need for it."

"How fantastic!" I said. "It's over. How old is he now?"

Thirty-four, she said.

"Still young," I said. "He's got his whole life ahead of him."

I relayed the news to Jamie, who was overjoyed and immediately started talking about how he was going to reunite Clayton and Violetta in London for a sequel. He wanted to film Clayton stepping out of the prison into freedom, and to film the Beauty Way chant at Big Mountain. I relayed this to Sally, who said she didn't want any cameras at the release and that she and Clayton and everybody else were going to be preoccupied at the ceremonial, and it would be much better if Jamie could come out two weeks later, but Jamie said he was on deadline and couldn't wait that long, so she finally said she couldn't speak for Clayton, but as far as she was concerned, she guessed it was all right if we just showed up at Big Mountain by the second, when the Beauty Way was starting, and play it by ear. After greeting Clayton, Sally was flying right back to get everything ready, and Clayton's father, Spencer, would be driving him down from Denver, where they were swinging by to see his grandfather, Sam Lonetree, a venerable Winnebago chief. I explained to Jamie that this was the best we were going to be able to do, and that if we were cool, everything was probably going to work out fine, but I couldn't guarantee the participation of the family. A clause to this effect was added to our agreement. Jamie wasn't worried. "All you have to do is get me alone with Clayton for ten minutes, and I'll take care of the rest," he assured me.

Jamie and I agreed to meet in New York City on the evening of the twenty-ninth. He swung by the lobby of the magazine I had delivered my piece to, and without even greeting me or offering to help me with my bags, he said, "Come on, hurry up; the cab is waiting." He seemed really agitated, and when we got in the cab he explained that the man who was doing the voice-over for the film was coming into the studio tomorrow, and he didn't even have a script. He was going to have to pull an all-nighter and fax the script to London the next morning from Albuquerque, and he hadn't slept at all last night on the plane from London. The guy was a complete wreck, one of those revved-up urban deadline junkies I was all too familiar with, a textbook case of Anglo *koyaanisqatsi*. It could be a big problem at Big Mountain unless he slowed down. I explained how it worked with Navajo, how you just had to sit and be with them and break through your own impatience barrier and enter their time before anything happens. If they sensed you were after something, you were dead. I remembered how Ray Morgan had rebuffed me on the Rio Puerco when I started probing him about Water Way.

My plan was to get out to Big Mountain on the first and to hang out with Tom and John and ease Jamie and his cameraman, whom we were picking up in Albuquerque, into the situation. "You have to be very cool about the camera," I explained. "If they tell you to put it away, you have to put it away immediately." Here I was, bringing to a private, emotionally charged family ceremonial two white male *bila-gaana* strangers with a movie camera, whose only interest in being there was a movie they were making about "sexpionage" in the former Soviet Union. I wasn't looking forward to it, especially because by the time we got to Albuquerque it was clear that Jamie lacked the requisite sensitivity. We had a few beers at a bar in La Guardia while waiting for the plane, and a pushy, belligerent side began to come out. His personal life, like that of many riders of the manic media merry-go-round, was in shambles.

Fortunately, the cameraman, Dale, was laid-back and completely professional. Dale was originally from Chicago, but you never would have guessed he wasn't a native southwesterner, so successfully had he reinvented himself. "I came here twenty years ago and got too poor to leave," he explained to Jamie as we sat in the lobby of La Posada, Conrad Hilton's first hotel in his home state, and Jamie was charmed.

The three of us set out west on I-40 in Dale's spanking-new, tinted Suburban, which was a little upscale for Big Mountain, I mused, but the four-wheel drive would come in handy. I sat in back while Dale regaled Jamie, in the passenger seat, with southwestern lore, most of which I had heard before. But some of it was new. I'll never get the whole enchilada, I mused; it's a never-ending process. Dale knew that the green patrol cars of La Migra, for instance, were known as *los cocohuates,* the avocados. As we sped past the malpais, the ancient black-lava badlands west of Acoma, Dale told us that he had filmed a segment for *CBS Sunday Morning News* about a lizard that turns black to blend in with the lava. We continued past Red Rock, New Mexico, one of the places where the hanta virus broke out, he told us. A Navajo girl had dropped dead at a dance there in 1993. The initial theory was that she must have absorbed some toxic chemical in the rock.

We stopped for lunch in Gallup at El Rancho, the old hotel where the stars of many classic Hollywood westerns shot in the surrounding desert stayed: Gene Tierney of the 1941 *Sundown,* William Holden and William Bendix of the 1948 *Streets of Laredo,* Dane Clark of the 1951 *Fort Defiance,* Burt Lancaster and Lee Remick of the 1965 *The Hallelujah Trail.* Dale told us that "drinking hair spray is big around here, especially Lady Clairol, which is the drug of choice for those who can't afford Thunderbird wine."

In Window Rock we loaded up on grub, including a lot of beer for Jamie, who was used to drinking six or eight beers a day. He also chain-smoked Dunhills. We had to stop every fifteen minutes or so because Dale wouldn't let him smoke in the Suburban. Finally, at dusk we hit Big Mountain. Our first stop was Tom's outfit. The last I'd heard from him was a letter inviting me to the Sun Dance last July. Tom's relatives welcomed us with some delicious soup. But Tom was in Tucson with a blond woman, his aunt told me. He had joined a troupe that was chanting and drumming and dancing its way around the Southwest. He could be back tonight, or next month. I explained that we had come for Clayton's Beauty Way. They hadn't been invited, even though they were cousins in several different ways. One of Tom's uncles, who was sitting on a sofa, had just had a chant done for him, for stress, and he needed to rest now, which we took as our cue to take our leave. Tom's aunt said that if we needed a place to sleep, we could stay in the hogan out back.

We continued to John's. He was there with his kid brother Leonard, whom I hadn't met before; his sister Louise's teenage son; and a one-armed Diné friend named Cortez, who rarely spoke. We hugged, and I asked John how the Sun Dance went. "Really intense, man," he explained. "They cut strips of flesh on my chest, and I hung from them for an hour." Louise had split up with George Crittenden, the Chero-kee friend of Leroy Jackson that Tom and I had gone to see Jackson's widow, Adella Begay, with. George was somewhere in California, and she was living with another activist named Mervin. John filled me in on the struggle. The Bureau of Indian Affairs had said the people of Big Mountain could repair their houses, then it said they couldn't, and now it was threatening to evict by the end of the year all those who didn't sign the so-called accommodation agreement, which bought them fifty more years on their ancestral homeland, but their hogans would be torn down and replaced with modern housing, and they would be fenced in—ten acres per family, thirteen if the family had livestock.

John's family, of course, was having none of it. "They want to kick us out, but we'll see," John said. If the BIA didn't back down, as it had with previous ultimatums, there would be a bloody showdown. This was renegade Indian land, off the modern grid, a pocket of wild resis-tance with no water or electricity and as little connection as possible to Sloganworld.

Meanwhile, the Big Mountain people had just won an injunction to shut down the nearby Kayenta Mine. Peabody Coal, which owned the mine, was obviously going to appeal; however, the Black Mesa Mine was still in operation, still pumping three million gallons a day from the Navajo aquifer to flush the crushed coal down the 273-mile slurry line to Laughlin, Nevada. "Peabody is taking the liver out of Black Mesa," Leonard told me. They were all looking forward to Clayton's arrival. "This is Lonetree's home," John said with satisfaction. "He can go anywhere."

John's mother, Alice, Clayton's grandmother, had moved to her win-ter hogan, on a knoll overlooking Dinnebito Wash, a mile up the road, and this was where the ceremonial was taking place. I drove up there alone in the Suburban, and there was Alice, the old wrinkled *shimi-*

shani who had borne eleven children, bustling around as usual. She beamed at me in greeting. She looked happier than I had ever seen her. Sally was there, too. She looked haggard, not having slept in days. I had left it that we would try to make it if we could. She didn't look at all happy to see me. She was a little freaked out on the media, she explained. At Fort Leavenworth, she and her daughter Valerie had wanted to take Clayton down to the Missouri River to do a ceremonial right after his release, but they never got a chance to, because as soon as he walked out the gate he was mobbed by "twenty-four camera crews. They were pressing their cameras to the car windows. It was terrible," she said. "And I got another problem—this writer Rodney Barker." Barker had just published a book about Clayton and was going around on the talk shows and "acting like he was the spokesman for the family." Sally had told him she didn't want him to write the book, but he had persisted, and he had finally won her cooperation, she claimed, by promising to split the proceeds with Clayton, but Clayton hadn't seen a penny. She hadn't gotten anything down on paper. (Barker, whom I happened to meet on a plane back East a year later, denied there was any such agreement.) "Why can't they leave us alone?" she asked.

Barker had written a previous book, *Broken Circle,* about the three Navajo drunks whose mutilated bodies were found in an arroyo outside Farmington in 1974. The book was partly sympathetic, partly lurid, and had left a bad taste in my mouth, particularly the discussion of how witchcraft may have been used to take revenge on the murderers. Sally characterized Barker as someone who "just wants to make money off us." And now we're jumping on Clayton the minute he gets out of prison, I thought. Wait till she meets Jamie.

The next morning we all drove up to the hogan. Everyone was busy with preparations. I helped move things out of the hogan so everyone could fit. It looked like the family had come to a decision about filming, and everything was going to be fine. Louise, who was used to dealing with the media who came to Big Mountain, came up to us and said she had a contract for Jamie to sign. I had suggested to Jamie that he make a contribution toward the cost of the ceremony, but he was trying to get his footage for free. The contract did not involve any payment, but there was one restriction: no filming inside the hogan. I had already explained to Jamie that he wasn't going to be able to film the ceremony, because according to Navajo belief, photography could affect the outcome. Jamie said no problem, and Dale set up and started to film the preparations: a sheep being slaughtered, skinned, and butchered and the pieces placed on a grill to roast on a piñon fire. Sally was in a beautiful outfit but completely preoccupied, and she didn't even greet me, so I didn't bother her.

Around ten-thirty a caravan of four trucks pulled up to the knoll and stopped two hundred yards from the hogan. Clayton got out of one of them with several old men who were his escort, and they stood waiting for the sign to approach. John had said Clayton was supposed to walk the last six miles to the hogan; it was part of the ceremonial. But apparently the walk had been abbreviated. Finally he started coming. It was very moving and dramatic, about fifty of his immediate maternal family beaming love at him as he approached. He wasn't supposed to talk to anyone. Dale had set up his camera and was shooting Clayton's approach, but suddenly Alice came up to him, obviously upset, and put her hand over the lens and indicated that he should stop. Very coolly, Dale removed the camera from its tripod, folded up the tripod, and, calmly, respectfully, withdrew to the Suburban, where Jamie was pacing distractedly, unable to conceal his exasperation. This sent a clear signal that he had no interest in what was going on except to get it down on film.

Some of the family went into the hogan, and I went with them. Inside were maybe thirty people, most of them elders done out in their finest silver and turquoise, and the women in velveteen blouses and pleated skirts, the men in colorful cowboy shirts and bandannas. We went around clockwise, greeting them, then took our seats. The next day Jamie told me that he had slipped a small multidirectional microphone into my pocket before I went into the hogan and secretly recorded the whole thing, and removed it after I emerged, and if I complained, he would say that I had agreed to do it.

While Jamie was holed up in his hotel room in Albuquerque, frantically writing his script, I went to see a retired anthropologist who had spent decades studying the Navajo. He explained that Beauty Way is a lengthy homecoming and harmony-restoring ceremonial. Later, if Clayton continued to suffer emotional problems, the family could do Prostitution Way, a chant for curing venereal disease and emotional disturbance contracted by sleeping with a prostitute; Violetta, he explained, would be considered a prostitute. They could also do Enemy Way. The anthropologist lent me the definitive book on Beauty Way, written in the fifties. Two of his colleagues had recorded every syllable of the four-day chant and presented it in full in Navajo with an accompanying English translation, a detailed commentary, and an appendix of the various sandpaintings that could be used during it. They had captured the whole thing, yet the book seemed curiously lifeless and desiccated and two-dimensional—the problem with most anthropology and with most attempts to convert non-Western, nonrational belief systems into scientifically credible prose.

I attended only the opening chant, which took about two hours. As far as I could see, it went exactly according to the book. The *hataali* was a delicate, rail-thin, birdlike old man with gray hair. First, he consecrated the hogan, smearing cornmeal on its walls in the four cardinal directions. Clayton came in, stripped to his skivvies, and John helped him place his feet along a thin line of cornmeal that led to a sand-painting sprinkled with red sand in the center of the hogan. The line symbolized the road home, and when Clayton got to the sand painting, he sat down directly upon it to absorb its curative energy. Later, John carefully collected the sand. Then an old woman smeared cornmeal over Clayton's body and bathed him in yellow yucca-root suds. The *hataali* chanted long, high-pitched phrases that went on for minutes, occasionally pausing to expectorate into a Styrofoam cup. Every once in a while, I caught the core Navajo word *hozho,* beauty or harmony. Finally, there was a break, and several of us slipped out of the hogan, followed after about an hour more of chanting by the others.

One of Sally's sisters, Mae Washington, a tall, good-looking, powerful woman in her forties, came over to Jamie, who was standing next to the Suburban drinking the first of many beers he would have that day, and asked him angrily what he was doing there. "You just want to make money off us, don't you?" she accused.

I let him defend himself. This was a crucial moment for his mission, but instead of becoming all sweetness and persuading Mae that he was different from the others, and offering, as I had suggested, to make a monetary contribution to the ceremony, which was setting the family back several thousand dollars, he got his hackles up and said with a confrontational glare, "Don't blame me for what others have done before me."

I went over to Clayton and gave him a long hug. He still had the clean-cut, slightly bewildered look he'd had in prison four years before. "You can be very proud of yourself," I told him. "You behaved honorably, as few would have. You turned yourself in when they never would have found out what you did otherwise, and you paid your debt in full. Now you can get on with your life with a clean conscience."

We spent the afternoon feasting and catching up—Sally; her husband, Kee Richard; her sister Lavine. I introduced Jamie to Sally, and he immediately tried to impress her with how important a filmmaker he was, how this was going to be for the BBC and *Frontline* and the most prestigious shows in Germany and France, none of which was true, and even if it had been, it wasn't the way to go about winning her over anyway. I could see her eyes narrowing. The next morning she came upon Jamie trying to force Clayton into giving an interview in the grove below the hogan, and she really told him off. "All you see is the dollar signs in your eyes," she told me she said. "This is Clayton's home. Where are you from?"

Sunday morning John and Leonard and Cortez and I walked down to the wash, which, when it is running, empties into the Little Colorado, which in turn joins the main Colorado above the Grand Canyon. Four miles up, jets were silently tracing white lines of vapor trail on different planes across the firmament. Not a bird peeped. "It's so silent it hurts your ears," John said.

Jamie and Dale had taken off late the previous afternoon to film the scenery and the mines and had said they'd be back that night, but they still had not returned. It turned out Jamie was out of beer, and they had driven two hours, all the way to Page, the nearest place they could buy some, and spent the night at a motel there. Clayton came down to see us at John's place after we returned from our walk. Jamie could have gotten his interview then and there, but he was nowhere to be found. Clayton said some of the guards were real mean, and a lot of the inmates were into Satanism and other weird stuff. The blacks were into black magic, the Aryan brothers were into Druidism. He had kept abreast of what was happening outside as best he could, followed the O.J. trial. "O.J. says he's going to find the real killer of Nicole and Ron, and what's he doing? Playing golf," he observed. I realized it was going to take more than a four-day Beauty Way to heal Clayton. He was like a kid who had been kept in a closet for years.

The question now was, should he see Violetta again? There had been no communication between the two of them since Clayton's transfer to Vienna in 1985, except for the letter from her that I had delivered to him in 1993 saying that she still loved him and was waiting for him. His aunt Lavine had said that the Navajo Way was when someone hurts you, you have nothing more to do with them, and she hoped Clayton would just forget about Violetta and find a nice Navajo girl to settle down with. But maybe he needed to see her again for closure. And this guy Jamie was offering to bring the two of them together, so it was worthwhile to at least talk to him. Clayton said, "But this is not the right time. I'm not supposed to do any business while I'm having this ceremony." (At this point Jamie had not told me that he was thinking of putting a hidden camera in Clayton and Violetta's bedroom, or about the hidden mike he claimed to have slipped into my pocket. Unaware of his utter sleaziness, I was still trying to put things together for him.)

Clayton and I and Cortez walked up the road toward Alice's hogan; the chant had resumed after dark and had gone on all night, and he needed some rest. Suddenly Dale's Suburban came rattling down. Jamie got out, and without greeting us, projecting frenzy and confusion into what had been a very pleasant and reflective stroll, he ordered Dale and me to return to John's to get him another pack of Dunhills. He also told me to "get rid of the one-armed guy," but Cortez refused to go with Dale and me; Sally, it turned out, had asked him to stick with Clayton at all times. So Jamie, Clayton, and Cortez continued up the road, and Dale and I returned to John's and waited. After maybe half an hour Jamie came walking down alone with a foul look on his face. How'd it go? I asked.

"Shut up," he said. "Shut up and let me think."

He got into the car, and we drove down to John's in silence. Finally he explained that he had almost gotten Clayton to agree to the interview on the spot, but we'd left with the camera. But you told us to go down and get your cigarettes, I reminded him. (I had suggested that he and Clayton and Cortez walk on up the road, and Dale and I would follow in the Suburban, several hundred yards behind.) But at that moment, he went on, Sally had showed up and told him to, as he put it, "fuck off."

It had ended with Clayton's agreeing to meet Jamie at John's house at seven on Friday morning. "He gave me his word of honor that he'd be there," Jamie said. "Do you think he's going to show?"

"Clayton strikes me as an unusually honest person," I said. "If he gave you your word of honor, you can bank on it." So we went back to John's and packed up. Of course Jamie didn't ask John whether it was all right if the interview took place at his place, and of course Clayton didn't show. I have no idea how Jamie's documentary ended. He said he had two scripts—script A was about Clayton the victim; script B about Clayton the person everyone trusted—and if Clayton didn't give him the interview, he was going with script B. Frankly, I hope Jamie scrapped all of his Arizona footage.

On the way back to Albuquerque, I realized that Jamie couldn't possibly have worked for the BBC. The BBC does its homework, and Jamie had been patently uninterested in Navajo culture, in the ceremony, and even in the details of Clayton's case. (I had brought along the original hundred-page draft of my *Esquire* story, which laid it all out and put it in the context of Big Mountain and the Navajo culture, how Sally believed Clayton was the victim of local witchcraft, but Jamie didn't even want to see it.) When I got home, I called the manager of the BBC's television-documentary division, who told me that no Jamie Doran had ever worked there, nor had he ever heard of such a person.

On the way back to Albuquerque I tried to explain to him that if he'd been a little more sensitive and attuned, he would have gotten the interview, and he said to me, "Don't tell me you give a shit about the Navajos. Don't play the angel. It doesn't become you. You're a journalist, and you're damn good at what you do. You saw the story, and you went for it. You used the mother to get to Clayton. That's all we journalists are interested in—the story. If by coincidence we do some good—great. But that's not what we're in it for."

I thought that over and decided the opposite was ideally true in my case. I chose my stories, when possible, not for their commercial possibilities, but for their potential to do good. If by coincidence I sold the story to Hollywood, as had happened a few times—great. Nothing gave me more satisfaction than to expose injustices committed on defenseless traditional peoples, which was why I had been drawn to Big Mountain. There I had stumbled on Clayton's story. My heart had gone out to him and his mother. He had obviously been shafted, and maybe if I wrote about it movingly enough and went to Moscow and tracked down Violetta, it might help get him out. That was my primary motive, incredible as it might seem to Jamie.

But it was also true, and I couldn't deny it, that I saw a great story of cross-continental, cross-cultural love, sex, and espionage, a lonely, frightened Indian in Moscow in the Cold War. If there was a movie that exposed the injustice to an even greater audience and made Clayton, Sally, and me some money in the process, why not? I got Robert Redford interested, but he ended up passing because there were, as my agent explained, "problems." The main problem seems to be Clayton's teenage infatuation with Hitler. Hollywood wants its Indians noble these days and isn't prepared yet to dignify them with complexity.

But was this really an honest self-assessment? I mused as we sped east through the moon-drenched desert toward the glittering lights of El Burque. The truth was that despite strenuous efforts to "blow my mind" in the sixties and long sojourns among traditional peoples, I was still the writer, the watcher. I was part vulture myself, and that was why I took such a dislike to Jamie, because in those three days of torment, for which I was handsomely paid, I came face-to-face with the vulture in me, with my own shadow. Jamie was a florid manifestation of my own defilements, a living caricature of the predatory Anglo. We belonged to the same species, the same tribe, and it was useless to pretend otherwise.

Selected Bibliography

The core of my good-sized library on the Southwest is several hundred books by the university presses of New Mexico (UNMP), Arizona (UAP), Nebraska (UNP), and Oklahoma (UOP). I thought I would be making my life easier by getting all these books. All I had to do was read them and regurgitate them in an entertaining fashion, and presto: one magisterial biography of the Southwest. But the joke was on me: many of the books are quite unreadable. For seven years I carted them with me on my various moves—from New Rochelle, to my office at the *New Yorker,* to Mexico City, to the Adirondacks, to Albuquerque, and back to the Ads. The books that follow are the ones that I got to, to which I owe another huge debt, à la de Voto, not to mention to the staffs of the presses themselves, which were extremely generous in many ways (starting with laying the books on me). The possibility exists that other crucial sources, written or verbal, may well have been lost in the shuffle and not been properly credited here or in the text; for any such instances, I deeply apologize in advance. I read numerous newspaper articles, mainly in the Albuquerque *Journal* and *The New York Times,* but they are not specifically cited.

NATURAL HISTORY

Abbey, Edward. *Cactus Country.* Time-Life, New York, 1973.
———. *Desert Solitaire.* Peregrine Smith, Salt Lake City, 1981.
Austin, Mary. *The Land of Little Rain.* UNMP, Albuquerque, 1974.
Benson, Lyman. *The Cacti of Arizona.* UAP, Tucson, 1969.
Brown, David E. *The Grizzly in the Southwest.* UOP, Norman, 1985.
Cockrum, E. Lendell. *Mammals of the Southwest.* UAP, Tucson, 1982.
Collett, Farrel R. *Mammals of the Intermountain West.* Univ. of Utah Pr., Salt Lake City, 1988.
Craighead, Frank C., Jr. *Track of the Grizzly.* Sierra Club, San Francisco, 1977.
Denhardt, Robert M. *The Horse of the Americas.* UOP, Norman, 1975.
Dobie, J. Frank. *The Mustangs.* Univ. of Texas Pr., Austin, 1984.

————. *The Voice of the Coyote.* UNP, Lincoln, 1961.

Dodge, Natt N. *Flowers of the Southwest Deserts.* Southwest Parks & Monuments Assn., Tucson, 1976.

Elmore, Francis H. *Shrubs and Trees of the Southwestern Uplands.* Southwest Parks and Monuments Assn., Tucson, 1976.

Garretson, Martin S. *The American Bison.* N.Y. Zoological Soc., New York, 1938.

Grater, Russell K. *Discovering Sierra Mammals.* Yosemite & Sequoia Natural History Assn., 1978.

Heald, Weldon F. *The Chiricahua Mountains.* UAP, Tucson, 1984.

Heinrich, Bernd. *Ravens in Winter.* Summit, New York, 1989.

Helms, Christopher L. *The Sonoran Desert.* KC Publ., Las Vegas, 1980.

Hornaday, William T. *Camp-fires on Desert and Lava.* UAP, Tucson, 1983.

Jackson, Donald Dale, and Peter Wood. *The Sierra Madre.* Time-Life, New York, 1975.

Jaeger, Edmund C. *Desert Wildlife.* Stanford Univ. Pr., Stanford, Calif., 1961.

Kluckhorn, Clyde. *To the Foot of the Rainbow.* UNMP, Albuquerque, 1992.

Krutch, Joseph Wood. *The Desert Year.* William Sloane, New York, 1952.

Larson, Peggy. *The Deserts of the Southwest.* Sierra Club, San Francisco, 1977.

Leopold, Aldo. *A Sand County Almanac.* Oxford Univ. Pr., London, 1968.

Leydet, François. *The Coyote.* UOP, Norman, 1977.

Limmerick, Patricia. *Desert Passages.* UNMP, Albuquerque, 1985.

McGinnies, William G. *Discovering the Desert.* UAP, Tucson, 1981.

McHugh, Tom. *The Time of the Buffalo.* UNP, Lincoln, 1974.

MacMahon, James A. *Deserts.* Knopf, New York, 1985.

Martin, Paul S., and Richard G. Klein. *Quaternary Extinctions.* UAP, Tucson, 1984.

Martin, William C., and Charles R. Hutchins. *Summer Wildflowers of New Mexico.* UNMP, Albuquerque, 1986.

Monson, Gale, and Lowell Sumner. *The Desert Bighorn.* UAP, Tucson, 1980.

Munz, Philip A. *California Spring Wildflowers.* Univ. of California Pr., Berkeley, 1961.

Munz, Philip A., and David D. Keck. *A California Flora.* Univ. of California Pr., Berkeley, 1959.

Nichols, John. *On the Mesa.* Peregrine Smith, Salt Lake City, 1986.

Parsons, Mary Elizabeth. *The Wild Flowers of California.* Dover, New York, 1966.

Russell, Larry, and Dick Canby. *Arizona's Red Rock Country.* Northland, Flagstaff, 1984.

Santee, Ross. *Men and Horses.* UNP, Lincoln, 1977.

Sears, Paul B. *Deserts on the March.* UOP, Norman, 1980.

Simanski, Richard. *Wild Horses and Sacred Cows.* Northland, Flagstaff, 1985.

Van Dyke, John C. *The Desert: Further Studies in Natural Appearance.* Ariz. Historical Soc., Tucson, 1976.

Walker, Bryce S. *The Great Divide.* Time-Life, New York, 1973.

Wallace, Robert. *The Grand Canyon.* Time-Life, New York, 1973.

Whitford, W. G. *Patterns and Process in Desert Ecosystems.* UNMP, Albuquerque, 1986.

Wyman, Luther E., and Elizabeth F. Burnell. *Field Book of Birds of the Southwestern United States.* Houghton, Boston, 1925.

Wyman, Walker D. *The Wild Horse of the West.* UNP, Lincoln, 1945.

GEOLOGY

Baars, Donald L. *The Colorado Plateau.* UNMP, Albuquerque, 1983.

Baldridge, W. Scott, and Kenneth H. Olsen. "The Rio Grande Rift." *American Scientist* 77, no. 3 (May–June 1989).

Fletcher, Colin. *The Man Who Walked through Time.* Knopf, New York, 1968.

McKee, Edwin D. *Ancient Landscapes of the Grand Canyon Region*. Northland, Flagstaff, 1985.

Nations, Dale, and Edmund Stump. *Geology of Arizona*. Kendall/Hunt, Dubuque, Ia., 1983.

Stokes, William Lee. *Scenes of the Plateau Lands and How They Came to Be*. Publishers Pr., Salt Lake City, 1983.

WATER AND WATER LAW

Bowden, Charles. *Killing the Hidden Waters*. Univ. of Texas Pr., Austin, 1977.

Broyles, Bill. "Desert Thirst: The Ordeal of Pablo Valencia." *Journal of Arizona History* 23, no. 4 (1982).

Clark, Ira G. *Water in New Mexico*. UNMP, Albuquerque, 1987.

Corle, Edwin. *The Gila*. UNP, Lincoln, 1964.

Dumars, Charles T., et al. *Pueblo Indian Water Rights*. UAP, Tucson, 1984.

Dunbar, Robert G. *Forging New Rights in Western Waters*. UNP, Lincoln, 1983.

Johnson, Rich. *The Central Arizona Project 1918–1968*. UAP, Tucson, 1977.

McGee, William. "Desert Thirst As Disease." *Interstate Medical Journal* 13 (1906).

Meyer, Michael C. *Water in the Hispanic Southwest*. UAP, Tucson, 1984.

Rea, Amadeo. *Once a River*. UAP, Tucson, 1983.

Reisner, Marc. *Cadillac Desert*. Viking, New York, 1986.

Weatherford, Gary D., and F. Lee Brown. *New Courses for the Colorado River*. UNMP, Albuquerque, 1986.

Worster, Donald. *Rivers of Empire*. Pantheon, New York, 1985.

DESERT SPIRITUALITY

Foster, Steven, and Meredith Little. *The Book of the Vision Quest*. Prentice Hall, New York, 1988.

Merton, Thomas. *Wisdom of the Desert*. New Directions, New York, 1960.

ETHNOASTRONOMY

Farrer, Claire R. *Living Life's Circle*. UNMP, Albuquerque, 1991.

Williamson, Ray A., and Claire R. Farrer. *Earth & Sky*. UNMP, Albuquerque, 1992.

ETHNOBOTANY

Nabhan, Gary Paul. *The Desert Smells Like Rain*. North Point, San Francisco, 1982.

———. *Gathering the Desert*. UAP, Tucson, 1985.

Naj, Amal. *Peppers: A Story of Hot Pursuits*. Knopf, New York, 1992.

ARCHAEOLOGY

Fagan, Brian M. *The Peopling of Ancient America*. Thames & Hudson, London, 1987.

Frison, George C., and Bruce A. Bradley. *Folsom Tools and Technology*. UNMP, Albuquerque, 1980.

Gittings, Kirk, and V. B. Price. *Chaco Body*. Artspace, Albuquerque, 1991.

Grant, Campbell. *Canyon de Chelly*. UAP, Tucson, 1978.

Gregonis, Linda M., and Karl J. Reinhard. *Hohokam Indians of the Tucson Basin*. UAP, Tucson, 1983.

Haury, Emil. *The Hohokam*. UAP, Tucson, 1976.

Haury, Emil, and Helga Teiwes. "First Masters of the American Desert." *National Geographic* (May 1967).

Kidder, Alfred Vincent. *An Introduction to the Study of Southwestern Archaeology*. Yale Univ. Pr., New Haven, Conn., 1962.

L'Amour, Louis. *The Haunted Mesa*. Bantam, New York, 1987.

Lekson, Stephen H. *Great Pueblo Architecture of Chaco Canyon, New Mexico*. UNMP, Albuquerque, 1984.

Lister, Robert, and Florence Lister. *Chaco Canyon*. UNMP, Albuquerque, 1981.

McNitt, Frank. *Richard Wetherill Anasazi*. UNMP, Albuquerque, 1957.

Nabokov, Peter. *The Architecture of Acoma Pueblo*. Ancient City Press, Santa Fe, 1986.

Noble, David. *Ancient Ruins of the Southwest*. Northland, Flagstaff, 1981.

Turner, Christy. "Dental Evidence for the Peopling of the Americas." Paper presented at 46th Annual Meeting, Society for American Archaeology, 1981.

———. "Sinodonty and Sundadonty." Paper presented at XIV Pacific Science Congress, Khabarovsk, 1979.

Wedell, Waldo R. *Prehistoric Man on the Great Plains*. UOP, Norman, 1961.

White, Tim D. *Prehistoric Cannibalism*. Princeton Univ. Pr., Princeton, N.J., 1992.

HISTORY
General

Beck, Warren A., and Ynez D. Haase. *Historical Atlas of New Mexico*. UOP, Norman, 1969.

Corle, Edwin. *Desert Country*. Dell, Sloane & Pierce, New York, 1941.

de Buys, William. *Enchantment and Exploitation*. UNMP, Albuquerque, 1985.

de Voto, Bernard. *The Course of Empire*. UNP, Lincoln, 1952.

Fradkin, Philip L. *A River No More*. Knopf, New York, 1981.

Frazier, Ian. *Great Plains*. Farrar, New York, 1989.

Hillerman, Tony, ed. *The Best of the West*. HarperCollins, New York, 1991.

———. *The Spell of New Mexico*. UNMP, Albuquerque, 1976.

Hollon, Eugene W. *The Southwest: Old and New*. UNP, Lincoln, 1969.

Horgan, Paul. *Great River*. Texas Monthly Pr., Austin, 1984.

Jackson, J. B. *The Essential Landscape*. UNMP, Albuquerque, 1985.

Jansen, Joan M., and Darlis A. Miller. *New Mexico Women*. UNMP, Albuquerque, 1986.

John, Elizabeth A. H. *Storms Brewed in Other Men's Worlds*. UNP, Lincoln, 1975.

Lavender, David. *The Southwest*. UNMP, Albuquerque, 1980.

Lingefelter, Richard E. *Death Valley and the Amargosa*. Univ. of California Pr., Berkeley, 1986.

Morris, John W., et al. *Historical Atlas of Oklahoma*. UOP, Norman, 1976.

Pearce, T. M., ed. *New Mexico Place Names*. UNMP, Albuquerque, 1965.

Perrigo, Lynn I. *The American Southwest*. UNMP, Albuquerque, 1975.

Roylance, Ward J. *Utah*. Utah: A Guide to the State Foundation, Salt Lake City, 1982.

Shelton, Richard. *Going Back to Bisbee*. UAP, Tucson, 1992.

Simmons, Marc. *Albuquerque*. UNMP, Albuquerque, 1982.

Sonnichsen, C. L. *Tucson*. UOP, Norman, 1982.

Wagoner, Jay J. *Early Arizona*. UAP, Tucson, 1983.

Walker, Henry P., and Don Bufkin. *Historical Atlas of Arizona*. UOP, Norman, 1979.

Webb, Walter Prescott. *The Great Plains*. Ginn, Boston, 1931.

Mexico

Cabeza de Vaca, Alvar Nuñez. *Adventures in the Unknown Interior of America*. UNMP, Albuquerque, 1984.

Corral vda. de Villa, Luz. *Pancho Villa an Intimacy*. Centro Librero la Prensa, Chihuahua City, 1981.

Diaz, Bernal. *The Conquest of New Spain*. Penguin, Baltimore, 1963.

Fuentes, Carlos. *The Old Gringo*. Farrar, New York, 1985.

García, Mario T. *Desert Immigrants*. Yale Univ. Pr., New Haven, Conn., 1981.

Prescott, William H. *History of the Conquest of Mexico*. Modern Library, New York.

Riding, Alan. *Distant Neighbors*. Vintage, New York, 1984.

Tuck, Jim. *Pancho Villa and John Reid*. UAP, Tucson, 1984.

Varner, John Grier, and Jeanette Johnson Varner. *Dogs of the Conquest*. UOP, Norman, 1983.

Villegas, Daniel Cósio. *Historio mínima de México*. El Colegio de México, Mexico City, 1974.

Weber, David J. *The Mexican Frontier, 1821–1846*. UNMP, Albuquerque, 1982.

Whitaker, Arthur Preston. *The Spanish-American Frontier: 1783–1795*. UNP, Lincoln, 1969.

THE NATIVE SOUTHWEST
General

Albanese, Catherine L. *Nature Religion in America*. Univ. of Chicago Pr., Chicago, 1990.

Beals, Ralph L. *The Comparative Ethnology of Northern Mexico before 1750*. Ibero-Americana 2, Berkeley, 1932.

Berkhofer, Robert F. *The White Man's Indian*. Vintage, New York, 1978.

Boas, Franz. Introduction to *Handbook of American Indian Languages*. UNP, Lincoln, 1966.

Clark, W. P. *The Indian Sign Language*. UNP, Lincoln, 1982.

Clifford, James. *The Predicament of Culture*. Harvard Univ. Pr., Cambridge, 1988.

Clifton, James A., ed. *The Invented Indian*. Transaction, New Brunswick, 1990.

Debo, Angie. *A History of the Indians of the United States*. UOP, Norman, 1970.

Dutton, Bertha P. *American Indians of the Southwest*. UNMP, Albuquerque, 1975.

Ellis, Richard N., ed. *The Western American Indian*. UNP, Lincoln, 1972.

Harrington, M. R. *Ancient Life among the Southern California Indians*. Southwest Museum Leaflets, no. 26, 1955.

La Barre, Weston. *The Ghost Dance*. Delta, New York, 1970.

Nabokov, Peter. *Indian Running*. Ancient City Pr., Santa Fe, 1981.

Nabokov, Peter, ed. *Native American Testimony*. Viking, New York, 1991.

Ortiz, Alfonso, ed. *Southwest*, Vols. 9 and 10 of *Handbook of North American Indians*. Smithsonian, Washington, D.C., 1979, 1983.

Parsons, Elsie Clews. *American Indian Life*. UNP, Lincoln, 1967.

Prucha, Francis Paul. *The Great Father*. 2 vols. UNP, Lincoln, 1984.

Rodin, Paul. *The Trickster*. Schocken, New York, 1972.

Roe, Frank Gilbert. *The Indian and the Horse*. UOP, Norman, 1955.

Spicer, Edward H. *Cycles of Conquest*. UAP, Tucson, 1981.

Spicer, Edward H., ed. *Ethnic Medicine in the Southwest*. UAP, Tucson, 1977.

Utley, Robert M. *The Indian Frontier*. UNMP, Albuquerque, 1984.

Wauchope, Robert, ed. *Handbook of Middle American Indians*. 17 vols. Univ. of Texas, Austin, 1964.

Welsh, Peter H. *People of the Southwest*. Southwest Museum, Los Angeles, 1984.

Williams, Walter L. *The Spirit and the Flesh*. Beacon, Boston, 1986.

Apache

Bourke, John G. *On the Border with Crook*. UNP, Lincoln, 1971.

Browne, J. Ross. *Adventures in the Apache Country*. UAP, Tucson, 1974.

Debo, Angie. *Geronimo*. UOP, Norman, 1976.

Goodwin, Grenville. *Western Apache Raiding and Warfare*. UAP, Tucson, 1971.

Lummis, Charles F. *General Crook and the Apaches Wars*. Northland, Flagstaff, 1966.

Momaday, N. Scott. *The Way to Rainy Mountain*. UNMP, Albuquerque, 1969.

Sonnichsen, C. L. *The Mescalero Apaches*. UOP, Norman, 1958.

Thrapp, Dan L. *The Conquest of Apacheria.* UOP, Norman, 1967.
———. *Victorio and the Mimbres Apaches.* UOP, Norman, 1974.
Worcester, Donald E. *The Apaches.* UOP, Norman, 1979.

Comanche
Wallace, Ernest, and E. Adamson Hoebel. *The Comanches.* UOP, Norman, 1952.

Havasupai
Hirst, Stephen. *Havsuw 'Baaja: People of the Blue-Green Water.* Havasupai Tribe, Supai, Ariz., 1985.
Whiting, A. F. *Havasupai Habitat.* UAP, Tucson, 1985.

Hopi
Bourke, John G. *Snake-Dance of the Moquis.* UAP, Tucson, 1984.
Huxley, Aldous. *Brave New World.* Bantam, New York, 1953.
Malotki, Ekkehart, and Michael Lomatuway'ma. *Hopi Coyote Tales.* UNP, Lincoln, 1984.
Sun Chief. *The Autobiography of a Hopi Indian.* Yale Univ. Pr., New Haven, Conn., 1942.
Waters, Frank. *Book of the Hopi.* Ballantine, New York, 1963.
Whorf, Benjamin Lee. *Four Articles on Metalinguistics.* Foreign Service Institute, Washington, D.C., 1949.

Mojave
Kroeber, Clifton B., and Bernard L. Fontana. *Massacre on the Gila.* UAP, Tucson, 1986.

Navajo
Barker, Rodney. *The Broken Circle.* Simon & Schuster, New York, 1992.
Beck, Peggy V., and Anna L. Walters. *The Sacred.* Navajo Community College, Tsaile, Ariz., 1977.
Benedeck, Emily. *The Wind Won't Know Me.* Knopf, New York, 1993.
Forster, Elizabeth W. *Denizens of the Desert.* UNMP, Albuquerque, 1988.
Headley, Lake, with William Hoffman. *The Court Martial of Clayton Lonetree.* Holt, New York, 1989.
Locke, Raymond Friday. *The Book of the Navajo.* Mankind, Los Angeles, 1976.
Luckert, Karl W. *Coyoteway.* UAP, Tucson, 1981.
New Mexico Advisory Committee, U.S. Commission on Human Rights. *The Farmington Report.* 1975.
Parlow, Anita. *Cry, Sacred Ground.* Christic Institute, Washington, D.C., 1988.

O'odham
Blaine, Peter, with Michael S. Adams. *Papagos and Politics.* Ariz. Historical Soc., Tucson, 1981.
Underhill, Ruth M., et al. *Rainhouse and Ocean.* Museum of N. Ariz. Pr., Flagstaff, 1979.

Pueblo
Champe, Flavia Waters. *The Matachines Dance of the Upper Rio Grand.* UNP, Lincoln, 1983.
Cushing, Frank Hamilton. *Zuñi.* UNP, Lincoln, 1979.
Hillerman, Tony. *The Boy Who Made Dragonfly.* UNMP, Albuquerque, 1972.
Minge, Ward Alan. *Ácoma.* UNMP, Albuquerque, 1976.
Ortiz, Alfonso, ed. *New Perspectives on the Pueblos.* UNMP, Albuquerque, 1972.
Tyler, Hamilton A. *Pueblo Gods and Myths.* UOP, Norman, 1964.

Seri

Felger, Richard Stephen, and Mary Beck Moser. *The People of the Desert and Sea.* UAP, Tucson, 1985.

Tarahumara

Artaud, Antonin. *Les Tarahumaras.* Gallimard, Paris, 1971.

Fontana, Bernard L. *Tarahumara.* Northland, Flagstaff, 1979.

Gonzàlez, Luis, et al. *Derechos culturales y derechos indígenas en la Sierra Tarahumara.* Universidad Autónoma de Ciudad Juárez, Ciudad Juárez, 1994.

Kennedy, John G. *Tarahumara of Sierra Madre.* AHM, Arlington Heights, Ill., 1978.

Lumholtz, Carl. *Unknown Mexico.* 2 vols. Dover, New York, 1987.

Merrill, William L. *Rarámuri Souls.* Smithsonian, Washington, D.C., 1988.

Pennington, Campbell W. *The Tarahumar of Mexico.* Univ. of Utah Pr., Salt Lake City, 1963.

Rodríguez, Luis Gonzáles, and Don Burgess. *Tarahumara.* Edición Privada de Chrysler de México, S.A., Mexico City, 1985.

Yaqui

Giddings, Ruth Warner. *Yaqui Myths and Legends.* UAP, Tucson, 1959.

Spicer, Edward H. *The Yaquis.* UAP, Tucson, 1980.

Zuñi

Green, Jesse, ed. *Zuñi: Selected Writings of Frank Hamilton Cushing.* UNP, Lincoln, 1979.

Wilson, Edmund. *Red, Black, Blond, and Olive.* Oxford University Press, New York, 1956.

THE HISPANIC SOUTHWEST

Anaya, Rudolfo A., and Francisco Lomeli, eds. *Aztlán.* UNMP, Albuquerque, 1979.

Bannon, John Francis. *The Spanish Borderlands Frontier 1513–1821.* UNMP, Albuquerque, 1974.

Bolton, Herbert Eugene. *Bolton and the Spanish Borderlands.* UOP, Norman, 1964.

———. *Coronado.* UNMP, Albuquerque, 1964.

———. *Rim of Christendom.* UAP, Tucson, 1936.

Briggs, Charles L., and John R. Van Ness. *Land, Water, and Culture.* UNMP, Albuquerque, 1987.

Campa, Arthur L. *Hispanic Culture in the Southwest.* UOP, Norman, 1979.

Chávez, John R. *The Lost Land.* UNMP, Albuquerque, 1984.

Conover, Ted. *Coyotes.* Vintage, New York, 1987.

Domínguez, Fray Francisco Atanasio. *The Missions of New Mexico, 1776.* UNMP, Albuquerque, 1956.

García, Ignacio M. *United We Win.* UAP, Tucson, 1989.

Gonzáles, Nancie L. *The Spanish-Americans of New Mexico.* UNMP, Albuquerque, 1967.

Hall, Douglas Kent. *The Border.* Abbeville, New York, 1988.

Kessell, John L. "A Broken Triangle: Maria de Agreda, Franciscans, and Jumanos." Manuscript.

La Farge, Oliver. *Santa Fe.* UOP, Norman, 1959.

Las Casas, Fray Bartolomé de. *Apologética historia de la Indies.* Madrid, 1909.

Miller, Tom. *On the Border.* UAP, Tucson, 1985.

Parsons, Francis B. *Early 17th Century Missions of the Southwest.* Dale Stuart King, Tucson, 1966.

Ross, Stanley R., ed. *Views across the Border.* UNMP, Albuquerque, 1978.

Simmons, Marc. *Witchcraft in the Southwest*. UNP, Lincoln, 1974.

Udall, Stewart L. *To the Inland Empire*. Doubleday, New York, 1987.

Urbanski, Edmund Stephen. *Hispanic America and Its Civilizations*. UOP, Norman, 1978.

Webb, Edith Buckland. *Indian Life at the Old Missions*. UNP, Lincoln, 1983.

Weisman, Alan. *La Frontera*. Harcourt, New York, 1986.

THE ANGLO SOUTHWEST

Altschuler, Constance Wynn. *Chains of Command*. Ariz. Historical Soc., Tucson, 1981.

Arrington, Leonard. *Brigham Young*. Knopf, New York, 1985.

————. *Great Basin Kingdom*. UNP, Lincoln, 1966.

Audubon, John Woodhouse. *Audubon's Western Journal*. UAP, Tucson, 1984.

Baker, T. Lindsay. *A Field Guide to American Windmills*. UOP, Norman, 1985.

Bartlett, John R. *Personal Narrative of Explorations and Incidents in Texas, New Mexico, California, Sonora, and Chihuahua, During the Years 1850, '51, '52, and '53*. 2 vols. D. Appleton & Co., New York, 1854.

Baugh, Virgil E. *Rendezvous at the Alamo*. UNP, Lincoln, 1960.

Bergon, Frank, ed. *The Journals of Lewis and Clark*. New York, Penguin, 1989.

Billington, Ray Allen. *America's Frontier Heritage*. UNMP, Albuquerque, 1974.

————. *The Far Western Frontier*. Harper, New York, 1962.

————. *Land of Savagery, Land of Promise*. UOP, Norman, 1981.

Boyer, Glenn G., ed. *I Married Wyatt Earp*. UAP, Tucson, 1981.

Brady, Cyrus Townsend. *Indian Fights and Fighters*. UNP, Lincoln, 1971.

Branch, E. Douglas. *The Hunting of the Buffalo*. UNP, Lincoln, 1962.

Brodie, Fawn M., ed. *The City of the Saints by Richard Burton*. Norton, New York, 1963.

————. *No Man Knows My History*. Norton, New York, 1945.

Brooks, Juanita. *John Doyle Lee*. Howe Bros., Salt Lake City, 1984.

————. *The Mountain Meadows Massacre*. UOP, Norman, 1985.

Cather, Willa. *Death Comes to the Archbishop*. Vintage, New York, 1971.

"The Chinese Experience in Arizona and Northern Mexico." Reprinted from *Journal of Arizona History*. Tucson, 1980.

Cleland, Robert Glass. *This Reckless Breed of Men*. UNMP, Albuquerque, 1976.

Connell, Evan S. *Son of the Morning Star*. North Point, San Francisco, 1984.

Dellenbaugh, Frederick S. *A Canyon Voyage*. UAP, Tucson, 1984.

Dick, Everett. *Vanguards of the Frontier*. UNP, Lincoln, 1965.

Drago, Harry Sinclair. *The Great Range Wars*. UNP, Lincoln, 1970.

Durham, Philip, and Everett L. Jones. *The Negro Cowboys*. UNP, Lincoln, 1965.

Erickson, John R. *Panhandle Cowboy*. UNP, Lincoln, 1980.

Faulk, Odie. *Land of Many Frontiers*. Oxford University Press, New York, 1968.

Frazer, Robert W. *Forts of the West*. UOP, Norman, 1980.

Gallagher, Carole. *American Ground Zero: The Secret Nuclear War*. MIT Press, Cambridge, 1993.

Garavaglia, Louis A., and Charles G. Worman. *Firearms of the American West*. UNMP, Albuquerque, 1984.

Garrett, Pat F. *The Authentic Life of Billy the Kid*. UOP, Norman, 1954.

Goetzmann, William H. *Army Exploration in the American West 1803–1863*. UNP, Lincoln, 1979.

Grey, Zane. *Tales of Lonely Trails*. Northland, Flagstaff, 1986.

Hahn, Emily. *Mabel*. Houghton, Boston, 1977.

Harrison, Jim. *Legends of the Fall*. Delacorte, New York, 1968.

Headley, Lake, and William Hoffman. *Loud and Clear*. New York, Henry Holt, 1990.

Hogrefe, Jeffrey. *O'Keeffe: The Life of an American Legend*. Bantam, New York, 1992.

Horsman, Reginald. *The Frontier in the Formative Years.* UNMP, Albuquerque, 1970.

Jackson, J. B. *The Essential Landscape.* UNMP, Albuquerque, 1985.

Jans, Pat. *The Frontier World of Doc Holliday.* UNP, Lincoln, 1957.

Jeffrey, John Mason. *Adobe and Iron.* Prospect Avenue, La Jolla, Calif., 1969.

Jordan, Terry G. *Trails to Texas.* UNP, Lincoln, 1981.

Kant, Candace C. *Zane Grey's Arizona.* Northland, Flagstaff, 1984.

Kramer, Jane. *The Last Cowboy.* Peter Smith, Magnolia, Mass., 1993.

Lavender, David. *Bent's Fort.* UNP, Lincoln, 1954.

———. *A Fist in the Wilderness.* UNMP, Albuquerque, 1964.

———. *The Trail to Santa Fe.* Trails West, Santa Fe, 1989.

LeBaron, Verlan M. *The LeBaron Story.* Keels, Lubbock, Tex., 1981.

Lively, John. "The Nicolai Fechin House." *Fine Homebuilding* (Feb./Mar. 1985).

Luhan, Mabel Dodge. *Movers and Shakers.* UNMP, Albuquerque, 1985.

Lummis, Charles F. *A Tramp across the Continent.* UNP, Lincoln, 1982.

McWilliams, Carey. *Southern California: An Island on the Land.* Peregrine Smith, Salt Lake City, 1973.

Martin, Douglas D. *Tombstone's Epitaph.* UNMP, Albuquerque, 1955.

Miller, Tom. *On the Border.* UAP, Tucson, 1985.

Morgan, Ted. *Literary Outlaw: The Life and Times of William S. Burroughs.* Henry Holt, New York, 1988.

Morison, Samuel Eliot, and Henry Steele Commager. *The Growth of the New Republic.* Oxford, New York, 1962.

Morris, Edmund. *The Rise of Theodore Roosevelt.* Coward, New York, 1979.

Nash, Gerald D. *The American West in the Twentieth Century: A Short History of an Urban Oasis.* UNMP, Albuquerque, 1977.

Neider, Charles, ed. *The Complete Travel Books of Mark Twain.* Vol. 1. Doubleday, New York, 1966.

Nichols, John. *The Milagro Beanfield War.* Ballantine, New York, 1974.

O'Neal, Bill. *Encyclopedia of Western Gun-Fighters.* UOP, Norman, 1979.

Pattie, James O. *The Personal Narrative of James O. Pattie of Kentucky.* Lakeside, Chicago, 1930.

Perry, Ralph Barton. *Characteristically American.* Knopf, New York, 1949.

Pilkington, William T., and Don Graham. *Western Movies.* UNMP, Albuquerque, 1979.

Pointer, Larry. *In Search of Butch Cassidy.* UOP, Norman, 1977.

Powell, J. W. *The Exploration of the Colorado River and Its Canyons.* Dover, New York, 1961.

Prassel, Frank Richard. *The Western Peace Officer.* UOP, Norman, 1972.

Prown, Jules David, et al. *Discovered Lands, Invented Pasts.* Yale Univ. Pr., New Haven, Conn., 1992.

Pyle, Ernie. *Ernie Pyle's Southwest.* Palm Desert, 1965.

Quaife, Milo Milton, ed. *Kit Carson's Autobiography.* UNP, Lincoln, 1966.

Randle, Kevin D., and Donald R. Schmitt. *UFO Crash at Roswell.* Avon, New York, 1991.

Redford, Robert. *The Outlaw Trail.* Grosset, New York, 1981.

Rittenhouse, Jack D. *A Guide to Highway 66.* UNMP, Albuquerque, 1946.

Ross, Stanley R. *Views across the Border.* UNMP, Albuquerque, 1978.

Rudnick, Lois Palken. *Mabel Dodge Luhan.* UNMP, Albuquerque, 1984.

Russell, Carl P. *Firearms, Traps and Tools of the Mountain Men.* UNMP, Albuquerque, 1983.

Sagar, Keith. *D. H. Lawrence and New Mexico.* Peregrine Smith, Salt Lake City, 1982.

Sandoz, Mari. *The Buffalo Hunters.* UNP, Lincoln, 1978.

Savage, William W., Jr., ed. *Cowboy Life: Reconstructing an American Myth.* UOP, Norman, 1975.

Savage, William W., Jr., and Stephen I. Thompson, eds. *The Frontier.* UOP, Norman, 1979.

Schneider, Bill. *Route 66 across New Mexico.* UNMP, Albuquerque, 1991.

Sherman, James E., and Barbara H. Sherman. *Ghost Towns and Mining Camps of New Mexico.* UOP, Norman, 1969.

———. *Ghost Towns of Arizona.* UOP, Norman, 1969.

Slotkin, Richard. *The Fatal Environment.* Atheneum, New York, 1985.

Smith, Henry Nash. *Virgin Land.* Harvard Univ. Pr., Cambridge, 1959.

Sonnichsen, C. L. *Tularosa.* UNMP, Albuquerque, 1980.

Sprague, Marshall. *A Gallery of Dudes.* UNP, Lincoln, 1979.

Stanley, Henry M. *My Early Travels and Adventures in America.* UOP, Norman, 1982.

Steffen, Jerome O., ed. *The American West.* UOP, Norman, 1979.

———. *Comparative Frontiers: A Proposal for Studying the American West.* UOP, Norman, 1980.

Stegner, Wallace. *Beyond the Hundredth Meridian.* UNP, Lincoln, 1953.

———. *Mormon Country.* UNP, Lincoln, 1981.

Stratton, R. B. *Captivity of the Oatman Girls.* UNP, Lincoln, 1983.

Tagger, Sherry Clayton, and Ted Schwartz. *Paintbrushes and Pistols.* John Muir, Santa Fe, 1990.

Tatum, Stephen. *Inventing Billy the Kid.* UNMP, Albuquerque, 1982.

Turner, Frederick Jackson. *The Turner Thesis.* Heath, Boston, 1956.

Wagoner, Jay J. *Arizona Territory 1863–1912.* UAP, Tucson, 1980.

Waters, Frank. *The Earp Brothers of Tombstone.* C. N. Potter, New York, 1960.

Watson, Douglas S. *The Santa Fe Trail to California 1849–52: The Journal and Drawings of H.M.T. Powell.* The Book Club of California, San Francisco, 1941.

Weber, David J. *Richard H. Kern.* UNMP, Albuquerque, 1985.

Wilder, Joseph Carleton, ed. *Inventing the Southwest. Journal of the Southwest* 32, no. 4, 1990.

Wiley, Peter, and Robert Gottlieb. *Empires in the Sun: The Rise of the New American West.* UAP, Tucson, 1982.

Acknowledgments

As Bernard de Voto wrote of his epic history, *The Course of Empire,* "this book is a clearinghouse for the books and ideas of others," and to repeat from the footnote on page 212 Victor A. Kover's remark as quoted in *The New York Times* several years ago, "Ultimately all history is based on the history of others." My sentiments exactly, except that I would take it further and ask, like a good Buddhist: To what extent does original thought even exist? The very title of this work may well be a case in point: I thought it was very lyrical and original when it came to me, seemingly out of the blue, one morning on the way to the post office in, as I recall, 1988, but a few years later I realized that it could very possibly owe a subliminal debt to Jim Harrison's *Legends of the Fall.*

This book has gone through several incarnations and has been the beneficiary of extensive editorial direction since its inception in 1985. It started as a relatively straightforward history of the Colorado River in the tradition of Alan Morehead's masterful books on the Nile. But at that point the Southwest was in the throes of a severe drought (as it is now again, eleven summers later), which brought home the basic fact of life about that part of the world: the *absence* of water—the non-Colorado, if you will—so the book became, as I would tell people, a sweeping hydrohistory or, more properly, an *an*hydrohistory. The waterlessness seemed to lend itself as an appropriate and sturdy clothesline on which all sorts of colorful wash could be hung.

By summer 1991, six editors had helped shape the work: John Herman (then at Simon and Schuster); Edward Burlingame and Ted Solotaroff (then of Harper and Row, which became HarperCollins); Sonny Mehta of Knopf and his erstwhile associates Jane Amsterdam and Lee Goerner. That summer, having back-burnered *Legends* for breaking stories in Africa and the Amazon, I rededicated myself. By now I had two hundred tight, fact-filled pages that brought the narrative up through the Spanish period. The writing was in the style of the old, William Shawn *New Yorker,* where I had been a "long-fact writer" since 1978, turning out every year or so a long piece that would later be published as a book. In fact the work was initially commissioned and generously supported by Mr. Shawn. Sadly, Mr. Shawn was retired in 1987, and by 1992 the long-fact genre was extinct. The densely detailed natural-history and archaeology passages toward the beginning are largely from this early draft.

Up to this point, on Solotaroff's orders, I had assiduously avoided the first person, but a new editor, the seventh, Bobbie Bristol, who inherited the project, wanted me back in it, which was fine by me, but the problem was, *which* me? By now I counted no fewer than twelve *mois*—as I called them, after Miss Piggy—who had interacted with the Southwest, beginning with the jejune twenty-four-year-old songwriter who blundered to the South Rim of the Grand Canyon in the fall of 1970. The challenge of marshaling these twelve selves of varying vintage into a single narrative was intriguing. I decided to go for it, to push the existing envelope of "nonfiction," and try to write the great book that was in me, in all of us, and in the fall of 1994 I finally delivered to Bobbie a frothy, unkempt, nonlinear 978-page manuscript titled "Legends of the Desert: Twelve Mois Prowl the Southwest." While very interesting in places, it fell considerably short of my hopes of its being the next *Ulysses* or *Let Us Now Praise Famous Men.*

Bobbie sent me a letter that essentially read me the riot act, and a few months later, she left Knopf. A new editor, the eighth and, as I would discover, the one *Legends* and I had been waiting for, George Andreou, took the work on and deftly oversaw the attainment of its final form, in which the *moi* concept has been cut back to a leaner and more wieldy multiple persona, but is not entirely absent, and the more outrageously experimental passages, which I must admit not even I miss, have been excised. The latter part of the work reflects the emphasis in the early nineties on the Southwest as a multicultural laboratory. At that time, thanks to (it was thought) the combined efforts of La Niña in the Pacific and the eruption of Mount Pinatubo in the Philippines, the climate of the region was cooler and moister, and there was less concern about water problems. My own interests had shifted from meticulous observation of the interplay of flora and fauna and man and nature to raw human drama, and so there is more of this toward the end of the book. After 1992, when people would ask what the book was about, I would no longer say that it was "a sweeping hydrohistory" of the Southwest; I would tell them that it was about "the whole enchilada." Hard as I've tried, it is not really a cohesive, sustained performance (as I'm sure critics will be quick to point out) as much as an accretive process, a chronicle of ten years of flux—in the perceptions of the Southwest, in journalism, anthropology, publishing, and not least in my own life—attempting to grapple with thousands of years of biogeographical and geopolitical flux in that part of the world. Not exactly a winning book idea, but not having the will to put in another ten years trying to get it right, I've reconciled myself to what it is. Eight gifted editors, themselves at various stages in their careers, contributed to the work in different and invaluable ways. To them I owe my first and largest debt of gratitude.

The saga of the book mimicked the boom-and-bust cycles of its subject. By 1992 my advance had run out, and I found myself in the awkward and stressful situation of having to support myself and my family solely by freelance magazine writing. Each six-week magazine project would buy me two weeks or so to work on the book, and so *Legends,* which should have been delivered in 1992, dragged on fitfully an extra three years. The only good thing about the book's being so late that I can think of is, as the nineteenth-century naturalist Alfred Russell Wallace said of his six-year-overdue *Malay Archipelago,* "Had the book been published six years ago, everyone would have forgotten it by now." Three friends lent me money at desperate junctures: William Woodward, Timothy Ferris, and Hector Vasconcelos. The only good part of this was that I found out who my real friends are. My father, from whom I had been financially independent since 1968, bailed me out on several occasions when I was on the brink of being repo'd, foreclosed, levied, or disconnected. I will never forget all of your kindness.

I am also deeply grateful to Beth Hadas of the University of New Mexico Press, who arranged for me to be a visiting scholar in the university's Department of Communications during the 1991–92 academic year. During these nine months, I made a number of new friends who were incredibly generous in helping with various aspects of the book: the Taos novelist John Nichols, the Albuquerque builder Patrick Markwith, the sculptor and Chicano water activist Nicásio Romero, Tom and John of Big Mountain, Paul Robinson of the Southwest Research Center, David Luján of Tonantzin, anthropologists Peter Nabokov and Jane Lancaster. I had already been picking Bernard Fontana's brain on ethnological questions since 1985. In addition to those cited in the text, the following experts provided invaluable input, although they may not wish to be associated with the use I ended up putting it to:

- Natural history: Gary Paul Nabhan, Caroline Wilson, Tom van Devender
- Water and water law: William Wheeler, Richard Johnson, Emelin Hall, Jane A. Cramer
- Archaeology: Emil Haury, Christy Turner, Chip Wills, Paul Martin
- Cowboys and shootists: Glenn Boyer, Michael and Stanley Marsh (who generously put me up at Toad Hall on three occasions)
- Anthropology: Alfonso Ortiz (Pueblos), Jay Levi (Tarahumara), Sylvia Rodriguez (Hispanic New Mexico), Keith Basso and Edgar Perry (Apache), Dr. and Mrs. Warren Perkins and Chuck Griffith (Navajo), Thomas Pena (Hopi)
- History: J. B. Jackson (who put me up in 1986), John Kessell, Ramón Gutiérrez, Guillermo Tovar y Teresa, J. Paul Taylor, Evan S. Connell, Leland Sonnichsen, Meredith Dodge, Andrés Romero, Bill Sanchez, Marc Simmons
- Tucson: Marjorie Sherill, Charles Bowden
- Hallucinogens: Richard Evans Schultes, Andrew Weil
- Solar energy: Steve Baer
- Radioactive spills: Mary Risley
- Environmental conservation: Joanie Berde, Sam Hitt
- Art: Peter Eller, Helen Ingram

I caution the serious reader that some of the information and scholarship presented herein, the latest thinking at the time I gleaned it, may well have been discredited or superseded by now. This is the peril of being an amateur and a generalist.

I am grateful to Robert Redford for underwriting Sally Tsosie's and my trip to Fort Leavenworth; to the *New Yorker* for sending me to write about Leroy Jackson. Reduced and altered versions of the sections on Edwin Bustillos and Los Alamos appeared in *Outside* magazine, and on Clayton Lonetree in *Esquire*.

Index

A Note About the Author

For twelve years a staff writer for *The New Yorker* and now a contributing editor of *Vanity Fair*, Alex Shoumatoff has been celebrated for his profiles of personalities from Chico Mendes to Dian Fossey, and for his reporting from the farthest-flung reaches of the world, from Africa to Tibet. In his nine previous books, his main concerns have been the Third World and the relation of humans to nature. Shoumatoff was born in Mt. Kisco, New York, in 1946. He lives on a mountain in the Adirondacks with his wife and four sons.

A Note on the Type

The text of this book was set in Sabon, a typeface designed by Jan Tschichold (1902–1974), the well-known German typographer. Based loosely on the original designs by Claude Garamond (c. 1480–1561), Sabon is unique in that it was explicitly designed for hot-metal composition on both the Monotype and Linotype machines as well as for filmsetting. Designed in 1966 in Frankfurt, Sabon was named for the famous Lyons punch cutter Jacques Sabon, who is thought to have brought some of Garamond's matrices to Frankfurt.

Composed by North Market Street Graphics,
Lancaster, Pennsylvania
Printed and bound by Quebecor Printing,
Fairfield, Pennsylvania
Designed by Anthea Lingeman